D1571190

Spiritual Radical

E D W A R D   K .   K A P L A N

Yale University Press / New Haven & London

Spiritual Radical

Abraham Joshua Heschel
in America, 1940–1972

Published with assistance from the
Mary Cady Tew Memorial Fund.

Set in Bodoni type by Binghamton
Valley Composition. Printed in the United States of America by
Sheridan Books, Ann Arbor, Michigan.

Library of Congress Cataloging-in-Publication Data
Kaplan, Edward K., 1942–
Spiritual radical : Abraham Joshua Heschel in
America, 1940–1972 / Edward
K. Kaplan.—1st ed.
p. cm.
Includes bibliographical references and index.
ISBN 978-0-300-11540-6 (alk. paper)
1. Heschel, Abraham Joshua, 1907–1972.
2. Rabbis—United States—Biography.
3. Jewish scholars—United States—Biography.
I. Title.
BM755.H34K375 2007
296.3'092—dc22
[B]   2007002775

A catalogue record for this book is available from
the British Library.

To my wife, Janna

Contents

Introduction

Abraham Joshua Heschel (1907–1972) became a prophetic voice for Christians and Jews during three momentous decades in the United States. In the 1940s he countered the horrors of war and genocide with vivid essays on prayer, faith, and holiness. In the 1950s he became a public intellectual, publishing books of constructive Jewish theology while launching a critique of religious and ethical life. And in the turbulent 1960s Heschel was a widely publicized activist in civil rights, interfaith dialogue, and opposition to the Vietnam War.

This volume is the sequel to *Abraham Joshua Heschel: Prophetic Witness*, written in collaboration with the late Samuel H. Dresner, which traced Heschel's European journey from Hasidism to modernity. Born in Warsaw, Heschel was reared in a devout Jewish community and went on to earn a Ph.D. in philosophy from the University of Berlin. He experienced firsthand the rise of

Hitler and taught at Martin Buber's Lehrhaus (school for Jewish studies) in Frankfurt. After he was expelled by the Nazis, he was able to return to Warsaw in 1938.

Heschel then sought an immigrant visa to the United States. In July 1939, just before Germany invaded Poland and the outbreak of World War II, he managed to obtain a position at Hebrew Union College in Cincinnati, Ohio, arriving there in 1940 after a brief stay in London, during which he founded the short-lived Institute for Jewish Learning. In the United States he mastered English with astonishing skill, rebuilt his career, and constructed a persona Americans could understand.

Spiritual Radical: Abraham Joshua Heschel in America traces how this observant Jew became a "spiritual radical" who judged contemporary life from the uncompromising viewpoint of a Hebrew prophet. In 1951 Reinhold Niebuhr, America's leading Protestant theologian, predicted that Heschel would "become a commanding and authoritative voice not only in the Jewish community but in the religious life of America." By 1966 even popular magazines like *Newsweek* recognized that he had "built up a rich, contemporary Jewish theology that may well be the most significant achievement of modern Jewish thought."

Socially progressive and theologically conservative, Heschel did not speak for any single denomination. Instead he applied traditional Jewish sources to clarify pressing issues of personal piety, religious education, the relation between Israel and the Diaspora, interfaith negotiations, the Holocaust, and more. In his biblical idiom, he denounced American racism, the cultural genocide of Soviet Jews, and the arrogance of military thinking.

It was during the civil rights movement, when he marched with Martin Luther King, Jr., that Heschel became a media icon. Between 1962 and 1965, he significantly influenced the debates that resulted in the declaration on the Jews of the Second Vatican Council, and his impact on Protestants was consolidated by his appointment as Harry Emerson Fosdick Visiting Professor at Union Theological Seminary. His final years were consumed by the religious movement to end the American intervention in Vietnam, a conflict he judged criminal.

There was a public and a private Heschel. The public figure was a teacher and scholar, an audacious social critic, and a master of poetic prose who opened people's consciousness to the divine presence. The private person was a mystic, inspired by the living God, a Hasidic prince, a man of prayer and inwardness, and a friend, husband, and father.

Heschel was also a vulnerable human being, who had been wounded by the destruction of the several cultures that made up his multiple Jewish identity. In Warsaw he was a child prodigy, in training to become a Hasidic rebbe who would succeed his father as the charismatic leader of their religious community. But he also embraced the Jewish secularism of the city and later that of Vilna, Lithuania. In Berlin, he came to appreciate modern Orthodoxy and mastered the Western humanistic canon. These cultures—along with numerous family members, teachers, and friends—were destroyed by Hitler. In the United States, although he was honored, even revered, by a variety of people, Heschel felt alone, torn by internal contradictions and ideological conflicts. Heschel did not keep a diary, though his emotions radiate from his prose, and it was only in his final book, *A Passion for Truth*, which was published after his death, that he admitted to the conflicting attitudes that drove him: sympathy and anger, reverence for all human beings and disgust at their untruth, mediocrity, greed, and violence.

The key to Heschel's personality lies in his two opposed "teachers": the optimistic, compassionate Baal Shem Tov, the eighteenth-century founder of Hasidism, and the melancholy, abrasive, judgmental rebbe of Kotzk, a dissident within this pietistic movement. Like the Kotzker rebbe, Heschel was dismayed by the pervasiveness of evil, moral apathy, and self-deception. Like the Baal Shem Tov, he remained awed by God's concern for humankind. As a writer and an activist, Heschel drew from both, devoting his life to safeguarding human holiness while confronting our resolute barbarism. But these internal conflicts caused tremendous stress and probably contributed to his premature death at age sixty-five.

There was no consensus among observers about Heschel's personality, which was intense and changeable. He was variously perceived as courageous and shy, ambitious and humble, saintly and vain, a captivating mentor and a careless classroom pedagogue. He cannot be reduced to an ideal image, nor can his philosophy be distilled into a static system.

This cultural and intellectual biography places Heschel's ideas and actions within the flow of the events through which he lived. He pushed the boundaries of Orthodoxy as well as of liberal Judaism, asserting the reality of divine revelation to the Jewish people at Mount Sinai and affirming the sacred authority of religious law (halakhah), while defending religious pluralism. This is why I call Heschel a spiritual radical. He went to the roots of faith in God, judging creeds as secondary. For Heschel, humility and contrition before the mystery, rather than dogma or institutional authority, was the standard for all religions.

During the more than thirty years I have been studying Heschel's works, I have remained fascinated by his literary style, by his gift for connecting mysticism and the moral life, and especially by his persistent faith in the living God and the relevance of religion to today's dilemmas. What he called "radical amazement" is a bulwark against the fanaticisms that tempt us to fear that all religion is destructive.

I was educated in the Reform Judaism of the 1950s. But what I experienced in Sunday School was spiritually arid, despite the Reform movement's interest in social justice. I also grew up immersed in the civil rights movement through my father, Kivie Kaplan, who was dedicated to the Reform movement and from 1950 was a leader of the NAACP (National Association for the Advancement of Colored People), serving as its national president from 1966 until his death in 1975. I met such personalities as Thurgood Marshall, Martin Luther King, Jr., Roy Wilkins, Constance Baker Motley, and Myrlie Evers, and I became close to Howard Thurman. These personal encounters behind the public stage helped me understand the dynamics of Heschel's charisma and his renown.

Yet the "prophetic Judaism" of Reform did not satisfy my spiritual yearnings. More attractive to me were Hindu philosophy, Buddhism, other forms of mysticism, and French poetry. Afraid that I would jump ship and hearing that "Rabbi Heschel was a mystic," my father wrote him asking him to send me some of his books. He did, and I was enthralled by *Man Is Not Alone*, the first Jewish book that convincingly evoked for me the presence of God. (Buber's *I and Thou* was stimulating, but it directed me more to Asian paths than to Judaism.)

I met Heschel in 1966 while earning a Ph.D. in French literature at Columbia University. He spoke with me for two hours in his office at the Jewish Theological Seminary, and we formed a special bond, not an uncommon experience, as I later learned. He invited me to walk with him on Shabbat afternoons, filled with long, ambulatory conversations, and I participated with him in the religious opposition to the Vietnam War. From Heschel I learned how worship, even mystical inwardness, could lead to, even incite, ethical commitment.

Even as I pursued a career as a teacher and scholar of French literature with a specialty in nineteenth- and twentieth-century poetry, I wrote articles on Heschel, starting in 1971, as well as studies of Buber, Thomas Merton, and Howard Thurman. In 1996 I published *Holiness in Words*, a study of Heschel's theory and practice of poetic language and its relation to prayer, mystical intuition, moral sensitivity and action, the Holocaust, and biblical interpretation. In 1987 Samuel Dresner invited me to write a biography of Heschel, and the first volume, under the co-authorship of Rabbi Dresner, appeared in 1998, published by Yale University Press.

Writing a biography requires a delicate combination of intuition, analysis, and research. Interviews and opinions are partial, and I have attempted to ground my portrait of Heschel on documents as well as personal testimonies. As I compared idealized public images with the real person, I took heart from Heschel's daughter, Susannah, who quoted a college classmate of Martin Luther King, Jr., "By idolizing those whom we honor, we fail to realize that *we* could go and do likewise." She continued: "I certainly appreciate the honor shown to [my father], but I also worry that we tend to romanticize when we need to demythologize."

Heschel had powerful charisma, and he inspired both right-wing and left-wing disciples. Prominent on the right were Seymour Siegel and Fritz Rothschild, who distrusted Heschel's participation in the antiwar movement, and Samuel Dresner, who initiated this biography. These and other social conservatives, blaming the liberation movements of the 1960s for undermining morality, appreciated Heschel's theology of the living God and his critique of American hedonism but considered his political activism misguided.

Heschel's left-wing disciples included two political militants who became rabbis: Michael Lerner, founder of *Tikkun* magazine and an interreligious network of spiritual progressives, and Arthur Waskow of the Shalom Center in Philadelphia. Heschel's daughter, Susannah, a feminist and professor of Judaic Studies at Dartmouth College, advanced her father's political tendencies and as a scholar exposed Christian theological roots of anti-Semitism during the Nazi period.

In the 1960s Heschel's spiritual radicalism inspired the *havurah* movement—inclusive communities outside the synagogue devoted to study, prayer, and social responsibility. Rabbi Zalman Schachter-Shalomi's Jewish Renewal was anticipated by Heschel's neo-Hasidism. Today pluralistic Jewish day schools carrying Heschel's name are being established around the country. Recently, in Boston, a transdenominational rabbinical school has opened, founded by Arthur Green, one of Heschel's students and pioneer of the havurah movement.

Heschel's century, the twentieth of the Common Era, a century of horrors and marvels, has come to a close. Increasingly, Jews, Christians, even Muslims look to his books and essays for spiritual guidance. Heschel's life story speaks to the culture wars of today, helping to clarify the contentious effects of religion in public life in the United States and around the world. The pertinence of Heschel's central concerns to the instabilities of today is too obvious to belabor: readers can make their own applications.

His true disciples are in the future.

Part One

Cincinnati: The War Years

*I grew up in an awareness that Jews are running away from Judaism
and religion. This was true in Poland, where I was born; in Germany,
where I studied; and in America, where I found refuge in 1940. In those
years spiritual problems were considered irrelevant, but during the last
seven or eight years I have been surprised by an extraordinary change.*
—Heschel, "Teaching Religion to American Jews," 1956

HESCHEL SPENT FIVE YEARS IN CINCINNATI, OHIO, WHERE HE ARRIVED EIGHT
months after war was declared in Europe. He was one of a group of eight
refugee professors known as the College in Exile who were brought to Cincinnati by Julian Morgenstern, president of Hebrew Union College (HUC), as part
of an initiative to rescue European Jewish scholars. Hebrew Union was a Reform institution dedicated to modernizing Judaism; as proclaimed in the
school's catalog of 1940–41, "a real and positive American Judaism" had to
"adapt itself to the life which its children must live as loyal citizens of this
American nation and participants in and eager contributors to evolving American culture."[1]

Heschel would have preferred to work at the Jewish Theological Seminary
(JTS, in those days called simply the Seminary), a Conservative rabbinical
school in New York City, but at the time the school refused or discouraged applicants from his institution, the Berlin Hochschule für die Wissenschaft des
Judentums (Academy of scientific historical Jewish scholarship), a Liberal
Jewish school, despite efforts by the Hochschule's distinguished professors
Leo Baeck and Ismar Elbogen, who considered Conservative Judaism more
compatible with European Liberal practice and thought than American Reform. As late as April 1938, JTS provost Louis Finkelstein wrote to Elbogen
that German rabbinical candidates could not meet the Seminary's high standards.[2]

Compounding the difficulties facing the European refugees in the late
1930s was the fact that immigrant visas to the United States were almost impossible to obtain. Morgenstern tirelessly appealed to the State Department on
behalf of the refugee professors. To A. M. Warren, chief of the Visa Division,
the HUC president stressed the utility of modern Judaism, justifying its study
as "a modern, liberal, and progressive religion." Even Heschel, the least sea-
soned of his group, was touted as a "very promising young scholar in the field
of Bible and Jewish philosophy [that is, medieval studies], who had been

teaching as successor to Professor Martin Buber at the Jüdisches Lehrhaus in Frankfurt."[3] The visas were finally granted, and Heschel and his fellow refugees began arriving at HUC in 1939–40.

Cincinnati in the 1940s was a typical American city with a large Jewish population dating to before the Civil War. The majority of these Jews were of German origin, and they had established the Reform movement in North America, whose academic center was HUC, founded in 1875 by Rabbi Isaac Mayer Wise.

While at HUC, Heschel lived in the Americanized, predominantly German Jewish Clifton neighborhood, but he preserved his emotional and spiritual health among the traditional Jews of the Avondale area, known as the Gilded Ghetto. This community of about twenty thousand fostered Jewish culture through religious schools for children from Orthodox and Conservative congregations (which did not have Sunday schools, as their Reform counterparts did), Zionist groups, meetings for Hebrew speakers, and theater activities. With these varied resources, Heschel began to forge a new life and a new, American, identity.

1

First Year in America (1940–1941)

But Einstein, the greatest physicist of our century, is neither a magician
nor a founder of a religion. . . . Convinced "of the living order
of all natural events," Einstein has dismissed the good Lord from
His dwelling place in the universe.
—Heschel, "Answer to Einstein" (1940)

ON 21 MARCH 1940, ABRAHAM HESZEL (AS HIS POLISH PASSPORT READ) STEPPED off the Cunard White Star liner *Lancastria* onto the dock at New York City. The *New York Times* reported evasively that among the ship's 480 passengers about 360 were "German refugees." In reality, they were Jews fleeing Hitler. The twelve-day voyage had been rough, marked by the terrors of war and storms that battered the vessel, shattering several portholes. On leaving the boat, Heschel was startled to see an African American kneeling to polish the shoes of a white man. Like many Europeans, he had never before seen a black person. Heschel was shocked by this view of America's racial hierarchy, a segmentation to which he remained particularly sensitive.[1]

Heschel was welcomed at the dock by his cousin Rabbi Mordecai Shlomo Friedman, the Boyaner rebbe, himself recently arrived from Vienna, and the rabbi's son Israel, both, like Heschel, Hasidic Jews and descendants of the rebbe of Ruzhin, the movement's most aristocratic figure. They took him to 132 Henry Street on the Lower East Side of Manhattan, where he lodged with his eldest sister, Sarah, and her husband (and first cousin), the Kopitzhinitzer rebbe, also named Abraham Joshua Heschel, refugees from occupied Vienna who had settled in New York the year before. A few days after his arrival the family celebrated *Shabbat Zakhor*, the "Sabbath of Remembrance," when Jews read the Torah portion about the Israelites' eternal enemy, Amalek. The occasion was made more poignant by the knowledge that Heschel's mother and sister Gittel remained confined in the Warsaw Ghetto, while another sister, Devorah Miriam Dermer, and her husband were enduring persecution in Vienna. The following day, 24 March, Heschel observed the festival of Purim, honoring the Jews' release from Haman's genocidal decree, a gripping reminder of the daily catastrophes occurring in Europe.

With no material resources, Heschel quickly looked to his professional obligations. On the ship's stationery (giving the American Express office on Fifth Avenue as his return address) he wrote to Julian Morgenstern, who had obtained his life-saving visa: "I have just arrived in New York! *Barukh hashem!* [Thank God.] I would like to make my respects to you. Thank you very much." He followed this with a diplomatic request for permission to remain in the city for a few days, closing, "With feelings of sincere gratitude, Your obedient, A. Heschel." The president of Hebrew Union College (HUC) graciously agreed to the request, encouraging Heschel to meet people, especially Ismar Elbogen, one of Heschel's professors at the Berlin Hochschule who had recently arrived in Manhattan and was the person who had placed Heschel on the list of scholars to be saved by HUC. (Elbogen himself was sponsored by five Jewish

Mordecai Shlomo Friedman, the Boyaner rebbe.
Courtesy of Yitzhak Meir Twersky.

institutions.) Heschel wrote Morgenstern that he had met some leading academics at the American Oriental Society, of which Morgenstern was a prominent
member. Among them were the archeologist William Foxwell Albright of the
Johns Hopkins University and Millar Burrows, professor of biblical theology at
Yale Divinity School, who had written a perceptive review of *Die Prophetie* (On
prophecy, the published version of Heschel's doctoral thesis) in 1937.[2]

But Heschel's plans went beyond Cincinnati. While in Europe he had confided to Martin Buber that he had accepted the HUC offer for pragmatic reasons,
as a way to obtain a visa and a place to stay while he sought a more compatible
institution. To further this aim, Heschel had mailed *Die Prophetie* to Louis
Finkelstein, provost of the Jewish Theological Seminary (JTS).[3] Now Heschel
strengthened his ties with JTS. Although grateful for his position in Cincinnati,
he already felt that New York would be his intellectual and spiritual center.

Heschel arranged a visit with the influential Mordecai Kaplan, dean of the
JTS Teachers Institute. He also met with Finkelstein, now the Seminary's

president, and the historian Alexander Marx, the librarian, speaking mostly in Hebrew because of his still halting English. They invited Heschel to address the JTS rabbinical students, for which Heschel candidly sought Morgenstern's approval: "I am too new in this country. I cannot know how to handle such a question. I therefore want to submit it to you asking you for your kind advice." Morgenstern willingly agreed. Heschel lectured to the JTS students in Hebrew and was pleased with their response, a fact he dutifully communicated to Morgenstern the following week.[4]

His New York business complete, Heschel took the night train to Cincinnati, arriving on 10 April and taking up residence in a small suite at the college dormitory with one bedroom and a living room. Even with free room and board, his material needs were barely met by his yearly salary of $1,500. He took meals in the dining room (which was not kosher) with the students but ate only vegetarian and dairy foods, including eggs and cheese, or kosher Osherwitz salami (an unhealthy diet for a man with incipient heart disease, as he later discovered).[5]

European Professors in America

The war and the persecutions of Jews continued in Europe while Heschel was adjusting to American life. Like most refugees, he closely followed events, poring over newspapers in Hebrew, Yiddish, German, and English (including the *New York Times* and the *Contemporary Jewish Record,* a monthly digest of European sources distributed by the American Jewish Committee in New York), which were readily available in Cincinnati. But as a foreigner without status or money, Heschel was in no position to sponsor visas for family or friends who remained in Europe. In any case, U.S. immigrant quotas were filled. He rarely mentioned his family's peril, but students noticed that he would sometimes sigh deeply in distress.[6]

Heschel did attempt to reestablish communication with his mentor and friend, the philosopher Martin Buber, whose program of adult Jewish education at the Frankfurt Lehrhaus he sorely missed. Soon after arriving at HUC, Heschel wrote to Buber in Jerusalem describing his new situation.[7] But there was no answer, and Heschel did not write again for almost two years. As if to compensate for Buber's silence, Heschel renewed his warm friendship with Eduard Strauss, a confidant from Frankfurt who was now living in Manhattan after escaping Germany. A biochemist by training, Strauss had been a popular teacher of biblical studies at the Lehrhaus. Strauss was one of the few people Heschel addressed in German with the familiar *Du* (thou) instead of the formal *Sie* (you).

Work was Heschel's antidote to despair, and he mailed Strauss some draft chapters of a book he had begun in Germany, asking for comments. He also shared his emotions and ideas with Strauss. He missed the passionate conversations of his Frankfurt years and told Strauss that he longed to speak about "so many heart-moving things."[8]

Heschel's initial community in Cincinnati consisted of European academics, the refugees like himself who were members of Morgenstern's College in Exile. The oldest and most noted of these was Eugen Täubler, who was accompanied by his wife, Selma Stern, herself a historian. Täubler was a specialist in Greek civilization. Born in Poznan, he came from a long line of rabbis and held a doctorate from the University of Berlin, where he had been an assistant to Theodor Mommsen, the nineteenth century's greatest authority on ancient history, before becoming a professor at the universities of Zurich and Heidelberg.

Other members of the College in Exile included Franz Landsberger, a professor of art from Breslau, and Isaiah Sonne, a professor of Jewish philosophy and postbiblical literature in Florence and director of the Rabbinical College on Rhodes until 1938. Most familiar with the American academic scene was the Assyriologist Julius Lewy, who had taught at the University of Giessen and headed its Oriental Seminar in 1937. In the United States, Lewy had taught at the Jewish Theological Seminary and Johns Hopkins before coming to HUC in 1936 as visiting professor. In 1939 Lewy settled in Cincinnati with his wife, Hildegard, also a Ph.D. in Assyriology, and founded the Department of Semitic Studies, which attracted outstanding graduate students.[9]

Alexander Guttmann, the Talmud scholar who had granted a degree to Heschel at the Berlin Hochschule, arrived in 1940. Next came Max Wiener, a professor of Jewish philosophy, and the Arabist Franz Rosenthal, who had won a prestigious international prize in 1938 though the Nazi government would not allow him to accept it.[10] Heschel and Rosenthal had waited together in London for immigrant visas to the United States.

The status of these Europeans at HUC was ambiguous, adding to their formidable cultural and linguistic obstacles. The school already had enough professors, and the refugees were not official members of the faculty; they could not attend meetings or make policy decisions. Heschel's position, for example, carried the title fellow in Jewish philosophy.

The academic community at HUC was small, American, and tightly knit. The 1940–41 catalog lists twelve professors, one professor emeritus, two visiting professors, and one "research professor" (not on campus), Ismar Elbogen. The HUC student body consisted of about sixty young men, most of them

Julian Morgenstern, president of Hebrew Union College, with his College in Exile:
scholars who had escaped Nazi-occupied Europe. Left to right: *Samuel Atlas, Heschel,*
Michael Wilensky, Eugen Täubler, Julius Lewy, Morgenstern, Alexander Guttmann,
Isaiah Sonne (hidden), Eric Werner, Franz Landsberger, Franz Rosenthal. Courtesy of
American Jewish Archives, Cincinnati, Ohio.

around eighteen years old and generally insulated by age and experience from life's distresses. To the surprise of Heschel and the other Europeans, few of them had even a basic Judaic foundation. The curriculum assumed little knowledge of Hebrew or the classical texts. The entrance examination was easy: applicants simply had to read passages from the Book of Genesis. Most students entered the Preparatory Department (the remedial level), which included four levels of Hebrew language instruction and introductory courses on the Bible, liturgy, Mishnah (the original oral law, the foundational book of Talmud), and Midrash (theological and creative rabbinic commentaries on the Bible), as well as public speaking. Students joked about the overemphasis on sermonizing, such as teaching them to pronounce *God* as a three-syllable word.

Students were supported by scholarships despite the stringencies of the post-Depression era. Tuition to HUC was free; dormitory residence cost $350 per year. To complete their rabbinical training, students were required to matriculate simultaneously as undergraduates at the University of Cincinnati, where tuition for three years was usually $740, often paid by HUC. Six to nine years was the normal course of study.

Most of the HUC faculty offered advanced courses that reflected the Reform emphasis on the ancient world and the history of Judaism as a culture and civilization. Morgenstern himself taught the introductory course on the beginnings of Judaism and the Hebrew prophets, as did his former student Sheldon Blank. Nelson Glueck gave classes on biblical archeology, Henry Englander taught medieval Bible commentaries, and Alexander Guttmann taught Talmud and the legal codes. Jacob Rader Marcus and Jacob Mann taught history, Samuel Cohon theology and Hasidism, and Isaiah Sonne philosophy.

Practical ethics was taught by Abraham Cronbach, a political and religious radical, who founded the Social Studies Department and trained students in the duties of the rabbinate. Courses on pedagogy and pastoral psychology were given by Abraham Franzblau. Cora Kahn, the only female on the teaching staff, taught mandatory classes on elocution, instructing the inexperienced rabbis-to-be on how to walk and talk in public.

Social graces were considered indispensable to these future Reform leaders, who were expected to minister to affluent, culturally assimilated, predominantly German Jewish congregations. Students received training in deportment, and most of them needed it; the majority came from western or midwestern lower- or middle-class families, often of East European origin. At HUC a matron provided gentility while maintaining order in the dormitory and, in keeping with Cincinnati's southern culture, the African American help made the beds daily, did the students' laundry, and, dressed in white coats, served meals in the dining room at tables spread with formal cloths.

Heschel, already horrified by European racism, befriended Larry D. Harris (addressed by HUC faculty and staff only by his first name), the black head-waiter of the dining hall who also supervised the staff. Harris was a devout Christian and a deacon of his church, and he was proud of his heritage.[11] Heschel became extremely interested in Harris's family and community, discussing with him the predicament of African Americans in the segregated city.

Heschel was out of his element at HUC, whose forms of observance were far more removed from traditional practices than German Liberal Judaism.[12]At the Berlin Hochschule, for example, and even in most progressive German synagogues, men and women still sat in separate sections, although they were not isolated by a *mechitzah* (partition). The Hochschule served kosher food, and professors followed halakhah (Jewish law) in much the same way American Conservative and Orthodox Jews did.

Worship at HUC did not conform to Heschel's traditional practice of prayer three times a day. What HUC called "divine services" generally followed classical Reform style, which was modeled after Protestant ceremonies and performed mostly in English, led by a "reader." The Torah and Haftarah texts in Hebrew were spoken, not chanted. A student choir was accompanied by an organ. The centerpiece of this ceremony was a sermon (not the Torah reading), often presented by a rabbinical student as a pedagogical exercise. Decorum was crucial.

Observance of the Sabbath, the holiest day of the week, while respected at HUC, was also far from traditional. Students were required to attend chapel services Friday evenings at 5:30 and Saturday mornings at 10:00, but the community largely disregarded the Sabbath prohibitions on work, travel, and the use of electricity. Indeed, for most students, the highlight of the week was Friday night, the time for off-campus dates. Weekday worship (at 3:50 P.M.) was optional, and there were no *Minha* (afternoon) or *Ma'ariv* (evening) services.

Similarly, in the Cincinnati Reform synagogues (called temples), an organ was played on the Sabbath, when traditional Jews are forbidden to produce music, and a backdrop to the service was provided by a choir, often made up of non-Jews. The rabbi and cantor performed the ritual, not the congregation. And the men did not wear a *kippa*, or yarmulke, or the *tallit* (prayer shawl).

Heschel was not the first European refugee to be taken aback by the practices of Cincinnati's Reform Jews. In 1935 five rabbinical students from the Berlin Hochschule had been culturally initiated on their first Sabbath morning. Unaware that Reform men worshiped without covering their heads, they sat in the front row of Rabbi David Philipson's prestigious Rockdale Temple wearing yarmulkes. After the service, when they wished Philipson "Shabbat Shalom," he admonished them, "If you ever come to my service again wearing hats, I will have you bodily thrown out."[13]

Indeed, Philipson, at that time the oldest living graduate of HUC, typified the stringencies of American Classical Reform. Following the principle that reason and science would keep Judaism from dying out by modifying tradition, the Pittsburgh Platform of 1885, which Philipson helped draft, directly challenged Orthodox beliefs. (Conservative Judaism did not yet exist.) The official platform dismissed the possibility of direct divine revelation, rejected the authority of the *mitzvot* (commandments), and abrogated the laws governing kosher food. Prayers and holidays judged to be obsolete were removed.

The positive focus for Philipson and other proponents of Classical Reform was "ethical monotheism." Reform Jews pursued social justice and replaced parochial conceptions of Jewish peoplehood with universal values. At the same time, the Pittsburgh Platform opposed the establishment of a Jewish homeland in Palestine, arguing that Jews were citizens of countries in which they lived.

Nevertheless, American Reform Jews were becoming more receptive to traditional practices as the generations of predominantly German Jews committed to assimilation were replaced by East European immigrants who maintained the ancestral religion. Thus, in 1937, the Central Conference of American Rabbis, the professional association of Reform spiritual leaders, promulgated a new policy, the Columbus Platform, which stated: "Judaism as a way of life requires, in addition to its moral and spiritual demands, the preservation of the Sabbath, festivals and Holy Days, the retention and development of such customs, symbols and ceremonies as possess inspirational value, the cultivation of distinctive forms of religious art and music and the use of Hebrew, together with the vernacular, in our worship and instruction."[14]

And yet an abyss remained between Reform and Heschel's own religious understanding. Reform still emphasized a nontheological approach that considered acts of holiness "customs, symbols, and ceremonies" with "inspirational value." Heschel believed that observance was a response to God's will: the Torah was divine revelation, not a human artifact. Although HUC saved Heschel from the catastrophe in Europe, it could not provide him with a spiritual home.

Adjustment

Heschel lived in the dormitory, where he took his meals, and attempted to live in two worlds, maintaining his observance publicly in awkward ways. He did not wear a kippa while eating, as would Orthodox men and even some Reform rabbinical students, but students noticed that when he said the *motzi* (the prayer over the bread at the beginning of the meal) he would cover his head swiftly with a handkerchief. They wondered whether he was embarrassed to wear a skullcap, because he feared ridicule, or whether he was just trying to fit in. He regularly attended chapel services but did not participate and did not wear a kippa, even though some students did. To preserve his privacy, he usually sat halfway up, at the extreme right of the chapel, where few people gathered, giving the impression of someone who was deeply preoccupied.[15]

But privately he fulfilled his devotions with fervor, a fact that was known among the students. Alone in his room, after (or before) chapel, Heschel would perform all three prayer services required by sacred law: *Shaharit* (morning), *Minha* (afternoon), and *Ma'ariv* (evening). In his room he wore the tallit and kippa, and every weekday morning he wrapped tefillin (phylacteries) around his head and arm. When praying he would *shukl* (sway), as was common among Hasidic Jews, with eyes tightly shut, or pace around with his tallit covering his head.

Shy and unfamiliar with American ways, Heschel was perceived as someone special, both intensely and discreetly observant. He attracted two students early on, the philosopher Lou Silberman and the spiritually oriented Dudley Weinberg. Years later Silberman remembered Heschel as "a diffident, soft-spoken young man on the second floor of the dormitory . . . sad-eyed and, despite what goodwill there may have been, sadly alone, not at home among our noisy crew. But there were so many things we did not, could not know."[16]

Heschel worked hard, goaded by necessity. The scholar's iron discipline, his almost photographic memory, and the joy of fierce concentration—skills he shared with other religious prodigies—served his drive to learn. His greatest strength was his mastery of languages. Heschel possessed remarkable linguistic gifts that had been reinforced by his rigorous upbringing. Through childhood and adolescence, as a Hasidic Jew whose mother tongue (*mame-loshn*) was Yiddish, he had studied biblical and rabbinic Hebrew, the Aramaic of the Bible, Talmud, and Zohar, and even modern Hebrew, both written and spoken, which was unusual among the anti-Zionist Hasidim. In Warsaw, Vilna, and Berlin he had learned Polish and German and developed a reading knowledge of Arabic, Latin, French, and some English. His earliest publications in Yiddish, Hebrew, and German displayed an artist's sensitivity to words.

People were astonished at his ability to write graceful and incisive English prose within a year of his arrival in America. While continuing to treasure Goethe's *Conversations with Eckermann* in the original German, he embraced English classics as well. Among the books in his dormitory rooms were Shakespeare's complete works, an unabridged English dictionary, and Roget's *Thesaurus*, which had to be replaced several times as it became thumbed and tattered beyond use.[17] Heschel delighted in learning new words, even remembering the circumstances of his acquisitions.

Heschel's intellectual sanctuary was the HUC library. One of the great Judaica resources in the world, it housed several important collections and more than 2,500 manuscripts. There he continued his research on medieval Jewish philosophy, a basic academic field that helped him formulate his own theological system. More significant, he found there rare Hasidic manuscripts and initiated a new project, closer to his heart than metaphysics: a history of the Baal Shem Tov, the founder of Hasidism, and the early Hasidic movement in Poland.[18]

Heschel established warm professional ties with the librarians, including Adolph S. Oko, a Russian Jew and a friend of Martin Buber's, whom Oko provided with English-language books that were hard to find in Palestine. One of HUC's colorful characters, Head Librarian Oko was only twenty-four in 1931 when the new HUC president, Kaufmann Kohler, directed him to expand the library. Oko succeeded, but he alienated students and faculty by his condescending attitude. Soon after the new library was dedicated, Oko fell in love with a married Christian woman. She divorced her husband, and they were married on the Sabbath eve in a Christian ceremony. This was the last straw for HUC. Dismissed for "moral offense," Oko left Cincinnati but remained active in the community of bibliographers.[19]

Michael (Michoel) Wilensky, the curator of manuscripts, who had immigrated from Berlin in 1935, was a more compatible companion for Heschel. A scholar of medieval Hebrew grammar, Wilensky was an East European Jew who was comfortable in several Jewish worlds: Orthodox, Liberal, and secular. And, like Heschel, Wilensky possessed a distinguished Hasidic *yikhus* (pedigree). Heschel may have met Wilensky in Berlin, where they both took a philosophy seminar with David Baumgardt at the university; Wilensky was also a friend (and the landlord) of Menachem Mendel Schneerson, the future Lubavitcher rebbe, who attended the University of Berlin from 1928 to 1931. In Cincinnati, Wilensky was close to Rabbi Eliezer Silver, a leader of the American Orthodox Jews, with whom Heschel soon established ties.[20]

Yet Wilensky, as a refugee, felt isolated at HUC. Students mocked him because he was afraid to speak and preferred to listen; he was nicknamed "mute Wilensky." Wilensky felt intimidated because his English was still poor, although he spoke fluent Yiddish and Hebrew, as well as German and Russian— languages most of the HUC students apparently did not need.[21]

Right before the summer vacation, just two months after settling in Cincinnati, Heschel initiated the process of naturalization. He obtained a certificate of arrival at the U.S. District Court. His declaration of intention, dated 29 May 1940 in the name of "ABRAHAM HESZEL (known as Heschel)," summarized his

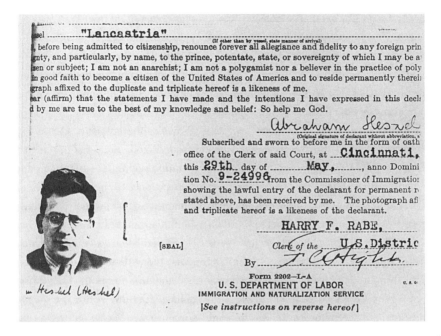

Certificate of arrival for Abraham Heszel (Heschel), 29 May 1940.
District Court of the United States, Cincinnati, Ohio.

civic identity and physical features: age, 33; eyes, brown; complexion, dark; height, 5'7"; weight, 160 pounds; nationality, Polish; religion, Hebrew; born, Warsaw, Poland, on 11 January 1907.[22]

Confronting Albert Einstein

At the end of his first term at HUC, Heschel began what would become his routine of spending the long summer recess from June through September in New York City. This time, rather than lodge with his sister's family in lower Manhattan, he rented a room at 362 Riverside Drive, apt. 10B, on the Upper West Side near the Jewish Theological Seminary and Columbia University. Heschel did research in the schools' libraries, met with faculty members, and furthered contacts with other immigrant groups. He also arranged to see his good friend Eduard Strauss, who was having difficulty adjusting to American life. The nearly five months Heschel spent in New York that summer opened important opportunities as he embarked on his new life.

At YIVO, the secularist research institute familiar to him from Warsaw and Vilna, Heschel recovered a Yiddish-speaking community. Founded in Vilna in 1925 to preserve East European culture—including Hasidic materials—YIVO had immigrated to 123rd Street in New York, which became the institute's center in 1940. There Heschel found respect as a poet who had appeared in the *Varshaver shriftn* (Warsaw writings) anthology in 1926 and in the New York Yiddish periodical *Zukunft* (Future) in 1929–30 and as the author of *Der Shem Hameforash: mentsh* (The Ineffable Name of God: Man), which was published in Warsaw in 1933. He joined the board of directors, one of its only religiously committed members.

That same summer, Heschel made two momentous professional decisions that advanced his sense of personal security and his sacred mission. First, he strengthened his ties with JTS president Louis Finkelstein, a scholar of the Talmudic period and a canny administrator, who had enlisted influential figures from the realms of science, the humanities, and different faiths for a think tank. Finkelstein's dream was to reconcile science and faith within America's academic and religious elite. To this end he inaugurated the "Conference on Science, Philosophy, and Religion in Their Relation to the Democratic Way of Life," to be held at JTS in September. The press release featured quotations from Harlow Shapley, director of the Harvard Observatory, and Albert Einstein, who urged, "Science can only be created by those who are thoroughly imbued with the aspiration towards truth and understanding. This source of feeling, however, springs from the sphere of religion. . . . [S]cience without religion is lame, religion without science is blind."[23]

Heschel, for his part, made a bold and surprising move, astounding for such a recent immigrant. Though not a speaker at the conference, he used it to challenge America's most prestigious Jew, Albert Einstein. The Nobel laureate did not present his talk in person at the opening session on the Natural Sciences (11 September 1940), but his paper, "Science and Religion," was read, distributed, and hotly debated. Einstein resolutely opposed the idea of a personal God—Heschel's primal certainty as a Jew. The interdisciplinary audience was polarized, despite Einstein's diplomatic suggestion that scientific curiosity included a spiritual motive.[24]

Heschel took immediate action. Through JTS and the German Jewish refugee community, he arranged to publish "Answer to Einstein" (Antwort an Einstein) in *Aufbau* (Reconstruction), a German-language newspaper dedicated to the "Americanization" of immigrants, with a readership of thirty thousand. The 13 September issue headlined the controversy "Einstein's Dismissal of Any Kind of Belief in a Personal God." Heschel's "detailed response" was announced for the following week.[25]

The editors of *Aufbau* abridged Einstein's original paper (which they translated into German) in a manner that heightened the polemic. Entitled "God's Religion or Religion of the Good?" it began dramatically by blaming "all the present conflicts between the spheres of religion and science" on the concept of a personal God "who interferes with natural events." Decrying the "juvenile period of mankind's spiritual development," Einstein admonished religious teachers to "have the courage to give up [this] teaching" and instead to cultivate the humanistic triad of "the Good, the True, and the Beautiful."[26]

The following week Heschel defended the reality and moral necessity of a personal God. He insisted that human beings, not God, were responsible for worldly evil. Attacking the famous scientist with sarcasm, Heschel derided Einstein's naturalistic faith as "a magical resurrection rite," while prudently noting that he was responding to "Einstein's communication to the Conference . . . as printed in *Aufbau*." He satirized Einstein as "a missionary for a forgotten confession" and rejected his premise that only "natural events" could be appropriately discussed. Heschel asserted that Einstein, as a Jew, should not revert to an outmoded paganism. With shaky logic, he associated the physicist's scientism with Nazi racial theories that led directly to "the view that all life and action are determined by natural factors, blood, soil, and race."[27]

Heschel's model for the sanctity of human life was the Hebrew Bible, not biology. Pointing to the dangers of deifying reason, he asserted that a morally neutral science "cannot be prevented from creating poisonous gas or dive-bombers; and rationalism is powerless once 'the magnificent blond beast' . . . takes arms in order to subjugate inferior races." He concluded that religion bounded by the limits of science could not guarantee morality: "Were Nature the source of all knowledge, we would have to accept bestiality and fatalism. But then there would be no freedom, no truth, no science." Spiritually speaking, pride or hubris was the greatest peril facing modern civilization.

Heschel's "Answer to Einstein" was audacious, and it inaugurated his lifelong campaign against secularized religion. In it he upheld his faith in the living God as essential to ethical sensitivity. Religion, not science, must clarify "why there is a world in the first place" and interpret "the meaning of life and death, the meaning of being and of history."

Back in Cincinnati, Heschel was called upon to further the scholarly mission of an East European immigrant very much like himself, Zevi Diesendruck,

HUC's specialist in medieval Jewish philosophy, who had passed away on 4 June 1940, soon after Heschel's arrival. Heschel accepted a request to complete Diesendruck's magnum opus in Hebrew, "The Idea of God in Maimonides," and to compose his obituary for the *American Jewish Year Book*, the annual digest of important developments in world Jewry.[28]

The obituary, a biography in miniature, was Heschel's first article in English, and in it he also mapped out his own aspirations as a modern Jewish thinker.[29] (Although Heschel had made noticeable progress in English, his style was at times cumbersome, though at others elegant.) He began by admitting that students found Diesendruck to be an "austere rationalist" in the classroom: a boring, overly meticulous expositor of texts. But more to the point, noted Heschel, Diesendruck was at once a rigorous scholar, a literary artist, and an ardent supporter of modern Hebrew culture. Heschel applauded Diesendruck's Hebrew essays for their "command of the vast stores of the language and an exceptional imagination in coining new expressions."[30] And he admired Diesendruck's translations into Hebrew of Plato's *Dialogues* and his philosophical writings (also in Hebrew) on language, prayer, and artistic and religious creativity.

Heschel concluded by describing the hardships of Diesendruck's last years, which anticipated problems he would later face as a teacher and thinker in the United States. He acknowledged Diesendruck's isolation and his unfulfilled ambitions. Diesendruck had died young, at age fifty, his scholarly masterpiece incomplete, his courses at HUC disparaged: "In his yearnings he remained lonely and unhappy. He did not achieve renown, nor did his writings ever become popular. The essays he finished were read by but few." Abraham Heschel, setting out in a new language and a new culture, would dedicate his prodigious energy to preventing his own creations from succumbing to a similar fate.

2

Hebrew Union College (1941–1943)

The pious man is possessed by his awareness of the presence and nearness of God. Everywhere and at all times he lives as in His sight, whether he remains always heedful of His proximity or not. . . . Awareness of God is as close to him as the throbbing of his own heart, often deep and calm, but at times overwhelming, intoxicating, setting the soul afire.

—Heschel, "An Analysis of Piety" (1942)

began on 19 October 1940, following the High Holy Days, a month after his re-joinder to Einstein appeared in *Aufbau.* As in his previous year, he held the lowest position open to the refugee scholars, who were not official members of the faculty: fellow in Jewish philosophy (his prize-winning colleague Franz Rosenthal was fellow in the Bible and Semitic languages). Similarly, Heschel's teaching was limited for the most part to basic courses. As the specialist in me-dieval Jewish philosophy, he offered an introductory course and an advanced seminar on Hasdai Crescas's *Or Adonai* (Light of the Lord, a major synthesis of Jewish beliefs and dogmas). Eleven students enrolled in his philosophy course. He also taught elementary Hebrew language—"cursory Hebrew reading" (sight reading of vocalized and unvocalized biblical and rabbinic texts) to six students. He found the classroom intellectually stultifying.[1]

The refugee professors were welcomed sympathetically, but it was no secret that they did not fit in. Although the next year the HUC catalog of 1941–42 (acknowledging the crisis in Europe for the first time) praised the presence on campus of "almost a dozen distinguished Jewish refugee scholars from all parts of the war-torn world"—which, it claimed, reaffirmed the principle that "if Judaism is to live and expand here in America it must be open to every positive influence of modernism, must square itself with every advance in sci-entific thought"—their standards remained far higher than the curriculum could offer. European students had mastered the Bible, Talmud, the commen-taries (like Rashi), and the legal codes from early youth. Julius Lewy, who had adapted to the new school better than the others, addressed the problem in the *Hebrew Union College Bulletin.* Lewy admitted that foreign professors were handicapped by having to teach in English but pointed out that they, in turn, were disturbed that American students lacked core knowledge and skills usu-ally possessed by European Gymnasium graduates, "accustomed to reading, if not Hebrew, at least a Latin or Greek text." As a consequence, he acknowl-edged, both refugee teachers and American students tended to perform poorly in class.[2]

Many recent immigrants from Germany compensated for their painful loss of prestige by excessive criticism of the school. An acerbic observer of these tensions was the American-born history professor Jacob Marcus, who blamed the Europeans for refusing to integrate: "They believed that as German Ph.D.s they were superior to the barbarians in America. Innately they felt superior and that they were not immediately given the recognition they felt they de-served."[3]

Connections and Alliances

Although Heschel shared many of the refugee professors' attitudes toward HUC, he tried wholeheartedly to adjust. He was not only an aspiring academic. His multicultural Jewish identity, more complex than that of most Americans, included his inner sense of status, his self-view as a Hasidic prince, heir to spiritual dynasties. If he had described himself this way, however, he would have been viewed with suspicion or contempt. At the same time, Heschel was prey to self-doubt, dating from his early years in Warsaw, when his tutor, Reb Bezalel, relentlessly chastised his ego with "the blessings of humiliation."[4] Throughout his life, with varying degrees of self-awareness, Heschel struggled with a sense of inferiority, even as he craved respect and even adulation from others.

On campus, Heschel aroused contradictory, often extreme, reactions. He was perceived as quiet, reserved, shy. He rarely spoke his mind, always listening, usually asking questions. Heschel sought acceptance, but he often did not know what to do to earn it. He developed an irenic personality, a diplomatic reserve, emphasizing the positive. First and foremost, he maintained a dignified, deeply respectful loyalty to President Morgenstern, who had saved his life. Heschel preserved a "reverent obligation" toward Hebrew Union College and for years to come sent Morgenstern warm letters of holiday greetings.[5]

Yet Jacob Marcus was suspicious of Heschel's strategic use of his (genuine) gratitude toward President Morgenstern. Ignoring the normal desire of most immigrants to seek acceptance, he judged Heschel opportunistic because of his "overriding ambition to get ahead in his new career in America." At the same time Marcus admitted, "Morgenstern wanted people to be deferential to him and Heschel [was]. Morgenstern was especially good to the refugee scholars, because they were dependent, indebted to him."[6]

Music presented Heschel with other opportunities to connect with the Americans. He once told a student that music was essential to his being and competed with prayer as his greatest joy. Even as an adolescent in Warsaw, Heschel had enjoyed secular songs; indeed, his mother had feared that he was becoming detached from his Hasidic roots.[7] As a student at the University of Berlin, enticed by great performances of ballet and opera, he decided that the arts were the ally of religion, not its foe.

His well-known passion for music helped Heschel establish ties with otherwise incompatible colleagues, among them David Philipson, the influential Reform leader who had rebuked the immigrant students for wearing yarmulkes to temple. As rabbi of Cincinnati's Rockdale Temple for fifty years (he retired in 1938), Philipson helped found the militantly anti-Zionist American Council for Judaism. Yet Heschel gladly accepted Philipson's invitations to ride in his chauffeur-driven car to the Cincinnati Symphony, directed by the internationally famous Eugene Goosens.[8] This contact was useful for professional reasons, too, since Philipson continued to teach at HUC and was the senior member of the board of governors.

Music even enabled Heschel to form a tie with Jacob Marcus, who considered him a fraud. And it was through Marcus that Heschel met the woman who became his wife. Heschel had been invited to the Marcus home by Marcus's wife, Antoinette, a concert pianist and singer, for a private recital. There he was introduced to Sylvia Straus, a talented pianist from Cleveland, Ohio. Exactly six years younger than Heschel (they were both born on 11 January), Straus was studying in Cincinnati with the eminent Severin Eisenberger. Her musical performance that evening enchanted Heschel.[9] The two dated before Straus returned to Cleveland, but she soon moved to Los Angeles with her parents. They exchanged letters but did not meet again until three years later, in the summer of 1945, in New York, after Heschel had joined the faculty of the Jewish Theological Seminary. They were married the following year.

Another faculty member who was unimpressed by Heschel was Samuel S. Cohon, the professor of theology, with whom Heschel might have expected to have much in common. Originally from Minsk, Belorussia, Cohon still spoke with a Yiddish accent even though he had been ordained at HUC in 1912, at age twenty-four, and had taught there since 1923. Like Heschel, Cohon took theology seriously (he served for a time as a congregational rabbi), considering Judaism an encounter with the holy, and he knew the works of nineteenth-century and more recent European thinkers, including Franz Rosenzweig and Martin Buber.

Heschel hoped that Cohon would become an ally, if not a spiritual companion. An intellectual leader of Reform Judaism, Cohon was the main drafter of the 1937 Columbus Platform, which supported a return to some traditional observances, the use of Hebrew, and the notion of Jewish peoplehood. At HUC, Cohon offered courses on Hasidism, comparative religion, and systematic and religious thought. But Cohon was put off by Heschel's confusion over American customs. Cohon's tough-minded wife, Irma, remembered that Heschel had asked for an invitation to a Reform conversion ceremony, out of a sincere desire to learn. But he refused to sign the document as a witness, "tremblingly declaring," reported Irma Cohon: "I sign my name to nothing." Even though no traditional Jew would ratify such a ritual, she reproached Heschel for his "nervous adjustment, fearful of personal commitment."[10]

Another time, Cohon was repelled by Heschel's request for personal guidance. According to Irma Cohon, Heschel beseechingly "cornered" her husband, as he would his rebbe. In her words: "Assuring Heschel of his readiness to confer with him, at any time, Cohon explained that he could not presume to stand as a divine intermediary." These two sons of Eastern Europe simply could not find common ground.[11]

But Heschel did develop a personal relationship with Sheldon Blank, the other Bible specialist, and especially with his wife, Amy, whom Heschel asked to witness his certificate of naturalization. The Blanks were Classical Reform Jews and belonged to Cincinnati's two leading temples, Rockdale and Wise (HUC faculty were given free membership at both institutions). They did not keep a kosher home, but in their way they celebrated the Sabbath and holidays devoutly, often inviting HUC students to join them.

Heschel appreciated Amy Blank's journey from tepid Orthodoxy to enthusiastic Reform Judaism. She was born and reared in London, but her parents were originally from Germany. Dissatisfied with their lax traditionalism, she joined the Reform movement. After she and her husband were married, they moved to Cincinnati, where they reared two daughters and Amy taught at the Rockdale Temple Sunday School. Heschel would come to take tea with her, and they would speak German together. They shared an interest in the arts: as Amy published poetry and was involved in theater and other creative activities.[12]

Less advantageous to Heschel's career was his admiration for the most radical member of the HUC faculty, Abraham Cronbach, the founder of the Social Studies Department. On the surface, theirs was a most unlikely alliance since Cronbach was a moral extremist who sought to Americanize Judaism far beyond Classical Reform. Cronbach actively opposed Zionism and the use of Hebrew in religious services and Jewish life. He was a pacifist during the First and Second World Wars, and spoke at the funeral of Julius and Ethel Rosenberg, who were executed for treason.[13]

Cronbach appealed to Heschel as a mensch, a human being of unusually strong character, and as an uncompromising dissident. At HUC, "Crony" taught courses on the Psalms, the Book of Proverbs, the chaplaincy, social welfare, refugee aid, public assistance, and civil liberties. He offered an advanced course on Jewish social ideals in the Bible, Talmud, Midrash, Maimonides, and other Hebrew sources (the catalog states that students were required to read the texts in the original). In class he invariably sided with the "villains" over conventional heroes.

For Cronbach, anything in the Jewish tradition that did not meet his standards was not Jewish, while anything outside the tradition that was ethical was. He and his wife chose not to have children but adopted the sickliest girl in the local orphanage. When traveling by train he would sit up all night in the coach, refusing a luxury that those who could not afford sleeping car accommodations could not share.[14]

Cronbach practiced the humanism of Felix Adler (founder of the Ethical Culture movement), who upheld the sanctity of the human personality. In his awkward style, Cronbach wrote in the *Hebrew Union College Bulletin:* "Psychologically analyze the devout worshiper, and social reactions appear at every turn. . . . 'He prayeth best who loveth best.'"[15] Heschel shared Cronbach's reverence for each human being as an image of the divine.

Heschel urged his closest student, Samuel Dresner, to accompany Cronbach to a home for unwed mothers so that Dresner could see how Cronbach made the Bible relevant to everyday life. There, in his high-pitched, nasal voice, Cronbach recounted the story of "a very prominent citizen," Abraham, and his "fancy wife," Sarah. They were proper and correct in their behavior. One of their servants, Hagar, became pregnant out of wedlock. (The young mothers became interested.) Enraged, Sarah drove Hagar out of the house; she wandered in the woods with her baby, Ishmael, and so on. (The mothers were in tears.) Cronbach had related the Bible's sympathy for victims of injustice to their own lives.[16]

At the Cronbach home, Heschel and HUC students met ministers, social workers, local Jews and Christians, and members of the African American community. One day Heschel complimented Maurice Davis, a rabbinical student who later married Cronbach's daughter, Marion, for befriending one of the black men on the janitorial staff without talking about it. (Maimonides considered anonymous gifts to be the highest form of charity.) Emotionally Heschel told Davis, "I want you to know that is what Judaism is all about," then walked away.[17]

Traditional Jewish Communities

Heschel often left the Clifton area where he lived and worked and walked the two or three miles to the Jewish neighborhoods of the Avondale section. There he bought kosher food and met people who shared his learning and observance, as well as his support for Jewish Palestine and modern Hebrew culture. Heschel became closest to Rabbi Louis Feinberg and his family: his wife, Rosa, and their two daughters, Bertha (Bertsie) and Miriam (Mimi). Feinberg was a self-effacing Conservative rabbi who integrated Orthodoxy and modernity into his life and ministry.[18] Feinberg's family had emigrated from Lithuania; he earned his B.A. at the University of Pennsylvania and in 1916 was ordained at the Jewish Theological Seminary. From the 1920s to 1950 he was rabbi of the Avondale synagogue Adath Israel, the leading Conservative congregation in Cincinnati.

Rabbi Feinberg's worship services were congenial to Heschel. The prayers were traditional, and men and women sat separately, but with no mechitzah dividing them. The synagogue was a large, impressive building of white limestone in neoclassical design with a Byzantine interior. Unique for that period, the circular ceiling of the sanctuary was decorated with Hebrew quotations from the Bible, Mishnah, medieval poetry, and works of the Jewish nationalist poet Hayyim Nahman Bialik, showing support for a homeland in Palestine and modern Hebrew. Heschel also appreciated the cantor's beautiful voice and expressive feeling.[19]

The Feinbergs were a warm, hospitable family. Rosa, from the Orthodox German Jewish community of Baltimore, spoke German, although her parents were born in America, and around 1935 the Feinbergs adopted a teenaged German Jewish boy. Heschel helped them host HUC students at their home on Shabbat for the Friday evening meal or the Saturday noon meal after services.[20]

Once, while staying overnight with the Feinbergs, Heschel accidentally glimpsed an intimate act showing Rabbi Feinberg's attachment to God. During the nine days leading into Tisha B'Av, commemorating the destruction of the ancient Temple in Jerusalem, devout Jews follow strictures of mourning, which include not wearing freshly laundered clothing. Heschel noticed Feinberg in his bedroom taking out several shirts, putting them on, and then taking them off again, thereby making them "used" shirts that could be worn during the nine days. This was true piety, according to Heschel, unusual in America and completely private, shared only with the divine.[21]

Heschel's other spiritual resource was a prominent Orthodox rabbi, Eliezer Silver, the forceful and flamboyant leader of the Kneseth Israel synagogue. Born and reared in the Kovno province of Lithuania, Silver mastered the Talmudic method of Brisk with Rabbi Hayim Soloveitchik and was affiliated with Rabbi Hayyim Ozer Grodzenski, head of Agudah (Agudat Israel, the Orthodox political party) in Poland and Lithuania. In 1907 Silver immigrated to the United States and served Orthodox congregations in Harrisburg, Pennsylvania, and Springfield, Massachusetts, before arriving in 1931 in Cincinnati, the stronghold of Reform Judaism. Silver despised Reform Judaism as a blasphemous source of assimilation and visited the HUC campus only once, to put the institution in *herem* (excommunication). In 1925 Silver was elected president of the Union of Orthodox Rabbis of the United States and Canada (the Agudat Harabonim), remaining a member of its presidium until his death.[22]

In 1939 Silver became founding president of the American branch of Agudat Israel, by that time an international organization of Orthodox rabbis opposed to Zionism and other forms of modernity, which included as leaders several of Heschel's close relatives. Mordecai Shlomo Friedman, the Boyaner rebbe, was a vice president. Another cousin, Rabbi Yehuda Aryeh Leib Perlow, the Novominsker rebbe of Williamsburg, in Brooklyn, opened the 1940 annual convention in Cincinnati, commemorating the death of Hayyim Ozer Grodzenski. Heschel's brother-in-law Abraham Joshua Heschel, the Kopitzhinitzer rebbe, was one of Agudah's most revered members.[23]

Heschel and the other refugee scholars also honored Silver's heroic role in helping to rescue Jews from Nazi Europe. After the Germans invaded Poland, Silver founded the *Va'ad Hazalah* (emergency committee), dedicated to saving Orthodox rabbis, scholars, heads of yeshivas, and students. Silver traveled to Warsaw and met with Poland's Hasidic leader, Rabbi Abraham Mordecai Alter, the once powerful Gerer rebbe, whose vibrant Hasidic community had attracted Heschel during his youth, though he did not study there. With aid enlisted from the Ohio senator Robert Taft, Silver rescued the Gerer rebbe from the Germans, enabling him to reach Jerusalem the following year. The Va'ad also sent life-saving packages of food and clothing to Jews under Nazi domination and advocated the controversial policy of ransoming individual Jews.[24]

Since it was close to a three-mile walk to Rabbi Silver's synagogue, Heschel did not go there regularly on Shabbat, but sometimes he prayed there during the week. Rabbis Feinberg and Silver both offered safe havens for Heschel's devotions: Feinberg embodied the traditional wellsprings of American Conservative Judaism and Silver the zeal of Lithuanian Orthodoxy.

Other ties were formed over the issue of Jewish Palestine. Heschel became friends with David Brodsky, a Zionist *shaliah* (representative or messenger) from Warsaw, whom he first met at a rooming house in the Avondale area. A twenty-six-year-old activist who had recently arrived from Europe, Brodsky earned money by pressing clothes for a Jewish tailor in nearby Kentucky. He came from a learned, Zionist, though antireligious family. His father was a Hebrew teacher who had created a youth community on an agricultural farm. Brodsky's sister Elonka Prozhabotsky (David modified his family name to Brodsky) became famous as a fighter in the Polish underground after the German invasion. (She later died of typhus in Auschwitz.) Brodsky became a delegate to the Zionist Congress in Baden in 1939. He raised money for the Resistance, trained pioneers in Lithuania, and escaped through Russia to Cincinnati in 1942, where he recruited for the Labor Zionist Youth Organization (*Habonim*).[25]

But most important for Heschel's emotional life during those years in Cincinnati was the chance to teach a Sabbath afternoon *Midrasha* (study group) sponsored by the Cincinnati Bureau of Jewish Education (BJE). The BJE was a nondenominational organization, which sponsored a Talmud Torah (afternoon Hebrew school), cultural activities like drama and music, courses on modern Hebrew, and a Zionist youth group, which was also supported by Rabbi Feinberg and his congregation.[26]

Each Shabbat afternoon until he left Cincinnati, Heschel walked to Bureau headquarters on Rockdale Avenue. Waiting for him were eight to ten young Hebrew speakers, high school or college students. Most of them had received scholarships for a year of study at the excellent Hertzlia Gymnasium in the Jewish city of Tel Aviv, and they returned fluent in Hebrew. Although he was opposed to secularizing the religion, Heschel was a cultural Zionist, committed to a Jewish state in Palestine and the use of Hebrew in the Diaspora. Like his students, he spoke impeccable modern Hebrew with the Sephardic accent of the Jewish pioneers.

For those precious hours of text study and personal communication in Hebrew, Heschel was freed from the tensions of life at Hebrew Union College. As one of his students, Hanna Rosen, remembered, when he arrived at class his face would be sad. After half an hour, he would shine, his whole bearing transformed.[27] With these students he could behave naturally. The group included Simcha Kling, who had recently returned from Jewish Palestine; Aviva and Shulamit Gootman; Nechama Tannenbaum; Nechama Weiner, who was born in Tel Aviv and came to America in 1940; Myra Yuhlfelder, who was from a relatively assimilated family; Nechama Levin, who had lived ten years in Palestine; Burt Berman; and Herbie Wechsler, the German Jewish student at the University of Cincinnati who lived with the Feinbergs. Pesach Krauss joined the following year, as did Bertsie Feinberg, the rabbi's elder daughter.

With this committed group, Heschel was an effective pedagogue who instilled critical thinking. They studied classical texts such as *The Kuzari*, Judah Halevi's philosophical dialogue; the Spanish fifteenth-century philosopher Joseph Albo's *Sefer ha-Ikkarim* (Book of principles), a treatise on faith; and the *Shir ha-shirim* (Song of songs), among others. Sometimes he would spend two hours on a few sentences. He also asked students to write essays on the *Tanakh* (the Hebrew Bible), a book they studied carefully. This was the first time they were invited to think about the Holy Book in its entirety, although Myra Yuhlfelder was the only one to complete her paper. This young scholar later became professor of Greek and Latin at Bryn Mawr College.

Heschel was unusually flexible in his teaching, combining the formal European lecture format with the student participation valued by Frankfurt Lehrhaus pedagogy. True, some students did not always pay attention, squirming, chatting, or making jokes. They did not all consider him a good teacher. Some did not appreciate his attention to details and his digressions: he never got to *The Kuzari* itself but remained with the introduction. But most students remembered with nostalgia chanting Hasidic melodies at sunset for the *havdalah* service separating the holy day from the rest of the week. As the room darkened, Heschel taught them wordless songs (*nigunim*) from his past. The mood was peaceful and melancholy.

With Pesach Krauss, Heschel felt a further affinity; he was not embarrassed to ask the older, male Midrasha student at the University of Cincinnati what color tie he should wear. The self-conscious Heschel was concerned about his clothing; he wanted to dress like a proper American. Decades later, Rabbi Krauss, chaplain at the Sloan-Kettering hospital for the treatment of cancer, recalled those classes with reverence as he chanted Heschel's nigunim to fortify dying patients and their grieving families.[28]

In addition to teaching at the Midrasha, Heschel joined the Ivriah Society, founded in 1911 by Yosef Gootman, father of his students Aviva and Shulamit, and Samuel Cohon of HUC. This group was associated with the Cincinnati branch of Poale Zion (Labor Zionists), organized to counteract the anti-Zionism at HUC. For decades they sponsored lectures and welcomed prominent Hebrew writers, poets, educators, and scholars to their monthly forums.

Even at HUC, Heschel had occasions to share his love for modern Hebrew. Interested students created the Mann-Diesendruck Society, named for two deceased HUC professors. They met every Sabbath and spoke only Hebrew.[29] Various HUC professors were invited to lecture, among them Samuel Cohon and Heschel.

Heschel also dated occasionally, although none of the acquaintances developed into a lasting relationship. Perhaps he reserved his warmest feelings for the captivating Sylvia Straus, who was continuing her musical studies elsewhere. But Heschel enjoyed female friendships, such as his relationship with Hanna Grad Goodman, a married woman with two brothers and a brother-in-law in the armed forces. Exceedingly active in the Jewish community, she gave singing classes at the community Talmud Torah and directed the BJE's theater group, as well as teaching acting to make extra money. In addition, she directed the BJE's extension activities and the Cincinnati Zionist Youth Council, and after the United States entered the war she wrote regularly to more than forty servicemen to help raise morale. She was as busy and preoccupied in her world as Heschel was in his.[30]

Perhaps because of its clear boundaries, this was a real friendship, respectful and affirmative. Heschel felt relaxed and natural with Goodman. They enjoyed frequent telephone conversations, and they argued a lot, a true marker of trust. Heschel was always patient with her, especially when they touched upon serious topics such as philosophy or religion. They even had an enthusiastic debate about God, although their discussions tended to focus on their work, such as the plays she was directing, some of which Heschel attended.

Yet there was a limit to what they shared. Heschel did not talk to Goodman about his social life, although a friend told her about a date with an attractive young professor at HUC. He did not mention the great Hasidic dynasties from which he was descended, and she did not tell him that one of her direct ancestors was the great Rabbi Israel Salanter, a *mitnagid* (opponent of Hasidism) and founder of the rigorous *Mussar* movement in Lithuania.

Heschel tended to hold back his most intimate emotions. He did not confide even to Goodman about his European experiences or speak of his close family members confined to the Warsaw Ghetto and Nazi-occupied Vienna. Perhaps he felt that no American could fathom his grief or his sacred calling.

The Consolations of Work

As HUC's second term began, on 6 January 1941, the war continued to rage in Europe. Heschel was dismayed at the indifference of most Americans to the situation abroad; newspapers like the *Cincinnati Post* and *New York Times* reported news of the war in detail, but even they usually relegated it to their inside pages. Around the time Heschel turned thirty-four, on 11 January, his world seemed to be collapsing. He acknowledged his pessimism in a letter to his friend Eduard Strauss, who had written to him after a four-month silence: "The good is not pleasant and 'the beautiful is nothing but the beginning of the horrible.'" Yet he affirmed his faith in God: "I think that, despite everything, we are not at all deserted. And this is what counts! We must heighten our awareness of what is beyond joy and pain."[31]

Work helped Heschel overcome his gloom. He continued his research on medieval Jewish philosophy while launching a personal project: essays in English on piety and holiness. He began by republishing earlier articles. He placed his Hebrew essay on prayer—originally prepared in Warsaw in 1939 for a volume commemorating Mayer Balaban—in *Bitzaron Hebrew Monthly*, an American periodical. Heschel then asked Strauss to reprint another essay he had written on prayer, this one in German, in the *Bulletin* of Congregation Habonim. That summer Heschel returned to New York and continued to make significant professional inroads. Now a master of English prose, his first major article in English, "An Analysis of Piety," was accepted by the *Review of Religion*, put out by Columbia University's Department of Philosophy and Religion. The editors also invited him to review a book edited by the eminent historian Salo Wittmayer Baron celebrating the eight hundredth anniversary of the birth of Maimonides. Heschel was being recognized by academic specialists.[32]

In the fall, Heschel put the finishing touches on "A Concise Dictionary of Hebrew Philosophical Terms," a mimeographed booklet (eighty-six pages) intended "primarily for the use of the students of the Hebrew Union College," which he described as "entirely pedagogical." Heschel and his students had gathered "English equivalents of medieval philosophical vocabulary" from several dictionaries, particularly Klatzkin's, to help beginners.[33]

As the spring 1942 term began, Heschel was worried about the renewed silence of Eduard Strauss, and he wrote inviting Strauss to visit Cincinnati so they could speak together. Four days later he wrote again from Chicago, trying to give Strauss an emotional boost by relating a conversation he had had with their mutual friend Fritz Kaufmann, another German Jewish refugee, who was teaching philosophy at Northwestern University. Heschel informed Strauss that Kaufmann had spoken of his delightful encounter with Strauss in 1933, "one of the two unforgettable conversations during those years." Strauss at his best, said Kaufmann, was "'pure fire without smoke.'" Heschel added, "This expression filled me with such profound joy, that I needed to share it with you."[34]

Heschel, too, found his spirits raised by Kaufmann, for they both practiced phenomenology, the analysis of consciousness established by Edmund Husserl in the 1920s. In Germany, Kaufmann had been Husserl's assistant at the University of Freiberg until he was expelled by the Nazis in 1936; he then taught at the Berlin Hochschule, publishing graceful articles on Ernst Cassirer, esthetics, and phenomenology. (Some ten years later, Heschel sent Kaufmann the manuscript of his first major book, *Man Is Not Alone*, soliciting his critical advice.)[35]

The meeting reinforced Heschel's efforts to launch his own scholarly program. Barely two years after arriving in the United States, he now felt ready to announce his grand design: the construction of a theology based on his studies of the metaphysics of the medieval Jewish philosopher Ibn Gabirol, which he had published in Europe in heavily footnoted German essays. These dry, technical monographs served a higher purpose, as he had confided to Buber and Henry Corbin, the French Islamic scholar, in 1938. Heschel envisioned a "systematology," a philosophical rendition of spiritual insight and Jewish living, and its creation became the intellectual enterprise of his American career.[36]

Heschel announced his ambitious goal in the March 1942 *Hebrew Union College Bulletin*, the official newsletter to alumni and potential donors, along with news of two other academic projects. The first was the completion of Heschel's revision of Zevi Diesendruck's manuscript on Maimonides; Rabbi Joshua Loth Liebman of Boston had been engaged to translate the introduction. The second was an English translation of Heschel's 1935 biography of Maimonides. As it happened, Diesendruck's book never appeared, while the English translation of Heschel's *Maimonides* did not come out until 1982. His most consequential declaration, however, would prove accurate. After informing readers that his first theological essay in English, "An Analysis of Piety," had appeared that month in the *Review of Religion* he proclaimed his mission as a Jewish theologian: "Dr. Abraham Heschel is now engaged in preparing a volume on a systematized study of the philosophy of the Jewish Religion."[37]

Bolstered by these projects, Heschel decided to pursue his relationship with Martin Buber more assertively. He knew that the previous year Buber had submitted the manuscript of a historical novel, *Gog and Magog*, to the Jewish Publication Society (JPS) in Philadelphia and was awaiting a response. Buber was seeking American readers, since he had financial problems and could no longer publish his books in their original German. Heschel believed that he could help with this, and he wrote to Buber, explaining that his twenty months of despair, and his distance from the suffering, prevented him from writing. Heschel yearned for the elder man's warmth and intelligence, adding in Hebrew the hope that God would allow them to be reunited in better times. He also reminded Buber that he could exert some influence at the Jewish Publication Society and sent regards to Buber's wife; perhaps most consequential, Heschel informed Buber that he was advancing his philosophy of religion, his system.[38]

Buber answered almost immediately, restoring their collegial communication. In the meantime, Heschel mobilized his contacts. He met with the former HUC librarian Adolph Oko and received accounts of the difficulties surrounding Buber's other new book, *Der Glaube Israels* (translated as *The Prophetic Faith*). Heschel contacted members of the JPS editorial board—Shalom Spiegel of the Jewish Theological Seminary, Salo W. Baron of Columbia, and David Philipson of Hebrew Union College—while keeping track of responses from the three outside readers. Heschel himself submitted a letter of support. *Gog and Magog* was finally accepted by the society under the title *For the Sake of Heaven,* translated by Ludwig Lewisohn.[39]

The experience taught Heschel that scholarly publishing in the United States was a bleak business, restricted by financial considerations. He wrote Buber that even William Foxwell Albright, the preeminent archeologist at Johns Hopkins, had to print his books at his own expense.[40] This situation may have encouraged Heschel to elaborate his religious philosophy in a less technical style.

Heschel designed his first major essay in English, "An Analysis of Piety," for a general audience. Describing Hasidic spirituality in modern terms, with no source references, he drew his ideal portrait of "the pious man" from his uncle, Rabbi Alter Israel Shimon Perlow, the Novominsker rebbe of Warsaw. Without focusing on Judaism as such, Heschel extended his phenomenology of prophetic inspiration to rescue the old notion of piety from its negative connotations, although he did confront the negative: "[The pious person] feels the hidden warmth of good in all things, and finds hints of God cropping up in almost every ordinary thing on which he gazes. It is for this reason that his words bring hope into a sordid and despairing world."[41]

Portraying "the inner life of a pious man," Heschel exhibited a personal style of writing: concise, harmonious, with a penchant for aphorisms and literary devices like antithesis and alliteration. His amalgam of analytic and poetic prose was unusual, and it had a pragmatic as well as stylistic function: to convey his foundational insight, the recentering of the self to God. The pious person, he wrote, "is not aiming to penetrate into the sacred. Rather he is striving to be himself penetrated and actuated by the sacred, eager to yield to its force, to identify himself with every trend in the world which is towards the divine." Religious thinking, that is, is recentered from the human "subject" in search of God to the ultimate subject, God.[42]

Other key ideas emerged that Heschel would elaborate in future writings: reverence, freedom and responsibility, the divine ownership of nature, the illusion of human mastery, conceit and vainglory, the externalization of religious life, the kinship of human and divine. He concluded with a vision of a "ladder leading to the ultimate," ascending from the ethical to the holy. Theology, for Heschel, was inseparable from ethics.

The final paragraph of "An Analysis of Piety" is like a prose poem, deftly constructed to resonate with modern religious aspirations: "Man's task is to reconcile liberty with service, reason with faith. This is the deepest wisdom man can attain. It is our destiny to serve, to surrender." He concluded by recognizing the holiness of life itself, defining death as "the ultimate self-dedication to the divine." The last line became one of Heschel's guiding ideas: "For the pious man it is a privilege to die."[43]

Shortly after the publication of "An Analysis of Piety," an enlarged, Hebrew version was accepted for publication in *Sefer Ha-Shanah*, the yearbook of the Histadrut Ivrit, an American organization devoted to modern Hebrew culture. In addition, the prestigious scholarly journal *Jewish Quarterly Review* accepted Heschel's monograph on reason and faith in the work of Saadia Gaon (882–942) for a special issue commemorating the millennium of the thinker's death. Heschel was earning recognition from established specialists as well as from general readers.[44]

His elegant monograph in English on faith and religious knowledge according to Saadia was a masterpiece of *Wissenschaft des Judentums* (scientific historical Jewish scholarship), a rigorous textual, philosophical, and linguistic study, with exhaustive references to sources in English, German, Hebrew, and Arabic. It appeared along with contributions by America's leading Judaic scholars, among them Salo W. Baron, Harry Austryn Wolfson of Harvard University, Abraham Halkin of the Jewish Theological Seminary, and Aron Freimann of the New York Public Library (whom Heschel knew from Frankfurt).

Heschel's study appeared in two installments, in 1943 and in 1944. He then reprinted them together as a pamphlet of sixty-seven pages with the Jewish publisher Philip Feldheim. Entitled *The Quest for Certainty in Saadia's Philosophy*, it became Heschel's first "book" in English. Heschel may have intended his title as an implicit challenge to the 1939 book of that name by the American pragmatist philosopher John Dewey, but he was more explicitly responding to current debates between neo-Orthodox and rationalist thinkers, both Jewish and Christian: "What [Saadia] attempted to convey amounted to the view that religion *is* knowledge and that secular knowledge itself cannot dispense with faith." It was as if Saadia were a precursor of Heschel's own program to promote closeness to God.[45]

Part 1 of "The Quest for Certainty" defined faith as compatible with reason. Although reason and "critical examination" served as guarantors, intuition or insight were the true modes of religious knowledge. Part 2, "Reason and Revelation," repudiated both complacent Orthodoxy (which promulgated obedience to law to the exclusion of critical thought) and shallow rationalism and empiricism, or pragmatism, the reigning American educational ideology. Heschel even found in the medieval thinker a proto-Hasidic witness: "While eliminating all anthropomorphic features of his concept of God, [Saadia's] mind eventually overflows in a song of praise, an outlet for his affection for God, that was welling up in his heart." Heschel's "critical postscript" justified his own intuitive certainty: "The preference for truth is implanted by God in our minds."[46]

During his first two years at HUC, Heschel had established his creative method, publishing essays that contained the seeds of fuller works to come. Starting with academic monographs on medieval Jewish philosophy, he added lyrical pieces in English that combined logic with poetic prose. Saadia's sophisticated apologetics *The Book of Belief and Opinions* (which Heschel retranslated as "Creed and Faith") became a conceptual model for *Man Is Not Alone* (1951). Almost instinctively, Heschel was constructing a treatise on spirituality and ethics, a modern and devout philosophy of religion.

3

Institutional Struggles and World War (1942–1944)

*Emblazoned over the gates of the world in which we live is the
escutcheon of the demons. The mark of Cain in the face of man has come
to overshadow the likeness of God. There have never been so much guilt
and distress, agony and terror. At no time has the earth been so soaked
with blood. Fellow-men turned out to be evil ghosts, monstrous
and weird. Ashamed and dismayed to live in such a world,
we ask: Who is responsible?*
—Heschel, "The Meaning of This War" (1943)

FOR HIS THIRD ACADEMIC YEAR AT HEBREW UNION COLLEGE, HESCHEL WAS promoted to instructor in Jewish philosophy and rabbinics, an acknowledgment of his expertise in Talmud and medieval thought. His assigned courses, however, remained mostly elementary: liturgy (in the Preparatory Department), Rashi's commentaries (for the lower and medium levels), and intermediate Hebrew.[1]

On campus he was perceived in contradictory ways. He still looked like an immigrant. Youthful and clean-shaven, he combed his dark hair straight back or in a pompadour. He dressed meticulously, wearing rimless glasses and a suit, sometimes sporting a bow tie. At times warm, at others distracted, he struck Jacob Marcus as calculating, "frightened and eager to be accepted, wanting to please everyone," while he seemed to many students to be a spiritual model.[2] Both views were valid. Heschel wanted to succeed, and he worked relentlessly to achieve his goals, which were themselves contradictory. He needed to secure himself professionally, and gain academic authority, to be able effectively to communicate his vision of human holiness.

Heschel felt professionally threatened when Samuel Atlas arrived at HUC in April 1942. Eight years older than Heschel, Atlas had taught philosophy at the Institute for Judaic Studies in Warsaw from 1929 to 1934 (Heschel was there during the 1938–39 academic year) and then moved to London. Heschel had known him there when he was awaiting his immigrant visa in 1940; in fact, he had enlisted Atlas to lecture at his Institute for Jewish Learning. At HUC, Atlas was a special instructor with the title of lecturer in Talmud and philosophy, a position that was higher than Heschel's. Heschel feared that Atlas would be given the advanced courses he himself hoped to teach.[3]

A silent rivalry developed between the two men, who represented two conflicting strains of European Jewish culture. Atlas was a classic mitnagid who hated Hasidism. Born in Kovno, Lithuania, he was educated at the famous Slobodka yeshiva but had left this narrow religious world as a teenager and, after witnessing the Russian Revolution, had completed his humanistic education at the universities of Berlin, Marburg, and Giessen. Like Heschel, Atlas was a man of contradictions. A neo-Kantian rationalist, Atlas practiced Orthodoxy, and his theology could be summarized, abstractly, as: "God is the idea of the ultimate coincidence of the 'ought' and the 'is' that occurs only in eternity."[4] He was just the sort of critical philosopher, steeped in the Talmud's legal discussions, likely to disdain Heschel's reverential manner of thinking.

Yet both men admired Rabbi Eliezer Silver, a fierce defender of Orthodoxy, and Heschel did try to make friends with Atlas, though he was more intrigued by Atlas's wife, Celia, a shrewd, attractive, cultured Russian Jew who had studied literature at the universities of Moscow and Berlin. The Atlases sometimes invited Heschel to dinner on Friday nights. On these occasions Heschel would speak only with Celia, who didn't like Heschel very much, considering him a *Schöngeist* (esthete), preoccupied with literature and other artistic subjects. The Atlases also saw Heschel as "secretive, planning, scheming," in part because both Heschel and Samuel Atlas wanted to leave Cincinnati and visited New York as often as possible. (Heschel was the first to make the break, resigning in 1945 to join the Jewish Theological Seminary, where Atlas also sought a position. In 1951 Atlas joined the Reform seminary in New York, the Jewish Institute of Religion, which had merged with HUC.)[5]

Heschel's curriculum worries were soon resolved. Concentrating on Talmud, Atlas took over Alexander Guttmann's class in Mishnah and only one of Heschel's classes in philosophy, while Heschel continued to offer two required courses on medieval Jewish philosophy and an elective seminar on Maimonides.[6] His deepest pedagogical aspirations, however, remained frustrated. It was Samuel Cohon who offered seminars on Hasidism, although there was little student interest.

The New Generation

Heschel's hopes were rekindled in the fall of 1942 by a group of twenty-two freshmen, the largest class ever to enter HUC. These candidates were, in many ways, a typical band of young American males. Eighteen came from large cities, mostly in the Midwest and the East; nine were college graduates, and one had a Ph.D., while thirteen were still undergraduates and required to matriculate simultaneously at the University of Cincinnati. These Reform Jews, many of whom became prominent rabbis or religious thinkers, presented both challenges and opportunities for Heschel.

Some had passed the HUC entrance examinations without any problems. These were Eugene B. Borowitz from Columbus, Ohio, who also entered the senior class at the University of Cincinnati, and Samuel Dresner from Chicago, Peter Lewinski from Watertown, Connecticut (a refugee from Germany), R. Lowell Rubenstein from New York (who became the radical theologian Richard L. Rubenstein), and Arnold J. Wolf from Chicago, all of whom entered the junior class at the university. Other students, including Robert Bergman from New York (a senior), were accepted provisionally because they lacked adequate preparation. Albert Plotkin from South Bend, Indiana (who had a Bachelor's degree in English from Notre Dame), was accepted because he "indicated some knowledge of Judaism."[7]

Heschel still lived in the dormitory, and he extended himself for his sympathetic students. They developed mutually helpful relationships. The students admired his determination to master the English language. Albert Plotkin, who lived across the hall, was fascinated by the way Heschel devoured literature, constantly seeking the right word in Roget's *Thesaurus,* and communicating his excitement about his progress: "Oh Albert! Today I learned ten new words." One day Heschel heard Plotkin typing and asked him for help preparing his manuscripts. The student agreed and continued this secretarial function for the next three years. In return, Heschel tutored Plotkin in Hebrew.

American culture fascinated Heschel. Some evenings he would exercise in the HUC gymnasium, and he went regularly to the corner theater on the hill down Clifton Avenue, where the feature film changed twice a week. Movies provided a good way for Heschel to increase his proficiency in English, and they helped him relax, but he felt guilty about spending his time this way. After one late show he lamented to Arnold Wolf, who often accompanied him, "When my grandfather was tired, he used to read Kabbalah; when I'm tired I go to the movies." It was hard for Heschel to let go, even after working for over twelve hours.[8]

Through his Hasidic upbringing Heschel had developed an exceptional ability to inspire a lasting spiritual commitment in his students. His first American follower was Samuel Dresner, an intense young man from a moderately observant Reform family in Chicago. In high school, Dresner had encountered a homeless woman in downtown Chicago, an experience that changed his focus from sports and girls to questions of evil, God, and moral responsibility. As part of this turn toward the spiritual, Dresner began to study the fundamentals of Judaism with his rabbi, Felix Levy, one of the Reform movement's intellectual leaders. Together with Levy's brilliant nephew Arnold Wolf they took up study of the Humash (the five books of Moses with Rashi's commentaries). Dresner became an undergraduate at Northwestern University, where he met Marvin Fox, an Orthodox Jew who was majoring in philosophy. Dresner eventually decided to become a Reform rabbi, against his parents' wish that he enter an uncle's business.[9]

At HUC, Dresner was ready to be inspired, and a breakthrough came that fall with a chance remark from Heschel, a quotation from *Pirkei Avot* (Ethics of the ancestors): "The shy person cannot learn and the impatient person cannot teach, so you don't be shy and I won't be angry."[10] After several conversations with Heschel outside of class, Dresner became convinced that Heschel was "the greatest Jew of his time"—the zaddik (holy man) of his generation. Dresner became a lifelong disciple of Heschel's. He organized a group of like-minded seekers and, prudently, invited Samuel Cohon, who had traditionalist sympathies, to be its adviser. Sensitive to Heschel's insecurity, they avoided associating him with their drive to introduce Orthodox practices at HUC.

Heschel helped these students understand Jewish spirituality through conversations and his own meticulous observance. He welcomed them to his room for *havdalah,* the haunting prayer ceremony that bids farewell to the Sabbath. He taught them nigunim, melodies without words, and told Hasidic stories as they lit the braided candle, chanting prayers, that separated sacred time from the work week.

Few of the rabbinical students, however, sympathized with this spiritual group, calling them, somewhat derisively, the "Kavanah Boys." (*Kavanah* is the Hebrew term for "intention," the spiritual fervor associated with prayer and Hasidism.) They gave the members satiric nicknames: Peter Lewinski (later changed to Levenson) from the Berlin Hochschule became "pious Pete," Robert Bergman was "mitzvah Bob," Albert Plotkin was "transcendental Al," and Sam Dresner, the ringleader, was "Kavanah Sam." On the fringes of this community were the class's bold intellectuals: Lowell (Richard) Rubenstein, Eugene Borowitz, and Sam's childhood friend, the gifted and sometimes caustic Arnold Wolf.

The other students were equally unimpressed by Heschel. Although Heschel inspired many students outside the classroom, his formal teaching almost destroyed his reputation—and his morale. Cultural differences were largely responsible for this hostility. The European Heschel was disconcerted by his American students' lack of respect. In European universities, students would rise when the professor entered the classroom. (In fact, members of Heschel's Hasidic community in Warsaw used to rise when he, the Hasidic prodigy, entered the room.) Teachers sat at a desk and lectured from notes, often without looking up, while students silently noted the material being presented to them. American students, however, expected to interact with their teachers, and they expressed themselves freely.

In addition, Heschel's teaching methods were old-fashioned. He did not present his lessons methodically but proceeded by means of digressions, a style more appropriate to a yeshiva than to an American college. He would begin by discussing a prayer, then he would move to its Talmudic background, then its

Hasidic background, then its sources in mystical literature, and so on. He referred to so many works that were unfamiliar to them that most students were lost, able to grasp only bits of the lesson. When he tried to arouse them to an awareness of holiness, his ultimate aim in teaching, he could not get through to them. He would ask the class, "Gentlemen, look at this prayer. What does it say to you?" but the students would only sit uncomfortably and smirk. "It's magnificent," he would say, attempting to convey its wonder, but to little effect.[11]

A minority of the students admired him, but most saw Heschel as an affront to their rationalism and their American ideals. They criticized him for being badly prepared, aloof, and sometimes hostile. And, in fact, Heschel often betrayed his frustration, indulging in sarcasm. He sometimes ended class with "Gentlemen, it was almost a pleasure." In retaliation, they made Heschel a butt of humor, even harassment. Students sniffed out his weaknesses and put him on the defensive. They teased him with questions about his faith in God, mocking his Yiddish accent and even taunting him. In the dormitory he was subjected to hazing. Once they put a water-filled condom on his door that splashed him as he entered the room. Another time they hung a dead chicken outside his window, calling it a *dybbuk*, a sarcastic reference to an East European superstition about evil spirits. Such pranks humiliated Heschel.

As Heschel began publishing pieces in English, the students started mocking his writing, especially his opulent literary style. The writer's grace and fervent piety were an affront to their narrow skepticism. During one *Purimspiel*, the comical play that celebrates the raucous holiday, they took aim at the aphoristic ending of "An Analysis of Piety"—"For a pious man it is a privilege to die." They chanted a series of parodies: "For a pious man it is a privilege to eat," ". . . it is a privilege to drink," ". . . it is a privilege to piss," and so on.

Heschel would occasionally retaliate. One day Dresner had introduced him to his Orthodox friend Marvin Fox, who had joined the army and was visiting Cincinnati on official business. Heschel and Fox talked for a while, and Heschel invited him to his class on medieval commentaries of the Bible, in which they were studying the Humash. No one paid attention to the visitor in military uniform, and when Heschel entered the class the students showed little respect. At first Fox was amused that six or seven senior rabbinical students were still learning this rudimentary text in traditional education, and he was even more surprised when they placed a "pony," an English translation, inside their Hebrew-language edition of the Humash. Heschel began the class by

asking a student to read the Hebrew text and translate; this was not so difficult, since the student had a pony. The Rashi questions that accompanied it as
commentary were more challenging. The student struggled with every word,
even with Heschel helping him. Heschel then presented Rashi's first principle: "So what is Rashi's question? Mr. ———?" The future rabbi was at a
total loss. Other students made snide comments. Heschel repeated the same
uncomfortable exercise with two others, with equal results. Yet they did not
seem embarrassed.

Then, with some malice, Heschel suggested, "Perhaps our visitor would
like to read?" The students began to laugh. When Fox respectfully declined,
Heschel looked at him pleadingly. Fox then agreed, and a student handed him
a Humash. Fox answered, "That's OK, I can do without," and he proceeded to
recite the next two verses from memory. Students were staggered. For the next
twenty minutes or so Heschel and Fox discussed Rashi and other commentaries, which they had long since memorized. Heschel was having a wonderful
time. When the class over, and they were walking out, Heschel exclaimed,
"You just gave me the happiest day I have had in this institution."[12]

There were students who appreciated the rigorous way Heschel taught
Rashi, however, and the way he would ask, "What is really bothering him?"
"What does the text really say to you?" His classes on liturgy were generally
appreciated, though many students had never participated in or even seen a
traditional weekday morning service. Heschel was able to convey his love of
worship, sometimes taking his classes to an Orthodox synagogue or to Rabbi
Feinberg's service at Adath Israel. Students who responded to these outings
were invited to the Feinbergs' home for Shabbat.[13]

Outside of class, Heschel counseled students; he listened to them, encouraged them, and often confided in them. He called them by their first names,
unlike most of the other professors, establishing a personal bond. Heschel
could find the right moment to open up to a student. Once he spoke of his
Berlin doctoral dissertation to Albert Plotkin, who had praised a lecture he
gave on the prophets. "Albert," he said, "you know I wrote this book during
the worst period of barbarism, beatings, and hatred, glorification of war. In this
atmosphere, I was writing my pathos." To comfort him Plotkin replied, "Well,
Doctor, some day, one of your students will visit Berlin and teach what you
have taught." And indeed, inspired by Heschel, Plotkin wrote a dissertation
on the prophet Jeremiah's language of pathos and sympathy and years later
lectured on Heschel's book *The Prophets* at a Judaic studies conference in
Berlin.[14]

Heschel could lead receptive students to religious insights. One day he walked into class and said, "Something very great happened today." "What?" asked Plotkin. Heschel responded, "The sun rose." "So what?" asked Plotkin. Heschel said, "Did you ever see the sun rise?" "No," Plotkin replied. Heschel suggested that the next morning they take a walk. He was demonstrating to the future rabbi how the most mundane event could evoke awe and radical amazement, the fountain of sacred sensitivity.[15]

Sometimes, Heschel inspired his students through gently proffered criticism. One day, returning to HUC from the Conservative synagogue with Eugene Borowitz, Heschel noticed that his student's shirt collar was frayed. Heschel reminded Borowitz that a *talmid hakham* (religious scholar) should always appear in public properly dressed so as not to dishonor the Torah. Borowitz was impressed by the way Heschel had spoken in spiritual terms instead of admonishing the rabbi-to-be about how congregants would expect him to dress.[16]

Coping with Catastrophe

Heschel and the other refugee scholars continued to have problems adjusting to life in Cincinnati. One way to alleviate their sense of alienation was to focus more on their research than on classroom techniques. Another means was humor; when they were gathered together they would sometimes joke about the American faculty. One night, at Abraham Cronbach's home, Julius Lewy, Samuel Atlas, Elias Epstein, and Heschel were debating the correct pronunciation of ancient Hebrew. Lewy, the Assyriologist, explained that Isaiah would not have understood any of them. Heschel then recalled that when he had received Morgenstern's invitation in Warsaw to join HUC, his English was so poor that he had had to hire an English letter writer to help compose his acceptance. Lewy leaned across the table, pointed his finger at Heschel, and said, "That is where you made your first mistake. You should have answered Morgenstern in Hebrew . . . And let him get the translator!"[17]

At other times Heschel allowed himself to poke fun at American Jewish customs he encountered in Cincinnati. One time an elderly Reform woman asked his blessing for a "confirmation." Heschel was unaware that the Reform temples had taken over the Christian term to describe graduation from Sunday school. Asking his European colleagues in Yiddish, "What is a confirmation?" Heschel roared with laughter. Privately, but good-naturedly, he joked about the slack Jewish observance at HUC. Heschel was friendly with the school engineer, a Seventh-day Adventist who lived on campus and refused to answer the bell or do any work after sundown on Friday, just like traditional Jews. Laughing, Heschel claimed that he was the only *shomer Shabbos* (true Sabbath observer) at HUC.[18]

But during these years of war, Heschel endured an estrangement from the American Jewish community that was far more bitter than his problems adjusting to Hebrew Union. He remained silent about this period for twenty years, opening up only when he was interviewed in 1963 by a Yiddish-speaking journalist, Gershon Jacobson, a Jewish refugee from the Soviet Union. That conversation in his mother tongue opened an emotional floodgate. Heschel explained that in 1941 he could not make American Jews understand the situation in Europe. He had tried unsuccessfully to persuade "a prominent person active in Jewish communal affairs and a devoted Zionist" to help Jews in the Warsaw Ghetto, who "live[d] with the belief that American Jewry [was] not resting [on their behalf]. If they [had known] about our indifference [to them] in Warsaw, the Jews there would [have] die[d] of despair. However, my words fell on deaf ears."[19]

The following summer in New York, Heschel witnessed a massive failure of American Jewry. On 21 July 1942, a huge rally supporting European Jews took place at Madison Square Garden, organized jointly by the American Jewish Congress, the Jewish Labor Committee, and B'nai B'rith. Reports had come from Poland of the mass murder of seven hundred thousand to a million Jews by the Nazis. Prime Minister Winston Churchill and President Franklin Roosevelt sent statements to the rally condemning the atrocities. The Synagogue Council of America urged rabbis and their congregations to dedicate the fast of Tisha B'Av to the victims. But few concrete measures were taken to rescue or even help the Polish Jews, for the American organizations remained divided over policy. Heschel was among thousands of Jews who were aghast at this disunity.[20]

Less than a week later, the Jewish Telegraphic Agency transmitted the first news of widespread deportations from the Warsaw Ghetto. By mid-August, reliable sources were reporting that "3,600 men, women, and children had been brutally deported in trains to internment camps in unoccupied southern France and sent off to an 'unknown destination' eastward, these representing the first contingent of a total of 10,000 Jewish refugees" who were being sent to their deaths. Heschel hoped that Reform Jews, whose rabbinic institution had saved him, might be more committed than the other agencies. He attended the annual meeting of the Central Conference of American Rabbis (CCAR), where a Quaker leader tried to persuade the organization to send food packages to Jews in ghettos and concentration camps. Heschel summarized: "The Rabbis declared that this could not be done officially because it would help the Germans if food was sent to the territories they controlled."[21]

Heschel was crushed. Prayer was his only recourse, as he admitted to Jacobson: "I went to Rabbi Eliezer Silver's synagogue in Cincinnati, recited Psalms, fasted, and cried myself out. I was a stranger in this country. My opinion had no impact. When I did speak, they shouted me down. They called me a mystic, not a realist. I had no influence on the Jewish leaders."[22]

Horror at the apparent apathy of American Jews was widespread in the immigrant community. By late 1942, it was clear to most that the next step in Nazi policy would be extermination. Hayim Greenberg, a prominent Jewish writer and activist, sounded the alarm. Settled in the United States since 1924, Greenberg was the editor of two widely circulated Labor Zionist publications, the Yiddish-language *Yidisher Kemfer* and the English-language *Jewish Frontier*. Heschel's connections with Greenberg were long-standing; in Russia and later in Berlin, Greenberg had collaborated with David Koigen, Heschel's mentor. On 19 November, Greenberg proclaimed in *Jewish Frontier*: "In the occupied countries of Europe a policy is now being put into effect, whose avowed object is the extermination of a whole people. It is a policy of systematic murder of innocent civilians which in its dimensions, its ferocity and its organization is unique in the history of mankind." A detailed article followed, amassing incontrovertible evidence.[23]

Greenberg's articles had little effect on the English-speaking Jewish community, and he next addressed Yiddish speakers, in the 12 February 1943 issue of *Yidisher Kemfer*, which Heschel certainly read. The editorial, entitled "Bankrupt," indicted Jewish leaders, accusing them of succumbing to a moral disease, "a kind of epidemic inability to suffer or to feel compassion . . . [a] pathological fear of pain, [a] terrifying lack of imagination." The unmistakable symptoms of this affliction were institutional rivalry and petty quarrels.[24]

Heschel was not the only East European to be derided as "a mystic" when he dared confront American Jews. Greenberg described one such incident during "a session of the Jewish Labor Committee." When "a colleague from Poland permitted himself to express a few sharp words of rebuke on the subject of their indifference and passivity, he was shouted down publicly as a 'hysteric'—as if a state of hysteria is today not more normal for Jews than dull, even temper and an attitude of 'business as usual.' "[25]

The written word was Heschel's only recourse. But instead of concentrating

*Hayim Greenberg, ca. 1950. From Hayim
Greenberg,* The Inner Eye: Selected Essays
*(New York: Jewish Frontier Publishing
Association, 1964)*

on political facts, he dwelt on the spiritual gifts of European Jewry, whose very
existence hung in the balance. During his December 1942 vacation in New
York, he spent a Shabbat evening at the home of Mordecai Kaplan, dean of the
Teachers Institute at the Jewish Theological Seminary and editor of *The Reconstructionist,* a widely read periodical whose masthead proclaimed its humanistic goals: "the advancement of Judaism as a civilization, . . . the upbuilding of
Israel's ancient homeland, and . . . the furtherance of universal freedom, justice and peace." Although Heschel's reverence for the living God contradicted
Kaplan's view of God as "an idea" serving human needs and aspirations, Kaplan had been deeply moved by Heschel's "Analysis of Piety." In his diary,
Kaplan composed a long poem inspired by one passage, planning to include it
in his new prayer book.[26]

After their Shabbat together in New York, Heschel wrote a note of thanks: "I
have often thought of our talk and felt like saying that the community of *kavanah* [inner devotion] is more decisive than the difference of *nusah* [custom]."
Despite Kaplan's sociological Judaism and his aversion to "supernaturalism,"

he was open-minded; he was even attracted to Heschel's piety. Kaplan soon invited Heschel to contribute an essay on spirituality to *The Reconstructionist*.[27]

Before writing the *Reconstructionist* article, which he entitled "Faith," Heschel reflected on the unfolding European catastrophe in the March 1943 *Hebrew Union College Bulletin*, his first such statement in America. In full control of literary English, he translated and adapted his 1938 talk to a Quaker group in Frankfurt, "Versuch einer Deutung" (Search for a meaning), retitling it "The Meaning of This War." The piece opened dramatically: "Emblazoned over the gates of the world in which we live is the escutcheon of the demons. The mark of Cain in the face of man has come to overshadow the likeness of God. There have never been so much guilt and distress, agony and terror. At no time has the earth been so soaked with blood."[28]

Heschel faced the theological challenge of these lethal persecutions by insisting that we could not blame God; rather, the disaster was the result of our lack of moral courage: "Let Fascism not serve as an alibi for our conscience. We have failed to fight for right, for justice, for goodness; as a result we fight against wrong, against injustice, against evil." Even the war against Germany was an evil, a consequence of social wrongs, weakened democracies, and the trivialization of religion. For Heschel the most appropriate action was authentic religious commitment. With a characteristic antithesis, he concluded by reminding Jewish readers that they were "either slaves of evil or ministers of the sacred." Citing a midrash on the covenant at Sinai, he summarized the present challenge: "Israel [the Jewish people] did not accept the Torah of their own free will. When Israel approached Sinai, God lifted up the mountain and held it over their heads saying, 'Either you accept the Torah or be crushed beneath the mountain.' The mountain of history is over our heads again. Shall we renew the covenant with God?"

While completing his essay, Heschel asked students in his dormitory to help him find the best words. Saul Kaplan found the rare term "escutcheon" (shield or insignia), which Heschel, yielding to his love for verbal harmonies, chose to translate the prosaic German *Wappen* (weapons) from the original speech. Albert Plotkin typed the manuscript.[29]

Heschel had found his militant voice. The following February (1944), he added some powerful phrases to the essay for a slight revision that was published in *Liberal Judaism*, the organ of the Union of American Hebrew Congregations (UAHC, the national lay organization of Reform Jewry). More directly than ever he chastised America's largest Jewish denomination as he urged them to act: "A messenger recently came and conveyed the following message from all the European Jews who are being slaughtered in the hell of Poland: 'We, Jews, despise all those who live in safety and do nothing to save us.'" Heschel continued to agonize over his own helplessness, and the evasiveness of American Jews elicited his fiercest condemnation.[30]

In April 1943, German soldiers began the liquidation of the Warsaw Ghetto. Heschel's mother and sister Gittel were among the seven hundred thousand Jews remaining in the district where he grew up. On 19 April, the day of the first Passover Seder, at 6:00 A.M., German troops entered the ghetto walls, where they were met by the heroic Jewish uprising. In early May the Germans assaulted the Jewish resistance command post; several of the leaders committed suicide to avoid capture. On 16 May the Nazi commander, General Jürgen Stroop, reported that "the Jewish section of Warsaw no longer exists."[31]

In Cincinnati, Heschel was on the verge of collapse. He couldn't sleep; he could hardly speak; he spent his days just walking in the Burnett Woods across the street from the college, sometimes accompanied by Plotkin. By telegram or telephone he learned that his mother had died of a heart attack when German soldiers stormed their apartment. He responded to the news as would any traditional Jew, gathering a minyan (a quorum of ten men) together to hold a service in his dormitory room to honor her. Later he was informed that his surviving sister, Gittel Heszel, had been deported to Treblinka, where she was murdered.[32]

The following month Heschel attended a memorial service at the college to honor the dead of the Warsaw Ghetto. Raw with emotion, he was distressed by a song from the pulpit that he felt was not appropriate. It would have hurt the Jews of Warsaw to hear it, he said.[33]

While the Warsaw Ghetto uprising was taking place, Heschel's second essay on spirituality, "The Holy Dimension," appeared in the *Journal of Religion*, published by the University of Chicago. The article introduced his foundational notion of "radical amazement," a mental shock that initiated a process of religious thinking; here he called it "wonder and awe." He explained that the phenomenology of wonder and awe could persuade us that God was near: "While penetrating the consciousness of the pious man, we may conceive the reality behind it." Heschel was refining his terminology. Once a person was ready to accept the wonder of God, that person would be ready for the final stage of religious thinking: perceiving the mutuality of human and divine. "This condition outlasts catastrophes and apostasies and constitutes God's covenant with mankind and the universe." Without referring specifically to Judaism, Heschel used the word *covenant* to convey a general precondition of faith. [34]

Heschel did not deny the reality of evil; quite the contrary. But free human beings must attune their actions to God's perspective, as he asserted in his rich, evocative prose: "Man is an animal at heart, carnal, covetous, selfish, and vain; yet spiritual in his destiny: a vision beheld by God in the darkness of flesh and blood. Only eyes vigilant and fortified against the glaring and superficial can still perceive God's vision in the soul's horror-stricken night of falsehood, hatred, and malice."[35]

Institutional Crisis

Faculty meetings at HUC reflected little of the global calamity. On 11 April 1943, a week before the ghetto uprising, the faculty discussed alumni responses to a questionnaire on curriculum and decided to make changes in the Department of Rabbinics. Heschel and Atlas were invited to attend, though still as non-faculty colleagues. On 23 April, after Heschel and Atlas had left for the Passover vacation in New York, a motion to approve Heschel's promotion to a full faculty position with the title of instructor was seriously debated. Jacob Marcus was the only person to vote against it, and he submitted a memorandum to justify his view that "no recommendations for appointments be made for the duration of the war, or until the financial future of the College is assured." For Marcus, opposition to Heschel's promotion was a purely practical matter: "Today we have a full time teacher for every nine students; we have a full time teacher or special instructor for about every three students."[36]

At that meeting, Heschel was highly praised. The motion to promote him was carried four to one, and the following month, the HUC Board of Governors, headed by David Philipson, approved the promotion. The minutes of their meeting included an impressive summary of his qualities—a perceptive portrait if we discount his well-known difficulties in the classroom: "[We recommend] that Dr. Abraham Heschel, who has been a refugee scholar here at the College for three and a half years, who has carried a steadily increasing teaching load in various Departments with unqualified success and has proven his teaching ability, and who gives rare promise, through his unique personality, of exerting a splendid, stimulating spiritual influence upon our students, be appointed as Instructor in Jewish Philosophy and Rabbinics for the academic year 1943–1944."[37]

There was significant evidence in favor of this enthusiastic forecast. In addition to his publications, Heschel was active on the library committee, and he accepted numerous speaking engagements around the country on behalf of the college. When he attended his first faculty meeting with full status on 20 May 1943, congratulations were recorded in the minutes, expressing "the best wishes of the Faculty for many years of happy mutual relationship."[38] A new era seemed ready to open at Hebrew Union College for Heschel.

President Morgenstern believed that American Judaism as taught at HUC would revitalize the religion, and he lauded his College in Exile in the *Hebrew Union College Bulletin*.[39] Regrettably, this optimism was bolstered by chronic self-deception. For several years, students had been frustrated by the faculty; even the Americans, they felt, valued pure scholarship over practical rabbinical training. Little in the curriculum prepared them to become religious leaders in the community. Elementary courses in Hebrew and basic texts were useful, but most of the advanced courses led to specialized research, not a vibrant pulpit.

Morgenstern candidly acknowledged this discrepancy as he explained that his students could never, as rabbis, teach the Bible to their congregants as they studied it at HUC: as a faulty historical document. In his own classes he corrected what he considered to be scribal errors in the sacred canon; but he also published an inspirational commentary on the Book of Genesis. Morgenstern managed to be at once a skeptical scholar and an inspirational rabbi.

By 1943 the crisis was fully exposed. Questionnaires sent to recent graduates about their HUC education came to a faculty subcommittee, which issued a scathing report. The overwhelming conclusion was that the HUC community was being undermined by the disillusionment of students who felt that the college was out of touch with contemporary Judaism—an identity crisis Heschel and the other refugees were enduring firsthand. The institution, urged the report, required drastic improvement in two essential areas: the curriculum and the religious atmosphere. Many of the recently ordained rabbis blamed the professors. As one graduate wrote: "Our studies were far too dull and too uninteresting for us to have concentrated on them long and still retained our sanity." Another rabbi deplored the effects of academic neutrality: "There is entirely too much German pedantic scholarship and too little living enthusiasm for the beauties of Jewish culture and life." The report cited a long, bitter letter from another young rabbi, who charged: "The Faculty is chosen only with a view to scholarship or to the balance of power in the politics in the rabbinate. . . . I left, feeling soiled, and degraded, as though I was no longer worthy."[40]

The solution, according to the report, was to find a spiritual role model, a "deeply inspirational man, who loves youth, and knows its yearnings and aspirations, who is at the same time a well-rounded scholar,—in other words, a great and compelling personality on the Faculty, to whom the average student can turn with confidence." Another alumnus dreamed of a college with professors who "would 'infect' students with interest, zeal and enthusiasm for Jewish studies and Jewish life."[41]

To be such a model was Heschel's goal, but he was able to touch only a few students in the Reform community of Hebrew Union College.

4

Architecture of a New Theology (1944–1945)

---

*Dark is the world to me, for all its cities and stars, if not for the breath of
compassion that God blew in me when he formed me of dust and clay,
more compassion than my nerves can bear. God, I am alone with my
compassion within my limbs. Dark are my limbs to me; if not for Thee,
who could stand such anguish, such disgrace?*
—Heschel, *Man Is Not Alone* (1951)

IN THE SUMMER OF 1943, HESCHEL ATTENDED THE AMERICAN JEWISH CONFER-
ence, a meeting of major organizations that took place at New York's Waldorf
Astoria Hotel from 29 August to 1 September. The delegates clashed, barely
managing to agree that Palestine should be designated the national homeland
for millions of Jewish refugees. (The American Jewish Committee resigned
from the Conference, the first important organization to do so.) Even more divisive was the problem of how to save Jews in Poland and Germany. Heschel
helplessly looked on as infighting brought a rescue resolution to defeat. These
notables of American Jewry could not even agree to support an interdenomi-
national emergency committee. He was appalled.[1]

Heschel was more heartened by the aggressive campaign of Rabbi Eliezer
Silver's emergency rescue committee, the Va'ad Hatzalah. By 1943, when the
full extent of Hitler's "final solution" had become widely acknowledged, Silver sought to rescue every Jew he could. Motivated by the sacred imperative of
pikuach nefesh (saving human life), the Va'ad supported controversial policies
such as ransoming Jews and cooperating with Revisionist Zionists, the terrorist Irgun organization, and other groups antagonistic to their religious conceptions. Rescuing as many Jews as possible, not just Orthodox rabbis and
yeshiva students, was paramount.[2]

It was at this moment that Heschel, who was not yet a naturalized citizen,
became a political activist. He joined Silver and Mordecai Shlomo Friedman,
his cousin the Boyaner rebbe, and other strictly Orthodox rabbis in a public
protest aimed at obtaining a meeting with President Roosevelt at the White
House. This Jewish march on Washington took place on 6 October 1943, three
days before Yom Kippur. It was the only rally in America's capital to save
European Jews.[3]

Heschel was among the four hundred rabbis, most of them formed in European yeshivas, bearded and dressed in traditional garb, who marched down
Pennsylvania Avenue, accompanied by Jewish War Veterans of America. But
the protestors were not received by the White House because Roosevelt's Jewish advisers had told him that these immigrants were not official community
leaders. Instead they were greeted on the Capitol steps by an uncomfortable
Henry Wallace, the vice president. Rabbi Silver intoned their petition in Hebrew, after which Rabbi David Burrack translated it into English. The protesters urged the U.S. government to deliver "the remnants of the people of the
Book" and to open Palestine and other nations to Jewish refugees. Wallace responded with vague expressions of sorrow but no plans to rescue the remaining victims.

The rabbis then took chartered streetcars to the steps of the Lincoln Memorial, where Rabbi Wolf Gold read the petition aloud. They prayed, sang the national anthem in Hebrew, and walked back to the White House, where a delegation that included Heschel's cousin (as president of the Union of Grand Rabbis of the United States and Canada) petitioned for a special government agency to save Jews.[4]

Despite a description of this dramatic event in the *New York Times*, the established Jewish community did not support the protesters. The rabbis returned home discouraged. Yom Kippur that year was especially grim.

The Esoteric Heschel

After the holidays, Heschel began his fifth and final academic year at Hebrew Union College, 1944–45, now as associate professor of Jewish philosophy and rabbinics. Despite his promotion, his course offerings remained elementary; he taught liturgy and Rashi in the Preparatory Department and a class on medieval exegesis of the Torah in the Collegiate Department. His scholarship, if not his teaching, met with success. He completed the groundwork for the systematology of Judaism he had announced to Martin Buber and Henry Corbin while still in Europe. He published the essays "Faith" and "Prayer," both aimed at general readers. For specialists he published a booklet reprint of his two-part "The Quest for Certainty in Saadia's Philosophy." Years later, Fritz Rothschild, who had become Heschel's groundbreaking interpreter, saw these works as the architecture of his new theology.[5]

Heschel's long-standing efforts to obtain a position at the Jewish Theological Seminary finally seemed likely to be fulfilled. He had regularly sent reprints of his articles to Louis Finkelstein, beginning with his "Answer to Einstein." The JTS president appreciated Heschel's special qualities; in thanking Heschel for a copy of "An Analysis of Piety," he recalled "with a great deal of pleasure" Heschel's lecture at the Seminary during his first week in New York, adding this forecast: "It seems to me that your coming to this country may help greatly in stimulating Jewish religious thought." The following year Finkelstein wrote that "The Holy Dimension" might provide an antidote to "the confusion of our day."[6]

In both quantity and quality Heschel's output was breathtaking. His distinction among Judaic scholars was confirmed by invitations to contribute to commemorative volumes, placing him among the leaders of the profession.

In January 1944, Heschel announced in the *Hebrew Union College Bulletin* that he had completed a monograph in Hebrew, "Did Maimonides Strive for Prophetic Inspiration?" for the *Louis Ginzberg Jubilee Volume* honoring the seventieth birthday of the JTS's most prestigious faculty member. Contributors to the Hebrew-language section included Heschel and Samuel Atlas of HUC; A. S. Halkin, Saul Lieberman, Alexander Marx, and Louis Finkelstein of JTS; Gerhard (Gershom) Scholem of the Hebrew University in Jerusalem; and Heschel's former teachers Chanokh Albeck, Julius Guttmann, and Harry Torczyner (Tur-Sinai) of the Berlin Hochschule. Contributors to the English-language section included W. F. Albright of Johns Hopkins, Salo W. Baron of Columbia, Leo Strauss of the New School for Social Research, Harry Austryn Wolfson of Harvard, and H. L. Ginsberg, Robert Gordis, and Shalom Spiegel of JTS. The following summer, Heschel completed a second monograph in Hebrew on divine inspiration, "Prophecy After the Cessation of Prophecy." This companion to the Maimonides piece reached print five years later in the *Alexander Marx Jubilee Volume.*[7]

The personal thrust of these foundational studies of divine inspiration— or *ruah ha-kodesh* (the Holy Spirit)—cannot be overstated. Heschel's exhaustively documented monographs deploy the academic neutrality of Wissenschaft des Judentums in the service of faith; hundreds of citations to rare and classical sources testified to the living reality of God and the continuing ability of human beings to receive divine inspiration. Heschel again asserted his spiritual agenda in his contribution to a volume memorializing Moses Schorr, the rabbi, scholar, and member of the Polish Parliament whom Heschel replaced at the Warsaw Institute of Jewish Studies in 1938–39. (Schorr was deported by the Russians and died in a prison camp in Central Asia.) The editors were Louis Ginzberg of JTS and Abraham Weiss, who taught Talmud and rabbinics at Yeshiva University. (Heschel knew Weiss from the Warsaw Institute.)[8]

In contrast to the luminaries from New York, Cincinnati, and Jerusalem who contributed articles on Mishnah and Talmud, in the Schorr tribute Heschel chose to present an anonymous Kabbalistic commentary on the prayer book, a thirteenth-century manuscript that he edited and introduced with a short bibliography. In addition to its value as a previously unknown historical document, it was compelling as a spiritual process, illuminating the manner by which kavanah associated with various ancient sacrifices was transferred to prayers after the destruction of the Temple.[9]

Finkelstein recognized Heschel as an authority on Jewish mysticism, inviting him in 1944 to contribute a chapter to a reference book he was editing,

The Jews: Their History, Culture, and Religion. Around that time, the editors of the *Journal of Religion* asked Heschel to review *Major Trends in Jewish Mysticism*, by Gershom Scholem, the world expert in that neglected area. Heschel's synopsis was neutral: "Scholem, who labored for more than twenty years in the field . . . has proved a master of philological analysis and historical synthesis alike." In contrast, Heschel favored a personal approach to Jewish mysticism.[10]

Heschel's scholarly writings advanced his esoteric agenda: to demonstrate that classic Jewish authorities validated his conviction that God's voice did not cease after the prophets, with the implication that divine revelation remained available. In this still indirect way, he justified his own spiritual counterdiscourse, an elevated rhetoric intended to initiate a mode of thinking centered on God.[11]

Heschel's writings in English also challenged conventional views of Judaism. Without footnotes or references to Hebrew sources, his elegantly written essays appealed to both the rational and intuitive faculties. As a writer he excelled in passages of poetic prose interspersed with philosophical assertions and striking aphorisms.

A prime example was his far-reaching essay "Faith," which Mordecai Kaplan solicited for *The Reconstructionist.* Heschel firmly contradicted the editor's dogmatic rationalism with his assertion: "Faith is a force in man, lying deeper than the stratum of reason[,] and its nature cannot be defined in abstract, static terms." True to the application of phenomenology he had developed at the University of Berlin, Heschel gave precedence to intuition, not reason, in religious knowledge: "In the realm of faith, God is not a hypothesis derived from logical assumptions, but an immediate insight, self-evident as light. To rationalists He is something after which they seek in the darkness with the light of their reason. To men of faith He *is* the light."[12]

Heschel posited a universally shared sense of the holy, an a priori structure of consciousness: "Each of us has at least once in his life experienced the momentous reality of God." Memory formed dispersed insights into a meaningful pattern, enabling the individual to join a historical continuity: "Faith is loyalty to an inspiration that has occurred to us. Jewish faith is recollection of that which occurred to our ancestors." Reiterating in literary prose the philosophical distinction he made between faith and creed in his monograph on Saadia, Heschel defined faith as an ineffable encounter with a real God, beyond words and concepts; creed referred rather to abstract formulations. Here Heschel celebrated insight with striking analogies: "Our creed is, like music, a translation of the unutterable into sounds, thoughts, words, deeds. The original is known to God alone."[13]

Heschel concluded the essay with his foundational principle, that God is in search of man. He assumed that readers could ultimately perceive themselves as *objects* of God's concern. The final phrases pulse with a sacramental fervor: "Faith does not spring out of nothing. It comes with the discovery of the holy dimension of our existence. Suddenly we become aware that our lips touch the veil that hangs before the Holy of Holies. Our face is lit up for a time with the light from behind the veil. Faith opens our hearts for the entrance of the Holy. It is almost as though God were thinking for us."[14]

Audacious in making these mystical claims, Heschel prepared readers to achieve openness to the living God. It is a tribute to Mordecai Kaplan's own open-mindedness that he solicited and published this essay. By 1944 Heschel had positioned his Trojan horse of spirit within the fortress of social science.

Transplanting the Holy Spirit

Heschel continued this research and writing amid catastrophic world events. During his customary summer in New York, from June to October 1944, the war took a decisive turn. The *New York Times* headlines of 6 June announced: "D-Day, Allied Invasion of Normandy: Allied Armies Land in France in the Havre-Cherbourg Area; Great Invasion Is Under Way." Two weeks later, on 22 July, the paper reported: "The Soviet battle for the liberation of Poland began in earnest yesterday as the Red Army smashed across the Bug River from Lyubomi on a thirty-seven-mile front and advanced up to nine miles beyond the west bank."

In August, worried about his fellow refugees, Heschel wrote informing President Morgenstern of his successful research and inquiring about two scholars whom the HUC president had unsuccessfully attempted to bring to Cincinnati at the same time he rescued members of the College in Exile. He learned that Albert Lewkowitz had arrived safely in Palestine, but that Arthur Spanier had perished. "It was my sad duty to convey this news to Dr. Spanier's sister, who lives in New York City," Morgenstern lamented. (In 1938, Spanier had fled to Holland from Germany and from there was able to help Heschel send money and supplies to his mother and sister in Warsaw.)[15]

Heschel went back to HUC for the fall semester, but when it ended he returned to New York, where he met with Louis Finkelstein and attended a meeting of a Yiddish-speaking group with him. Heschel remained in the city beyond the opening of the second semester at HUC in order to deliver a speech that was to mark a decisive turning point in his public career. At the final session of YIVO's nineteenth annual meeting, he spoke in Yiddish on "The East European Era in Jewish History" (Di mizrekh-eyropeishe tkufe in der yidisher geshikhte). The event took place on Sunday afternoon, 7 January 1945, at the Park Central Hotel, Seventh Avenue and 55th Street. (Heschel was originally scheduled to address the opening session on Friday evening at Hunter College, but he postponed his talk until after the Sabbath.)[16]

Heschel became an epoch-defining orator for Americans that afternoon, just as he had become for Quaker leaders when he spoke to them in Frankfurt in 1938 and blamed human indifference, not God, for the increasing persecutions of Jews. As he had on that occasion, he took an oppositional stance, countering—judiciously, though forthrightly—the strict empirical methods of Max Weinreich, YIVO's notable research director and a firm secularist. (Heschel frequently consulted with him by telephone from Cincinnati.) At the same time, Heschel subsumed Jewish secularism into a religious process, relegating to the background "the spread of Enlightenment, Haskalah, the spread of Hasidism, the revival of the Hebrew language, the modern Hebrew and Yiddish literatures, Zionism, Jewish socialism, the establishment of new centers, the building of Palestine." As a religious thinker Heschel judged these social movements "adventitious" (in Yiddish, *tofldik*), secondary (even accidental!) to the God-centered way of life that inspired them.[17]

Heschel pledged to transplant the Holy Spirit to the soil of modern America. To illustrate this solution, he contrasted the rational, orderly mindset of the Golden Age of medieval Sephardic Jewry with the spontaneous, intuitive turn of mind that characterized his own Ashkenazi origins. He even sought to rehabilitate traditions such as *pilpul*, the oft-ridiculed excessive analysis of Talmudic texts: "It is easy to belittle such a mentality and to dub it with unworldliness. The soul is sustained by impracticality. . . . A civilization that concentrates merely on the utilitarian is essentially not greatly different from barbarism," he asserted polemically.[18]

Heschel judged that the very existence of Judaism was at stake. He distilled the "essence" of East European Jewish culture as sanctification. To his fellow speakers of Yiddish he issued a prophetic call: "In the dreadful anguish of these days, a bitter question sears our lips: What will become of us, the survivors? Shall we, Heaven forbid, be subject to the fate of Sephardic Jewry after the catastrophe of 1492: fragmented groups in Turkey and Morocco, stray individuals in Amsterdam, magnificent synagogues and fossilized Jewishness?"[19]

Insisting upon the "hidden light" of Jewish piety, he concluded: "This era was the Song of Songs (which according to the rabbis is the holiest of Holy Scripture) of Jewish history in the last two thousand years. If the other eras were holy, this one is the holy of holies."[20]

The English-language YIVO newsletter published a summary of Heschel's speech that highlighted its ethnographic dimension: "The historical value of an era should not be estimated by its publications or works of art but according to the folkways of the people and the cultural substance of its daily life. . . . The democratization of Talmudic learning, the influence of the Kabbalah and the renascence in Jewish life through the Khassidic movement," he was reported to have said, "created new social patterns and brought forth a Torah from the heart." Heschel had firmly taken sides in the Jewish cultural competition between piety and secularism as he asserted the primacy of holiness over "new social patterns."[21]

Indeed, religious and secular Jews were divided over Heschel's speech, which quickly became legendary. His words were rousing, his presence charismatic, and he fully deserved the acclaim he received for uttering them as a prelude to his American life of spiritual rescue. But the historical record soon became exaggerated. Heschel was credited with inspiring the audience "of several thousands" at the opening session of the conference to rise spontaneously in prayer. (In reality, he spoke at the final session to an audience of hundreds.) A more realistic, though equally compelling description was published in a review of Heschel's book emerging from that event: "His audience listened spellbound. A noted Yiddish publicist who was present reported that when Dr. Heschel had concluded his address an Orthodox rabbi in the audience was moved to recite the 'Kaddish d'Rabbanan' [memorial prayer in honor of scholars]: 'Magnified and sanctified be His great Name.' "[22]

Heschel's YIVO speech defied the Catastrophe (the word Holocaust was not yet used) by absorbing both secular and religious Yiddish culture into his holy history. At the least it aroused admiration as more than a Kaddish; it was a eulogy, a hesped, a poetic sublimation of his lost heritage.

Following his creative process from insight to speech to essay to book, he first revised his Yiddish discourse for the March–April 1945 YIVO Bleter and the following year published an English translation in the inaugural volume of the Yivo Annual. Heschel then expanded the Yiddish version into a forty-five-page booklet published by Schocken. By 1948, he had elaborated his Yiddish essay into the English manuscript of *The Earth Is the Lord's*. Transforming his Yiddish speech into an English book, Heschel completed a metamorphosis from European immigrant to American Jewish intellectual.[23]

The same month that he gave the YIVO speech, as the Red Army was liberating Warsaw, Heschel was in touch with Melekh Ravitch, the editor and Yiddish poet from that city who had published some of his early work. Now settled in Canada, Ravitch directed programs at the Montreal YIVO as well as a Yiddish-language "People's University" for adult education. He invited Heschel up to lecture.[24]

In his letter Heschel had enclosed offprints of his essays on prayer, faith, and Saadia. An epistolary debate ensued. Replying in Yiddish, Ravitch acknowledged candidly: "The Greco-Arabic quotations [from the Saadia paper] I could not, of course, follow. . . . The essays on Faith and Prayer are filled with wonderful, small and quiet poetry woven into them. Through them I learned to understand you. Reading them caused me great esthetic pleasure. However, I would love to talk with you, talk a great deal, for my ways lead in an altogether different direction." Ravitch sought reciprocal communication: "I have understood you with deep piety, and I hope that you will reward me with a little understanding on your part." He inserted his own biographical sketch of Zevi Diesendruck, whom he knew from "the good old days in Vienna," along with thoughts about a "revised Bible for Jews," probably a secular manifesto. "I am extremely interested in your attitude toward my demand for a new Bible. I am really anxious about it," he wrote Heschel. [25]

Heschel replied quickly, refusing to sympathize with Ravitch's nonreligious mission. The very idea of creating a "New Testament," especially a Jewish one, was anathema. Leave that to Christians. This generation of Jews was certainly not capable of producing one. Nor would Heschel excuse the audacity of Jesus for claiming to improve upon his revealed tradition. Heschel did concede that the tree of Judaism had significantly dried, but he insisted that the Hebrew Bible retained immense power, mainly from the Jewish people who sustained it, as well as through certain individuals. Authentic Judaism was like a bush disguised by ornaments. Heschel trusted that today's Jews would be able to separate the valid from the false and thus preserve its eternal vitality. But Ravitch was not open to Heschel's program to convince nonbelievers that God was present in Jewish tradition.[26]

Also in January 1945 Heschel's essay "Prayer" appeared in the *Review of Religion,* again bringing his analysis of the inner life to an English-speaking readership. This time Heschel's presentation was explicitly Jewish, though his goals remained universal. He introduced the "essence" of worship with a story about the Gerer rebbe, Rabbi Isaac Meir Alter, who cherished the sigh of a shoemaker who had bewailed his lack of time to make his morning prayers. Heschel suggested, "Perhaps that sigh is worth more than prayer itself." Then, without mentioning the Hebrew terms, he examined the classic problem of law (halakhah), or outward acts, versus intention (kavanah), emotion, and inner awareness. Foremost in the latter was the desire to pray. Authentic prayer, according to Heschel, was the proper vehicle of religious insight and theocentrism its hallmark. Implicitly, but without naming Buber, he rejected the popular notion of dialogue: "It is incorrect to describe prayer on the analogy of human conversation; we do not communicate with God. We only make ourselves communicable to Him."[27]

Heschel addressed readers without faith, agnostics, or those who rejected religion, as he elucidated the ethical consequences of recentering the self: "Prayer takes the mind out of the narrowness of self-interest, and enables us to see the world in the mirror of the holy. For when we betake ourselves to the extreme opposite of the ego, we can behold a situation from the aspect of God."[28]

Heschel also clarified his other key notion, the idea of the "ineffable": the impossibility of finding words adequate to spiritual reality. He drew upon his 1939 German-language essay "Prayer as Expression and Empathy" (Das Gebet als Äusserung und Einfühlung) to delimit "two main types of prayer": the prayer of self-expression, which comes from the heart; and the prayer of empathy, in which we project ourselves into prescribed words. "A certain passage in the morning prayer was interpreted by the Kotzker Rabbi to mean that God loves what is left over at the bottom of the heart and cannot be expressed in words. It is the ineffable feeling which reaches God rather than the expressed feeling."[29]

While stressing his confidence in the divine, Heschel admitted to his overwhelming sense of isolation: "The thirst for companionship, which drives us so often into error and adventure, indicates the intense loneliness from which we suffer. We are alone even with our friends. . . . In the hour of greatest agony we are alone. It is such a sense of solitude which prompts the heart to seek the companionship of God."[30]

Characteristically, Heschel ended on a practical, even edifying note. He urged readers to imitate the divine, to the point of transforming the world: "We anticipate the fulfillment of the hope shared by both God and man. To pray is to dream in league with God, to envision His holy visions."[31] Humankind carries the burden, and the privilege, of a messianic vision. Prayer must be fulfilled in action.

Finding a Professional Home

In the meantime, while pursuing contacts at the Jewish Theological Seminary, Heschel continued to negotiate for a position at Yeshiva University, the modern Orthodox institution. The previous summer he had proposed some courses to Jacob I. Hartstein, Yeshiva's academic director, and they exchanged letters in February. By late March, Heschel was settling on a teaching schedule, including Jewish mysticism and the history of Jewish philosophy.[32]

One problem remained. Hartstein, a prudent administrator, made a note to himself to consult Yeshiva's most influential faculty member, Rabbi Joseph Baer Soloveitchik, before hiring Heschel. He probably did so, although we have no evidence of what Soloveitchik advised. In any case, Heschel's candidacy was apparently supported by Samuel Belkin, Yeshiva's president. By 10 April, Hartstein had tentatively offered Heschel two courses in the college and perhaps a seminar in the graduate school. "I would very much like you to meet with President Belkin on your next scheduled brief trip to the city," he added. Then the correspondence stopped; it continued only after Heschel received an offer from JTS.[33]

This was probably the first contact, indirect as it was, between Heschel and Soloveitchik, the two men who became America's preeminent traditionalist Jewish thinkers. Heschel and Soloveitchik came to represent opposite approaches to Jewish observance. Although both had earned doctorates in philosophy from the University of Berlin—Soloveitchik in 1930, Heschel in 1933—Soloveitchik was heir to the great Talmudic dynasty of Brisk and considered obedience to halakhah to be the essence of Jewish life. Whereas Heschel, the scion of Hasidic dynasties, emphasized the necessity of inner experience and love of God to fulfill accepted observance, which he also upheld.[34]

Heschel spent the Passover recess, 15–22 April, in New York, at the beginning of a period of extraordinary international turmoil that started with the death of President Roosevelt on 12 April. Two weeks later (2 May), the *New York Times* headlined: "Hitler Dead in Chancellery, Nazis Say; Doenitz, Successor, Orders War to Go on; Berlin Almost Won; U.S. Armies Advance." Less than a week later, on 7 May, the war in Europe was over. Amid these world events, Heschel's courtship of the Jewish Theological Seminary neared its consummation. President Finkelstein and his star professors, Alexander Marx and Louis Ginzberg, saw in Heschel a counterforce to Mordecai Kaplan, a tireless proselytizer, whom they felt was sabotaging the Conservative rabbinate with his humanistic religion. Ironically, Kaplan himself urged the Seminary to hire Heschel. He wanted to devote more time to his synagogue, the Society for the Advancement of Judaism, and his new movement, Reconstructionism. The plan was for Heschel to teach Jewish philosophy and traditional worship to future Jewish educators.[35]

Seminary officials made tactful inquiries about Heschel's fitness as a classroom teacher, for they had heard about problems at HUC. Moshe Davis, the incoming dean of the Teachers Institute, questioned Pesach Krauss, Heschel's former Midrasha student, a companion from youth movements who was now at JTS preparing to be a rabbi. Krauss portrayed Heschel as an ideal "teacher and friend," who had been marvelous at the Sabbath afternoon Midrasha. Negative rumors might be partially true, he admitted, but most HUC students were unteachable anyway because of their poor Jewish background.[36]

Decisive support came from Louis Ginzberg, a founding father of the Seminary and Finkelstein's teacher and closest adviser. Ginzberg was the first professor hired by Solomon Schechter when he assumed the presidency of JTS in 1902, and he helped Schechter recruit the Seminary's top scholars: the historians Alexander Marx and Israel Friedlander, Mordecai Kaplan, and Israel Davidson, a specialist in medieval Hebrew literature. The triumvirate of Ginzberg, Davidson, and Marx consolidated the reputation of JTS as an academic center.[37]

It might seem surprising that Ginzberg would appreciate Heschel's special talents since, like Soloveitchik, Ginzberg believed that halakhah was the essence of Judaism, despite his expertise in Jewish legends, and he was not interested in the dynamics of religious belief. By origin and temperament, he was a mitnagid. Born in Kovno, Lithuania, in 1873, he had received advanced training in the yeshivas of Kovno, Telz, and Slobodka. Like Heschel, he took pride in his yikhus: he was the great-grandnephew of the Vilna Gaon, Rabbi Elijah ben Solomon Zalman, a Talmudic genius and fierce adversary of the Hasidic movement.[38]

But Ginzberg was a modern Jew: open-minded, highly educated, cosmopolitan. From the University of Berlin he had transferred to Strasbourg to study with the great Orientalist Theodore Noeldke, earning his doctorate at the University of Heidelberg with a dissertation on *Aggadot* (rabbinic stories and speculations) in the Church Fathers. Ginzberg's vast erudition led to his *Legends of the Jews* (7 vols., 1909–38). As a master of Talmud and authority on halakhah, he became an unofficial *posek* (authoritative decider) for the Conservative movement and wrote many responsa on problems of contemporary Jewish practice. In addition, Ginzberg was proficient in Kabbalah, Hellenism, and several modern European languages and literatures.

Ginzberg recognized Heschel as an authentic Jew who, like himself, possessed wide erudition and an intelligence sharpened by European culture. Ginzberg decided that Heschel should be invited to join the JTS faculty during one of the latter's frequent visits to the city. Ginzberg's wife, Adele, impressed by a lecture Heschel gave at Congregation B'nai Jeshurun, rushed home to tell her husband, "*Shatze* [my darling], this is the man we must bring to the Seminary because Kaplan is ruining all the students." Ginzberg telephoned Heschel at his hotel to invite him for Shabbat at their apartment on 114th Street, but Heschel had already made plans to spend the holy day with his Hasidic relatives. He came on Sunday instead. After lunch the men walked in Riverside Park, along the Hudson River. Ginzberg was astonished that Heschel knew so many obscure Kabbalistic writings and other rare sources, and he enjoyed displaying his own erudition to Heschel. Ginzberg called Finkelstein with a strong recommendation.[39]

There was additional pressure to hire Heschel from other sources. An internal battle was raging at JTS, not unlike the crisis at HUC. Finkelstein was under fire from his fellow rabbis for featuring academic scholarship at the expense of practical professional training. The rabbis also objected to Finkelstein's outreach to wider Jewish and Christian constituencies through his "Institute for Religious and Social Studies" and his "Conferences on Science, Religion, and Philosophy." Some disgruntled faculty had demanded his resignation. From February through April 1945, Finkelstein's authority was in question. He finally gained support from the Board of Directors at their 17 April meeting.[40]

Even so, Heschel was not Finkelstein's only candidate. The president was also considering the brilliant and versatile Shlomo Pines from Paris and Jerusalem, an expert in medieval Arabic and Jewish philosophy with a specialty in Maimonides, who knew over sixty languages. Outside authorities were consulted, such as Harry Austryn Wolfson, an expert on medieval philosophy who knew both Heschel and Pines. In the end, Heschel was deemed the better teacher, more attuned to issues of worship and contemporary theology, and he was offered the position. On 24 May, Finkelstein sent Heschel an official letter of appointment as associate professor of Jewish ethics and mysticism in both the Rabbinical School and the Teachers Institute. Heschel courteously responded: "In accepting this great task and high distinction I am fully aware of the responsibility it implies. *I pray that no one may be caused to stumble through my teaching* [in Hebrew, from Mishnah Berachot 4:2]. I thank you from the bottom of my heart. Cordially yours, Abraham Heschel."[41]

While the negotiations with JTS were going on, Heschel had tactfully kept President Morgenstern apprized of his approaching decision to leave Hebrew Union College. Three weeks before receiving Finkelstein's letter of appointment, Heschel sent his official letter of resignation to Morgenstern, recalling their previous discussions "in a spirit of friendship and understanding." Heschel declared his respect for the institution and alluded to his efforts on its behalf: "I have tried to contribute everything within my power to the scholastic and spiritual development of my pupils." He then admitted his reservations about the "distinctive philosophy of Judaism" practiced at the college: "While I find that there are ideals and obligations which I whole-heartedly share, I do not feel that my own interpretation of Judaism is in full accord with the teachings of the College." He concluded by expressing his loyalty to the school: "The College has become very dear to me and I cherish the aspiration to be of service even after my departure from Cincinnati, and to be considered by its Board, Faculty, and Alumni a staunch friend of this illustrious institution."[42]

The following week Morgenstern relayed Heschel's message to the Board of Governors. As he wrote to Heschel, "A deep appreciation of the motives of honor and integrity which prompted you to reach this decision was expressed by the Board of Governors. It was their feeling, too, that under the circumstances you were doing the right and honorable thing. It was in this spirit that your resignation was accepted."[43]

Heschel's departure was perceived by many faculty colleagues as abrupt, however. Samuel Atlas and Jacob Marcus were especially taken by surprise and felt betrayed, perhaps because Heschel had said nothing to them of his plans. Others considered Heschel disloyal to the institution that had saved his life, and his reputation in later years suffered for it. In addition, some HUC faculty believed, erroneously, that Heschel had encouraged other students to leave. Samuel Dresner did follow Heschel to JTS, but Heschel did not urge that decision. However, he did advise Richard Rubenstein to leave HUC and pursue an academic career. Rubenstein had been more interested in philosophy at the University of Cincinnati, and his vocation as a congregational rabbi was uncertain; in fact, HUC had requested him to leave.[44]

In early May, soon after the collapse of Germany, there was an awkward farewell ceremony for Heschel. The students were represented by Jay Kaufman, who did not like Heschel. After some humorous remarks, Heschel responded with an undiplomatic quip: "Gentlemen, it is often said that only students graduate. That is not true. It is also possible for professors to graduate."[45]

Curiously, Heschel kept his options open with Yeshiva University. It was not until 3 June that he wrote to inform Hartstein, without naming the Jewish Theological Seminary, that he was no longer a candidate at Yeshiva: "I have resigned from the Hebrew Union College and accepted a new position," he stated vaguely. Even so, Hartstein was not put off, responding by airmail special delivery: "My interest . . . continues in the same measure as before. If the appointment which you accepted [crossed out: *expect*] is in an institution whose idealogy [*sic*] is compatible with our own, and if you are interested in teaching for a few weeks during the summer, I would like to talk with you thereabout immediately." He urged Heschel to telephone him collect or wire his response. Hartstein obviously knew about Heschel's contacts with JTS and hoped that he would remain interested in a possible position.[46]

Heschel's most positive closure to his Cincinnati years, before he left, was to complete his naturalization as an American citizen. He had signed his declaration of intention on 29 May 1940 "Abraham Heszel (known as Heschel)." Five years later, almost to the day, on 28 May 1945, with the same two American friends, Amy Blank and Bertha Feinberg, as witnesses, "Abraham Heschel" certified his oath of allegiance to the United States of America.[47]

Part Two

Rescuing the American Soul

We are God's stake in human history. We are the dawn and the dusk,
the challenge and the test. How strange to be a Jew and go astray
on God's perilous errands. . . . We carry the gold of God in our souls
to forge the gates of the kingdom.
—Heschel, *The Earth Is the Lord's* (1950)

AT THE END OF WORLD WAR II, WITH THE REVELATION OF THE FULL HORROR OF
the Holocaust, Heschel grappled with how to reconcile his love for the living
God with the suffering of his people, the relative detachment of bystanders,
and his own sense of helplessness. In his final book, *A Passion for Truth*, he
was able to describe his inner conflict between anguish and confidence in
God's caring presence: "To live both in awe and consternation, in fervor and
horror, with my conscience on mercy and my eyes on Auschwitz, wavering between exaltation and dismay."[1] Heschel struggled to keep these conflicting
emotions under control.

He hoped to find a spiritual and intellectual home at the Jewish Theological Seminary. Founded in 1886 to counteract the effects of American Reform,
this Conservative academy reached national prominence under Solomon
Schechter, who served as president from 1902 to 1915, and his successor,
Cyrus Adler. Louis Finkelstein assumed the presidency in 1940, after Adler
retired.[2]

When Heschel joined the faculty in the fall of 1945, the institution championed Schechter's ideals of Wissenschaft des Judentums. Its religious practice was traditional, identical with that of Orthodoxy. President Finkelstein
reigned over a hierarchical community. An official faculty photograph depicts
the relative status of its members. Seated in the front row at the center are
Finkelstein, with Louis Ginzberg, professor of Talmud, to his left and Alexander Marx, librarian and professor of history, to his right. To Ginzberg's left is
Mordecai Kaplan, professor of philosophies of religion and founding dean of
the Teachers Institute, and to Marx's right is Saul Lieberman, the supreme
Talmud scholar, who later became the president's main confidant.[3]

In the 1950s, a period Americans defined as "the age of anxiety," Heschel
became a public intellectual. He responded to the crisis of meaning that accompanied postwar affluence as the country plunged into the Cold War, a troubled competition with the Soviet Union that was aggravated by fears of nuclear
destruction. Heschel believed that, after the Holocaust, Jews were in dire

need of a spiritual and moral revolution. Although Jewish communities were expanding to the suburbs, he found that religious education and observance, as well as personal faith, were impoverished. Convinced that the soul of American Jewry was in a state of emergency, he expanded his first articles in English into inspirational books for a wide audience (*The Earth Is the Lord's* and *The Sabbath*) and works of religious philosophy (*Man Is Not Alone* and *God in Search of Man*). He addressed all Americans, bearing witness to his own faith and interpreting the classic Jewish sources for all seekers.

5

First Years in New York (1945–1949)

---

*Aaron Zeitlin is one of the few individuals whose Jewish mystical
thinking has become part of his inner essence, an element of
imagination, with which he lives his life, from which he forms his
poetic instruments. The Evil One is as real for him as "nature" is for
others and the* sefirot *of God are as comprehensible to him as modern
sociology is for others.*

—Heschel, "After Majdanek" (1948)

IN JUNE 1945, HESCHEL RENTED ROOMS AT 214 RIVERSIDE DRIVE AND IMMEDI-
ately took up his responsibilities as a member of the faculty of the Jewish Theological Seminary. By the end of the month he had submitted his chapter,
"The Mystical Element in Judaism," for JTS president Finkelstein's edited
volume *The Jews: Their History, Culture, and Religion*, explaining, "I had to
confine myself to the Zohar in order to give the reader a somewhat comprehensive idea of one phase of Jewish mysticism." In July, Heschel participated
in the JTS alumni summer session, a symposium on the theme "My Faith as
a Jew."[1]

In the meantime the war in the Pacific was coming to an end, prosecuted
with unequaled brutality and destruction of human life.

> First Atomic Bomb Dropped on Japan; Missile Is Equal to 20,000 Tons of
> TNT; Truman Warns Foe of a "Rain of Ruin"
> > [*New York Times*, 7 August 1945]
> Soviets Declare War on Japan; Attack Manchuria, Tokyo Says; Atom Bomb
> Loosed on Nagasaki
> > [*New York Times*, 9 August 1945]
> Japan Decides to Surrender, the Tokyo Radio Announces, as We Resume
> Heavy Attacks
> > [*New York Times*, 14 August 1945]

From that time forward, nuclear annihilation and the Holocaust became
indelibly associated in Heschel's mind.

Heschel was able to relax briefly when he joined the Ginzbergs for a two-
week vacation in Maine. On his return he took a room at 362 Riverside Drive.
At the end of August, a week before Rosh Hashanah, he wrote to Julian Morgenstern about his respite with the Ginzbergs and concluded grimly: "The
stirring events that took place during the last weeks are tragically contrasted
with the silence of death that hovers over Poland." He ended the letter with
a quotation from the prophet Isaiah: *Akheyn atah el mistater* (You are indeed
a God who concealed Himself).[2]

The Finkelstein Academy

In the fall, Heschel settled into the Seminary, which was more congenial to
his needs than HUC. He took meals at the kosher cafeteria, developed ties
with students, and took full advantage of the Seminary's outstanding collection of books and manuscripts. Worship at the JTS chapel followed traditional

lines: women and men sat on opposite sides of the aisle, but with no mechitzah between them.

The faculty was predominantly European by birth and training, and they were observant Jews; but, eschewing spiritually committed writing, they engaged almost exclusively in meticulous historical and textual scholarship. Most rabbinical candidates were well prepared in Judaic studies. More than a third had studied in yeshivas or the high school of Yeshiva University. But a great many had entered the Conservative Seminary to escape the narrowness of Orthodoxy. Such efforts to find an appropriate American Judaism were widespread.

President Finkelstein seemed an ideal figure to help resolve these conflicts. He was a towering figure: strikingly handsome, with his dark beard and disheveled hair, and ambitious for his institution and himself. Committed to "the great experiment of modern Judaism," he would rise at 5:00 A.M. to study sacred texts. He was seen as a sage who combined deep Judaic knowledge with a keen responsibility to the world at large.[3]

Finkelstein was born in Cincinnati of immigrant parents from Lithuania and grew up in the Bronx. He studied with his father, an Orthodox rabbi, and by age sixteen he had mastered the Bible and several tractates of the Babylonian Talmud. After public high school he earned degrees at both the City College of New York and the Jewish Theological Seminary, where he studied the Talmud under Louis Ginzberg. In 1918 he earned a Ph.D. in religion from Columbia University. The following year he earned an advanced rabbinical degree from the Seminary, which gave him authority to make decisions of Jewish law. He became the rabbi of an Orthodox congregation in the Bronx while teaching Talmud at JTS, to which he soon returned for good.

In 1940 he became President Roosevelt's adviser on Judaism and its application to world peace. Finkelstein often said that Judaism was "the least-known religion" (an expression Heschel later used). To remedy the general ignorance, he organized educational projects, including the multivolume reference *The Jews: Their History, Culture and Religion*, to which Heschel contributed his essay on Jewish mysticism, a relatively new field at the time.

Finkelstein was a historian and a philologist, focusing on the social and economic conditions of ancient Jewish life. He studied documents scientifically, with close attention to detail, and published monographs on well-known prayers such as the *Amidah* and *Birkat Ha-Mazon*. His several books included a biography of the first-century sage Akiba ben Joseph and a two-volume account of the Pharisees. He also wrote works that reached beyond the scholarly community.

Finkelstein had what might appear to be conflicting hopes for the Seminary. He envisioned it as a world-class academic institution that produced important scholarship and also trained rabbis for the pulpit. He wanted his faculty to be acclaimed as specialists while appealing to a wide readership. But the reality was that JTS professors were rewarded for producing technical monographs or critical editions of classic texts, not for their ability to inspire students. Finkelstein expected Heschel, who combined spirituality with modern thought, to be a role model for the future rabbis. He valued Heschel's versatility, his ability to be at once an academic researcher, a literary virtuoso, and a defender of tradition. Moreover, Heschel's challenge to Albert Einstein had enhanced the Seminary's public visibility. Heschel seemed to be a dream candidate. Finkelstein and Ginzberg's first thought was to place Heschel in the Teachers Institute to counteract the influence of Mordecai Kaplan, the Seminary's most impressive classroom personality.[4]

Kaplan was an intellectual adventurer who attacked the students' belief in miracles and a personal God, which he termed "supernaturalism." Ordained by the Seminary in 1902 (before Solomon Schechter had reorganized the Seminary), Kaplan was appointed founding dean of the Teachers Institute in 1909. He also taught at the Rabbinical School. Unlike most professors at JTS, he enjoyed engaging students in discussion, and he prepared his lessons carefully.

But traditionalists worried that Kaplan was undermining the religious faith of the rabbinical students. His foundational work, *Judaism as a Civilization: Toward a Reconstruction of American Jewish Life*, furnished pragmatic explanations of customs, ceremonies, and beliefs. His movement, the Society for the Advancement of Judaism (later called Reconstructionism), put forward a sociological view of religion that allowed nonbelievers to feel comfortable about their Jewishness. God was an "idea," or a "process," not a transcendent "person" revealing the divine will to Moses on Mount Sinai. The joke circulated: "There is no God and Kaplan is His prophet."

Although Kaplan was marginalized by the Seminary authorities, his central idea, that Judaism was a civilization, was widely accepted. Under his energetic leadership, the Teachers Institute became a model for Hebrew high schools, colleges, and Jewish day schools throughout the country. Since Kaplan was a fervent Zionist, the Teachers Institute espoused Jewish nationalism and the Hebrew language. The arts also flourished there, with courses and performances of dance, theater, and music.

Heschel enjoyed the Teachers Institute, a vital community, though subordinate to the Rabbinical School, with students of both sexes from all Jewish backgrounds. Heschel loved to teach in modern Hebrew, which was not common practice at the Rabbinical School. And Heschel admired Mordecai Kaplan as a person, without overlooking his vastly opposed views on religion.

Heschel expected to divide his teaching evenly between the Rabbinical School and the Teachers Institute. The Rabbinical School was the more prestigious program, and its faculty were elitist, men whose scholarly specialties were prized above their skill in the classroom. The Teachers Institute was more democratic and practical; its mission was to train instructors of Hebrew and Jewish culture. But Heschel was severely disappointed with his teaching assignments. As junior faculty he taught classes at the Teachers Institute eight to ten hours per week, including elementary courses on medieval Jewish philosophy and Humash, much the same as he had done at HUC. And he was given only one required course in the Rabbinical School, for one hour a week, alternating between Maimonides and Judah Halevi. Heschel had limited access to rabbinical students, and his courses remained basic.[5]

In 1945 the Teachers Institute faculty consisted of nine men and three women, including Judith Kaplan Eisenstein, the dean's daughter, who taught music. (She was the first bat mitzvah in North America.) Also on the Teachers Institute faculty were H. L. Ginsberg, Abraham S. Halkin, Sylvia Ettenberg, Moshe Davis, Zevi Scharfstein, and Hillel Bavli. Heschel did not get along with Halkin, an expert in Judeo-Arabic literature and the medieval period, who had just joined the faculty to preside over courses in history, the school's prime subject. (He also taught at the City College of New York.) Born in Russia, Halkin immigrated to the United States in 1914. Although he read the Torah at Seminary services with consummate skill, he was a secularist and railed at students who believed that God inspired the biblical text. He did not like Heschel.[6]

Heschel became close to Hillel Bavli (originally Rashgolski), a completely different personality. Bavli was a widely published Hebrew poet and literary critic, born in Lithuania, who had studied at yeshivas in Kovno and Vilna. He immigrated to the United States in 1912, attended Columbia University, and began teaching Hebrew literature at JTS in 1918. Bavli was involved in American literary life, translating Dickens as well as several African American writers, including W. E. B. DuBois and Claude McKay, into Hebrew. Most notably, Bavli promoted Bialik's mission to encourage Hebrew culture and found a Jewish state in Palestine. Heschel shared Bavli's literary commitment and his outrage at the neutrality of American Jewish academics toward the nascent state of Israel. Bavli published a protest poem in *Hadoar*, the New York Hebrew-language newspaper, condemning the neglect of Zionism of many Seminary officials, including Finkelstein: "Vain and barren you tread on hushed carpets in the sealed-off halls of learning, sporting your crown of complacency and cloaked in your mantle of self-importance." [7]

Above all, Heschel appreciated Bavli as a passionate Jew with an inclusive spirit, "a marvelous blend of poetry and piety, of artistry and religious discipline, of sacred stubbornness in defending the traditions of our people and enthusiastic openness to the new and unprecedented in the world of poetry. He was one of the few men in whom the great experiment of modern Judaism did not end in failure."[8]

Heschel's own "great experiment of modern Judaism" began officially six months after he arrived at JTS. On Monday, 1 April 1946, he gave his inaugural lecture, "A Jewish Philosophy in a Time of Crisis," which was followed by a reception. The institutional guest list included Seminary benefactors, as well as representatives of the Rabbi Isaac Elchanan Theological Seminary (of Yeshiva University), Boston Hebrew Teachers College, Dropsie College, Hebrew Union College, Herzliah Hebrew Academy, and Union Theological Seminary. This was also a prime opportunity for Heschel to honor friends, many of whom were immigrants, and to reinforce professional contacts. His personal guest list defined his wide community as it then stood. Included from Cincinnati were Rabbi and Mrs. Feinberg and Julian Morgenstern. Guests from New York included Aron Freimann, bibliographer and former chief librarian of the city of Frankfurt's Judaica collection; Freimann's son-in-law, the physician Menny (Moshe) Rapp; Erich Reiss, Heschel's editor in Berlin, now living in New York with his new wife, the portrait photographer Lotte Jacobi; and Eduard Strauss from the Frankfurt Lehrhaus.

Heschel also invited the Zionist leader Hayim Greenberg; Max Weinreich and Solomon (Shlomo) Noble from YIVO; Jacob Klatzkin and Solomon Liptzin, specialists in Yiddish literature; and the publisher Theodore Schocken. From Yeshiva University came Jacob Hartstein and Abraham Weiss, the Talmud professor. Invitations also went to Simon Halkin, the Hebrew poet and brother of Abraham; Moshe Maisels of the New York Hebrew PEN Club, who was the editor of *Hadoar;* Simon Bernstein of the Zionist Organization of America; and Joshua Bloch, from the Jewish Department of the New York Public Library.[9]

The Seminary did not preserve copies or accounts of Heschel's inaugural lecture, but we can reconstruct it with a degree of plausibility from a typewritten draft of a paper on the postwar revival of Judaism prepared around that

Heschel lecturing at the Jewish Theological Seminary, 1946. Photograph by Virginia F. Stern. Courtesy of the Ratner Center for the Study of Conservative Judaism, Jewish Theological Seminary of America.

time by the JTS faculty. (It was never completed.) The typescript included some corrections in Heschel's handwriting, while many passages echo "The Meaning of This War" and other Heschel essays, recent or to come. It opened with a characteristic flourish: "The horrors of the second World War have filled the hearts of all upright men with reproach and shame. Never has there been so much guilt and distress on this earth. The catastrophe has left its indelible mark on the soul and body of many peoples. Israel [the Jewish people], however, has been most grievously wounded. One-third of its members were exterminated and many of the survivors impoverished, facing starvation, disease, and even persecution."[10]

Practical considerations followed. The Seminary could send a study commission to Europe, improve religious education in the United States, support scholarly research projects and adult education, strive for a Jewish homeland in Palestine, and generally broaden its concerns: "There can be no religious piety without social justice, no lasting economic prosperity without the sense for the spiritual." Heschel's unique idiom emerged most strongly at the end,

Louis Ginzberg introducing Heschel to a lecture audience, Jewish Theological Seminary, 1946. Photograph by Virginia F. Stern. Courtesy of the Ratner Center for the Study of Conservative Judaism, Jewish Theological Seminary of America.

with the focus on holiness: "Let us never forget that the sense for the sacred is as vital to us as the light of the sun. There can be no nature without the Torah, no brotherhood without a father, no humanity without God."[11]

Heschel frequently jotted down insights on scraps of paper. This draft included one note, in which he indulged his fondness for antithesis and alliteration: "The world is not a vacuum. Either we make it an altar for God, or it becomes an arena for atrocities. There can be no neutrality. Either we are ministers of the sacred or slaves of evil."[12]

Remnants of European Community

In New York, Heschel was able, through immigrant friends and acquaintances, to re-create a community that incorporated some of the varied Jewish cultures from the life in Europe he had lost. He retrieved a bit of literary Warsaw with his friend Aaron Zeitlin, a Yiddish writer whose father, Hillel, had been murdered in the ghetto by the Germans. Before the outbreak of the war Aaron had been invited to New York to direct one of his plays for the Yiddish theater. His wife and children had died in Auschwitz. Zeitlin now published poems that forcefully evoked the Catastrophe.

Heschel recovered the spirit of Vilna with Leyzer Ran, an acquaintance from his years at the Realgymnasium, who invited him to contribute to a memorial book (*yizkor bukh*), *The Jerusalem of Lithuania*, a collection of essays and photographs published by YIVO. The YIVO secularists respected Heschel as a Yiddish writer who had published several series of poems in Warsaw, Berlin, and New York.[13]

Heschel also saw several friends from Germany, among them Stephen Kayser, an art critic from Frankfurt who became the first curator of the Jewish Museum, recently established by JTS. And Heschel urged the Jewish Publication Society to commission translations of novels by Soma Morgenstern, who was now living in New York.[14]

By mail Heschel communicated with friends who had immigrated to Palestine, especially Yehiel Hofer, the closest confidant of his youth in Warsaw. Hofer's wife and children had been murdered by the Nazis, while the Russian "liberators" had deported him to a work camp in Siberia. After the war, Hofer reached Tel Aviv, where he remarried, practiced medicine, and became a writer in Hebrew and Yiddish. Heschel, whose own financial means were limited, periodically sent him money. Heschel also kept in touch with his elders in Jewish Palestine, including Martin Buber, who was rebuilding his career as a teacher and writer in Jerusalem, and Fishl Schneersohn in Tel Aviv, Heschel's Warsaw mentor, who was a specialist in psychiatry and child development. Schneersohn now worked in the Ministry of Education, developing principles of ethical training.[15]

Heschel remained close to the members of his extended Hasidic family to varying degrees. On his mother's side, the Perlows, Hasidim from Novominsk near Warsaw, were the first to arrive in America, around 1924. Heschel's uncle, Rabbi Yehuda Aryeh Leib Perlow, the brother of the Warsaw Novominsker rebbe (Rabbi Alter Israel Shimon, his mother's twin brother), immigrated to the Williamsburg section of Brooklyn. Two years later, a son of the Novominsker rebbe, Rabbi Nahum Mordecai Perlow, settled in Borough Park, also in Brooklyn. Both men took the title of Novominsker rebbe.[16]

Most of these Hasidim, whose dynasty was formed in Lithuania, were skeptical of Heschel. Although they recognized his learning in Talmud, they faulted him for teaching at a non-Orthodox institution, which they saw as undermining

Heschel's Hasidic family, paternal branch, ca. 1955. Standing, left to right:
Heschel; Israel Heschel; Rabbi Abraham Joshua Heschel, the Kopitzhinitzer rebbe.
Courtesy of Yitzhak Meir Twersky.

the Torah-true religion. In addition, they judged that his writings did not adequately emphasize the demands of halakhah. Heschel's book on the Sabbath, for example, was philosophical; it did not even mention the thirty-nine types of work to be avoided on the holy day.[17]

Among the Perlows, Heschel was closest to Aaron, a first cousin with whom he grew up in Warsaw. In 1930 Perlow and his wife, Malka Twersky (from another Hasidic dynasty), settled in Brooklyn. In 1936 Aaron became a naturalized American citizen, able to help Heschel during his escape from Europe. (When Heschel reached London in 1939, he urged another Perlow cousin, Bernard, to bring immigration documents to Aaron in America.) In New York Aaron and Heschel renewed their friendship, enjoying long conversations together. Perlow was strictly Orthodox, but he was modern, "a shaven man," with an established position in the diamond trade. He worked in the early morning so he could study in the New York Public Library Judaica section from 11:00 A.M. to 8:00 P.M. every day.[18]

Heschel reserved his deepest feelings, however, for his paternal cousins, by whom he was more readily accepted. They were descendants of the rebbe of Ruzhin, Rabbi Israel Friedman. In 1927 Rabbi Mordecai Shlomo Friedman,

Heschel's Hasidic family, maternal branch, late 1950s. Left to right: *Aaron Perlow; Rabbi Yehuda Aryeh Leib Perlow, the Novominsker rebbe of Williamsburg, Brooklyn; Rabbi Nahum Mordecai Perlow, the Novominsker rebbe of Borough Park, Brooklyn. Courtesy of Yitzhak Meir Twersky.*

the Boyaner rebbe, left Vienna with his family and established his Hasidic court on the Lower East Side of Manhattan. (Rabbi Friedman's son Izzy [Israel] was a social worker in Harlem, another Hasid in modern dress, as it were.) Heschel cherished his visits to the *shtibl* (prayer house) of his first cousin and namesake, Rabbi Abraham Joshua Heschel, the rebbe of Kopitzhinitz, husband of his oldest sister, Sarah.[19]

The Kopitzhinitzer rebbe exemplified the "pious man," for he possessed exceptional warmth and loving-kindness (*hesed*). Ethics was inseparable from the ritual commandments for the rebbe, who devoted much of his time to collecting money for needy Jews. For example, he refused contributions from people who were not shomer Shabbos (Sabbath observers). Once a friend introduced a prospective donor, assuring the rebbe that the man was shomer Shabbos, but the rebbe went further, asking, "Are you *shomer hol?*" (honest and kind during the week [*hol*] in business and personal relationships). For the rebbe, righteous behavior every day made it possible to aspire to God on Shabbat.[20]

The wedding of Israel Friedman and Natalie Lookstein, 1966. Left to right:
*unidentified man; Heschel; Samuel Belkin, president of Yeshiva University; Rabbi
Joseph Lookstein, founder of the Ramaz School. Courtesy of Yitzhak Meir Twersky.*

With them Heschel recovered the enveloping family of his youth. The
Kopitzhinitzer rebbe had ten children (who were both Heschel's cousins and
his nieces and nephews): Israel (Sruel), Leah Rachel, Chava, Batsheva, Mira,
Miriam, Malka, Chaya Pearl, Moses Mordecai (Moyshe), and Meshullam Zusya.
Heschel had been close to Israel in Europe, writing from Vilna to encourage him
in his Talmud studies. Now Heschel often spoke with Israel, an intense, somewhat shy young man, who was ill at ease with people but revered for his purity
of heart.

The Friedman-Heschel clan welcomed "Professor Heschel," as he was
known in their community. While they profoundly disagreed with the tenets of
Conservative Judaism, their love for him, and for all Jewish people—*ahavat
yisrael*—was central to their observance, as was the commandment of hospitality (one meaning of the name "Heschel"). Nonetheless, the Kopitzhinitzer
rebbe, who could not read German, wanted to evaluate Heschel's European writings. He asked Rabbi Shraga Feivel Mendolowitz, the head in the 1920s of a
community in Williamsburg that became a citadel of Orthodoxy, whether there
were any *apikorsus* (disbelief or non-Orthodox ideas) in them. The authoritative
Rabbi Mendolowitz pronounced Heschel's writings to be kosher.[21]

Heschel spoke on the telephone with his brother-in-law every weekday, usually between 1:00 and 2:00 P.M., using the Warsaw dialect of their native Yiddish. People who observed these conversations said that they had never seen Heschel so relaxed, so natural, as he was at these times. The intimacy of the mother tongue liberated him from the American persona he had developed to communicate his sacred vision to outsiders.

As in prewar Europe, when he had navigated between diverse Jewish cultures, Heschel was tested in North America, by secularists as well as his Orthodox connections. Melekh Ravitch, Heschel's editor in Warsaw, was keen to understand how his former protégé had remained devout. In March 1946, Heschel traveled to Montreal to lecture at Ravitch's Yiddish Folk School. On Sunday, after Heschel's presentation, they debated issues of Judaism, the Holocaust, and faith in a living God. Ravitch described the encounter in his Yiddish-language memoirs, reminiscing about his first meeting with the adolescent Heschel in 1925. "Everything about his face is as it was twenty-one years ago. With the exception of the beard which he shaved smooth with an electric apparatus. Also the cigar, brown and fragrant, which the guest smokes from time to time, in rabbinic fashion, even rebbe-like." Ravitch was one among several Warsaw acquaintances who understood the gestures, the body language, that Heschel "behaved like a rebbe."[22]

Ravitch began the essay by describing his lifelong battle "against religious forms and anthropomorphic conceptions of God which is, in essence, the way of the pious." For Ravitch, who remained unmoved by Heschel's spiritual writings, the Holocaust only confirmed his atheism: "With deep sorrow I reflected that if *belief* and *prayer* had not stood so exalted among Polish Jewry, even among Polish Jewish Socialists, the unexpected tragedy would not have dealt them such a deep and sudden blow. For the pious it is enough when they deceive themselves that God hears them. Nonbelievers want God to listen to them seriously." [23]

The conversation continued for several hours. It was Purim, when Jews are commanded to hear the reading of the *Megillah* (the Scroll of Esther). Heschel excused himself in order to complete this mitzvah, but Ravitch asked him to remain. Heschel "put on a yarmulke and read the *Megillah* with a cantillation and Warsaw accent to the well-known tune which I haven't heard in nearly half a century." Then they returned to their debate, which was never resolved. Ravitch rejected Heschel's "stubborn piety," which could not explain, let alone justify, the suffering and death of innocent people. For his part, Heschel persistently maintained that compassion for God's suffering (his theology of God in exile) could incite responsible citizens to act and so save lives in the future.

Heschel in Love

In the summer of 1946, following his first academic year at JTS, amid unceasing professional activity and inner anguish about the war, Heschel met up again with Sylvia Straus. She had come to New York for an audition with Arthur Rubinstein, the virtuoso pianist. Rubinstein appreciated her talent, advising her to remain in the city to study with the composer and pianist Edward Steuermann, and promising to assess her progress a year later. Straus moved to New York, where she continued to study piano and took courses in philosophy at Columbia University. She and Heschel began to date again.[24]

Heschel was always drawn to music, and several of his early Yiddish poems evoke its amorous effects:

> Your fingers caress the piano keys—
> an army of white, long bird beaks—
> I've gathered stillness for the shrines
> Of my nights, and light for your wild secrets.[25]

The night he first met Straus he had been attracted to her as much for her skilled playing as her personal qualities. Straus was beautiful, with deep dark eyes, lush hair, and a classic Semitic nose. Spirited and clever, she was interested in ideas, and Heschel found something naive and pure, and quite appealing, in her enthusiasms. She was unfamiliar with Orthodox Judaism, however, and did not know Hebrew. Although Heschel would teach her Jewish laws and customs, the halakhic way of life that was second nature to him, they could not share much of his life experience.

Heschel was fascinated by this artistic woman and her happy, Americanized family. Her parents were immigrants: her father, Samuel, came from Russia, and her mother, Anna, from Poland. The family spoke some Yiddish at home, but they were minimally observant; Sylvia's father was a secular socialist, although her mother lit the Shabbat candles on Friday nights. Sylvia had three brothers, who doted on her. The youngest, Jack, was away in the army, Morris had taken over the family grocery store, and Reuben, the eldest, became a pathologist, a medical researcher, and a gifted violinist.[26]

Abraham Joshua Heschel and Sylvia Straus on their wedding day,
Los Angeles, 10 December 1946. Courtesy of Barbara Straus Reed.

Sylvia found Heschel handsome, and she enjoyed his playful sense of
humor, a quality Heschel shared with close friends and relatives during moments of freedom from his cares. She was also attracted to his European culture
and his Jewish piety. Heschel was thirty-nine years old, Sylvia thirty-three,
both primed for marriage. After Sylvia accepted Heschel's proposal, they went

to Louis Ginzberg and his wife for their endorsement. President Finkelstein asked the acting president of Columbia University, Frank D. Fackenthal, to use his influence to find them an apartment.[27]

Sadly, after the wedding was arranged, Sylvia's mother, Anna, suddenly passed away, and they postponed the wedding a short time for the initial mourning period. They were married in Los Angles on 10 December 1946 in an Orthodox ceremony. There was no honeymoon, and the couple returned to New York and began their life together, renting an apartment on Riverside Drive.[28]

Each of them had serious professional goals, and they agreed that Sylvia would pursue her performance career, which demanded long hours of practice, while Heschel would remain in his JTS study late into the night to continue his research and writing. Like many two-career couples, each supported the other's autonomy. With his marriage, Heschel also accepted the gulf between himself and his wife, and their two fundamentally different Jewish identities.

Confronting the Holocaust

A month after Heschel and Sylvia were married, on 18 January 1947, Heschel gave another major address in Yiddish at YIVO. The topic of the twenty-first annual conference was the revival of Judaism and the Jewish people after the war. Owing to the dramatic effect of his first appearance two years earlier, Heschel was featured at this larger convocation. Nearly 3,000 persons heard Heschel speak at the Hunter College assembly hall on "The Meaning of Jewish Existence." Heschel focused on the spiritual dimension, in contrast to the other predominantly historical papers, this time even more forcefully than in his previous address: "Judaism . . . is the merging of the worldly with the heavenly, the elevation of man to a state higher than man, in which a minor offense becomes a crime against heaven, and an unethical act, a denial of the divine."[29]

Using this speech as a springboard, Heschel began developing essays for publication. "To Be a Jew: What Is It?" appeared in September 1947, around the High Holy Days, in the Yiddish-language *Yidisher Kemfer*, the Labor Zionist newspaper edited by Hayim Greenberg. In it Heschel warned: "We are the only channel of Jewish tradition, those who must save Judaism from oblivion, those who must hand over the entire past to the generations to come." At the same time, his notion of Jewish philosophy was humanistic, not parochial or ethnocentric: "to set forth the universal relevance of Judaism, the bearings of its demands upon the chance of man to remain human."[30]

Soon he placed a second essay in *Yidisher Kemfer,* exposing his vulnerability as a Jew who had survived the Holocaust. Reviewing two substantial volumes (638 pages total) of Yiddish verse by Aaron Zeitlin that had been published the previous year in New York, he proclaimed that the Jewish people were enduring a mourning process. First came shock: "We still feel the blow to our heads. It feels like the heavens above have dropped in chunks. We have not yet grasped the disaster that has befallen us. We are still before the funeral—ready to sit *shiva,* bewildered, confused and petrified." Then followed a glimmer of self-awareness, anxiety, questioning: "When I think of my people, burned in the crematoria of Poland, a shudder begins to course through my veins. I feel the claws of insanity." Ineffable agony isolated Jews from the rest of humankind, and only poetry like Zeitlin's could indicate the magnitude of grief. What, asked Heschel, "is the task of a Jewish poet in our times?"[31]

As he reflected upon his own vocation in America, Heschel denounced assimilation, and perhaps his own youthful aspirations, citing Zeitlin:

> "As for me, I was a man of letters in Warsaw,
> who believed like all the others
> in the same Goethe
> and in other such brilliant egoists."

Heschel went on to condemn the antireligious cult of the Jewish Enlightenment, with its surrender to worldly values, denouncing "the plate-lickers of non-Jewish culture." A solution for Heschel, as for Zeitlin, was to integrate modern and mystical thought, including Kabbalah and Hasidism. Heschel concluded by citing a terrifying poem of Zeitlin's that depicted "a large gloomy rat" inspecting a ruined world, "a world without God and without Jews." Another Holocaust was possible. Such was the terror Heschel carried within himself for the rest of his life.[32]

Students, Skeptics, and Disciples

Heschel did not share his rich literary life with most of his students. His classroom demeanor at JTS mirrored that at HUC. Dissatisfied with his course assignments, he withdrew his interest from formal teaching. He deserved his poor reputation. Heschel's required philosophy course at the Rabbinical School was the worst. It met at 9:00 A.M. on Mondays, too early for most students. Heschel would begin by calling the roll, so the class would start ten minutes late, and he usually finished before 10:00. Sometimes he would stop his lecture in mid-sentence when the bell rang.[33]

Heschel rarely prepared his lessons, often asking students what subjects they had discussed in the previous class, making them feel devalued. His assignments could be inconsistent and demeaning, for example, requiring them to summarize one of his own books or chapters of Maimonides. For most of the term he might give no written assignment and then demand an extensive paper for the following week, or require three papers and a final examination for a class that met only one hour a week.

It was obvious that Heschel cared most for his writing. Although he made an exception for favored students, his mind and his audience were elsewhere. He often brought in galley proofs of articles or books and read them to the class, sometimes penning in corrections while he talked. Many students felt insulted. Others, however, considered themselves honored to be among the first to hear his words. To some students Heschel was disorganized, to others he taught the way a Hasidic rebbe would, telling stories aimed at producing dramatic insights. He could be extremely generous to receptive students, to whom he gave hours of his time, inviting them to his office for probing conversations, advising them on personal problems, and nurturing their spiritual growth. For them, despite dreary or alienating moments in class, he was a brilliant teacher who shared his thoughts in progress. The younger students at the Teachers Institute, in particular, who were less burdened with required courses, appreciated Heschel's lessons on Rashi, the sage who democratized Jewish learning, making the holy texts available to everyone. Heschel helped these students understand the classic commentator for the first time. By contrast, few students in the Rabbinical School were attached to Heschel in the same way. Many were skeptical or disappointed. But each member of that first Heschel generation preserved stories and, over the years, helped create his legend.

Although Heschel was not allowed to teach courses on Hasidism, he tried to create special worship opportunities, one of which was a 10:00 P.M. weekday evening service, a Ma'ariv minyan. His most successful project was the late Shabbat afternoon *seudah shlishit* (third meal) in the cafeteria, modeled after the Hasidic *sholosh sheudos*. At sundown, with lights extinguished, students would sit around the rebbe's table in silence, then begin chanting nigunim.

Although Heschel was generally a failure in the classroom, he did fulfill Finkelstein's expectations in one important respect. Most rabbinical students were followers of Mordecai Kaplan; they felt comfortable with his sociological approach to religion and appreciated his passion for proselytizing. Heschel, with his opposed views and his own followers, was able to reinvigorate serious theological debate and spirituality among the students, as Kaplanians and Heschelians vied with one another in the cafeteria and dormitories.

Outside the classroom, Heschel acquired a devoted student following whose leader was Samuel Dresner, his adherent from HUC.[34] Dresner revered Heschel as a genuine zaddik. As a self-proclaimed disciple, Dresner took notes on Heschel's classes and conversations, hoping one day to write a biography of his master. In 1951 Dresner was ordained and pursued a distinguished career as a Conservative congregational rabbi, an ethical activist, and a cultural critic, publishing essays on Jewish practice, books critical of the funeral industry and atomic warfare, and a volume of meditations, *Prayer, Humility, and Compassion* (1957), that was directly inspired by Heschel. As a scholar of Hasidism, Dresner received the degree of Doctor of Hebrew Letters (DHL) under Heschel's direction, writing his dissertation on Rabbi Yaakov Yosef of Polnoy. His book *The Zaddik* (1960), for which Heschel wrote a preface, became a classic study of spiritual leadership. For many years Dresner was the editor of *Conservative Judaism*, the movement's rabbinic journal, wielding considerable influence.

Heschel also formed a strong tie with Wolfe Kelman, another rabbinical student. Kelman was born in Vienna in 1923 and came from distinguished Hasidic stock. His family immigrated to Toronto, where he grew up in a thriving Orthodox community. During the war Kelman joined the Royal Canadian Air Force. Still in uniform, he came to New York seeking admission to the Rabbinical School, but he missed the entrance examination. Shalom Spiegel, a member of the Admissions Committee, agreed to test him on the Talmud—as they rode in the elevator. Kelman easily passed.

Yet he was unhappy at the Seminary. He found the courses elementary and the professors aloof. He wanted to quit, but his classmate Dresner insisted, "You have to meet Heschel." "What do I have to do with some little Hasidic rebbe from Poland," he answered. But Sam set an appointment with Heschel for the next day. Kelman knocked on the door, and Heschel ushered him into his small office, filled with cigar smoke. While Heschel continued a telephone conversation, Kelman picked up a *sefer* (religious book in Hebrew) and started to read it, absorbed. A few minutes later, Heschel put down the telephone and asked, "So you know that book?" Kelman smiled, "I know that book very well. My grandfather wrote it." Heschel looked at him. "Excuse me young man, what is the grandson of the Dinover Rav doing at the Jewish Theological Seminary?"

Heschel and Wolfe Kelman, Jewish Theological Seminary commencement, 1971.
Courtesy of the Ratner Center for the Study of Conservative Judaism, Jewish
Theological Seminary of America.

Kelman answered, "I will tell you, if you tell me what the grandson of the *Ohev Yisrael* [the Lover of Jews, his ancestor the Apter Rav] is doing at the Seminary." Heschel jumped up from his desk and hugged Kelman, an embrace that inaugurated Heschel's closest American friendship.

The two men had much in common, despite the difference in their ages. Both were descended from Hasidic dynasties and chose to leave their loving but restrictive Orthodox families for the larger Jewish world and beyond. They shared the trauma of having abdicated their ancestral charge while remaining Hasidim in spirit. And they had an easy rapport, for both enjoyed telling stories. During Kelman's days as a rabbinical student, Heschel was "a friend, a helper, a shoulder to lean on." He was a nurturing presence in the dormitory and helped care for Kelman when he was recovering from a painful cyst operation.

Kelman was ordained in 1950. But instead of taking a pulpit, he became executive vice president of the Rabbinical Assembly, the professional body of Conservative rabbis. His office was housed in one of the Seminary buildings,

Left to right: *Seymour Siegel, Heschel, and Samuel Dresner, ca. 1949.*
Courtesy of the Ratner Center for the Study of Conservative Judaism,
Jewish Theological Seminary of America.

and he and Heschel would spend time together every day. They would lunch together if neither had other appointments. Many evenings they would speak on the telephone and meet at night to pick up the early edition of the *New York Times.* Sometimes one would walk the other home, but they would be talking so earnestly that they would both continue on to the other's doorstep.[35]

Their friendship was close, but both Kelman and Heschel preferred to maintain a certain formality. Kelman never called Heschel by his first name. Although Heschel opened his heart to Kelman, who was involved in most of his major life decisions, in their conversations and letters he was always "Professor" or "Dr. Heschel." Kelman was the younger Jewish professional, Heschel the rabbi and scholar. In fact, only acquaintances and a few Christian friends called him Abraham. Even his wife, Sylvia, called him Heschel, from his full first name, Abraham Joshua *Heschel* Heschel. Heschel's normal mode of relating to people, even intimates, was to guard his inner self, maintaining a distance from others.

Faculty and graduating class, Jewish Theological Seminary, 1948. Faculty,
first row (left to right): Bernard Mandelbaum, Boaz Cohen, Alexander Sperber,
Hillel Bavli, Shalom Spiegel, Alexander Marx, Louis Finkelstein, Saul Lieberman.
H. L. Ginsberg, Heschel, Robert Gordis, visiting professor Ernst Simon. Photograph
by Gedalia Segal. Courtesy of the Ratner Center for the Study of Conservative
Judaism, Jewish Theological Seminary of America.

Some of the students in whom Heschel showed deep interest—conversing
with them for hours in his office, asking them to walk him home, inviting them
to his apartment for holidays, even taking some of them to visit his brother-in-
law, the Kopitzhinitzer rebbe—later became his supportive colleagues at the
Seminary or opened doors for him beyond the Jewish community. One such
was Seymour Siegel, who came to JTS in 1947. Siegel grew up in Chicago in a
close-knit Yiddish-speaking family and community. His yeshiva education
prepared him to become an Orthodox rabbi or a Talmud scholar, but after
graduating from the University of Chicago, he gravitated toward the Conservative Seminary. His friends Samuel Dresner and Wolfe Kelman urged him to
study with Heschel. Although Siegel was disappointed in Heschel's Jewish
philosophy course, the two developed a warm relationship, often conversing
in Heschel's office or at his home.[36]

Siegel was struck by Heschel's compassion. Once in April 1948, while Israel's War of Independence was going on, Heschel came in and announced, "This morning I've read about the Deir Yassin incident. If Jews can do that, I'm so disturbed that I'm calling off the class." Heschel was referring to the massacre the day before of more than two hundred Arab civilians, most of them women and children, in the village of Deir Yassin, west of Jerusalem. The murderers were Jews, illegal terrorist forces of the Irgun, to which Menachem Begin belonged, and the Lehi, also known as the Stern Gang. Heschel's support of Israel did not blind him to the sufferings of Israel's enemies or to the inevitable injustices of war.[37]

Siegel did brilliant work in the Rabbinical School and earned several prizes. In the 1951–52 academic year he joined the faculty as teaching fellow in Talmud and a student adviser. In 1958, Siegel became an instructor of Talmud. Under Heschel's inspiration, he developed a special competence in religious thought and helped further the theology program at the Seminary.

Also close to Heschel was Marc Herman Tanenbaum, who came from a Yiddish-speaking Orthodox family in Baltimore. Tanenbaum's mother welcomed Christian neighbors into their home, however, and Tanenbaum became comfortable with people of other faiths and ethnicities. The precocious Tanenbaum entered Yeshiva University at age fourteen, graduating in 1945. He then entered JTS, seeking a less restrictive but still devout Judaism. He studied Jewish history with Alexander Marx, learning about the interaction of Judaism and early Christianity. He also took one class with Heschel, but he didn't appreciate Heschel's defensive teaching style.

During Tanenbaum's last year at JTS, however, the two formed a lifelong bond, almost accidentally, as a result of Heschel's instinctive warmth. One day Tanenbaum found himself in the elevator with Heschel, who noticed that he seemed worried. When Tanenbaum admitted to having family problems, Heschel invited the student to his office, where they sat for two hours, while Tanenbaum poured out his distress. His father had suffered several heart attacks, and his mother was managing the family store with only her daughter to help. Tanenbaum expected his father to die, and he felt guilty for remaining in New York while his mother was in such difficulties.

Suddenly, Heschel picked up the telephone and called Tanenbaum's mother in Baltimore, speaking to her gently in Yiddish and English. To Tanenbaum, Heschel was giving his mother *nehamah*, a traditional Jewish form of consolation. Heschel encouraged her, "Be strong, and you will be strong." She knew of Heschel through the Yiddish press as a "sage," a "great teacher;" yet this important man was telling her how pleased he was to have her son as a student, promising to pray for her husband's recovery, and urging her to feel free to call him. Tanenbaum developed a reverence for Heschel as a person, overwhelmed that his teacher would willingly spend his valuable time with a student and comfort his mother. To Tanenbaum, Heschel embodied the essence of Jewish life.[38]

Ordained at the same time as Wolfe Kelman, his roommate and close friend, Tanenbaum never became a pulpit rabbi but returned to New York and worked at *Time* magazine in public relations. He then joined the small publishing house of Henry Schuman, where he helped publish *The Earth Is the Lord's*, the book that established Heschel's renown among speakers of English as the voice of East European Jewish piety.

Another student, from an entirely different cultural background, provided Heschel with another critical perspective. Fritz A. Rothschild was born in 1919 in Bad Hamburg, Germany, and grew up in a middle-class Orthodox family. As a rebellious young man he joined the religious Zionists (Mizrahi), studying Hebrew so that he could become a typesetter in Palestine. The anti-Jewish laws prevented Rothschild from completing a Gymnasium degree, without which he could not enter a university. Instead, this venturesome thinker attended classes taught by Martin Buber and others at the Jüdisches Lehrhaus in Frankfurt.

One day Rothschild heard a young professor named Abraham Heschel lecture on the Bible at a conference for Jewish youth leaders. He was quite taken with Heschel, who spoke German elegantly (though with a marked Yiddish accent) and took the Bible seriously, arousing respect in his skeptical audience.

After the Kristallnacht pogrom in November 1938, Rothschild was arrested and confined for seven weeks in Buchenwald, but he managed to get a visa to Northern Rhodesia to work in an uncle's business. From Africa, Rothschild wrote a long letter to Martin Buber in 1943, asking about the future of Jewish culture and inquiring whether "Dr. Abraham Heschel is still alive and how he is." In his pessimistic reply Buber informed Rothschild that Heschel was "a lecturer at Hebrew Union College in Cincinnati, and he is doing all right. I have written to him that you inquired about him."[39]

Five years later, in 1948, Rothschild arrived in New York from Northern Rhodesia, alone, without any means of support, hoping to study at JTS. He consulted a secretary at the Seminary about the entrance examination, which she took upon herself to administer. She asked Rothschild to translate the first line of an article in elementary journalistic Hebrew, "The refugees stand on the deck of the vessel that carries them to Palestine," which Rothschild read with much faltering. She failed him. Discouraged, Rothschild got a job with a Hebrew publisher on Delancey Street. Later he learned that Heschel was now at JTS. He visited him at his office, and they spoke in English. Heschel took the initiative: "Let's take practical matters first; why don't you study here?" When Rothschild explained that he had failed the reading test, Heschel chose a scholarly journal from a shelf and asked him to read an article in academic Hebrew by Mayer Balaban, a historian from Warsaw. Rothschild knew this technical vocabulary and read fluently. "No need to translate," said Heschel, "you have just passed your entrance examination. You can enter the Teachers Institute in the fall, and we shall see."

Rothschild qualified to enter the Teachers Institute as a third-year student in the five-year degree program. He struggled at first for he had never heard Hebrew spoken, and all courses were given in Hebrew. He took a course with Heschel, who taught from his recent booklet in Hebrew, "Pikuach Neshama" (To Save a Soul, 1949). But Finkelstein refused to admit Rothschild into the Rabbinical School. Standards were rigid: because he had not been educated in America, Rothschild could never work as a congregational rabbi. Finkelstein finally allowed Rothschild to enroll in text courses at the Rabbinical School along with a number of intellectuals interested in graduate work, university

Heschel and Fritz Rothschild, Jewish Theological Seminary commencement, 1971.
Courtesy of the Ratner Center for the Study of Conservative Judaism,
Jewish Theological Seminary of America.

teaching, and research. The "Institute for Theology," as the special group was called, included Arthur Cohen, Moshe Greenberg, David Winston, and Arthur Hyman. They had a special course in Mishnah and studied with Saul Lieberman and other JTS luminaries, including Heschel.[40]

In 1951, after receiving a Bachelor of Religious Education from the Teachers Institute, Rothschild entered Columbia's graduate program in philosophy, hoping to write his doctoral dissertation on Heschel. John Herman Randall, his adviser, asked for a sample chapter before approving or rejecting the topic. Rothschild submitted a systematic essay on Heschel's religious thought, which was eventually accepted. Later, Rothschild joined the faculty of the Teachers Institute. He and Heschel developed a salutary working relationship: Heschel would show his manuscripts to this brilliant, strong-willed German Jew who, in turn, would help his teacher clarify his thoughts, providing both men with critical perspective and intellectual stimulation. In 1959 Rothschild published an anthology of Heschel's writings with an insightful introduction, making his teacher's life and thought available to a wider public.[41]

Another German Jew testified privately to the impact of Heschel's work. While a student at the Berlin Hochschule, Heschel had studied with Dr. Leo Baeck, the revered leader of Berlin's Jewish community. During the Nazi years, the Liberal rabbi and scholar had heroically refused to abandon his community; he remained in Berlin and was deported to Theresienstadt. It was rumored that he had perished there, but he had survived, earning an even greater reputation for courage and spiritual dignity. Heschel admired Baeck's piety and considered him "the most cultured [*hochgebildet*] man" he had ever met.[42]

One day Heschel heard that Baeck was visiting New York, staying at the Biltmore Hotel. Heschel was anxious to see him again and telephoned the hotel. Baeck picked up, answering in German, "Ja, Baeck hier." Heschel was so overcome with emotion that he couldn't speak. Baeck waited, then, thinking it must be a wrong number, began to hang up. Heschel finally stammered, "Dr. Baeck, I'm coming down to see you at the hotel." On the subway with his student Wolfe Kelman, Heschel wondered, "What am I going to say to this man? What can I say to my old teacher who has just been liberated?" When they entered the hotel, there stood Rabbi Baeck with his cane, dignified as ever, stiff as a ramrod. Baeck immediately went to Heschel, grasped his hand, and said, "Heschel, in the last issue of the *Monatsschrift* there was your article on the essence of prayer. I smuggled it with me into Theresienstadt and

I want to thank you. That article was a great comfort to me in those dark days."[43]

One cycle of Heschel's life was complete. In Germany, before the war, he began as a philosopher to define the power of prayer. In the United States, as a spiritual interpreter, he helped a wider public deal with despair by celebrating holiness.

6

Books of Spiritual Rescue (1948–1951)

In this hour we, the living, are "the people of Israel." The tasks, begun by the patriarchs and prophets and continued by their descendants, are now entrusted to us. We are either the last Jews or those who will hand over the entire past to generations to come.
—Heschel, *The Earth Is the Lord's* (1950)

---

launched his new mission, to educate American Jews on two levels: theological and cultural. The foundation of both was what I call a sacred humanism, already embedded in his essay "The Mystical Element in Judaism," which was completed in 1945 but not published until 1949. Unlike Martin Buber, whose brief, memorable, and essentially secular notion of "I-Thou dialogue" could be grasped by a wide readership, Heschel sought to inculcate a more complex ethos that combined reverence for the living God, traditional observance, and universal ethics.[1]

For Heschel, Jewish mysticism sanctified human life and was intrinsically this-worldly. His interpretation of the Zohar, mysticism's basic text, emphasized the "exaltation of man" based on a reciprocal relationship (or covenant) with the divine: "Jewish mystics are inspired by a bold and dangerously paradoxical idea that not only is God necessary to man but that man is also necessary to God, to the unfolding of His plan in this world." The Zohar's theology of divine pathos, as Heschel defined it, minimized the supernatural aspects of this source, also known as "The Book of Splendor."[2]

Adding references to the Talmud and the Bible (especially Psalms) to his article, Heschel elaborated the rabbinic and Kabbalistic doctrine of the Shekhinah, the divine presence that accompanies Israel in exile.[3] He concluded by fitting mysticism into the prophetic experience with a footnote reference to his 1936 thesis, *Die Prophetie.*

A Spiritual Emergency

In 1949 Heschel put forth his vision of authentic Jewish survival in a Hebrew-language booklet entitled "To Save a Soul" (Pikuach Neshama), addressed to religiously literate Jews. Originally delivered as a speech to the heads of day schools and yeshivas in the New York metropolitan region, this booklet echoed Heschel's YIVO speeches and his 1947 Yiddish essay "Who Is a Jew?" which were all intended for Jewish secularists. The rich Hebrew style of "To Save a Soul" alluded to the Bible, the Talmud, prayers, and religious doctrines that only Jews close to traditional sources could properly appreciate. The title played on the well-known commandment of pikuach nefesh (saving human life): if necessary, one must suspend religious law in a life-threatening situation. The term *nefesh* refers to the vital principle; *neshama* is the divine soul within the human.[4]

After Auschwitz, wrote Heschel, Jews had to do whatever was necessary to preserve the soul from extinction. The essay's subtitle, "From the Kiln of Jewish Existence," evoked both the Nazi crematoria and the furnaces of creativity. According to Heschel, "The very existence of a Jew is a spiritual act. The fact that we have survived, despite the suffering and persecution, is itself a sanctification of God's name [*kiddush ha-shem*]." To be Jewish was to perceive the spiritual dimension, "to feel the soul in everything." Its essence was the quality of "Sabbathness," spiritual refinement, which led to a universal morality: "Objectively, one could [or must] say to every person: If you want to live a spiritual life that is complete and righteous, then go and live as a Jew. Our fate is a sign and a mission. What happened to Israel [the Jewish people] will happen to the whole world." Jews must go beyond restrictive, ethnocentric conceptions: "Judaism teaches us that to remain a people we must be more than a people. Israel is destined to be a holy people."[5]

Heschel also opposed those Orthodox Jews who judged the Nazi genocide as God's punishment for neglecting divinely commanded laws. He interpreted Sabbath observance, for example, not as a system of rules of Jewish behavior but rather as a vehicle for developing sensitive concern for the sanctity of human life. Heschel even implied that if everyone, not just Jews, observed the Sabbath another Holocaust might be prevented. The spiritual imperative rang clear: Jewish educators had a divine calling to rescue the human soul by helping Jews to live as Jews. He concluded with an apocalyptic warning: "Perhaps people have never been as much in need of Judaism as they are in our generation. The human species is on its deathbed."[6]

Heschel himself dealt with the crisis by following the spirit of halakhah. As he explained in *Man's Quest for God*, "'There are three ways in which a man expresses his deep sorrow: the man on the lowest level cries; the man on the second level is silent; the man on the highest level knows how to turn his sorrow into song.' True prayer is song." He confided to Samuel Dresner that in his daily devotions he did not recite the *Tahanun* prayer, a confession of sin and supplication that was usually omitted only on the Sabbath and festivals. Heschel explained that it was a Hasidic custom to omit these woeful entreaties on the *Yahrzeit* (anniversary of a death) of a rebbe, for such was not a day of sorrow but a mark of renewal and celebration. Because almost every day after the war was the Yahrzeit of a rebbe, Heschel did not say Tahanun at all. By means of his silence, each day he memorialized another leader, acknowledging his heartbreak before God alone. Publicly, however, Heschel would sing, literally and figuratively. He loved nigunim, and he wrote English essays in musical prose that praised—and idealized—East European Jewry.[7]

The cultural battle among American Jews was as arduous as the spiritual one. Heschel believed that mainstream Jewish organizations had stayed relatively uninvolved during the Nazi exterminations because of their bias against Polish immigrants. Years later, he explained: "Everybody respected German Jewry. They produced a Heine, an Einstein, but Polish Jews, they are ne'er-do-wells. I have great respect for German Jews, but for me personally, the Baal Shem Tov is much more important than Einstein." That was one reason why Heschel justified the personal God against the naturalism of Einstein, America's most prestigious modern Jew.[8]

Heschel wished to reach a national audience, and for that he would have to publish in English in respected, widely circulated magazines. The most prominent forum for Jewish readers was *Commentary*, a liberal, nonsectarian journal founded in 1945 by the American Jewish Committee. Controversial issues of cultural, political, and religious import, to both Jews and Americans generally, were debated in its pages in sophisticated, often highly emotional articles.[9]

In May 1948 (the month Israel declared its independence), an essay by Heschel appeared in *Commentary*, "The Two Great Traditions: The Sephardim and the Ashkenazim"; the text was introduced as a chapter from his forthcoming book on East European Jewry. This polemical piece was Heschel's first critique of American Jewish values. His rhetorical strategy was to draw broad oppositions, antitheses that seemed impossible to reconcile. He set up stark, oversimplified contrasts between the Sephardic culture of medieval Spain and the Ashkenazic culture of Eastern Europe. Each category represented a distinct approach to thought and society: Sephardic culture emphasized rationalism, scientific scholarship, and cultural elitism; Ashkenazic culture favored intuition, a sense of the holy, and a democratic community.

Heschel forcefully advanced the latter. He began by praising Sephardic culture, "distinguished not only by monumental scientific achievements but also by a universality of spirit. [The Sephardic] accomplishment was in some way a symbiosis of Jewish tradition and Moslem civilization." Heschel's appreciation was sincere and well grounded; he had written extensively on Sephardic thinkers like Saadia, Ibn Gabirol, Maimonides, and Isaac Abravanel. But here he chose the other way.[10]

Heschel's preference reflected his own intuitive manner and literary style: "Ashkenazic writers forego clarity for the sake of depth. The contours of their thoughts are irregular, vague, and often perplexingly entangled; their content is restless, animated by inner wrestling and a kind of baroque emotion." He praised the Yiddish language as the natural instrument for the Jewish masses of Eastern Europe, elevating it to a spiritual plane: "In this language you say 'beauty' and mean 'spirituality'; you say 'kindness' and mean 'holiness.'" Heschel excelled in a fluid, musically repetitive style, rather than in systematic linear exposition. He crafted his manuscripts so that tone was as important as content.[11]

But his critical agenda was always clear. Here his purpose was to denounce the tendency of American Jews to slip into mediocrity. He reproved Sephardic ethics as "at times bourgeois, full of prudence and practical wisdom . . . [taking] a middle course and avoid[ing] extremes," while he welcomed "Ashkenazic ethics" as aiming at the absolute, "never compromising, never satisfied, always striving." Acknowledging the imminent recognition of the state of Israel, Heschel warned Jews everywhere not to succumb to pride: "Magnificent synagogues are not enough if they mean a petrified Judaism. Nor will the stirrings of creative life in Palestine find any echo if brilliance is held more important than warmth."[12]

Heschel concluded by faulting the German tradition of Wissenschaft des Judentums for perpetuating negative stereotypes. His example was an unnamed "prominent Jewish historian, in a work first published in 1913 and reprinted in 1931," who dismissed Hasidism for "the preposterousness of its superstitious notions and of its unruly behavior." (He was alluding to the major work on Jewish liturgy by his former teacher Ismar Elbogen.) This judgment typified the contempt of German Jews for the *Ostjuden*, East European Jews.[13]

Some readers disputed Heschel's idealizations of Eastern Europe in letters to the editor of *Commentary*. Rabbi Theodore Wiener of Corsicana, Texas, deemed Heschel's model unrealistic "in an area of high cultural development." Ernst Simon, visiting professor at JTS from the Hebrew University, praised Heschel's "illuminating and discriminating remarks" but reminded readers that not all great German Jewish scholars were ethnocentric: Leopold Zunz, Abraham Geiger, Hermann Cohen, and Franz Rosenzweig all appreciated the spiritual treasures of East European Jewry. Jacob Sloan, a poet and translator of Hebrew and Yiddish literature, rejected Heschel's defense of the "inevitability" of Jewish religion as "a piece of rhetoric." Sloan's solution to the crisis of faith, printed in *Commentary* the following year, was a vague nihilism: "Going deeper, we need consciousness—of the inevitability of all human failure."[14]

Other Jewish intellectuals, however, were receptive to the potential of spirituality. The year following Heschel's *Commentary* essay, Leslie Fiedler, then an assistant professor of literature at Montana State University, wrote incisively about Martin Buber's interpretation of Hasidism. Fiedler sought to harmonize religion and ethics while rejecting the optimism that had become widespread in the late 1940s, fostered in part by Rabbi Joshua Loth Liebman's best seller, *Peace of Mind* (1946). It was Buber, argued Fiedler, who had translated religion into humanistic terms, into a "mysticism become *ethos*," for Jews "without adequate Hebrew or Yiddish, even . . . the utterly un-synagogued." Buber's stories made Hasidism palatable to assimilated Jews since he presented it as the secular idea that "all things are the potentialities of joy," without requiring fidelity to Jewish law. Heschel's authentic "neo-Hasidism" had not yet entered Fiedler's range of vision.[15]

Will Herberg became the first prominent Jewish intellectual to recognize Heschel's significance. Herberg had gained renown for a 1947 *Commentary* essay describing his return to his Jewish roots after years as a Marxist ideologue and Communist Party activist. Influenced by the Protestant neoorthodox theologian and activist Reinhold Niebuhr, Herberg had set out to acquire at the Jewish Theological Seminary the religious education he lacked. In his essay Herberg elaborated a Jewish "crisis theology," a vibrant mixture of Niebuhr's emphasis on sin and corrupt human nature with the existentialism of Rosenzweig and Buber. But in 1949, in the same issue of *Commentary* as Fiedler's essay, Herberg launched a mordant critique of American Jewish life. Now he vehemently rejected secularism and saw the age of Buber and Rosenzweig as "hardly more than an isolated episode in the almost unrelieved mediocrity of Jewish religious thinking in recent decades." For Herberg, Jews needed to recognize that Judaism was a God-centered religion of crisis.[16]

Herberg and Heschel met at the Jewish Theological Seminary. The repentant Marxist admired the way Heschel translated Hasidism and other forms of traditional Judaism into a bold way of thinking and living that was at once observant, open-minded, and morally courageous.

Bridging the Cultures

The Earth Is the Lord's marked Heschel's metamorphosis from Yiddish speaker and essayist to American author. The book grew organically from several pieces, his Yiddish review of Zeitlin's poetry, his chapter "The Mystical Element in Judaism," his essay in *Commentary,* and "To Save a Soul." (He reserved his writings on prayer, piety, faith, and Saadia Gaon for *Man Is Not Alone.*)

By 1948 the manuscript of *The Earth Is the Lord's* was complete, at least in preliminary form. But no publisher was interested, not even the Jewish Publication Society, with whom Heschel was negotiating on Buber's behalf. Heschel showed the manuscript to Marc Tanenbaum, who worked as a publicist for Henry Schuman, a small publisher of quality. Tanenbaum was overwhelmed by the book's beauty and touched by its personal application. Heschel "had captured the spiritual and cultural essence of European Jewry. I began to understand my parents," he felt. Tanenbaum proposed the book to Schuman, who was "something of an esthete." Schuman responded, "This is absolutely exquisite! I would be honored to publish it." Heschel joyfully thanked Finkelstein, who had also put in a good word, and reported the publisher's enthusiasm: "Particularly since Mr. Schuman is a very cultured and erudite gentleman but thoroughly uninformed about Judaism, I feel rather happy about it."[17]

Henry Schuman decided to create a literary work of art. He commissioned Ilya Schor, a Polish Jewish silversmith and graphic artist who had studied in Paris, to embellish the book with wood engravings. Tanenbaum arranged for the noted writer Ludwig Lewisohn to provide advance comments. *The Earth Is the Lord's* was printed on special paper, with an attractive dust jacket and evocative illustrations.[18]

In form and content, the book was designed to bridge cultures. The jacket copy described both author and illustrator as Jewish immigrants who had trained in Europe. Heschel was an "eminent Hebrew scholar, philosopher of religion, . . . whose ancestors were among the founders of the Hasidic movement." Schor combined "the flavor of an ancient folklore with the fresh inventiveness of his highly individual imagination." The jacket also had a blurb from Lewisohn: "It is years since I have read anything so exquisite, so profound, so overwhelmingly necessary to the soul."

The Earth Is the Lord's became one of America's first post-Holocaust books. Schuman's preface (eliminated in subsequent editions) underscored the Catastrophe (as the Holocaust was then called), a "tragedy of a magnitude never before experienced in the world's history." Heschel's preface stressed the positive, the spirituality of prewar Jewish Poland: "I am justified in saying that it was the golden period in Jewish history, in the history of the Jewish soul." The first page displayed a woodcut of a Hasid holding a Torah, while the final page noted the book's origin in the January 1945 lecture at YIVO. It was Heschel's first American book, literally and figuratively translating a Yiddish world into an elegant English idiom.[19]

The Earth Is the Lord's comprised fifteen short chapters, each self-contained and introduced by a woodcut and ending with a *cul-de-lampe* (typographical ornament). Chapter 1, "The Sigh" (in Yiddish *krechts*, the Jewish "Oy!"), evoked the flow of sadness underlying the celebration of spirituality. Heschel then established another key idea, the opposition of time and space, inner and outward existence: "Pagans exalt sacred things, the Prophets extol sacred deeds." (Heschel's insistence that Judaism was not a religion of space, that it was concerned with a life beyond the physical—synagogues, land, technology—would provoke insistent opposition.)[20]

Heschel accentuated the spiritual ideal of East European Jewish culture, what he called its essence. Chapter 2, "'With All Thy Heart,'" evoked the "individual stamp" people put on all their acts. Chapter 3, "The Two Great Traditions," was a slightly revised version of the article published in *Commentary* two years earlier. In chapters 4–9 Heschel lauded study as a means of attachment to God, the commentaries of Rashi for providing access to the Talmud for ordinary laborers, and even pilpul, excessive Talmudic interpretation, as training in intellectual audacity: "Thinking became full of vigor, charged with passion."[21]

Heschel's own vision emerged most fully in chapters 10–11, the book's center. "Kabbalah" was an adaptation of his piece for Finkelstein while "Hasidim" introduced his own role model, the Baal Shem Tov, who "brought heaven down to earth. He and his disciples, the Hasidim, banished melancholy from the soul and uncovered the ineffable delight of being a Jew." Joy in Jewishness was desperately needed, then as now.[22]

The final chapters (12–15) defined the Judaism Heschel wanted moderns to emulate. Divine revelation was still available, and Sabbath observance could lead to a spiritual life. A sacred space, however, was unimportant: "Jews did not build magnificent synagogues; they built bridges leading from the heart to God." He then claimed that Jewish revolutionary secularism derived its energy from religious tradition: "The fervor and yearning of the Hasidism, the ascetic obstinacy of the Kabbalists, the inexorable logic of the Talmudists, were reincarnated in the supporters of modern Jewish movements. Their belief in new ideals was infused with age-old piety." Heschel's concluding pages repeated the warnings articulated in his Yiddish and Hebrew essays: "The alternative to our Jewish existence is spiritual suicide, disappearance, not conversion into something else. Judaism has allies, partners, but no substitute. It is not a handmaiden of civilization but its touchstone."[23]

The Earth Is the Lord's challenged the preference of most American Jews for assimilation. Heschel's religious stance was questioned by reviewers in both the popular press and Jewish newspapers. The contentious issues, as Heschel knew, were a prevailing disdain for East European Jews and a bias against traditional religion. They were not purely academic: two of the major preoccupations of postwar Americans were World War II and the quest for identity. John Hersey's novel *The Wall*, depicting the heroic Warsaw Ghetto uprising of Jewish resistance, was a national best seller. *The Earth Is the Lord's*, by contrast, presented the Jewish past in an incongruously spiritual manner.

Some readers excused Heschel's bias. Writing in the academic journal *Jewish Social Studies*, Heschel's friend the Yiddish expert Sol Liptzin recognized his approach as "intentionally one-sided," but claimed that only antiquarians would be interested in "the filth and folly, the superstitions and delusions, the neglect of manners and the provincialism, which prevailed in eastern communities." Alfred Werner in the *New York Times* admitted that Heschel exaggerated slightly, but "he is right in asserting that these Yiddish-speaking wretched laborers, artisans and traders . . . were linked by a pattern of life which stressed spiritual rather than mundane pleasures."[24]

The real battle was launched by Irving Kristol, book editor of *Commentary*. Kristol's review, entitled "Elegy for a Lost World," condemned what he perceived to be the world-denying consequences of spirituality. Kristol dismissed Heschel's attempt to endow the profane with a holy dimension: "This radical confusion of universes can be found in non-Jewish thinkers, too, but it is only in Judaism that the confusion is the religion itself. To be more exact, it is the Jew himself." Developing his assimilationist stance, Kristol explained that Heschel's dazzling literary style was dangerous because it was so seductive: "a fervor that is unrestrained and a piety that is immoderate." He degraded the writer's skill by faulting his immigrant origins: "English is not Dr. Heschel's native tongue, and his command of it is impressive. But he has, I think, made an error in trying to achieve an archaic splendor which sits uneasily on the rude Anglo-Saxon that is at the base of the language." Kristol framed his argument over a question of style, but his underlying fear was that "romantic" images of the old country might cultivate, in America, a return to "the rebbe, the Hasid, the ghetto." Kristol was irked that Heschel apparently denied the "enlightened" view that Jewish life in the Pale of Settlement was miserable. American Jews must reject the religion, the reviewer strongly implied.[25]

Heschel's position was also distorted by some rabbis who equated mysticism with negation of the world. Immanuel Lewy, writing in *The Reconstructionist*, placed Heschel among "those modern Jews who regard our present civilization as empty."[26]

For Heschel and his reviewers, the stakes were nothing less than the survival of Jewish culture in the postwar period. Typical of Heschel's unsympathetic opponents was Marvin Lowenthal. In a negative review in the *New York Herald Tribune* the author, translator, and Zionist political figure praised the philosopher Morris Raphael Cohen at Heschel's expense: "[Cohen] is cool, logical, and sensible. He eschews the Orphic phrase which is too often a profound way of saying nothing. . . . A poet and mystic while under the spell of his inspiration is above the realities of life." Unlike Heschel, Cohen advocated "a reasonable course between the extremes of assimilation and an exclusively Jewish culture."[27]

Heschel decided to respond. His answer exposed his vulnerability in being a spiritual polemicist in the pragmatic climate of the day. In a letter to the editor, he insisted upon his inclusiveness and refuted Lowenthal's charge of bias against Sephardic culture by citing such phrases as "brilliant epoch in Jewish history, distinguished not only by monumental achievements but also by universality of spirit." Heschel stood his ground while admitting, "I did by implication 'disparage' those aspects of life which defy the basic spiritual values of Judaism and Christianity and which are the cause of the world's unrest today, and for this I have no apologies to offer." In reply Lowenthal charged that Heschel "belittle[d] the totality of Sephardic life" based on errors of fact: Ashkenazic Jews did borrow from other cultures; formal philosophizing, "which Heschel imputes as a non-Jewish and hence somewhat reprehensible trait to the Sephardim," entered Ashkenazic culture in the seventeenth century from Germany; popular Judaism among Sephardim today is "just as simple and naive as any humble mass-culture can be; the Jews of Morocco will yield nothing on that score to the Jews of Galicia," and so on.[28]

Maurice Samuel was the only reviewer to share Heschel's vision of spiritual renewal. Samuel was a popular novelist, translator of Hebrew and Yiddish literature, and interpreter of relations between Jews and Gentiles. He supported Heschel's mission "to build into tomorrow's American Jewry an everlasting, living and organic recollection of the Yiddish-speaking civilization through which it received its Jewishness." Samuel's brief but sophisticated essay in *Congress Weekly*, the widely read journal of the American Jewish Congress, explained that *The Earth Is the Lord's* successfully transmitted the elusive quality of *Yiddishkeit* (Jewishness). American Jews, noted Samuel, should become more, not less, identified with their ancestors. Samuel recalled the example of a Hasidic rebbe who refused to say his prayers until God promised to spare his town from pogroms. Such stories illustrated a particular "Yiddish-Jewish turn of thought," what Heschel called the *knaitch*.[29]

Most original was Samuel's insight into Heschel's method of evoking holiness. In direct contrast to Kristol, Samuel appreciated the writer's "inversion" of ordinary perception, his focus on the transcendent: "Life is no longer the substance, it is only the shadow of a substance; this world is not the reality; it is a parable for the reality." In Heschel's words, holiness is "the subtle shading of a thought, or a fervent gesture, which puts a situation, as it were, in God's quotation marks."[30]

Heschel's appeal to assimilated Jews was tested around 1946, when Simon Greenberg, a professor at the Jewish Theological Seminary and the rabbi of a large Conservative congregation in Philadelphia, asked Heschel to meet with Maurice Friedman, a young intellectual militant. Friedman was reared as a Reform Jew in Tulsa, Oklahoma. A socialist and pacifist, he graduated from Harvard in 1942 planning to become a labor organizer and educator. But he was also fascinated by mysticism, especially Asian and Christian traditions. Friedman's mother, alarmed that he might abandon Judaism, sent him to Rabbi Greenberg, who introduced him to the works of Martin Buber. Friedman was impressed. Greenberg then sent him to meet Heschel.[31]

In his office at JTS, Heschel acted as a rebbe would; after listening to Friedman pour out his life story, he made strong demands of the young man, advising him to learn Hebrew, study at the Seminary, and become observant. Heschel was not indulgent toward Friedman's personal complaints. He was shocked when Friedman spoke of being angry with his mother, an insight released by group therapy: " 'If I could find my mother to tie her shoestrings,' Heschel answered, 'I should be the happiest man on earth!' " Heschel told Friedman that "his family and friends and, indeed, the whole of Polish Jewry in which he had grown up, had disappeared almost without a trace. He chided me for my unhappiness over my short-lived and ill-fated first marriage. 'Hasidism teaches joy,' " he said.[32]

Heschel followed up on this encounter, urging President Finkelstein to accept Friedman as a special Seminary student.[33] In the summer of 1950 Friedman arrived in New York to study Hasidism with Heschel. But the teacher's insistence on observance was too stringent, and Friedman left New York, choosing instead to earn a doctorate in the history of culture at the University of Chicago. Friedman's doctoral dissertation, "Martin Buber: Mystic, Existentialist, Social Prophet," became a foundational introduction to Buber's thought.

Although Friedman devoted his professional life to Buber, becoming Buber's translator and one of his first interpreters in the English-speaking world, he did publish perceptive reviews of Heschel's books.

Power Shift at the Seminary

While Heschel's career advanced outside his home institution, there were conflicts within it that he could not successfully navigate. The JTS faculty and administration made up a tightly knit community in which professional and personal relationships were intertwined. The institution sometimes resembled a miniature shtetl, where everyone knew each other, worshiped in the same synagogue, ate together in the cafeteria, invited one another over for Sabbath and holiday meals. Several faculty members were related by marriage.

Louis Finkelstein reigned over this hierarchy, and for years his primary adviser (and scholarly ideal) was Louis Ginzberg, one of the few key faculty members, along with Mordecai Kaplan, who esteemed Heschel while vehemently opposing his theology. Then a major power shift occurred in 1946, a question of personality as much as distribution of power. Heschel lost his two main allies. Kaplan retired as dean of the Teachers Institute to devote more time to his Society for the Advancement of Judaism, although he continued to influence Seminary policy. Ginzberg, who was seventy-three and frail, fell ill; he gradually reduced his teaching load, coming less frequently to the Seminary, and eventually remaining at home.

More than from the loss of his allies, Heschel suffered from the effects of a change that had occurred in 1940, when Finkelstein brought Saul Lieberman from Israel to take over the Talmud program from Ginzberg. Lieberman, gifted with a photographic memory, was generally acknowledged to be the greatest Talmud scholar of his generation.[34] Some claimed he was equal to the Gaon of Vilna. And Talmud was the area that defined JTS scholarship.

Born in Belorussia, Lieberman was educated at the Mussar (strict, ethical) yeshivas of Malch, Slobodka, and Novaredok, institutions in which Talmud was studied for its own sake, a principle known as *Torah lishma*. (Usually, Talmud study was for practical purposes, to make legal and ethical decisions.) He attended the University of Kiev, continuing his studies in Palestine and France. In 1928 he immigrated to Jerusalem, committing himself to the historical-critical method of correcting scribal and other errors in sacred texts.

Lieberman applied his prodigious range of knowledge to purely technical scholarship. He knew by heart not only the Palestinian and the Babylonian

Louis Finkelstein (left) and Saul Lieberman.
Courtesy of the Ratner Center for the Study of
Conservative Judaism, Jewish Theological Seminary
of America.

Talmuds (in itself an astounding accomplishment) but also variant readings, and he had mastered their background, along with Greek and Latin classics and early Christian literature. As an editor he restored the Talmud texts by comparing manuscripts and sources outside the Jewish canon, such as Greek and Latin legal literature. At the same time, Lieberman followed Orthodox observance and defended traditional values.

Finkelstein revered Lieberman, who supplanted Ginzberg as his confidant and closest adviser. From the start, Finkelstein gave Lieberman privileged status, a relatively large salary, only four hours of teaching a week in the Rabbinical School, and a spacious office with two large rooms. In 1949 he appointed Lieberman rector of the institution and rabbi of the Seminary synagogue, responsible for supervising the service and assigning honors. From then on what historians call "the Finkelstein-Lieberman axis" dominated the institution.[35]

Heschel was caught up in the traditional clash between Hasidim and their opponents, the mitnagdim, which appeared at JTS as the disdain of the textual scholars for piety and religious thought. As Lieberman's standing at the Seminary rose, Heschel's declined. Lieberman despised Heschel's mixture of erudition and fervor. He was not interested in philosophy and was hostile to theology, which he considered a Christian subject. He never changed his conviction that Jewish mysticism was *narishkeit* (nonsense).[36]

The tension was exacerbated by personality conflicts, largely the result of professional jealousy. The rift between Lieberman and Heschel developed gradually, following years of goodwill. Heschel and Sylvia were originally friends of Lieberman and his wife, Judith, herself born in Europe and the daughter of Rabbi Meir Berlin (Bar-Ilan), a prime exponent of religious Zionism. The couples took walks together, the men discussing passages from the Talmud. In August 1948, the Heschels enjoyed a three-week vacation with the Liebermans at their summer cottage on Martha's Vineyard. Sylvia Heschel enjoyed Lieberman's company and was able to speak frankly to him, teasing him about his reputation for cynicism and for humiliating students in the classroom. As a personal favor, Lieberman made halakhic adjustments to Sylvia's Sabbath observance to enable her to use the elevator and to practice the piano by using a silent keyboard.[37]

But in 1951, as Heschel's books began to be widely praised in the media, Lieberman cooled considerably toward him. (Sylvia noticed a change the following year, after the birth of their daughter.) Making matters even more difficult, the couples lived in the same building, at 425 Riverside Drive near 115th Street.

A New Theology in the Making

By the summer of 1948, the manuscript of Heschel's long-planned systematology, his religious philosophy, was beginning to take shape. It was still a rough draft, however, consisting of his articles on piety, holiness, faith, and prayer, with a new introduction on approaches to God. At this early stage, the book included only nine chapters (the completed work, *Man Is Not Alone*, had twenty-six). Heschel submitted his manuscript to Louis Ginzberg, who was enthusiastic. He recommended the book, which he described as "concerning the soul of the Jew" to Maurice Jacobs, executive vice president of the Jewish Publication Society (JPS). Jacobs told Heschel to send it to Solomon Grayzel, the JPS president and an expert editor. In fact, Jacobs urged Heschel to send Grayzel two copies, one to his vacation home and the other to the Philadelphia headquarters of the firm.[38]

This was a great opportunity for everyone concerned. The JPS, a venerable institution founded in 1888, was America's leading Jewish publisher, with a subscriber list of thousands. Its books (including the authoritative English translation of the Hebrew Bible) were sold to reading clubs and individuals throughout North America. And the public was beginning to crave works with an element of the sacred.[39]

Nonetheless, the book that embodied the theological revolution Heschel hoped to achieve first went through a rigorous evaluation. After Grayzel decided the topic was suitable for the JPS list, three members of the Publications Committee evaluated the manuscript. Only after their reports were discussed at the committee's general meeting would a decision be made about whether to publish. Heschel was impatient and anxious, eager for an early decision. He enlisted support from Finkelstein and Ginzberg, who were influential members of the Publications Committee. Both pressured Grayzel to bypass the normal procedure. Finkelstein wrote that Heschel's book was "in many respects unique," while Ginzberg argued that it offered an exceptional opportunity for JPS, which neglected books on religious aspects of Judaism in favor of history and literature.[40]

Outside readers who knew Heschel's work expressed high regard for it, even before they saw the manuscript. Julian Morgenstern admitted, "I know that my judgment would be favorable," while Milton Steinberg, the influential young rabbi of the Park Avenue Synagogue, looked forward to examining it: "Anything that he writes interests me." But some evaluators had difficulty with Heschel's intuitive approach and poetic style. The eminent Reform rabbi Solomon Freehof of Pittsburgh, unfamiliar with Heschel's publications, read the "chapters" with an open mind: "Many of them are beautiful; some of them are dull; all of them are substantial. They are worth publishing." But he raised a policy question, one typical of the time: "Is it within the scope of our work to publish essays on religion?" If it is, he added, "Simplify some of the more difficult and duller essays, such as the essay on piety."[41]

Louis L. Kaplan, head of the Baltimore Board of Jewish Education and dean of the Baltimore Hebrew College, perceptively defined Heschel's good qualities—which were also his shortcomings: "It is perhaps more poetry than philosophy and there are occasions when the style is a bit florid, but this is in harmony with the author's thesis and his approach to religion."[42]

The Publications Committee met on 7 November 1948 to discuss these reports. They appreciated Ginzberg's early support for Heschel's manuscript—at this point entitled "Jewish Faith and Piety"—as a pioneering work of spiritual awakening: "I am fairly convinced that there must be thousands of Jews and Gentiles alike who, like me, would like to know something about the subjects just enumerated. The author, a first rate scholar, has succeeded in putting the results of his studies in a very attractive and popular way." The project was accepted, and Heschel signed the contract on 15 February 1949. But the publisher was short of cash and could not send him an advance.[43]

Heschel had matured as a writer, but he needed an active editorial guide. His creative process was organic, not linear; he proceeded from insight to insight, phrase to phrase, sentence to sentence. He continued to write short notations on pieces of paper, placing them in folders, later composing paragraphs or chapters. Now he needed someone to help him organize a book from this collection of essays.

Heschel was receptive to criticism, and he improved his manuscript considerably under Grayzel's careful direction. By profession a historian and a meticulous editor, Grayzel candidly informed Heschel that several readers had trouble following his "poetico-mystical approach." One outside reviewer typified the average reader of goodwill whom Heschel had to reach: "As for me generally, I admire Dr. Heschel's warmth, imagery, and his security in the realm which transcends our 'mediate' experiences. But I confess that as I read his work I find his flight too steep for me and I tend to fall way behind him in the experiences he tries to portray."[44]

Revising and finishing the manuscript was arduous. In good faith Heschel expected to send Grayzel half the manuscript in May, but only in July did he submit chapters on God (eighty-three pages), on piety (twenty-five pages), and on prayer (twenty-seven pages). He worked constantly, uncertain how to order the chapters, never satisfied. Heschel and Grayzel communicated by mail weekly during the following months, as the author completed his chapters piecemeal and then revised them. [45]

It was a tense process. Grayzel found his "copy reading" task much more difficult than simply marking a manuscript for the printer, as he admitted to the author: "I do not know whether because of my inability to comprehend the mystical approach or because of the lack of clarity in your writing, there are passages that I do not understand." Both men were contending with the production schedule, which included deadlines for marketing and distribution. Thoroughly engrossed in refining his text, Heschel wrote to Grayzel every few days, sending pieces of manuscript.[46]

Grayzel met with Heschel in New York to discuss how best to clarify the narrative. Grayzel suggested a technique that Heschel would use for the rest of his career: to divide each chapter into brief sections with subtitles so that readers could more easily follow the sequence. This arrangement accommodated Heschel's lyrical repetitions while highlighting the coherence of paragraphs and the overall narrative.[47]

By mid-November 1949 it was time to announce the book, with a brief description, for the list of 1950 titles going out to JPS subscribers. Heschel had not yet chosen a title; Grayzel suggested *Between Man and God.* But in May 1950 the manuscript was still unfinished, although it was nearing completion.[48]

Then Heschel made a startling announcement. His manuscript had swelled so much that he needed to publish a second volume. Grayzel was worried because the financial situation of JPS was precarious. He was afraid that the whole deal might collapse. Only copublication with a trade house might save the project.

At this point Roger W. Straus, Jr., president of the prestigious literary firm Farrar, Straus and Company, entered the negotiations. An urbane, artistically sensitive publisher of fine books, Straus (not related to Heschel's wife, Sylvia) combined high culture with a canny business sense. Descended from a wealthy, influential New York family, he had a strong and appealing personality. Heschel and Straus enjoyed each other's company, and Heschel respected the publisher's practical advice. Most of all, perhaps, Heschel shared Straus's regard for good literature.[49]

Straus advised Heschel to persuade JPS to incorporate a second volume into the original contract. Anxious, Heschel made a tactical mistake; he tried to put pressure on the publisher by asking his colleague Simon Greenberg, vice chancellor of the Seminary and Grayzel's personal friend, to intercede with Judge Louis E. Levinthal, a member of the JPS executive committee, to add this volume to the original contract. Grayzel was angered by Heschel's interference, but he was a consummate diplomat. Heschel's manuscript had reached six hundred pages, and Grayzel supported the author's request, reminding the executive committee that JPS had published "almost nothing on Jewish theology since the days of Solomon Schechter."[50]

Heschel was still far from completing the book, however. When in July 1950 he sent Grayzel a table of contents, the editor realized that he had never seen the eleven chapters of part 2. He joined forces with Straus to prod Heschel to reduce his manuscript or to divide it into two books of publishable size.[51]

Then Straus took over. After much discussion, it was decided that Farrar, Straus would publish the book jointly with JPS. Straus offered Heschel a new contract that included an advance and supported his intention to publish two sizable volumes. Heschel signed the contract with Farrar, Straus and Company on 27 July 1950, with the proviso that volume 1 of his "philosophy of religion" would be delivered by 15 October, and volume 2 a year later. In mid-August a new contract was signed by JPS and Farrar, Straus.[52]

Grayzel congratulated Straus on his successful negotiation, while faulting Heschel: "It seems to me a case where apparently a man's conceit— in his desire to write a big book—won over his wisdom. For I am still convinced that it would have been to Heschel's advantage, and certainly to the advantage of his subject and his readers, if he had condensed his material into a single volume of moderate size."[53]

Heschel's motives for insisting on the longer book were complex, a mixture of personal ambition, ethical urgency, and intellectual and spiritual passion. He delivered the completed manuscript to Straus on 5 October 1950, the day after Simchat Torah, the joyous celebration of God's revelation. Heschel's new book, now entitled *Man Is Not Alone*, was included on the 1951 JPS subscriber list, with the second volume planned for 1952.[54]

In November, Heschel assured Grayzel that he expected to complete volume 2 within the year, by "the fall of 1951." Heschel was being unrealistic; he could not even stop making changes in the galleys and page proofs of volume 1, delaying publication for an additional week. He was still seeking an unattainable perfection.[55]

7

Theological Revolution (1950–1952)

*But, then, a moment comes like a thunderbolt, in which a flash of the
undisclosed rends our dark apathy asunder. It is full of overpowering
brilliance, like a point in which all moments of life are focused or
a thought which outweighs all thoughts ever conceived of. . . . Apathy
turns to splendor unawares. The ineffable has shuddered itself
into the soul. . . . We are penetrated by His insight.*
—Heschel, *Man Is Not Alone* (1951)

WHILE HESCHEL WAS WRITING AND PREPARING *MAN IS NOT ALONE* FOR PUBLI-
cation, Sylvia Heschel was launching her own career. She had practiced
every day for years, preparing for her concert debut at Manhattan's Town
Hall. The date was set for 15 February 1951, a month before the official publication of *Man Is Not Alone*. Heschel zealously supported his wife's professional

Sylvia Heschel, from the program of her Town Hall debut,
15 February 1951. Photograph by Lotte Jacobi. Courtesy of the Lotte Jacobi
Collection, University of New Hampshire.

aspirations. He sent out numerous letters with tickets and copies of the program, urging relatives, friends, colleagues, and students to attend the recital. He even enlisted students to distribute tickets.[1]

Sylvia Heschel, as the playbill named her, would be performing pieces by Bach, Schumann, Mozart, Chopin, and Maxwell Powers, ending with Stravinsky's "Danse Russe" from *Petrouchka*. It was a challenging mixture of composers and musical styles. Everyone was extremely nervous, not least her husband. The hall was not filled. Heschel's supporters from the Seminary were there, but Louis Finkelstein was conspicuously absent, having excused himself in advance. This hurtful pattern of neglect would continue.[2]

Sylvia's performance touched many in the audience, her expressive body movements heightening the musical emotions. After the concert, people remained to congratulate her. Sylvia was not able to enjoy their praise, however; she had contracted a bad cold and had taken medication that made her sluggish. The next day the critics diluted their praise with serious reservations. The *New York Times* stated that she had "overreached herself." The *New York Herald Tribune* described her renditions as "rather stodgy" and "a bit wooden." Appreciation of her technical mastery was mixed: "She has fleet fingers which did not permit more than a casual error, and she is able to spin a clean and rounded phrase, but for the most part the demands of the program taxed her skills beyond their present resource." The March issue of *Musical Courier* also balanced criticism and praise: "Miss Heschel [sic] plays as if she were carefully listening to herself, in happy contrast to other young artists whose minds and fingers go separate ways."[3]

Sylvia considered her public debut a failure, and she and Heschel were devastated. She abandoned her plans for a performance career and took up teaching. Until well into her eighties, she was a respected piano teacher at the 92nd Street Young Men's Hebrew Association. She continued to give smaller recitals and participated in private chamber music groups.

A Theological Revolution

Less than a month after his wife's Town Hall concert, Heschel received his author's copy of *Man Is Not Alone*. Several weeks before publication, he had received an appreciative prognosis from Finkelstein, to whom he had sent a copy of the proofs. The JTS president predicted that Heschel's "lucid, easily-read, poetical prose" would inspire readers "in this day of widespread religious and philosophical confusion."[4]

Man Is Not Alone was given a sophisticated marketing campaign, organized by Farrar, Straus and Young (as the company was now called). The Jewish Publication Society as copublisher secured broad distribution from its subscription lists. The yellow dust jacket displayed a detail from Michelangelo's Sistine Chapel fresco, "The Creation of Adam," which showed the first man reaching toward God's outstretched finger. On the back was a photograph of the author by Lotte Jacobi, the German Jewish wife of his Berlin publisher. Heschel looked like a modern intellectual—young, clean shaven, in rimless glasses, with his dark, wavy hair combed back.

The dust jacket downplayed the transcendent element. Below the author photograph was a blurb from the Kirkus review service: "The author is neither a rationalist nor a mystic, but comes at his theistic position through an analysis of the human personality and through finding basic wonder there, awe and reverence, a 'sense of the ineffable.' The second part of the book deals with man's needs and his satisfaction through religious faith." The jacket copy also deemphasized the book's theological agenda, reducing Heschel's religion of a living God to a banal, pragmatic humanism; Heschel's philosophy of religion, it claimed, was useful "not in terms of beliefs and practices but in terms of a satisfying philosophy of life."

In reality, Heschel intended the book as a blueprint for a theological revolution. *Man Is Not Alone* claimed that readers could encounter God's presence directly. In this he vied implicitly with Franz Rosenzweig's *Star of Redemption* (1921) and Martin Buber's *I and Thou* (1923)—both of which were barely known to the American public (*Star of Redemption* was not published in English until 1971)—which emphasized the human side of the religious quest. Heschel's spiritual itinerary was more straightforward and elegant than Rosenzweig's philosophical masterpiece and more authentically biblical than Buber's lyrical dialogue with the sacred. Heschel's "Philosophy of Religion"—the book's subtitle—trained readers to receive divine revelation. (Part 1 explored "The Problem of God" and part 2 "The Problem of Living.") He appealed to thoughtful, open-minded seekers, introducing the "cognitive emotions" of awe and wonder as a way to discover "radical amazement."

Rigorous self-questioning, he argued, would shatter conventional categories of knowledge. The person who abandoned preconceptions would first reach a state of despair, but radical amazement would lead the seeker from despair to radical insight. Heschel recapitulated the entire journey in chapter 9, "In the Presence of God." The process began with "dark apathy," a loss of ego that allowed the living God to enter human consciousness: "But, then, a moment

Author photo of Heschel for the jacket of Man Is Not Alone, *1951.*
Photograph by Lotte Jacobi. Courtesy of the Lotte Jacobi Collection,
University of New Hampshire.

comes like a thunderbolt, in which a flash of the undisclosed rends our dark apathy asunder." Normal, ego-centered thinking was reversed: "We are penetrated by His insight. We cannot think any more as if He were there and we here. He is both there and here."[5]

This paradigm shift was Heschel's theological revolution: the recentering of human thought from the self to God as subject. (Immanuel Kant's "Copernican revolution" in philosophy had placed the emphasis on the human subject.) Heschel believed that all thoughtful people could achieve such insight. Using philosophical terms, he did not describe it as a mystical encounter with God but rather as a "categorical imperative" analogous to Kant's rational categories. The mind endured a radical "turning" (in Hebrew, *teshuvah*) to God-centered or theocentric thinking. Readers would eventually achieve "certainty" in the reality of God.

Heschel also examined basic theological problems such as doubt, the nature of faith, the notion of one God, God as the subject, and the divine concern. In chapter 16, "The Hiding God," he confronted the problem of evil and human responsibility, borrowing from and revising his 1943 article "The Meaning of This War."

Part 2, "The Problem of Living," applied Heschel's paradigm shift to religious observance and ethics. Rather than explain religion as a fulfillment of human needs (the jacket copy notwithstanding), he saw the essence of being human as a need of God. The Bible was not human theology but God's anthropology. The concluding chapter, "The Pious Man," portrayed an ideal awareness of God's presence, inspiring readers to lead a holy and righteous life.

Heschel was in full command of his literary craft, displaying an original manner of thinking and writing, and calling for an imaginative reading strategy. He combined incisive philosophical analysis and lyrical passages vivified by comparisons and images appealing to memory and emotions with aphorisms that condensed insights into easily grasped concepts. In this way he sought to provoke a complete transformation of consciousness. But it took years for scholars to delineate his multilayered discourse and narrative approach.[6]

On a popular level, however, Heschel achieved national renown, set off by a review by Reinhold Niebuhr, America's leading Protestant theologian, in the *New York Herald Tribune*. The founding editor of *Christianity and Crisis* and a professor at Union Theological Seminary, Niebuhr dramatically predicted that Heschel would "become a commanding and authoritative voice not only in the Jewish community but in the religious life of America."[7]

Niebuhr admired the way Heschel evoked the living God. In contrast to Irving Kristol, the Protestant thinker appreciated Heschel's elegant narrative as "the work of a poet and mystic who has mastered the philosophical and scientific disciplines and who with consummate skill reveals the dimension of reality apprehended by religious faith." He praised Heschel's mastery of English as remarkable for "an immigrant scholar."[8]

Niebuhr's gratifying words were followed by a longer, more detailed review in *Congress Weekly* by Jacob B. Agus, a leading thinker in the Conservative rabbinate and author of *Modern Philosophies of Judaism,* the first major presentation in English of the work of Rosenzweig and Buber. Agus underscored the book's immediate relevance: "A profound hunger for faith is now felt in every walk of life." He associated Heschel with such Christian thinkers as the nineteenth-century philosopher Friedrich Schleiermacher in Germany and Niebuhr in America, and with Rabbi A. I. Kook in Palestine, in addition to Buber and Rosenzweig. Pointing to the "pragmatic spirit of America [that] seems to have discouraged the attempt to analyze religious feeling and to expound the deeper reaches of Jewish mystical piety," Agus directed readers to look beneath Heschel's poetic style: "With some effort the underlying logical argument may be disengaged from the rich and haunting imagery." Agus concisely summarized Heschel's analysis of consciousness as an "objective" sense of the ineffable, "a compulsion from outside our ego." Heschel's ethics derived from an "inner call" from God, what he called "transitive concern" in both human beings and in God: "Thus God needs man as man needs God."[9]

If Judaic Studies had been an established academic discipline, Agus's review might have initiated a systematic interpretation of Heschel's works. But in 1951 there were only general forums such as *Commentary* in which new works of Jewish philosophy could be carefully examined.[10] Heschel needed allies to help overcome resistance to his God-centered vision.

Behind the scenes of *Commentary,* however, a conflict was brewing between Irving Kristol, the book editor, and Marvin Fox, an Orthodox Jew who taught philosophy at Ohio State University, whom Kristol had invited to review *Man Is Not Alone.* The battle began when Kristol read the typescript of Fox's laudatory evaluation and became convinced that Fox had been "taken in." Defensively, Kristol wrote to Fox and asked him to revise the review, assuring him that he did not consider it "unfair, incompetent, or badly written; on the contrary, it is quite the reverse of all these. But I *do* think it is profoundly wrong in its ultimate estimate of Heschel's book." Kristol questioned the "quality" of Heschel's writing, which he felt did not meet a high-enough level on "objective aesthetic-religious grounds." (With this term Kristol conflated two distinct realms of experience, the esthetic and the religious.) Heschel, argued Kristol, was "a prisoner of his own notion of religious rhetoric; this may be explained by his basic unfamiliarity with the English language, but it is there nevertheless."[11]

Kristol's overreaction uncovered the competition over defining an American Jewish identity. Unwittingly, he revealed that his standard, even for works of Jewish piety, was the Christian literary canon. While admitting that *Man Is Not Alone* was better than Liebman's *Peace of Mind,* he insisted that Heschel was still a lesser writer: "If you compare Heschel's writing with, let us say, [John] Donne's sermons, I think you will see what I mean," he snapped.[12]

For his part, Fox was shocked by Kristol's demand, which breached norms of intellectual freedom, and replied at once, sending a carbon copy to the *Commentary* editor-in-chief, Elliot Cohen. Mutual recriminations between Kristol and Fox continued for months, moving beyond the issue of Fox's review. Finally Kristol gave in. He allowed Fox to resubmit his text, "without altering a comma" if he so wished. In June, Fox received galley proofs to correct, "edited slightly for style and brevity." His review, "A Modern Mystic," appeared in the August 1951 issue.[13]

Fox touted Heschel's potential as an effective interpreter of modern Orthodoxy. He presented *Man Is Not Alone* as an antidote to the mediocrity of American Judaism, "in which almost every conceivable kind of activity is given precedence over Torah and worship." Heschel would inspire religious commitment: "It comes as a breath of fresh air in an atmosphere which has grown heavy with triviality."

Fox appreciated Heschel's "phenomenology of the religious life," quoting a passage from chapter 9 ("A tremor seizes our limbs . . . our whole being bursts into shudders") that could incite readers to experience "the moment of high ecstasy" in which God penetrates our consciousness. He was less receptive to the "poetic" or experiential aspects of *Man Is Not Alone,* however. As a philosophy professor he regretted that Heschel had not provided "a complex systematic structure in terms of which we might organize a coherent picture of the religious life."

In the self-defined rationalist camps, Reconstructionists and their associates were goaded into action by Heschel's seeming rejection of social science. These pragmatic Jews struggled to wrap their minds around Heschel's poetic style and his firm faith in the living God. A sustained and respectful critique of *Man Is Not Alone* was published in *The Reconstructionist* by Rabbi Eugene Kohn, a leader of Reconstructionism and the journal's editor. The American-born Kohn had been ordained in 1912 at the Jewish Theological Seminary, and his antipathy to "supernaturalism" typified American Jewish thinking in the 1940s. Yet Kohn appreciated Heschel's cultural potential. Referring to Gershom Scholem's *Major Trends in Jewish Mysticism,* Kohn agreed that Americans could benefit from a modern Jewish book like *Man Is Not Alone,* which could help them "ponder on the ultimate mysteries of life." Heschel's approach was mystical, but it did not represent "a flight from reality and a denial of empirical fact."[14]

Although Kohn believed that the "mystical experiences to which the author referred were psychological reactions shared in greater or lesser degree by all human beings," he supported Heschel's interpretations of the ineffable, awe, and radical amazement. Moreover, Kohn grasped that Heschel's "indicative style" overcame the logical contradiction of speaking about the inexpressible. But "Heschel's fundamental fallacy" was the assumption "that ineffability is a criterion, indeed *the* criterion of religion."

The key issue was the authority of social science, and Rabbi Kohn, as would many of his colleagues, reproached Heschel for "disparaging" discursive reason. Judaism was a realistic civilization, concerned "only with what lies before us. . . . Radical amazement must not leave us in a maze." Kohn concluded: "The sociological and psychological approach to religion followed in the writings of [Mordecai] Kaplan and others offer[s] many more clues than does the mystical approach of Heschel."[15]

Heschel was swimming against a mighty current. Closer to home, Alexander Burnstein, writing in the official bulletin of Conservative rabbis, candidly admitted that "many of the author's metaphysical presuppositions and his highly speculative mysticism I am unable to accept."[16]

Systematic evaluation of Heschel's works became possible with the inception of a new scholarly review, *Judaism,* a "Quarterly Journal of Jewish Life and Thought." This nondenominational forum, sponsored by the American Jewish Congress, was intended to complement—or compete with—*Commentary,* which was more attuned to secular culture and politics than to religion and philosophy. North America's leading Jewish academics and rabbis contributed. The editor-in-chief of *Judaism,* Robert Gordis, a luminary of the Conservative movement, announced the journal's goal as nothing less than "a Renascence of Judaism." Heschel soon became a prime model for that renewal.[17]

The inaugural issue of *Judaism* (January 1952) placed Heschel's work at the center while questioning his claim to write a "philosophy of religion." In addition to an essay by Heschel (discussed below), the journal published a sophisticated review of *Man Is Not Alone* by Emil Ludwig Fackenheim, assistant professor of philosophy at the University of Toronto and already a notable religious thinker. Fackenheim had studied philosophy at the University of Halle and was ordained in 1939 by the Berlin Hochschule. He immigrated in 1940 to Canada and began teaching at the University of Toronto in 1948, publishing articles on Jewish philosophy and existentialism in both popular and academic venues. His essays in *Commentary* had defended both Jewish faith and religious thought.[18]

Fackenheim praised Heschel's challenge to "those who consider religion only from a pragmatic angle such as its psychological or sociological effects." More important, he defined for the first time Heschel's three modes of writing and cognition—"the aphoristic, the descriptive, the philosophico-argumentative"—although he asserted that "they will not mix." He reproached Heschel for subordinating logical argumentation to bursts of pithy sayings, "not a few of which are trite, and some even in poor taste." As an academic philosopher, Fackenheim valued linear continuity over Heschel's literary mixture of styles. But he felt that the book's "most solid" sections effectively portrayed "the religious man enthralled by the Ineffable and the Holy, the man who tries to live in the sight of God."[19]

Surprisingly, Fackenheim misinterpreted what he called Heschel's "mysticism," a word Heschel had not used. With no textual proof, he deemed Heschel "frankly pantheistic," experiencing God as identical to the natural world, a way of thinking that Fackenheim felt could lead to moral indifference. (In fact, the opposite was true: Heschel's 1949 essay on Jewish mysticism stressed how the Kabbalists subordinated personal salvation to redemption of the world.)[20]

Still another misreading flawed this important review. Fackenheim, haunted by the atrocities of the Hitler period, regretted that Heschel had not taken into account sin, the tragic, evil, and history. Fackenheim had ignored chapter 16, "The Hiding God," which opened with the words: "For us, contemporaries and survivors of history's most terrible horrors, it is impossible to meditate about the compassion of God without asking: Where is God?"[21]

Although Fackenheim reproached Heschel for transgressing the "sharp distinction between religious and philosophical writing," he praised *Man Is Not Alone* as "one of the few genuinely religious books in contemporary

Judaism, one of the few books which have the power to speak to a soul in search of God."

The most perceptive analysis of *Man Is Not Alone* came from another philosopher, Shmuel Hugo Bergman, the first rector of the Hebrew University in Jerusalem and a close associate of Martin Buber's. In the May 1951 *Mitteilungsblatt*, a German-language journal published at the Hebrew University, Bergman clarified Heschel's basic assumptions. He focused on Heschel's aim of transforming the reader's consciousness in a moment of divine revelation. Relating Heschel's American writings to his German dissertation and studies in Hebrew and Yiddish, Bergman explained that Heschel's philosophy of religion was neither a self-contradiction nor a pretentious subterfuge, "because the nature of religion lies in experience rather than in conceptual thought." Reason played a significant, though subordinate role in Heschel's exposition: "Faith borrows from philosophy the language and the expressions which make it possible to express the unspeakable in some way."[22]

Citing the revelation in chapter 9 ("The ineffable has shuddered itself into our soul . . ."), Bergman asserted that Heschel considered "the central thought of the Jewish religion [to be] the B'rith, the *covenant*. It obligates God, and it obligates man. We need to read the Bible from the perspective of this covenant, for 'the Bible is not the story of the people of Israel, but the story of God in search of the righteous man.'" Pointing out how Heschel stressed God's initiative, Bergman's perceptive review (which was never translated) may have influenced Heschel to name his second volume *God in Search of Man*.[23]

Judaism and Civilization

Heschel's ambition sometimes led him to neglect professional courtesies. In June 1951, while absorbed in composing the second volume of his religious philosophy, he also managed to complete another small book. Simon Greenberg had requested an essay on the Sabbath to be used by the United Synagogue, the national organization of Conservative congregations. Heschel conceived of a larger work.[24]

Heschel was uncomfortable breaking the news to Solomon Grayzel, to whom he was obligated by contract for the larger philosophical project. So when he agreed to evaluate a manuscript by Leo Baeck, he seized the opportunity to inform Grayzel "immediately" that he had just finished writing "a lengthy section of the second volume, dealing with the idea of the Sabbath," which could be published separately for the United Synagogue as "an offprint of the second volume." Heschel was being disingenuous. He had already arranged for Roger Straus to publish it as a small book with woodcuts by Ilya Schor, and Greenberg was preparing to use it.[25]

Grayzel was "surprised" (as he put it) by Heschel's news, worried that this extended essay would compromise the sales of volume 2 of the "Philosophy," which had been accepted with misgivings by the JPS Publications Committee. Yet clearly *The Sabbath* was a fait accompli. Roger Straus joined with Heschel in placating Grayzel, by letter and telephone. They explained to him that the two books would not compete; each appealed to a different readership. Grayzel, outmaneuvered, protested to Straus with diplomatic restraint: "At the very time that we are supposed to be working towards an increase in our membership by broadening our base, we are committed to the publication of a rather abstruse volume, while the author gives a more popular volume on more or less the same subject to someone else."[26]

Heschel followed up with a telephone call. Straus wrote to Grayzel to close the "discussion" and made this point: "We are pushing right ahead with the manuscript and will be going to press next Monday, the 16th. I hope it isn't too much of a burden for you to work out the details with the other members of the publication board."[27]

The struggle between publishers continued into the High Holy Days. At the end of September, Straus dealt Grayzel another blow, informing him that volume 2 would not be available for the 1952 JPS subscription list. On 2 October the galley proofs of *The Sabbath* were mailed to prospective buyers, such as the National Conference of Christians and Jews. Accepting his defeat, Grayzel wrote to congratulate Heschel, wishing him and his wife a happy New Year. Once more absorbed in volume 2, Heschel was relieved by Grayzel's courteous capitulation.[28]

As a part of the Farrar, Straus publicity campaign, Heschel published a chapter of *The Sabbath* in the October 1951 issue of *Commentary,* which the editors introduced with praise for his previous publications. Heschel's essay, entitled "Between Civilization and Eternity: An Ancient Debate and an Allegorical Interpretation," put forth his key idea that Judaism was a religion of time as opposed to a religion of space. (This notion might have rivaled Buber's "I and Thou" as an entry to spiritual living.) Heschel urged modern Jews to observe the Sabbath in order to harmonize the integrity of inward meditation and social responsibility in the world of space: "This, then, is the answer to the tragic problem of civilization: not to flee from the realm of space; to work with things of space but to be in love with eternity. Things are our tools; eternity, the Sabbath, is our mate."[29]

"Architecture of Time," a second selection from the forthcoming book on the Sabbath, appeared in the inaugural issue of *Judaism*. Here Heschel opposed the view of "Judaism as a civilization." The idea of space was limiting, individualistic; it referred only to the technological realm. The idea of time included the divine as continuous creation. The distinction was vital: "This is the task of men: to conquer space and sanctify time." Heschel sought to train spiritual consciousness. Regular observance of the Sabbath would enhance "a spiritual presence" and sanctify the world.[30]

Heschel's tendency to draw antitheses polarized critics. He attempted to forestall misunderstandings by explaining: "Our intention here is not to deprecate the world of space. To disparage space and the blessing of things of space is to disparage the works of creation, which God beheld and saw that 'it was good.' . . . Time and space are interrelated. . . . What we plead against is man's unconditional surrender to space, his enslavement to things."[31] But the response continued to be sharply divided.

The Sabbath: Its Meaning for Modern Man appeared the next month under the imprint of Farrar, Straus. The preface, "Architecture of Time," introduced the ten brief chapters, each illustrated by one of Schor's expressionistic wood engravings; an epilogue, entitled "To Sanctify Time," closed the book. *The Sabbath* took its place alongside *The Earth Is the Lord's* as a classic introduction to Heschel's thought.[32]

Heschel had become so significant in Jewish circles that he dominated the third issue of *Judaism* (July 1952), which included two responses to his new book, one hostile (Trude Weiss-Rosmarin), the other supportive (Nahum Glatzer). Heschel's answer to criticisms of his spiritual approach to time was presented in a rather technical essay, "Space, Time, and Reality: The Centrality of Time in the Biblical World-View." (Heschel placed this essay as an appendix to the second edition of *The Sabbath*.)[33]

The quarrel centered on whether time was a valid Jewish category. Trude Weiss-Rosmarin, the learned, combative editor of the *Jewish Spectator*, refuted Heschel, insisting that Heschel's thesis "rests on untenable premises and is supported by faulty props." She denounced his apparent "disdain of space" and claimed that there was "no proof whatsoever for his theory." She averred, "the evidence of the most authoritative Jewish sources proves on the contrary that Judaism identifies God with space, viz., the usage of *makom*—space—as a synonym for God in the Mishna, Talmud, medieval literature, and colloquial Hebrew speech."[34]

The essay was the onset of Weiss-Rosmarin's lifelong campaign against Heschel. She objected to his "mysticism," his manner of thinking, and especially his ornate writing: "Dr. Heschel's prose is strongly tinged with poetic images and he freely draws on the privilege of poetic license."[35]

The July 1952 issue of *Judaism* also featured a review essay by Nahum N. Glatzer, a professor at the recently founded Brandeis University. Glatzer was a Polish Jew who had been educated in Germany. He had studied the classical Jewish texts as a youth and had participated in Rosenzweig and Buber's movement of Jewish education before and during the Hitler period. Glatzer placed *The Sabbath* within the context of a "major problem of Jewish intellectual history," namely, "the attitude of post-biblical Judaism to the worldly civilizations with which it came into contact—and to civilization in general." According to Glatzer, the scientific issue of the "space-time continuum" was irrelevant to Heschel's interpretation of holiness in time.[36]

Glatzer placed Heschel alongside Hermann Cohen, Leo Baeck, and Franz Rosenzweig as thinkers who were "united in their attempt to reach down into the innermost recesses of Judaism in order to explain the Sabbath[,] which entered civilization as a revolutionary idea and remained since a corrective force in religious thought. Heschel's characteristic is that he accepts the challenge of our world today at its keenest."[37]

Underlying the controversy was the real objection to *The Sabbath:* it was theological in content and poetic in style. At that moment in American Jewish history, the lines were firmly drawn between intuitive and analytical modes of thought. Even so, some reviewers admitted to feeling ambivalent, attracted to Heschel's spirituality in spite of their objections.

Rabbi Ira Eisenstein, a leader of Reconstructionism along with his father-in-law, Mordecai Kaplan, and Eugene Kohn, wrote in *The Reconstructionist* that a minority of readers would appreciate Heschel's "impeccable and epigrammatic style" while the majority would be "bewildered." Heschel's narrative, he claimed, was ambiguous: despite repeated declarations "that one should not disparage space—things; nevertheless, one gets the impression that he is always doing just that." At the same time, Eisenstein was moved by the "semi-mystical quality" of Schor's woodcuts, "which with a modified abstract treatment, preserve the flavor of old-world Jewry."[38]

Jacob Agus, writing in the bulletin for Conservative rabbis, took a pedagogical slant. He saw Heschel as a "mystic" who remained "in the lofty domain of 'pure' piety and singing its praises, hoping that the strains of the melody will awaken sympathetic resonance in the hearts of men." *The Sabbath* was "a modern 'midrash,' addressed to intellectuals and searching souls," but not to the majority of readers.[39]

Will Herberg in *Commentary* offered a bold theological verdict. He praised Heschel's philosophical task: to define "the central categories of Biblical faith." Heschel's ideas were inseparable from his eclectic method, "a creative combination of theological analysis and rabbinic Haggadah." Above all, Herberg admired Heschel's almost exclusive focus on holiness. The will of God was the heartbeat of Heschel's address to "moderns." This was why Heschel, at this early stage in his career, provoked such fervid, contradictory opinions. He appealed to "the *post-modern* generation which is seeking for the substance of life on a level far deeper than the superficialities of yesterday's 'modern thought.'" Herberg supported Heschel's challenge to "the secularist clichés of a half century ago," which persisted to the present day.[40]

Academic Ups and Downs

These intellectual debates in the Jewish media were reflected in, indeed exacerbated by, the hothouse atmosphere of the Jewish Theological Seminary. As Heschel gained stature outside the Seminary, his alienation from most of his colleagues increased. He was never accepted as a peer by the faculty, principally because he did not practice the historical text scholarship honored by the institution. Heschel was a generalist in an academy of specialists.

Even in the JTS chapel, Heschel did not fit in. At the 7 A.M. morning service, he was the first to arrive; wrapped in his tallit and tefillin, he paced around as he prayed, swaying back and forth, eyes tightly closed in ardent concentration. The other professors sat stiffly, dignified, and did not move when they prayed.[41]

An unsympathetic witness to Heschel's alienation, Hillel Halkin (son of the history professor Abraham Halkin) admitted that most faculty members rejected Heschel, or even mocked him behind his back, because "matters of the spirit did not much concern them." Colleagues earned respect by establishing accurate texts.[42]

Heschel's standing at JTS was undermined actively by Saul Lieberman and more covertly by Louis Finkelstein. Lieberman had enormous influence with Finkelstein and had become demonstrably malicious toward Heschel. He mocked his Hasidism, disparaging him to colleagues and even to students. With a subtle sadism, Lieberman enjoyed demeaning Heschel in ways that Heschel would not recognize but others would. As rabbi of the JTS synagogue Lieberman was charged with giving honors, such as *aliyot,* being called up to recite the blessing over the Torah. Once Lieberman admitted why he regularly gave Heschel the sixth aliyah, *shishi,* the least prominent of the seven: "Hasidim think that the sixth is the most honorable *aliyah* . . . but only he knows it!"[43]

On the surface, Heschel's relationship with Finkelstein remained cordial. Habitually aloof, Finkelstein continued to treat Heschel with courtesy, communicating mostly through letters. He routinely wrote to praise Heschel's achievements, while avoiding direct conversations. Like most faculty members, they addressed each other as "Professor Finkelstein" and "Professor Heschel." Finkelstein was at the height of his powers. He had reorganized the administration and retained his full authority as chancellor, creating positions of vice chancellor for specific administrative areas. He was honored nationally by having his portrait on the cover of *Time* magazine in October 1951, during the High Holy Days. A laudatory article, entitled "A Trumpet for All Israel," praised the Seminary as being in the forefront of a return to Judaism. Finkelstein was described as almost a holy figure.[44]

Yet for all his academic and worldly success, Finkelstein envied Heschel's even greater celebrity in the world outside the Seminary. Finkelstein had fully supported Heschel's first publications, making beneficial contacts for him. Then *Man Is Not Alone* received national acclaim through the attention of Reinhold Niebuhr. Finkelstein had been cultivating a relationship with Niebuhr for years, and he found Heschel's dramatic success galling. Finkelstein remained silently resentful as Heschel gained greater prominence in the Gentile world.

Unlike Lieberman, with his campaign of subtle denigration, Finkelstein undermined Heschel in more insidious ways, through neglect. Without abandoning the appearance of respect, he would not improve Heschel's teaching schedule, despite repeated requests to do so. And he refused to find Heschel a more roomy office. Heschel's bookcases were filled to the ceiling, his cabinets overstuffed with folders and manuscripts. The dark, crowded study was picturesque but an uncomfortable place to spend long hours of study or writing, to welcome students and other visitors, or to teach private seminars.

Heschel remained acutely sensitive to, even obsessed by, his colleagues' poor regard for his academic work, even blaming himself, though he knew that the real problem was a matter of values. He never lost his yearning for approval from them, and he tried to compensate by seeking adulation from his favorite students. Although he rarely complained of the indignities he endured, close friends, colleagues, and even some students were aware of them. They would listen to him on the occasions he did confide in them, and they would offer him consolation.[45]

Ironically, Heschel shared this fragile self-esteem with his nemesis, Saul Lieberman. They were cultural and intellectual rivals, but they were also both products of a harsh East European Jewish pedagogical tradition. Both men were child prodigies who suffered from scarred egos aggravated by craving for approval.

Lieberman's father was a learned rabbi who had tutored him at home before sending him to study with eminent scholars. Like many stern East European Jewish fathers, he had attacked his son's pride, calling him "idiot" and other humiliating names. This brutality was reinforced when Lieberman began training in Mussar yeshivas, where the harsh discipline sometimes led to pathological self-loathing in the students, who reciprocated by censuring others. Years later Lieberman applied Mussar pedagogical methods at JTS, humiliating students for their own good.[46]

Heschel shared Lieberman's need for adulation, as well as an inferiority complex that originated from the same period of his life. Heschel's father had died before his tenth birthday, and the boy's education was entrusted to a disciple of the rebbe of Kotzk. Heschel's self-confidence was subject to constant rebuke, so that his joy in the Baal Shem Tov was offset by the mortification he endured under the teachings of the Kotzker rebbe. The young Heschel came to magnify his own weaknesses: "I owe intoxication to the Baal Shem, to the Kotzker the blessings of humiliation."[47]

Heschel's relationships with his students continued to be mixed: many were put off by his indifferent teaching, but others found him stimulating, warm, and deeply spiritual—a true rebbe. Heschel was a central figure on the Seminary Admissions Committee, influencing some students even before they began their rabbinical training. The high point of the committee's work was the interview with prospective students by a group of professors. Although Vice Chancellor Simon Greenberg was the official chair and other faculty members regularly participated, for most students Heschel was masterful; he could be intimidating but also attentive to spiritual issues, strongly supportive of those he valued, even funny.

At one such session, the distinguished professors were seated around the table. Finally, Heschel, who had remained quiet during the interview, stroking his beard, as he often did, turned to the candidate and asked, "If you were going to Alaska, what two things would you take with you?" Thinking that his answer should be Jewishly appropriate, the aspiring rabbinical student answered, "Tallis and tefillin." Dr. Heschel looked at him and asked, "Wouldn't you take a warm coat?" Another time, Heschel was seated at the head of the table with a junior faculty member, Avraham Holtz, at his left. When the candidate saw Heschel he was paralyzed with fright. Realizing this, Heschel asked him the name of the college he was attending, the name of his home town, his rabbi, and so on. The young man could not answer. To put him at ease, Heschel suggested that the two of them exchange places and the candidate do the asking and Heschel the answering. Finally the young man found his voice: "Professor Heschel, what are you doing at the Seminary?" Heschel joked, "I'm here to be very close to my very good friend Avraham Holtz." Everyone laughed, and the interview proceeded as usual. That student is now a rabbi.[48]

A number of rabbis owe their profession to Heschel. He frequently supported applicants considered unsuitable by other members of the committee. He also assumed the unpleasant task of soothing the ruffled feelings of sons of prominent rabbis, or even faculty members, who were rejected. He put hours into each case, calling applicants on the telephone and meeting with them privately.[49]

There were also illuminating classroom moments. The Law Committee of the Conservative movement had recently debated whether gelatin was kosher. Heschel came into class and asked, "Gentlemen, what is your opinion, is gelatin kosher or not?" The rabbinical students became engrossed in discussion for several minutes. Heschel interrupted, "Gentlemen, can you tell me if the atomic bomb is kosher?"[50]

Heschel was often careless with his required classes, but sometimes his neglect produced unexpected benefits. One day he interrupted his lecture on Maimonides and left the room to fetch his morning mail. When he returned, he read the class a letter he had received: a synagogue in an old Jewish area of the Bronx was about to be sold. There were two potential buyers: a black Baptist church and a large bank. The synagogue board knew that according to tradition a synagogue should not be converted into a church. Nonetheless, they asked Heschel for his opinion.

"So, gentlemen, you are soon to be rabbis, what is your *pesak,* your decision?" After several seconds of uncomfortable silence, a student approvingly quoted the traditional *pesak:* "Never to a church!"

Heschel listened politely, then rose, stroked his beard, and spoke: "May I insult you? If it is sold to a bank then it will become a temple of capitalism; if sold to a church, it will continue to be a temple of God. Should a rabbi endorse a *shul* being converted into a temple of capitalism!"[51]

In 1951 Heschel formed a lifelong bond with Marshall Meyer, like Maurice Friedman a gifted young man with a deficient Jewish education. (Heschel seemed to be especially receptive to such intellectually enterprising outsiders.) Entering his final year at Dartmouth College in the honors program, Meyer was planning a special research project. He was a committed Jew, but he lacked the knowledge to answer what he felt were attacks on Judaism by his professor, Eugen Rosenstock-Huessy, a renowned philosopher and theologian who had been close to Rosenzweig and Buber in Germany before immigrating to the United States. (Rosenstock-Huessy, who converted to Christianity at age sixteen, debated with Rosenzweig and influenced the latter's embrace of Judaism.) Rosenstock-Huessy had been at Dartmouth since the 1930s and had a great deal of influence over the students.[52]

Meyer's rabbi from home, Zev K. Nelson, urged him to meet Heschel. Meyer went to the Seminary, took the elevator up to the sixth floor, and entered Heschel's office, where he was overwhelmed by the piles of books and papers. Heschel sat at his desk, smoking a cigar. Their first conversation was decisive. They spoke for two hours. Heschel was extremely interested in Meyer's struggle with Rosenstock-Huessy: "Do you want to fight this man, or defend your Judaism?" Meyer said that he wanted to learn more about Judaism. "How is your German?" asked Heschel. "Nonexistent," admitted Meyer. The same was true of his Hebrew and Aramaic. After discussing Meyer's readings in philosophy and Jewish writings in translation, Heschel agreed to sponsor his senior project.

He instructed Meyer to attend a Camp Ramah (Conservative Jewish camp) that summer to improve his Hebrew. For the 1951–52 academic year, under Heschel's tutelage, entailing frequent visits to New York for meetings that lasted hours, Meyer wrote a paper on the doctrine of love in *Genesis Rabbah*, the prime Midrash commentary on the Bible. That project helped Meyer counter Rosenstock-Huessy's Christian critique of Judaism as a religion that lacked a loving God and allowed no personal freedom within the law.

Meyer thus made his commitment to Judaism and to Heschel. In the fall of 1952 he entered the JTS Rabbinical School, where he worked with Seymour Siegel, who gave remedial classes for students with faulty Hebrew, and he took all of Heschel's seminars. Meyer went on to the Hebrew University to study with Buber, Scholem, and Ernst Simon; later at Union Theological Seminary he took courses with Paul Tillich, Wilhelm Pauck, and Reinhold Niebuhr; he also attended classes at Columbia University.

Meyer worked as Heschel's student secretary until he was ordained in 1958. He was able to discuss all his problems with Heschel, psychological as well as religious and moral. His relationship with Heschel was as close in its own way as Wolfe Kelman's was. Meyer eventually founded the Abraham Joshua Heschel Rabbinical Seminary in Buenos Aires; he also revitalized the Congregation B'nai Jeshurun in Manhattan in the spirit of his mentor and friend.

Martin Buber's American Lecture Tour

In the fall of 1951 Louis Finkelstein arranged for Martin Buber to make a six-month lecture tour of the United States. It was Buber's first visit, and about seventy lectures were planned at prominent locations around the country, including the Jewish Theological Seminary. Heschel would have been the appropriate person to appoint as JTS faculty host, for he had been in close communication with Buber since 1935. But this was Finkelstein's project, an exceptional public relations opportunity for the Seminary and for the chancellor, who was still elated over the cover article in *Time*. Heschel was put aside, snubbed.[53]

Seymour Siegel, a junior faculty member, was chosen to be Buber's caretaker, his *shammes*. Siegel welcomed Buber and his wife Paula at Idlewild (now John F. Kennedy) Airport on 1 November 1951. Buber wanted to see Heschel as soon as possible. When they met they embraced warmly. The following day, a gala dinner was held for Buber with the JTS faculty. Then Buber took the train to Dartmouth College, where he spoke on 13 November, staying at the home of his friend Eugen Rosenstock-Huessy. This was a great occasion for Marshall Meyer, who witnessed their first embrace after decades. That evening Buber lectured on Carl Jung and religion, criticizing "omnipotent psychology." Students were especially impressed by Buber's answers from the floor, his "spontaneous sense of humor. . . . Such qualities were a great aid in overcoming the effect of a thick, German accent," wrote the undergraduate newspaper reporter.[54]

Buber's lecture tour was successful, inaugurating his American career and helping him publish his books in English translation. People were inspired by his oracular presence, fascinated by his thinking on various issues,

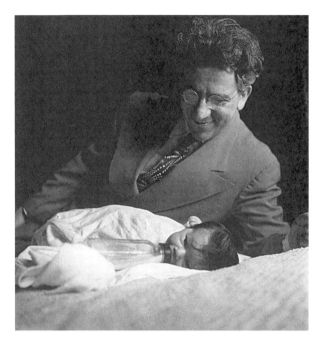

Heschel with daughter Susannah, born 15 May 1952.
Photograph by Lotte Jacobi. Courtesy of the Lotte Jacobi
Collection, University of New Hampshire.

Heschel and Susannah, ca. 1958. Courtesy of Yitzhak Meir Twersky.

and excited by the prospect of reading his books. On the eve of his return to Israel, JTS hosted a farewell tribute at Carnegie Hall. The program that Sunday evening, 5 April 1952, did not include Heschel. On the contrary, it featured the Reconstructionist wing of Conservative Judaism: Ira Eisenstein gave the invocation, and there were brief tributes by Paul Tillich and Mordecai Kaplan, each in his own way an exponent of symbolic religion. Buber's farewell lecture, "Hope for This Hour," referred to the Cold War and denounced "the demonic power which rules our world, the demonry of basic mistrust." Dialogue, acceptance of the other's true needs, was the solution, the hope.[55]

About three weeks after Buber and his wife returned to Jerusalem, Meyer welcomed Heschel to Dartmouth College to lecture as part of the Great Issues Course on 28 April 1952. It was Heschel's first invitation to speak at an American college. Since Sylvia was expecting a baby at any time, he did not stay long.

Heschel's treatment of the topic "What Is Wrong with Western Civilization?" impressed both faculty and students. According to the daily campus newspaper, Heschel especially enjoyed exchanges with the audience: "When asked a question, he waits. He delivers his answer with precision and conviction. . . . As Americans, he says, 'we have an additional responsibility through our power and our influence. We must know what we stand for. Whatever goes on here affects all men.' "[56]

About two weeks later, on 15 May, Sylvia Heschel gave birth to a baby girl. It was a difficult delivery: the mother had wanted a midwife, but doctors had to remove the baby with forceps. Heschel, relieved and ecstatic, wrote immediately to several friends, and to Louis Finkelstein, who was visiting Jerusalem: "The father is very grateful to *hashem* [God]." To Meyer he wrote: "I wish I would know how to be grateful to God for that gift." The child was named Channa Shoshanah ("Anna" for Sylvia's mother; "Shoshanah," "rose" in Hebrew, for Reizel, Heschel's mother). A naming ceremony took place at the Kopitzhinitzer shtibl at 132 Henry Street on the Lower East Side of Manhattan.[57]

Heschel doted on Susie, who was precocious and lively, and he loved to play with her. Heschel dedicated his next book, *God in Search of Man*, "To Sylvia." (The only previous book he had dedicated was his 1933 collection of Yiddish poetry, in memory of his deceased father.) In this way Heschel publicly honored his wife and their American family.

8

Critique of American Judaism (1952–1954)

The idea of revelation remains an absurdity as long as we are unable to comprehend the impact with which the reality of God is pursuing man. Yet, at those moments in which the fate of mankind is in the balance, even those who have never sensed how God turns to man, suddenly realize that man . . . is important enough to be the recipient of spiritual light at the rare dawns of his history.

—Heschel, "A Preface to an Understanding of Revelation" (1954)

JUDAISM AS A CULTURAL FORCE WAS ENTERING THE AMERICAN MAINSTREAM. On 20 January 1953, for the first time, a rabbi, the tall and eloquent Abba Hillel Silver, leader of Reform Judaism and a Zionist, offered a prayer at a presidential inauguration, that of Dwight David Eisenhower. Eisenhower's landslide victory over Adlai Stevenson helped bring the Korean conflict to an end, ushering in an era of relative peace. (Eisenhower's vice president, Richard Nixon, would overshadow Heschel's final years.)

But even as they enjoyed the postwar prosperity, Americans were becoming increasingly shaken by the Cold War and the pervasive suspicion it generated. An atmosphere of intimidation was fueled by the ongoing anti-Communist hearings being held by Joseph McCarthy's Senate Committee on Governmental Operations and the House Committee on Un-American Activities. The nuclear arms race with the Soviet Union created further anxiety.

All the while, Heschel concentrated on problems of spiritual authenticity. He deplored the prevailing American trend of interpreting religion in terms of social science. When he was invited to address national constituencies, Jewish or interfaith, he usually took a confrontational stance: dramatic, extreme, uncompromising. In the face of American Jews' emphasis on Judaism as a culture, he defended the religion of the living God; Judaism was not merely a civilization or a secular humanism. And God-centered reality was ultimate truth.

Restoring the Spirit of Jewish America

The relation of symbolism to the sacred was a lifelong concern of Heschel's, dating from his debates with Buber in the 1930s. In June 1952 he gladly accepted an invitation to present his views at the "Institute for Religious and Social Studies," an interfaith conference organized by Louis Finkelstein. Heschel spent the summer in Hanover, New Hampshire, working on this paper, in addition to volume 2 of his "Philosophy" (the "Philosophy of Judaism") and other, related essays. He was saddened to learn of the death of Eduard Strauss on 24 August, by which he lost another link to the Frankfurt Lehrhaus and its program of spiritual renewal.[1]

At Finkelstein's conference that November, Heschel defied the majority of participants—Catholic, Protestant, and Jewish—who argued that symbolism could renew religious life in the same way it had energized psychology, architecture, dance, drama, and literature. For them, the divine had been replaced by an "idea" of God; symbolic ritual had salutary psychological and social effects. By viewing Judaism and Christianity as cultural forms of action rather than reverent responses to divinely revealed laws, modern practitioners would be moved to turn outward together, into social action. Religious law and the divine presence, which inspired the individual's relationship to God, were deemed no longer relevant to contemporary life. Quite the contrary, Heschel systematically denied the value of symbolism in Jewish theology and practice.[2]

Carefully defining his terms, he began with spatial symbols, such as the Holy Ark, in which God's presence was felt. He distinguished between a "real symbol," in which something of the divine inhered in the image, and a "conventional symbol," which stood for something but did not partake of it, such as a flag. According to Heschel, even the created world was not a symbol of God: "The world speaks to God, but that speech is not God speaking to Himself." Images must not be confused with the transcendent. In terms of practice, ritual objects possessed "no inherent sanctity." Candles, Torah ornaments, special garments, even the Holy Ark, served only psychological or esthetic functions, "to add pleasure to obedience, delight to fulfillment." It was the person's inner relationship with God that gave meaning to the act.[3]

For Heschel, authentic religious knowledge had to be direct and experiential, not simply rational. He countered the claim of Kant and his followers like Salomon Maimon that "only *symbolic* knowledge is possible." He denounced the doctrine of a religion limited to concepts, a view that "regards religion as *a fiction*, useful to society or to man's personal well-being."[4]

Heschel's specific target was American Reconstructionism. He shared the Reconstructionists' goal of revitalizing observance, but he held that their focus on symbols denied its sacred essence: "Symbols are relevant to man; *mitzvot* are relevant to God. Symbols are folkways; *mitzvot* are God's ways." For Heschel no compromise was possible with divine reality; the mitzvot expressed God's will. He boldly concluded with this alternative, a challenge to his listeners to decide: "The will of God is either real or a delusion."[5]

Typically, Heschel overstated his position, a risky strategy. Bent on demonstrating that "nothing is more alien to the spirit of Judaism than the veneration of images," he ignored the vast poetic and mythical resources of Kabbalah, Zohar, and mystical tradition that he had studied from his youth.[6] (The research of Gershom Scholem on Jewish mysticism was sufficient to refute Heschel's claim.) Why did Heschel expose himself to easy criticism?

For Heschel, faith was the issue at the heart of the Jewish culture wars. His polemic against symbolism was aimed at protecting authentic observance; in his words, symbolism "reduces beliefs to make-believe, observance to ceremony, prophecy to literature, theology to esthetics." Moreover, he rejected symbolism on ethical as well as theological grounds. There was only one "symbol" of the divine, namely, each and every human being, body and spirit: "Human life is holy, holier even than the Scrolls of the Torah. Its holiness is not man's achievement; it is a gift of God rather than something attained through merit."[7]

At the conference, however, Heschel's competitors had the last word. Mordecai Kaplan reiterated his advocacy of symbolism, which he considered to be the necessary vehicle of human communication and collective action. For Kaplan and his followers, Heschel's insistence upon revelation from a transcendent God was simply supernaturalism or "primitive religion . . . in other words, magic." Old "rites and observances" needed to be reinterpreted. Sociology provided a rationale to counter religious apathy.[8]

This interfaith conference underscored the division between Jews who viewed Judaism primarily in cultural terms and those who viewed it princi-

Heschel in his office at the Jewish Theological Seminary, ca. 1954. Photograph by John Popper. Courtesy of the Ratner Center for the Study of Conservative Judaism, Jewish Theological Seminary of America.

Mordecai Kaplan, ca. 1955. Courtesy of Mel Scult.

pally in religious terms. For Heschel, of course, authentic Judaism derived from God, who was real, a God of pathos, emotionally involved with humankind, and his writings of this period concentrate on humans' relation with the divine. In addition to the new work he was doing, he looked into the possibility of reissuing his doctoral thesis, *Die Prophetie* (On prophecy), in English translation.

Several years earlier, Heschel had come across a book entitled *The Hebrew Prophetic Consciousness*, by Harold Knight, a Protestant scholar in Great Britain who translated German and French theological works into English. The book was a paraphrase of Heschel's Berlin dissertation, which Knight had appropriated, perhaps believing that Heschel had been murdered by the Nazis. Dismayed, Heschel had consulted H. L. Ginsberg, the JTS Bible specialist, and contacted a lawyer in London about the possibility of filing a lawsuit. But compassion intervened. When Knight threatened to commit suicide if he were disgraced by exposure, Heschel decided not to press charges; in any case, Heschel did not want to destroy the reputation of an otherwise worthy scholar.[9]

Seeking to publish his own book in English, early in 1953 Heschel negotiated another joint venture between the Jewish Publication Society and a trade
house. He chose Charles Scribner's Sons, which published the works of Reinhold Niebuhr. Heschel mailed a packet of reviews of his 1936 German book to
William Savage of Scribner's, urging him to encourage Grayzel to copublish
a translation.[10] Grayzel answered immediately, expressing interest.

Grayzel sent copies of Heschel's German book for evaluation to Julius A.
Bewer, a Christian Old Testament scholar, and H. L. Ginsberg, both recommended by Heschel. Grayzel also wrote to Sheldon Blank, professor of the
Bible at Hebrew Union College. Everyone responded quickly and positively.
Ginsberg praised Heschel's thesis as "a serious phenomenological study,
which was favorably received when it came out." He added that a translation
"would obviate the temptation to plagiarize the comparatively unknown German original." Blank recalled his appreciation of Heschel's book several
years earlier, adding a wry comment: "Whether JPS should publish it or not is
a matter of JPS policy. I do not know of anything better on the subject. Perhaps
this book is too good."[11]

In October, the JPS Publications Committee decided "to accept copublication of the translation with the commercial publisher." They also recommended copublication of *God in Search of Man* with Farrar, Straus and Young,
since "Dr. Heschel reported that the manuscript would be ready in the Spring
of 1954." But Sheldon Blank had been right: Heschel's book on the prophets
was "too good"—that is, too technical—for a commercial success. Reconsid-
ering its initial support, JPS turned it down, as did Scribner's. The translation
of *Die Prophetie* returned to Heschel's files, later to be revised and expanded.[12]

In the meantime, Heschel extracted material from his thesis and the manuscript he was still working on for his "Philosophy of Judaism," and fashioned
them into three articles, which he placed strategically to reach different read-
erships.

For religiously engaged modern Jews, he arranged to publish "The Divine
Pathos: The Basic Category of Prophetic Theology" in the January 1953 issue
of *Judaism*, translated by William Wolf. *Pathos* referred to God's concern or
"emotional" reactions to "what happens in the world." The human-divine relationship was "transitive" and not immutable. Heschel adapted the vocabulary of Rosenzweig ("correlation") and Buber ("dialogue") to explain the
meeting of divine and human: "In sum, the divine pathos is the unity of the
eternal and the temporal, of the rational and the irrational, of the metaphysical

and the historical. It is . . . the correlation of Creator and creation, of the dialogue between the Holy One of Israel and His people."[13]

The next month another programmatic essay, "The Moment at Sinai," appeared in *American Zionist*, the journal of the Zionist Organization of America. In this analysis of revelation Heschel urged politically oriented Jews not to abandon their spiritual heritage. Striking out against secularization, he distinguished between the God of the philosophers, "a concept derived from abstract ideas," and the God of the prophets, "derived from acts and events." To clarify the unprecedented character of revelation, Heschel rejected Alfred North Whitehead's "process theology," favored by Mordecai Kaplan and his followers, as he asserted the reality of a divine "event"; Heschel understood "divine event" to mean that such inspiration remained available to human beings, "that there is a voice of God *in the world*—not in heaven or in any unknown sphere—that pleads with man to do His will."[14]

Heschel prepared a third essay, "A Preface to an Understanding of Revelation," for a special volume published in England to honor Leo Baeck's eightieth birthday. The contributors were a distinguished international array of historians and philosophers: Martin Buber, Albert Einstein, Karl Jaspers, Thomas Mann, Jacques Maritain, Ernst Simon, Gershom Scholem, Julian Morgenstern, Selma Stern-Tauebler, Norman Bentwich, and Nicholas Arseniev. In the essay Heschel challenged the liberal view of Judaism represented by Leo Baeck's *Essence of Judaism* (1936), drawing his justification of divine revelation from the manuscript of *God in Search of Man*.

He began by validating the supernatural communication: "We have never been the same since the day on which Abraham crushed his father's symbols, since the day on which the Voice of God overwhelmed us at Sinai." Insensitivity to the reality of God, according to Heschel, placed humankind in mortal jeopardy, since human beings are born with "a passion and drive for cruel deeds, which only the fear of God can soothe." He graphically evoked the apathy among bystanders during the Holocaust, while suggesting that there yet remained enough religious faith to save civilization from complete destruction: "If man can remain callous to a horror as infinite as God, . . . [can] make soap of human flesh, then how did it happen that nations did not exterminate each other centuries ago?" For Heschel the living God was the ultimate corrective: "Unless a new source of spiritual energy is discovered commensurate with the source of atomic energy, a few men may throw all men into final disaster."[15]

Heschel's rejection of process theology and his tendency to draw excessive contrasts provoked firm but amiable criticism from Arthur A. Cohen, one of the gifted students in the JTS "Institute for Theology." Cohen wrote to his teacher, cautioning him not to "employ whipping boys, the major ones being your distinction between philosophy and prophecy, process and event." He urged Heschel to demonstrate more sympathy for his opponents: "Beggars such as us cannot be choosers. To make our audience we cannot risk surrendering half." Rather, he felt that Heschel should seek common ground between competing conceptions. For Cohen, "revelation was the focus of a process, that God continues to expand out of that process, that God gains from having revealed. . . . As it was suggested to me today by Jack Riemer, my conception is of the great moved mover." Cohen concluded with genuine admiration: "Need I add that as always I find your writing brilliant, penetrating and always valuable? Criticism is too rare an event for anybody that I could withhold it."[16]

Heschel appreciated this bold, and brilliant, evaluation, but not enough to alter his characteristic style. He chose to maintain his polemical approach instead of developing a more nuanced analysis. He was willing to alienate academic interpreters in order to assert more forcefully principles he considered of ultimate import.

A crucial part of Heschel's mission was to revive the sacred in American Jewish life through bold religious education. He had been teaching in American seminaries since 1940, and he was dismayed by the compromises they made in their curricula. He had been shocked to discover how ill-prepared his students were in what he considered the fundamentals of their religion, and he challenged Jewish educators to confront this problem. Perhaps his demands on others reflected his own disappointments in the classroom.

In February 1953, Heschel was a featured speaker at the eleventh annual conference of the Jewish Education Committee, as the New York Bureau of Jewish Education was then known. More than three hundred teachers and school principals debated the theme "Teaching Jewish Values." Rabbi Alexander Steinbach of Brooklyn opened the meeting by defining the conference goal as the creation of group cohesion; his approach favored the principles of psychiatry and social science. Heschel, in his plenary address, took the opposite stand, rejecting the sociological model. Speaking on "The Spirit of Jewish Education," he emphasized the individual, inwardness, and faith and criticized reductionist, exclusively humanistic approaches.[17]

Heschel took to task what he called "the autocracy" of psychology and sociology: "Human existence cannot derive its ultimate meaning from society, because society itself is in need of meaning." His negative example was Nazi

Germany, which defined as right "what is useful to the German people." He then spoke as a prophet, anticipating by ten years his social activism and demanding the highest ethical standards: "How can one preserve one's integrity in a world filled with intrigue, flattery, and falsehood? . . . What is the value of being moral in spite of the defeats of the moral man in the atmosphere of cynicism in which we live?" To counter the current negativity, teachers must help young people discover "the ultimate significance" of their lives.[18]

Heschel claimed that truly biblical ethics was largely absent from Jewish education. He spoke of a student who attended Jewish schools for fifteen years yet still believed that Judaism sanctioned revenge and that the statement "Love thy neighbor as thyself" was from the New Testament. Bar mitzvah boys learned to bless the Torah but were not taught to appreciate the meaning of "He has planted within us eternal life," part of the benediction. With a sarcastic edge, Heschel acknowledged the enormity of his goals: "I am committing a heresy, I know, if I suggest that we ought to teach them a phrase such as 'Ye shall be holy,' the vision of a '*neshamah yethera*' [according to tradition, observant Jews receive an additional soul on Sabbath], the meaning of '*Shekhinah*' rather than words such as '*kaddur basis*' [baseball], but heretical I must be."[19]

Heschel had begun his talk by repudiating the debased image of the *melamed* (a Hebrew teacher of children) found in Jewish popular literature. He did not mince his words: "The fact that [the melamed receives little respect] seems to be nothing but blasphemy, and I am a *melamed* myself. It is treason to the spirit of Judaism, for in our teachings there is no higher distinction than that of being a teacher." He concluded by challenging the modern teacher to be "either a witness or a stranger. To guide a pupil into the promised land, he must have been there himself. . . . What we need more than anything else is not *text-books* but *text-people*. It is the personality of the teacher which is the text that the pupils read; the text that they will never forget." Heschel allied himself with his audience, admonishing them for being like the blacksmith's apprentice who had learned all the skills except how to kindle the spark.[20]

Heschel's "spark" did not burst forth immediately. The following day the educators discussed prayer, history, contemporary Jewish life, and the state of Israel. Most participants continued to follow psychological approaches and expressed "considerable doubt" as to "whether it is possible to teach abstract principles and values directly at the elementary level."[21] Heschel revised his speech for publication, creating an educational manifesto, a germinal article (like "An Analysis of Piety") from which further essays grew. But he also went directly to the rabbis.

The Soul of Conservative Judaism

That summer, Heschel delivered his fullest critique of American Jewish practice. Recognizing that the bourgeoning of synagogues in suburbia had not enhanced the quality of observance and religious learning, leaders of the Reform and Conservative rabbinates separately invited Heschel to define his ideal of prayer to colleagues in the field. During the week of 22–27 June 1953, he embarked upon a sort of shuttle diplomacy, delivering his most detailed outline of what he thought rabbis of all denominations should strive for.[22]

To each group, Heschel asserted exactly what its members did not want to hear. Conservative Judaism, like Orthodox, emphasized law (halakhah) and ritual observance over cultivation of the inner life; Reform rejected the authority of halakhah in favor of rational philosophy and individual choice. To the leaders of each movement Heschel tailored his counterdiscourse to restore the fullness of Judaism, contradictions and all.

Heschel first admonished his Conservative colleagues at their fifty-third annual convention at the Breakers Hotel in Atlantic City, New Jersey. Ira Eisenstein, a leader of Kaplan's Society for the Advancement of Judaism, was president of the Rabbinical Assembly (R.A.) that year. Hoping to cultivate a mutually illuminating exchange of views, he organized the program around Heschel and Eugene Kohn, the other leader in Kaplan's Reconstructionist movement.

Eisenstein opened the meeting on 22 June. He reported improvements in the R.A. administrative machinery and welcomed impending recommendations from the Prayer Book Commission headed by Rabbi Jacob Agus. Surveying the bleak political landscape, Eisenstein condemned the tactics of Senator Joseph McCarthy as "terror and intimidation." And he reminded his colleagues how he and other Reconstructionists sought to unify the Jewish people.[23]

Heschel's keynote speech, "The Spirit of Jewish Prayer," followed the presidential report. Heschel began diplomatically, anticipating some hurt feelings: "In advancing some critical remarks I do not mean, *God forbid* [in Hebrew], to take a superior attitude. In all honesty, my criticism will be to a considerable degree self-criticism." But those criticisms of the congregational rabbis were harsh: "Our services are conducted with pomp and precision. The rendition of the liturgy is smooth. Everything is present: decorum, voice, ceremony. But one thing is missing: *Life*." Heschel's images were graphic and his tone was caustic: "Has the synagogue become the graveyard where prayer is buried? Are we, the spiritual leaders of American Jewry, members of a *chevrah kadisha* [burial society]?"[24]

To define the substance of authentic prayer Heschel denounced "the habit of *praying by proxy*," letting the rabbi and the cantor do the work: "Our prayers have so little charm, so little grace, so little *chen* [grace; Hebrew]. What is *chen?* The presence of the soul. A person has *chen* when the throbbing of his heart is audible in his voice; when the longings of his soul animate his face." He deplored the *"spiritual absenteeism"* of congregants who simply attended services without truly participating. Faulty thinking, he claimed, was to blame for such apathy.

Heschel summarized the four "prevalent doctrines" of God and Judaism, measuring each view by the standards of a living God. His analyses were stark, provocative, and verging on caricature. First was "the doctrine of agnosticism," which considered "prayer [to be] a fraud." Heschel condemned those who believed that "the only way to revitalize the synagogue is to minimize the importance of prayer and to convert the synagogue into a center. It is something which the Talmud characterizes as *sin: 'To call a Holy Ark a chest and to call a synagogue a community center* [in Hebrew].'" These strictures were obviously directed at Reconstructionists and their secularizing sympathizers.

Second, he denounced "the doctrine of religious behaviorism," widespread among Orthodox and some Conservative Jews, in which people "seem to believe that religious deeds can be performed in a spiritual wasteland, in the absence of the soul, with a heart hermetically sealed." Heschel was alluding to the foremost exponent of modern Orthodoxy, Rabbi Joseph B. Soloveitchik, who defined the ideal Jew as "Halakhic Man."[25]

Heschel then targeted Reform (and numerous Conservative) Jews imbued with the view of Judaism as a civilization. They were proponents of the "doctrine of prayer as a social act," which "is built on a theology which regards God as a symbol of social action, as an epitome of the ideals of the group, as 'the spirit of the beloved community.'" Although Heschel strategically did not name the obvious author of this faulty ideology, Mordecai Kaplan, his condemnation of what he called the "sociological fallacy" could not be more explicit.[26]

Heschel's fourth and final target was a variant of "process theology," which he caricatured as "the doctrine of religious solipsism." According to that view, "the individual self of the worshiper is the whole sphere of prayer-life. The assumption is that God is an idea, a process, a source, a fountain, a spring, a power. But one cannot pray to an idea, one cannot address his payers to a fountain of values." Once more, Heschel avoided singling out specific thinkers within his community by attacking a 1911 book by the French psychologist Joseph Segond.[27]

Heschel warned that American Jews were undergoing a crisis of belief. The problem among their leaders too was widespread: "I have been in the United States of America for thirteen years. I have not discovered America but I have discovered something in America. It is possible to be a rabbi and not to believe in the God of Abraham, Isaac and Jacob." Most American rabbis, according to a survey he cited, conceived of God as "the sum total of forces which make for greater intelligence, beauty, goodness." Heschel demanded faith in a personal God, for "if the presence of God is a myth, then we are insane in talking to Him." The risks of such intransigence were enormous.[28]

Once again Heschel refused to compromise. God's presence in the world was at stake: as he had noted in *Man Is Not Alone*, "Great is the power of prayer. For to worship is to expand the presence of God in the world. God is transcendent, but our worship of Him makes him immanent."[29] Heschel concluded with several suggestions on how to maintain the centrality of prayer. Jews should concentrate on "how to pray," not "what to say." Poking fun at the Prayer Book Commission, Heschel called for a "*Prayer* Commission." He also suggested that the rabbi and cantor stop facing the congregation, an innovation that had been made for the sake of decorum: "It is embarrassing to be exposed to the sight of the whole congregation in moments when one wishes to be alone with his God. A cantor who faces the holiness in the Ark rather than the curiosity of man will realize that his audience is God." Finally, urged Heschel, rabbis, teachers, and cantors must embody the "absolute significance" of being a Jew.

In "The Spirit of Jewish Prayer," Heschel bore radical witness to the need for an American Jewish theology. But his was a lonely voice. With his demand for absolute integrity, how could he expect support from the majority? He himself had cited statistical proof that most American rabbis did not believe in God. In addition, Heschel's insistence on the magnitude of human evil undercut the optimism of American Jews in the 1950s. His view, compatible with Hasidic tradition and the recent cataclysm of the Holocaust, was that humans' alienation from God reflected "the soul-stirring awareness that God Himself was not at home in a universe, where His will is defied, where His kingship is denied. *The Shekhinah is in exile*, the world is corrupt, *the universe itself is not at home.*" Many in Heschel's audience were offended by his sarcasm; they felt like "whipping boys," as Arthur Cohen had warned him could happen, and were hurt and angry.

The next evening, one of Heschel's theological adversaries took the floor. In "Prayer and the Modern Jew," Eugene Kohn presented the classic Reconstructionist position. While agreeing with Heschel that "modern man has largely lost the art of prayer," he dismissed the traditional belief that God hears our prayers. Kohn asserted that people have "rejected the idea that God is a transcendent person"; they needed an updated "idea of God" in order to embrace prayer once again.[30]

Kohn contradicted Heschel at every turn. His talk blended process theology, sociology, and Buber's I-Thou dialogue, all popular trends in American Judaism. He justified the revision of the prayer book by arguing that traditional liturgies retained too many ethical and scientific "errors," such as "ideologies designed to exalt the group at the expense of other groups, authoritarian appeals to obedience to hierarchical dignitaries, obsolete interpretations of nature and history." Prayer did not influence God but only the worshiper, "by illuminating his moral vision, deepening his appreciation of life's values." There was no room for a biblical God in Kohn's religion.[31]

After Kohn's speech, some support for Heschel came from the audience. Recognizing that many of his colleagues regarded Heschel as "a mystic and a dreamer," Irving Lehrman defended him with Abraham Lincoln's famous witticism in response to complaints that General Grant's excessive drinking made him unfit to lead the Union Army: "Ah, if I only knew the brand of liquor he uses, I would feed it to my generals." Rabbi Lehrman continued: "If Dr. Heschel is a mystic and a dreamer, intoxicated with the idea of God, and the heights to which man can ascend in approaching Him,—then I would like to know the source from which he derives his intoxication, so that we can imbibe it ourselves, and feed it to our congregations. I have come to the conclusion that this is the greatest need of our times and our generation."[32]

Then Heschel stood up. He was surprised, "puzzled," "amazed," and even "distressed" that his call for authentic prayer in Conservative synagogues had provoked such indignation. But even as he attempted to engage in a sympathetic discussion, he revealed his stubborn, insensitive side. He began defensively, insisting that he had postponed his own research to examine "the details of a problem which is specifically and uniquely yours." But he then acknowledged that "your problems, too, are mine. The assurance that I was speaking in the spirit of self-criticism was not an empty phrase. All my life I have been deeply bothered by my own miserable failure to attain *kavanah* in prayer." Heschel then tried to justify his polemical style. He explained that sharp phrases such as "the separation of synagogue and God," "decapitated prayer," or "prayer without God" were intended simply to make his position clear.

The rabbis, too, went on the defensive. Several protested that their congregations resisted a theological approach to worship. Harry Halpern of Brooklyn vented the frustration of many as he explained that he would like to use services as a means of attaining kavanah but that it was impossible to do so with a congregation that confused *davening* [praying] with entertainment. They would begin chattering "when the high-priced warbler" (the cantor) stopped singing. Under such conditions, how could rabbis turn the synagogue into a place for true piety and silent meditation?

As the evening concluded, Ira Eisenstein, the R.A. president, took the floor and explained that he had planned Heschel's and Kohn's opposing presentations in the hope that they would lead to fruitful discussion. Although he could "recognize the validity" of Heschel's approach, he was disappointed that Heschel demanded that everyone "accept his theological dogma, [otherwise] you can't pray at all. I deny that."[33] He invited the principal speakers to have the final word.

Heschel spoke first, asserting that most misunderstandings were matters of emphasis and repeating his avowal that true prayer was difficult for him to achieve: "I am profoundly embarrassed by the inadequacy of my praying. I have no peace of mind, nor do I submit to despair." Then he made an astounding admission, which drew him closer to some of his listeners: "I have been wrestling with the problem all my life as to whether I really mean God when I pray to Him, whether I have even succeeded in knowing what I am talking about and whom I am talking to. I still don't know whether I serve God or I serve something else." This was not a confession of agnosticism; Heschel did not doubt the reality of God. But, as a sophisticated thinker, he realized that he was handicapped by the inadequacy of language to evoke the ultimate. Religious reality was essentially "ineffable." The task of his *philosophy* of religion, systematic reflection on the experience of piety, was to elucidate the dilemma of faith.

He also attempted to modify some of his criticisms. He had not dismissed decorum in the synagogue as such, nor did he condemn interpretation of the liturgy. He only questioned approaching the problem of prayer with "historic information rather than commitment, rather than inner identification." A rabbi must be able to discover "something new, something fresh" in his heart: "I do not refer to any supernatural events or to any scholarly discoveries. I refer to countless moments of insight which can be gained from communing with the individual words."

But he continued to assert the authority of his own intuition, thereby cutting himself off from rationalists who preferred intellectual constructs. Heschel denied that he had spoken of "*a concept* or demanded the acceptance of a definition. We Jews have no concepts; all we have is faith, faith in His willingness to listen to us. We have no information, but we sense and believe in His being near to us." Heschel seemed to accept only one answer to his own question: "Whom am I serving when I use the word God?"

Heschel did attempt to recover some common ground by respecting his "opponents" as human beings: "The strange thing about many of our contemporaries is that their life is nobler than their ideology, that their faith is deep and their views shallow, that their souls are suppressed and their slogans proclaimed." Discreetly but unmistakably Heschel was alluding to Mordecai Kaplan: "We must not continue to cherish a theory, just because we have embraced it forty years ago." In the end, his response did not advance the dialogue, for all his attempts to do so.

Eugene Kohn had the final word, and it was both generous and uncompromising. The Reconstructionist leader refused requests from some of his partisans to "refute" Heschel. He was not offended by Heschel's critical comments; he viewed them as "motivated by love and I take them in that spirit." Kohn then reaffirmed his loyalty to God as a cosmic process: "I can talk in the same way and with the same freedom with that cosmic process which I regard as the very source and fountain of my own being."

As the conference ended, the core problem remained unresolved: Did Reconstructionism deny a transcendent Deity? Was it a disguised form of atheism or a genuine belief in the living God? Did religious naturalists—as they were also known—recognize a holy reality beyond human conceptions?

All in all, Heschel felt that his challenge to the Rabbinical Assembly was a mixed success, as he wrote to Marshall Meyer: "My talk created quite a stir. Many rabbis expressed gratitude, many more were disturbed—and admitted: we are disturbed because we feel guilty. I feel it was worthwhile." The *New York Times* summed up Heschel's radical critique: "Religious Places Held Devoid of Spirit"; "Rabbinical Assembly Is Told That Only Spiritual Revolt Can Save Humanity."[34]

That fall, Fritz Rothschild, pursuing his graduate studies in philosophy at Columbia University, discussed Heschel's role at the R.A. convention in *Commentary*. Rothschild cited JTS vice chancellor Simon Greenberg's definition of the ideal modern Jew: "We wanted and want to match the most ardent *Hebraist* in knowledge of Hebrew, the most ardent *Orthodox Jew* in the practice of piety, the most ardent *Reform Jew* in determination to make Judaism aesthetically attractive, and the most militant *secularist* in making Judaism contemporaneous and relevant" (emphasis mine). Rothschild thus suggested that Heschel was uniquely capable of realizing that synthesis.[35]

A more positive postscript to the conference was the warm personal relationship that developed between Heschel and Ira Eisenstein. Their friendship was similar to that of Eisenstein's father-in-law, Mordecai Kaplan, and Heschel, two ideological opponents who felt genuine affection for each other. A love for Judaism, and the joy of being Jewish, united these ideological competitors.[36]

Philosophies of Reform Judaism

The next day Heschel flew to Estes Park, Colorado, to address the sixty-fourth annual convention of the Central Conference of American Rabbis (CCAR). This group was more receptive to contemporary thought—secular, Christian, and Jewish—than their Conservative and Orthodox colleagues. Adapting his approach but retaining his stringencies, Heschel challenged their humanistic assumptions and emphasized the need for a return to traditional observance.

Heschel spoke at the session on "Contemporary Currents in Jewish Theology." The other presenters were Rabbis Samuel Cohon, his former HUC colleague, and David Polish of Evanston, Illinois. Their papers were both slanted toward existentialism, an ethical philosophy of anxiety, courage, and commitment that was prevalent in Europe at the time. Each sought to identify the best model for contemporary American Judaism, and their references were basically the same: Kant, Kierkegaard, Hermann Cohen, Karl Barth, Rosenzweig, Buber, Will Herberg, Reinhold Niebuhr, and Mordecai Kaplan. Neither saw Heschel as a potential guide for alienated contemporaries, either "rational" or "mystic."

Cohon's paper, "The Existentialist Trend in Theology," began by evoking the "climate of the catastrophic events of two world wars." He traced the current "disillusionment with man, human reason and with human goals" back to

Kierkegaard's radical faith through Jean-Paul Sartre's atheistic existentialism and Martin Heidegger's grim ontology of mystery. In Christianity, the crisis (also called dialectical) theology of Karl Barth posited God as "Wholly Other," with "an abyss separating human and divine." Cohon considered Will Herberg the most influential contemporary Jewish thinker in the existentialist vein, but although Herberg's *Judaism and Modern Man* claimed "to systematize the fundamentals" of Buber and Rosenzweig, Cohon deemed him overly influenced by Christianity and thus not an appropriate model for American Judaism. Cohon favored the kind of neo-Hasidism to be found in "Rosenzweig's philosophy of experience and Buber's theocentric mysticism—despite all their ambiguities and artificialities." He recommended that his audience explore two recent books, Nahum Glatzer's intellectual biography of Rosenzweig and Buber's *Eclipse of God*. (Apparently Cohon did not know Heschel's *Man Is Not Alone*, for he made no reference to it.) [37]

David Polish's survey, "Current Trends in Jewish Theology," similarly neglected Heschel. Polish began by considering Herberg's potential as a model for modern Jewish theology, but, like Cohon, he objected to Herberg's Christian neo-orthodox influences, "a theology which is foreign and repugnant to liberal Judaism." According to Polish, Mordecai Kaplan provided a remedy to Herberg, since the "idea of God" as a process immanent to the natural world favored humankind's self-liberation, but Kaplan's impersonal system did not "assuage the hunger for union with God and fulfillment in Him." In the end, Polish touted Buber as the most appropriate model, since Buber emphasized human responsibility: "God's entrance into the world is contingent upon man." Polish then cited a Hasidic master: "Said the Rabbi of Kotzk: 'God dwells wherever man lets Him in.' Here the whole crucial position of man is summarized." Polish concluded that Rosenzweig and Buber remained the prime examples of present-day spirituality, quoting Kaplan against his own slogans: "Faith in God cannot come to us by the mere process of reasoning" and "No religious experience is genuine without elements of awe and mystery."

In fact, Polish had adduced from Buber's writings on Hasidism many key notions that Heschel shared, but Heschel entered Polish's discussion only through a citation from his monograph on Saadia: " 'An essential disagreement between reason and revelation,' says Heschel, 'would presuppose the existence of two divine beings. . . . Faith can never compel reason to accept that which is absurd.' " (Polish was apparently unaware that Heschel had integrated his interpretation of Saadia into *Man Is Not Alone*.)[38]

Then came Heschel's turn. He spoke as a traditionalist, admonishing the Reform rabbis to observe the mitzvot as expressions of God's will. His paper, "Toward an Understanding of Halacha," justified the need to return to consistent observance as the primary means of enhancing the spiritual potential of American Reform. Heschel stressed his solidarity with the plight of Reform rabbis: "I, too, have wrestled with the difficulties inherent in our faith as Jews." For the first time in his public life, Heschel discussed his own path toward renewed religious commitment. Through an autobiographical parable he sought to form a model for reinvigorating American Judaism: "I came with great hunger to the University of Berlin to study philosophy. I looked for a system of thought, for the depth of the spirit, for the meaning of existence. Erudite and profound scholars gave courses in logic, epistemology, esthetics, ethics and metaphysics. They opened the gates of the history of philosophy. I was exposed to the austere disciplines of unremitting inquiry and self-criticism."[39]

Heschel did not lose his theological convictions in Berlin, although his teachers, academic philosophers, did not admit religious thinking: "They spoke of God from the point of view of man. To them God was an idea, a postulate of reason. They granted Him the status of being a logical possibility. But to assume that He had existence would have been a crime against epistemology."[40]

Heschel was excavating the neo-Kantian foundations of American Reform. In Berlin his professors "were prisoners of a Greek-German way of thinking. . . . My assumption was: man's dignity consists in his having been created in the likeness of God. My question was: how must man, a being who is in essence the image of God, think, feel and act? To them, religion was a feeling. To me, religion included the insights of the Torah which is a vision of man from the point of view of God." He repeated passages from his 1952 talk on symbolism and his paper to the Rabbinical Assembly as he insisted upon the reality of God, driving his point home with the memory of how, walking on "the magnificent streets of Berlin" one evening, he had suddenly realized that he had forgotten to recite the evening prayer. The words of Goethe's famous poem rang in his memory: "Über allen Gipfeln ist Ruh" (Over all the hilltops is quiet now). Memories of lifelong observance transformed this pagan poem into a Jewish prayer: "Over all the hilltops is the word of God." This moving story summarized his advice to Reform spiritual leaders: "How grateful I am to God that there is a duty to worship, a law to remind my distraught mind that it is time to think of God, time to disregard my ego for at least a moment!"[41]

Knowing his audience, Heschel anticipated a number of standard objections to religious law. First, he rejected "the assumption that either you observe all or nothing." He dismissed "the assumption that every iota of the law was revealed to Moses at Sinai." He emphasized "the role of the sages in interpreting the word of the Bible and their power to issue new ordinances." In these respects, progressive Judaism could be compatible with a modern Orthodoxy. He also defined the limits of rationalist philosophy. He formulated a phrase, based on Kierkegaard's famed "leap of faith," in which "[a] Jew is asked to take *a leap of action* rather than *a leap of thought:* to surpass his needs, to do more than he understands in order to understand more than he does. . . . Through the ecstasy of deeds he learns to be certain of the presence of God."[42]

Prayer was too grave a responsibility, he insisted, to depend upon impulse, or even kavanah: "I am not always in the mood to pray. I do not always have the vision and the strength to say a word in the presence of God. But when I am weak, it is the law that gives me the strength; when my vision is dim, it is duty that gives me insight."[43]

Then Heschel made a tactical error, giving in to his polemical impulses and offending many listeners. To a recent survey by Rabbi Morton Berman that asserted, "'Reform Judaism is determinedly engaged in helping to meet a fundamental need of every human being for *symbolism* and *ceremonialism*' and 'for the poetry and beauty, for the mysticism and drama' which these provide for the satisfaction of man's emotional hunger," Heschel responded with sarcasm: "I must confess that I have difficulty translating 'ceremonies' into Hebrew. Customs—*minhagim*—have given us a lot of trouble in the past. *Minhagim* have often stultified Jewish life. According to Rabbenu Tam, the word *minhag* [Hebrew, *MNHG*] consists of the same four letters as the world *gehinom* [Hebrew, *GHNM*, hell]." This was a dig at American Reform, whose founder, Isaac Mayer Wise, as Heschel well knew, had published in 1856 a radically revised prayer book entitled *Minhag America.*[44]

For Heschel, the ideology of "customs and ceremonies," a staple of Reform religious education, was heresy, no substitute for "Torah": "Too often a ceremony is the homage which disbelief pays to faith. Do we want such homage? Judaism does not stand on ceremonies." Jewish observance was justified only by reference to the real, living God. Heschel concluded by supporting the growing tendency toward accepting "a code of practice required by every Reform Jew." He quoted from the movement's *Union Prayer Book:* "Help us, O God, to banish from our hearts . . . self-sufficient leaning upon our own reason," and

"Enlighten our eyes in Thy law that we may cling to Thy commandments." And he ended: "May it be a *return* to a *halachic way of life*, not to customs and ceremonies."[45]

Reactions to Heschel's address were swift, as they had been at the Conservative meeting earlier that week. Several rabbis rose to their feet and berated him for rejecting the humanistic tenets of Reform so violently. Heschel was again stunned, naively expecting his audience to be capable of greater self-examination.[46]

The following year several HUC students who had heard Heschel's controversial address at the CCAR meeting invited him to Cincinnati for a speech and a frank discussion. Heschel addressed them informally, mixing warmth, disdain, and hope for American Reform Judaism. Heschel made his most pointed critique through a humorous story from the Hasidic rebbe Simha Bunem of Przysucha, citing the Mishnah "If a beggar evokes pity, pretending that he is lame or blind, then he will really become lame or blind" as punishment because he deceives people.[47]

Heschel went on:

Simha Bunem then told this story about Mishka, a Russian peasant. Once the other peasants decided to play a joke on him and got him dead drunk. They took him to a church, dressed him in priest's garb and sat him in the priest's chair near the altar. When Mishka awoke, still groggy from alcohol and barely able to move, he noticed that he looked like a priest. But he vaguely recalled that he was just a peasant. He must still be asleep, dreaming of being a priest. But maybe it was the other way around.

Mishka was thoroughly confused. Being very shrewd, he recalled that when he went to church, the priest would read from a big book, for only a priest was able to read. So he decided to open the book; if he could read it, he was a priest; if not, he would be a peasant. When he opened the book, saw many letters in it, and could not read a single one. Aha! That meant he was a peasant and was just dreaming of being a priest. But how could that be, since he was fully awake?

Then the truth dawned on him. He was a priest; being a peasant was a dream. And as to his being able to read like priests, who says priests can read? They only pretend to!

Simha Bunem's parable posed the supreme question: Who is an authentic rabbi? Heschel's point was painfully clear: though most Reform rabbis could not read the Book of Tradition, they still believed that they were rabbis.

9

A Jewish Summa Theologica (1952–1956)

We have to press the religious consciousness with questions, compelling
man to understand and to unravel the meaning of what is taking place
in his life as it stands at the divine horizon. By penetrating the
consciousness of the pious man, we may conceive the reality behind it.
—Heschel, *God in Search of Man* (1955)

THE 1950S WERE THE YEARS OF HESCHEL'S MOST INTENSE CREATIVITY. THE
manuscript of *Man Is Not Alone* had expanded to include a second, more massive volume, a global interpretation of Judaism that was eventually entitled
God in Search of Man. In the meantime, he fashioned his speeches of 1952–53
into *Man's Quest for God: Studies in Prayer and Symbolism.* (Some students
teasingly referred to these titles as "Heschel's hide-and-seek.") As he consolidated his theological revolution, various branches of American Judaism were
exploring his answers to their problems of Jewish identity.[1]

Orthodoxy on the Defensive

In addition to his encounters with the Conservative and Reform movements, Heschel was engaging with the worlds of American Jewish Orthodoxy.
Among these traditionalist thinkers, Heschel found a more sympathetic audience, in addition to implicit criticism.

Jewish Forum, a New York monthly founded in 1917, was the first to introduce Heschel to the strictly observant public. The journal's byline—"Devoted
to safeguarding democracy by the united aid of Jew and non-Jew"—suggested
an editorial policy of open-mindedness. But the editors sometimes protected
Orthodoxy with extremist zeal. In the July 1952 issue they featured a severe
polemic, "Judaism and the 'Lost' Intellectuals," which denounced many of
Heschel's friends.

The author, Charles Raddock, was a Jewish journalist and "managing editor
of the leading anti-Communist labor newspaper in the United States." According to Raddock, genuine Judaism had to measure up to Talmudic rigor and Maimonides' thirteen principles of faith. He ranted against what he called "social
butterflies, with literary genius, residing in Jewish New York, from which they
send out their brain-bled books to an indifferent Mid-western, Southern Anglo-
Saxon intelligentzia [*sic*]." Among Raddock's targets were Hayim Greenberg,
whom he accused of "sentimental Jewishness," and Martin Buber, who advocated "vacuous, inconsequential and unpragmatic 'Godliness,' or pseudo-
Christian, Zend-Avestaic religiosity."[2]

Responses to Raddock's piece appeared in the September 1952 (Rosh
Hashanah 5713) issue. Generally favorable to his standards for religious
learning were Aaron Zeitlin, identified as a columnist for *Jewish Day,* who
supported Torah study but made an exception for English translations, and
Erich Gutkind, a German Jewish thinker, who presented a cogent defense of
"outsiders" to religious tradition; he praised scholars and philosophers such

as Hermann Cohen, Franz Rosenzweig, and Gershom Scholem, who attracted readers to Judaism, as well as Buber, whose Bible translation with Rosenzweig "reveals an extraordinary insight into the ultimates of the Torah." Less indulgent reactions arrived from Irving Howe, the secularist literary critic, who denounced religion as such, deploring "that desiccating sentimentality which prevails in the American Jewish world," and Fritz Kaufmann, who dismissed Raddock's defensive Orthodoxy as "the grave of an ossified idol." Emil Fackenheim, in rejecting Raddock's "virulent attacks on respected thinkers," nonetheless urged traditionalists "to show that Orthodox Judaism is capable of resolving [the problems of modern intellectuals]." Recognizing that halakhah was the issue on which many Jews split, Fackenheim was seeking ways to reconcile observance and modernity. In this he was joined by Heschel, who had not been targeted by Raddock's harangue.[3]

That same issue of *Jewish Forum* carried a major review essay on Heschel, however. The author, calling himself "Dayyan Al-Yahud" (Judge of the Jews, a title attributed to Abraham ben Nathan, the twelfth-century Talmudic scholar and *dayyan* in Fostat, Egypt), proclaimed Heschel the new voice for modern Orthodox Judaism, as Niebuhr had pronounced him for the Gentile public. The pseudonymous reviewer, widely learned in the classic sources, described Heschel as both devout and worldly, "unconventional." Displaying intimate knowledge of Heschel's upbringing in "the Warschawiansky milieu" as well as the contemporary American Jewish scene, Al-Yahud carefully examined *The Earth Is the Lord's, The Sabbath,* and *Man Is Not Alone.* He judged that Heschel's chief "weakness" was his tendency to exaggerate antitheses: "This extreme presentation is, to put it mildly, more than a bit on the *overwrought side.*" The critic then corrected some of Heschel's scholarly references, citing Philo, Plato, medieval Jewish philosophy, and Talmudic, Midrashic, Kabbalistic, and Hasidic literature. (Previously only Trude Weiss-Rosmarin had challenged Heschel's learning.)[4]

Al-Yahud highlighted two of Heschel's central ideas, the sanctity of time over space and the partnership of God and humankind. He looked forward to Heschel's next book, which he hoped would be "a more comprehensive and adequate exposition of Judaism," concluding, *"Heschel alone*—with a vision aimed at the infinite, never compromising, never satisfied, always striving—is the fitting contemporary thinker to give the world this long felt desideratum." Although the review was complete in itself, Al-Yahud published three more parts in later issues, consisting of "minor corrections, chosen at random" from Heschel's three books, again backed up with references. He also analyzed their literary style. Overall, he praised Heschel as a source of holiness: "One has to be blind not to see the inner hidden light and not to perceive the Shekhinah, which may be revealed to us in the land of Medinat Israel" (the state of Israel).[5]

Although Heschel was not yet ready to produce the "comprehensive" account of Judaism envisioned by Al-Yahud, by the fall of 1953 he had begun to envisage a scholarly history of the early Hasidic movement (1720–72) that would reach beyond the Jewish world. The life, teachings, and influence of the Baal Shem Tov and his disciples were at the core of Heschel's identity, and since the late 1940s, while completing his first American books, he had been laying the groundwork for this chronicle.

In fact, Heschel had begun his project of preserving the Hasidic ideal even earlier, in Europe, when he started collecting Hasidic books and manuscripts. (He was forced to abandon most of them in Warsaw.) In the United States he found significant holdings at the library of Hebrew Union College in Cincinnati as well as at the Jewish Theological Seminary and YIVO in New York. He acquired many precious volumes for his personal collection from rare booksellers like Yakir Beigeleisen and Samuel Kestenbaum in New York. To supplement these resources, Heschel conceived the idea of establishing a Hasidic archive to be housed at YIVO, and the project was inaugurated in 1949.[6]

Heschel enlisted four prominent Hasidic rebbes, three of them close relatives, to solicit documents and testimonies for the archive. Rabbis Yehudah Aryeh Leib Perlow, the Novominsker rebbe; Mordecai Shlomo Friedman, the Boyaner rebbe; Abraham Joshua Heschel, the Kopitzhinitzer rebbe; and Chaim Halberstam, the Czechover rebbe (who was not related to Heschel), jointly signed a letter that acclaimed Heschel's high standing, referring to him as *Ha-Rav Ha-Hasid* (Hasidic rabbi). In their eyes, Heschel was a worthy descendant of his namesake, the Apter Rav. As researchers Heschel hired Israel Friedman, a cousin, and Moses Shulvass, professor of history at the College of Jewish Studies (later Spertus College) in Chicago, a friend from Warsaw and Berlin. They helped recover oral traditions and made photostats of manuscripts, letters, stories, and sayings; the originals remained in the owners' reverential care.[7]

As the basis for the history Heschel began to publish biographical monographs in Yiddish and Hebrew for scholars with the requisite cultural knowledge. Unlike his writings in English for a general readership, he conceived these biographies in the Wissenschaft manner: factual accounts supported by hundreds of footnotes. Perhaps these academic studies, in which matters of detail could not be disputed, were attempts to impress Gershom Scholem and other historians and so pave the way for scholarly acceptance of a lyrical book that would be more detailed than *The Earth Is the Lord's.*[8]

Heschel inaugurated his series in the 1949 *Yivo Bleter* with a study in Yiddish on Rabbi Pinchas of Koritz, a close associate of the Baal Shem Tov's. He outlined the earliest ideology of the movement and the tense relations between Reb Pinchas and the Baal Shem Tov's successor, Dov Baer, the Maggid of Mezeritch. (Heschel published a slightly different version of the article in Hebrew in a volume honoring the publisher Salman Schocken.) In 1950 Heschel's extensive study in Hebrew of Rabbi Gershon of Kuty, the Baal Shem's brother-in-law and confidant, appeared in the *Hebrew Union College Annual.* He detailed Gershon's immigration to the Land of Israel in 1747 and documented his international contacts with Jewish community leaders from Poland to Constantinople.[9]

A third monograph, in Yiddish, was the most personal. "Unknown Documents in the History of Hasidism" appeared in the 1952 *Yivo Bleter.* In it Heschel explained how he came to establish the archive. He printed eleven family documents, among them a letter from his maternal ancestor, Rabbi Levi Yitzhak of Berditchev, dated 1801, that referred to Rabbi Abraham Yehoshua Heschel, later the rebbe of Apt, praising his initiatives in collecting money for Jews in the Land of Israel. Even more intimate was the *Tenai'im* (engagement contract) of the Apter Rav, dated 1764, which contained intriguing details of books, clothing, finances, and the dynasty's genealogy. One footnote described the special Sabbath clothing (a satin *kapote* [robe] with *strokas* [silver clasps]) of his uncle, the Novominsker rebbe of Warsaw, whom Heschel had visited almost daily as a child. With utmost discretion, and only for readers of Hebrew or Yiddish, Heschel began to display his family's sacred linen. Together these erudite monographs, with their passion for particulars, bear witness to his drive not only to preserve the historical influence of his ancestors but also, more important, to resurrect their spiritual presence.[10]

To support his project of turning these monographs into a book-length history, Heschel applied for a Guggenheim Fellowship in the fall of 1953. He chose his most prestigious supporters to write letters of recommendation, each of whom addressed a different aspect of his activities. Reinhold Niebuhr asserted: "I regard Dr. Heschel as one of the most creative Jewish theologians of our day." Julian Morgenstern, now president emeritus of HUC, praised Heschel as "an earnest, high-minded and competent scholar." The artistically handwritten letter from Martin Buber authoritatively summarized Heschel's qualifications: "a vast and authentic knowledge, a reliable intuition into the phenomena of religious life, the true scholarly spirit of text interpretation, and independent thinking."[11]

The most restrained assessment came from Herbert Schneider, philosophy professor at Columbia University: "I would be inclined to give him a chance. He is good chiefly for writing. Teaching and lecturing are not congenial to him and would distract him." Schneider added that the danger of Heschel's being "over-sympathetic" to his subject would be mitigated by other scholars, such as Buber, who could help him maintain objectivity.[12]

Inside help came from Roger Straus, a member of the Guggenheim Foundation's Board of Trustees, who wrote an official recommendation and also a personal note to Henry Allen Moe, who administered the awards: "I consider Dr. Heschel an absolutely first rate philosopher and writer and my belief is that he will achieve in wider circles what he has already achieved in certain academic circles."[13]

Heschel received the award in April 1954 as he was completing the manuscript of *God in Search of Man*. His stipend of four thousand dollars would cover the next academic year, September 1954 through August 1955. Finkelstein immediately wrote to congratulate him: "Such public recognition of your work will aid in education of the whole community and will be a source of joy to your many friends and admirers all over the country."[14]

Heschel worked on the book well into the 1960s. Over the years he placed slips of paper in numerous Hasidic books stored in the JTS special collections, planning to retrieve them as he wrote. But in 1966 a fire at the JTS library destroyed more than fifty thousand volumes and priceless manuscripts. As Heschel watched, with tears flowing down his cheeks, he told his student Arthur Green: "That is the end of my book on the Baal Shem Tov." Heschel never completed the project, nor did he finish the Hasidic Archive. In 1985 Samuel Dresner gathered translations of Heschel's articles in a collection entitled *The Circle of the Baal Shem Tov*. The archive project was revived in 1999, in another form, when Heschel's grandnephew, also named Abraham Joshua Heschel, established with YIVO the Zamler Project in Hasidic Communities in New York.[15]

"Heschel's Hide-and-Seek"

For two years Heschel had been struggling with his most ambitious project. He was under growing pressure to complete the "Philosophy of Judaism," whose title, *God in Search of Man*, had been generally accepted though it was still somewhat fluid. In May 1954 the Jewish Publication Society once again conveyed its impatience at the delay, and Heschel promised to deliver the manuscript in June, in time for publication the following year. It was about 70 percent prepared, he claimed, adding ominously: "But I know the book will only gain if I spent more time on it." Roger Straus and Solomon Grayzel continued to press him, but the author stubbornly maintained his independence. Grayzel was especially worried about the JPS marketing schedule, which had to take into account huge subscriber lists, book clubs, the Jewish holidays, and more.[16]

Heschel's intellectual challenges had been compounded by the need to provide documentation. Fritz Rothschild, now teaching at the Teachers Institute of the Seminary, had urged his senior colleague to add footnotes to his copious Judaic sources, many of which were quite rare. Rothschild correctly judged that the paucity of notes in *Man Is Not Alone* lent credence to the charge by careless or malicious critics that Heschel's thought was idiosyncratic or more compatible with Christianity than with Judaism. Heschel had undertaken the tremendous labor of supplementing the material supplied by his outstanding memory. A year had passed, and almost another.[17]

An unexpected worry was a matter of personal dignity. Heschel was offended that the JPS editorial board still required three outside readers to approve his manuscript before publication. Heschel appealed to Roger Straus and his JTS colleague Shalom Spiegel, professor of medieval Hebrew literature, both of whom dispatched indignant letters to Grayzel. Grayzel's prompt answer to Spiegel was conciliatory, but firm: "I must say that if the book had not been delayed for three years, this problem would never have arisen." Heschel brooded. Two weeks later he thanked Grayzel for his support for the book, but he was still annoyed: "Does [Salo W.] Baron submit each volume to readers?" Grayzel placated his author by reporting that the JPS Publications Committee had accepted the manuscript at its June meeting. In addition, Heschel was invited to join the committee, an invitation he accepted, attending his first meeting on 31 October.[18]

By July 1954 Heschel had completed his book on prayer and symbolism. This was a much easier project because most chapters were adapted from previous publications: his 1945 essay on prayer from the *Review of Religion;* his paper on symbolism for Finkelstein's JTS interfaith colloquium; and his two 1953 speeches to American rabbis. Heschel added a preface, and for chapter 2, "The Person and the Word," he revised two early articles on prayer that were originally written in German and Hebrew. Scribner's officially launched

Man's Quest for God in November 1954, and the Jewish Publication Society placed an order for two thousand copies to offer to its members. Finkelstein wrote to congratulate Heschel: "This book will help bring many back to our faith."[19]

Man's Quest for God, consolidated Heschel's critique of American Judaism, which he judged to be handicapped by lack of attention to the inner life. Enhancing the practice and understanding of prayer would complete the social aspects of observance, bringing people to a fuller awareness of the holy dimension of life.

Sensitivity to words was the key to this transformation of consciousness; words had independent dignity and power. By projecting our emotions into inherited prayers, we could bring out their richness and, reciprocally, enrich our perception of the world and of ourselves: "A word is a focus, a point at which meanings meet and from which meanings seem to proceed. In prayer, as in poetry, we turn to the words, not to use them as signs for things, but to see things in the light of the words." Poetry, for Heschel, was prayer in potential. Prayer might begin as an act of empathy, identification with a printed text. But the next phase of worship surpassed imagination. A person praying with kavanah, with deep intention, could actualize an immanent force: "It is the spiritual power of the praying man that makes manifest what is dormant in the text." Heschel sought to convince readers that "words of prayer are repositories of the spirit."[20]

At the same time, he emphasized "the ineffable," that which lay beyond the connotations of poetry. In prayer one realized most acutely the outer limits of language: "In no other act does man experience so often the disparity between the desire for expression and the means of expression as in prayer. . . . What the word can no longer yield, man achieves through the fullness of his powerlessness." Assuming the distance between divine and human, the achieved human "fullness" was a more forceful longing for the absolute.[21]

At Samuel Dresner's suggestion, Heschel used a slightly revised version of his 1944 essay on World War II as the final chapter of *Man's Quest for God*. Now entitled "The Meaning of This Hour," it had been updated with an allusion to the ongoing McCarthy hearings, which were being broadcast on television: "God will return to us when we shall be willing to let Him in—into our banks and factories, into our Congress and clubs, *into our courts and investigating committees* [emphasis mine], into our homes and theaters." Heschel exemplified the spirit of genuine prayer, which fostered ethical responsibility, by defending civil liberties, the heart of American democracy.[22]

The same month that *Man's Quest for God* was published, Heschel became active in interfaith dialogue under the auspices of the Religious Education Association, an academic and professional forum founded in 1903 that held yearly conventions and published a quarterly journal. Heschel joined round-table discussions at Columbia University on Judeo-Christian values in higher education. Representing the theology section, along with Wilhelm Pauck of Union Theological Seminary and John J. Dougherty of Immaculate Conception Seminary, he impressed the academic elite. George N. Shuster, president of Hunter College, chaired the meeting, which included presidents or ranking administrators from Columbia, Hamilton College, the City College of New York, and Fordham University. Others included faculty in the natural sciences, the social sciences, history, classics, philosophy, religion, medicine, law, education, journalism, engineering, and theology.[23]

The reviews of *Man's Quest for God* confirmed Heschel's appeal to Christians. Some general praise appeared in advance notices, then Will Herberg reviewed the book in *Theology Today,* a Christian periodical aimed at a well-informed readership, in which he highlighted Heschel's spiritual radicalism: "Heschel moderates his drastic criticism of the present-day synagogue—more in the printed version than in his spoken addresses—but in the end he cannot help exclaiming: 'Better prayer without a synagogue than a synagogue without prayer.' No more shattering judgment of American religious life—and not merely Jewish—can be imagined."[24]

Maurice Friedman, whose recent book on Buber was gaining acclaim, developed an overview in the widely circulated *Congress Weekly,* published by the American Jewish Congress. Trained in literature and culture as well as philosophy and theology, Friedman underlined the connection between Heschel's writing method and the dynamics of religious reflection: "What was new about these books was not so much their subject matter as their way of thinking and their style."[25]

And for the first time comments on Heschel appeared in a publication whose main purpose was interfaith understanding. An admiring though impressionistic essay, "Heschel's Conception of Prayer," by Edward Synan, S.J., appeared in the inaugural volume of *The Bridge: A Yearbook of Judeo-Christian Studies.* Edited by John M. Oesterreicher, a priest from a German Jewish background, this Catholic initiative aimed to publish articles by scholars of both faiths.[26]

Within the Jewish world, the ideological battle lines were already drawn. Ira Eisenstein's forthright review in *The Reconstructionist* announced candidly: Heschel has "never before come out so clearly against what we believe and for what we have ceased to believe." Heschel's major failing, he noted (as did Dayyan Al-Yahud), was a tendency to exaggerate oppositions, which Eisenstein himself further exaggerated as "a choice between a return to orthodox acceptance of literal revelation and a flight from religion altogether." The majority of the present generation, he claimed, "are repelled" by that approach. What galled Eisenstein the most were Heschel's attacks against psychology and rationalism, which "'symbolized' God out of existence altogether." Eisenstein's final judgment was negative: Heschel "is doing religion in our time no service."[27]

A Jewish Summa Theologica

God in Search of Man was the turning point in Heschel's life and thought. The years spent writing it were necessary to enable him to sharpen his notions of depth theology, situational philosophy, awe, wonder, the ineffable, and insight that had emerged from *Man Is Not Alone*. Heschel's numerous source notes validated the book's subtitle, "A Philosophy of Judaism." An entire Judaica library, of both classic and rare sources, seemed to be cataloged in its pages. In subsequent years Heschel developed essays, articles, and speeches from sections of this germinal book.[28]

The saga of Heschel's tardy completion of *God in Search of Man* repeats the pattern set with the first volume. Following acceptance of the book by the JPS Publications Committee in July 1954, Heschel promised in November (when *Man's Quest for God* appeared), that he would deliver a completed manuscript by the following April, in time for the JPS production schedule and promotions geared to the High Holy Days. Straus masterminded the arrangements from his side of the copublication. [29]

In March 1955, Heschel assured Straus that the manuscript would be ready "early in June." But he caught his sponsor by surprise: "The book will be some 20,000 words longer than MAN IS NOT ALONE." Finally, on 27 April, Heschel signed the contract with Farrar, Straus and Cudahy; Seymour Siegel was the author's witness.[30]

There were additional delays. The pressures of completing *God in Search of Man* did not prevent Heschel from bringing out translations of some of his European writings. In June 1955 he placed "The Last Years of Maimonides," the final chapter of his 1935 biography, in the *National Jewish Monthly*, a B'nai B'rith publication.[31]

By August, he still had not completed the manuscript of *God in Search of*

Man. Lesser Zussman, in charge of production at JPS, commiserated with Pat Van Doren, the production manager of Farrar, Straus: "A December date will throw our Fall schedule completely cockeyed, but I know that this is Heschel's fault and not yours. Heaven protect us from its own mystics." More delays ensued. Grayzel read the galley proofs during the High Holy Days, reassuring Heschel on 4 October, during Sukkot, "I was delighted to see that this book reads more easily than *Man Is Not Alone.* Needless to say I liked it." The official publication date was postponed until 23 January 1956. In the meantime, Heschel turned to yet another major project, an expanded translation of his doctoral thesis on the prophets for JPS, which took him several years to complete.[32]

Roger Straus and Lesser Zussman saw *God in Search of Man* into print; they ironed out the finances, launched a publicity campaign, and distributed the book. Early in October 1955 Straus sent out proofs for advance reviews or magazine excerpts. Among the first to receive them was *Commentary*, which without explanation declined to print a selection. The Jewish Publication Society published a few passages in its "Bookmark" announcement and in November ordered 5,500 volumes for JPS members.[33]

Advance reviews, published in journals for librarians, emphasized the book's wide appeal. The *Library Journal* praised Heschel's universality. From *Kirkus* came a vague but enthusiastic overview: "This is an extraordinarily stimulating book both to the mind and to the spirit, and to Jews and Gentiles alike."[34]

In *God in Search of Man*, Heschel perfected the style and narrative strategy needed for his broader scope. The book is divided into three parts, "God" (chapters 1–16); "Revelation" (chapters 17–27); and "Response" (chapters 28–42). Chapters were further divided into subtitled sections, which facilitated slow, meditative reading.

The intellectual itinerary traced in part 1, "God," culminated in a dramatic performance of divine inspiration. The central chapter, 13, "God in Search of Man," reiterated the mystical encounter of *Man Is Not Alone*, but with textual sources added as validation. Heschel began with a theological assertion: "For God is not always silent, and man is not always blind. His glory fills the world; His spirit hovers above the waters. There are moments in which, to use a Talmudic phrase, heaven and earth kiss each other; in which there is a lifting of the veil at the horizon of the known, opening a vision of what is eternal in time. Some of us have at least once experienced the momentous realness of God. Some of us have at least caught a glimpse of the beauty, peace, and power that flow through the souls of those who are devoted to Him. . . . The voice of Sinai goes on for ever: 'These words the Lord spoke unto all your assembly in the mount out of the midst of the fire, of the cloud, and of the thick darkness, with *a great voice that goes on for ever.'* "

Integrating intuition and sacred history, he testified that Holy Spirit (ruah hakodesh) was still available. A footnote cited the rabbinic authority: "Deuteronomy 5:19, according to the Aramaic translation of Onkelos and Jonathan ben Uzziel and to the interpretation of *Sanhedrin,* 17b; *Sotah,* 10b; and to the first interpretation of Rashi." Heschel's rendition of divine revelation combined experience, logic, and multiple textual references like these. He repeated sources cited in his 1950 Hebrew monograph on medieval manifestations of ruah hakodesh in which he had pledged himself to "guide other beings."[35]

Heschel detailed his theory of biblical interpretation in part 2, "Revelation." As a flexible traditionalist who rejected literal readings, he understood prophetic utterances as "understatements" pointing to God's overwhelming reality: "Who shall presume to be an expert in discerning what is divine and what is but 'a little lower' than divine?" He rejected the notion that the words of Scripture were "coextensive and identical with the words of God." Unambiguously, he insisted that "the surest way of misunderstanding revelation is to take it literally, to imagine that God spoke to the prophet on a long-distance telephone." Rather, God still spoke through sacred texts: "the Bible is *holiness in words.* . . . It is as if God took these Hebrew words and breathed into them of His power, and the words became a live wire charged with His spirit. To this very day they are hyphens between heaven and earth."[36]

Heschel's own language, like that of the Bible, was not literal and descriptive but rather responsive, often poetic, seeking to inspire the reader. His philosophy of religion was accordingly situational, taking into account the total human condition before God. His notion of what he called depth theology, still relatively undeveloped, focused on intuitions that precede reflection and statements of faith.

Heschel applied depth theology to his consideration of Jewish observance in part 3, "Response." He surveyed basic principles such as the mitzvot (in the chapter "A Science of Deeds") and the polarities of inwardness and law, spontaneity and regularity, and the like. He again took a stand against the thoughtless performance of rituals, what he called "religious behaviorism." He backed up his view with an erudite survey of the "ancient controversy among scholars of Jewish law about the necessity of kavanah to validate religious acts," which he relegated to a note.[37]

Heschel justified his acceptance of the irreconcilable inner conflicts of Judaism, as well as his own contradictions and his pluralism, in chapter 33, "The Problem of Polarity." A distinctive summary sentence defined authentic Judaism in terms of oppositions such as "the polarity of ideas and events, of mitzvah and sin, of kavanah and deed, of regularity and spontaneity, of uniformity and individuality, of halakhah and agada, of law and inwardness, of love and fear, of understanding and obedience, of joy and discipline, of the good and the evil drive, of time and eternity, of the world and the world to come, of revelation and response, . . . of man's quest for God and God in search of man." Antithesis continued to be his key mode of argument. In later essays and speeches, Heschel applied apparent opposites to help resolve ideological clashes within the community.[38]

Heschel's probing analysis of "The Problem of Evil" (chapter 36) emphasized the ever-present danger of moral indifference: "Modern man may be characterized as a being who is callous to catastrophes. . . . All that is left to us is our being horrified at the loss of our sense of horror." Good and evil are always mixed. The inevitable "confusion of good and evil" can be overcome only by a striving for holiness.[39]

The three concluding chapters—"Freedom," "The Spirit of Judaism," and "The People Israel"—were brief and relatively undeveloped, but they set forth ideas that Heschel would elaborate in later years. Among them were his argument that the essence of human freedom was the transcendence of vanity and self-interest in service to God; that the Sabbath, as "the art of surpassing civilization," would help people to return to Judaism; and that Diaspora Jews had a "unique association" with the Jewish state: "Even before Israel became a people, the land was preordained for it. What we have witnessed in our own days is a reminder of the power of God's mysterious promise to Abraham." National events such as the civil rights struggle and world crises like the Six-Day War and America's intervention in Vietnam would lead Heschel to develop many of these terse formulations.[40]

In the book's concluding words, Heschel proclaimed "the universal relevance of Judaism, . . . its demands upon the chance of man to remain human." To be a Jew, part of "the chosen people," was to serve God's vision of justice and compassion for the entire world: "We do not say that we are a superior people. . . . It signifies not a quality inherent in the people but a relationship between the people and God." It was only later, after he became involved in political protests, that Heschel further refined this theme.[41]

National Renown

After last-minute shipping problems, *God in Search of Man* became available to the public soon after the New Year. As Heschel had hoped, it found an audience among Gentile as well as Jewish readers. On 16 January, the publicity department of Farrar, Straus and Cudahy launched the book at a luncheon featuring as guest speaker the Episcopal bishop James Pike, dean of the Cathedral of Saint John the Divine in New York, and "a select group of theologians and religious editors." A month later Heschel was acclaimed in the Sunday *New York Times* book section. The Unitarian A. Powell Davies, of All Souls Church in Washington, D.C., praised Heschel's Jewish response to "the perpetual emergencies of human existence, the rare cravings of the spirit, the eternal voice of God to which the demands of religion are an answer."[42]

More widespread recognition came with a feature article in *Time* magazine on 19 March 1956, embellished with a photograph of the author. Heschel was portrayed as a modern Jewish sage, joining the pantheon of Rosenzweig and Buber: "Twinkle-eyed Dr. Heschel, a small man located beneath a bush of grey hair, labors in a blue haze of cigar smoke, and writes prose that sings and soars in the warm, intuitive tradition of the great 18th-century Hasidic leaders from whom he is descended. His just published book, *God In Search of Man* (Farrar, Straus and Cudahy; $5) is subtitled 'A Philosophy of Judaism,' but it speaks to all those men for whom the Bible is a holy book." Heschel had fulfilled Reinhold Niebuhr's prediction of 1951, becoming an authoritative source for Christians seeking to penetrate the spirit of Judaism. The following month, Niebuhr himself, prodded by Roger Straus, published an appreciative essay on the new book in the *Saturday Review of Literature*.[43]

A number of substantial review essays by both Christians and Jews confirmed the importance of Heschel's most ambitious book. In the influential Protestant journal *Christian Century,* Will Herberg cited Niebuhr to explain that Heschel's "philosophy" was really a "a kind of higher phenomenology of religion linked with a critical self-examination." Herberg agreed that Heschel stood alongside Rosenzweig and Buber in "calling for a return to authentic Jewish faith in a form relevant to contemporary life." Heschel's former students Marshall T. Meyer and Jack Riemer both published glowing reviews. Riemer, now assistant rabbi at the East Midwood Jewish Center in Brooklyn, summarized the book for *The Torch*, a magazine of the National Federation of Jewish Men's Clubs. Meyer, now studying at the Hebrew University, placed a review entitled "A Matter of Life and Death" in the English-language

Jerusalem Post. Meyer hoped that Heschel's approach to Judaism would "aid in awakening that most important spirit of self-examination in those who have long since lolled themselves into a deep sleep of spiritual inactivity as a result of a purely mechanical obeisance to the letter of the Law."[44]

The interfaith journal *Religious Education* published two reviews simultaneously, one by the Christian James Muilenburg, an Old Testament expert at Union Theological Seminary, and the other by Heschel's former student Maurice Friedman, who was now teaching at Sarah Lawrence College. (The reviews were followed by a review of *The Bridge*, which contained the article on Heschel by Edward Synan.) The Christian scholar was quite generous. Muilenburg praised *God in Search of Man* as "the greatest of [Heschel's] books," claiming, "By any standard it is a *great* book . . . a symphony, a literary classic like Dante's *Divine Comedy*, an epic or even, if I will not be misunderstood, a kind of *summa theologica*. What relieves such a characterization from extravagance is that the writer is heir to a great tradition, which he has appropriated and assimilated."[45]

Friedman was more measured in his praise. Considering Heschel in the light of the conflict between American liberalism and neo-orthodoxy, Friedman found *God in Search of Man*, "better and more tightly organized than the earlier volume" and Heschel's belief in the reality of divine revelation "a useful corrective to the tendency of much liberal Judaism to see historical events as merely symbols of a general idea, e.g., the Exodus as a symbol of liberty." But he regretted Heschel's "repeated emphasis on man's loneliness, his relatively little concern with the self's relations to other selves, and his tendency to speak as if the self stood in relation only to God."[46]

Herbert Schneider, who had urged the Guggenheim Foundation to give Heschel's Hasidic project "a chance," seemed to feel that the author had fulfilled his promise. Although his *Review of Religion* article outlined the central philosophical argument that, he wrote, "may be concealed in the book under scattered 'insights' and technical, rabbinical idioms," it ended with the firm statement that Heschel's theology, "though impressionistic in form of expression, is a sustained, philosophical analysis." Schneider's conclusion prepared the ground for Fritz Rothschild's systematic interpretation of Heschel's several books.[47]

In addition to enlarging his Christian audience Heschel had finally found a way to reach progressive or even nonreligious Jews. But he did so without alienating traditional Jews. Two intellectual leaders of modern Orthodox Jewry, Joseph H. Lookstein and Emanuel Rackman, both congregational rabbis and professors at Yeshiva University, found in what they called Heschel's neo-Hasidism a potential model for "Torah-true" Jews during the Cold War.[48]

In the summer 1956 issue of *Judaism*, Lookstein, a professor of sociology and practical rabbinics, judged that Heschel, with his Hasidic experience, responded more authentically than Buber to the current religious crisis. Heschel had an "orientation to life which enables man to feel the unfailing presence of God"; this was "the only genuinely Jewish variety of Existentialism." Practically, this orientation led to ethical awareness, noted Lookstein, quoting this dramatic phrase from *God in Search of Man:* "One does not discuss the future of mankind in the atomic age . . . in the same way in which man discusses the weather."[49]

In 1954 Emanuel Rackman, assistant professor of political science, had published an essay in *Commentary* deploring the reduction of the holy Sabbath to a day of rest. Now, Rackman praised *God in Search of Man* in the religious Zionist magazine *Jewish Horizon*. Humorously defining himself as a repentant mitnagid, he admitted: "In the past the Chasidic movement enriched Judaism; in the present it is saving Judaism. Without Chasidic thought and commitment, Torah-true Jews would simply not be able to cope with the challenge of modernism." Heschel, he argued, spelled out "in detail" how "Jewish intellectuals" might successfully live in two civilizations, their ancestral one and the secular world.[50]

But Rackman also offered significant criticisms of Heschel that indicated why most Orthodox Jews preferred the halakhic approach of Joseph Soloveitchik. Although Heschel successfully demonstrated that halakhah "involved not only precise analysis of legal concepts but also an amalgam of *Aggadic* elements," he did not provide adequate illustrations, Rackman admitted. In addition, Heschel did not say enough about the Land of Israel, its holiness, "as unique in Jewish commitment as Torah and People." Rackman concluded on a positive note, however, praising Heschel for connecting "man's theology" and "God's anthropology." With the appreciative reviews by first Dayyan Al-Yahud and now Rackman and Lookstein, Heschel had the potential to become established as a thinker who could speak to and for modern Orthodox Jewry.[51]

As Heschel's influence grew in America, he was attracting students from abroad as well. Around 1953 Heschel met an Israeli student named Rivka Horwitz, who was seeking a sponsor for a Ph.D. dissertation on Jewish philosophy. A German Jew who had settled in Palestine in the 1930s with her family, she had been reared by her grandparents and sent to Mizrahi (religious Zionist) schools. In 1948 she attended the Hebrew University, where she studied with Julius Guttmann, Heschel's philosophy teacher at the Berlin Hochschule, and then Gershom Scholem. Horwitz became part of Scholem's inner circle of students, which also included Isadore Twersky, Ya'akov Levinger, Rivka Schatz Uffenheimer, and Yael Nadav. Scholem tried to persuade Horwitz to return to Germany to purchase libraries of defunct Jewish communities for the Hebrew University. When she had done this, he would agree to be her dissertation director. But Horwitz refused, seeking more independence, and came to New York instead.[52]

Horwitz knew Jack Riemer, who told her about Heschel, candidly warning her about his moodiness: "You have to meet Heschel. So simple, sometimes he's nice and sometimes he ignores people." She agreed, not knowing that Heschel and Scholem saw themselves as antagonists. Years earlier, in *Major Trends in Jewish Mysticism* (which Heschel reviewed in 1941), Scholem had denigrated Heschel's ancestor Rabbi Israel Friedman of Ruzhin. Writing about the last phase of Hasidism and its second-rate leaders, he described Heschel's regal forebear bluntly as "the greatest and the most impressive figure of classical Zaddikism, . . . the so-called Rabbi of Sadagora, . . . [who was] nothing but another Jacob Frank who has achieved the miracle of remaining an orthodox Jew." Despite Heschel's repeated requests, Scholem refused to alter his accusation, which identified his revered ancestor with the leader of a heretical eighteenth-century sect.[53]

When Horwitz came into Heschel's office, he tested her by asking about a number of Kabbalistic concepts and was impressed by her scholarly knowledge. "I am ready to work with you," he said, but first he wanted her to write a research paper on Baruch Kosover, an eighteenth-century Hasidic rabbi and Kabbalist. Horwitz's paper, written in excellent Hebrew, deeply impressed Heschel, who told others how brilliant she was, though to her he only said that the work was "fine."

Horwitz was accepted at the Teachers Institute to do a Master's degree (women were not allowed to do doctoral work at the Rabbinical School), but she chose instead to study religion at Columbia University, where she wrote a dissertation on Franz Rosenzweig. While she was in New York, she and Heschel formed a bond, but she was never close to him, or one of his disciples, perhaps because she was a woman, or perhaps because of Scholem's implicit presence. Horwitz and Heschel did not have long conversations or take walks together, and she was not invited to the Heschel home for Shabbat.

Nevertheless Horwitz's own work maintained a balance between Scholem, who preferred sober historical studies, and Heschel, who was more interested in constructing his own metaphysics and urged her to concentrate on theological issues, not factual details. But she remained Heschel's friend after she returned to Israel, promoting his works as a religious alternative to the authoritarian and politicized Judaism of Israel. As a professor at Ben Gurion University in the Negev, she reviewed the first two volumes of *Torah min ha-shamayim be-aspaklaryah shel ha-dorot* (Theology of Ancient Judaism, 1962, 1965; later translated as *Heavenly Torah*) and promoted Hebrew translations of Heschel's works.[54]

Part Three
Spiritual Radical

The prophet knew that religion could distort what the Lord demanded of man, that priests themselves had committed perjury by bearing false witness, condoning violence, tolerating hatred, calling for ceremonies instead of bursting forth with wrath and indignation at cruelty, deceit, idolatry, and violence.

—Heschel, *The Prophets* (1962)

THE EVENTS OF THE 1950S ELEVATED THE ASPIRATIONS OF AN INCREASINGLY restless American public. National prejudices, fears, and hopes tested the moral foundations of democracy. Internal insecurities, the Cold War, segregation and civil rights, and the obsessive space race further challenged Americans. President Eisenhower began his first term in 1953, following the conclusion of the Korean War but in the midst of the congressional anti-Communist hearings. In 1954 the Supreme Court ruled against segregation in public schools as coalitions of blacks and whites began insisting on equal rights for all Americans. The Soviet Union launched the satellite *Sputnik* in 1957, aggravating the Cold War and undermining confidence in the quality of American technology and education. As the decade advanced, these issues and the persistent fear of nuclear annihilation caused many Americans to seek novel means of spiritual renewal.

As the 1960s began, the national mood became more confident. At his presidential inauguration on 20 January 1961, John Fitzgerald Kennedy promised Americans that they were on the edge of a new frontier. Civil rights for African Americans became a mass movement under the banner of Martin Luther King, Jr., and his Southern Christian Leadership Conference (SCLC); their slogan, "Redeem the Soul of America," reflected a widespread commitment to the political process.

It was during these decades that Heschel found his public voice, speaking effectively to Jewish, interfaith, and national audiences. He adapted many of these speeches into essays for a wide audience on religious education, Jewish observance, and Israel and the Diaspora. In 1960 he made his White House debut at a conference on children and youth. In 1963 he was featured at the first "National Conference on Religion and Race," where he met King. Heschel's commitment to civil rights guided his pioneering support for Jews persecuted in the Soviet Union.

As Heschel became more visible, his physical appearance became more dramatic, which gave him further prominence in the visual media. A photograph of Heschel with civil rights leaders, including Ralph Bunche, Nobel laureate and undersecretary of the United Nations, and King at the historic Selma–Montgomery march of 1965 became his most enduring emblem: a bearded man with long, shaggy white hair, the image of a Hebrew prophet.

Heschel also began working with officials of the Roman Catholic Church, using his authority as a consultant for the American Jewish Committee to influence historical discussions on Jews and Judaism at the Second Vatican Council. Between 1961 and 1965 he was involved in intricate negotiations with Vatican officials, a story that will be told in Part 4.

Yet throughout this period of increased public activity, Heschel continued to advance his scholarly work, publishing four substantial books: *The Prophets* (1962), *Torah min ha-shamayim be-ispaklaryah shel ha-dorot* (Heavenly Torah As Refracted Through the Generations, 3 volumes, 1962, 1965, 1990), *Who Is Man?* (1965), and *The Insecurity of Freedom* (1966). The man who had sought to be a prophet to the Jews was becoming an "apostle to the Gentiles," an authoritative voice for all people.[1]

10
Building Bridges (1956–1959)

Man is on the verge of spiritual insanity. He does not know who he is.
Having lost a sense for what he is, he fails to grasp the meaning
of his fellow-man.
—Heschel, "Sacred Images of Man" (1958)

reflections. After his *Time* magazine profile, Christians as well as Jews began to regard him as an authentic biblical voice for social change. He influenced these constituencies through essays and lecture tours; he also began to take part in national interfaith organizations such as the Religious Education Association (REA), whose annual conventions in Chicago attracted participants from all backgrounds. He adapted his message to his different audiences, but always it focused on how authentic religion might transform every aspect of life.

For Jews, Heschel stressed the need to renew spiritual sensitivity. In 1956 he initiated a series of writings on pedagogical values with an article in *Adult Jewish Education,* "Teaching Religion to American Jews." Alluding to the tendency toward secularization throughout the Jewish world, he noted that in prewar Poland, Germany, and America, "spiritual problems were considered irrelevant." Now people were returning to their religion, but Judaism remained in a precarious state. He warned that most efforts to teach Judaism failed because educators did not ask the right questions. They had to impress upon students that nothing less than spiritual survival was at stake: "Am I anything more than just a physical being? What does it mean to be a Jew? What does it mean to be responsible for three thousand years of living experience?"[1]

For a wider, primarily Christian readership, he published "The Biblical View of Reality" in a collected volume, *Contemporary Problems in Religion.* This synthesis presented his depth theology in less specifically Jewish terms, focusing on "concrete events, acts, insights, of that which is immediately given to the pious man." Just as the biblical person sees the world "in relation to God," so too radical amazement can allow all people to achieve insight. Heschel played on the Christian idea that to those who deny Christ, faith is "foolishness" and "scandal" as he referred ironically to "the *foolishness of unbelief,* . . . the *scandal of indifference to God.*"[2]

Interfaith Initiatives

Heschel also popularized his views on the lecture circuit. In February 1957 he spoke at the annual Interfaith Religious Forum sponsored by Smith College, the eminent women's school in Northampton, Massachusetts. On three consecutive evenings he lectured on "God in Search of Man," "Man Is Not Alone," and "Sanctification of Time," followed by a coffee hour and discussion.

Heschel enjoyed these interactions, which allowed him to summarize his approach to Judaism and to religion in general. The Smith College student newspaper, the *Sophian*, quoted him as stressing his interfaith theme, what we now call pluralism: "There are many ways to God; it is the height of arrogance to deny the sanctity of any great religious tradition." When the reporter asked about "the current religious revival in the United States," Heschel responded with barbed wit, declaring that he noticed "only a revival of religious interest, not of religion."[3]

At the same time Heschel's standing among Christian intellectuals was confirmed by an invitation to present "A Hebrew Evaluation of Reinhold Niebuhr" in a volume of the Library of Living Theologians, an authoritative series of scholarly studies of leading thinkers. For the article Heschel adapted several pages from the manuscript of *God in Search of Man*, still in progress, into an incisive study of moral ambiguity, which he called "the confusion of good and evil." He began by emphasizing elements common to Judaism and Christianity: Niebuhr's harsh theology of original sin, "the mystery of evil," and his antagonism to "sentimentality" and "unrealism" were congruent, wrote Heschel, with certain Jewish mystical texts, the biblical books of the prophets Isaiah and Habakkuk, and the Psalms. Yet although he agreed that the world remained unredeemed, Heschel rejected Niebuhr's contention that human beings were incapable of acts of goodness without divine grace.[4]

Good and evil were mixed; they were not entirely separable, according to Heschel: "More frustrating than the fact that evil is real, mighty, and tempting is the fact that it thrives so well in the disguise of the good, and that it can draw its nutriment from the life of the holy." Hasidism, with its sensitivity to inwardness, was particularly open to acknowledging the ambiguities of human virtue. He refined Niebuhr's dualistic analysis with the notion of "polarity," which posited simultaneous discord, paradox, and unresolved mysteries. For Heschel, self-centeredness or "vanity" was humankind's basic flaw, allowing ego needs to take precedence over the demands of righteousness. Self-interest could be "redeemed," however, by action, fulfilling the mitzvot. This was the hope offered by Judaism: "The holiness of Abraham, Isaac, and Jacob, the humility of Moses [is] the rock on which they rely. *There are good moments in history that no subsequent evil may obliterate.*" Heschel concluded diplomatically: "It is, therefore, difficult from the point of view of Biblical theology to sustain Niebuhr's view, *plausible and profound as it is.*" In the end, Niebuhr's life and deeds were more authoritative than his theology.[5]

In 1957, Heschel was also honored by Protestant colleagues at the first joint meeting of the faculties of the Jewish Theological Seminary and Union Theological Seminary, arranged by Louis Finkelstein. Papers were delivered by two Union professors, the Old Testament scholar James Muilenburg and Niebuhr, both of whom praised Heschel's writings, unintentionally provoking some resentment among his JTS colleagues, especially Finkelstein, who considered Heschel a rival. Despite all Finkelstein's efforts toward interfaith collaboration, it was Heschel who was compelling the interest of the Christian public.[6]

But the most significant statement to come out of the joint meeting, in what turned out to be a historic moment in Jewish-Christian relations, was Niebuhr's denunciation of the Christian mission to convert the Jews as simply "wrong." He justified the spiritual autonomy of Judaism by applying the "two covenant theory": the view that God had revealed his will both at Mount Sinai and in the incarnation of Jesus, and that these were separate but equally valid incursions of the divine. In addition, Niebuhr hailed "the thrilling emergence of the State of Israel."[7]

This interfaith triumph cemented the firm (and mostly undocumented) friendship of Niebuhr and Heschel, two genuine American spiritual radicals. Until Niebuhr's first stroke in February 1952, Heschel's relationship with his influential reviewer had been formal: he signed a copy of *The Earth Is the Lord's* to "Dr. Reinhold Niebuhr, in friendship and esteem." But after Niebuhr gave his historic paper to the joint faculty meeting, the two saw each other regularly, frequently taking long walks together along Riverside Drive or Broadway. With amusement and some anxiety Niebuhr's wife, Ursula, a professor of religion at Barnard College, would watch her tall, stooping husband walking beside Heschel and worry that the smaller rabbi would not be able to hold him up if he toppled. Ursula Niebuhr considered Heschel her husband's closest friend during the last twelve years of his life.[8]

The November 1957 convention of the Religious Education Association afforded Heschel an ideal opportunity to define what I call his "sacred humanism." Academics and leaders of the nation's three major faiths (Judaism, Protestantism, and Catholicism) gathered to reflect upon the year's topic, "Images of Man in Current Culture and Tasks of Religion and Education." It was a summit meeting of religiously engaged thinkers, many of whom would become part of Heschel's spiritual community.

At the assembly on sacred images Heschel advanced his view that in order to resolve the present crisis of meaning we needed to develop a philosophy of the human: "Post-modern man is more deeply perplexed about the nature of man than his ancestors. He is on the verge of spiritual insanity. He does not know who he is." Pointing to the danger of defining humanity in physical terms, he drew an analogy between a materialistic definition in the *Encyclopaedia Britannica* ("Man is a seeker after the greatest degree of comfort for the least necessary expenditure of energy") and a view held in pre-Nazi Germany, which he had experienced in Berlin: "The human body contains a sufficient amount of fat to make seven cakes of soap, enough iron to make a medium-sized nail."[9]

For Heschel, the chief need in religious education was to "become aware of the sacred image of man." Borrowing from *Man's Quest for God*, he stated that a human being was the only "real symbol" of the divine, a combination of dust and the divine spark. Human life was thus holy. This theological insight held immense consequences: "The fate of the human species depends upon our degree of reverence for the individual man."[10]

Heschel argued that such a vision was already present in the Bible's universalistic vision of world peace. He cited a daring assertion in Isaiah (19:23–25) that anticipated the reconciliation of Egypt, Assyria, and Israel: "Our God is also the God of our enemies, without their knowing Him and despite their defying Him. The enmity between the nations will turn to friendship. They will live together when they will worship together. All three will be equally God's chosen people." Heschel would often quote this passage in future speeches, and he included it in his 1969 book on Israel.[11]

Beyond the conference Heschel hoped to elaborate, in book form, an anthropology (a philosophy of the human) from the perspective of the Hebrew Bible. He began by expanding the speech on "Sacred Images of Man" into an article, which first appeared in *Christian Century*, an "undenominational journal of religion" established in 1884. He then carefully revised the piece for the convention issue of *Religious Education*. He added many passages to the essay to represent the Jewish viewpoint alongside Greek, Chinese, Christian, and Hindu views in a collection called *The Concept of Man*, edited by the Indian philosophers, the statesman Sarvepalli Radhakrishnan and P. T. Raju. Heschel's goal was to find common ground for Judaism and Christianity—even Islam and Asian religions—on the foundation of a sacred humanism.[12]

By 1958 the role of religion in a free society had become a national concern. That May, Heschel joined more than a hundred distinguished lawyers, professors, clergy, educators, and publicists to participate in an interfaith colloquium organized by the Fund for the Republic, a noninstitutional think tank. They met for several days at the World Affairs Center in New York, located at East 47th Street and United Nations Plaza.

Among the conference participants were some old friends, including two Jesuit priests from Woodstock College, John Courtney Murray, editor of *Theological Studies*, and Gustave Weigel, who had been Heschel's fellow speaker at the REA conference's assembly on sacred images. Also participating were Paul Tillich, professor of systematic theology at Harvard Divinity School; Will Herberg, who taught Judaic Studies at Drew University; and Reinhold Niebuhr, a member of the Fund's Committee of Consultants. Forums were held on religious pluralism and civic unity, church and state, the question of religion in the public schools, the secular challenge, and other issues. Heschel spoke at the session on religion and the free society with Weigel and Tillich.

By this time Heschel had worked through his religious critique of contemporary politics. Religion, he observed, must rise above expediency to represent absolute values, the first of which was the holiness of humankind. Social ills were due in large part to the trivialization of the human image and the degradation of language, a debasing of words, which must remain truthful repositories of the spirit. Heschel proclaimed the necessity of cultivating reverence. Above all, religion must challenge the status quo: "Religion is spiritual effrontery. Its root is in the bitter sense of inadequacy, in the thirst which can only be stilled by a greater thirst, in the embarrassment that we do not really care for God."[13]

Alluding to the ongoing civil rights struggle, he asserted his support for pluralism and faulted the narrowness of institutions: "It is an inherent weakness of religion not to take offense at the segregation of God, to forget that the sanctuary has no walls."[14]

Most audacious was Heschel's challenge to America's consumer culture. With questionable logic, he associated the economic depression of pre-Nazi Germany with the worship of comfort and success prevalent in the United States. Referring to sociologist Vance Packard's best-selling exposé of advertising strategies, *The Hidden Persuaders* (1957), Heschel implied that both fascism and capitalism could lead to the abandonment of basic human values: "The insecurity of freedom is a bitter fact of historical experience. In times of unemployment, vociferous demagogues are capable of leading people into a state of mind in which they are ready to barter their freedom for any bargain. In times of prosperity hidden persuaders are capable of leading the people into selling their conscience for success." For Heschel, public life must advance truth, personal integrity, and the divine vision of justice and compassion.[15]

Finally, Heschel attacked government policies that were justified by self-interest rather than democratic generosity: "Foreign aid, when offered to underdeveloped countries, for the purpose of winning friends and influencing people, turns out to be a boomerang. Should we not learn how to detach expediency from charity?"[16]

Heschel's analysis was extremely well received. George N. Shuster, president of Hunter College (who had chaired the 1954 REA meeting at which Heschel spoke on Judeo-Christian values) wrote enthusiastically to Louis Finkelstein, his fellow academic executive: "[Heschel] was magnificent. Indeed, it seems to me that I have never heard a better statement about basic religious considerations in our time." One can imagine Finkelstein's ambivalence about his colleague's success.[17]

Nevertheless, in January 1959, Finkelstein was authorized to promote Heschel to full professor. The recognition was long overdue. Despite his achievements as author and public speaker and almost twelve years on the faculty, Heschel had remained an associate professor, a tenured but subordinate rank. He was now Seminary Professor of Jewish Ethics and Mysticism.[18]

Teaching the Prophets

In the meantime, Heschel continued to pursue his goals to turn American Jewry back toward the "religion of Abraham, Isaac, and Jacob," promoting religious education and completing his masterwork on the Hebrew prophets. In February 1958, at a conference organized by the Cleveland Bureau of Jewish Education, he explained his radical pedagogy to religious school teachers; later, in a seminar session, he discussed the prophets, using material from his manuscript in progress. In this relatively informal setting, with a sympathetic and knowledgeable audience, Heschel was relaxed, a master teacher. The talk was not revised for publication, and the mimeographed transcription conveys his trenchant style at its best, as well as some of his diplomatic failings.

He came right to the point. Judaism had been "trivialized." The chief problem facing religious teachers was to confront "spiritual illiteracy" by raising the level of thinking among their students. Heschel denounced "intellectual vulgarity" that detached Judaism from "the living issues of the human soul." He condemned Americans' hedonism and their tendency to view religion in pragmatic terms: "The body is the supreme object of worship. Of course, God is also served, because He is useful. Why not let there be a God? It's nice," he said sarcastically. Heschel provoked his fellow educators, hurting some feelings:

"Sometimes I wonder whether bad Jewish education isn't worse than no education at all."[19]

But he also offered solutions. Teachers should revive specifically Jewish terms to confront hard issues of faith. The word *mitzvah*, for example, was not the same as "customs and ceremonies," it "abound[ed] in connotation": "Man is not alone in doing the good, in carrying out the holy. Man responds to God when he does the good." Echoing his writings of the 1940s, Heschel asserted that education needed to address the individual's inner life to "save the soul from oblivion."

In his battle with the wary mediocrity of religious education, Heschel urged teachers to concentrate on spiritual insight: the "authentic Jewish teacher [is] a person in whom God is not a stranger. . . . But remember, it isn't easy." He was absolute in his reverence: "God is He whose regard for me I value more than life." Above all, he explained, teachers should cultivate awe: "The real theme of most of my books is the problem, why have faith at all? . . . The first step is the sense of wonder in the face of all existence, the entrance to faith."

In his seminar "The Relevance of Prophecy," Heschel discussed ideas he was developing in his new book (which he described as forthcoming, although it was still five years from publication) that he felt could inculcate genuine religious thinking.

He began by admitting that it was almost impossible to "understand" prophecy. There were practical obstacles. First, "modern man is conditioned by all sorts of factors in such a way as to reject, *a priori*, any claim raised by the prophets of Israel to have been inspired by God." In addition, Jewish scholarship had not investigated seriously "the dogma of prophecy or the dogma of revelation." Third, "the act of prophetic inspiration" needed to be distinguished from a system of belief. The solution was to define what the prophet teaches us about "God's relation to man." Most important was "the prophetic personality," the total person we could strive to understand and even to emulate.[20]

As he focused on the prophet's personality, he expressed his own, describing the ironic contrast between speculative philosophy and moral concern he himself had confronted, even as a student in Hitler's Berlin: "Instead of dealing with definitions and demonstrations, one is suddenly thrown into orations about widows and orphans, about the corruption of judges, and the affairs of the marketplace." His words on "prophetic indignation" could have been a description of his own volatile temperament, his outrage at the tepid conscience: "The prophet's words are outbursts of violent emotions. His rebuke is harsh and relentless. But, if such sensitivity to evil is to be called hysterical, what name should be given to the deep callousness to evil which the prophet bewails?" But he also showed how adept he had become at tuning his words to specific audiences, ending his speech to the educators with the humorous invitation, "I have been impolite enough to shock you into the realization of how difficult it is even to raise questions about what is involved in being a prophet. Having performed a most unpedagogical act, making it difficult for you to ask questions, I am asking and inviting you to do so."

In the question-and-answer session that followed, Heschel, at ease among these committed Jews, skillfully clarified some practical issues.

> Question: "In regard to the content of prophecy, how can it be better understood by the teacher and presented to the pupils?"
>
> Heschel: "Remember one thing. Don't adjust the prophets to yourself, nor yourself to the prophets. You find words in the prophets which are totally unintelligible to us; namely, God cares. . . . But our authenticity as Jews depends upon this decision, on whether God cares for what goes on in a particular home in Cleveland."
>
> Question: "How can one make this subject concrete and real to the eighth grade children?"
>
> Heschel: "I think one can. But first of all let us ask: "Is this subject concrete and real to us?" . . . I have said this to teachers many times: Important as technique is, the *neshoma* [the soul] is more important than technique."

Heschel once again elevated a practical problem to a spiritual challenge.

Heschel responded to other questions with equal clarity. When asked about Christians who quoted prophetic predictions concerning the end of the world, he warned against oversimplifying and pulling passages out of context. But he also recognized their fear as relevant: after World War II and the advent of the atomic bomb, it was easy to believe that the world could be destroyed. "What is Jewish law and what is Jewish piety, if not an expression of that consciousness, that life is a very serious business?"

Heschel was pressed about divine revelation, the main dividing line between traditional and progressive religionists. What did he think of "intuitive" knowledge? In response, he recalled that "in a book on prophecy published a great many years ago" (his doctoral thesis), he had made "a rather careful study of the differences between intuition and prophetic insight." Revelation was bestowed by God, intuition was a human mode of knowing. When asked whether prophecy was possible today, he affirmed it, expanding on a crucial source he had first cited in his 1950 Hebrew essay on the Holy Spirit:

> In the Book of Deuteronomy [5:19], after describing the voice the people heard at Sinai, there occurs the following phrase: *kol Gadol v'lo yasaf*, a great voice, and *v'lo yasaf*. What does *v'lo yasaf* mean? Two interpretations are found in rabbinic literature. One, a great voice was at Sinai, but nevermore. The second interpretation is, a great voice that never ceased. The voice of Sinai goes on forever. I am very excited about the fact that we have both interpretations. If we only had one interpretation; namely, a great voice but nevermore, we would have petrified Jews. If we had only the second interpretation, a great voice that never ceases, we would have slippery Jews, relativists. How marvelous that we have both interpretations. They supplement each other.[21]

Traditionalists, Heschel was saying, could also be pluralists, tolerant of and recognizing contradictory views. He affirmed the factuality of divine revelation but also highlighted the necessity of interpreting its human rendition. Through this application of depth theology, he hoped to bridge the abysses dividing secular, liberal, and "Torah-true" Jews. Pluralists, he wanted to show, could also become traditionalists.

Israel and the Diaspora

In addition to exploring issues of religion for both interfaith and Jewish audiences, Heschel was broadening his audience politically, through a series of lectures on the relation of Israel to the Diaspora. The foundation of his commitment to the Jewish state was religious, as he asserted in *God in Search of Man*, coming to him through the ancient claims of the Bible as well as through modern Hebrew literature. Yet he was not a Zionist in the classical sense, intending to settle in the new state of Israel. He considered that entity culturally and religiously inseparable from Jewish communities in the Diaspora, where he chose to remain.[22]

Growing up in prewar Europe, Heschel had encountered virtually all approaches to Zionism. His elders in Warsaw were leaders in the Agudah, the ultra-Orthodox organization that resisted modernity and opposed settlement in Palestine before the coming of the Messiah. Yet his daily prayers, like those of all observant Jews, called for the eventual ingathering of the dispersed people to the Holy Land. In Poland, Heschel became close to dedicated Zionists such as Fishl Schneersohn, Schneur Zalman Rubashov (as Zalman Shazar, the first president of Israel, was then known); in Germany, his friends included the Zionists David Koigen and Martin Buber.

In America, Heschel's zeal for the Jewish state was tempered by his spiritual radicalism. In 1951 he published his programmatic essay "To Be a Jew" in the inaugural issue of *Zionist Quarterly*, founded by the Zionist Organization of America. In it he unequivocally proclaimed the priority of God: "Why is my belonging to the Jewish people the most sacred relation to me, second only to my relation to God? Israel is a spiritual order in which the human and the ultimate, the natural and the holy, enter a lasting covenant, in which kinship with God is not an aspiration but a reality of destiny."[23] Over the years he urged religious and secular Israelis, as well as Jews in the Diaspora, to sustain universal ethical standards.

Yet Heschel longed to visit the Holy Land, and in August 1957 he was finally able to do so. His friend Zalman Shazar, as acting chairman of the Department of Education and Culture in the Diaspora, a government agency, invited him to speak at the "Ideological Conference" in Jerusalem, an international gathering of Zionist representatives. (This was a tremendous gift because Heschel could not afford the trip without institutional support— his salary at JTS remained low despite his growing prominence.) With the approach of the tenth anniversary of Israel's Declaration of Independence and the controversial Sinai invasion of October–November 1956, in which Israel, Great Britain, and France unsuccessfully attempted to wrest the Suez Canal from Egypt, Israelis felt the need to reflect on their past—and their future. Heschel and others would help evaluate the spiritual health of the developing Jewish state.[24]

Shazar's invitation also gave Heschel an opportunity to augment his religious image by growing a beard. "How could I visit the Land of Israel without a beard?" he told Wolfe Kelman. Heschel formed his appearance prudently, beginning with a neat goatee.[25]

Heschel, Sylvia, and the five-year-old Susannah first flew to London, where they spent a week visiting Heschel's brother Jacob Heshel (the British spelling of the family name); he also met with a member of the prominent Jewish Montefiore family and other distinguished Jews. The Heschels went on to Paris for another week, where they probably saw Heschel's first cousin Tova Perlow, who had left Warsaw for Palestine about the time Heschel moved to Vilna. Heschel wrote enthusiastically to Kelman: "Such experiences add perspective and scope even to a parochial mind." The Heschels then flew to Jerusalem on 5 August and settled in a pension on Abravanel Street.[26]

*Susannah, Sylvia, and Abraham Heschel leaving
for Israel, ca. 1960.*

The Israeli press expected substantial insights to come out of this international Zionist meeting, especially from Heschel, whose reputation as a unique religious thinker had preceded him. After ten days in the country, he was featured in an article in the English-language *Jerusalem Post* as a "fusion" of "Jewish mystic" and "modern scholar." The reporter summarized his life and writings, mentioning his enthusiasm for Israel as well as his provocative stance on the "Ideological Conference": Heschel hoped that it might help "emancipate people's minds from the clichés and banalities in which so many of us are involved." Old ways of thinking were "completely stale and out of date."[27]

The same day the article appeared, 15 August, Heschel brought his challenging spiritual perspective to the conference participants at the Hebrew University. Speaking in Hebrew, he sought to persuade intransigent nationalists that Jews in the Diaspora were one with the Israeli people and to persuade belligerent secularists that authentic Judaism demanded more than just acquiescence to ritual law.

In the shadow of the Holocaust, Heschel claimed, the historical conscious-ness of Jews in Israel and in the Diaspora was identical: "Disaster, deliver-ance, dismay—these three words mark the supreme issues of Jewish existence in our day. Yet though involving the heart and center of our existence they re-main at the periphery of our thinking. The memory of the disaster is being ef-faced from our minds, the deliverance we take for granted, and dismay we suppress." Forgetfulness was the gravest threat. Speaking as an American Jew, and true to his oppositional stance, he defended Jews outside the Holy Land: "The people of Israel is a tree whose roots are in Israel and the branches in the Diaspora. A tree cannot flourish without roots. But how can it bear fruit with-out branches? Be careful with the branches!"[28]

He then examined the relationship of the religion to the nation and to God: "Only in Israel are the people and Torah one. . . . The depravity of civilization is proof that a godless people [the Nazis] is bound to become a satanic peo-ple." Jews must carry the message of holiness to the world. He evoked Zechariah's image of the brand plucked from the fire (Zech. 2:3): "Every one of us alive is a spark of an eternal candle and a smoldering ember snatched from the fire. Without his knowing it, every one of us is crowned with the Holy. Let us learn to be aware of the majesty which hovers over our existence."[29]

Opposing Israel's reigning secularism, Heschel focused on religion for all Jews. He subordinated the "national problem" of establishing a Jewish home-land to "the spiritual plight of the individual . . . , especially in the Dias-pora." In order for Judaism to survive, rabbinical authorities must become more flexible: "A Judaism confined to the limits of *halakhah*, with all due re-spect be it said, is not exactly one of the happiest products of the Diaspora. Such condensation and parochialism has little of the sweep and power of the prophets."[30]

Although his demand for religious commitment was radical, even quixotic, he admitted that few individuals enjoyed "perfect faith." He cited the example of Ezra the Scribe, "of whom the Rabbis said that he was worthy of receiving the Torah had it not been already given through Moses, [who] confessed his lack of perfect faith." Heschel was both modest and defiant. He pressed his audience, many of whom were fierce atheists, to cultivate humility and a yearning for God: "A religious revival will come from inner embarrassment, from the agony of the intellect as it stands overwhelmed in the face of the mys-tery which lies hidden in all things and the inscrutable mystery of the mind it-self." Religion and nation were interdependent, but there was a definite scale of importance: "Judaism stands on four pillars: on God, the Torah, the people of Israel, and the land of Israel. The loss of any one of these entails the loss of the others; one depends on the other."[31]

The reactions to Heschel's speech were mixed. The *Jerusalem Post* reported the next day that Yitzhak Tebenkin, a leader of the Ahdut Ha'avoda (a radical labor party), had been furious at the religious speakers who maintained that Jews who did not believe in the *Shulhan Arukh* (Code of Jewish Laws) were "traitor[s] to the Jewish people." Heschel had objected, "No one said that," and Tebenkin responded, "Word for word." Then, according to the article, Heschel modified his assertion: "After the speech, Prof. Heschel rushed over to Mr. Tebenkin and said that the words he had used were: 'A Jew who does not believe in God denies the Jewish people.' After a brief exchange, Mr. Tebenkin walked away saying: 'And what if I don't believe in God? I believe in man!' "[32]

After the conference, there was a meeting with several leaders at the home of Prime Minister David Ben-Gurion that for Heschel confirmed the importance of his focus on spiritual values. In his report to the Rabbinical Assembly the following April, Heschel explained that Ben-Gurion had not asked his visitors about "forming new organizations or arranging national demonstrations," but rather: "*Why do you believe in God?*" A distinguished cabinet member and ranking leader of Mapai (the workers party) explained that he hoped the conference would help him advise his daughter, a brilliant, successful student and "proud to be an Israeli," who was "*confused and bewildered about the meaning of being a Jew.*"[33]

Returning to the United States, Heschel refocused his speech and presented it in English for the annual convention of the Rabbinical Assembly, 27 April–1 May 1958. After morning and afternoon panels in honor of Saul Lieberman, Heschel joined Mordecai Kaplan in the session on the state of Israel, which focused on the relations between "the people" (*Am*), "the land" (*eretz*), and "the community or state" (*medinah*).

Heschel expressed his own reverence and radical amazement at the very founding of the Jewish state: "Dark and dreadful would be our life today without the comfort and the joy that radiate out of the land of Israel. Crippled is our people, many of its limbs chopped off, some of its vital organs torn out—how strange to be alive, how great is our power to forget." But Israel's mere existence was not enough; what mattered was the quality of Jewish life everywhere: "The question is not how to make the State meaningful to the Jews of America but how to make the State worthy of 2,000 years of waiting."[34]

He applied the notion of *galut* (exile), which usually pertained to Jews who lived outside the Holy Land, to "the spiritual condition" of all Jews, especially

Americans: "Some Bar Mitzvah affairs are *galut*. Our timidity and hesitance to take a stand on behalf of the Negroes are *galut*." But Americans were not the only "exiles": "There is *galut* whenever Judaism is judged by the standards of the market-place and whenever the sense of the holy is replaced by spiritual obtuseness." Even in the Jewish state, "The vital, unquestionable, and indisputable need of maintaining an Israeli army is *galut* too. The fact that the State of Israel must celebrate its birthday by demonstrating its guns and tanks in the streets of Jerusalem, cries out tragically that redemption has not come. In a world which is dark and enmeshed in evil, Israel is not redeemed." Heschel's love for Israel was inseparable from his agonized, prophetic vision of peace. [35]

Yet he had been impressed by the spiritual thirst throughout Israel, the desire for God: "It is present among the uncommitted, and the official representatives of religion are unable to cope with it. Soldiers complain that the chaplains are concerned with the *kashrut* of the kitchen rather than with the questions of the mind and the longings of the heart." He suggested that American Jews (less prone to a similar obtuseness) might show Israelis the right path. Rabbis and laity could cooperate in bringing "the spirit of the Sabbath into the Jewish home, or in trying to build day-schools, or in establishing the habit of studying Torah." A ladder of observance, flexibility, was the way.[36]

Religion, Politics, and Jewish Identity

Heschel's views were faced with a practical test five months later. On 27 October 1958 (13 Heshvan 5719), Prime Minister Ben-Gurion called on authorities worldwide—writers, academics, and rabbis—to evaluate the status of children of mixed marriages, in which the mother was an unconverted non-Jew. Were such children Jews? The religious parties in Israel were so powerful that civil and religious jurisdictions were not independent, and these Orthodox groups were categorical in defending strict halakhic norms, which denied "Jewishness" to such offspring. The pressing, politically divisive issue was the "Law of Return," the right of Jews everywhere to immediate citizenship if they immigrated to Israel.[37]

Along with forty-six other *hachmei Yisrael* (Jewish sages or scholars) from Israel, Europe, and North America, Heschel welcomed the challenge. In his answer, derived from "both the Halakhah and reality," he attempted to reconcile the values of pluralism and Orthodoxy. He affirmed traditional law but judged with compassion those who wished to be recognized as Jews yet did not qualify under strict rabbinic standards. At the same time he rejected those who "tried to base Jewish existence on nationality alone, and to make a distinction between people and religion." A "schism" would spell disaster.[38]

He regretted the Israeli government's loose secular definition: "A theory which proposes that there is a Jewish people without a religion necessarily implies that there is a Jewish religion without a people." Heschel sought to preserve both peoplehood and Torah, proposing this compromise: "The religion and nationality of an adult will be recorded as 'Jew' if he declares in good faith that he is a Jew and not a member of any other religion."[39]

Heschel sympathized with the anguish of those for whom the confines of the law were too restrictive. Legislation or authority could not resolve a person's spiritual disquiet: "We cannot force people to believe. Faith brought about by coercion is worse than heresy. But we can plant respect in the hearts of our generation." This was Heschel's lifelong task.[40]

To resolve the civil issue of Jewish identity, he formulated an administrative definition that did not undermine the authority of halakhah. First, he distinguished between spirit and politics: "The term 'Jew' is a concept both religious and national. As a religious concept it has a fixed definition; as a national concept its meaning is obscure." Therefore, for immigrants whose mother was not Jewish, it would be better not to define the term "Jew." "If for security reasons a legal resident of Israel needs a document to identify himself, it might be possible for those unable to identify themselves as 'Jews' to be registered as 'Hebrews.' As for the 'Law of Return,' we need not impose rigorous tests."[41]

Heschel's generous position contrasted with the legalistic approach of Rabbis Joseph Soloveitchik and Hayyim Heller, who presented their response together; for them halakhah was the nation's buttress: "We are indeed perplexed that the State of Israel now seeks to hew down our traditional branches and thereby smear the ancient glory of Israel which has long been sanctified through the spilt blood and sufferings of preceding generations."[42]

Like Heschel, Louis Finkelstein took a more moderate view, though his answer differed from Heschel's in some respects. Refusing to make a halakhic pronouncement, he counseled patience and compassion for non-Jews who asked to be considered Jewish: "In such matters, our Sages taught us that even if the left hand has to reject one, the right hand should be used to draw him near." Mordecai Kaplan, more radical, questioned the assumption that Israel was a Jewish state. The child of a non-Jewish mother, he wrote, should be registered as a "Jewish resident" in the hope that at maturity he or she would convert ritually.[43]

The year following Ben-Gurion's survey, in November 1959, Heschel took center stage in an American controversy about politics, Zionism, and religion. "The Great Debate," as it was called, occurred at the biennial convention of the United Synagogue of America, the lay organization of the Conservative movement, which had about a million members. Heschel unexpectedly provoked discord among the 1,300 delegates when, speaking at a session on "the future of Zionism and its role in Judaism," he opposed the United Synagogue's joining the World Zionist Organization (WZO), a political action group founded in 1898 to help establish a Jewish state. Since the creation of Israel, the WZO had concentrated on education and problems affecting new immigrants.

Heschel opposed the involvement of religious institutions in politics as firmly as he judged politics according to spiritual standards. He declared that the United Synagogue should remain independent of any political movement, even one as intimately connected with Jewish survival as the WZO: "The primary function of the synagogue is to inspire the soul and to instruct the mind; its task is to cultivate faith in God, love of man and understanding of Torah; its goal is holiness; its methods are personal, intellectual, spiritual. The primary function of a political organization is to serve the self-interest of the group it represents; its goal may be holy, yet its methods are adroitness, opportunism and expediency." Even sacred ends could not justify some means.[44]

After Heschel finished his speech, Mordecai Kaplan immediately demanded the floor to give a strong rebuttal. The *New York Times* reported, in "Jewish Split over Zionist Ties," that Kaplan "denied that the World Zionist Organization was a political party in any sense, and expressed 'amazement' at Dr. Heschel's views." Nahum Goldmann, president of the WZO, similarly rejected Heschel's reasoning as "an empty excuse." But Simon Greenberg agreed with Heschel that support for Israel did not require a religious entity to join the WZO, and the delegates decided against affiliation.[45]

Interpreting Heschel

Heschel maintained a hectic schedule of public debate without neglecting his research and writing. In January 1959 he optimistically announced that two new books were "scheduled to appear in the near future"; their provisional titles were *The Idea of Mosaic Revelation in Jewish History* and *The Prophets of Israel*. Meanwhile, sympathetic readers published substantial studies of his writings, principally in Jewish journals such as *Congress Weekly, Commentary, Conservative Judaism,* and *Judaism.* Yet even they frequently filtered Heschel's eclectic mode of reflection through the stereotypical opposition of "mysticism" versus "reason." This simplistic approach limited an otherwise astute exchange of interpretations in *Commentary* between Jakob J. Petuchowski, assistant professor of rabbinics at Hebrew Union College, and Edmond La B. Cherbonnier, professor at Trinity College in Hartford, Connecticut, the first Christian to write systematically on Heschel's significance as a thinker.[46]

Petuchowski asserted that Heschel "has become for many the leading Jewish theologian in this country," but he reproached him for sacrificing "conceptual thinking" to "situational thinking." Cherbonnier's defense appeared a few months later, refuting the familiar claim that Heschel disparaged reason: "The Biblical philosophy that Heschel develops is intellectually more satisfactory than the conventional theology which Petuchowski defends."[47] This debate provided significant insights but failed to clarify the fuller context of Heschel's method and system.

Fritz Rothschild undertook that enterprise by selecting essential pages among Heschel's many writings for a volume that made Heschel more widely known and better understood. Heschel told Rothschild, with some regret, that he was not a systematizer, like Paul Tillich; and he appreciated Rothschild's native intelligence, acerbic wit, broad literary culture (in English and in German), and especially Rothschild's ability to organize the basic concepts dispersed throughout his writings. He was happy to cooperate in Rothschild's project, an anthology called *Between God and Man*, one of the titles Heschel had rejected in the course of preparing *God in Search of Man*. This title also alluded to Buber's collection, *Between Man and Man*, but it placed God first.

A version of Rothschild's introduction to the volume appeared in the spring 1959 issue of *Judaism*, serving as a publicity notice for the forthcoming anthology. The publication of *Between God and Man* in May made the systematic study of Heschel possible, and it became a prime textbook for courses in modern Jewish philosophy. Readers could now evaluate Heschel for what he was actually trying to accomplish. The anthology included forty-one selections taken from most of Heschel's published works and the manuscript of *The Prophets*. A bibliography of Heschel's writings in Europe, Israel, Argentina, and in the United States made it a valuable research tool as well.[48]

Rothschild's careful introduction to Heschel's life and works explained his terminology and theological system. Heschel assumed "the fact" of God's concern for humankind and the world; that was what Rothschild called "the *root metaphor* of his ontology." This divine concern became Heschel's "conceptual tool to render intelligible such different fields of inquiry as theology, ontology, and ethics." Rothschild also coined a phrase that Heschel happily adopted (with Rothschild's permission): "The pathetic God [that is, the God of pathos] as distinguished from the God of Aristotle is not the Unmoved Mover but the *Most Moved Mover*."[49]

All in all, Rothschild's anthology provided scholars with evidence that Heschel's "exposition is a masterly synthesis in which elements from the whole of Jewish religious tradition from the Bible, Talmud, Midrash, medieval philosophy, Kabbalah, and Hasidism are welded into an organic whole that is held together by the central framework of his philosophy of religion." As John Herman Randall, Rothschild's philosophy professor at Columbia University, exclaimed, to Rothschild's delight: "You have succeeded where God himself has failed: making a consistent, systematic philosopher out of Heschel."[50]

The most astute critique of Rothschild's presentation came from his friend Arthur A. Cohen, writing in *Christian Century,* who found that "Heschel proves greater and wilder than the anthologizing tamer can manage." Only years later did interpreters confirm Cohen's insight into Heschel's esoteric agenda: "Language and thought are for him devices for piercing the veil which separates the living God from creation. Intuition . . . is for Heschel rather a mode of coaxing truth out of the universe."[51]

11

A Prophetic Witness (1960–1963)

The prophet is an iconoclast, challenging the apparently holy, revered,
and awesome. Beliefs cherished as certainties, institutions endowed
with supreme sanctity, he exposes as scandalous pretensions.
—Heschel, *The Prophets* (1962)

---

national scene. Still more comfortable in his office or in the library, he was pushed into public events by former students who now held influential positions. Wolfe Kelman was executive vice president of the Rabbinical Assembly (the "civil servant" of Conservative rabbis, as he put it), and Marc Tanenbaum, Kelman's close friend, was executive director of interfaith relations at the Synagogue Council of America, an umbrella group that represented all Jewish denominations. Separately and together, the two acted as Heschel's impresarios.[1]

Also supporting Heschel was Samuel Dresner, now a pulpit rabbi and editor of *Conservative Judaism* (a position he held for ten years). Two former students had joined the faculty of the Jewish Theological Seminary: Seymour Siegel, assistant professor in the Rabbinical School, and Fritz Rothschild, instructor in philosophy of religion in the Teachers Institute. Although Heschel still lacked institutional support, he did have a network.

But he still needed encouragement as an orator. To Kelman and others he confided his shyness and fragile self-confidence, especially in front of large, unfamiliar audiences. Heschel had a charismatic presence, but some listeners sensed his awkwardness, as when he would interrupt his talk to ask the audience teasingly whether he should continue. Some of his jokes fell flat and could provoke discomfort. Heschel took pointers in elocution from Marshall Meyer, who possessed a strong theatrical presence. Usually the substance of Heschel's speeches would carry the day, especially when he developed them in written form.

Secular Meeting Grounds

One of the most prestigious forums he was asked to address in these years was the president's "Conference on Children and Youth," initiated in 1909 by Theodore Roosevelt and held every ten years. Heschel was chosen to represent the Jewish perspective by Marc Tanenbaum and John Slawson, head of the American Jewish Committee (AJC), who were members of the national group that was organizing the fiftieth-anniversary gathering. From 27 March through 2 April 1960, more than seven thousand delegates attended to represent a variety of professional fields and religious origins.[2]

President Eisenhower opened the convocation at the University of Maryland in College Park. He asserted his "unshakable faith" that "today's youth would find peace with freedom in the space age." In keeping with the tenor of the time, he supported any religious faith that would convey "such truths as the transcendent value of the individual and the dignity of all people, the futility and stupidity of war, its destructiveness of life and its degradation of human values." The deliberations began the next day with five large assemblies.[3]

Heschel's message was received with enthusiasm. He applied "moral and spiritual values" to social issues. Echoing resolutions against discrimination based on race, color, or creed, he stood behind the civil rights movement: "How can we speak of reverence for man and of the belief that all men are created equal without repenting the way we behave toward our brothers, the colored people of America?" In the language of a spiritual revolutionary, he thrilled the audience with a call for "*a radical reorientation of our thinking.*" The next day many of his striking formulations were featured in the *Washington Post:* "the greatest threat" was not the atomic bomb but our "callousness to the suffering of man." His denunciation of American consumerism was highlighted: "The basic problem of today's youth is today's parent, who has shoved aside his moral responsibilities while questing [for] wealth and comfort." The solution he offered was to strengthen the family; devoted and responsible parents would create a morally sensitive environment.[4]

In addition to the newspaper coverage, the AJC interfaith relations department distributed hundreds of mimeographed copies of Heschel's speech around the country. He was pleased that his words also appeared in *Law and Order: The Independent Magazine for the Police Profession,* reaching yet another constituency.[5]

Heschel was also successful as a visiting professor. His first invitation came from the University of Minnesota, which offered him a nine-week appointment (April–May 1960) at the prestigious religion program sponsored by the Danforth Foundation. Soon after his electrifying speech at the White House conference, Heschel, Sylvia, and eight-year-old Susannah moved to Saint Paul. Heschel offered an undergraduate course on Maimonides, a graduate seminar on the prophets, and nine public lectures under the general topic "The Intellectual Relevance of Judaism."[6]

The lectures and other events were arranged by the philosophy department with support from the Hillel and Wesley Foundations, a Jewish and Christian group, respectively. Each week Heschel presented one of his basic themes: depth theology; God in search of man; freedom and existence; a symbol of God; religion and public education: a church-state problem; needs, ends, and deeds; empathy and expression; pathos and sympathy; sanctification of time.

The evening events attracted large crowds, for his reputation as a national speaker preceded him. Fewer people had attended previous Danforth lectures, but Heschel consistently drew full audiences of five hundred. Heschel and his listeners had to be moved to larger venues: the Mayo Memorial Auditorium and the Bell Museum of Natural History. Heschel shared his delight with Kelman: "The echoes of my Washington address are quite extraordinary. *I am quite unworthy of all God's mercy* [in Hebrew]."[7]

Heschel was able to influence receptive faculty members, among whom was a group of nonobservant Jews. Many had read his books, and although they did not harbor extraordinary expectations, they were open-minded, wondering how Heschel would differ from the Catholic and Protestant scholars who had previously been brought to campus. Two people became especially close to Heschel during his stay: Louis Milgrom, the Hillel rabbi, and David Cooperman, a sociology professor. Milgrom, who knew Heschel, was already favorably disposed; Cooperman, more skeptical, met Heschel for the first time in Minnesota and learned to appreciate his religious manner of thinking.

Heschel could be a deft communicator. He wove Jewish parables into his talks, and he had a knack for revealing the religious depth of everyday events. What some faulted as a digressive, anecdotal style could, when successful, elicit transforming insights. During one question period, for example, a listener demanded compelling evidence of God's existence. The audience tittered uncomfortably, and there was an awkward pause while Heschel considered the matter. He stroked his beard, looked around, and breathed in, quieting the large audience. Then he explained: If you were to look at a beautiful painting and want to know who painted it, you could find the name of the artist on the canvas. If the artist were famous, you would feel justified in admiring the handiwork. But if you look about the world, and you want to know who made it, you don't look at the sun to see God's signature. Nature is a divine creation, but it is not identical with God. This analogy satisfied both questioner and audience, who breathed sighs of relief.

Cooperman was especially moved by the story. Heschel's mention of artwork had jogged an emotion-laden memory of a Marc Chagall etching of the prophet Isaiah receiving divine inspiration in which the Holy Name of God was inscribed on the sun. Later, Cooperman described to Heschel his reactions to the uneasy pause, Heschel's poetic response, and the crowd's sighing in unison. Then he mentioned his memory of the Chagall etching. Heschel looked at him intently and said that he had been thinking exactly along those lines. The conversation sealed the bond between them.[8]

Heschel could also use humor effectively. At one Sunday talk for faculty, when he was discussing insensitivity to holiness, which he called "spiritual obtuseness," he told this joke: An old woman had saved up for a trip to the Wailing Wall in Palestine (this was decades before it became accessible to Jews, after the June 1967 war). Upon her return, she met with her friends, who sat around her in a circle. "What is the Wailing Wall like?" they asked excitedly. Her answer: "It's a Wailing Wall like any other Wailing Wall!"[9]

Heschel also found light-hearted ways to explain why it was necessary to believe in God. He had returned briefly to New York to address the annual meeting of the American Jewish Committee at the Hotel Commodore on "The Moral Challenge to America." He told a story of a wealthy businessman from Leipzig who had found a perfect son-in-law from a matchmaker. When his wife objected, "'We don't even have a daughter,' . . . he said to her in Yiddish, *'What's the harm? Let there be a son-in-law around the house.'* Let there be a God around the universe, it costs so little."[10]

As Heschel's residency ended and the family prepared to return to New York, a large number of Jewish faculty gave them a farewell reception. These intellectuals had not been converted to religious observance or transformed radically, but they now began to consider the world in terms of Judaic categories.

During his two months in Minnesota, Heschel had done one other thing that was to affect his public image in the years to come. He had let his goatee and graying hair grow longer after Rabbi Milgrom had joked that he did not look "mystic enough" to be an expert on Kabbalah and the prophets. With his salt-and-pepper waves and full whiskers, Heschel looked more the way his public expected a major Jewish thinker to look. Later in life, Heschel cultivated this image, especially during his civil rights and antiwar activities, when the appearance of an "Old Testament prophet," as Christians called him, gave him increased recognition as a "rabbi" in the mass media.

Back in New York, Heschel turned his first University of Minnesota lecture, "Depth Theology," into a well-constructed rationale for religious pluralism. He published it in *CrossCurrents*, an interfaith quarterly, at a delicate moment in American history. It was the fall of 1960, and John F. Kennedy was attempting to become the first Catholic president of the United States. Upset by the media obsession with Kennedy's minority faith, *CrossCurrents* editor Joseph E. Cunneen focused the issue on the national problem of religious bigotry. He placed the essay by "Rabbi Heschel," as he was described, emphasizing his Jewish perspective, directly after his own editorial pointing to possible solutions to the political prejudices of the majority of Americans.[11]

Heschel's notion of depth theology assumed that there was a firm distinction between dogma and experiential, intuitive awareness of the living God. Excessive attachment to concepts undermined authentic religion. Referring to the dangers of fundamentalism, he described dogma as "a poor man's share in the divine. A creed is almost all a poor man has. Skin for skin, he will give his life for all that he has. Yea, he may be ready to take other people's lives, if they refuse to share his tenets." Depth theology, on the contrary, finds common ground. Heschel again used analogies to art to explain why "pre-theological" intuition could favor connections between people of different beliefs: "Theology is like sculpture, depth-theology like music. Theology is in the books; depth-theology is in the hearts. The former is doctrine; the latter an event. Theologies divide us; depth-theology unites us." The cognitive emotions of embarrassment, indebtedness, a sense of mystery, and wonder could lead to shared celebration before God.[12]

Owing to the continued efforts of Heschel's former students, Heschel was being asked to supply the "Jewish perspective" on a number of issues. On 9 January 1961, two days before his fifty-fourth birthday, he returned to Washington to deliver a paper to the "White House Conference on Aging." Attending the four-day meeting at the Mayflower Hotel were more than seven hundred activists in the fields of gerontology, religion, family life, education, medicine, and social welfare. Organized by the outgoing administration of President Eisenhower, the conference was strongly influenced by the agenda of President-elect Kennedy, especially his far-reaching plan to broaden health care for the elderly by tying it directly to the Social Security system. In addition to his triumph the year before, Heschel owed his presence on the program to Marc Tanenbaum, a cochairman of the section on religious approaches to old age.[13] He gave one of his most insightful analyses of the human condition at the session on "The Older Person and the Family in the Perspective of Jewish Tradition." He began by elevating the ethical commandment to honor your father and mother to its spiritual essence: "There is no reverence for God without reverence for father and mother." He then deplored widespread attempts to disguise age: "You find more patients in the beauty parlors than in the hospitals. We would rather be bald than gray. A white hair is an abomination." People instead should honor "the authenticity and honesty of existence."[14]

Most grievous was the spiritual crisis of old age, the "sense of emptiness and boredom, the sense of being useless to, and rejected by, family and society, loneliness and the fear of time." For this Heschel offered some practical solutions. By attending to their own inner growth, older citizens could transform society: "What the nation needs is *senior universities*, education toward wisdom in the value of time. . . . *Just to be is a blessing, just to live is holy. The moment is a marvel;* it is in evading the marvel of the moment that boredom begins which ends in despair." In an era where religion and ritual no longer enrich family communication, parents need to find ways to share "moments of exaltation" with their children, so that they will willingly remain connected to their elders as they enter their final years.[15]

Heschel was the star of the conference. His audience was transfixed by his analyses, his original solutions, and his eloquence. For several days, participants discussed his speech excitedly, and Arthur S. Fleming, retiring secretary of the Department of Health, Education, and Welfare, referred to it several times in his closing remarks. Several of Heschel's formulations were included in the policy statement drawn up by the religion section. After the conference the Synagogue Council of America distributed the speech as an attractive pamphlet, "To Grow in Wisdom." It also appeared in two issues of the *Congressional Record* and became one of Heschel's most widely reprinted occasional writings.[16]

Heschel now turned his attention to his upcoming visiting professorship at the University of Iowa's School of Religion. In February, he made a two-day preparatory visit to campus. He met with his graduate seminar on rabbinic theology and assigned them readings, had dinner with professors and local rabbis, and gave a lecture on "The Prophets of Israel" to an overflow crowd. The student newspaper, the *Daily Iowan*, described Heschel's sensitivity to current concerns, as when he discussed juvenile delinquency in terms of "justice" and "pathos." Heschel also denounced the monstrosity of evil, but insisted: "God is not indifferent to evil. He is always concerned." Repeating a favorite biblical passage, Heschel ended his talk with a vision of peace and reconciliation, alluding to current tensions in the Middle East: "Egypt and Assyria are locked up in deadly wars. Hating each other, they are both enemies of Israel." And then he concluded, as reported in the student paper: "Our God is also the God of our enemies, without their knowing Him, and despite their defying Him. The enmity between the nations will turn to friendship."[17]

After three months in New York, Heschel returned to the University of Iowa in May. He met with his graduate seminar six hours a week (double the usual time), delivered public lectures, and consulted with the local Jewish community. He evaluated the Judaica collection of the university library and agreed to help augment their holdings by organizing a fund-raising committee of rabbis and professors. Particularly successful was a seminar for rabbis who came from five surrounding states.

Heschel's experience in the classroom was apparently as gratifying for him as were the public events, and he was attentive to the needs of individual students. (Among the many people Heschel inspired was a young instructor of Christian ethics, Franklin Sherman, who later published the first book-length study of Heschel.) After his departure, a problem remained with an undergraduate who had missed the final examination and was late in submitting his term paper, claiming that he had written it but forgotten to hand it in. Writing to Dean Michaelsen, Heschel explained that he had spoken with the student several times, "and he impressed me as a person who is honest and who suffers from a deep sense of insecurity. My failure to trust him would come as a great shock to him." Heschel did enclose some questions for a makeup examination in case the administration required it. But the wise dean followed Heschel's advice and gave the student credit without requiring additional work.[18]

During this period, two of Heschel's close friends, both East European Jews, passed away. Ilya Schor, who had illustrated Heschel's first two American books, died on 7 June 1961 at age fifty-seven. A month later, Hillel Bavli, the Hebrew poet and translator from the JTS Teachers Institute, died at age sixty-eight. Heschel delivered the eulogy in English at Schor's funeral and wrote an obituary in Hebrew for Bavli for the weekly *Hadoar*. From these versions he developed deeply personal memorial essays in English reflecting his own ethical passion, love of art, and spiritual tact informed by Hasidism.[19]

Of Schor, Heschel wrote that he was a painter, silversmith, and woodcut artist who represented a "sober intoxication with truth." Above all, Schor's art embodied the Jewish style, which Heschel strove to evoke through words: "Schor knew the central secret of the Jew: how to hold a Sefer Torah. In his paintings you sense the warmth, the intimacy, the joy, but also the sadness and the anguish, and a craving that goes on for ever. He has deposited for posterity the spirit of a world that is no more."[20]

In Hillel Bavli, Heschel celebrated the essence of modern Jewish literature: "the beauty he created in his poetry, the dignity and force he lent to the life and literature of Hebrew in America, . . . the radiant vitality of his understanding of human beings, for works of art, for subtleties of words, and above all the integrity, the purity of his character, his unassuming and magnificent piety, his power to revere and to love." Heschel felt most affected by Bavli the person: "Whenever I stood in his presence, I felt ennobled. My heart was never empty when I left him."[21]

Bavli also embodied Heschel's lifelong mission to bridge cultures, achieving this through his original poetry and translations into Hebrew: "Most souls are too narrow to contain both the world of Judaism and the world of secular beauty. In the soul of Hillel Bavli both worlds were at home. He was a marvelous blend of poetry and piety, of artistry and religious discipline, of sacred stubbornness in defending the traditions of our people and unprecedented openness in the world of poetry. He was one of the few men in whom the great experiment of modern Judaism did not end in failure."

Spiritually Radical Pedagogy

In the spring and fall of 1962, advancing his own "great experiment of modern Judaism," Heschel took up the fight for religious education at three conferences, outdoing his shuttle diplomacy of 1953. His standard was "spiritual audacity," a phrase he used throughout. In mid-May he addressed the annual convention of the Rabbinical Assembly; the following week (29–31 May) he spoke at the biennial convention of the World Council of Synagogues in Jerusalem; and in November, he addressed the annual meeting of the interfaith Religious Education Association.

That year the Rabbinical Assembly devoted its convention to institutional self-examination. Simon Greenberg, vice chancellor of the Jewish Theological Seminary, spoke on the role of the rabbinate in primary and secondary religious schools. Samuel Schafler, a pulpit rabbi and educator who had been ordained at JTS, discussed how to teach Jewish teenagers. According to Wolfe Kelman, in his yearly report as R.A. executive vice president, the main problem for American Jews was not assimilation or intermarriage but rather the quality of education.[22]

Heschel was featured at a session on the "The Values of Jewish Education" chaired by Seymour Fox, associate dean of the JTS Teachers Institute, with Rabbis Simcha Kling and David Lieber as discussants. Heschel immediately challenged his colleagues: "The disease from which we suffer is *intellectual* as well as *spiritual illiteracy; ignorance* as well as *idolatry of false values.* We are a generation devoid of learning as well as sensitivity. . . . I insist that the *vapidity of religious instruction* is a major cause of this failure."[23]

Building on his earlier critiques of symbolism and his 1958 talks to the Cleveland Bureau of Jewish Education, he deplored the "trivialization" of Judaism, in which sacred "mysteries" were replaced with "customs and ceremonies," demoting God's commandments to folkways. Teachers must learn to inspire the inner person, unlock the reverence and awe contained in our most common prayers: "People recite the Kaddish [the prayer for the dead]. Why not call attention to the spiritual intoxication and the endless craving in the words *yisgadal v'yiskadash* [exalted and hallowed be God's great name]?" Education must become an event. At the same time Heschel acknowledged his own inadequacy, a feeling that all teachers shared: "I have been a *melamed* [teacher] all my life. I know how hard it is to teach. The first moment of each class is like the hour in which the Jews stood at the Red Sea."[24]

Heschel sought to promote a sacred humanism, a global reverence for all individuals. Living in a manner compatible with God's presence must be accompanied by a radical sense of human dignity: "May I offer a formulation of value? 'Better to throw oneself alive into a burning furnace than to embarrass a human being in public.'" What greater affirmation of the person could there be? Challenging the death-of-God ideologies then current among thinkers like his former HUC student Richard Rubenstein, he demanded a renewal of faith in the sacred potential of human striving: "The central issue is not man's decision to extend formal recognition to God, to furnish God with a certificate that He exists, but the realization of our importance to God's design; not to prove that God is alive, but to prove that man is not dead."[25]

At the biennial convention of the World Council of Synagogues Heschel delivered essentially the same speech. He maintained that Jewish educators in both Israel and the Diaspora needed to stress values over content. Pedagogy must be personal, so that students could experience the "living moment" of knowledge: "For an idea to happen, the teacher must relive its significance, and become one with what he says." The future might depend on the spiritual potential of students, "that man has a soul, that the community has a soul. Did we not witness how entire nations lost their souls?" Referring again to Hitler's Germany, Heschel fought to find positive measures of the human potential.[26]

Responses to Heschel's talk by Rabbi Bernard Segal, who had replaced Marc Tanenbaum as executive director of the United Synagogue Council, and Alfred Hirschberg, editor of a Jewish newspaper in São Paulo, pointed to well-grounded obstacles to Heschel's towering goals. Like Heschel, Siegel deplored the "strange phenomenon" in the United States in which religious teachings were eliminated or downplayed in order to protect the "unity" of the Jewish community. Hirschberg carefully analyzed Jewish life in Brazil, pointing out that "the maximum demands Dr. Heschel put before you are, for the time being, impossible to realize in our midst." In fact, nonreligious projects such as beautiful new buildings did attract young people to the Jewish community.[27]

The following November, Heschel adapted his Jewish educational manifesto for the more than eight hundred predominantly Christian delegates at the Religious Education Association convention in Chicago. His speech, entitled "Idols in the Temples," used no Hebrew quotations, deleted most of his references to Jewish problems, and clarified many sentences. His message, however, remained the same: the Hebrew Bible was for everyone a source of divine presence, a model of sacred humanism, and a call to action.[28]

Talmudic Pluralism and the Prophets

Heschel did not let his enterprising public life hold back his specialized scholarship. Drawing from his lifelong memory of the Bible, medieval and modern commentaries, Kabbalah, and the Talmud, his new book in Hebrew, *Heavenly Torah as Refracted Through the Generations* (Torah min ha-shamayim b'aspaklariah shel ha-dorot), traced the classical sources of his pluralistic theology. In his own modern voice he asserted: "There is a grain of the prophet in the recesses of every human existence."[29]

After initial difficulties in finding a publisher, he published the first volume of his encyclopedic study of the Talmud in 1962 with Soncino Press in London and New York. His scholarly agenda was again oppositional, first to demonstrate how the Talmud conveyed dynamic theological reflections (*aggadah*), not just legalistic dialectics (halakhah), and, more important, to show the congruence of rabbinic theology and prophetic inspiration.

Nonetheless, Heschel was worried about being accepted by authoritative Judaic scholars. He discussed with Fritz Rothschild his plan to write a study that no traditional rabbi could refute. Rothschild warned him that few academics or traditionalists dared to think beyond conventional boundaries. The only people capable of reading such a book would be scholars with a thorough grounding in the Hebrew and Aramaic sources. And most of these, he predicted, would be incapable of appreciating Heschel's eclectic method. Text scholars like Saul Lieberman had no interest in theology; philosophers like Will Herberg did not know enough Hebrew.[30]

This project was so intrinsic to Heschel's identity that he remained undeterred by the prospect of an unreceptive audience. He had mastered the immense rabbinic literature as an adolescent in Warsaw, and when he began to write, texts kept returning to his memory. His friend Moshe Maisels, editor of *Hadoar*, remarked that Heschel's manuscript must have taken ten years of tremendous research, but Heschel told his wife, Sylvia, that he had needed only two and a half years, since he did not have to look up most of the sources (although Gordon Tucker, who later translated the book, noted that many of Heschel's citations had to be corrected). This period of composition was a great pleasure, he told his wife, as the Talmudic prodigy within him joyfully reemerged.[31]

True to his system of polarities, he organized the vast rabbinic corpus around two opposing "schools" and personalities, those of the first- and second-century Talmudic sages Rabbi Akiva (Akiba ben Joseph) and Rabbi Ishmael (Ismael ben Elisha). Both rabbis, of course, believed that Moses received the Torah at Mount Sinai. But they diverged on how to interpret the meaning of this divine revelation. According to Heschel's contrast, Akiva was a mystic for whom every word, jot, and tittle of the Torah scrolls, even the crowns on the Hebrew letters, held hidden meaning. For Akiva, "the true Torah is in Heaven." Rabbi Ishmael, on the other hand, was a rationalist who emphasized the text's plain meaning. For him, "the Torah speaks the language of human beings." Together, these two personalities reflected Heschel's complex temperament and theological inclusiveness, which welcomed contradictions: "Rabbi Ishmael's qualities were modesty and punctiliousness, restraint and caution, moderation and patience. By contrast, Rabbi Akiva was all yearning and striving, insatiable appetite, unquenchable thirst." Heschel believed that these opposing tendencies remained constant throughout the history of Judaism.[32]

However, Heschel's sympathy with Rabbi Akiva, a "poet at heart, and at the same time a razor-sharp genius," was obvious. He found his own synthesis of intellect and intuition in Akiva, and his activism as well. Akiva sought to "arouse the public, to demand action from them, to be their guide. . . . He was a man of action, a spokesman for his people, a public servant, and a traveler to lands beyond the sea." Above all, Heschel located his own theology of divine pathos in Rabbi Akiva's teaching. A classic interpreter of normative Judaism, Akiva also anticipated Heschel's "veritable revolution in religious thought." In writing this book on the Talmud, Heschel was seeking a *hekhsher* (certificate of kashrut) for his open-minded philosophy of religion. The study he had provisionally called the "Battle of the Books" defined rabbinic Judaism as both supernatural in its orthodoxy and open to diverse interpretations.[33]

Heschel was impelled to write *Heavenly Torah* for reasons even more intimate than validating his theology. At the heart of his approach to Talmud was a desire for attachment to God, as he stated in the introduction to volume 2, published in 1965. Like his uncle the Novominsker rebbe of Warsaw, who each day recited by heart chapters of the Mishnah, Heschel felt that the process of interpretation created a relation to holiness, even a state of *devekut*, "cleaving to God."[34]

The book's dedication implied yet another poignant motivation, as it recalled his most acute personal losses: "To the memory of my mother, the saintly Rivka Reizel, and to the memory of my sisters, Devorah Miriam, Esther Sima, and Gittel, who perished in the Shoah. May their souls be kept among the immortals." He then cited a Midrashic reflection on Deuteronomy 32:4: "The Rock! His deeds are perfect, / Yea, all His ways are just." In this manner, both explicit and discreet, cloaked in irony, Heschel advocated Akiva's affirmation of God's justice despite the horrible state of the world.[35]

There remained still another motivation, sad, self-defeating, but touchingly human. Admired by his Hasidic relatives as a *lamdan*, a learned and brilliant Talmudic scholar, Heschel could not suppress his longing to be acknowledged by Saul Lieberman, despite the obvious fact that Lieberman was incapable of appreciating his way of thinking. At the Jewish Theological Seminary one studied Talmud only for its own sake, not for a theological or practical purpose. Moreover, for Lieberman, Judaism was essentially law, not spiritual insight. For Heschel, all sacred study could lead to deeds of righteousness. Heschel gave a signed copy of *Heavenly Torah* to Lieberman, hoping for some appreciation of its value. The great Talmudist wrote Heschel a mean and denigrating note: he called it a nice volume, full of quotations, but pointed out that the great Hungarian Semitic scholar Wilhelm Bacher had already organized the rabbinic corpus so as to highlight Rabbis Akiva and Ishmael. Heschel confided this insult to Wolfe Kelman, who insisted that Heschel return the note to Lieberman. Heschel did so, and Lieberman answered with a more civilized acknowledgment and an implicit apology.[36]

There were few reviews of Heschel's monumental book, but those that appeared all touched upon questions of method. Praise came from the eminent Louis Jacobs of Jews' College in London, writing in *Conservative Judaism*. For Hebrew readers of *Hadoar*, David Shlomo Shapiro, a Bible scholar and Orthodox rabbi from Milwaukee, commended Heschel as a historian of Jewish thought who had rehabilitated the intellectual relevance of aggadah. Jacob Neusner, a former student secretary of Heschel's at JTS and now an assistant professor at Dartmouth College at the beginning of a remarkable career as a textual scholar and cultural critic, was the first to understand that *Heavenly Torah* was the key to Heschel's entire work; it was an exploration of religious knowledge, "the ways in which God makes himself known."[37]

It took Israeli scholars three years to take notice of *Heavenly Torah*. After the second volume appeared in 1965, Ya'akov Levinger, in the religious periodical *De'ot*, raised the inevitable question of Heschel's scholarly approach. The book's format was one of standard academic erudition, with footnotes, abundant citation of authorities, and the rest of the scholarly apparatus, but the author's orientation was personal, organized by topics, and without a discernable logical order. Rivka Horwitz wrote an exposition in the Israeli periodical *Molad*. Aware that conventional academics would mistrust Heschel's mixture of textual, conceptual analysis and personal involvement, she explained: "Often . . . we have the sense that we are facing an impassioned poet who speaks of matters that tug at his own heartstrings."[38]

While writing *Heavenly Torah*, Heschel also completed another long overdue project, transforming his German doctoral dissertation on the prophets into an inspiring book for Americans. In early 1957 he believed that his revised manuscript was almost ready, as he wrote to Solomon Grayzel, on the assumption that the Jewish Publication Society would publish it. The following year he completed several chapters, but the book remained unfinished. Two years later, in fall 1960, Harper and Row agreed to bring it out with JPS.[39]

In the meantime, Heschel published excerpts from the manuscript. He placed one selection in *Judaism*, another in a volume honoring Rabbi Leo Jung, an intellectual leader of modern Orthodoxy, and translations in journals in France and a Yiddish magazine in Buenos Aires. But he once more missed the JPS deadline for *The Prophets of Israel*, as the book was still entitled. Finally, in May 1962, he delivered the manuscript to Harper and Row, complete except for a brief chapter on the prophet known as Second Isaiah. But the publisher had to hire an outside consultant to reorganize and edit the manuscript, which was repetitious and too long. After additional postponements, *The Prophets* came out in February 1963. It was an impressive volume of more than five hundred pages.[40]

In his introduction, dated August 1962, Heschel defined his preference for phenomenology over the historical-critical methods favored by most scholars. He drew an exaggerated contrast between the scientific approach he had practiced as a doctoral candidate in Berlin—"pure reflection" on prophetic consciousness—and his present stance of personal involvement. A detached, academic approach was impossible, even irresponsible, he now insisted.[41]

In some of his most compelling prose, replete with alliteration and assonance, Heschel justified his empathy with these ancient radicals: "The situation of a person immersed in the prophets' words is one of being exposed to a ceaseless shattering of indifference, and one needs a skull of stone to remain callous to such blows." He wanted readers of all faiths to experience "communion with the prophets," who illustrated his religious philosophy by providing models of *"exegesis of existence from a divine perspective."* This was the biblical groundwork of Heschel's activism.[42]

Most salient was the moral urgency of *The Prophets*, beginning with the dedication "to the martyrs of 1940–45." Heschel's dedicatory epigraph from Psalm 44 ended with the bitterest question to God: "Why dost Thou hide Thy face?" Heschel continued to ask, as he had a decade earlier in *Man Is Not Alone*, What is the meaning, if any, of the Holocaust?[43]

The preface and chapters 1–8 introduced individual prophets with sketches of their personality, historical background, and message. Chapters 9–18 defined biblical notions of history, justice, chastisement, the theology of pathos, and the religion of sympathy. The final section, chapters 19–27, carried over technical expositions on method from *Die Prophetie* that were meant to shield the mystery of divine revelation from being minimized by psychological or anthropological explanations of ecstasy, poetic inspiration, or psychosis. Heschel concluded with the notion of God as divine subject, the keynote of his theology.

The author's voice took on vehement tones as he showed how the prophets criticized opportunistic religion and power politics: "Few are guilty, but all are responsible. If we admit that the individual is in some way conditioned or affected by the spirit of society, an individual's crime discloses society's corruption." Heschel presented prophetic Judaism as radical and subversive. Politics must be applied spiritually in order to augment moral sensitivity as well as to produce correct action: "The purpose of prophecy is to conquer callousness, to change the inner man as well as to revolutionize history." The prophet was not a diplomat, and he stood outside social norms: "The prophet hates the approximate, he shuns the middle of the road. . . . The prophet is strange, one-sided, an unbearable extremist."[44]

The book's psychological dimension was perhaps its most original, and personal, contribution. Close to Heschel's own sensibility were Hosea, Isaiah, and Jeremiah, in part because they voiced something of his own piercing loneliness: "[The prophet] alienates the wicked as well as the pious, the cynics as well as the believers, the priests and the princes, the judges and the false prophets." Hosea, especially, suffered because of his sympathy for God's anger at unfaithful Israel. God ordered him to marry a loose woman named Gomer, whom Hosea then rejected after discovering that she had several lovers; but God insisted that Hosea take her back. Hosea's suffering, according to Heschel, was an experience of God's own suffering because of Israel's infidelities.[45]

Later, during the Vietnam War, Heschel emulated Isaiah, denouncing the U.S. government's arrogance and the moral apathy of most Americans: "Callousness is sovereign and smug; it clings to the soul and will not give in. The crack of doom is in the air, but the people, unperturbed, are carried away by a rage to be merry." Isaiah rejected tactical politics and military power, devoting himself instead to "the day when nations 'shall beat their swords into plowshares and their spears into pruning hooks.' "[46]

Most intimately, the prophet Jeremiah reflected Heschel's inner, emotional combat; both men were raw, hypersensitive, overly vulnerable. Jeremiah (and Heschel) endured a "hypertrophy of sympathy" in which emotions carried him away: "Such excess of sympathy with the divine wrath shows the danger of sympathy grown absolute." Sometimes Heschel seemed to lose control of his indignation, as when he defended the highest standards of feeling and commitment in the presence of ranking government officials.[47]

The prophet known as Second Isaiah was Heschel's model of faith after the Holocaust: "It is a prophecy tempered with human tears, mixed with a joy that heals all scars. . . . No words have gone further in offering comfort when the sick world cries." The people Israel, who were God's "suffering servant," were thus prepared to accept the mystery. In the end, God's love would prevail. Human agony could be given meaning.[48]

The book's final sentences reaffirmed Heschel's view of the human self as something "transcendent in disguise," a reflection of God's consciousness: " 'Know thy God' (I Chron. 28:9) rather than 'Know Thyself' is the categorical imperative of the biblical man. There is no self-understanding without God-understanding."[49]

Of all Heschel's books to date, *The Prophets* received the widest critical attention in both academic and general publications, Christian and Jewish. Christians admired his dramatic account of their Old Testament precursors. In fact, Harper and Row had promoted *The Prophets* with this in mind, using advance praise from Reinhold Niebuhr and James Muilenburg on the jacket. *Christian Century* praised Heschel's rendition of "divine pathos" and his "beauty of language . . . profundity of analysis and . . . subtlety of insight." A reviewer in the Jesuit magazine *America* promised, "There is not a dull page in it."[50]

The most thorough academic reviews came from Brevard S. Childs of Yale Divinity School and Samuel Terrien of Union Theological Seminary. These

Christian Old Testament experts recognized that Heschel had sidestepped conventional scholarly issues to focus on the inner life of the prophets. Terrien lauded the book's virtues while pointing to a number of omissions, among them neglect of literary examination of the authorship of the book of Amos and the lack of form-critical analysis. Nevertheless, Terrien concluded: "It would be difficult, if not impossible, to find elsewhere a more lucid and compelling appreciation for the reality of the divine pathos."[51]

Jewish critics involved in public debates were more divided. In *Commentary*, David Daiches, professor of literature at the University of Sussex, England, judged *The Prophets* in light of the Holocaust. Objecting that Heschel avoided the enigma of why the righteous suffer, he dismissed the author's contention that "History is a nightmare" as another of his "vague generalizations." On the positive side, Daiches appreciated Heschel's poetic instinct for the prophet's compassion for God: "Dr. Heschel is at his best in analyzing (though with a good deal of repetition) this unique feature of Hebrew prophecy."[52]

Confusion about Heschel's views on (and use of) metaphorical language aroused the ire of Daiches, a secularist, as well as of Eliezer Berkovits, an Orthodox Jew. Daiches was irked by Heschel's support for the notion of divine revelation: "One may appreciate the greatness and uniqueness of the Prophets without committing oneself to this literal belief." Writing in a new journal, *Tradition: A Journal of Orthodox Thought*, Berkovits rejected Heschel's notion of divine concern as un-Jewish: "The boldness of Dr. Heschel's thought consists, first, in taking literally all biblical expressions that ascribe to God emotions of love and hatred."[53]

On the other side of the argument, David Shlomo Shapiro, who had favorably reviewed *Torah min ha-shamayim*, upheld Heschel's emphasis on the pathos of God. Writing in Hebrew in *Hadoar*, Shapiro praised Heschel's synthesis of theology and ethics: "There is no dichotomy of pathos and ethos, of motive and norm. . . . It is because God is the source of justice that His pathos is ethical; and it is because God is absolutely personal, devoid of anything impersonal, that His ethos is full of pathos."[54]

The Prophets was widely perceived, especially in Protestant theological seminaries, as a reanimation of the Hebrew spirit. The book soon provided Heschel himself with inspiration—and quotations—as a defender of civil rights and, especially, as an opponent to America's intervention in Vietnam.

12

We Shall Overcome (1963–1966)

Racism is an evil of tremendous power, but God's will transcends all powers. Surrender to despair is surrender to evil. It is important to feel anxiety, it is sinful to wallow in despair. What we need is a total mobilization of the heart, intelligence, and wealth for the purpose of love and justice. God is in search of men, waiting, hoping for man to do His will.

—Heschel, "The Religious Basis of Equality of Opportunity: The Segregation of God" (1963)

THE YEAR 1963 WAS A WATERSHED, WHEN HIGHEST HOPES TURNED TO BITTER disillusionment. That January, Americans celebrated the centenary of the Emancipation Proclamation. Pope John XXIII passed away on 3 June, but hopes for the renewal of the Roman Catholic Church through the ongoing Second Vatican Council remained strong. Later that summer, on 28 August, more than two hundred thousand citizens gathered in Washington, D.C., to support equal opportunity for blacks and were uplifted by Martin Luther King's "I Have a Dream" speech. Then, on 22 November, President John F. Kennedy was assassinated in Dallas, Texas, a catastrophe that threatened to destroy the nation's self-confidence. Soon afterward, Heschel took sober measure of the historical moment: "Our world, which is full of cynicism, frustration, and despair, received in 1963 a flash of inspiration; 1963 was a noble year, a triumph of conscience, a triumph of faith. It will depend upon us whether 1963 will remain a chapter in sacred history."[1]

Racism and Religion

Having experienced the ravages of European anti-Semitism, Heschel had an abhorrence of American racism that began when he stepped off the boat in 1940 and deepened with his friendships with Larry Harris and Abraham Cronbach in Cincinnati, through which he learned more about the prejudices African Americans endured. In 1958 he began to speak out publicly, making a sharp pronouncement to the Rabbinical Assembly deploring "our timidity and hesitance to take a stand on behalf of the Negroes." In 1963, as the civil rights movement increasingly dominated national attention, he realized that his time to act had arrived.[2]

Again it was Marc Tanenbaum, seconded by Wolfe Kelman—both forceful supporters of civil rights—who brought Heschel to the fore. Tanenbaum presided over a planning meeting for the first "National Conference on Religion and Race," due to take place in Chicago in January 1963. Heschel was chosen to be the keynote speaker at the opening plenary session, where he would provide "the prophetic inspirational statement," according to an internal memorandum.[3]

For the first time in American history, leaders of the country's three major faiths—Catholicism, Judaism, and Protestantism—were meeting for a candid discussion of race relations. The process was coordinated by Mathew Ahmann, director of the National Catholic Conference for Interracial Justice. Sponsors were the Department of Racial and Cultural Relations of the National

Council of Churches of Christ; the Social Action Department of the National Catholic Welfare Conference; and the Social Action Commission of the Synagogue Council of America, in addition to sixty-eight other national groups. More than 650 voting delegates and 200 local observers were present at the opening plenary on 14 January 1963 at which the conference chairman, Dr. Benjamin E. Mays, president of Morehouse College, read greetings from President John F. Kennedy. Mays then presented Abraham Joshua Heschel.[4]

Heschel's address, "The Religious Basis of Equality and Opportunity," stirred the predominantly Christian audience with its dramatic biblical analogies. Alluding to international summit meetings of the Cold War era, he associated the current racial situation with the Israelite epic of liberation: "At the first conference on religion and race, the main participants were Pharaoh and Moses. Moses' words were: 'Thus says the Lord, the God of Israel, let my people go that they may celebrate a feast to me.' While Pharaoh retorted: 'Who is the Lord, that I should heed this voice and let Israel go? I do not know the Lord, and moreover I will not let Israel go.' The outcome of that summit meeting has not come to an end. Pharaoh is not ready to capitulate. The exodus began, but is far from having been completed. In fact, it was easier for the children of Israel to cross the Red Sea than for a Negro to cross certain university campuses." On theological grounds Heschel denounced racism and the moral insensitivity that made it possible: "Racial or religious bigotry must be recognized for what it is: Satanism, a blasphemy." (He added these last words by hand to the speech manuscript, having originally written: "*Racial or religious bigotry* must be recognized for what it is: atheism.") Quoting Reinhold Niebuhr he declared, "'Race prejudice, a universal human ailment, is the most recalcitrant aspect of evil in man,' a treacherous denial of the existence of God."[5]

Drawing on lively formulations from *The Prophets*, Heschel sought to galvanize his hearers. He believed that detachment was the problem keeping whites from embracing the cause of what he described as universal human dignity. He restated one of his radical injunctions from the Talmud: "It is better . . . to throw oneself alive into a burning furnace than to humiliate a human being publicly." What was needed was a transformation of the nation's soul: "*The Negro problem is God's gift to America*, the test of our integrity, a magnificent spiritual opportunity." Hopeful, even optimistic, he cited Pope John XXIII, who had opened the twenty-first Ecumenical Council with the words "Divine Providence is leading us to a new order of human relations." Heschel concluded: "History has made us all neighbors. The age of moral mediocrity and complacency has run out. This is a time for radical commitment, for radical action."[6]

Not all participants were swayed. First to respond was William Stringfellow, an Episcopalian and an activist poverty lawyer. Himself a political radical, Stringfellow had lived in Harlem for several years after graduating from Harvard Law School. Bluntly, and with bitterness, he said that the time had come for more than what he called Heschel's "lamentation." The historical struggle was not only between the individual and God but between the institutions and ideologies of this world. The "Conference on Religion and Race" "was too little, too late, and too lily white," he insisted. The white majority in the audience was stung, even offended, when Stringfellow wryly expressed gratitude that the solution to the country's racial crisis did not depend on the church. He challenged the conference to support the Black Muslim movement; Malcolm X (not just Martin Luther King, Jr.) should have been invited to give an address.[7]

But Albert Vorspan, director of the Commission on Social Action, Union of American Hebrew Congregations (the Reform Jewish lay organization), spoke for many who saw hope in the religious alliance. Annoyed by Stringfellow's negativity, Vorspan tempered his original intention to chastise the ills of institutional religion by emphasizing the black-white alliance. We should not yield to despair nor send for sackcloth and ashes, he warned.[8]

The final speech was to be given by Martin Luther King, Jr., whom Heschel met for the first time at the conference. The two quickly became allies, realizing that they shared basic ways of perceiving the world, not least a biblical theology grounded in the Israelites' liberation from slavery in Egypt, and a commitment to nonviolence. Both men were charismatic orators at the fullness of their powers, Heschel as a writer and speaker, the younger King as a preacher and movement leader. Each had been influenced by the activist theology of Reinhold Niebuhr and used it to help communicate his minority experience to the American mainstream.[9]

Both men had grown up in a hostile environment, experiencing the indignities of racism and its lethal effects on their people, Heschel in Poland and Germany, King in the segregated American South. Each was the heir to a religious dynasty, primed from childhood for sacred obligations. King's father, the Reverend Martin Luther King, Sr., was pastor of the prestigious Ebenezer Baptist Church in Atlanta; Heschel's father and ancestors were Hasidic rabbis. Like Heschel, King was intellectually precocious. At age fifteen he entered Atlanta's Morehouse College, and he was later ordained at Crozier Theological

Seminary in Chester, Pennsylvania. King went on to earn a Ph.D. from Boston University, and in 1954 he became pastor of the Dexter Avenue Baptist Church in Montgomery, Alabama, from which he launched his civil rights campaigns.

In their private lives, each had married a musician: Heschel's wife, Sylvia, was a pianist; King had met his wife, Coretta Scott, when she was studying voice at New England Conservatory of Music in Boston. The two men even shared physical characteristics: both were relatively short (5'7") and stocky, weighing about 170 pounds.

Now, in Chicago, King closed the conference with an authoritative "Challenge to the Churches and the Synagogues." Several times bringing the audience to its feet, King offered a harsh diagnosis: "We must face the melancholy fact that one hundred years after the Emancipation Proclamation, the Negro is still dominated politically, exploited economically, and humiliated socially. Negroes, North and South, still live in segregation, housed in unendurable slums, eat in segregation, pray in segregation and die in segregation." In much the same way as Heschel, who deplored the mediocrity of institutional religion, King chastised organized Christianity as untrue to its root values: "If the Church does not recapture its prophetic zeal, it will become little more than an irrelevant social club with a thin veneer of religiosity." King shared Heschel's focus on the sanctity of the human being in the eyes of God: "Segregation denies the sacredness of the human personality. . . . Human worth lies in relatedness to God. An individual has value because he has value to God."[10]

Time magazine published a brief, pessimistic account of the Chicago event: "The dominant mood of the four-day meeting . . . was what one participant called 'that awful fatalism.'" However, the issue devoted two columns to Heschel's recent book, *The Prophets*, accompanied by a photograph. Touting him as "one of the world's most illustrious Jewish theologians," *Time* praised Heschel for his "prophetlike" intervention at the conference: "He was a mordant critic of religious ineffectiveness in U.S. race question [*sic*]."[11]

One consequence of this conference for Heschel was that he was invited to join four hundred Christian and Jewish clergy for a meeting with President Kennedy and his brother Robert, the attorney general, in the East Room of the White House. On 16 June 1963, the day before the event, Heschel sent the president a telegram, proclaiming: "Let religious leaders donate one month's salary toward fund for Negro housing and education. I propose that you Mr. President declare a state of moral emergency. A Marshall Plan for aid to

Negroes is becoming a necessity. The hour calls for high moral grandeur and spiritual audacity."[12]

One result of the Chicago assembly was that similar conferences were instituted across the country. These local events became the most practical manner of forming coalitions among people of different races, religions, and classes. In February 1964 Heschel addressed one such interfaith meeting at the America Hotel in Manhattan, under the auspices of the "Metropolitan New York Conference on Religion and Race." The sponsors included the New York Board of Rabbis, the Protestant Council of the City of New York, the Queens Federation of Churches, the Roman Catholic Archdiocese of New York, and the Roman Catholic Diocese of Brooklyn. More than two thousand clergy and laity participated in the day-long series of meetings.[13]

Heschel spoke at the dinner session, along with New York mayor Richard Wagner and Francis Cardinal Spellman, the archbishop of New York. Heschel updated his Chicago speech with an even bolder presentation: "The White Man on Trial." With the memories of the March on Washington the preceding August still vivid, Heschel again cited the exodus from Egypt. This time he compared the grumbling of the Israelites wandering in the desert to the legitimate complaints of African Americans: "The Negroes of America behave just like the children of Israel. . . . Now three months later they have the audacity to murmur: what shall we drink? We want adequate education, decent housing, proper employment. How ordinary, how unpoetic, how annoying!" Sharpening his criticism of the complacency of whites, Heschel mockingly condemned the national mood: "Life could be so pleasant. The Beatles have just paid us a visit. The AT&T is about to split its stocks. Dividends are higher than ever. Vietnam has a sensible government. Castro is quiet and well-mannered. Khrushchev is purchasing grain from us. Only the Negroes continue to disturb us: What shall we drink?"[14]

Heschel's rhetoric was radical, but so were his goals: he demanded nothing less than a "spiritual revolution." He distinguished between the "major legal and social revolution," which was a necessary precondition, and its underlying meaning, "a spiritual emergency, the need for all of us to change our image of the Negro as well as the need of the Negro to enhance his own proper image. . . . It is a psychological law that people will only respect a person who has self-respect and entertain contempt for a person who has self-contempt." Religion, which demanded inner integrity of its adherents, was the most authentic vehicle for ideals of social transformation. Legislation was, of course, necessary, but "true fellowship" and "democratization" of education must be founded not only on "riding on the same bus" but on the ability to share "moments of joy, cultural values, insights, commitments." The civil rights revolution required a spiritual revolution, intuitive communication. World history was at a turning point, and Heschel believed that he was speaking for all persecuted peoples, not only American blacks and Jews in Soviet Russia, but also "the people in Tibet, the hungry masses in India and Brazil, the sick and the poor, the wetbacks, the Braceros in our own country."[15]

More locally, Heschel involved himself in the strife in New York City between local black leaders and the predominantly Jewish Teachers Union. He opposed school boycotts threatened by community activists, but he also supported a busing system for the higher grades. Along with John Bennett, president of Union Theological Seminary, and Monsignor Gregory L. Mooney of the Catholic Interracial Council, Heschel signed a letter to the *New York Times* urging that the city provide superior integrated education to all its children. Heschel remained active in the Coalition for Integrated Education and forcefully expressed his views at meetings.[16]

In 1965 Heschel moved beyond giving speeches, publishing essays, and attending meetings condemning racial discrimination to joining protests in the streets. His fuller involvement was instigated by a brutal police assault on nonviolent black protesters in Selma, Alabama, on 7 March. John Lewis, chairman of the Student Non-Violent Coordinating Committee (SNCC), and Hosea Williams of the Southern Christian Leadership Conference (SCLC) had initiated a small, unorganized march from Selma to the state capital at Montgomery. As the hundred or so demonstrators started to cross the Edmund Pettus Bridge to the highway, they were attacked by mounted state troopers with dogs and tear gas, who severely beat them with clubs. The attack immediately acquired the name Bloody Sunday.

That evening an ABC television documentary, "Trial at Nuremberg," was interrupted by graphic footage of the current American violence. Heschel was not alone in recognizing the parallels with Nazi Germany, proclaimed in nationwide headlines the next day. (The Kristallnacht pogrom of the night of 9–10 November 1938 was originally known as Bloody Thursday.) Horrified, President Lyndon Johnson pressed Attorney General Nicholas Katzenbach for solutions, while members of Congress championed legislation to secure voting rights for blacks.[17]

Americans could no longer deny the racial crisis. There was tremendous moral outrage, sparking hundreds of demonstrations around the country. Mayors, governors, and religious leaders condemned the segregationists and championed the nonviolent activists. In this atmosphere of upheaval Heschel became a co-leader of a demonstration on 9 March in New York City to protest the attack. Along with young activists from SNCC and the Congress for Racial Equality (CORE), two groups considered "militant" (code word for extremist) by more established groups, Heschel took part in a "freedom march" to the New York FBI headquarters to deliver a petition demanding protection for voting rights workers and the arrest of violators of federal law. The approximately eight hundred marchers—students, clergy, doctors, and others—staged a two-hour protest in front of the headquarters at 69th Street and Third Avenue. Agents had erected barricades around the entrance to control the demonstrators, who held up traffic, marching and singing protest songs. Several leaders demanded to see John F. Malone, assistant director of the New York office. But the government agents refused to let the protestors enter, fearing a sit-in.

The report of Director Malone noted that he agreed to meet the leaders in the lobby; there the SNCC representatives demanded that two additional members be included in the meeting. The shabby appearance of the newcomers aroused his suspicion, as summarized in a memorandum to J. Edgar Hoover: "An experienced eye would immediately size them up as troublemakers." Heschel calmly mediated this dispute. After Malone "explained to the Rabbi that certain representatives of the group had obviously deceived him," Heschel was able to persuade the delegation to respect the original agreement. The report continued: "The two last-arrived individuals, the heavyweight Negro male and the woman, protested vigorously at this exclusion but finally accepted Rabbi Heschel's suggestion that they agree to Mr. Malone's suggestion that three would be sufficient to come upstairs." This action led to Heschel's inclusion on the FBI list of potential subversives, although the report had highlighted his calm and moderation during the confrontation and forty-five minute meeting.[18]

Once the FBI had identified Heschel as a troublemaker, the agency was swift to investigate him. The next day Heschel's name was recorded among the three hundred signers of an advertisement in the *Washington Post* calling for the repeal of the McCarran Act, which, "born in panic and productive of fear, adds nothing to our security and diminishes the honor of a democracy." (The 1950 McCarran Act required that Communists and other suspected "subversives" register with the attorney general; Senator Joseph McCarthy used it as the basis for his anti-Communist hearings.) From that time Heschel appeared on the wide-ranging FBI list of citizens to track. His public stands were documented, through direct observation by special agents, reports from informants, and newspaper accounts. Reports marked "secret" were then distributed to several security agencies, as well as to J. Edgar Hoover, who was widely known to be hostile to civil rights.[19]

Heschel was not long in giving them more to note down. In the two weeks after Bloody Sunday, a call went out nationwide for a massive march from Selma to Montgomery. This time the five-day march was carefully planned with the cooperation of the major civil rights organizations, including the SCLC (which raised most of the money and prepared the local people), SNCC, the National Association for the Advancement of Colored People (NAACP), and the Urban League. From around the country thousands of people chartered airplanes and buses to join the march at Selma or on the road to Montgomery. This protest had the protection of the Johnson administration. Under orders from the president, more than 1,800 armed Alabama National Guardsmen patrolled the route, with the help of the U.S. Army and about a hundred FBI agents. Helicopters hovered overhead.[20]

Heschel contributed to this historical witness. As an American citizen, he was exercising his constitutional rights; as a voice of biblical justice, he felt commanded to protest conspicuously. He had accepted his public role as Hebrew prophet. Despite fears for his safety from his wife and the twelve-year-old Susannah, he agreed to join the march at the urging of Rabbi Everett Gendler, a pacifist and former student. Gendler had led a group of rabbis to Birmingham, Alabama, to work for voting rights and remained in touch with the Reverend Andrew Young, King's executive assistant at the SCLC.

One week after his confrontation with the New York FBI, on 20 March, Saturday night after the Sabbath, Heschel and Wolfe Kelman took an airplane to Atlanta, where they stayed overnight. On the flight to Montgomery the next morning they met up with Maurice Davis, whom Heschel knew from HUC. Davis was now a Reform rabbi and married to the daughter of Abraham Cronbach. Andrew Young met them at the airport, and they drove to Selma in time to begin the march. Young was excited to meet Heschel, whose book on the prophets he had admired as a seminary student. He was struck that an academic scholar and theologian of Heschel's stature and age would participate in this march. "It lent a tremendous degree of credibility to our effort to have him join," he recalled. Heschel appeared in the light of a grandfather, as well as a prophet, for he enjoyed playing with Young's two children, who accompanied them. [21]

Heschel joined King on Sunday morning at a religious service at Brown's Chapel, where about two hundred people had spent the night, while more than three thousand waited outside. King welcomed the out-of-state participants;

then Heschel read from Psalm 27: "The Lord is my might and my salvation; whom shall I fear? / . . . When evil-doers came upon me to eat up my flesh, / Even mine adversaries and my foes, they stumbled and fell." King ended the service with a sermon on the wandering of the Israelites in the wilderness after the exodus from Egypt.[22]

While King was calling out names of people he wanted with him in the first three rows of the march, Heschel insisted that he be placed in the first row. Although Heschel had a sense of his own importance, his wish to be in front was not simply a question of ego; he understood the practical benefit of media images. With his yarmulke, white hair, and beard, Heschel knew that he looked like what the popular imagination thought of as a "rabbi." He joined Ralph Bunche, former undersecretary of the United Nations, King, and the Reverend Ralph Abernathy, King's key aide. On Heschel's right was the Reverend Fred Shuttlesworth of the SCLC. Also in front were Archbishop Iacovus of the Greek Orthodox Church, Walter Reuther of the AFL-CIO labor union, and John Lewis, the SNCC chairman, who had been one of the protestors beaten in the previous demonstration. All wore Hawaiian leis, a gift from one of the participants. Kelman marched in the second row with Andrew Young, who remained attentive to Heschel's well being.[23]

Heschel's instincts were correct. The essence of his brief, but deeply felt, participation in the Selma–Montgomery march was captured by a UPI photograph of him standing with King, Bunche, Shuttlesworth, and Lewis. Heschel's yarmulke, white hair, and beard made him the perfect media symbol of the Hebrew prophet. This image has been reproduced countless times as an icon of the civil rights movement and testimony to the black-Jewish coalitions of the 1950s and 1960s.

Fears for Heschel's safety on the march had been realistic. The onlookers expressed bitter anti-Semitism in addition to racial bigotry. As the demonstrators of all races and faiths, though mostly black, filed slowly through the white section of Selma, hostile onlookers cursed and jeered, and old women with sour looks sat in rocking chairs on their porches. Above them were displayed banners bearing such messages as: "Koons, Kikes and Niggers Go Home!" Adding to the intimidation, the police drove by, filming the marchers, many of whom found the National Guard presence as intimidating as it was protective. After four or five hours the procession stopped to rest. Many prominent individuals had planned to return home before reaching the end, after making their gesture of solidarity, among them Heschel, Kelman, and Davis. (King himself left temporarily for a speaking engagement in Chicago.)

Other witnesses joined the march along the way or went straight to Montgomery for the culmination.

After they left the march, Heschel, Kelman, and Davis went to the Montgomery airport, arriving quite late, hungry, and tense, and stopped at the snack bar to get something to eat. There Heschel's sense of humor and courage defused a nasty situation. The woman behind the counter was surly and rude, and she did nothing to hide her dislike of them. She looked at the white-bearded Heschel and said sarcastically, "Well, I'll be damned. My mother always told me there was a Santa Claus, and I didn't believe her . . . until now!" Heschel merely smiled. The men asked for food. She said there was none. They asked for bread. She said there was none. Heschel kept smiling.[24]

Gently he asked her, with his soft voice and Yiddish accent, "Is it possible that in the kitchen there might be some water?" She admitted there was. "Is it possible that in the refrigerator you might find a couple of eggs?" She thought it possible. "Well, if you take the eggs, and boil them in the water, that would be just fine."

She glowered at him, "And why should I?"

"Why should you? Well, after all, I did you a favor."

"What favor did you ever do me?"

"I proved there was a Santa Claus."

She burst out laughing and went to make them some dinner.

While they were waiting, Heschel turned to Rabbi Davis and asked him whether he had called his wife, Marion, whom Heschel also knew. Davis explained that he and Marion had an arrangement: he never telephoned unless something was wrong. Heschel shook his head in disagreement. Davis explained that otherwise Marion would be apprehensive if she did not hear from him, or if he was delayed in calling. Again Heschel shook his head.

Heschel said, "Maurie, I called my wife. Now you do the same." Davis answered, "Yes, sir," and called Marion. As she answered the phone he knew something was wrong. Her father, Abraham Cronbach, had just suffered a stroke and was hospitalized in Cincinnati.

Davis dashed to the airline counter to get a ticket to Cincinnati, but no scheduled flights were going there. Heschel told him to request a seat on a plane to Cincinnati that a Rabbi Goldman had chartered. There were no vacant seats. Heschel insisted, "Then tell Goldman to get off the plane, and give you his seat." It seemed clear to him.

A woman on the flight overheard their conversation and exchanged her seat for his ticket to Atlanta, while Davis gave her some money to fly home the next day. Davis flew directly to Cincinnati and spent the night at the hospital with his wife and father-in-law.

The Selma–Montgomery march ended four days later. Close to fifty thousand people had poured into the capital for the final speeches. Flags of the state of Alabama and the Confederacy flew above the capitol building of segregationist governor George Wallace, but not the colors of the United States of America. After speeches by Ralph Bunche, Roy Wilkins of the NAACP, James Farmer of CORE, Whitney Young of the Urban League, Rosa Parks, Bayard Rustin, and others, King gave a magnificent oration. Back in New York, in a private memorandum, Heschel formulated the spiritual meaning of the protest. He wrote about "having walked with Hasidic rabbis on various occasions. I felt a sense of the Holy in what I was doing. . . . Even without words our march was worship. I felt my legs were praying."[25]

Four months later, on 6 August 1965, President Johnson signed the Voting Rights Act.

Saving Soviet Jewry

While expressing his solidarity with African Americans, Heschel was foremost among Jewish leaders in speaking out against the catastrophic situation of Jews in the Soviet Union. Through the lens of the Holocaust, he perceived the persecutions they were undergoing as a form of cultural genocide. The Soviet constitution guaranteed freedom of religion to all peoples, but in reality this applied only to the Russian Orthodox Church and a few Protestant denominations. Roman Catholics had been expelled, while the Jewish population of more than 3 million was beset by restrictions. Jews were forbidden to operate religious schools; only one theological seminary was operating, and it was foundering. In addition, around four hundred synagogues had been forcibly shut down, leaving only ninety-five remaining. Jewish cemeteries were closed in Moscow, Kiev, and Minsk. There were no prayer books. The baking of Passover matzoh was outlawed. Anti-Semitic propaganda proliferated in newspapers.

In America, the Jewish establishment was slow to respond to the situation, held back by political caution, simple ignorance, or moral lethargy. But in 1961 the Synagogue Council of America (the Conservative congregational group) established a policy to pressure the Soviet authorities. Wolfe Kelman reported that the plight of Soviet Jewry was high on the list of priorities of the Rabbinical Assembly: he noted that the previous year the Synagogue Council and the

Rabbinical Assembly had made widely publicized efforts to establish exchange visits between the Russian Jewish and the American Jewish communities. "I feel we can be justifiably proud of our role in that situation," said Kelman, without reporting the poor results.[26]

In reality, bolder diplomacy was imperative. Launching another initiative, the Synagogue Council sent a delegation to the "political counselor" of the Soviet Embassy, Georgy Kornienko, with a list of "concerns," including the recent death sentences for Jews accused of "economic crimes," as well as the Soviets' refusal to allow contacts between American and Soviet Jewish leaders and the prohibitions on baking matzoh and other religious observance. When the Soviet authorities did not respond, the Synagogue Council enlisted help from the National Council of Churches.[27]

The interfaith effort met with better success. A delegation of American Christians visited the Soviet Union and reported that the Jewish community was suffering from "poor, run-down" synagogues and "a lack of rabbis." A group of Soviet Christians then came to New York, where they met with Jewish groups; later they visited Jewish leaders throughout the country. On 3 July 1963 Jewish and Christian activists met with Anatoly Myshkov of the Soviet Embassy in Washington. Formal negotiations on the Jewish question had begun.

Heschel was scheduled to address Conservative rabbis on the general topic of moral responsibility shortly after the August 1963 March on Washington (which Heschel did not attend). He proposed to repeat his address on civil rights, but Kelman insisted that he concentrate on the persecution of Jews in Soviet Russia. Heschel welcomed this opportunity to open his heart. At the meeting, which took place on 4 September, he was uncompromising, unusually severe. He judged that the soul of American Jewry was once again threatened, as it had been in 1940–43, by apathy. He inveighed against this apparent unconcern: "There is a dreadful moral trauma that haunts many of us: The failure of those of us who lived in free countries to do their utmost in order to save Jews under Hitler." Russian Jewry was "the last remnant of a spiritual glory that is no more," and it was in danger of annihilation.[28]

Heschel's civil rights coalitions gave him hope that the conscience of America had been "electrified" by the mass demonstrations and victories in the Supreme Court. Idealistically, he was "sure that the Negroes will be ready to join us on behalf of equal rights for Jews in Russia." But he directed his principal message to the rabbis. After seeking to arouse their compassion by citing a Hasidic master, he described the "strange rite" in which the neck of a red heifer, a flawless, unworked young cow, was broken, and the body burned to atone for a murder. For Heschel, abandoning Soviet Jewry was equivalent to murder. He bitterly named several ways American Jews tried to assuage their consciences, concluding: "We are busy in 1963 just as we were busy in 1943." Finally, Heschel cited other instances of indifference to the mass persecution of Jews. He recalled that as a boy he had been amazed that there was "no moral indignation in Europe, when a whole people was driven out of Spain in 1492. Was there no outcry, no outburst of anger when human beings were burned alive in the auto-da-fé?" He then cited another, more ancient failure, "the indifference of our people to the Ten Tribes." Soviet Jewry, he insisted, must not be lost as well, consigned to oblivion.[29]

Heschel recognized the political hazards of his position: relations between the United States and the Soviet Union were unstable, although the Nuclear Test Ban Treaty had recently been signed, and there was danger in provoking the Soviets. But he considered politics secondary to moral issues, concluding with the outcry: "Let the 20th century not enter the annals of Jewish history as the century of physical and spiritual destruction!"

Kelman carefully publicized Heschel's message. He had arranged for Gershon Jacobson, a Russian Jewish immigrant and journalist writing in both Yiddish and English, to attend the address, which Jacobson printed in English in the Yiddish-language newspaper the *Day-Morning Journal* two weeks later (following the Holy Days) in three installments.

The next fall, again during the High Holy Days, Heschel challenged the conscience of American Jews even more aggressively. At the 28 October 1964 meeting of the New York Conference on Soviet Jewry at Hunter College, in front of an audience of more than two thousand, he delivered a relentless condemnation of the Soviets. There was some hope that Leonid Brezhnev, who had replaced the deposed Nikita Khrushchev as general secretary of the Communist Party, would bring in new leaders, more favorable to Jews. Yet Heschel insisted that Stalinism was not dead. Reaching unprecedented heights of invective, Heschel excoriated the disease of official racism, so familiar to him: "Malice, madness and blind hatred had combined in Stalin's mind to produce a foul monster whose work goes on to this very day. It is a sinister fiend whose work is a kind of blood-sucking cruelty in depriving Jewish citizens of their pride, of their human dignity, of their spiritual authenticity." With mordant sarcasm he inquired why Soviet leaders worried so much about the baking of matzoh, or the importation of a few prayer books from abroad; why they forbade the teaching of Hebrew, the language of the prophets. Jewish civilization was being undermined by petty bureaucrats, stupidity, even corruption within the Soviet Jewish community itself.[30]

Heschel ended with a prod at the conscience of American Jews, who still were not doing enough, in his opinion, to help their Soviet brothers and sisters. The very presence of God was at stake, he told them, illustrating this claim with a commentary on Isaiah 43:12 ("I have declared, and I have saved, and I have announced, and there was no strange god among you; therefore ye are My witnesses, saith the Lord, and I am God"): "A rabbi of the second century took the statement to mean, if you are my witnesses, I am God; if you cease to be my witnesses, there is no God to be met." Soviet Jewry was an ultimate test of the free world: "To fight for human rights is to save our own souls."[31]

Two years later, Heschel was not satisfied with the progress made by two national conferences on Soviet Jewry. At the 1966 annual convention of the Rabbinical Assembly, held for the first time in Toronto, he ignited a controversy that spread beyond the conference when he condemned the American establishment for "spending their energy on dealing with marginal non-vital issues rather than on the most important emergency of our day." In his zeal Heschel made a serious tactical error by targeting the Conference of Presidents of Major American Jewish Organizations, set up years before to represent twenty-four religious and secular groups.[32]

In point of fact, Heschel spoke twice, first on his announced topic of interfaith dialogue, then at the session on Soviet Jewry (at which Elie Wiesel, who had recently returned from the Soviet Union, gave Heschel credit for impelling him to action: "I went for a very simple reason. I was moved by what Rabbi Heschel, the first to raise his voice, had said and written about the Jewish tragedy in Russia."). Like Heschel, Wiesel spared no words as he indicted Jews around the world for abandoning the 3 million Soviet Jews, drawing a parallel with the Holocaust. As the *New York Times* reported the next day, Wiesel "charged that the Soviet Jewry issue 'was being utilized by some Jewish leaders for self-aggrandizement and fund-raising and not in an effort to evoke the conscience of the world to the plight of Soviet Jews.'" The same article quoted Heschel, ensuring that his accusations against the American Jewish establishment would be widely disseminated.[33]

The establishment immediately struck back as Rabbi Joachim Prinz, chairman of the Conference of Presidents, publicly targeted Heschel's criticism, dismissing his accusation. (Prinz, a refugee from Germany, a congregational rabbi in Newark, New Jersey, and president of the American Jewish Congress, had been the Jewish speaker at the 1963 March on Washington.) A more personal attack came from Rabbi Israel Miller, chairman of the American Jewish Conference on Soviet Jewry, who denounced Heschel for "vocal demagoguery." Miller's words were picked up by Jewish newspapers all around the country.[34]

However, even among the Jewish establishment, many felt that Heschel had been justified in his criticism. The Rabbinical Assembly officially expressed "dismay" at the repudiation of Heschel, "who has been a prime mover in awakening the conscience of American Jewry about the conditions of our brothers in the Soviet Union." An editorial in *Jewish Week* of Washington, D.C., developed a realistic view of the dispute: "When the Conference on Soviet Jewry accused its critic, Rabbi Abraham Joshua Heschel, of 'demagoguery' it sounded very much like the indignation of a disturbed conscience." Heschel was a prophet of truth, not a cautious politician. At a high personal cost he attempted to spur self-criticism among Jewish leaders, pointing out organizational weaknesses that later were largely corrected.[35]

Heschel's persistent support for Soviet Jews also attracted FBI scrutiny. On 7 December 1966, the first night of Hanukkah, he participated in a vigil at Columbia University led by the controversial Hillel rabbi C. Bruce Goldman. The Newark FBI office took the account from the *New York Times* and, classifying it as relevant to the "CP [Communist Party], Counterintelligence Program," forwarded it to the national director with this note: "Bureau authority is requested to mail this clipping on four CP subjects of Jewish background."[36]

A Sacred Humanism

While actively pursuing a politics of witness, Heschel clarified his ethical and religious philosophy for the Raymond Fred West Memorial Lectures at Stanford University. This endowed series was intended to enable outstanding thinkers to address issues of "Immortality, Human Conduct, and Human Destiny." Heschel's appointment as the West lecturer represented significant academic recognition; his predecessors included the social philosopher Joseph Wood Krutch, Reinhold Niebuhr, and the biologist Julian Huxley.[37]

Heschel delivered three lectures, "In the Likeness and the Unlikeness of God," "In Search of Meaning," and "Existence and Exaltation," on 5, 7, and 8 May, arousing considerable interest among Stanford's activist students and faculty. He charmed and motivated the packed audiences in Dinkelspiel Auditorium, as reported in the student-run *Stanford Daily*, which highlighted his epigrammatic style in its summaries.

In "In the Likeness and Unlikeness of God," Heschel focused on the inner nature of human beings, drawing an ironic contrast between people and unreflective animals: "Man is a beast who knows he will die; he is cultivating the doubt that man is worthy of being saved. Thus he has a 'superior sense of inferiority.'" The second lecture, "In Search of Meaning," stressed the cultural menace brought about by "the liquidation of the inner man." Developing ideas from previous speeches, Heschel insisted that a life without commitment was not worth living. In his final lecture, "Existence and Exaltation," he directed thinkers in this age to "save the inner man from extinction." Social responsibility should be strengthened: "Millions are starving while new hotels are being built in Las Vegas."[38]

That same week the outspoken African American novelist James Baldwin was also visiting Stanford. On 7 May, during Heschel's second lecture, Baldwin gave a talk that was sponsored by the Civil Liberties Caucus. On the day of Heschel's final lecture, Baldwin spoke at noon to an overflow crowd, while students and faculty from the Socialist, Civil Liberties, and Peace Caucuses formed a mass rally; they sent a telegram to President Kennedy protesting police action against blacks in Birmingham. Reviewing Heschel's and Baldwin's appearances, the head of the student body wrote to Allard Lowenstein, a political activist and former teacher at Stanford, "Last week was perhaps the single most exciting week at Stanford."[39]

Heschel revised his Stanford lectures into *Who Is Man?* which appeared in 1965, published by Stanford University Press. By this time Heschel had significantly clarified his theology of humankind, and his preface marked the slim volume as a "prolegomen[on] to a more comprehensive study in which I have been engaged for some time"—the "philosophical anthropology" he had called for in speeches on education. Reversing his usual creative process, in which he expanded paragraphs into essays and essays into books, in *Who Is Man?* Heschel distilled the arguments of *Man Is Not Alone, God in Search of Man,* and *The Prophets* into six chapters.[40]

His dedication of the book to Hannah Susannah (his daughter, Susie), followed by the biblical citation I Chronicles 28:9–20, signaled this book as his spiritual legacy to the next generation. Referring to King David's last words to his son Solomon, the Bible passage concludes: "David said to his son Solomon, 'Be strong and of good courage and do it; do not be afraid or dismayed, for the Lord God my God is with you; He will not fail you or forsake you till all the work on the House of the Lord is done.'" (At her bat mitzvah that May, Susannah received the ancestral torch.)

Who Is Man? analyzed the Holocaust in terms of metaphysical absurdity. Heschel defined his key terms, a clarification that was urgent, for he believed that the denigration of human ideals had contributed largely to the century's atrocities: "Massive defamation of man may spell the doom of all of us. Moral annihilation leads to physical extermination."[41] It was the closest Heschel ever came to writing a systematic theology, couching his religious analysis in terms of existential philosophy and, for the first time, referring explicitly to Martin Heidegger, the influential philosopher who had supported Nazi ideology. (Heschel usually left unnamed his ideological adversaries.) The main topic of each of the six untitled chapters emerged from the subheads that outlined the conceptual armature of his system. Heschel's readers might even review its main lines simply by reading the table of contents, which listed all the subheads.

Chapter 1, for example, defined how to "think of man in human terms" or "the logic of being human." Chapter 2 criticized two inappropriate notions: materialistic and hedonistic "definitions of man" that led to "the eclipse of humanity." Heschel began constructing his alternative system to existentialism in chapter 3 with the category of "preciousness," as he asserted: "Human life is the only type of being we consider intrinsically sacred, the only type of being we regard as supremely valuable." Each person was an example of "ultimate preciousness."[42]

In chapter 4 Heschel focused on wonder and radical amazement as means to achieve religious insight. Acknowledging that his theology could respond to the Holocaust, he named Heidegger as he refuted the (abstract) ontological approach in favor of biblical thinking: "The first seeks to relate the human being to a transcendence called being as such, whereas the second, realizing that human being is more than being, that human being is living being, seeks to relate man to divine living, to a transcendence called the living God." Heschel returned to this technical discussion in chapters 5 and 6 as he rejected Heidegger's rhetorical question, the foundation of atheistic existentialism: "Has the Dasein [Being], as such, ever freely decided and will it ever be able to decide as to whether to come into existence or not?" Heschel asserted his own faith in God the creator: "I have not brought my being into being. Nor was I thrown into being. My being is obeying the saying, 'Let there be!'" The two final chapters emphasize the ethical demands of religion, the power of appreciation, and the human need for celebration.[43]

Heschel thus laid the foundations for an alternative model to existentialism, which he summarized with this elevation of Descartes's rationalist dictum: "I am commanded—therefore I am." Human "embarrassment" in face of the "ineffable" was a form of religious sensitivity and "celebration" a culmination of conscious existence. Human responsibility was his last word: "By whatever we do, by every act we carry out, we either advance or obstruct the drama of redemption; we either reduce or enhance the power of evil."[44]

This little volume whetted the appetite of some critics for a fully elaborated philosophy of humankind. *Booklist* recognized that Heschel's perspective was "strictly antithetical to existentialism . . . rooted in recognition of the divine sanctity of human life." Marvin Fox, now professor of philosophy at Ohio State University, in a favorable review in *Tradition,* asserted that Heschel, "known to be an observant Jew," had provided a humanistic theology appropriate for the modern Orthodox.[45]

Heschel's other book of sacred humanism, *The Insecurity of Freedom,* which documented the author's political, social, and religious activism, was a collection of essays and speeches. For several years, Wolfe Kelman had been urging him to collect these works into a single volume. By late 1963, Heschel had sent several pieces to Roger Straus, who passed them on to Edmund Epstein, the editor of Noonday Press, a subsidiary of Farrar, Straus. Epstein was enthusiastic about the project, but it took two full years to complete.[46]

In January 1964, Heschel and his editor discussed possible titles, although the contents were still in flux. Heschel signed a contract in February, now working with Robert Giroux to complete the project, and they agreed on the title, expecting it to appear the following January. But in April 1965, anticipating a visit to the Holy Land, Heschel asked for an extension so that he could include an essay on Israel. He finally met the deadline for a March 1966 publication.[47]

The Insecurity of Freedom: Essays on Human Existence documented Heschel's spiritual radicalism. Heschel dedicated it, simply, but with deep appreciation, "To Wolfe," the man who, with Marc Tanenbaum, had helped launch his public career. Although the book was divided into three (untitled) sections, it had no preface or introduction to unify or contextualize the diverse pieces. Part 1 focused on national issues, beginning with "Religion in a Free Society" and including addresses on youth, aging, the patient as a person, racism, and civil rights. Part 2 contained theological essays, on depth theology, Reinhold Niebuhr, Protestant renewal, Jews and Catholics, and the "sacred image of man." Part 3 dealt with Israel and the Diaspora, religious education, and Soviet Jewry, ending with an essay called "The Last Years of Maimonides."[48]

By concluding the book with this chapter on the medieval Jewish sage,

*Heschel in his office at the Jewish Theological Seminary, ca. 1963. Photograph
by John Popper. Courtesy of the Ratner Center for the Study of Conservative
Judaism, Jewish Theological Seminary of America.*

Heschel ratified his own transformation from pure scholar to activist, or, more
accurately, his integration of the two. The author of *The Insecurity of Freedom*
was a professor of Jewish ethics and mysticism who, like Maimonides, recon-
ciled the inward, meditative life with public action: "Contemplation of God
and service to man are combined and become one." And like Maimonides,
Heschel spent his final years consumed by his service to God, to the Jewish
people, and to humankind.[49]

Farrar, Straus and Giroux launched *The Insecurity of Freedom* on 25 April 1966 at a luncheon at the Lotus Club on 86th Street. Heschel then left for a lecture tour of theological seminaries as part of his visiting professorship at Union Theological Seminary; he also began giving antiwar lectures as a member of Clergy Concerned About Vietnam.[50]

UNITED SYNAGOGUE

REVIEW

Part Four

Apostle to the Gentiles

"Summit" Meeting

See page 2

> *Religion is a means, not an end. It becomes idolatrous when regarded as*
> *an end in itself. Over and above all being stands the Creator and Lord of*
> *history, He who transcends all. To equate religion and God is idolatry.*
> —Heschel, "No Religion Is an Island" (1966)

TRADITIONALISTS OF MANY FAITHS WERE FINDING WAYS TO ABSORB THE BENE-fits of modernity. Within the Roman Catholic Church, the prospect for developing positive relationships with other religions—especially Judaism—looked brighter in 1958 after the election of Angelo Giuseppe Roncalli as Pope John XXIII. A warm and compassionate man of peasant origins, Roncalli, as Apostolic Delegate to Turkey and Greece, had saved thousands of Jews during World War II from deportation, and certain extermination, by providing them with forged baptismal papers. More broadly, the Vatican diplomat recognized that accounts of the crucifixion of Jesus were often used to justify, and even inspire, Christian anti-Semitism and the persecution of Jews.

The Jewish initiative for mutual understanding with the church began with research by the Frenchman Jules Isaac, a historian and an inspector of schools. Isaac documented the Christian roots of anti-Semitism in his 1947 *Jésus et Israël* (Jesus and the Jewish people). Isaac attempted to influence Pope Pius XII, who had made changes favorable to the Jews in the Good Friday liturgy. (The traditional Easter liturgy had characterized Jews as a "treacherous" [*perfidus*] people. Now *perfidus* was understood more objectively as "unbelieving," not accepting Christ.)[1] In 1960, the elderly Isaac provided Pope John XXIII and three members of the Curia, the church's doctrinal authority, with examples of the pernicious "teaching of contempt," such as the notion that the Jews were a "deicide" race, responsible for killing Christ, and had been scattered around the world as punishment for their crime.

These facts became essential to Pope John's renewal of the church. Acutely sensitive to Jewish suffering, he personally charged Augustin Cardinal Bea (pronounced bay-A), president of the Secretariat for Christian Unity and an Old Testament scholar, to prepare a draft on "the inner relations between the Church and the people of Israel." This would be a key document to be considered by the upcoming Ecumenical Council (as the Second Vatican Council was originally called). Bea sought the advice of the American Jewish Committee and other Jewish organizations.

Marc Tanenbaum, as incoming director of interreligious affairs at the American Jewish Committee, believed that his former teacher Heschel was supremely qualified for the theological negotiations with Cardinal Bea and other Vatican officials. Despite severe opposition from some Jews at the idea of debating doctrine with church officials, Heschel was inspired to launch a powerful defense of Judaism, a task that probed his deepest personal wounds and led him to expose his most intimate vulnerabilities as a person. He had not healed from the ravages of World War II and Nazism. But he significantly influenced the drafting of *Nostra Aetate* (In our times), the "Declaration on the Relation of the Church with Non-Christian Religions" (1965), which for fifty years has promoted a positive relationship between Catholics and Jews.

On a professional level, Heschel's involvement with the Vatican Council, as well as his participation in the civil rights movement, led directly to his most gratifying academic position, as Harry Emerson Fosdick Visiting Professor at Union Theological Seminary. In this sympathetic, politically engaged religious community, Heschel excelled as a teacher and colleague, embodying for these Christians the vital relevance of the Hebrew Bible.

13

Confronting the Church (1961–1964)

We must insist upon loyalty to the unique and holy treasures of our own tradition and at the same time acknowledge that in this aeon religious diversity may be a providence of God.

—Heschel, "The Ecumenical Movement" (1963)

DURING THE YEARS THAT HESCHEL WAS ACHIEVING NATIONAL PROMINENCE AS a public intellectual, he was also playing a largely confidential role in a great international drama. As the primary theological consultant to the American Jewish Committee (AJC), he represented the interests of the Jewish people to the Second Vatican Council (popularly known as Vatican II), the epoch-making conclave convened in 1962 by Pope John XXIII to update the teachings of the Roman Catholic Church and to redefine its relationship with other forms of Christianity and with non-Christian religions, especially with Judaism. Heschel felt that his mission to the Vatican was his greatest opportunity to save Jewish lives.

Spiritual Diplomacy

Heschel began the process in 1961 as he established a close working relationship with Augustin Cardinal Bea, to whom Pope John had entrusted the future declaration on the Jews. That project had its most dedicated sponsor in the octogenarian Bea, a learned and saintly scholar of the Old Testament. Born and reared in Germany (his father changed their family name from Behan to Bea), he had studied philosophy and theology at Freiberg University, entered the Jesuit order in 1912, and continued his biblical studies in Berlin and Holland, settling permanently in Rome in 1929. A professor of biblical exegesis and the history of the people of Israel, he was appointed rector of the Pontifical Biblical Institute and editor of the academic journal *Biblica*, positions he held until Pope Pius XII chose him as his confessor. Bea was fluent in Hebrew, Aramaic, ancient Greek, Latin, Italian, French, and of course his native German; he had recently learned English. Bea not only had profound scholarly knowledge of the Hebrew Bible, he cherished Judaism as a living religion.[1]

The cardinal formed a subcommittee of his Secretariat composed of like-minded priests: Gregory Baum was a Protestant convert to Catholicism of Jewish background; John M. Oesterreicher, a Jewish convert to Catholicism, was director of the Institute of Judeo-Christian Studies at Seton Hall University; and Leo Rudloff, abbot of the Benedictine Priory in Weston, Vermont, spent six months each year at Dormition Abbey in Jerusalem. This group drafted a statement according to which Paul's Epistle to the Romans (chapters 9–11), which addresses the "mystery of Israel" and its relation to Christ, could be interpreted positively toward the Jews.

Bea also consulted with the American Jewish Committee and other organizations, asking them to prepare memoranda on issues they wished the Secretariat to examine. Although the AJC already enjoyed access to Vatican officials through the International University for Social Studies "Pro Deo" in Rome, Bea was offering more direct influence. (Pro Deo University, as it was called, had been founded in 1950 to foster joint research programs among different faiths and to promote democracy and religion in Europe and the developing world.) The AJC contacted Elio Toaff, chief rabbi of Rome; Jacob Kaplan, chief rabbi of France; Joseph B. Soloveitchik, professor of Talmud at Yeshiva University; Louis Finkelstein, chancellor of the Jewish Theological Seminary; Salo W. Baron, professor of Jewish History at Columbia University; and philosophy professor Harry A. Wolfson of Harvard University. Heschel, however, was the most active of the AJC's advisers.[2]

At the AJC, in addition to Marc Tanenbaum, Heschel dealt with Zachariah Shuster, the European director, stationed in Paris, who informed New York headquarters of events occurring at the Vatican. Shuster was an East European Jew, educated in yeshivas but otherwise self-taught, who spoke and read several languages. He immigrated to New York in the 1920s and worked as a Yiddish journalist for *Der Tog* (The Morning). In the early 1940s, the AJC sent him to Paris to work in Jewish international relations. In 1960 Shuster visited Jules Isaac at his home in Aix-en-Provence and learned about Isaac's audience with Pope John and the upcoming council, which had just been formally announced. Cardinal Bea had written to Isaac of his charge to develop a declaration on the Jews, and Isaac repeated to Shuster the cardinal's encouraging words: "You are assured of more than hope," echoing a phrase the pope himself had used when meeting with Isaac.[3]

Heschel welcomed the project, hopeful that the church was finally ready to abandon its millennial anti-Jewish teachings. The AJC provided him with information, secretarial and logistic support, and constructive criticism. He enjoyed working with Tanenbaum in New York and Shuster in Rome, two dedicated and worldly-wise professionals. In May 1961 Tanenbaum asked his American team to evaluate a draft of the AJC report on Catholic teachings. He sent copies to Soloveitchik, who lived in Boston while commuting to Yeshiva University in New York (asking him to pass one on to Wolfson at Harvard), to Finkelstein, and to Heschel, who was in Iowa City on his visiting professorship at the University of Iowa. For Soloveitchik, work on the draft led to a conflict with his Orthodox constituency; publicly he and the Rabbinical Council (the official body of modern Orthodoxy) opposed direct contact with the Ecumenical Council. Privately, Soloveitchik's son-in-law, Aharon Lichtenstein, associate professor of literature at Yeshiva University, wrote and signed a perceptive and detailed critique of the draft.[4]

In July 1961, Pro Deo University arranged a confidential meeting in Rome between Cardinal Bea and the AJC's Shuster and Ralph Friedman, head of the AJC Foreign Affairs Department. The cardinal informed the AJC officials that his subcommittee was working on the declaration on the Jews and that he wished to work closely with the AJC. Within a year, the AJC had completed two documents: "The Image of the Jew in Catholic Teaching," based on a critique of church textbooks co-sponsored by AJC and St. Louis University; and "Anti-Jewish Elements in Catholic Liturgy," which focused on the deicide accusation and other elements in the liturgy degrading to Judaism. These studies substantiated the Secretariat's original policy paper on the Jews.[5]

Heschel made his first substantial contacts that November. He flew to Rome, met Zachariah Shuster, and arranged "fortuitous" encounters with several Vatican officials, including Father Felix Morlion, president of Pro Deo University and the AJC's most highly placed ally. Heschel spent four hours with Morlion, a personal friend of the pope and Cardinal Bea, who gave Heschel pointers on Vatican etiquette, suggesting that he send his writings on biblical theology to the pope and other officials.

Heschel was introduced to Cardinal Bea on Sunday, 26 November 1961. He was accompanied by Shuster and Professor Max Horkheimer, the AJC's German consultant and co-director with Theodor Adorno of the Institute for Social Research in Frankfurt. (The original appointment, on Saturday morning, was changed so as not to violate Heschel's Sabbath observance.) Also present were the cardinal's closest associates, Monsignor Johannes Willebrands, secretary of Bea's committee; Father Stefan Schmidt, Bea's personal secretary, a German-speaking Croatian; and Father Morlion. Both Heschel and Bea had prepared carefully for this formal encounter. Heschel had studied Bea's introduction to a critical edition in Hebrew of the Song of Songs. Bea, who admired Heschel's Berlin dissertation on the prophets, reviewed references to Heschel's writings in Catholic academic sources.[6]

Shuster's memorandum to the AJC Foreign Affairs Department meticulously recounted the orchestrated event. Heschel was the presenter, speaking in German. There was an immediate rapport between Heschel and Bea, two devout biblical scholars. Heschel gave the cardinal "two large Hebrew volumes of *Midrash Rabba* [the basic rabbinic commentary on the Torah] with place markings indicating commentaries on The Song of Songs." He expressed admiration for the cardinal's scholarly edition of the Song of Songs, "even including subtle points of punctuation. Cardinal Bea was obviously very pleased." Heschel also referred to Bea's introduction and asserted his personal view that "prophetic thinking was a responsibility to history and an alertness to the requirements of the present moment."[7]

After creating this "warm and friendly" atmosphere, Heschel mentioned the two AJC memoranda, which offered "specific suggestions regarding changes in Catholic liturgy and catechism." He asked the cardinal for permission to send another, more affirmative memorandum, urging the church to "bring about a greater knowledge of Jewish religion and Jewish teaching." When Heschel had taught Christians he "had been astonished to discover how little Christian denominations knew about each other, much less about Jews." Above all, he added, "Jews want to be known, and understood, and respected as Jews (*Als Juden*)."

An informal conversation followed. Horkheimer spoke about the religious situation in Germany. The cardinal condemned anti-Semitic incidents in Argentina. Heschel deplored the persecution of Jews in the Soviet Union. Bea expressed pleasure at an apparent increase of religious interest among youth in Israel. At the end, the cardinal invited Heschel to submit the memorandum on improving Jewish-Christian relations and reminded the AJC delegation of his strong support for a declaration on the Jews.[8]

During his visit to Rome, Heschel also met with Willebrands, who was soon afterward elevated to cardinal. For an hour they discussed the mission to convert the Jews, a central Christian principle that Heschel vehemently opposed. Testing the waters for compromise, Heschel conceded, "No one asks the Church to abandon its hope for converting the world," and he proposed a rabbinic strategy in which an obsolete custom or tradition could be ignored without abrogating the law. Willebrands nodded in understanding.[9]

Heschel soon became the principal AJC interpreter of Jewish views to the Vatican. Shuster was elated by Heschel's visit, as he reported to Tanenbaum: "I personally found Dr. Heschel a most charming, inspiring and delightful personality. He is a man of spirit and understanding." Upon returning to Paris, Shuster wrote to Heschel to ratify their partnership in helping inaugurate an era: "The beginnings of a new spirit are clearly visible." The gregarious Shuster cultivated contacts with a number of participants in the Ecumenical Council. Returning periodically to his Paris headquarters, he spent long periods in Rome, stationed conspicuously in the lobby of the Hotel Mediterraneo, reading various international newspapers and trading facts and impressions with council members.[10]

Less overtly, Shuster found other ways to obtain restricted information, and even copies of secret documents. He developed a clandestine source of information, a "mole" within Cardinal Bea's Secretariat. This secret agent was an Irish Jesuit, Malachi Martin, a voluble, larger-than-life figure variously referred to as "Forest," "Pushkin," and Heschel's "young friend" in Shuster's confidential reports and transcripts of transatlantic phone conversations. Martin, a highly educated Old Testament scholar at the Pontifical Institute in Rome, was sympathetic to the Jewish position. He held degrees in ancient Semitic languages and biblical archeology from the University of Louvain and had studied at Oxford and the Hebrew University in Jerusalem. Martin also knew modern Hebrew, Arabic, and several European tongues.

With a mixture of motives, lofty and ignoble, Martin became close to Heschel and Shuster. He enjoyed their company immensely, especially when they vied with each other in telling jokes in Yiddish. Heschel felt close to Martin as well, confiding details of his childhood in Poland, the privations of his student years in Berlin, and his immigration to the United States. Martin primarily advised the AJC on theological issues, but he also provided logistical intelligence and copies of restricted documents.[11]

Soon after returning to New York, Heschel hurried to draw up what became known as "The Third Memorandum," which he had promised to Cardinal Bea. Informants inside the Vatican were urging the AJC to submit the text soon since Bea's statement on the Jews was nearing completion. In December, Heschel sent his draft to Shuster and Morlion, and in March 1962 he submitted a later version to a working committee made up of Shuster, Tanenbaum, Judith Hershcopf of the AJC, Finkelstein, Soloveitchik, and officials of Pro Deo. They and others offered further refinements. On 22 May, with a covering letter in German, Heschel sent the final report to Cardinal Bea.[12]

Heschel's memorandum, "On Improving Catholic-Jewish Relations," became the foundational AJC contribution to the Vatican Declaration on the Jews. Tanenbaum summarized its content for his AJC colleagues: "1) A declaration rejecting the deicide charge; 2) Recognition of the Jews as Jews; 3) A statement calling for more knowledge and understanding, to be prompted through; a) A forum to make knowledge of Judaism available to Catholic priests and theologians; b) Joint Cath[olic]-Jewish research projects and publications; c) Encouragement of interreligious cooperation in civic and charitable endeavors. 4) Explicit rejection of anti-Semitism by the Church; a) A permanent high-level commission at the Vatican, for eliminating prejudice and watching over Christian-Jewish relations; b) Similar commissions in all dioceses." Shuster and Tanenbaum directed Heschel to emphasize point 1 (the deicide issue), "because it was learned that the draft being prepared by Bea's working group did not cover it."[13]

The AJC was pleased with Heschel's initiative. He had elevated this functional document into a prophetic proclamation, conveying to Vatican officials its religious significance for Jews. The memorandum opened by proclaiming the universal necessity to serve the divine: "With humility and in the spirit of commitment to the living message of the prophets of Israel, let us consider the grave problems that confront us all as the children of God." The Hebrew prophets were a vital source for both religions: "Both Judaism and Christianity live in the certainty that mankind is in need of ultimate redemption, that God is involved in human history, that in relations between man and man God is at stake."[14]

Asserting that the strained relationships between Jews and Christians constituted "a divine emergency," Heschel allowed himself some rhetorical excess: "The prophet is sleepless and grave. The frankincense of some deeds of charity fails to fumigate the cruelties. Perhaps the prophet knew more about the secret obscenity of sheer unfairness." Among the multiple causes of anti-Semitism, he judged the foremost to be "the slanderous claims that 'the Jews' are collectively responsible for the Crucifixion of Jesus, that because of this the Jews were accursed and condemned to suffer dispersion and deprivation throughout the ages. This charge has been used by anti-Semites for centuries, to justify the most cruel and inhuman treatment of Jews; it has even been advanced to justify the fate of six million Jews during the Nazi Holocaust." The upcoming Ecumenical Council, Heschel averred, should "issue a strong declaration stressing the grave nature of the sin of anti-Semitism as incompatible with Catholicism and, in general, with all morality." His preambles to the three other proposals returned to this theme with equal indignation.

Cardinal Bea's subcommittee completed a forty-two-line Latin document, *Decretum de Iudaeis* (Statement on the Jews), to be submitted to the Central Preparatory Commission; if approved, it would then go to the council prelates for open discussion. There were great hopes on both sides.

Now other forces entered the negotiations. Vatican II was a spiritual milestone, but it was also a political minefield. Typifying the pitfalls, in May 1962, several months before the council was due to open, Nahum Goldmann, president of the World Jewish Congress, without consulting the Vatican or other Jewish organizations, announced that he was sending, uninvited, a former member of the Israeli Ministry of Religious Affairs, Dr. Chaim Wardi, to Rome as "an unofficial observer and representative." Jewish colleagues and church officials were outraged. All sides perceived Goldmann's unilateral decision as a betrayal of trust. The "Wardi incident" provoked political resistance, irritating Arab leaders and Catholic clergy alike. The Egyptian president Gamal Abdel Nasser and others protested, reinforcing the already strong minority opposition of Vatican conservatives to Cardinal Bea's efforts. These pressures forced the Preparatory Commission to remove the draft statement on the Jews from the agenda of the opening session.[15]

The AJC officials were dismayed. In September, Shuster and Friedman obtained a meeting in Rome with Bea and Eugene Cardinal Tisserant, dean of the Sacred College of Cardinals and a member of the Preparatory Commission. Stefan Schmidt, Bea's personal secretary, also present, confided that the Wardi incident was tragic, but Bea reassured the Jewish officials. He reported on his discussion of the matter with Pope John, who had declared, "The Jews also have immortal souls, and we have to do something for them too." Bea admitted, however, that other church officials would need more persuasion.[16]

Vatican II: The First and Second Sessions

Spiritual generosity was in the air as Pope John XXIII opened the Ecumenical Council on 11 October 1962. The day before, Richard Cardinal Cushing of Boston, a friend of the Jews and the Kennedy family priest, spoke with an open heart: "We must stand together, love each other and know each other. . . . The Jewish community and the Protestants have sent their best wishes for our Council's work." Yet the council's first session ended two months later, on 8 December, without having considered two progressive statements, on religious liberty and the Jews. To make matters worse, a few days before the session ended a scurrilous, nine-hundred-page anti-Semitic attack entitled *Il complotto contro la Chiesa* (The plot against the Church) was distributed to every prelate. The anonymous volume claimed to have unmasked a worldwide Jewish conspiracy, including infiltration of the Vatican by Jews (an allusion to Fathers Gregory Baum and John Osterreicher). Uncertainty about the outcome of the council increased when the pope fell ill in November; he died six months later.[17]

As fears among Jews intensified, the AJC mobilized its information system. Shuster closely monitored the sensitive, sometimes contentious intrachurch maneuvers, keeping Heschel up to date. AJC officials paid special attention to the astute reports of the journalist Gershon Jacobson, who was covering the council for the Yiddish-language *Day-Morning Journal*. Heschel had become close to Jacobson during the movement to save Soviet Jewry. Now on assignment at the Vatican, Jacobson was especially adept in appreciating the nuances of the impression Heschel was making on church officials: "Professor Heschel spoke to them in a language that captivated them and made them, at the same time, feel ashamed." Moreover, he "did it in a way that gained even more respect and appreciation on the part of Catholic leaders in regards to Jews and Jewish values." Heschel had become a consummate religious diplomat.[18]

Jacobson also discovered that Heschel had unwittingly revealed his susceptibility to flattery to Hans Küng, a theological adviser to the council. After speaking with Heschel for almost an hour at a reception, Küng was impressed by Heschel's tremendous memory, his learning, and his spiritual orientation, but also found him to be gullible. "With a smile, with a compliment, and with brotherly love, you can buy him off, and bury him, too," the canny priest was reported as saying.[19]

After the initial failure to persuade the council to consider the Declaration on the Jews, Cardinal Bea tried to rally support by a promotional visit to the United States in March 1963. The American bishops were strong advocates of religious freedom and favorable views of Judaism. The centerpiece of the trip would be an unpublicized meeting at AJC headquarters in New York of the cardinal and about ten "national Jewish religious and cultural personalities." The AJC sent a memorandum in German to the cardinal setting out the agenda. Heschel, Finkelstein, and Soloveitchik were the first to approve it and agree to participate. Heschel would chair the meeting, which the AJC proudly termed "unprecedented."[20]

Cardinal Bea, Father Schmidt, and Monsignor Willebrands arrived in Boston with Father Morlion; their official host was Cardinal Cushing. On 26 March, Bea kicked off his tour by presiding over a joint meeting of Catholics and Protestants at Harvard University. The next morning Heschel and Marc Tanenbaum, who had been invited to meet privately with Bea, arrived at the chancery. Several weighty conversations took place. Heschel and Bea first spoke alone for about thirty minutes, like old friends. Then Tanenbaum, Schmidt, and Willebrands joined them. Heschel said a few formal words of appreciation for their common goals, and Bea warned the group not to publicize these contacts, since "bitter enemies of the Jews in Rome," and outside the church, might turn that information to their advantage.[21]

Center: *Heschel with Rabbi Marc H. Tanenbaum and Augustin Cardinal Bea,
ca. 1963. Courtesy of the American Jewish Committee.*

Heschel introduced specific requests, some of them quite exacting, all
recorded in a confidential AJC report. Informally, Heschel suggested that
Pope John might "condemn the charge against the Jews of deicide as a heresy
or as a blasphemy. . . . Cardinal Bea said that he thought something like this
might be possible." Heschel pressed for Bea's plan to establish a permanent
organization, after the Vatican Council, for interfaith study projects. Bea next
astonished his Jewish guests by asking them what they would think if the Vatican were officially to recognize the state of Israel? The stunned rabbis took
a moment to catch their breath, answering that Jews all around the world
would welcome such news. (Three months later this great-hearted idea died
with Pope John XXIII. The state of Israel was not accorded Vatican recognition until 1993.)[22]

Returning to New York, Tanenbaum and Heschel completed arrangements
for the confidential meeting of prominent rabbis with Cardinal Bea. On 31
March at 3:30 P.M. at the AJC headquarters on East 56th Street (known as the
Institute for Human Relations) the cardinal spoke with representatives of all

*Lawrence Cardinal Shehan of Baltimore and
Zachariah Shuster, 1965. Foto Lampo, Rome.
Courtesy of the American Jewish Committee.*

branches of American Judaism, including the modern Orthodox. Participants included Heschel, as chairman; Louis Finkelstein; Albert Minda, the president of the Central Conference of American Rabbis (Reform); Theodore Friedman, the president of the Rabbinical Assembly of America (Conservative); Emanuel Rackman, former president of the Rabbinical Council of America (Orthodox) and assistant to the president of Yeshiva University; Julius Mark, the president of the Synagogue Council of America; and officials of the AJC. Rabbi Soloveitchik could not attend since his wife was undergoing surgery the following day. (The minutes noted that the group offered a prayer "for her speedy and complete recovery.")

Heschel opened the formal program in German by introducing the cardinal and his associates and then the Jewish leaders, who, he said, were there in a personal capacity. Heschel introduced in absentia Solomon Freehof, a Reform rabbi and specialist in Jewish law, and Soloveitchik, adding: "Both of these scholars have studied the materials which I will mention shortly, and are in full agreement concerning the contents." He reminded his colleagues that the meeting was "informal and unpublicized." Heschel then read in English questions that had been submitted in advance to Bea. The rabbis wanted the Ecumenical Council "unequivocally" to declare that the Jews were not cursed or collectively responsible for the death of Jesus; the church should condemn as "sins against charity" descriptions of Jews as evil or greedy or other harmful images; it should "translate the dogmatic and moral principles above into concrete regulations"; and finally, it should create an institute for intergroup study and the furthering of Christian-Jewish relations.[23]

Bea responded in German, saying that he was very pleased to meet with Jewish scholars and theologians since he was an Old Testament scholar himself; more to the point, his "activities on behalf of a Jewish-Christian understanding are not the result of some temporary situation or political opportunism, but based on a very deep conviction held for many years." After these opening remarks, the cardinal's presentation was forthright and elegant. Speaking in English, he demonstrated that the notion of an accursed people, and other negative teachings, were not justified by the Gospel texts. And he gave advice on how to pursue theological dialogue with the church: "It is therefore neither necessary nor wise . . . to attack either the claim to be divine which Jesus made or the credibility of the Gospels. In so doing one comes into headlong collision with what Christians believe. One must treat the convictions and beliefs of his fellow men with respect and veneration."[24]

The cardinal answered every question, reminding his Jewish colleagues not to expect too many specifics as the council was dealing with some seventy documents totaling more than two thousand pages. He acknowledged "the great political difficulties which have arisen and some protests" that the Vatican had received, and he thought that "conversations should be started with some people in Israel." Bea concluded by reiterating that the pope "fully endorse[d]" his views.[25]

The next morning, Bea publicly addressed Jewish concerns at a press conference in the apartment of J. Peter Grace, president of the American affiliate of Pro Deo. Significantly, the cardinal borrowed phrases from Heschel's 1962 memorandum: "It is in fact both error and heresy to charge the Jewish people with 'deicide.' Through the centuries the Jewish people have paid a high price in suffering and martyrdom for preserving the Covenant and the legacy of holiness in faith and devotion." He made clear his "sincere desire that the Catholic Church and its faithful will acknowledge the integrity and permanent preciousness of Judaism and the Jewish people." This was just the statement that Jews hoped the Vatican Council would ultimately approve.[26]

By now, Heschel had become the model Jewish spokesman. Bea emphasized his hope for "the continued cooperation of Rabbi Heschel and members of the American Jewish Committee who have contributed so significantly thus far to removing the bases of misunderstanding between Catholics and Jews."[27]

That evening, at the Plaza Hotel in Manhattan, local, national, and international leaders gathered for a ceremonial feast of agape (fraternal love), an interfaith banquet to honor Cardinal Bea. Sponsors were the Pro Deo University in Rome and its affiliate, the American Council for the International Promotion of Democracy Under God. Prominent politicians lent their authority to representatives of the three biblical faiths, Christianity, Judaism, and Islam. U Thant, secretary general of the United Nations, was on the dais. The invocation was offered by Cardinal Spellman, followed by salutations from Mayor Robert Wagner and Governor Nelson Rockefeller. Cardinal Bea spoke on "Civic Unity and Freedom Under God." Responses were given by the Reverend Henry Pitney Van Dusen, president of Union Theological Seminary; Sir Muhammad Zafrulla Khan, president the U.N. General Assembly, on behalf of Islam; Rabbi Abraham Joshua Heschel; and Steven Gill Spottswood, bishop of the African Methodist Episcopal Zion Church. Father Felix Morlion summarized the proceedings, and the final prayer was offered by Archbishop Iakovos, primate of the Greek Orthodox Diocese of North and South America, a stalwart of interfaith cooperation.

Heschel's speech was warm and generous, but also politically audacious. He began with his classic image of spiritual emergency, the Midrashic story of God's suspending the mountain of history over the Israelites. Interreligious dialogue was imperative, he insisted, because of the Cold War and the possibility of nuclear annihilation: "Is it not true that God and nuclear stockpiles cannot dwell together in one world?" he asked. People of all faiths were faced with the same "dreadful predicament [which] is not due to economic conflicts. It is due to a spiritual paralysis." As a necessary precondition, Heschel called for radical humility and a revival of reverence for all human beings. Heschel also paid tribute to Bea and expressed enthusiasm for the Ecumenical Council and Pope John's encyclical, *Pacem in Terris* [Peace on Earth], which promoted religious freedom. He then affirmed his commitment to religious pluralism by citing the prophet Malachi (1:11) and rabbinic sources: "God's voice speaks in many languages, communicating itself in a diversity of intuitions. The word of God never comes to an end. No word is God's last word."[28]

The immediate outcome of Cardinal Bea's American tour was modest: the decision to create an Institute for Judaic Studies to be part of, or associated with, the Institute for Social Studies Pro Deo in Rome. The larger goal—a declaration on the Jews—would take three more years to accomplish, owing in part to human mortality. Pope John XXIII passed away on 3 June 1963 at age eighty-one. Three days later, after a million mourners had passed by his bier, he was buried in the grottos beneath Saint Peter's Basilica. Although he had held the Throne of Saint Peter for only four years and seven months, Pope John had redirected the tide of church history forever.[29]

One of the key issues raised by his death was the fate of the Ecumenical Council, which his successor could choose to suspend or resume. Two weeks later, on 21 June, the liberal-minded Giovanni Battista Cardinal Montini, archbishop of Milan, was elected pope. At age sixty-five Montini was an experienced diplomat who had been close to the previous pontiff. He took the name of Paul VI, "after the apostle who transformed Christianity into a world religion." He was said to possess "the intellectual clarity of Pope Pius XII and the open-heartedness of Pope John XXIII." Progressives worldwide were encouraged by the selection. The new pope was crowned at a majestic outdoor ceremony on Saturday, 30 June. After a blessing in Latin, the pope in his native Italian stated his intention to reconvene the Ecumenical Council. The AJC team could continue its mission.[30]

For Heschel personally an unfortunate miscommunication marred the grand event. The *New York Herald Tribune* reported that Vatican officials were "somewhat surprised by President Kennedy's designation of Rabbi Louis Finkelstein as a US representative to Pope Paul's coronation." The clear implication was that Heschel had not been chosen. By this omission Heschel was conspicuously humbled in favor of Finkelstein, his unspoken rival at the Jewish Theological Seminary. AJC and Pro Deo officials were concerned, not only because of the blow to Heschel's dignity but also because his not being appointed to the American delegation had "harmed his [public] stature," and thus his negotiating power. Father Morlion explained to David Danzig, the chairman of AJC public relations, that he had arranged for Finkelstein to be received by Cardinal Bea "only in the presence of Rabbi Heschel[,] who was elected to head the scholarly groups." Heschel would visit Bea another time for more substantial consultations.[31]

It was only later, after much embarrassment, that Heschel learned that he had indeed been invited to the coronation by Cardinal Bea himself, but the invitation had arrived late, after Heschel had already canceled his Thursday airplane reservation, which would have enabled him to reach Rome before the Sabbath. Both the AJC and their Pro Deo allies in Rome apologized to Heschel for the faulty communication.[32]

Supporters of the Declaration on the Jews had great hopes for the second session of the Ecumenical Council, which Pope Paul VI had called for 29 September 1963. Some time before that, Shuster learned "from reliable sources" that Bea's Secretariat had drafted an excellent text that dealt with most of the Jewish concerns. Having obtained a copy of this top-secret document, he summarized its essential elements in a letter to Heschel: "A solemn affirmation that Christianity has emerged from Judaism and originated from the Jewish religion and history. . . . It then says in clearest terms that the Church rejects the accusation of deicide made against the Jews; that it deplores anti-Semitism in past and present times; and concludes with a statement deploring the persecutions of Jews and declaring anathema any person who has contempt of or persecutes the Jews." Shuster went on to explain that "friends in Rome" advised against making any aspect of the document public, especially before the council opened.[33]

Impressed by these details, Heschel replied to Shuster's glad tidings in very large script: "Just received your letter of 9.12, and I am overjoyed! Let us pray that the draft may receive the necessary votes." But these ecstatic expectations suffered a check when a public relations calamity blew up, confirming Shuster's fears. Milton Bracker, the Rome bureau chief of the *New York Times*, using his own sources (including someone from the AJC), published an article on 4 October revealing the existence of the revised declaration. Two weeks later Bracker outlined the proposed text in a front-page article with the headline: "Vatican Council Paper Decries Blaming of Jews in Jesus's Death." Bracker also divulged Cardinal Bea's contacts with Heschel and other Jewish representatives, and reminded readers of the mortifying Wardi affair.[34]

These unauthorized disclosures provoked formidable responses, both negative and positive, storms of antagonism and support that took months to subside. The favorable draft statement now faced more concerted opposition. For the Jewish negotiators, damage control was the first priority. Adopting a positive approach, AJC president A. M. Sonneband mailed Bracker's article to Jewish community leaders around the country with a memorandum that highlighted AJC efforts to influence the council's declaration. The memo even mentioned the confidential 31 March meeting of the rabbis with Cardinal Bea under Heschel's chairmanship.[35]

Inside the AJC officials looked for reassurance. On 22 October, Heschel shared a confidential letter from "a Catholic friend in Rome whom he described as an intimate of Cardinal Bea" (probably Malachi Martin) that expressed guarded optimism: "The *New York Times* article by Milton Bracker went too far and was premature. But we hope and are confident that nothing pejorative will result from this story. It would take a lot, a mighty lot, to stop the march of events during the next ten days or so."[36]

The draft document, "On the Catholic Attitude Toward Non-Christians, and Especially Toward Jews," was finally distributed to the council members at the meeting of 8 November. They received it with favor, even enthusiasm. When it was announced that Cardinal Bea would present chapter 4 (the declaration on ecumenism and the Jews) and Bishop Emile de Smedt of Bruges chapter 5 (the declaration on religious liberty), the prelates applauded loudly. Heschel, Shuster, and their team were confident. Since the text had been widely discussed in the press, Shuster believed that Heschel should meet with Bea and try to persuade him to fine-tune some of the details. Heschel flew immediately to Rome. But Bea, cautiously avoiding internal battles, judged it impolitic to receive a Jewish representative at that sensitive moment. Heschel and Shuster met with Willebrands instead, and Heschel "made a very forceful and effective plea for the alteration of . . . two passages" that might be misinterpreted as blaming the entire Jewish people for the death of Jesus.[37]

The Jewish lobbyists were being unrealistic. Conservative forces within the Vatican strengthened their opposition to the document. Another anonymous anti-Semitic tract, *Gli Ebrei e il Concilio alla luce della Sacra Scriturra e della tradizione* (The Jews and the Council in the light of Scripture and tradition), was stealthily distributed to the council members. This pamphlet advocated retaining the deicide charge and called for the conversion of the Jews. As a result of these pressures, Vatican conservatives were able to maneuver behind the scenes to delay the vote on chapters 4 and 5. The second session of the Ecumenical Council ended on 4 December 1963 without even considering these progressive policies.[38]

Heschel felt the failure of the declaration keenly, as Shuster reported to Tanenbaum: "I know that he left [Rome] in a state of depression. Unfortunately, he happened to arrive at the lowest ebb of developments. I trust, however, that he has succeeded in overcoming his pessimism and [is] seeing matters now in a more balanced perspective." Heschel never achieved that equanimity.[39]

Now the risk was that before it came up again, the draft might be revised by a less sympathetic committee. The AJC and its allies launched an international campaign to save the Declaration on the Jews. In public, Cardinal Bea blamed the delay on lack of time in the council meeting. Heschel and the AJC knew better. Alarmed that their project was in jeopardy, they tried political tactics. Heschel probed friends at Union Theological Seminary to see whether they would be willing to sign a protest ad for the *New York Times*. In addition, he enlisted his friend Gustave Weigel, a Jesuit priest, professor of ecclesiology at Woodstock College, church liberal, and consultant to the council. Late at night on 2 January 1964, Heschel spoke with Weigel in his JTS office. Equally discouraged, the two planned to ask the American cardinals Spellman, Albert Meyer, and Joseph Ritter to send supportive messages to Cardinal Bea. The next day Weigel died of a heart attack in the offices of the Jesuit magazine *America*.[40]

Some maneuvers were questionable. In mid-March, Heschel arranged with Roger Straus for Malachi Martin, who was now at the Biblical Institute in Jerusalem, to publish his "kiss and tell" book about the internal workings of the Ecumenical Council in the hope that it would influence the present deliberations. In May, Farrar, Straus published *The Pilgrim* (referring to Pope Paul VI) under the pseudonym of "Michael Serafian." With a treacherous blend of fact, overstatement, and invention, it characterized the pope in unflattering but essentially accurate terms as sincere and intelligent but indecisive, weak, and beholden to the Curia. Martin's identity was soon uncovered, and many protested his betrayal. The book was removed from circulation, at considerable financial loss to the publisher. Heschel and Roger Straus eventually ended their friendship with Martin.[41]

Conflicts increased within the Jewish camp as well. In February 1964 the *London Jewish Chronicle* reported that Joseph Soloveitchik, forcefully opposing "theological discussion" with Christians at the midwinter conference of the Rabbinical Council of America, had repudiated the Vatican document as "nothing more or less than evangelical propaganda." Moreover, the article continued, "Rabbi Soloveitchik's sharpest words were reserved for Jewish efforts to have Christian texts changed." Tanenbaum attempted to mediate. Several times he communicated with Soloveitchik, by letter and in person, and he finally dissuaded him from spurring the Rabbinical Council formally to reject the declaration: "It would play directly into the hands of the Arab states and anti-Semitic elements in the conservative Curia who are determined to forestall this declaration," he warned. Soloveitchik agreed not to act, but other Orthodox colleagues criticized unnamed "Jewish laymen" (certainly the AJC), as reported in the *New York Times* on 23 June.[42]

The AJC did everything possible to support Cardinal Bea and other forward-looking clerics. Over the succeeding months, AJC officials contacted American cardinals and bishops favorable to the declaration and distributed their speeches to the press. But in May rumors circulated that the draft had been seriously "watered down" and the repudiation of the deicide charge removed, a critical failing. In desperation the AJC called three exceptional meetings. On 11 May, about twenty-five Jewish, Protestant, and Catholic representatives gathered at the Human Relations Institute to discuss the decree. As before, Heschel chaired that exchange of views. In the evening a small dinner was arranged with Cardinal Tisserant, dean of the Sacred College of Cardinals.[43]

The AJC then arranged an audience of its highest officers—President Morris Abram, Ralph Friedman, Philip Hoffman, John Slawson, and Zachariah Shuster—with Pope Paul in Rome. Before flying to Italy, they met with Secretary of State Dean Rusk, who endorsed their endeavor. Accompanying them was the wife of Leonard Sperry, whose family was donating money for an Intergroup Center at the Pro Deo University in Rome. The papal audience took place on 30 May, a Saturday. Cardinal Tisserant was also present. The conversation, at which the pope commended Cardinal Spellman's support for the Jewish declaration, was publicized the next day in *L'osservatore romano*, the quasi-official Vatican newspaper.[44]

Unfortunately, this audience provoked disapproval in several quarters. The Rabbinical Council was incensed that the AJC leaders had agreed to meet with the pope on the Sabbath. Bea and the recently elevated Cardinal Willebrands were also offended at the AJC's public violation of religious law; to their knowledge it was the first time a Jewish group ever had an audience on the Holy Day. Privately, Bea also regretted that the meeting with the pope had not been cleared with him, since the topic was his major responsibility. Bea assured his Jewish consultants, however, that the new text of the declaration was an improvement on the old and admonished them not to seek "more complete statements" of its contents.[45]

It was soon learned that the text had indeed been revised, but in a manner detrimental to Jewish interests. The press again was responsible for the exposure. On 12 June the *New York Times* described the secret document with an article headlined: "Text on the Jews Reported Muted." The reporter, Robert C. Doty, who had replaced Bracker in Rome, detailed several adverse changes, citing "a combination of political and theological considerations."[46]

The bad news received further confirmation. On 24 June Heschel addressed the Catholic Theological Association at its annual meeting in New York City. There he spoke privately with Father Thomas Stransky, an American Paulist and executive secretary of Cardinal Bea's Secretariat, a warm, informal man. For an hour, "in strictest confidence," Stransky expressed his "profound chagrin," which he shared with Cardinal Willebrands, "over what he called Cardinal Bea's 'capitulation' to Cardinal Cicognani and his allies" in the Curia. (Cardinal Cicognani was the Vatican secretary of state, a powerful conservative, who objected to Bea's liberal declaration on the Jews.) Stransky informed Heschel that the Jewish decree had gone to the Coordinating Commission, which made changes, sending it on with other documents to Pope Paul. The pope approved everything for council discussion except the text on the Jews.[47]

All in all, these various "informants" from Rome were giving Heschel and the AJC conflicting views about whether the declaration would even be considered at the third session. The Jews feared the worst.[48]

Adding to Heschel's stress was the death, on 30 June 1964, of his only surviving sister, Sarah Bracha Heschel, the wife of his cousin the Kopitzhinitzer rebbe. While still in mourning for his sister, Heschel spent the night of 13 July at the Trappist Abbey of Gethsemane in the hills of Kentucky as the guest of Thomas Merton, the monk and poet. Heschel's writings were familiar as spiritual readings among monastics, and Heschel and Merton had corresponded since 1960. As master of novices, Merton used *God in Search of Man* and *The Prophets* as teaching texts, and he wanted to meet the man behind the author. Their encounter, under the pall of the Ecumenical Council, confirmed Merton's deep sympathy for, and even identification with, Judaism and the Jewish people.[49]

Taking over for the strict Abbot James Fox, who was away, Father Flavian Burns, the young prior, allowed Merton to leave his hermitage and accompany him to the Louisville airport, where they met Heschel. The exuberant Merton and Heschel connected immediately. Listening to a broadcast of the Republican National convention at the airport, where the militaristic Barry Goldwater was sure to be nominated for the presidency, Heschel was reminded of the Nazi period in Germany. In the hour-long ride back to the monastery, he and Merton joked about German Jewish family names, such as Gold and Silver, which adopted precious metals, and they spoke about mystical theology and other spiritual matters.

Central to their conversation was the Declaration on the Jews at the Ecumenical Council, soon to convene its third session. Affected by Heschel's pessimism, Merton noted in his diary that the rabbi was "convinced that Serafian's *Pilgrim* is perfectly right," and that "the Jewish Chapter will never be accepted in the Council." Merton felt that it was time for the church to repent, but Heschel "thinks [Cardinal] Bea is really finished, that he suffered a crushing defeat in the Second Session (obvious). The envy aroused by his American trip brought him many enemies, and he had plenty before that."[50]

Heschel ate dinner in the guest house with Merton and Father Flavian. The monks' unfamiliarity with Jewish dietary laws created quite a stir when the rabbi refused the steak (because it was not kosher), provided as a special supplement to the monks' normally vegetarian diet. As Merton noted: "Heschel did well on cheese, lettuce, etc. He enjoyed the wine and smoked a couple of long cigars." The convivial atmosphere led Heschel to joke with Brother Edwin, who was serving them, by inviting him to sit down and let the rabbi serve him. The embarrassed monk demurred. "Didn't you enjoy serving?" asked Heschel. "Yes," replied the monk. "Then why deprive me of the same pleasure?" They remained at the table until 10:30, a late hour for monks, who rise at 2 A.M. to start the day with the office of Vigils.[51]

The immediate upshot of this brief but poignant visit (which is still remembered at the monastery) was Merton's vigorous letter the next day to Cardinal Bea. In supporting the Declaration on the Jews, Merton declared, "I am personally convinced that the grace to truly see the Church as she is in her humility and in her splendor may perhaps not be granted to the Council Fathers if they fail to take account of her relation to the anguished Synagogue." Heschel soon felt compelled to expose his own anguish.[52]

14

Vulnerable Prophet (1964–1965)

Nothing is easier than to deceive oneself. As the mind grows sophisticated, self-deception advances. The inner life becomes a wild, inextricable maze. Who can trust his own motivations? His honesty? Who can be sure whether he is worshiping his own ego or an idol while ostensibly adoring God?
—Heschel, *A Passion for Truth* (1973)

AS THE THEOLOGICAL ADVOCATE FOR THE AMERICAN JEWISH COMMITTEE, Heschel struggled to reconcile his public persona as a voice of the Hebrew prophets with his human weaknesses. Faced with the possibility of failing in his mission to end the Catholic Church's anti-Jewish teachings, he was filled with tension, as were most Jewish advocates and their allies. Opposition from within the Jewish community exacerbated his normal uncertainties. The situation worsened on 3 September 1964, two weeks before the opening of the Ecumenical Council's third session, when another crisis occurred.

Supporters of the Jewish cause were disconcerted by the unauthorized publication of the revised draft of the Vatican text on the Jews in the *New York Herald Tribune*. An anonymous "special correspondent," probably Gershon Jacobson, published a translation of the Latin original, "Schema of the Doctrine on Ecumenism, Second Declaration: On the Jews and Non-Christians." The following day another version of the draft appeared in the *New York Times*.[1]

This leak showed all the signs of being calculated. Perhaps the well-meaning perpetrators assumed that public exposure before the official discussion would disarm opponents of the more liberal declaration. Two passages of this new draft were especially offensive:

> It is also worth remembering that the union of the Jewish people with the Church is a part of the Christian hope. Accordingly, and following the teaching of Apostle Paul (cf. Romans 11, 25), the Church expects in unshakable faith and with ardent desire the entrance of that people into the fullness of the people of God, established by Christ.
>
> Everyone should be careful, *therefore* [emphasis added], not to expose the Jewish people as a rejected nation, be it in Catechetical tuition, in preaching of God's word or in worldly conversation, nor should anything else be said or done which may alienate the minds of men from the Jews. Equally, all should be on their guard not to impute to the Jews of our time that which was perpetrated in the Passion of Christ.

Jews could only interpret the church's "ardent desire" to be united with the Jewish people as a call for conversion. The word *therefore* strongly implied that toleration of the Jews assumed this motive.[2]

Internal AJC reaction to this revised draft was temperate, but urgent. A memorandum dated the same day, 3 September, probably written by Zachariah Shuster, detailed the draft's shortcomings and urged the Ecumenical Council to restore the previous document, "eliminating any spirit of conversion, condemning in unequivocal terms the charges of deicide against the Jews of Christ's time or of later times, and repudiating anti-Semitism." Heschel, however, abandoned diplomacy, sending a personal rebuke to several Catholic friends that was picked up by the *New York Times* and, the following week, *Time* magazine. His indignation led him to use unusually strong language: "Since this present draft calls for 'reciprocal understanding and appreciation, to be attained by theological study and fraternal discussion,' between Jews and Catholics, it must be stated that *spiritual fratricide* is hardly a means for the attainment of 'fraternal discussion' or 'reciprocal understanding.'"[3]

In particular, he assailed the notion that Jews were "a candidate for conversion." That Christian "hope" was tantamount to annihilation. Recalling that his people had "paid a high price in suffering and martyrdom for preserving the Covenant and the legacy of holiness, faith and devotion to the sacred Jewish tradition," he spurned church triumphalism with a bitterness that shocked even some of his closest Christian allies: "As I have repeatedly stated to leading personalities of the Vatican, I am ready to go to Auschwitz any time, if faced with the alternative of conversion or death."[4]

No compromise was possible. Christianity must answer to history, he continued: "Jews throughout the world will be dismayed by a call from the Vatican to abandon their faith in a generation that witnessed the massacre of six million Jews and the destruction of thousands of synagogues on a continent where the dominant religion was not Islam, Buddhism or Shintoism."[5]

Among the friends to whom Heschel mailed mimeographed copies of this statement was Thomas Merton. In the solitude of his Kentucky hermitage, the monk confronted his own conscience. Answering Heschel on 9 September, Merton declared his solidarity: "My latent ambitions to be a true Jew under my Catholic skin will surely be realized if I continue to go through experiences like this, being spiritually slapped in the face by these blind and complacent people of whom I am nevertheless a 'collaborator.'" He wrote in his diary the following day: "It is precisely in prophetic and deeply humiliated and humanly impoverished thirst for light that Christians and Jews can begin to find a kind of unity in seeking God's will together."[6]

At home, however, Heschel's prophetic rebuke was itself rejected. On 16 August the *New York Times* reported that the Rabbinical Council of America (the modern Orthodox organization) had reinforced its interdiction of interfaith theological discussions. The article also announced the imminent publication of Soloveitchik's essay "Confrontation," which argued for the establishment of barriers between Christians and Jews. Henceforth Soloveitchik spearheaded his movement's rejectionist line.[7]

Secret Summit Meeting

The third session of the Ecumenical Council was due to convene on 14 September 1964. As the day approached, tensions were almost unbearable. The timing was particularly bad for Jews, who were entering the hallowed ten-day period between Rosh Hashanah and Yom Kippur known as the Days of Awe. The council's opening date, the day before Yom Kippur, seemed to symbolize the theological abyss between Jews and Christians.

Still desperate to save the Declaration on the Jews, the AJC as an emergency measure pressed its highest Vatican contacts to obtain a private audience for Heschel with Pope Paul himself. The political risks involved were high. If advertised, Heschel's meeting with the pope could compromise the AJC's long and deliberate lobbying efforts and discredit the initiatives of Cardinal Bea, himself beset by church conservatives. Heschel's prestige within the Jewish community was also at stake. By meeting with the pope during the High Holy Days, he might appear to be demeaning himself and Jews everywhere.[8]

Heschel consulted with several people, more for support than for permission or advice. He spoke with Louis Finkelstein, the Kopitzhinitzer rebbe, and his brother Rabbi Jacob Heshel in London. They all agreed that meeting with the pope would be a kiddush ha-shem, a sanctification of God's name.

Cardinal Cushing expedited the arrangements, but difficulties in scheduling increased the stress on Heschel. Vatican officials first set the meeting on the Jewish Sabbath. Heschel refused to violate the holy day. Through Monsignor Edward Murray, Cushing's chief adviser and a council *peritus* (expert), the audience was moved to Monday, 14 September, the opening day itself.[9]

Before the Sabbath, Heschel flew to Rome, where his presence remained covert. He did not attend synagogue on *Shabbat Teshuvah*, the solemn ceremony of repentance before Yom Kippur; he was deprived of this sacred resource. Nor did he dine at his favorite kosher restaurant.[10]

Around noon on Monday, Heschel and Shuster entered the pope's private study in the Vatican. Heschel brought a new memorandum for consideration and a copy of his recent book *The Prophets*. Although the pope spoke English well, a translator was present, an American monsignor, Paul Marcinkus. While nervous, Heschel seemed to be well prepared.

Shuster drew up two distinct accounts of Heschel's secret audience with Pope Paul VI, one the official memorandum to the AJC leadership drafted by himself and Heschel, the gist of which entered the historical record, the other Shuster's brutally candid description of Heschel's shortcomings at the meeting. Shuster shared this version only with John Slawson and Marc Tanenbaum, who kept it under lock and key.[11]

Shuster's official report distilled the substance of Heschel's thirty-five-minute discussion with the pontiff. It began with the ceremonial framework: "Heschel opened with a prayer in Latin, which he translated into Hebrew. The Pope responded, 'It is a beautiful prayer, I was happy to hear it.' Heschel then acknowledged Cardinal Cushing's help and prayers, and the Pope showed him Cushing's cablegram [requesting the appointment]. Heschel replied, 'I pray that this visit will also have the blessing of our Father in Heaven,' to which the Pope nodded."[12]

After these formalities, Heschel introduced his topic, "the paragraph [of the new draft declaration] stating that the Church has 'unchanging hope' and 'ardent desire' that the Jews will enter the Church." The pope "expressed his bewilderment" at Heschel's remark that such a hope "would defeat the purpose" of the declaration, which, the pontiff explained, "was conceived in a spirit of benevolence and abundant friendship to the Jew and does not contain anything offensive. As a matter of fact, the Pope said, there are some people who consider the proposed declaration as being too favorable to the Jews." Obviously, Heschel and the pope viewed the declaration from opposing, perhaps irreconcilable, theological assumptions.

A brief debate on conversion (Heschel's most contentious topic) ensued. Diplomatically, Heschel asked the pope to respect "the sensitivity of the Jewish people and [recognize] that any reference to the eventuality of the acceptance by Jews of the Christian faith might create misunderstanding." The pope's "firm" answer was unmistakable: "The declaration is a religious document, addressed to all the Catholic world and cannot be guided by political or journalistic motivations. He said that unsolicited counsel and advice from elements outside the Church cannot influence the position of the Church." Heschel reiterated his point about possible misunderstanding and agreed that "it was not our intention to question the right of the Council to proclaim its beliefs." Responding to Heschel's request that he intervene personally on the wording of the declaration, the pope refused: "The Council is a democratic body and follows democratic procedure. The appropriate commission of the

Council will have to consider this text and whether any modifications should be made in it."

Heschel then appealed to the pontiff's compassion, attempting to convey the extent of Jewish suffering at the hands of Christianity; he urged the pope to condemn anti-Semitism ("a unique evil and unlike any other kind of discrimination") and to remove it once and for all from church teachings. At that point, Shuster spoke for the first time and "called the Pope's attention to the passage on deicide and said that . . . the implication is that the Jews of ancient times and of subsequent generations *were* responsible for [Christ's death]."

As the discussion ended, the pope accepted Heschel's memorandum, saying that he would submit it to the appropriate commission of the council.[13] Heschel presented the pope with a copy of *The Prophets* that contained an inscription to him citing three verses from the prophet Malachi. The pope read the inscription and said, "It is very beautiful." The official AJC report concluded with Heschel's offering his services to the pope as an adviser on Jewish issues: "The Pope graciously listened but did not commit himself. He then mentioned that Rabbi Zolli was a good friend of his. At the end of the audience, he presented Dr. Heschel and Mr. Shuster with souvenir medals."

Shuster added: "The entire conversation was conducted in a spirit of give-and-take without any restrictions. While the Pope was firm and definite in his remarks, he was most cordial and friendly to us." Heschel and Shuster had indeed placed the essential issues before the pope, but they were apparently unsuccessful in enlisting him to their side. It remained for the AJC to highlight the positives in this theological impasse.

Shuster's superconfidential report (consisting of twenty-one numbered points) expressed the desperation of a devoted Jewish diplomat who had staked all his hopes on this one, top-level encounter. Ashamed by its apparent failure, Shuster stressed the negative aspects of Heschel's performance, blaming Heschel entirely and not taking circumstances enough into account. But as later accounts confirm, Heschel was overwhelmed during this meeting by his charge as emissary of the Jewish people.[14]

Shuster's disgruntled version set the scene with body language: "The Pope was at ease, while Dr. Heschel sat on the edge of his chair, fidgeting, extremely tense, betraying great nervousness." Heschel's introductory remarks were "too long, obsequious in manner, repetitious in addressing the Pope innumerable times as 'Your Holiness,' and lacked point and clarity." The pope reminded his visitors that "he was ready to listen but that we should remember that the

Council was a deliberative body, one that made its own decisions, and that he cannot impose on it in any way. However, he said, he would be willing to transmit any viewpoint to the appropriate commission for ulterior consideration."

Despite that reminder, Heschel attempted to persuade the pope to support the previous statement on the Jews, because, according to Shuster's report, the revised text "would create a bad impression on public opinion." The pope answered by reminding Heschel that the document was addressed to believing Catholics, not outsiders. Refusing to drop this line of argument, Heschel repeated his view, probably thinking of the Talmudic principle by which some religious laws can be subordinated to the higher good of maintaining peace.[15]

Shuster found this part of Heschel's performance particularly shameful: "My eyes sank to the ground because I heard a Jew speaking to the head of the Catholic Church and bring in such irrelevant, unsuitable and alien considerations as *public relations* in a matter of the highest religious import and significance." Heschel was in a state of panic; unable to introduce further arguments, he "return[ed] again and again to obsequious remarks, pointing out the great public role the Council had assumed in the world, and that the passage, as it stood, would be misunderstood."

Heschel was stymied when the pope warned him that already too much pressure had been exerted from the outside, "and if such were to continue, then there would be *danger* (the Pope's very words) that the entire declaration would have to be tabled." At this point a grotesque breach of etiquette occurred that, recalled the humiliated Shuster, brought "great pain and distress for me personally": "the young interpreter, Monsignor Marcinkus (whose actions I do not condone in any way) could no longer contain himself in view of the ludicrous behavior of Dr. Heschel, and he began to mimic and imitate Dr. Heschel's gestures and manner of talking." (The 6-foot-4 Marcinkus, known for his athletic swagger and acerbic wit, soon became the pope's advance man and bodyguard.)[16]

Unable to endure the conversation any longer, Shuster interrupted Heschel to bring up the Jewish objections to the charge of deicide. Persuading the church to repudiate this charge had been a primary goal of the audience, but Heschel had neglected it to pursue the issue of conversion. Using French, which the pope spoke better than English (and perhaps to neutralize Marcinkus), Shuster submitted that the new draft was "quite catastrophic because it practically came out and accused the Jews of Christ's time, all the Jews of his time, of being Christ-killers." The pope replied that "this view of the Jews was again based on the Scripture." Shuster was forced to accept defeat: "Hearing this

Left to right: *Monsignor Paul C. Marcinkus, Pope Paul VI, Martin Luther King, Jr., and Ralph D. Abernathy at the Vatican, 18 September 1964. AP/Wide World Photos. Reproduced with permission.*

point of view, I knew that there was no point in continuing our discussing this subject."

Frustration overcame both emissaries, and Heschel concluded the audience awkwardly. Shuster believed that the pope was "ready apparently to listen to further arguments and discussion, but none were forthcoming. Finally, in a state of near exhaustion, Dr. Heschel presented a copy of his own book on the Prophets."

Heschel's parting gesture led to one final rebuff. He approached the pope and offered his "advice on matters affecting Jews and Judaism." Shuster reported: "The Pope was silent for a moment as though not grasping the meaning of Dr. Heschel's remarks. Then he said: 'Yes, Rabbi Zolli was a very good friend of mine and I knew him very well.' Dr. Heschel was flabbergasted and visibly taken aback at this reaction of the Pope to his remark, and obviously did not know how to respond to it."

Shuster grasped the pope's non sequitur all too well, as Heschel probably did, taking it as an insult: Zolli had been chief rabbi of Rome until he converted to Catholicism soon after the war. This was another example of theological misunderstanding: the apostate Zolli was not going to win favor with Jews, but he could serve as an expedient resource for Christians. The Holy Father did not want Heschel's advice. Shuster "felt a deep distress at the apparently pointed indelicacy of the Pope's reference to Rabbi Zolli. But Dr. Heschel had no justification in offering his services; it was tactless and uncalled for and lacking in self-dignity."

Both men left the pope's study extremely agitated. Soon after, Malachi Martin saw them arguing, Shuster, his face ashen, exploding at Heschel. As Shuster admitted in his top-secret report: "I recall definitely that on leaving the Vatican, the words that came spontaneously to my mind and lips were *chillul ha-shem v'yisrael* (the desecration of God's name and of Israel)." Shuster's warm and impassioned alliance with Heschel had collapsed in bitterness.[17]

Shuster's devastating criticism of Heschel confirmed the fragility of self-esteem even among the most dedicated Jews, himself as well as Heschel. Completing his candid report the next day, Shuster noted with horror that the pope's intimates had already learned of Heschel's poor performance. From then on the AJC relegated Heschel to the background while Shuster, Tanenbaum, John Slawson, and especially their numerous Catholic allies at the council carried the battle forward.

The Day of Atonement began the next evening at sunset. Heschel, like Jews worldwide, faced God's judgment with these words on his lips: "Do I have the right to survive this year without *teshuvah*" (repentance, lit. "return")? "And your life shall hang in doubt before you."[18]

Ironically, on the day of Heschel's secret audience with the pope, Rabbi Joseph Soloveitchik publicly reasserted his opposition to interfaith theological discussions. As reported by the *Jewish Press Agency*, the leader of modern Orthodoxy alluded negatively to Heschel's earlier "Auschwitz" memorandum without naming him: "The situation does not call for hysteria and readiness to incur martyrdom. All it requires is common sense, responsibility, dignity and particularly a moratorium on theological 'Dialogue' and pilgrimages to Rome."[19]

Behind the scenes, Vatican leaders who supported the Declaration on the Jews still valued Heschel's authority. Father Morlion helped repair the immediate damage of his inept performance by explaining to the pope that Heschel "had been profoundly impressed by the saintly religious spirit and frank realistic explanations of His Holiness, last Monday, and that he probably would be able to influence the Orthodox Rabbis of USA and Israel, in the sense of reasonable hope and moderation." Heschel's disrepute within the American Orthodox establishment remained an internal Jewish matter.[20]

But during the ensuing weeks, the turmoil within Jewish circles spilled into the public sphere, much of it due to Heschel himself. Wounded in his self-esteem, he attempted to bolster his reputation as an uncompromising prophetic voice. Apparently heedless of the diplomatic dangers, and despite his pledge of secrecy, he began to release hints about his confrontation with the head of the Catholic Church. The first rumors of Heschel's papal audience were aired by the *Religious News Service,* a worldwide press outlet reporting on issues concerning all religions. Two weeks later a few distorted pieces of information reached print. In the 2 October 1964 issue of the *Day-Morning Journal,* an article in Yiddish by the ubiquitous Gershon Jacobson traced the outlines of the still-confidential meeting.[21]

The following week, more details reached the London *Jewish Chronicle* "from our correspondent, New York," probably Jacobson, who announced: "Rabbi Dr. Abraham Joshua Heschel, who has been in close touch with Cardinal Bea . . . was invited by Pope Paul VI to an audience on the Monday before Yom Kippur, it is now disclosed." The reporter emphasized Heschel's refusal to discuss what was said but added that he "has reason to believe that Pope Paul was greatly impressed by Rabbi Heschel's statement."[22]

Alarmed and outraged at these violations of confidentiality, Shuster feared that the entire AJC project might collapse. Immediately he dispatched a "personal and confidential" memorandum to John Slawson, as ever carefully explaining his reactions. Only Heschel could be the source of this "flagrant breach of faith," Shuster asserted. The rabbi's reported claim that the pope was "greatly impressed" was especially shocking. Fearing that opponents would accuse the pope of allowing himself to be unduly influenced, Shuster urged that Heschel be silenced and the papal audience "be kept in total secrecy."[23]

Shuster was correct in his anticipation that the news would spread beyond the control of the AJC. The brief *Jewish Chronicle* article quickly led to a cover story in the October issue of the *Jewish World,* an independent illustrated monthly published in New York. Again the author was anonymous, but he was as well informed as Jacobson. This longer account was provocative, calculated to nettle its partisan readership. The magazine cover featured photographs of Heschel and Pope Paul along with the misleading headline, repeated inside: "What Happened on Yom-Kippur Eve at the Vatican?" (The article did explain that Heschel, refusing to meet with the pope on the Sabbath, had rescheduled the audience for the following Monday, the day *before* Yom Kippur eve.) The reporter explained that "Heschel himself declined to talk about his trip. He told his friends that he'd been sworn to secrecy by the Vatican. After piecing together every bit of information the following may be reported."[24]

That report was a mixture of fact and distortion, not necessarily attributable to Heschel, and it caused consternation at both the Vatican and the AJC. The reporter "guessed" that the AJC's Interreligious Department had arranged the meeting, despite the admonitions of several staff members that "if this should become public knowledge it would jeopardize the foundations of the Ecumenical efforts." Above all, "Heschel claimed that he had not requested the audience. He implied that *he had been invited* to go there."[25]

The article also exposed the tactics of lobbyists for the Jewish declaration. It recalled that before the third session opened on 14 September 1964, "both versions [of the declaration] were leaked to the *New York Times* and reprinted widely. . . . *The new draft threatened the collapse of the interfaith movement.*" Soloveitchik's suspicions were mentioned: "The merest hint of 'conversion' is of course offensive to Jewish ears because it recalls dark *ancestral memories* associated with forced professions of faith and unwanted proselytism." Powerful adversaries, including President Nasser of Egypt and other Arab leaders, had worked to suppress the document.[26]

The report went on to cite some anti-Semitic innuendoes expressed at the council itself while praising the supportive American bishops, especially Cardinal Cushing: "A new tone was introduced by a plea from several Church Fathers asking for *an act of contrition* by the Church on behalf of the Jews." The conclusion alluded sarcastically to Hitler (emphasized by italics): "[This Vatican source] added that the Most Holy Father still has not made up his mind on the Jewish issue at this time, the *final solution* is still to come." Such rhetoric could only upset Jews and Christians motivated by trust or magnanimity.[27]

Vatican II: The Third Session

For all practical purposes, even if Heschel had performed according to expectations, he could not have changed the draft declaration on the Jews. Its fate was sealed well before his papal audience. The pope could have done very little, if anything, to modify it even had he wished to. The text was discussed on 18 and 19 September 1964 and, predictably, it was opposed by prelates from Arab countries and church conservatives. All sorts of maneuvers were deployed to stall consideration of the issue. The Curia even attempted to remove the document from Cardinal Bea's Secretariat, though without success.

A vote on the Declaration on the Jews was scheduled for 19 November and the vote on religious liberty for the following day. Using a suspect parliamentary tactic, council president Cardinal Tisserant announced that both votes would be postponed. There was a tremendous outcry among supporters, and more than a thousand bishops signed a petition urging Pope Paul to reconsider the decision. The pope refused to do so, but he promised that the issues would be treated in the fourth and final session.

Hopes rose on 20 November, the last Friday of the third session, when Cardinal Bea was allowed to introduce the draft statement on the Jews for preliminary approval. It passed enthusiastically with 1,770 in favor, 185 opposed. (The text on non-Christian religions was adopted by a similar majority.) Pope Paul promised that the definitive text would be presented at the final session the following year. Grateful AJC officials thanked their allies at the Vatican for their efforts on behalf of the vote. Shuster wrote to Cardinal Willebrands and Father Thomas Stransky, and sent a telegram to Cardinal Bea and others, expressing joy and the gratitude of the AJC. It was a triumph for church progressives; but the text, approved for discussion yet arousing vehement dissent, was still subject to revision.[28]

By early December, Shuster judged that Heschel had become a major liability. He telephoned Marc Tanenbaum, following up with a firm but tactful letter; revealing that "Dr. Heschel is now a *persona non grata* to the highest Vatican authorities," Shuster urged Tanenbaum to keep the matter confidential: "The only other person with whom you could discuss this matter is Dr. Slawson." Heschel must not only be removed from the ongoing process, his name must be expunged from the official record.[29]

Tanenbaum, at home in bed with a bad cold, had a secretary read him Shuster's personal letter over the telephone. A consummate professional, Tanenbaum consented: "I understand exactly what you are saying and I will see to it that your point of view is reflected in the final document." Heschel's role was minimized in the AJC "White Paper," the draft of an internal history that detailed the still covert AJC involvement in the negotiations with the Vatican. It was a dismal demotion from the heroic narrative of the summit meeting of the rabbi and the pope.[30]

Internally, Heschel was engulfed in an emotional maelstrom. On the day following the preliminary vote on the Jewish declaration, the evening of 21 November, he accorded an in-depth interview in Hebrew to a visiting Israeli reporter from the widely circulated Tel Aviv newspaper *Ma'ariv.* Geula Cohen, a formidable personality and right-wing Zionist, notorious as a "girl terrorist" and "unyielding Israeli warrior," had worked as a radio broadcaster in the early 1940s for the Stern Gang, a paramilitary organization that was outlawed by both the British and the Zionists. Captured by the British and sentenced to nine years in prison, she escaped two years later. After independence in 1948 she became a teacher and a journalist.[31]

Prodded by this adroit interviewer, Heschel elaborated a personal narrative of his audience with the pope, suppressing the humiliation, and making another diplomatic blunder. The attractive, charismatic activist had won the confidence of the fifty-eight-year-old professor, whom she described as handsome and a Jewish sage. As she directed his attention to his memories of helplessness during the Holocaust she unleashed the emotions that had underlain his mission, spurring both his successes and his failures. (When Heschel first arrived in Rome for the papal audience, Shuster had warned him that his statement about Auschwitz had been very badly received among Catholic friends. Undaunted, Heschel replied, "I had my *own private* reasons for making this remark.")[32]

Heschel felt a sense of responsibility to all the Jews slaughtered in Europe. His mission to Rome was to save future Jewish lives, he explained; it was

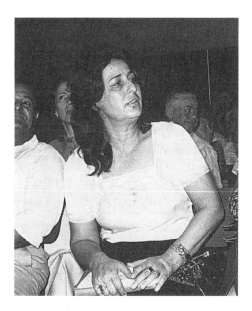

*Geula Cohen, ca. 1964. Courtesy of Geula
Cohen, Israel.*

Rabbi Marc H. Tanenbaum, ca. 1963.
Courtesy of the American Jewish Committee.

a response to that obsession: "I live in Auschwitz. Since Auschwitz I have only one rule of thumb for what I say: would it be acceptable to those people who were burned there."[33]

Cohen then explored Heschel's public statement about being "ready to go to Auschwitz" if faced with conversion or death. Appealing to his ego, she goaded him about Christian anti-Semitism: "This statement of yours made me proud. Yet, I would have written it differently, saying: 'if this were the only way in which I would be permitted to live, I would have endeavored to send *them* [Christians] to Auschwitz.'" According to Cohen, Heschel did not seem "shocked by [her] words" and openly, and naively, displayed his vanity: "Permit me to avoid modesty at this moment. Frankly, I assert that the statement on Auschwitz, of which you are proud, is the strongest statement possible, and it has shaken many people throughout the world."[34]

Heschel then explained the strategy behind his reference to Auschwitz: "[Christians] correctly understood that I was comparing them to the Nazis. If I had made the statement in a straightforward fashion saying 'you are Nazis,' it would have sounded ridiculous. My style of writing is by hinting, because truth is in the depths." This was the way Heschel confronted his adversaries. "There are those who would like to attack their bodies. I want to attack their souls. Today, there is no longer any place for religious wars as such. Today, there is occasion for conversation and discussion. Do you consider the desire to discuss a sign of weakness?"[35]

Cohen highlighted their diametrically opposed perspectives. She pushed beyond the brink of common sense by voicing her own contempt for Christianity: "But they are the murderers. For they are guilty not only of killing Jews but of killing God." Heschel did not rise to this particular bait, avoiding direct attacks; he was a pragmatic negotiator who rejected the position of Soloveitchik, without naming him, and other Jews who refused to engage with the Vatican: "The moment I became convinced that I could contribute toward the death of the Christian myth about the Jewish killing of God (which was the cause of so much sacrifice and suffering) I rose and went to the Pope."[36]

Cohen did not agree. For her, the solution to anti-Semitism was a well-armed Jewish state, not debate and compromise. Heschel chose the more dangerous goal of reconciliation: "Has the Israeli army succeeded in protecting the Jews of the Diaspora who are deprived of such protection? . . . The only legitimate dignity, even when you go to the rescue, you do not forget who you are; and this I have not forgotten. When I stood before the Pope, I did not forget for one moment my forefathers."[37]

Heschel then switched topics, proudly recalling his first meeting with Cardinal Bea in November 1961. He set central importance on the memorandum he prepared at the cardinal's request, which led, he claimed, to his meeting with the pope: "At the initiative of very important theologians, I was invited to an audience by the Pope."[38]

Cohen then elicited Heschel's version of the papal audience, which he now felt freer to embroider. In this wishful, post-facto account, he claimed to have offered, in his solution to the conversion issue, a theological concession: "Inasmuch as this Christian hope is a hope for the end of time, and since what will happen at the end of time is God's mystery, . . . one can therefore formulate this hope in an eschatological form which would be acceptable also to Jews, expressing the hope that at the end of time all men will worship our Father in Heaven." Heschel reported the pontiff as answering, " 'I shall do what I can, but you know that the Council is a democratic body.' "[39]

As Heschel described his part in the negotiations, Cohen observed signs of his narcissism: "Professor Heschel's voice was raised at this moment not so much in an outburst of triumphant joy as in joyful concern with the final victory—'have you noticed that what was introduced into the final text of the declaration is in the spirit of the words that I suggested to the pope?'"[40]

When Cohen's blockbuster interview with Heschel appeared in *Ma'ariv* on Christmas Day, 1964, Vatican officials were stunned. The news spread quickly, touching off a firestorm. The first intimation came from Vatican Radio, which picked up a short notice from Radio Cairo about the interview, stressing Heschel's supposed inference that church officials were comparable to Nazis. Some council members, adversaries of the Declaration on Judaism, prepared a strong rebuttal for *L'osservatore romano*, but Cardinal Bea was able to stop it. Less than a week later, Shuster received the appalling report from Vatican informants that Heschel's indiscretion had reached the highest authorities: not only Cardinal Bea but Cardinal Cicognani, the Vatican secretary of state and a powerful conservative, and the pope himself. Cooperative ties between Jews and Catholics, so cautiously cultivated for years, were severely menaced. Shuster was horrified that the AJC project was again threatened.[41]

Cardinal Bea, whose bond with Heschel was particularly deep, suffered excruciatingly. On 31 December 1964, the octogenarian was summoned to the Vatican secretary of state, where for an hour and a half, Cicognani bitterly reproached him about the Heschel interview, and for maintaining contacts with the American Jewish Committee, even accusing Bea of being "behind the article." Shuster quoted Bea's words: "'This article has been the direct cause of the most distressing time I have been called upon ever to spend in the Eternal City. Perhaps the time of ultimate catastrophe for many of my dearest plans.'"[42]

Bea relayed Cicognani's eyewitness account of the pope's reactions: "The Pope was angered and chagrined by the presumption of the tone used in the article; by the distortion of actual historical facts as he, the Pope, knows them; the implied insults to Christianity; the puerile disrespect and contemptuous attitude towards other most worthy, most beloved, and most righteous men, who have spoken more authoritatively, more worthily, of their religion, and their dignity, then he, Dr. Heschel, ever did or seemingly could do. . . . *'Who can say now that the Jewish document is not the direct product of Jewish pressures?'* the Pope asked" (Shuster's emphasis). Bea also reported that the Vatican secretary of state "is convinced that Heschel and his visit was the AJC in person. *The entire faithlessness of this man is ascribed totally to the AJC*" (Shuster's emphasis). Bea concluded that the AJC must dissociate itself completely from Heschel, privately and publicly.[43]

Shuster dissected Cohen's interview with Heschel in light of the expressed horror of Vatican officials, including the pope, who had read it. Heschel's vainglorious claim that the revised text of the declaration followed "in the spirit of my words to the pope" had enraged the pontiff, threatened to undermine the authority of Cardinal Bea, and gave "unqualified support to the major charge of the Arabs that the Jewish document is a direct product of Jewish pressure on the Holy Father and on the Vatican," he lamented.[44]

The Jewish diplomat was especially mortified by Heschel's apparent tolerance of the Israeli journalist's "violent, blasphemous attack on Christianity and on Christ himself." Shuster considered the remarks to be "entirely unparalleled in modern Jewish writings." Most damning to Heschel's character was his "deliberately proffered insult to every other Jewish personality who previously approached the Vatican, the Pope, or Cardinal Bea." Heschel referred to these professionals "contemptuously as 'mere social workers and politicians.'" The pope himself had "made specific reference to Heschel's humiliation of other Jewish personalities." Heschel had indeed violated the basic tenet of his own sacred humanism: reverence for every person as an image of God. By demeaning the network of dedicated Jewish diplomats, he had lost a major battle in his struggle against ego.[45]

Frantic AJC officials, disassociating themselves from Heschel, sought to repair the damage. In March 1965 Morris B. Abram, in his capacity as AJC president, wrote a comprehensive letter of apology to Cardinal Bea, promising that the AJC had no further association with Heschel, even though Heschel had subsequently repudiated his remarks: "He has assured us that his views have been misrepresented, that these invidious statements reflect the personal biases of the writer, and that these hostile expressions are contrary to the well-known positions toward the Church and Christianity which he has expressed on numerous other occasions."[46]

Although I cannot justify the betrayal Heschel unthinkingly inflicted on his AJC and Vatican partners—foremost among them Cardinal Bea—I can try to understand why he, the authoritative "Rabbi Abraham Joshua Heschel," was rendered almost speechless by his enormous responsibility when he met with the pope. Heschel was vulnerable on many levels. First and foremost, his memory had absorbed almost two thousand years of persecution of Jews by the Catholic Church: periodic killings, expulsions, demeaning public disputations, papal burnings of the Talmud. Moreover, the AJC had been unrealistic in expecting a single papal audience to resolve an issue that had been hotly contended for many years. It was a plausible political gamble, but it was based on the faulty assumption that Pope Paul could (and would) interfere with the "democratic" process in which over a thousand cardinals from around the world discussed, amended, and voted on legislation.

The immediate pressures on Heschel were immense. The Vatican had repeatedly put him in a position whereby he had to refuse to meet with the pope by scheduling the meetings for the Sabbath. Heschel was already exposed to Jewish attacks for agreeing to meet with the pope between Rosh Hashanah and Yom Kippur. In addition, he was still mourning his sister. At the meeting, he behaved like a wounded, traumatized Jew from Warsaw, and not a young and fearless prophet admonishing kings and nations to repent.

Finally, Heschel's self-esteem as an ordinary man was wounded in his Achilles' heel, his pride and his narcissism. He compensated for his shame (which remained a secret) by gradually constructing a public narrative with himself at the center. He probably did this unconsciously. Subsequent interviews demonstrate a consistent pattern of self-deception.[47]

Vatican II: The Grand Finale

In the historical record, however, Heschel's "failed" audience with Pope Paul VI and his alarming indiscretions were soon transformed into victory. When the fourth session of the Ecumenical Council opened on 14 September 1965, the revised texts of the Jewish declaration and the statement on religious liberty were examined quickly. On 21 September the statement on religious liberty was adopted by a large majority. On the 30th, Cardinal Bea's Secretariat distributed a version of the Jewish declaration that was somewhat less favorable than the previous one (for example, the charge of *deicide* was not explicitly condemned). Publicists in the United States took action.

As a last attempt to strengthen the declaration, Heschel, now his own agent, rallied his polemic skill to denounce this lack of specificity: "The deicide charge is the most dreadful calumny ever uttered. It resulted in rivers of blood and mountains of human ashes. . . . It is absurd, monstrous, and unhistorical, and the supreme repudiation of the Gospel of love." He took his hyperbole even further: "Not to condemn the demonic canard of deicide . . . is a defiance of the God of Abraham and an act of paying homage to Satan." Moderate Jewish diplomats did not appreciate Heschel's biblical extremism.[48]

But the four-year battle had exhausted all the possibilities. On 14 October, Cardinal Bea presented the revised text to the council. That afternoon the prelates approved a number of clauses: the assertion that the death of Jesus was not to be blamed on all Jews collectively; elimination of the word *deicide;* a passage that "deplored" anti-Semitism. The entire Declaration on Non-Christian Religions was also accepted. Page 1 of the *New York Times* announced: "Council's Final Approval Voted for Text on Jews."[49]

On 28 October 1965, the anniversary of John XXIII's election to the papacy, the final version of *Nostra Aetate* (In our times) was adopted, 2,312 to 88, with 3 invalid votes. Pope Paul VI promulgated the text immediately as official church doctrine. A solid foundation was established for future decades of Jewish-Christian dialogue and cooperation.[50]

Abraham Joshua Heschel became an inspirational symbol of the Jewish involvement in helping to formulate *Nostra Aetate.* The shortcomings of his secret audience were buried, while his major role (especially at the early stages) entered the historical record with the deliberate cooperation of the Vatican. Heschel soon emerged as an honored Jewish critic of the church and a unique spiritual resource for progressive Christians (Protestants and Catholics) seeking to advance the momentum of renewal.[51]

Competition for the official story of the Jewish partnership with Catholic progressives began soon after the promulgation of *Nostra Aetate.* A dangerously misleading article appeared in *Look* magazine, "How the Jews Changed Catholic Teaching," written by senior editor Joseph Roddy, who gave credence to the claim that without pressure from the Jews, the declaration would not have been accepted. He also reported, conversely, that the presence of Jewish lobbyists in Rome had invigorated the declaration's conservative opponents. The article revealed secret information (much of it obtained from Malachi Martin, who was given the pseudonym "Fitzharris O'Boyle"), along with numerous errors of fact and egregious distortions.[52]

Any historical narrative must remain incomplete, a product of interpretation. After studying the archival documents and comparing them with published accounts and interviews with several of the actors, I have concluded that the Jewish input was important but not decisive. The machinations behind the scenes should not blind us to facts: Pope John XXIII purposely appointed Augustin Cardinal Bea, a learned scholar and a priest of saintly integrity, to rectify the church's millennial injustices toward Judaism and the Jewish people. When all is said and done, the positive effects of Vatican II are owing to humble, compassionate, and intelligent Christians—Merton, Cushing, Bea, and thousands of others—who were inspired by what was "Godly and right."[53]

15

Interfaith Triumphs (1963–1966)

A Christian ought to realize that a world without Israel will be a world without the God of Israel. A Jew, on the other hand, ought to acknowledge the eminent role and part of Christianity in God's design for the redemption of all man.
—Heschel, "No Religion Is an Island" (1965)

WHILE HE WAS PURSUING HIS ACTIVITIES AT VATICAN II, HESCHEL HAD ALSO been gaining prominence in the American Protestant community. Starting with Reinhold Niebuhr's laudatory review of *Man Is Not Alone* in 1951, Heschel's authority as a spiritual voice had grown, reinforced by articles in *Time* magazine, responses to *God in Search of Man*, his participation at interfaith conferences, and his invited articles. In 1956 he published "The Biblical View of Reality" and "A Hebrew Evaluation of Reinhold Niebuhr" in essay collections. Two years later "Sacred Images of Man" appeared in the journal *Religious Education* and "The Religious Message" in John Cogley's edited volume *Religion in America*. The *Union Seminary Quarterly Review* published Heschel's talk on "Prayer and Theological Discipline" in 1959. With the publication of *The Prophets* late in 1962, Heschel's biblical theology became required reading in many Protestant seminaries.

Heschel found a major Protestant ally in John Coleman Bennett, since 1955 dean of faculty at Union Theological Seminary. Bennett was the Reinhold Niebuhr Professor of Social Ethics and had replaced the elderly Niebuhr as the theologian of progressive, politically engaged Protestantism. The Canadian-born Bennett was admired for his intelligence and humility, his support for the ecumenical movement, and his dedication to practical issues of justice. He and Heschel had become friends by 1962, when both were speakers at the annual conference of the Religious Education Association. Bennett spoke on ethics and military power in international relations, while Heschel delivered his critique of religious education, "Idols in the Temples," adapted from previous talks to Jewish groups.[1]

In December 1963, anticipating the triennial General Assembly of the National Council of Churches, editors of the *Christian Century*, the preeminent Protestant journal, devoted an issue to religious renewal, inviting Heschel to present a Jewish view. Protestants at this time were especially attentive to the Second Vatican Council, and discussions among the Roman Catholic clergy had roused them to intensive self-questioning.

Niebuhr, whose imperative was "to establish justice for all men," provided the issue with a radical critique, "The Crisis in American Protestantism." He faulted his coreligionists, "the owners of modern industry," for their complacency. The "Negro revolt," Niebuhr charged, challenged "the abject capitulation of American Protestant Christianity" as a betrayal of the social gospel movement of Walter Rauschenbusch and others. Heschel's theological answer to the call for religious renewal was equally bold. Still keenly involved in the machinations of Vatican II, he detailed, for the first time in print, deficiencies in Christian observance and thought. He deplored two trends, both connected with Judaism: "the age-old process of dejudaization of Christianity, and the modern process of desanctification of the Hebrew Bible." He went so far as to scold those he was trying to reach: "How dare a Christian substitute his own conception of God for Jesus' understanding of God and still call himself a Christian? . . . Only a conscious commitment to the roots of Christianity in Judaism could have saved it from such distortions."[2]

Heschel's criticism of Christian theology did not bother John Bennett. After Bennett's inauguration as president of Union in April 1964, one of his first acts was to invite Heschel to join the faculty as the Harry Emerson Fosdick Visiting Professor. On 5 November he offered Heschel two courses for the first semester; for the second Heschel would tour the country as a "roving profes- sor under the auspices of the Seminary." Bennett expected Heschel to embody Jewish tradition as well as to teach it. It was time for Protestants to have a share of him along with the Catholics, he added. Heschel accepted the offer enthusiastically the following week, adding a personal touch: "My gratitude for it is enhanced by the genuine admiration for you which I have felt for so many years."[3]

This was a tremendous opportunity for Heschel to influence Protestants, who dominated American social and political life. Located on Broadway across from the Jewish Theological Seminary, Union was proudly liberal, as the catalog announced: "Union Seminary was established in 1836 on the prin- ciple of freedom—freedom for the institution to determine the type of life and training that would best fit students for Christian service without ecclesiastical or university domination or dictation." The Fosdick Visiting Professorship had been established in 1953 by John D. Rockefeller III to honor one of America's great religious progressives and a member of the Union faculty from 1908 to 1946, when he also retired from the pulpit of Riverside Church.[4]

Heschel was the first Jew to be honored with this position. Bennett tele- phoned the news to Reverend and Mrs. Fosdick (the day of her death, as it turned out), and they both expressed "much satisfaction" at the news. An in- stitutional drama made the Heschel appointment even more noteworthy. Union's constitution required all faculty members to identify with a specific Christian denomination. Previous recipients of the Fosdick Professorship had all been Christians. It was necessary formally to change that rule in order to appoint Heschel.[5]

The faculty discussed the possibility of amending the constitution to elimi- nate the requirement. Some suggested that it would be simpler to insert the word *permanent* before "member of the faculty" in the requirement clause to allow non-Christians to become visiting professors. The Board of Directors met on 15 January 1965 and voted to amend the section of the constitution and bylaws to define *permanent* members of the faculty; on 9 March this vote was ratified unanimously. At the same meeting, Heschel was officially appointed Harry Emerson Fosdick Visiting Professor for the academic year 1965–66.[6]

The next day, a press release went out that quoted Niebuhr on Heschel's "commanding and authoritative voice," along with a page-long biography, including Heschel's European background, his abundant American publications, and a list of fifteen lecture topics. Invitations to speak soon arrived. The Pacific School of Religion in Berkeley, California, wanted to feature Heschel at their annual Pastoral Conference in February 1966. By July, more than a dozen events across the country had been organized. Heschel's national teaching tour would include twenty-five institutions.[7]

In the meantime, Heschel's family was preparing to celebrate Susannah's bat mitzvah on 15 May 1965, her thirteenth birthday. Susannah herself, independent and strong-willed, had requested the ritual, contrary to the custom prevailing among JTS faculty, who did not mark their daughters' bat mitzvahs, and her parents were quick to support her. (At the time, only about half of the Conservative congregations followed Reform and Reconstructionist Jews in dedicating girls to Judaism in this way.) The Heschels decided not to involve their Hasidic relatives, who would neither accept the idea of a bat mitzvah nor enter a Conservative synagogue.[8]

Hoping that JTS would host, if not welcome, their milestone event, the Heschels invited Louis Finkelstein to their home one Shabbat afternoon to discuss the matter. As Susannah remembered, "I broached the topic, arguing that his commitment to Civil Rights ought to extend to women. [Finkelstein] was friendly but patronizing and offered to make a party for me in his home, instead of anything in the [JTS] synagogue." Instead they held the service at Ansche Chesed, a Conservative synagogue on West End Avenue and 100th Street, within walking distance.

Invitations in Hebrew and English went out for the Sabbath morning ceremony. Heschel chanted the blessings, Susannah chanted the Haftarah and gave two speeches, one in Hebrew, the other in English. After the service there was a kiddush (a light lunch with blessings) at the synagogue, and the next day a reception at the Heschel apartment. Several obligations at the Seminary that day prevented Finkelstein, Saul Lieberman, and others from attending, and

The Heschels at home, ca. 1965. Photograph by Lotte Jacobi.
Courtesy of the Lotte Jacobi Collection, University of New
Hampshire.

their absence reinforced Heschel's sense of isolation from the tight-knit JTS community.[9]

Union Theological Seminary

An entirely different feeling reigned at Union. Heschel's inaugural lecture, "No Religion Is an Island," took place on 10 November 1965. Invitations were mailed to a wide public, including the administration and faculty of JTS. Union fittingly celebrated this major interfaith event in the grand manner, recording Heschel's speech on tape and publishing it in the *Union Seminary Quarterly Review.*

Heschel was worried that the Christian audience would be offended by his strictures against mission to the Jews. His strained relations at JTS also distressed him; once again the chancellor had chosen not to attend. Finkelstein had written to both Heschel and Bennett explaining that he had a previous commitment with the United Synagogue. (Heschel may not have received the note before the speech because the previous day the great Northeast blackout had left the city without power and in chaos for close to twelve hours.) Two days before the event, Heschel heard that Jessica Feingold, Finkelstein's administrative assistant, had not received an invitation, so he personally delivered one to her. She attended, as did some of Heschel's JTS colleagues. When the evening came, the auditorium was filled, and loudspeakers had to be set up in another room for the overflow crowd. They were not disappointed.[10]

Heschel delivered a magnificent oration, a wide-ranging and eloquent analysis of the foundations of Jewish-Christian cooperation. His dramatic opening defined the historical moment:

> I speak as a member of a congregation whose founder was Abraham, and the name of my rabbi is Moses.
>
> I speak as a person who was able to leave Warsaw, the city in which I was born, just six weeks before the disaster began. My destination was New York, it would have been Auschwitz or Treblinka. I am a brand plucked from the fire, in which my people was burned to death. I am a brand plucked from the fire of an altar of Satan on which millions of human lives were exterminated to evil's greater glory, and on which so much else was consumed: the divine image of so many human beings, many people's faith in the God of justice and compassion, and much of the secret and power of attachment to the Bible bred and cherished in the hearts of men for nearly two thousand years.

As "a brand plucked from the fire of an altar of Satan," Heschel asserted that the Holocaust was a catastrophe for all civilization. Judaism and Christianity shared a common fate, he proclaimed, and a common legacy: the living God, the Hebrew Bible, and the sacred image of humankind.[11]

Heschel repeated his contention that "the fate of the Jewish people and the fate of the Hebrew Bible are intertwined." Jews and Christians were united against the menace of nihilism, he contended, illustrating his point with a reference to the blackout: "The people of New York City have never experienced such fellowship, such awareness of being one, as they did last night in the midst of darkness." Religious people were threatened not by competing theologies but by alienation from the living God: "The supreme issue today is not the *halakhah* for the Jew or the Church for the Christian—but the premise underlying both religions, namely, whether there is a *pathos*, a divine reality concerned with the destiny of man which mysteriously impinges upon history."[12]

Heschel saw depth theology as the common ground of interfaith dialogue. After summarizing "four dimensions of religious existence" (creed, faith or inwardness, the law, the community), he evoked in one long sentence the existential situation preceding religious commitment and statements of belief: "I suggest that the most significant basis for meeting of men of different religious traditions is the level of fear and trembling, of humility and contrition, where our individual moments of faith are mere waves in the endless ocean of mankind's reaching out for God, where all formulations and articulations appear as understatements, where our souls are swept away by the awareness of the urgency of answering God's commandment, while stripped of pretension and conceit we sense the tragic insufficiency of human faith." This "tragic insufficiency of human faith," according to Heschel, coupled with an acute yearning for God's presence, could foster the spiritual companionship of "humility and contrition," open-mindedness, as a precondition of true interfaith dialogue.[13]

Taking up the issue of the Christian mission to the Jews that had so vexed his audience with Pope Paul he proclaimed, "No religion is an island"; no tradition holds the monopoly: "Thus any conversation between Christian and Jew in which abandonment of the other partner's faith is a silent hope must be regarded as offensive to one's religious and human dignity. . . . Is it not blasphemous to say: I alone have all the truth and the grace, and all those who differ live in darkness, and are abandoned by the grace of God?" Heschel cited Niebuhr and Tillich, who also rejected the idea of converting Jews.[14]

Heschel explained his own pluralism, "In this aeon diversity of religions is the will of God," quoting a Talmudic source: "The ancient Rabbis proclaim: 'Pious men of all nations have a share in the life to come.'" He cited other Jewish sages, including Judah Halevi and Maimonides, who affirmed the legitimacy of Christianity and Islam, along with Judaism. He concluded with a flourish that combined Christian and Jewish ideas in a pluralistic call to cooperative action: "to bring about a resurrection of sensitivity, a revival of conscience; to keep alive the divine sparks in our souls, to nurture openness to the spirit of the Psalms, reverence for the words of the prophets, and faithfulness to the living God."[15]

After thunderous applause, there was a reception, at which Heschel's theological rival, Mordecai Kaplan, came up and threw his arms around him, calling the event a kiddush ha-shem (heroic action that honors God's name). Ironically, it was Kaplan, the devout old Reconstructionist, and not Finkelstein, the traditionalist, who most earnestly applauded Heschel's defense of Jewish spirituality. For Kaplan, openness to the common ground of all religions triumphed over ego and ideology. Not all Heschel's JTS colleagues were so generous: the Bible scholar H. L. Ginsberg remarked to his colleagues in

Yiddish that Heschel's speech was not bad, but no speech at all would have been better. He considered Heschel a crypto-Christian who espoused a non-Jewish theology.[16]

Heschel revised his speech for publication in the *Union Seminary Quarterly Review;* it became his classic defense of religious pluralism, and a forthright rejection of mission to the Jews, strengthening his spiritual authority among Catholics, Protestants, and eventually Muslims.[17]

Heschel was happy and at ease at Union. From October 1965 through January 1966, he gave two courses and made himself available for private conversations. His classroom performance there was quite successful, for several reasons. For the first time in his life, a religious academy had asked him to offer courses based on his own books. And most of his Christian divinity students were disposed to be impressed by him, as were their professors. He was immensely popular. More students signed up for his classes than for those of any previous Fosdick visiting professor.

In addition, Union had sensitively accommodated Heschel's adherence to kashrut, religious dietary laws. A draft memorandum, quaintly entitled "Dr. Heschel's dietary scruples," advised prospective hosts: "Dr. Heschel, being of the Conservative branch of the Jewish Faith, follows their dietary regulations. Meals may include tuna fish, salmon, vegetable or fruit salads, cheeses or fish broiled in foil." (Union made greater efforts in this area than Hebrew Union College had in the 1940s!)[18]

Union had three major areas of the curriculum: the Biblical Field, the Historical Field, primarily church history, and the Theological Field, which included philosophy of religion, systematic theology, and Christian ethics. Heschel offered one course in the Biblical Field, in the Theology subdivision: New Testament 377: Theology of Ancient Judaism (Tuesdays, 11:00–12:50). The catalog was precise: "The authenticity and importance of rabbinic theology in the history of Judaism. *Halacha* (law) and *Agada* (theology). Two trends in Jewish theology: the school of Rabbi Akiba and the school of Rabbi Ishmael. Different categories and perspectives. The Battle of the Book. Different conceptions of the nature of the Torah, of the meaning of inspiration, of the role of Moses, of the language, authorship and hermeneutics of the Pentateuch, the nature of miracles, the meaning of suffering, God's presence, sacrifices, experience of God, life, piety, tradition." Heschel developed these topics from his two Hebrew volumes on rabbinic theology, *Heavenly Torah,* volumes 1 and 2. A total of thirty-nine students, including several auditors, attended.[19]

Heschel's second course, Philosophy of Religion 203: A Philosophy of Judaism, attracted an exceptionally large number of students, eighty-six including auditors. It was in the Theological Field, subdivision Philosophy of Religion, and met on Wednesdays, 4:10–6:00. The catalog again summarized Heschel's basic themes: "An attempt to explore the prerequisites and demands of faith, the polarities of meaning and mystery, the modes of being human, depth-theology, symbolism and immediacy, the theology of pathos, the confusion of good and evil, justice and compassion, the Law: obedience and celebration, study and prayer, holiness in time, the community of Israel, faith and interfaith." Most of these topics were encompassed in *God in Search of Man*. Students were required to read that book plus *The Earth Is the Lord's, The Sabbath*, and the chapter on "theology of pathos" from *The Prophets*.[20]

Heschel's popularity among the Protestants can be explained, in large part, by their appreciation of his charisma. For them he was an embodiment of Judaism. These committed Christians were eager to discover the Hebrew forerunners of their faith. They valued the fact that Heschel was a rabbi who believed in God. Moreover, he was frequently available to them: he kept the door of his office open, welcoming students (and faculty) who wanted to speak with him.

In the classroom he transmitted a religious sensibility, a dynamic, personal presence that endured in memories. One student found his course on first-century Judaism "less intense" than academic courses of other professors; Heschel was "more interested in how a student was 'feeling' the subject than in the scholarly minutiae and footnotes and closely woven arguments. . . . From an academic perspective he was easy. But from a spiritual perspective he was a delight and a challenge."[21]

Heschel's larger course on philosophy of Judaism required a lot of reading, but his teaching was often informal. In the introductory lecture he jokingly announced: "In this course I am not going to give you a bird's eye view of Judaism. I am not a bird; I'm a Jew!" Students remembered many ideas that were new to them: Heschel explained that Jews never write the word *God* on the blackboard "because you could erase it." "Just as material things remind us of their reality by their resistance to our wills, so we become convinced of the reality of the ineffable by its resistance to our categories." In illustration he told the story of a rabbi who continually studied the first words of Genesis. When his disciple returned six months later to find him reading the same text, he asked, "You haven't moved from that one verse yet?" The rabbi answered, "Well, I still haven't grasped everything in it."[22]

Generously, Heschel invited every one of his eighty-six students to meet with him. One young man was surprised that such a famous man would take this time and trouble. (He had never before met a rabbi.) Another student, William Lad Sessions, perceptively explained why Heschel's digressive and inspirational classroom manner might fail at an unsympathetic Jewish institution and succeed at a receptive Christian one: "It was a wonderful though frustrating experience. I found it hard to pin down any precise *ideas* Rabbi Heschel sought to communicate; instead, I primarily gained an intriguing and fascinating sense of the *person*."[23]

That person had "a kindly manner of teaching." His storytelling was "charming in a manner that was typically tender, persuasive, and enticing." At other times, when "an impolite graduate student [would] persist in reductively mistranslating Rabbi Heschel's discourse into some preferred contemporary jargon," the professor could be "tough-minded." But Heschel's sincerity and kindness were evident: "My dominant impression is of a passionately honest and kind man who sincerely wished to communicate the depth of the truth he lived."[24]

As had happened with some JTS students, some Union students found their conversations with Heschel life transforming. Heschel persuaded Sessions, who became a philosophy professor, that tradition was not "a constraint . . . but the necessary source of life." In later years, he realized that Heschel was disputing the tendency, common among youth in the 1960s, to repudiate the past: "I found that I could honestly devote myself to a life of philosophical scrutiny of my own religious tradition, without thereby losing my self-identity or integrity (prized possessions to a child of the '60s!)."[25]

Heschel's final examinations were fair but challenging. Students had ten minutes to develop each topic: 1) reasons for taking prophetic inspiration seriously; 2) the polarity of law and inwardness; 3) the main aspects of Jewish existence in Eastern Europe; 4) aspects of the Sabbath meaningful to a Christian.[26]

The irony was inescapable, and it must have aggravated Heschel: Jewish seminaries did not allow him teach his original scholarship and constructive theology. Union, on the other hand, cherished his interpretations of the Bible and rabbinic Judaism as the original sources of Jesus' teachings.

Most gratifying for Heschel during his year at Union were the warm relationships he and his wife developed with several colleagues. In addition to their ongoing friendship with Niebuhr and his wife, Ursula, the Heschels became close to John and Anne Bennett, Dora and James Sanders and their children, W. D. Davies and his family, and others. Particular friends were Samuel

Terrien, professor of Hebrew and cognate languages, and his wife, Sarah. The French-born Terrien was a specialist in the Psalms and the Book of Job, and his passion for art and music took him well beyond his expertise in ancient Near Eastern languages. He and Heschel had many discussions about theology and the Hebrew Bible.[27]

Heschel became closest to W. D. Davies, Edward Robinson Professor of Biblical Theology, and James A. Sanders, the recently appointed professor of Old Testament. Both scholars were ordained Christian ministers with a profound knowledge of biblical and rabbinic texts who revered Judaism. Heschel's friendship with these devout scholars combined personal affection and faith in the one God, which allowed them to negotiate their disagreements, some serious.

Heschel's relationship with the "precise and prolific" Davies had begun soon after the latter's arrival at Union in 1959 to take up the Chair of Biblical Theology, a position he held until 1966, when he moved to Duke University. He began his career as a specialist in the New Testament, but the discovery of the Dead Sea Scrolls persuaded him of the necessity of studying the Judaic origins of Christianity.[28]

Davies recognized that Jews and Christians viewed the Jewish state differently. His Israeli colleague Ephraim Urbach, professor of Talmud at the Hebrew University in Jerusalem, had urged him to write a letter to the *New York Times* supporting Israel against threatened Arab aggression. He did so but realized for the first time that Urbach, an Orthodox Jew, had assumed that Davies, as a Christian immersed in Hebrew Scripture, shared his belief "that Jews had a divine right to the Land of Israel." Responding to Urbach's surprising assumption, Davies developed a scholarly specialty in the relation of Judaism and early Christianity to the Holy Land.[29]

Davies appreciated Heschel's ability to convey Jewish spirituality and liturgical sensibility to Christians. He considered Heschel essentially a Hasidic rebbe, a personification of Torah and Jewish tradition with a modern European way of thinking. At the same time, Davies judged that Heschel's scholarship "lacked critical austerity." He appreciated the theological thrust of Heschel's works on the Talmud but was disappointed to find that many of the source notes in *Heavenly Torah* lacked historical perspective. Similarly, *The Prophets* neglected the finer points of historical research, though the book was illuminating.[30]

Heschel formed another abiding friendship with James Sanders, a warm, genial man from Memphis, Tennessee. Sanders, an ordained Presbyterian minister, was an expert in ancient Jewish texts; he had earned a Ph.D. in Bible from Hebrew Union College as well as degrees from Vanderbilt and Colgate Rochester Divinity Schools. Sanders revered Judaism while appreciating the situation of Arabs in the Middle East. Thoroughly conversant with the Hebrew Bible and its historical background, he was motivated by reverence for Judaism as an "incarnation of the Holy Spirit" (a formulation at odds with Jewish thought). As a specialist in the Dead Sea Scrolls, he spent the 1961–62 academic year at the American School of Oriental Research on the Jordanian side of Jerusalem, forming sympathetic bonds with Palestinian Arabs.[31]

Like Davies, Sanders admired Heschel as a biblical witness: "For Heschel, God was overwhelmingly real and shatteringly present." He first read *The Sabbath* during his seminary years, when neo-Orthodoxy had taken hold, and was impressed with its depiction of time rather than space as holy. Sanders considered Heschel "a *shalliah la-goyim*, an apostle to the gentiles." Sanders's wife, Dora, was a concert pianist, like Sylvia Heschel, and the couples enjoyed one another's company. Heschel and Sanders studied texts together and spoke about Bible, interfaith theology, and the state of Israel. Sylvia and Dora sometimes played duets.[32]

In spite of these friendships Heschel's Christian colleagues found shortcomings in his approach to interfaith dialogue. In gatherings of JTS and Union faculty, there were matters Heschel refused to discuss, such as the Christian mission to the Jews. In this regard Heschel was both inflexibly conservative and respectful of other religions. He also refused to discuss the current fascination with "death of God" theology, even as an academic hypothesis. To pronounce the very words was blasphemous, he felt, even if they were uttered with intellectual detachment. These reticences disappointed Davies, who had no intention of converting Jews to Christianity but held that true dialogue should exclude no issue, no matter how obnoxious. Yet the Protestant scholar recognized that Christians might not fear such discussion because of their cultural and political dominance, whereas Jews could not help feeling anxiety about it. In this understanding Davies touched on some of the agonized emotions deep within Heschel that had overcome him when facing the pope.[33]

Interfaith Theologian

Heschel launched his lecture tour for Union on 10 January 1966 (the day before his fifty-ninth birthday) with an interfaith panel on the Bible in the Union chapel. His appointment had received national attention. An article in the 31 January issue of *Newsweek* by the religion editor, Kenneth Woodward, a progressive Catholic, featured Heschel's "radical Judaism." Woodward cited the dramatic opening of the inaugural lecture, "I speak as a member of a congregation whose founder was Abraham, and the name of my rabbi is Moses," and brought up Heschel's controversial visits to Rome during the Second Vatican Council and his critique of American Judaism. A sketch of Heschel's life in Europe included his Hasidic background, his doctorate from the University of Berlin, even his book of Yiddish poems published in 1933.[34]

Of greatest interest to *Newsweek*'s broad readership, however, was Heschel's preeminence in interfaith dialogue: "With his appointment to Union, Heschel has become the center, and in a sense the source, of a new understanding between Christians and Jews which transcends the superficialities of conventional brotherhood." Woodward cited a number of striking phrases from *Who Is Man?* concluding with an enthusiastic historical appraisal: "To recover the prophetic message of ancient Judaism, Heschel has built up a rich, contemporary Jewish theology that may well be the most significant achievement of modern Jewish thought."

That same month Heschel was featured in the progressive Catholic monthly *Jubilee,* whose editor Edward Rice and "roving editor" Robert Lax were college friends of Thomas Merton's. Along with photographs of Heschel on the cover and inside, the magazine published his essay "Choose Life!" which surveyed his philosophy of humankind, civil rights, Jewish-Christian relations, and peace. The rabbi received the highest compliment from this devout, and dissident, magazine: "Heschel is a scholar whom Thomas Merton has called the world's greatest living theologian."[35]

Heschel's message to this Catholic audience was that spirit cannot be separated from ethical responsibility. He deplored the loss of transcendence, which led to a lack of reverence for human beings and for the world: "We are getting used to scandals, to outrage, even to terrible danger. There is apathy about nuclear bombs, for example, and about Vietnam." Public morality could not be handed over to politicians: "We have delegated our conscience to a few diplomats and generals, and this is a very grave sin."[36]

While Heschel was lecturing under the auspices of Union, he was also gaining prominence in the Catholic academic world. In March, Saint Michael's College in Winooski, Vermont, awarded him his first honorary doctorate. (He was the first Jew to receive this honor from the Catholic institution.) Two weeks later the University of Notre Dame also bestowed an honorary degree on Heschel. He had come to participate in a week-long international conference

(20–25 March 1966) on Vatican II marking the opening of the Graduate School of Theology and Institute for Advanced Religious Studies, the type of program for which Heschel had pressed strongly in Rome.[37]

Notre Dame intended this highly publicized event to launch the postconciliar era. On Sunday, 20 March, President Theodore M. Hesburgh welcomed the distinguished speakers, including Karl Rahner and Bernard Häring from Germany, Yves Congar and Henri de Lubac from France, Protestant observers such as Robert McAfee Brown, representatives from the Eastern Orthodox Church, Heschel and Marc Tanenbaum (the only Jews), and more than four hundred conferees. The proceedings were broadcast by closed-circuit television to an overflow crowd at the university and in several cities. Heschel and Tanenbaum participated with Thomas Stransky, their ally from Cardinal Bea's Secretariat, in the Monday evening session on the Declaration on Non-Christian Religions. The panel was chaired by Bishop John J. Wright of Philadelphia.[38]

On Wednesday evening Heschel and eighteen of the other participants received honorary doctorates (there were thirteen Roman Catholics, four Protestants, two Eastern Orthodox, and one Jew). Heschel's citation read, in part, "A leader of men deeply concerned with contemporary social problems, and consistently involved in efforts to increase mutual understanding between Christians and Jews." Heschel developed such a warm relationship with Father Hesburgh at the conference that the president invited him the following year to give the invocation at a Notre Dame alumni dinner.[39]

During his week in South Bend, Heschel gave a candid interview to a young priest, Patrick Granfield, OSB. Heschel's willingness to be critical was evident from the beginning, when Granfield asked the rabbi for his reactions to the lecture by Father Bernard Häring, a German moral theologian who had been active in Vatican II. Heschel's answer was blunt: "Father Häring, by saying that the act of worship is an act in Christ, indicated that there is only *one* acceptable form of prayer. As a Jew, I must reject that, and I also consider it dangerous to Christians." God must not take second place to Christ. Granfield also pressed Heschel about Martin Buber, whom Heschel usually avoided discussing so as not to criticize his teacher. (Buber was the modern Jewish thinker generally associated with Hasidism.) Heschel made it clear that he was not influenced by Buber, since he, Heschel, had known Hasidism from the inside long before he met Buber. "I can trace my family back to the late fifteenth century. . . . For seven generations, all my ancestors have been Hasidic rabbis."[40]

Heschel gave credit to Buber for several important cultural contributions, among them, bringing Hasidism to the West, supporting Zionism, and translating "the Hebrew Bible into German in a creative way." Nevertheless, Heschel reproached Buber for emphasizing aggadah (dynamic theological reflections) to the detriment of halakhah. Most important, he rejected Buber's notion of divine revelation as "a vague encounter. . . . A Jew cannot live by such a conception of revelation. Buber does not do justice to the claims of the prophets. So I have to choose between him and the Bible itself." Another major weakness in Buber's view of Judaism, according to Heschel, was that "he was not at home in rabbinic literature. That covered many years. A lot has happened between the Bible and Hasidism that Buber did not pay attention to."[41]

Granfield also probed Heschel for his personal response to the most agonizing topic, the Holocaust. Heschel acknowledged, "I am really a person who is in anguish. I cannot forget what I have seen and have been through. Auschwitz and Hiroshima never leave my mind. Nothing can be the same after that." He made a point of explaining to the priest his fear, shared by most European Jews, of officially sanctioned anti-Semitism: "I have been beaten up many times in Warsaw by young boys who had just come out of church. What do you expect Jews to feel? Do you think I can forget the long history of my people and the horrible things that have happened to us in the last thirty years. The Jew is afflicted with anxiety." The interview went far toward revealing what Heschel had been experiencing when he debated with the pope on behalf of the Jewish people.[42]

Heschel completed his visiting professorship at Union Theological Seminary in May 1966, but he continued his interfaith efforts. In August 1967 he addressed an international gathering of Catholic leaders in Toronto. The meeting was a veritable summit of Catholic theologians, who came from France, Germany, Holland, the United States, and Canada. Forty-three papers were given to some two thousand participants and outside spectators via closed-circuit television, broadcast television, and radio. The Reverend L. K. Shook, CSB, president of the Pontifical Institute of Medieval Studies in Toronto, had invited Heschel to present "a major paper" far beyond the standard academic fare: "I have in mind that you might even venture to tell Christian scholars what Jewish theology has to tell them about the Lord, the Holy One," he wrote.[43]

Heschel's panel took place on 31 August. Other participants were Catholic and Anglican priests from Montreal and Toronto, the Toronto publisher Bernard Neary, and the philosophy professor Emil Fackenheim, who had reviewed

Heschel's first major books. The chair, Father Edward A. Synan of the Toronto Pontifical Institute, who had written on Heschel and prayer, introduced Heschel as "a true son of the prophets, . . . a man who is moved by the love of God embedded in the love of all men. Heschel developed his paper, "The Jewish Notion of God and Christian Renewal," from previous speeches, but he added a critique of Christian approaches to Jerusalem and the state of Israel.[44]

Attentive to his listeners' theological sophistication, Heschel first explained that the original title of his talk, "*The God of Israel* [my emphasis] and Christian Renewal," which he preferred, had been "emasculated" on the way to the printer: "The difference between the two is perhaps the difference between Jerusalem and Athens," he complained. Faith was not a "notion" or an ideology or a system of ideas but a relationship with a real God.[45]

Christians must accept the continuity of their tradition with the Hebrew Bible: "The saying 'God of Israel' has no possessive or exclusive connotation: God belonging to Israel alone. Its true meaning is that the God of all men has entered into a Covenant with one people for the sake of all people." Heschel criticized Christianity for reducing theology to Christology, placing Jesus the Son (rather than God) at the center of the faith. This emphasis not only excluded Jews; it created hazards for believing Christians: "It is significant that quite a number of theologians today consider it possible to say, 'We can do without God and hold on to Jesus of Nazareth.'" In the printed version of his speech, Heschel added a note referring to the 1966 book by Thomas Altizer and William Hamilton, *Radical Theology and the Death of God,* to argue that nihilism was the gravest possible substitute for loyalty to God the Father.[46]

Heschel also justified the restoration of Jerusalem to the Jewish people by interpreting the response of Jesus to his disciples who asked: " 'Lord, will you at this time restore the kingdom of Israel?' And he said to them: 'It is not for you to know times or seasons which the Father has fixed by his own authority'" (Acts 1:6–7). Citing commentaries by Augustine, Calvin, and modern Christian scholars, Heschel supported "the expectation that the kingdom will be restored to Israel—an expectation expressed again and again in ancient Jewish liturgy."[47]

Heschel's talk was followed by astute questions. Father Adrien M. Brunet of the University of Montreal asked him to define the "precise connection" between his vision of God in the Bible and the renewal of Christian theology, while the Anglican priest Roland Corneille asked how Christians should understand the Jewish claim of restoration of Jerusalem, if exile was not conceived as a punishment. Heschel answered Brunet by criticizing the failure of

Christianity to make demands on its followers and to offer instead too many promises. He cited the rephrasing of Descartes he had used in *Who Is Man?:* "I am commanded—therefore I am." To Corneille, Heschel emphasized the necessity of "profound mutual respect" in interfaith dialogue; he would not hold the priest responsible for foolish statements made by other members of the church.[48]

As to whether the Jewish exile should be regarded as a punishment, an idea that Christians favored, Heschel recalled the recent restoration of Jerusalem to the Jews, suggesting that exile could be both punishment and an occasion for repentance: "Restoration is a profound event in the history of redemption for the Jewish people, and because it came about so unexpectedly, time will be needed to assimilate it." Emil Fackenheim, stating that he was in "complete agreement with the stand taken in Rabbi Heschel's paper," insisted that "it is impossible to interpret the murder of millions of innocents as divine punishment." Christians should join with Jews in rethinking the meaning of Jewish exile.[49]

Heschel had consolidated his central position among Roman Catholics committed to the spiritual revolution of Vatican II, as he had with the liberal Protestant establishment. These interfaith alliances would soon be sorely tested.

Part Five
Final Years

To live means to walk perpetually on the edge of a precipice. The human
predicament is a state of constant and irresolvable tension between
mighty opposites. Piety and prudence, Truth and self-interest, are
irreconcilable. Tension and conflict can no more be eliminated
from thought than from life.
—Heschel, *A Passion for Truth* (1973)

HESCHEL KEPT CLOSE WATCH ON PUBLIC EVENTS. ON 20 JANUARY 1965 LYNDON Baines Johnson was inaugurated president of the United States, elected in a landslide over Barry Goldwater. That February he stepped up the war in Vietnam. The United States unleashed massive bombings on North Vietnam while the Marines arrived in South Vietnam on 8 March. The U.S. escalation became Johnson's war, an affair of relentless military destruction. Yet he was still hoping to achieve his "Great Society" of greater economic and racial equity. "Guns and Butter" became his slogan.

Heschel frequently found the intensity of events and emotions he experienced in his last years almost unbearable, but he continued to teach, write, give speeches, and travel to conferences. His opposition to the Vietnam War sapped his health, as he rebuked the silent American majority for their apathy: "If . . . deep sensitivity to evil is to be called hysterical, what name should be given to the abysmal indifference to evil which the prophet bewails?"[1]

Catastrophe, and the threat of catastrophe, were ever present. In the midst of his anti–Vietnam War activities, Heschel was again called upon to represent the Jewish soul to Christians in June 1967, when Israel won a quick victory over invading Arab armies in what became known as the Six-Day War. Heschel traveled to Israel immediately after the conflict, sharing in the Israeli experience of anxiety and triumph. The following year Martin Luther King, Jr., and Robert Kennedy were assassinated.

Although prized by activists as a model of piety and biblical dissent and praised in mass circulation magazines like *Time* and *Newsweek,* Heschel endured personal isolation. Some of his Jewish critics believed that he gave himself so fully to interfaith work, the civil rights movement, and the Vietnam protest because they brought him acceptance and admiration from Christians. But vanity had little to do with his engulfing commitments. For the sake of truth and compassion he jeopardized his health, compromised his writing and teaching, and undermined his prestige within the Jewish community, which was turning toward the ideological right. He paid an exorbitant price for maintaining his witness on these several fronts—his untimely death.

16

Vietnam and Israel (1965–1967)

America has been enticed by her own might. There is nothing so vile as
the arrogance of the military mind. Of all the plagues with which the
world is cursed, of every ill, militarism is the worst: the assumption
that war is an answer to human problems.
—Heschel, "The Moral Outrage of Vietnam" (1966)

---

movement. Like thousands of Americans he opposed U.S. military support for the corrupt Saigon regime, but his dissent had no institutional backing. He was not associated with Reform Judaism, whose leaders were in the vanguard of social action, civil rights, and the antiwar movement. Orthodox rabbis, closer to his observance, either rejected political protest or upheld the government's prosecution of the war. A majority of JTS faculty dissociated themselves from Heschel's involvement. Although some detractors (and friendly conservatives) considered him naive politically, he kept himself well informed of events. He read the *New York Times* every day, followed other news sources, and studied books on the international situation. But he chose to judge events according to sacred values. He entered the antiwar movement in 1965, after an inner struggle that led him to conclude that the U.S. assault on North Vietnam was "an evil act."

Heschel had necessarily been aware of political currents since his youth in Warsaw and Vilna, and his university years in Berlin, but while revising his 1933 doctoral thesis into *The Prophets* he had moved from a stance of academic neutrality to one of engaged political commitment. At heart he was a contemplative who craved solitude for prayer, study, and reflection, as he wrote later: "Loneliness was both a burden and a blessing, and above all indispensable for achieving a kind of stillness in which perplexities could be faced without fear."[1]

As a U.S. citizen, however, he realized that "in regard to the cruelties committed in the name of a free society, some are guilty, all are responsible." Citing Leviticus 19:15 [actually 19:16], "Thou shalt not stand idly by the blood of thy neighbor," he declared that public opposition to the Vietnam War was a religious obligation, "a supreme commandment." He judged the Johnson administration misguided, wedded to the Cold War notion that "Communism [is] the devil and the only source of evil in the world." He believed that U.S. forces could not defeat North Vietnam without destroying the country's natural and human resources; the United States should withdraw immediately. Above all, Heschel feared for the American soul. In his judgment most citizens were indifferent to what he described as the criminal behavior of their elected government. Although religious law required Jews to obey the rules of the country in which they lived, it also decreed that "whenever a decree is unambiguously immoral, one nevertheless has a duty to disobey it." Militaristic thinking was the immediate peril: "I have previously thought that we were waging war reluctantly, with sadness at killing so many people. I realize that we are doing it now with pride in our military efficiency."[2]

Community of Faith and Dissent

In the fall of 1965, while still teaching at Union Theological Seminary, Heschel joined a protest rally organized by a local committee of clergy, both Christians and Jews. At issue were the maneuvers by the Johnson administration to stifle dissent. (At a Chicago news conference Attorney General Nicholas Katzenbach had threatened to prosecute "some Communists" involved in nationwide demonstrations against the war.) Along with a Jesuit priest and a Lutheran minister, on 25 October (about two weeks before his Fosdick inaugural lecture), Heschel spoke out at the United Nations Church Center, 777 U.N. Plaza. The Lutheran Richard John Neuhaus, pastor of St. John the Evangelist in the poor and predominantly black Bedford-Stuyvesant section of Brooklyn, expressed shock that "the President should be amazed by dissent." The Jesuit Daniel Berrigan, a poet and ardent pacifist, insisted that it was the duty of religious persons to involve themselves in politics. During the question-and-answer session, Heschel proposed a national religious movement to end the war. He told a *New York Times* reporter that the group would establish an official body to continue its opposition. Neuhaus and Berrigan were taken by surprise, but they approved of the idea.[3]

In November, Heschel participated in a "teach-in" on Vietnam with more than five hundred clergy. Absent was the charismatic Daniel Berrigan, "who had been sent to South America by his superiors in an effort to prevent his further participation in protests against the Vietnam war," as noted by the FBI. Francis Cardinal Spellman, who in addition to being archbishop of New York was a longtime archbishop for the military services, had begun wielding his authority against Catholic dissenters. It was probably Heschel's idea to represent the exiled Jesuit with an empty chair on stage. The Hasidim of Bratslav, after the death of their revered leader Rabbi Nahman, reverently placed this chair in their Jerusalem synagogue.[4]

The National Emergency Committee of Clergy Concerned About Vietnam (CCAV) was founded on 11 January 1966 (Heschel's fifty-ninth birthday) at the apartment of Union president John Bennett. Elected co-chairs were Neuhaus, Berrigan, and Heschel—a Protestant, a Catholic, and a Jew. Liberal Protestants dominated the movement; Catholic priests and nuns were slower in coming to the fore because of their submission to American bishops and authorities in Rome who objected to their participation. But soon, incited by students in Catholic universities, thousands of Catholic clergy—even a few bishops— joined the protests as individuals of conscience. By April, the co-chairmen of the Emergency Committee consisted of Bennett, Heschel, John MacKenzie, S.J., and the Catholic publisher Philip Sharper. The committee obtained office space from the National Council of Churches at its center on 475 Riverside Drive. Volunteers helped establish nearly 165 local committees in more than 20 states. With the energetic William Sloane Coffin, Jr., the Yale University chaplain, as acting executive secretary, this network of notables soon achieved national outreach.[5]

The committee's first act was to send a telegram to the recently inaugurated President Johnson urging him to extend the bombing halt that had begun the previous Christmas and to pursue negotiations with the National Liberation Front and the North Vietnamese. Among the twenty-eight signatories were Philip Berrigan, a Josephite priest and brother of Daniel; presidents of the Reform and Conservative rabbinical associations; Reinhold Niebuhr; Martin Luther King, Jr.; and editors, theologians, and national and international religious leaders. The religious mainstream was mobilized. For the next few months, the group added members and organized or sponsored acts of spiritual resistance to the war, such as rallies, fasts, vigils, and other forms of nonconfrontational protest. Their approach was moderate, cautious, and patriotic, rejecting even peaceful violation of laws, the staple of nonviolent civil rights actions. The means had to be compatible with the ends.[6]

Heschel was considered by many to be "the most influential Jewish leader on the National Emergency Committee" and "its prophetic voice." As had been the case during the Vatican II negotiations, his philosophical training and immense knowledge of Christian and Jewish sources prepared him to interpret the religious significance of current issues. Far more than a photogenic figurehead, Heschel was a regular participant in meetings who helped draft position papers and even raised money. He sent letters to rabbis and prominent Jewish laity, such as Hans Morgenthau of the University of Chicago and the Council on Foreign Relations and J. Robert Oppenheimer of the Institute for Advanced Studies in Princeton, asking them to join as sponsors. Morgenthau was pleased to add his name as one of the only nonclergy.[7]

The CCAV combined piety and political action. John Bennett displayed his professional authority in politics as well as theology. A "quiet and methodical" man, as president of Union Theological Seminary and chair of the editorial board of *Christianity and Crisis*, he was seen as "the most important of the early anti-Vietnam voices." Another Protestant eminence was the dynamic Robert McAfee Brown, a liberation theologian and champion of civil rights who had been arrested as a freedom rider. Born in Carthage, Illinois, Brown had served as a navy chaplain in the Pacific. He abandoned his early pacifism after learning of the atrocities perpetrated against the Jews by the Germans and Poles. Brown taught at Union for ten years before moving to Stanford University in 1968.[8]

Richard John Neuhaus was the youngest national board member. Born in Canada, ordained a Lutheran minister at Concordia Seminary in St. Louis, Missouri, he was theologically conservative but politically progressive, one of the rare activists from the Missouri Synod. From his parish in Brooklyn, he worked for civil rights while remaining suspicious of left-wing thinking and ideology.[9]

Daniel Berrigan soon moved beyond the committee, to more radical acts of opposition to the war. (Berrigan's first arrest for civil disobedience took place in October 1967 at the Pentagon.) But even after their paths diverged he remained an admirer of Heschel's; over the years Berrigan visited Heschel at his office at the Jewish Theological Seminary, sometimes debating with rabbinical students in the corridors or in one of Heschel's classes. Without advocating his tactics, Heschel respected Berrigan's spiritual radicalism, which was compatible with the poet's personality they shared.[10]

The two other Jews on the National Emergency Committee came from the Reform movement. Rabbi Maurice Eisendrath, the fiery president of the Union of American Hebrew Congregations (UAHC), the Reform lay organization, was a champion of civil rights and other progressive causes. Participating more directly in the committee's planning was the youthful Rabbi Balfour Brickner, director of UAHC interfaith activities and a member of its Social Action Commission. Brickner was responsible for building Christian-Jewish relations and was among the hundreds of Reform rabbis active in the civil rights movement of the 1950s. He had been arrested in the South.[11]

Heschel had finally found his true community. He relished these religious activists, who admired him as an embodiment of the biblical vision of peace and prophetic outrage they shared. His closest bond was with William Sloane Coffin, Jr., a charming, immensely talented, devout Presbyterian minister, zealously committed to social justice. Ethics and piety were inseparable for Coffin. As a student at Yale Divinity School, he was inspired by courses on Christian ethics by H. Richard Niebuhr, Reinhold's brother. He also emulated the theologian Karl Barth, who had said: "A Christian goes through life with a newspaper in one hand and a Bible in another." Yet Coffin was fascinated by Judaism. He had married a Jewish woman, Eva Rubinstein, the daughter of the pianist Arthur Rubinstein (who had once evaluated the artistry of Heschel's wife, Sylvia; Coffin himself was a pianist of professional caliber). Coffin's sense of justice was outraged by anti-Semitism, which he found conspicuous at Yale.[12]

During their first week of organizing the Emergency Committee, Coffin and Heschel connected almost immediately. Charisma played an important part. The activist pastor felt himself to be in the presence of a venerable prophet, "the most rabbinic figure I had ever seen or heard." With teasing affection, Coffin described their meeting. Heschel emerged from an elevator in the CCAV headquarters, "a totally inadequate beret on the top of his massive head of white hair."

> He proceeded to walk about the floor, his hands behind his back, listening to the score or so of seminarians talking animatedly into phones in the various offices we had taken over. Eventually he came to a stop in front of the map, where he seemed to be counting the number and noting the location of red pins.
>
> "Good evening, Father Abraham," I said.
>
> He turned. "Why do you call me Father Abraham"? he asked.
>
> "Because you are patriarchal and ecumenical, and because I am sure the original Abraham, father of us all, looked just like you."
>
> "You are very quick," he said, returning my smile through a beard whose hairs were as numerous and white as those on the top of his head. "Tell me, why are there no pins in Alabama, Louisiana and Mississippi?"
>
> "Because so far in all three states we have found only one Unitarian minister in New Orleans who is openly opposed to the war."
>
> "And what about Dallas? Why is there no pin there? Did you talk to Rabbi [Levi] Olan?"
>
> I replied that I had. When I said, "I hear you're the only clergyman in town who is willing to speak out against the war," the rabbi had replied, "Come to think of it, that's both true and not funny."
>
> Then Heschel wanted to know if I had persuaded any cardinal to join our board. I reported that I had spent four days trying to work my way through a seemingly endless line of monsignors in order to reach the two most likely candidates: Ritter in St. Louis and Cushing in Boston. I had reminded the monsignors that our position on the war was also that of the Pope, but that seemed to impress them little. However, they sounded sympathetic—as well as Irish and jovial—and had promised to do their best. But so far there were no results.[13]

Heschel was intrigued and invited Coffin to share the family Sabbath dinner the next evening. Coffin was impressed by Sylvia Heschel, with whom he shared musical affinities, and their "precocious fourteen-year-old daughter," Susannah. Coffin felt enough at ease with Heschel to press the volatile issue of conversion. Wouldn't it be "to the greater glory of God" (*ad majorem Dei gloriam*, the Jesuit motto) if the Jewish people accepted the divinity of Christ? asked Coffin provocatively. Heschel countered with a personal, rather than a theological question: "Tell me, my friend, were the Sabbath never again welcomed in this fashion, were the Torah and Talmud no longer studied, were the ark of the covenant of the Lord no longer opened in synagogues the world around, tell me, would that be *ad majorem Dei gloriam?*" Taking this stirring testimony as a test of wits, Coffin answered indirectly: "Father Abraham, you are not only a great philosopher and theologian, you're a shrewd old Jew."

Heschel was "taken aback" at this unaccustomed familiarity and asked for an explanation. Coffin replied from a less dogmatic viewpoint: "Well, I have a question for you. Do you think it is *ad majorem Dei gloriam* that God's chosen people should not have recognized God's love, in person, on earth?" Heschel was silent for some time. "Then raising his shoulders and turning up the palms of his hands, he said: 'Put it that way and we have a dilemma.' Then he proceeded to prove how possible and interesting it is to live with that dilemma. We talked of nothing but religion until one o'clock in the morning. Heschel wasn't out to convert me, and I couldn't see why any Christian would want Heschel to accept Jesus Christ as his Lord and Savior. Wasn't it enough that he was close to [being] a saint?"

Protest and Political Action

The National Emergency Committee continued its "middle ground" strategy of attempting to persuade the government to decrease bombings and press for a negotiated settlement. Deciding that the organization should remain in existence until the end of the war, a group composed of Bennett, Heschel, Coffin, Neuhaus, and David Hunter (the deputy general secretary of the National Council of Churches) hired a full-time executive director, Richard Fernandez. This young, brash, witty minister had served in the army; later, as part of his campus work, he had participated in the civil rights movement. In May 1966 the committee changed its name to Clergy and Laymen Concerned About Vietnam (CALCAV) to become more inclusive. A new era of religious resistance began.[14]

Richard Fernandez and Heschel at a meeting of Clergy and
Laymen Concerned About Vietnam, ca. 1968.
Photograph by John Goodwin.

Fasting and prayer were Heschel's favored tactics of spiritual opposition. Through such acts of repentance, he hoped to bring others to a recognition of error or sin, and thus to positive acts of restoration. The clergy were innocent of the crimes they "repented," but as Heschel often insisted, "in a free society, some are guilty, all are responsible." One such occasion was the Fourth of July 1966, at which CALCAV transformed a secular holiday into a national religious rite by staging a public fast in New York. There they called for an immediate end to the bombing of North Vietnam.

Heschel, Daniel Berrigan, and Richard Neuhaus led the two-day observance, in the sweltering heat of the Community Church. Heschel introduced the actions with the dire warning: "We have gone beyond the policy of brinkmanship; we may have started to descend into the abyss. America has been enticed by her own might. There is nothing so vile as the arrogance of the military mind." Neuhaus and Berrigan also spoke. The *New York Times* and local media regularly reported on the event, as they did at many CALCAV protests, increasing their political impact.[15]

Heschel and William Sloane Coffin, Jr., ca. 1968.
Photograph by John Goodwin.

After spending the customary summer vacation in Los Angeles, Heschel returned to New York in time for the High Holy Days, where he continued his CALCAV activities. The letters he wrote to enlist the support of Jewish leaders verged on the apocalyptic: "We are faced with the terrifying realization that events appear to be marching inexorably towards a third world war which may bring about by fire the universal destruction that God covenanted with Noah would not come about by water." In September, he published a fierce sermon, "The Moral Outrage of Vietnam," in *Fellowship*, the magazine of the interfaith pacifist organization Fellowship of Reconciliation. To these readers Heschel offered graphic images to dramatize the national dilemma. He opened with this surrealistic scene: "It is weird to wake up one morning and find that we have been placed in an insane asylum while asleep at night. It is even more weird to wake up and find that we have been involved in slaughter and destruction without knowing it." Heschel was obviously shaken to the roots of his being.[16]

His feeling for the God of pathos magnified his empathy with the Vietnamese victims: "God is present whenever man is afflicted, and humanity is embroiled in every agony wherever it may be," Heschel wrote in the *Fellowship* article. The idea of an enemy was "obsolete," he asserted, since "yesterday's enemy is becoming today's ally." In addition to developing political criticisms of U.S. policy deploring its habitual support of dictators, he praised the rise of "engaged Buddhism, as evidenced in the growing involvement of the Vietnamese monks in the daily life of the people."

CALCAV frequently featured Heschel at mass meetings, all documented by the FBI. At a June 1966 event sponsored by the Fellowship of Reconciliation, close to 1,200 people gathered at New York's Town Hall to honor Thich Nhat Hanh, an activist Vietnamese Buddhist monk. Included in the tribute were speeches by Heschel, Daniel Berrigan, Robert McAfee Brown, the poet Robert Lowell, the playwright Arthur Miller, and the playwright and poet Ishmael Reed. The FBI was present and reported Hanh's moderate message: "He stated that he wants the United States to end the bombing in Vietnam and have all shooting cease, leaving the United States troops for defense purposes only. . . . HANH commented that his presence in the United States indicated the Vietnamese still had faith in the Americans; however, he feared for his life when he returned to his country." "There were no incidents or arrests," another FBI report concluded blandly.[17]

The FBI also documented Heschel's participation in another political protest, at which some two hundred people marched from Bryant Park, at Sixth Avenue and 42nd Street, to the New York offices of Senators Robert F. Kennedy and Jacob K. Javits at Lexington Avenue and 45th Street. A delegation of two women and two male clergy delivered messages to the senators' offices, after which the parade went on to U.N. Plaza.[18]

When CALCAV wanted to play political hardball, Heschel generally exercised a moderating influence. Early in 1966, the Columbia University engineering professor Seymour Melman, an expert on international disarmament, proposed that CALCAV commission a book documenting American "war crimes" in Vietnam. A representative group of clergy, he reasoned, had a special obligation to condemn an American policy that violated not only international law but also basic ethical norms (the law being defined as the lowest standard of morality that civilized people agree to live by). Such a book would convincingly publicize "the erosion of moral constraint in Vietnam." Heschel, an acquaintance of Melman's, immediately vetoed the project, thinking that it would deflect the organization from its focus on the war itself. Melman, who saw himself as "a non-institutional religious Jew," was upset and asked Fernandez to persuade Heschel to authorize the project.[19] For more than two hours, Heschel resisted Fernandez's arguments because he feared that to accuse the president of the United States and his highest officials of being war criminals might provoke a public backlash.

The disagreement between Heschel and Melman persisted for the next five months. Heschel finally agreed to back the project after speaking with John Bennett. When the book was completed a year later, the only publisher who would take it was the Turnpike Press of Annandale, Virginia, run by Quakers. Although 38,000 copies were sold, and Heschel's acquaintance Harry Wachtel from Long Island (who was also close to Martin Luther King, Jr.) sent copies to all the members of Congress, there was no backlash. But despite extensive publicity, the book, *In the Name of America*, failed to incite the moral revolution the sponsors had hoped for.[20]

In the meantime, CALCAV was planning its first national mobilization, to be held in Washington, D.C., 31 January–1 February 1967. Using the 1963 March on Washington as its model, the mobilization included action workshops, visits to representatives and high government officials, and picketing in front of the White House. More than two thousand clergy and laity from forty-five states participated, arriving by airplane, train, bus, and automobile. Most of them had sleeping gear, planning to spend the night on the floors of local churches.[21]

The assembly marched to the White House, where a silent vigil was held. The marchers had been refused a parade permit and had to keep moving in circles. Nearby an anti-Communist zealot displayed signs and sang "God Bless America." When he pulled out a poster that read, "Communism Is Jewish from Beginning to End" the police carried him away. But he had managed to monopolize the newspaper photographers. Also protesting the protesters were about 250 people from a well-organized Christian fundamentalist group carrying signs that read, "Victory," "Communist Stooges," and the like. After the picketing, the CALCAV group walked silently to the Capitol.

The significance of CALCAV's Washington mobilization far surpassed the mammoth media event. At the center was a solemn interfaith worship service at the New York Avenue Presbyterian Church that combined ethics, politics, and spiritual transformation. The "Service of Witness in Time of War" crowned the first day of lobbying. It was led by an array of leaders: Robert McAfee Brown; Donald R. Campion, S.J.; William Sloane Coffin; Paul Moore, Jr., bishop of the Episcopal Diocese of Washington, D.C.; Jacob J. Weinstein, president of the Central Conference of American Rabbis; and Abraham Joshua Heschel. The worship for peace created an atmosphere of harmony, despite striking theological differences and its overwhelmingly Protestant content.[22]

Heschel electrified the audience with the speech from his *Fellowship* article, "The Moral Outrage in Vietnam." He began with a reading from Ezekiel 34:25–30 ("I will make with them a covenant of peace, and will cause evil beasts to cease out of the land . . . And they shall know that I the Lord their God am with them"), whose poignancy was heightened by his sing-song manner, plaintive, high-pitched voice, and Yiddish accent. Heschel contrasted Ezekiel's pastoral utopia protected by the loving care of God with the ravaging "wild beasts" of Vietnam: "Ours is an assembly of shock, contrition, and dismay. Who would have believed that we life-loving Americans are capable of bringing death and destruction to so many innocent people? We are startled to discover how unmerciful, how beastly we ourselves can be. So we implore Thee, our Father in heaven, help us to banish the beast from our hearts, the beast of cruelty, the beast of callousness. . . . In the sight of so many thousands of civilians and soldiers slain, injured, crippled, of bodies emaciated, of forests destroyed by fire, God confronts us with this question: Where art thou?"

The address climaxed with Heschel's story of "a child of seven" whose rabbi was teaching him the biblical account of the sacrifice of Isaac. He seemed to evoke his own childhood, switching to the first person: "My heart began to beat faster; it actually sobbed with pity for Isaac. Behold, Abraham now lifted the knife. And my heart froze within me with fright. Suddenly, the voice of the angel was heard: 'Abraham, lay not thine hand upon the lad, for now I know that thou fearest God.'" At the end the child asked the rabbi, "'Supposing the angel had come a second too late?' The rabbi comforted me and calmed me by telling me that an angel cannot come too late." Heschel concluded: "An angel cannot be late, but man, made of flesh and blood, may be."[23]

The next day, a CALCAV delegation met with Secretary of Defense Robert McNamara. The group included Heschel, John Bennett, William Sloane Coffin, Robert McAfee Brown, Richard John Neuhaus, Jacob Weinstein, and Michael Novak (the Catholic chaplain at Stanford University). As reported in the *New York Times*, they spent forty minutes with McNamara in his Pentagon office, attempting to persuade him to suspend the bombing of North Vietnam and begin peace negotiations. "Mr. McNamara's reply to the clerics' requests was not disclosed," the newspaper vaguely concluded.[24]

The inside story of the meeting reveals an emotional drama beneath the diplomatic give-and-take. A fifteen-minute appointment had been made with McNamara by Alfred B. Fitt, an assistant secretary of defense who was thought to harbor doubts about the war. On the way to the meeting, riding in Pastor Neuhaus's old Volkswagen bus, Heschel turned from the front seat and told Coffin, "You will be our spokesman." But Coffin felt too angry about the war, too exhausted, to do the job. Heschel nodded and said, "You will control your emotions." They were met at the Pentagon information desk by a pompous guide, who introduced himself as "Dr. Smith." Coffin worked off some of his emotion by grilling this former academic, who had taught speech at a small Midwestern college, before his rise in stature at the Pentagon. Then a uniformed full colonel met them, stating testily that the defense secretary had expected four visitors, not seven. Coffin further betrayed his anxiety with an unsuitable quip: "Never mind, Colonel, three of us can lie under the tires of the Secretary's car" (as Harvard students had done the previous week).[25]

Weinstein, too, was irritable and nervous. So he picked up on Dr. Smith's embarrassment by telling an old Jewish joke about a rabbi on the Day of Atonement who wanted to inspire his apathetic congregation to repentance by throwing himself to the synagogue floor, pleading with God, "Have mercy on my soul, a sinner!" Then the cantor, emulating the rabbi, lay down beside him, beating his breast and praying, "O Lord, if the holiest of rabbis is a sinner, how much more am I in thy sight!" Then the *shamas* (the sexton, a humble job) rushed down as well, beating his breast, "O Lord, if both the holiest of rabbis and the cantor are sinners, how much more my sins must exceed theirs!" Whereupon the cantor nudged the rabbi with his elbow and, nodding toward the shamas, murmured, "Look who's trying to be a nothing." (This produced tension-releasing laughter.)

Smith slipped away after the colonel returned with seven passes. Television cameras and reporters were now swarming about while the delegation was led to McNamara's office. In his later account Coffin savored every detail: "Over the far door the clock registered 4:13. There was no question in my mind that at exactly 4:15 the door would open. At 4:15 it did, revealing a handsome woman in an Air Force uniform who announced, 'The Secretary of Defense.' We turned to see the immaculately dressed man we had seen so often on television and in the newspapers. But news photos could never do justice to the energy that literally bounded into the room. Nor could they do more than hint at what I sensed immediately—his decency. It was disconcerting."[26]

The conversation started awkwardly. McNamara shook everyone's hand and began by thanking the clergy for their concern. He then remarked that he wished they had done more for civil rights. (A strange comment, since it was generally understood that the clergy had been deeply involved in civil rights and slow in responding to Vietnam.) Coffin then summarized the CALCAV position paper and handed McNamara a copy. At that moment, without visible cause, Heschel erupted with indignation. He was out of control, believed Coffin, as "he poured forth his anguish, his hands gesticulating pathetically." The secretary of defense showed no emotion and listened carefully, "more with astonishment than understanding." But, sympathizing with the rabbi's anguish and righteous anger, McNamara was moved to extend the meeting another fifteen minutes.[27]

Coffin and his colleagues were not impressed by McNamara's arguments. He claimed to favor restraint in the bombing while hoping that the North Vietnamese would be more willing to negotiate. But he maintained the right of American forces to bomb North Vietnam without an official declaration of war. The clergy, for their part, considered McNamara a war criminal because of his actions. On the human level, however, they found him to be "a nice guy," a man of decency and integrity, "a true innocent." The meeting ended unsatisfactorily for the CALCAV group, but it had provided another chance to influence government officials to favor peaceful solutions.[28]

As the antiwar movement gained momentum, plans were forming for a broad-based mobilization set for 15 April 1967. But CALCAV and other moderate groups feared that negative publicity about extremists who intended to take part might compromise their hard-earned respectability among the middle class. So the leaders of CALCAV did not officially endorse the April mobilization. Instead they enlisted Martin Luther King, Jr., a sponsor of CALCAV from its inception, to mark a turning point in opposition to the war. Along with Heschel and other highly regarded figures, King would deliver a major address against the war at New York's imposing Riverside Church on 4 April. The spiritual alliance of King and Heschel was renewed before an audience of more than three thousand.[29]

CALCAV guaranteed that King's historic address would reach the largest audience possible. The executive committee arranged for the text to be written by Andrew Young and Allard Lowenstein, the New York political activist, and edited by Richard Fernandez and the publicist Fred Sontag. Advance copies were distributed to newspapers and other media outlets. King had criticized the government's Vietnam policy as early as 1965, but up to this time he had been reluctant to jeopardize public and government support for civil rights and President Johnson's War on Poverty by taking too vocal a stand. Now he decided to end what he called his "shameful silence."[30]

When King rose to speak in Riverside Church, he was greeted by a stand-ing ovation, as he began: "I come to this magnificent house of worship tonight because my conscience leaves me no other choice. I join you in this meeting because I am in deepest agreement with the aims and work of the organization which has brought us together: Clergy and Laymen Concerned About Viet-nam." King answered his critics from the civil rights camp, who opposed his pronouncements on foreign policy. The Vietnam War had become "the enemy of the poor" when President Johnson's poverty program was "broken and evis-cerated as if it were some idle political plaything of a society gone mad on war." Black soldiers were being killed in disproportionate numbers. Violence in the urban ghettos, primarily black crime, was a symptom of a larger Ameri-can ill; his government, he sweepingly asserted, had become "the greatest purveyor of violence in the world today."[31]

Three talks followed, equally stirring, though more concise. The venerable Henry Steele Commager, professor of history at Amherst College, placed "this monstrous war in Vietnam" in perspective, pointing to the "defiant determina-tion" of a "self-righteous" administration and its supporters who "proclaim to an incredulous world that we are fighting the battle of freedom and of peace." John Bennett praised Commager's knowledge of "the history of American self-deceptions" and cited a number of opponents to the war: the Swedish sociolo-gist Gunnar Myrdal, the National Council of Churches, and more than two hundred presidents of college student organizations.[32]

For Heschel, the Vietnam War threatened our very humanity. He appealed to common sense: "This war is a supreme example of extreme absurdity . . . while those who participate in it are plagued by the awareness of being in-volved in a bitter Sisyphean battle." Deploring the betrayal of America's ideals, he offered compassion as the guide to action: "Has our conscience be-come a fossil? Is all mercy gone? If mercy, the mother of humility, is still alive as a demand, how can we say 'yes' to our bringing agony to that tormented country?"[33]

CALCAV printed 10,000 copies of these speeches as a thirty-five-page pamphlet (for which payment was optional), adding questions and answers, a letter from Dr. Benjamin Spock linking the civil rights and peace movements, a preface by Reinhold Niebuhr, who had been too ill to attend the event, and *New York Times* interviews with King, accompanied by a handsome, full-page photograph. In addition, CALCAV prepared a slim volume, *Vietnam: Crisis of Conscience*, which appeared in May. A guide for voters who wanted to pressure the government to negotiate a settlement to the war, it was an ecumenical effort, published jointly by Association Press of the Young Men's Christian Association, the Jewish publisher Behrman House, and the Catholic publisher Herder and Herder. It featured essays by Michael Novak, Robert McAfee Brown, and Heschel.

Heschel offered "The Moral Outrage of Vietnam," the piece he had earlier published in *Fellowship.* He framed the short essay as "an appeal to the individual conscience." Among his striking formulations was a denunciation of militarism as "whoredom, voluptuous and vicious, first disliked and then relished." The religious antiwar movement now had its official sourcebook. Within the year *Vietnam: Crisis of Conscience* sold more than 50,000 copies.[34]

A Voice for Zion

There was, of course, no unanimity about Vietnam in any camp. Many supporters of Israel feared that if American Jews opposed the Vietnam War too blatantly, the United States would withdraw its economic and military aid to the Jewish state. Tensions were mounting in the Jewish community. Heschel was especially saddened that his closest friends and colleagues, Wolfe Kelman, Fritz Rothschild, and Seymour Siegel, were in favor of a victory in Vietnam. They disagreed with Heschel not only for the sake of Israel but because they believed that the American military would crush Communist aggression.[35]

Meanwhile, Heschel received direct pressure from Israel to end his antiwar activities. A member of the Israeli embassy came to his office to speak with him, but he refused to abandon public protest. Another influential Israeli telephoned Elie Wiesel and asked him to talk to Heschel. Wiesel and Heschel spent an entire afternoon together, walking back and forth, discussing what a Jew should do in this situation. At one point Heschel stopped in the middle of the street: "Listen, there are people in Vietnam who have been bombarded for years and years and years and they haven't slept a single night. How can we simply go on and not try to help them sleep at night?" This vivid image stayed with Wiesel, and he took Heschel's side.[36]

Similar debates were becoming more urgent as anguish over Vietnam was heightened by threats in the Middle East. The leaders of Egypt, Syria, and Jordan were menacing Israel. Nasser, the pan-Arabist luminary, had repeatedly broadcast his pledge to drive the Jews into the sea. The Israelis were forced to take these declarations seriously, despite the Arabs' penchant for rhetorical excess. For Heschel, as for most Israelis and Jews around the world, the threat to Israel brought back memories of the Nazi genocide. The situation reached its crisis point on 23 May 1967 when Nasser blockaded the Straits of Tiran, effectively cutting off Israel from Africa and Asia and defying international law. This act of aggression also increased the peril of war between the Soviets and the Americans, who supported opposite sides in the conflict.[37]

During the weeks of Arab military build-up and terrorist raids on Israel, a number of prominent Christians signed an advertisement that ran in the Sunday *New York Times* supporting the Jewish state and opposing the Arab blockade. Headlined "The Moral Responsibility in the Middle East," it appeared on 4 June 1967, the day before the war began. Among the signers were John Bennett; Robert McAfee Brown; Reinhold Niebuhr; Thurston N. Davis, S.J.; James O'Gara; John B. Sheerin, CSP; Martin Luther King, Jr.; and Steven Gill Spottswood. These allies from the civil rights and antiwar movements urged the U.S. government to "recall that Israel is a new nation whose people are still recovering from the horror of the European holocaust." But it was too late. The Six-Day War (as sympathizers called the Israeli victory of 5–11 June) was launched the next day, and its bitter legacy has yet to be resolved.

Around the world Jews rediscovered their identity. On the American continent, in Europe, in North Africa, in Soviet Russia, even assimilated or nonobservant bystanders were seized by an unexpected, passionate sympathy. Thousands of Jews, young and old, flew to Israel to help or settle in the homeland. Heschel, too, renewed his commitment to Zion, as he once again bore witness to Israel's miraculous survival. In July he spent a month in Jerusalem. Among the people he saw were Pinchas Peli, an Israeli writer, journalist, and religious teacher, and his American-born wife, Penina. Heschel stayed at the President Hotel near their home. With Peli or by himself, Heschel walked all around Jerusalem, especially in the Old City, newly liberated by the Israeli Army. As he touched the stones of the Western Wall, previously denied to Jews by the Jordanian authorities, he recovered the Holy City of his daily prayers.[38]

Heschel translated this event using all the poetic instruments at his disposal. To a group of Conservative rabbis at Beit Berl, the teachers college near Tel Aviv, he expressed his amazement at what had occurred. Addressing them in Hebrew, he stressed the worldwide renewal of a Jewish sense of identity. The Six-Day War was "a time of a religious resurrection, . . . as if the Bible were continuing to be written." In a more analytical mode, Heschel attributed the Israeli victory to three factors: "the heroism of the Jews in Israel; the Jews in the Diaspora; and divine power. These three sources enabled the Jews to survive the Holocaust, the 1948 War of Independence, and the Six-Day War."[39]

Assuming the interconnection of Israel and the Diaspora, Heschel stressed the importance of historical memory: "The citizens of Israel have been overcome with amnesia. They look at the Hilton of Tel Aviv and forget the Battle of Tel Hai" (the Labour Zionist settlement in the Upper Galilee that was attacked by Arabs in 1920, a symbol of the Jews' determination to defend the Jewish homeland with their lives). American Jews, Heschel continued angrily, especially the young, have lost their connection with Israel: "The Achilles' heel of the Jews is civil war and disunity." Aliyah (immigration to Israel) for young Americans would help "to redeem Diaspora Jews." Jews everywhere have a moral obligation to the world at large, he concluded, citing a passage from Isaiah he had been using since the 1950s: "Another part of this vision is a peaceful Jewish state, which should stand as a model to the Gentiles. This is why we should aspire toward peace. Now is the time to start negotiating with the Arabs; the God of Israel is the same as the God of the Arabs."[40]

In August, Heschel returned to the United States to advance this demand. Addressing Hebrew speakers, he published his talk, "The Hidden Sources of Redemption," (Ginzey ha-yesha) in Hadaor. He also prepared a poetic essay in English, "An Echo of Eternity," for a special issue on Jerusalem of *Hadassah* magazine, the organ of the Women's Zionist Organization of America. Heschel provided the only religious perspective in the issue, whose illustrious contributors included James Michener, best-selling author of *The Source;* General Chaim Herzog, the first military governor of the West Bank; Colonel Mordecai ("Mota") Gur, the liberator of Jerusalem, in an interview with Elie Wiesel; and Teddy Kollek, the mayor of Jerusalem.

For Heschel, the Holy City was a symbol of Jewish unity. Israeli armed forces had opened the Arab sector of Jerusalem, known as the Old City, that had been occupied by the Jordanians since the 1948 war. Photographs of Jewish soldiers ecstatically praying at the Western Wall were distributed worldwide, and the Israeli popular song "Jerusalem the Golden," became the anthem of an unheard-of Jewish pride. Heschel celebrated the resurrection of Israel and his messianic hope for peace among all peoples: "There is great astonishment in the souls. It is as if the prophets had risen from their graves." In poetic rhythms he voiced the yearning of Jews over the centuries: "The Wall. At first I faint. Then I see: a Wall of frozen tears, a cloud of sighs. The Wall. Palimpsests, hiding books, secret names. The stones are seals." The liberation of Jerusalem had inspired a liturgy of return for modern Jews.[41]

For many Christians, however, the swift Israeli victory aggravated existing disagreements. Almost immediately after the war's end, many Christians of goodwill expressed their sympathy for the newly occupied Palestinians while attempting respectfully to scrutinize the disparity of views among the participants and observers. *Christian Century* introduced its 26 July 1967 issue with an almost desperate humor: "It occurred to us as we planned this potentially incendiary issue on the Middle East crisis that it might be wise to have it printed on asbestine paper. The juxtaposing of several conflicting articles on the Arab-Israeli dispute generates a highly inflammable situation."[42]

But others contributing to this *Christian Century* issue were more partisan. Willard G. Oxtoby, associate professor of religious studies at Yale University and a Presbyterian minister, condemned Israel's preemptive strike and occupation of Arab territories. The essay's tagline made his position clear from the outset: "Outright disagreement with Israel's well planned conquest of June 1967 is required of Christians." Oxtoby blamed Christians for succumbing to Jewish propaganda, such as "Intourist-type treatment for ecclesiastical V.I.P.s visiting Israel." And he extended his skepticism to the entire interfaith enterprise, deploring the tendency of American Jews to demand total support for Israel and equate criticism of Israel with anti-Semitism.[43]

Powerful essays by Jews presented a completely different experience. The Reform rabbi David Polish wrote that Jews were "disillusioned" because "the world once again refused to give credence to the warnings of Israel's impending annihilation." Above all, Christians must "summon up the courage to speak unambiguously to the world about Israel's unconditional claim to life— a claim whose justice is symbolized by its own unchallenged sovereignty in Jerusalem, paradigm of Jewish renewal."[44]

In a scrupulous essay, "Urbis and Orbis: Jerusalem Today," James Sanders, Heschel's friend from Union Theological Seminary, sought to be impartial. Sanders explained that he and his wife had been in Beirut, Lebanon, during the war. They felt stunned by the hostilities, sharing the attitude of many Westerners familiar with Arab politics: "Many more words are said than meant." After the victory, Sanders opposed Israel's annexation of the Holy City, fearing "a more serious Arab crusade." At the same time, mindful of the fragility of interfaith dialogue, Sanders explained: "I am as 'pro-Jewish' as any Christian in print. Not only have I disavowed all forms of the Christian mission to the Jews; I have publicly defended the view that Christianity needs Judaism to perform and fulfill her 'Mission of Israel' to the world and to the church." But he felt duty bound to reject the idea of a Palestinian state

James A. Sanders and Heschel at the Union Theological Seminary
commencement, May 1971. Courtesy of James A. Sanders.

under Israeli domination. He called for the internationalization of Jerusalem, even urging that it revert to "Jordanian administration under massive UN presence."[45]

The summer of 1967 was a low point in Heschel's Christian friendships. Sanders's article pained him, and the two did not speak for some time. Then, running into Sanders in the Union bookstore, Heschel brought up the issue. They took a walk and, as Sanders recalled: "I asked about the issue of holy space. He said that he knew I would ask, and we were back on track."[46]

Trusting in the power of direct communication between Christians and Jews, they organized another meeting on Jewish-Christian relations, inviting faculty from both JTS and Union to Sanders's apartment. Among the participants were Sanders, Paul Lehman, and Daniel Day Williams from Union; Heschel came with Fritz Rothschild. But Heschel, overcome with distress, missed his opportunity. Instead of building on their common devotion in one God, or on "the tragic insufficiency of human faith," he discomfited his

Christian colleagues by urging them to lend their names to a public statement of support for the Jewish state. As Sanders described it, "the Christians simply fell silent. They had not thought they would be asked to sign, as some later put it, a political document about Near Eastern foreign policy."[47]

Heschel had succumbed to the tensions of the moment. A more sophisticated approach was needed to bridge the abyss between Christians and Jews. Because he was much more effective as a writer or as an orator delivering a prepared speech, he welcomed the opportunity when B'nai B'rith invited him to write a book on Israel that would be meaningful to both Jews and Christians.[48]

17

Dismay and Exaltation (1968–1969)

Men slaughtering each other, cities battered into ruins: such insanity has plunged many nations into an abyss of disgrace. Will America, the promise of peace to the world, fail to uphold its magnificent destiny?
If I forget you, O Vietnam,
let my right hand wither.
—Heschel, "The Moral Outrage of Vietnam" (1966)

THE PROPOSED BOOK ON ISRAEL HAD TO WAIT, HOWEVER, AS THE ANTIWAR movement continued to consume Heschel's time. The second CALCAV national mobilization was scheduled for 5–6 February 1968 in Washington, D.C., and the FBI domestic intelligence division carefully monitored the preparations, although the details were readily available: Martin Luther King had announced them at a press conference in New York City on 12 January. In addition, CALCAV had sent out a registration flyer for the mobilization, which tallied horrifying statistics: "2 million South Vietnamese, or almost one eighth of the population, have become official refugees . . . 110,960 tons of napalm have been dropped over South Vietnam since the end of 1963. 150,000 acres of crop-producing land as well as 500,000 acres of jungle and brush have been defoliated by 5 million gallons of herbicide in 1967 alone."[1]

The day before the mobilization, on 4 February, Heschel and twenty-nine other religious leaders presented the CALCAV-commissioned book, *In the Name of America*, at a press conference in New York. A report of this account of American "war crimes" in Vietnam appeared on page 1 of the *New York Times*.[2]

Jewish Soul Searching

The following day, Heschel met with protestors at the Religious Action Center of Reform Judaism in Washington, D.C., right before the mobilization. He was featured along with Rabbis Maurice Eisendrath, the Reform movement's president, and Balfour Brickner. Heschel stood up to ask, "Why are there so few of us here?" Indeed, the room was almost empty. He continued: "*America* used to be a word of hope, of opportunity, for the world; now the word *America* has become *Shame*. Where are our Jews? We cannot limit the religious conscience. Isn't the word *rachmonos* [compassion, Yiddish] Jewish? The Vietnamese are our Jews and we as Americans are letting them die needlessly."[3]

During the discussion, Heschel was asked why he was willing to join coalitions associated with the New Left that opposed Israel. In answer, he told one of his favorite stories: "There was a Russian Jew whose son was drafted into the Czarist army, a tour of duty that might last 25 years. The father was alarmed. His son would be forced to eat *chazer* [pork, Yiddish], since that was the only meat available to Russian soldiers. This would be an appalling desecration. He explained the situation to his rabbi: If his son didn't eat the pork he would starve to death. What did the rabbi decide?—He can eat the *chazer* but he shouldn't lick his lips." This forced eating of *trayf* (ritually impure food) represented the compromises required by the Vietnam emergency. According to Jewish law, mitzvot such as kashrut and Sabbath observance are primary, but they must be suspended for the sake of pikuach nefesh, saving a human life.[4]

Eisendrath spoke about his recent worldwide peace mission. There were enormous tensions in the heart of American Jewry. Despite the need for U.S. support for Israel, he deplored the refusal of many Jews to oppose the Vietnam War. Some Conservative and Reform rabbinical students were thrilled that, for the first time, the two movements were sharing official communication. But they complained that most of their teachers were not interested in the Vietnam protest, and they begged Eisendrath and Heschel to speak at their schools. These young leaders feared that institutional Judaism might become one of the casualties of the Vietnam War.

After the meeting at the Jewish Center, Heschel joined other CALCAV leaders for the opening plenary and interfaith worship. There, after a litany of repentance, Heschel struck out at the indifference of too many to the sufferings in Vietnam: "The agony continues, the stubbornness increases. . . . The agony of God in Vietnam, the infamy of man in Vietnam! God's voice is shaking heaven and earth, and man does not hear the faintest sound. The Lord roars like a lion. His word is like fire, like hammer breaking rocks to pieces, and people go about unmoved, undisturbed, unaware. . . . A nation so rich in the appreciation of human dignity, in generosity and compassion, is destroying its own integrity in order to perform a game of power in the theater of absurdity." Heschel sought to goad the nation's conscience: "We must not seek refuge in personal dissent. We must endeavor to reach the hearts of all Americans." In the typed manuscript of his speech, he added and underlined the final sentence: *"This is a war against America!"*[5]

The next morning, 6 February, a memorial service at Arlington National Cemetery completed the liturgical protest. Forty chartered buses brought people to honor the war dead. They were forced to stand outside the cemetery walls because CALCAV had been denied a permit to use the amphitheater. Heschel and other leaders joined "a procession of agony" led by Martin Luther King. The march included James Shannon, the auxiliary Roman Catholic bishop of Minneapolis, who carried a cross; Rabbi Eisendrath, carrying a Torah scroll; Heschel, King, Ralph Abernathy, Jesse Jackson, Andrew Young, Everett Gendler, and others were carrying miniature American flags. It was an impressive, and photogenic, event.[6]

The weather was beautiful, a crisp day; the sky was clear and sunny on the white steps in front of the Tomb of the Unknown Soldier. The only sounds were the slap of rifle butts and clicking of heels during the changing of the guard. Marching eight abreast half a mile down Arlington Ridge Road, the two thousand protestors passed row upon row of white tombstones, mostly bearing crosses but some with Stars of David, straight and orderly, with mounds of fresh earth here and there. The service was simple. As the procession stopped, Dr. King intoned, "In this moment of complete silence, let us pray." All heads were bowed in soundless prayer for six minutes. Heschel broke the stillness with a lament in Hebrew from Psalm 22, which the Gospel of Mark also gives as the last words of Jesus: *Eli, Eli, lamah 'azavtani* (My God, my God, why hast Thou forsaken me?). Bishop Shannon closed the ceremony: "Let us go in peace. Amen."[7]

Soon after the mobilization, Heschel signed two full-page advertisements in the *New York Times*, one supporting a negotiated settlement of the war and

Antiwar mobilization at Arlington Cemetery, 6 February 1968.
Left to right: *Bishop James Shannon, the Rev. Martin Luther King, Jr., the Rev. Ralph Abernathy, Rabbi Maurice Eisendrath, Heschel. Photograph by John Goodwin.*

the other urging Americans to safeguard dissent and freedom of speech. As he pushed forward with his antiwar efforts, his alienation from his Jewish associates increased. Forthrightly prowar, David C. Kogan, administrative vice chancellor of the Jewish Theological Seminary, Wolfe Kelman, Seymour Siegel, and Arthur Hertzberg of the American Jewish Congress signed a protest letter to the editor of the *New York Times:* "To point an accusing finger only at our armed forces and that of our allies creates the impression that all the evil is on one side. This lack of balance will no doubt serve the Communist cause well."[8]

Heschel was especially vulnerable to criticism among Orthodox Jews. When photographs of the interfaith mobilization appeared in newspapers around the world, angry letters poured into the headquarters of the Union of American Hebrew Congregations (Reform) at 838 Fifth Avenue. Heschel was blamed for allowing Rabbi Eisendrath to desecrate a Torah scroll by carrying it into a cemetery, forbidden by Jewish law.

Leaders of Reform Judaism took this objection seriously. Eisendrath, post facto, consulted Solomon Freehof, the eminent Reform rabbi from Pittsburgh, and Heschel. Freehof cited the basic rule that "as long as you are not within four cubits of the dead (which is about three yards) you contravened no law. Besides, it is not sure that the Torah was kosher, not having [been examined] for errors in recent years. The Torah has to be regularly proofread." Heschel rallied his vast halakhic knowledge and telephoned his responsa to Rabbi Richard Hirsch, director of the Religious Action Center. Heschel drew six judgments from traditional sources:

> 1) In *B'rakhot* 18a, it says that "a man should not walk in a cemetery with *tefillin* on his head or a scroll of the Law in his arms and recite the *Shema.*" [Heschel added:] "or read the Torah," but it does not say that it is prohibited to hold the Torah if a man does not read from it. 2) Maimonides maintains that even holding the Torah is prohibited. 3) The above applies to a Jewish cemetery, but in this instance, Arlington Cemetery is non-sectarian and obviously the same rules would not apply as in the instance of a Jewish cemetery. 4) The reciting of the *Shema* (and the reading of the Torah) is forbidden within four cubits of the dead, but in Arlington Cemetery, at no time was the Torah within four cubits of a grave. [Heschel further justified the protest as within the limits of Jewish law.] 5) The noted Yechezkel Landau, in his commentary *Nodah bi-Yehuda* [a collection of more than 860 responsa, Prague, 1776] interpreted a passage in the Zohar to signify that at a time of great stress, the Torah should be taken by the

community to the cemetery to pray, for example, for rain or to stop a plague. 6) In the 1956 Suez Campaign, Rabbi Goren, chief chaplain of the Israeli army, was photographed taking the Torah in one hand and a rifle in the other to wage war. Is it not proper for us to use the Torah (without a rifle) to pray for peace? Heschel asked rhetorically.[9]

Hirsch's memorandum to Eisendrath further exonerated Heschel for his part in the procedure. Hirsch explained that the idea of using the Torah at Arlington Cemetery was first introduced at a CALCAV board meeting in New York, at which time Heschel opposed it on grounds that the Torah was not a symbol for Jews in the sense that a cross was a symbol for Christians. But shortly before the prayer service began at Arlington Cemetery, when the Christians said that they were going to march behind a cross, Heschel, put on the spot, realized that for Jews to march behind a cross would represent a real *issur* (prohibition). He decided that in terms of public perception, it was better to march behind a Torah; the appearance of compromise was the lesser evil.[10]

Honored as a Prophet

Along with severe criticism, Heschel experienced personal triumph in 1968. Most significant was the honor given him by rabbis of the Conservative movement at the annual meeting of the Rabbinical Assembly. (The Rabbinical Assembly was a larger, more flexible body than the Jewish Theological Seminary.) At the Assembly's convention, which met 24–28 March at the Concord Hotel, the rabbis celebrated Heschel's sixtieth birthday, honoring both his social activism and his contributions to Jewish scholarship.

This recognition was long overdue. Eminent scholars are usually honored at their fiftieth, jubilee birthday and given a Festschrift, a collection of essays by colleagues and former students. Heschel had turned sixty on 11 January 1967, a milestone now celebrated a year later. To honor Heschel, Martin Luther King was the keynote speaker at the celebration, reaffirming the alliance of African Americans and Jews. Sympathy and cooperation between these groups remained strong, despite growing concerns about black anti-Semitism, the emerging issue of affirmative action, and divisive views on Israel and the Vietnam War.

The convocation was highly charged. It was the rabbis' first national gathering since the Six-Day War. Eli A. Bohnen, as outgoing president of the

Heschel is honored at the 1968 annual convention of the Rabbinical Assembly by outgoing R.A. president Rabbi Eli Bohnen and guest speaker Martin Luther King, Jr. Courtesy of Michael and Joyce Bohnen.

Rabbinical Assembly, stressed the convocation's double focus: gratitude for Israel's victory over the Arabs and concern for conflict among Americans because of the escalating Vietnam war. Bohnen also criticized Jews who withdrew from civil rights: if American Jews ignored the problems of black Americans, they "would have no right to condemn anyone in Germany who went along with Hitler's program. We would have no right to blame the Pope [Pius XII] of those days for remaining silent in the face of the extermination of the Jews."[11]

That evening, the rabbis paid tribute to King by singing "We Shall Overcome" in Hebrew. Then Heschel introduced the honored guest, praising him as an authentic prophet: "Where in America do we hear a voice like the voice of the prophets of Israel? Martin Luther King is a sign that God has not forsaken the United States of America. God has sent him to us. His presence is the hope of America." In his address honoring Heschel, King returned the compliment, stating how deeply moved he was to hear the civil rights anthem sung in the language of the prophets. He acclaimed Heschel's speech at the 1963 Chicago "Conference on Religion and Race" and his participation in the

Selma–Montgomery march. King considered Heschel "a truly great prophet"; he hoped to return to the Rabbinical Assembly to celebrate Heschel's hundredth birthday.[12]

After King's speech, the rabbis and pastor engaged in a frank exchange of views, characterized by candor and mutual respect. The moderator was Everett Gendler, a longtime friend of King's and of Andrew Young, who was also present. Most important, perhaps, was King's support for Israel: peace was the issue, but security came first. "We must stand with all our might to protect its right to exist, its territorial integrity," he proclaimed. For the Arabs, peace required another kind of security, basic economic stability: "These nations, as you know, are part of the third world of hunger, of disease, of illiteracy. I think that as long as these conditions exist there will be tensions, that there will be the endless quest to find scapegoats." King called for "a Marshall Plan for the Middle East" that would bring impoverished Arabs "into the mainstream of economic security."[13]

King urged the rabbis to support economic justice by opposing the war in Vietnam, which was undermining the War on Poverty, and by supporting, both financially and with their participation, the Poor People's Campaign that June: "We need a movement to transmute the rage of the ghetto into a positive constructive force."[14]

The following day was devoted to Heschel. Formal papers by Edmond Cherbonnier, chairman of the Religion Department at Trinity College, Hartford, and Fritz Rothschild and Seymour Siegel of the Jewish Theological Seminary explored Heschel's thought. Cherbonnier contended that Christianity must be understood in relation to Judaism. The Hebrew Bible provided ways of thinking relevant to the modern dilemma. Surveying the abstract approaches of Thomas Aquinas, Paul Tillich, and Karl Barth, who had imposed Greek philosophical categories on the Bible, he pointed out that Heschel, on the contrary, spoke of the living God, the God of pathos. Heschel's biblical idiom provided a prophetic alternative to secular humanism.[15]

Rothschild, now assistant professor at the JTS Teachers Institute, explored Heschel's eclectic manner of writing. Heschel strove to convey "the certainty of the realness of God" using three expository methods: empirical materials from classical Jewish texts, including evocations of religious experience; phenomenological description and analysis of consciousness; and philosophical criticism. Heschel often mixed these modes of discourse to frame his central task of depth theology, the fostering of preconceptual knowledge of the living God.[16]

Heschel's other star pupil, Seymour Siegel, now professor of theology at the JTS Rabbinical School, highlighted five areas of Heschel's scholarship: the Bible, rabbinics, medieval philosophy, Hasidism, and mysticism. He emphasized Heschel's approach to the God of pathos and religion of sympathy, as well as his studies on ruah ha-kodesh (Holy Spirit) in Maimonides and others. Siegel then predicted that Heschel's two Hebrew volumes on rabbinic theology would "change the fundamentalist-traditionalist confrontation in Israel and in the United States." Heschel's books on the Talmud demonstrated that theological pluralism flourished among the founders of rabbinic Judaism.[17]

That afternoon Heschel gave the annual Rabbinical Assembly lecture. This was the first time in his twenty-three years on the JTS faculty that Heschel had been accorded this honor (usually reserved for Mordecai Kaplan). Heschel's topic, "The Theological Meaning of *Medinat Yisrael*" (the state of Israel), was fueled by memories of his summer in the Holy Land. The speech provided the groundwork for his new book on the Jewish state. Speaking to supportive rabbis, Heschel looked back to distinguish among the people, the land, and the state, as he clarified some basic theological issues. He opened by celebrating the Six-Day War as a vindication of an exiled people: "Unprecedented. A people despised, persecuted, scattered to corners of the earth as though dust, has the audacity to dream regaining authenticity, of being free in the Holy Land. . . . There is a covenant, an engagement of the people to the land. We could not betray our pledge or discard the promise."[18]

The "existential fact" of being a Jew necessarily included "attachment to the land, waiting for the renewal of Jewish life in the land of Israel." Israel's astounding victory inspired a revival of faith, even "a new certainty." Heschel believed that Israel's survival was providential, reinforcing his view that the "Bible lives on, always being written, continuously proclaimed." Heschel foresaw decades of post-Holocaust theology as he reminded his colleagues that "faith in God [is] on trial." He disputed the "death of God" theologians, mostly Christians, who blamed the Nazi extermination on divine absence, a view he had repudiated as early as *Man Is Not Alone:* "We all died in Auschwitz, yet our faith survived. We know that to repudiate God would be to enhance the holocaust. . . . At that moment in history we saw the beginning of a new awakening, the emergence of a new concern for a living God theology."[19]

Heschel also rejected the notion that the state of Israel was God's "atonement" for not intervening to stop Hitler and his murderers: "It would be blasphemy to regard [Israel] as a compensation. However, the existence of Israel reborn makes life in the West less unendurable." The two warring extremes of Heschel's personality—melancholy and awe, dismay and exaltation—found a troubled unity in the Holocaust and Israel. From one perspective, Hitler darkened the world irremediably, wounding his heart forever: "If I should go to Poland or to Germany, every stone, every tree, would remind me of contempt, hatred, murder, of children killed, of mothers burned alive, of human beings asphyxiated." From the other, the rebirth of Israel offered a counterbalance: "When I go to Israel, every stone, every tree is a reminder of hard labor and glory, of prophets and psalmists, of loyalty and holiness. . . . Jews go to Israel for renewal, for the experience of resurrection." Heschel thus revitalized his Zionism while remaining true to the Diaspora. Jews should reevaluate their commitment to the Holy Land; he urged Americans to absorb the holiness of Israel into their daily lives.[20]

In the discussion that followed, sharp questions came about Heschel's views on aliyah, the advisability of challenging the U.S. government on Vietnam, and his grim view of the twentieth century "in terms of horror and destruction." In response, Heschel pointed out that his research on members of the State Department and the Pentagon had convinced him that their decision to persist in Vietnam was a "perfect example of dehumanization of judgment." Today, America was known around the world as "the largest purveyor of violence. . . . America doesn't have a single ally." Heschel came close to endorsing pacifism, recalling how, as a child, he had felt contaminated by being in a room with a man suspected of murder: "I have to be afraid of God. I don't want to be responsible for murder, for the killing of innocent people." At the same time, he reassured critics that he was "rather careful and moderate in my protest work in the peace movement." He concluded with the idea he had made the center of his mission: faith in the living God. "Without God man is a lost soul, and it is in a lost soul that the demonic comes to life."[21]

Two weeks after Martin Luther King saluted Heschel at the Rabbinical Assembly, he was gunned down in Memphis, Tennessee, at the age of thirty-nine. As riots, destruction, and looting broke out in more than a hundred American cities, the nation prepared to honor its fallen prophet.

Heschel was asked to participate in King's funeral. On Tuesday, 9 April, accompanied by Seymour Siegel, he flew to Atlanta, where the two went to King's house, meeting with King's bereaved family, Robert Kennedy, Jacqueline Kennedy Onassis, and other national leaders. Two services were to be given that day, and Heschel attended both: a morning service at the Ebenezer Baptist Church, where King was co-pastor with his father, and an afternoon service at Morehouse College, where King had been an undergraduate. King's widow, Coretta Scott King, had invited Heschel to read from the Old Testament at the Morehouse service.

The passage she had chosen, on the Suffering Servant from Second Isaiah (53:3–5), was dear to both Jews and Christians. A stirring portrait of Israel as the afflicted beloved of God, it was interpreted by Christians as a prefiguration of the betrayal of Christ. Dramatically, in his plaintive, sing-song voice, Heschel paid a final tribute to his friend and ally:

> He was despised and rejected by men;
> A man of sorrows, and acquainted with grief;
> And as one from whom men hid their faces
> He was despised, and we esteemed him not.[22]

National and International Platforms

Soon after the King funeral, in early May, Heschel was the featured speaker on "Teaching Jewish Thought" at a meeting of Solomon Schechter Day School principals. With this congenial audience, educators from the Conservative movement who revered tradition, he was relaxed and personal, instinctively using Hebrew or Yiddish expressions. Recognizing the special problems of Jewish education in modern America, he began by explaining the advantages of his Hasidic upbringing: "I do not come from an assimilated background. The atmosphere in which I grew up was full of theology. Day and night I heard them speak only about 'prayer' and 'kavanah,' and about '*Hakodesh boruch hu'* [God, the Holy One, Blessed Be He] and about '*mesirat nefesh'* [extreme devotion; lit. giving over of one's soul]. What is this? It is Jewish theology. Of course, we believed in all the *dinim* and *minhagim* [laws and customs]."[23]

Responding to questions, Heschel emphasized that the foundation of Jewish teaching was to "establish a certainty about man being precious in the eyes of God." He sympathized with people who questioned faith, however: "Who am I to speak about this when I have my own doubts? . . . I myself am not ready. There is a statement by the Kotzker Rebbe, "*az a mensch meint az er iz fartig—iz er op'gkocht!*" [If a man thinks he is ready, he is finished!] No one is ready. I have to grope and study all my life." Heschel also praised the piety of African Americans as models for Jewish teachers, alluding (without naming him) to his friend Larry Harris, the headwaiter at Hebrew Union College: "I told him that he was the finest human being that I [had] met during the five years that I was in America."[24]

Heschel's national stature as theologian of the inner life was recognized in the year-end issue of *Newsweek*. In a comprehensive article on prayer that cited the archbishop of Canterbury, Michael Ramsey; the Greek Orthodox archbishop Iakovos; and Fulton J. Sheen, bishop of Rochester, Heschel was described as "perhaps the most knowledgeable theologian on the meaning of prayer."[25]

In mid-January 1969 Heschel embarked upon a speaking tour of Italy at the invitation of Elémire Zolla, a prolific writer and professor of Anglo-American literature. Zolla was a vibrant personality, admired for his vast knowledge of Hinduism and Buddhism, literature, and the arts. Neither a secular leftist nor a member of the Catholic establishment, he was a broadminded Christian who had published Italian translations of Heschel's work in his journal *Conoscenza religiosa* (Religious knowledge).[26]

They had first met in Rome during Vatican II, at Heschel's favorite kosher restaurant, Tenenbaum's, in the via Cavour. Zolla often went there to discuss Kabbalah with a mysterious, erudite man who was doing research at the Vatican library, whose name he never learned. One evening as he was sitting with Cristina Campo, a poet and critic interested in mysticism, the strange man announced that he would not discuss Kabbalah that evening: someone with superior knowledge was present. He silently pointed to Heschel, who was having a drink "in the Polish manner" (straight up) with Zachariah Shuster of the American Jewish Committee. Heschel and Zolla were introduced, and Heschel asked, "Why are you interested in the Kabbalah?" Zolla answered, "It is the Kabbalah that is interested in me." Heschel responded, "Fine, that's something like the title of one of my books." Thus began many conversations and a lasting friendship.[27]

The two men shared identical perceptions of art; Zolla was attuned to Heschel's intuitive personality and felt "a flow of sympathy that made conversation intoxicating. . . . The same idea would arise at the same time in both of us, we often understood one another without having to complete a phrase, or even without having to utter it." They appreciated similar thinkers, such as Henry Corbin, the French scholar of Islamic mysticism whom Heschel first met in prewar Berlin. Heschel and Zolla even appeared together on an Italian television program about prayer. With them was an Egyptian Muslim author who impressed them with his "unusual psychic concentration and earnestness." Afterward, the three men discussed the Hebrew prophets as precursors of Islam. The Muslim insisted that Islam was self-contained in the prophet Muhammad's revelation and not "in essence" derived from any previous

prophetic tradition. Later, Zolla suggested to Heschel that the Muslim's striking composure flowed from his belief that the Islamic revelation was au-
tonomous. Heschel took the side of continuous revelation, alluding to the divine
presence: "Someone is always with me, to remind me of this."[28]

During Heschel's 1969 visit, Zolla introduced him to literary and academic
people, among them Elena Mortara Di Veroli, a young professor who specialized in American Jewish authors, and whose Italian translation of *God in
Search of Man* had recently appeared. She came from a prominent family active in the Jewish community of Rome. (One of her ancestors was the object
of the infamous "Mortara Case," still remembered with bitterness. In 1858,
Edgardo Mortara, a six-year-old Jewish boy, was abducted by papal police after
being baptized by a Christian servant.) On behalf of Gianfranco Tedeschi,
president of the Haim Weizman Center, Rome's Jewish cultural organization,
she invited Heschel to lecture about the Sabbath. It was the first time Heschel
had addressed an Italian Jewish audience. He spoke in English, with Mortara
translating. The talk was a resounding success.[29]

The event gave Heschel the opportunity to influence the spiritual life of
Tedeschi, a nonobservant Jew and Jungian psychoanalyst. They first met at a
Friday night dinner. In discussing various approaches to Jewish observance,
Heschel asserted that "Rabbinism was parochialism," meaning that Jewish
life was governed by rules; for example, the Shulhan Arukh (Code of Jewish
Law) was different from Talmudic Judaism, which required interpretation.
The Jungian analyst, trained in an analytical discipline, was intrigued by this
way of thinking. But Tedeschi could not fathom the apparent contradiction
between Heschel's open-mindedness, his resistance to narrow-minded religion, and his strict Sabbath observance. Heschel's religious thinking rose
above the defensive strictures of Jews in most European countries where
there was little if any mediation between secular and strictly Orthodox ways
of life. After this encounter with Heschel, Tedeschi began to observe some of
the mitzvot, said the *motzi* (the blessing over bread that begins a meal), eliminated his office hours on Shabbat, and ate no bread on Passover. He married
a non-Jewish woman (in a civil ceremony) but gave his daughters a Jewish
education.[30]

The culmination of Heschel's trip to Italy was the "First International Conference on the Genesis of Sudden Death and Reanimation" held in Florence.
It was a wide-ranging interdisciplinary meeting that included physicians,
medical researchers, philosophers, and religious thinkers from Italy, France,
Russia, Japan, South Africa, and the United States. Heschel addressed the

"religious-philosophical" session on the last day, 14 January 1969, in the Sala Bianca of the ornate Pitti Palace. Other papers at Heschel's session included "Science and Fable at a Medical Congress," "Death and Zen Buddhism," "The Christian Facing Death," and "Death, Judgment, Hell, Heaven." Elémire Zolla spoke on "The Transplant and Western Religion."[31]

Heschel's talk, "Reflections on Death," refocused material from previous writings and developed the idea that death was an essential component of human life. He surveyed attitudes toward death in biblical, Talmudic, and Hasidic sources, which all led him to his God-centered thinking: "Man's being is rooted in his being known about. It is the creation of man that opens a glimpse into the thought of God, into the meaning beyond the mystery." According to Heschel, there was no doctrine of death in Jewish tradition; rather, varied beliefs about death led to ethical commitment: "The cry for a life beyond the grave is presumptuous, if there is no cry for eternal life prior to our descending to the grave. Eternity is not perpetual future but perpetual presence. . . . The world to come is not only a hereafter but also a herenow." Rejecting speculation about the afterlife, he quoted from his first American article, "An Analysis of Piety" (1942), the line with which he had also concluded *Man Is Not Alone:* "For the pious man it is a privilege to die."[32]

Soon after Heschel's return from Italy, on 20 January 1969, President Richard Nixon and Vice President Spiro Agnew were inaugurated. For Heschel, it was an unsavory climax to a sad period in American politics that began with the shameful spectacle of police beating antiwar demonstrators at the Democratic National Convention in Chicago the previous August. Heschel had little time to brood, however. From 3–5 February he played a major role in the third CALCAV mobilization in Washington. This time he was cautious in his endorsement of the radical theme announced for the gathering, "Vietnam and the Future of the American Empire." But he did agree with other leaders of CALCAV, whose membership had reached twenty-five thousand, that "Americans cannot be the policeman of the world nor impose [America's] social system on other nations."[33]

Heschel stood for the new focus on healing, highlighted in the mobilization position paper: "Not since the Civil War have Americans been so divided or has the continuance of our society been so seriously challenged. Reconciliation, if it be genuine, requires painful honesty in the diagnosis of our wounds." Discussions would focus on the future of Vietnam, American victims of the war, amnesty for draft resisters or conscientious objectors within the military, and the draft itself: "Conscription is a form of involuntary servitude. As such it is incompatible with the democracy for which we hope."[34]

In addition to its grassroots program, CALCAV tried to arrange meetings with government officials. An initial request to meet with President Nixon was denied, although a half-hour meeting with Stanley Resor, secretary of the army, was arranged for the next day. To protest the mutiny trial of six soldiers from San Francisco, CALCAV presented Resor with a statement signed by prominent religious leaders, including Heschel.

Heschel had hopes for a meeting with Henry Kissinger, Nixon's new national security advisor, scheduled for the final day of the mobilization. At the last moment, Kissinger had agreed to meet with a group made up of Coretta Scott King, Heschel, Richard John Neuhaus, Richard Fernandez, and William Sloane Coffin (who was appealing his recent federal conviction for counseling young men against the draft). The *New York Times* reported the next day that "leaders of a group that has supported defiance and evasion of the draft as a form of protest against the war in Vietnam said they were given a 'very respectful hearing' at the White House today when they pleaded for amnesty for draft resisters." The visit appeared to be a public relations success for both sides.[35]

As with the McNamara visit, the inside story revealed greater tension. The group met with Kissinger in his office in the White House basement. The national security advisor did not appreciate Coffin's quip, "Our job is to have justice roll down like a rolling stream. Yours is to fix the irrigation ditches." During a discussion in which Kissinger expressed frustration with the bureaucracy he had inherited, Heschel broke in, goaded by emotion: "How could you as a good Jew prosecute a war like this?" Kissinger was tongue-tied but remained respectful toward Heschel, whose tone was more pastoral than accusatory, and muttered something in return. As with the meeting with McNamara, the visit ended in a stalemate.[36]

The final interfaith worship at the Metropolitan A.M.E. Church was a fitting climax to the lobbying, and it was crowned by a symbolic media event when Heschel and Coretta Scott King led a solemn procession out of the church. Hundreds of people walked slowly to the Constitution Avenue entrance of the Justice Department. Father Richard McSorley, chaplain at Georgetown University, gave the invocation. There were three brief speeches, including an address by Evelyn Whitehorn, who was held legally responsible when her three sons refused to register for the draft. Heschel asked President Nixon to pardon all those who had refused induction. Jail must not be the price for those who disagree with national policy. Then he watched as Coretta Scott King and Pastor Neuhaus put their hands on the head of Thomas Lee Hayes, a young pastor working with American draft resistors in Sweden, as the group recited: "I pledge myself to the ministry of reconciliation. To seek the release of those in prison for conscience's sake, the return in freedom of those in hiding and abroad, and to work for the rebuilding of America in a world of enduring peace."[37]

Heschel continued to speak at demonstrations, despite the pressures of teaching, writing, peace meetings, and the publication of his book on Israel. On Memorial Day, 30 May, Heschel joined a march and rally in New York organized by Veterans for Peace in Vietnam (VPV), a group that had been classified by the House Committee on Un-American Activities as "another spe-cialized 'peace' front of the Communist Party." FBI special agents noted that the parade was orderly, but mentioned that "five Negro males who appeared drunk" carried a sign for the Student Non-Violent Coordinating Committee. The rally ended with no incidents, and the FBI estimated that about 500–700 persons had participated, with numerous onlookers.[38]

Pastor Richard John Neuhaus and Coretta Scott King bless the Reverend Thomas Lee Hayes, a counselor to draft resistors, 5 February 1969, as Heschel looks on. Photograph by John Goodwin.

Interpreting Israel to Christians

As the Vietnam protests continued, Jewish-Christian relations were being undermined by conflicting views on the Jewish state, the Six-Day War, and the occupation of Arab territories. Heschel persisted in his support of Israel along with his ongoing domestic protests. Soon after the June war, recognizing his scholarly credentials and renown in the civil rights and antiwar movements, the Anti-Defamation League (ADL) of the B'nai B'rith had commissioned him to write a book explaining to Christians the passionate attachment of Jews to Israel.[39]

Heschel agreed to interrupt his work on the Kotzker rebbe after the ADL sent him a dynamic helper, Judith Herschlag. She spent late afternoons and early evenings in Heschel's JTS office being his "ear." Heschel would give Herschlag manuscript pages, some with only one or two sentences, or dictaphone recordings to be typed. Their editorial collaboration worked smoothly, although Heschel was dogged by the pressure of events and constant telephone calls, to which he responded politely and patiently.

As was often the case, he constructed this book from essays, the first of which had appeared in the *Hadassah* magazine of September 1967. In January 1968 he submitted this piece to Roger Straus, who encouraged him to expand it into a book, which his company would eventually publish. Heschel developed the piece further for the Rabbinical Assembly convention that March, at which he was honored, and then again for an interfaith symposium on "Theology in the City of Man" on 15–17 October, sponsored by Saint Louis University, a Catholic institution.[40]

The Saint Louis audience offered a perfect test for his arguments. Heschel was the lone Jew among leading Protestants and Catholics, who included the historian Jaroslav Pelikan of Yale University, Harvey Cox of Harvard Divinity School, and Eugene Carson Blake, general secretary of the World Council of Churches. Adapting his Rabbinical Assembly presentation for a broad Christian audience; Heschel announced forcefully: "The survival of mankind is in the balance. One wave of hatred, callousness, or contempt may bring in its wake the destruction of all mankind."[41]

Aware that his listeners might not share his views, he echoed words from *God in Search of Man:* "Even before Israel becomes a people, the land is preordained for Israel. . . . The election of Abraham and the election of the land came together." He surveyed historical claims to Palestine and found "no such attachment to a land anywhere else in the world." Heschel defended

Israel's right to some of the newly conquered territories or, at the least, the entire city of Jerusalem. From Christian Scripture he took the passage that he had used when addressing the Catholic bishops in Toronto, Acts 1:6–7, in which the disciples of Jesus express their expectation that "Jerusalem will be restored to Israel." Heschel concluded: "Some commentators, indeed, see in these words a prediction of 'the reestablishment of Jerusalem as a capital of the Jewish nation.' "[42]

Even before he addressed his Christian audience in Saint Louis, by June 1968, the book had been substantially finished, submitted to Farrar, Straus, and its title set, *Israel: An Echo of Eternity.* In October, anticipating publication the following year, the original sponsor, the Anti-Defamation League, ordered a print run of two thousand copies. The book was illustrated by the American expressionist artist Abraham Rattner, a strongly identified Jew who worked in both Paris and New York. Israel's victory in the Six-Day War had inspired Rattner to create a gigantic canvas in honor of Jerusalem, which corresponded brilliantly to Heschel's lyrical celebration of the Holy Land. Rattner's modernistic line drawings were a fitting successor to Ilya Schor's nostalgic woodcuts for *The Earth Is the Lord's.*[43]

Israel: An Echo of Eternity was promoted aggressively. The official launch, a large event that included about seventy-five Christian leaders in addition to Jewish dignitaries, took place on 20 February 1969 at ADL headquarters on Lexington Avenue. The main speaker was Philip Sharper, an editor at Sheed and Ward and an acquaintance of Heschel's. Copies were sent to Father Theodore Hesburgh, president of Notre Dame; Levi Eshkol, prime minister of Israel; Yitzhak Rabin, Israeli ambassador to the United States; Abba Eban, Israeli ambassador to the United Nations; John Elson, religion editor of *Time*; Arthur Goldberg, U.S. ambassador to the United Nations, and other political and academic luminaries.[44]

Heschel's interfaith project was threatened, however, by a brief, provocative critique by Jim F. Anderson in the *National Catholic Reporter.* Anderson could not reconcile Heschel's anti–Vietnam War stand with his justification of Israel's attack. Illustrating the article with a photograph of Heschel, Neuhaus, and Coretta Scott King blessing Thomas Lee Hayes, Anderson denounced what he perceived to be Heschel's view that the Jewish state's "theological reality" implied the idea of "holy war." The antiwar writer continued, "The expression ['holy war'] is as repulsive within the Jewish framework as it is within Cardinal Spellman's Catholic-American theological thought or the Arab's call to the holocaust in God's name."[45]

The ADL sought to minimize the potential damage of this widely circulated essay by asking Rabbi David Lieber, vice president of the Jewish Theological Seminary, to write to Robert G. Hoyt, editor of the *National Catholic Reporter*, explaining Heschel's peaceful vision. Lieber cited Heschel's concern for "the loss of lives, the devastation, the fruits of violence" and his approval of General Rabin's remarks immediately after the war that many Israelis, wary of its consequences, did not celebrate the victory.[46]

A more effective media defense of Heschel's intentions was provided by a perceptive essay in *Time* magazine, unsigned but probably written by the religion editor, John Elson. "Jews: A Plea for Love Without Cause," opened with an anecdote taken from the book about "a Christian friend" who had asked Heschel why he was so "dreadfully upset" during the months preceding the June war. "Heschel thought for a moment. Then he replied gently: 'Imagine that in the entire world there remains one copy of the Bible, and suddenly you see a brutal hand seize this copy, the only one the world, and prepare to cast it into the flames." The article concluded: "Heschel insists that Israel must be more than usually benevolent for a secular nation, and should extend an open hand of friendship to its Arab neighbors."[47]

Many readers remained confused by the complexity of Heschel's moral positions, which some perceived as mutually exclusive. The reality was that Heschel subordinated ideological considerations (for example, political rights to territory) to the defense of eternal values. In this instance, he asserted his commitment to the reconciliation of Jews and Arabs; at the same time, Heschel clearly favored the Jewish perspective, placing blame for the June war and the Palestinian refugee problem exclusively on the Arabs. And yet, while stressing the historical and theological claim of Jews to the Land of Israel, he was convinced that his book would promote peace; he tried to have it translated into Arabic.[48]

Heschel continued to demand that Israel measure itself according to prophetic standards. And he reaffirmed his view—first expressed in *The Sabbath*—that "we meet God in time rather than in space, in moments of faith rather than in a piece of space." *Israel: An Echo of Eternity* was directed at readers of every background. It was another effort to prove his lifelong claim that the Hebrew Bible was a sacred source, and a moral challenge, to all people.[49]

18
Stronger Than Death (1969–1971)

Reb Mendl's demands for self-sacrifice that condemns self-seeking, for total honesty that tolerates no pretensions, for excellence that rules out mediocrity or compromise were merciless. They were compatible neither with what we commonly consider to be human nor with the divine attributes of love and compassion.
—Heschel, *A Passion for Truth* (1973)

IN THE LAST YEARS OF HIS LIFE HESCHEL FOCUSED ON HIS SPIRITUAL AND ETHI-
cal legacy, while continuing his fervent antiwar activities. To that end he accepted a great many speaking engagements and gave numerous interviews.
His two books on the Kotzker rebbe, his last, were his most personal, almost
confessional in tone and content. In them Heschel expressed his negative
feelings more freely than he ever had previously.

The Vietnam War showed no sign of ending. It remained a constant source of
pain to Heschel even as he persisted in dispersing his energies among several
projects. But he could not maintain the intensity of his life without bringing on
a crisis. The constant, sometimes frantic, activity of his final years ended in his
untimely death.

Late in August 1969, Heschel was the sole Jew among leading Protestants
and Catholics to address a mass meeting of the National Liturgical Conference
(an unofficial Catholic organization) in Milwaukee, Wisconsin. The audience
was composed of progressive Catholics, most of them young. The agenda
called for a fusion of inwardness and action: political change, social justice,
and the virtues of prayer. The theme, as described by Robert McAfee Brown in
his opening address, was that hope must emerge from dissent. Former senator
Wayne Morse urged participants to launch a "religious crusade" against the
Vietnam War. Andrew Young of the Southern Christian Leadership Conference
spoke of "hope in the quest for economic justice" and the revolutionary power
of the Gospels.[1]

The press paid special attention to Heschel. Before the event, he was reported to have criticized repressive tendencies within the Catholic Church,
defending activists such as Archbishop James Shannon, "who recently resigned because of conservative pressure against his questioning of the War,
Papal authority and the pill ban." At the same time, Heschel pleaded "that re-
formers not throw out positive religious traditions, such as reserving time for
daily prayer." In his address, Heschel offered "hope in the midst of alienation,
chaos, and destruction." How could this be found? Through prayer.[2]

In rhythmical cadences, Heschel demonstrated that prayer was a sanctuary
for the "weary, sobbing soul," as he continued: "How marvelous is my home. I
enter as a suppliant and emerge as a witness; I enter as a stranger and emerge
as next of kin." Prayer was a cosmic drama, with human beings responsible for
redeeming the divine: "I pray because God, the *Shekhinah*, is an outcast. I
pray because God is in exile, because we all conspire to blur all signs of His
presence in the present or in the past. I pray because I refuse to despair. . . . *I
pray because I am unable to pray.*"[3]

The focus on prayer even explained his political dissent: "Religion as an establishment must remain separated from the government. Yet prayer as a voice of mercy, as a cry for justice, as a plea for gentleness, must not be kept apart." Religious observance braces us to reject the status quo, even if it means toppling the authorities: "Prayer is meaningless unless it is subversive, unless it seeks to overthrow and to ruin the pyramids of callousness, hatred, opportunism, falsehoods. The liturgical movement must become a revolutionary movement, seeking to overthrow the forces that continue to destroy the promise, the hope, the vision." Thrilled at Heschel's "terse, proverbial insights," the audience gave him a standing ovation.[4]

Death and Reanimation

Returning from the conference, Heschel suffered a massive heart attack on the airplane back to New York. When the plane landed he was immediately put into intensive care at New York University Hospital on 32nd Street in Manhattan. For several days Heschel remained close to death. His wife, Sylvia, and daughter, Susannah, soon to enter Trinity College, kept vigil with Wolfe Kelman. There were moments when the doctors lost hope. At one point a young intern reported to Mrs. Heschel that the monitors had briefly gone flat: her husband had been clinically dead for some minutes, but the doctors were able to revive him. The physician did not expect Heschel to survive. Sylvia answered that they must save him, thousands of people depended on him. The next day Heschel improved slightly.[5]

Richard Fernandez informed the CALCAV Steering Committee of Heschel's condition, while David Kogen assured the JTS faculty that Kelman was in "constant contact with the situation." Kelman spent his waking hours at the hospital with Heschel, looking after Sylvia and Susannah. When he and Heschel were alone together, they shared moments of delicate tenderness. Unable to speak and hardly able to hold a pencil, Heschel, in a shaky script, wrote this note: "I love you Wolfe. Kiss Me."[6]

Heschel remained in serious condition. Before Rosh Hashanah (the Jewish New Year 5730 began on 13 September 1969), at Kelman's request, Rabbi Joshua Shmidman, who lived on 32nd Street near the hospital, invited Sylvia and Susannah to stay at his apartment during the Holy Days, when they would not be able to ride to the hospital. On Rosh Hashanah, Shmidman visited Heschel, who looked frightening, hooked up to monitors and medication drips, gray faced. Shmidman was afraid to speak, but he began to address Heschel in Yiddish—not the formal Lithuanian Yiddish of YIVO, but the earthy Yiddish of Warsaw.[7]

Heschel stirred and awakened. He asked his visitor to blow the shofar, which Jews are commanded to hear when Rosh Hashanah does not fall on Shabbat. Heschel was extremely feeble, but he whispered the blessings and began softly to name the blasts: *Teki'ah* . . . (Shmidman began blowing the shofar) . . . *Shevarim* . . . *Teru'ah* . . . *Teki'ah* . . . Heschel called the thirty blasts. Now he was sitting up, growing stronger. As the invocation ended Heschel "received" his visitor. Still speaking Yiddish, he asked, "Who are you?" Shmidman explained that he was teaching Jewish philosophy at Stern College, the women's branch of Yeshiva University. They spoke about the *Akedah* (the sacrifice of Isaac, read on Yom Kippur) as interpreted by Kierkegaard in *Fear and Trembling*. Heschel recovered his intellectual energy, describing his writing projects in which the Christian existentialist played a large part.

By 15 September, Heschel had recovered enough to be transferred from the intensive care unit to a private room, but he was still allowed only one visitor per day. When his cousin Rabbi Jacob Perlow, son of the Novominsker rebbe of Williamsburg and a leader of the Agudah, came to see him, Heschel was unable to speak, but he wrote a note in Hebrew with a quotation from the Psalms, *'anokhi tola'at v'lo ish* (I am a worm and not a man). Rabbi Perlow erased the middle word. Heschel then wrote, *kashe lihyot* (it is difficult to live), and finally, *Im kitzi b'Nu York, ani rotze lalun etzel dodi* (if my end is to be in New York, I want to rest next to my uncle). In choosing his final resting place, Heschel was reaffirming his Hasidic roots.[8]

Heschel must have sensed that his years were limited. His doctor recognized that his heart had been irreparably damaged, and a tremendous amount of scar tissue remained. Heschel had been prone to cardiac disease for most of his life, and he knew it. His mother's twin brother, the Novominsker rebbe of Warsaw, had died at age fifty-eight of an aneurysm. His mother had died of a heart attack in the Warsaw Ghetto. Heschel himself suffered from high blood pressure and was somewhat overweight. He admitted to Sylvia soon after they married that he could not eat salted food because of his heart condition.[9]

Heschel had returned home by early October but was unable to resume his teaching duties. On 15 October the JTS students organized a Moratorium Day "in protest of the war in Vietnam," endorsed by the Student-Faculty Committee of the Rabbinical School and the Teachers Institute. Although Heschel applauded this stance, a change from the earlier faculty opposition to antiwar protest, he was too weak to attend.[10]

For the winter Heschel and his wife rented a furnished hotel apartment in Miami, while Susannah attended Trinity College in Hartford. Friends brought the Heschels meals, drove them to market, took them for rides or to the library. Sylvia practiced piano every morning at a local synagogue. But in early March, Heschel was hospitalized with hepatitis, further delaying his recovery.[11]

Heschel gave up smoking cigars and was ordered to moderate his liquor intake, having only a single glass of alcohol before dinner. Yet he continued to drink two or three. When his wife complained, his sense of humor came to the rescue. "But Sylvia, after I drink one glass, I become another man!"[12]

More than anything else, writing helped restore his life. He was engrossed, obsessed even, with completing two books, one in Yiddish, the other in English, on the life and personality of Menahem Mendl Morgenstern (1787–1859), the rebbe of Kotzk. Sensing, probably, that these would be his last works, he returned to his childhood identity as a Yiddish-speaking Jew of Warsaw. For the first time in his life, he revealed his inner struggles—psychological, cultural, even theological. Heschel's life had been a constant battle between the kindness of the Baal Shem Tov and the harshness of the Kotzker rebbe. As he wrote in the preface to the Yiddish volume: "I am the last of a generation, perhaps the last Jew of Warsaw, whose soul lives in Medzibozh [the final home of the Baal Shem Tov] and whose mind in Kotzk."[13]

The Kotzker rebbe, impelled by disgust for conventional religion and self-serving politics, was the model for Heschel's own dissent. His portrait of the Kotzker highlighted his own rebellious side: the doubter, the modern intellectual, the angry dissident underlying the loyal, compassionate prophetic witness.[14]

Heschel distilled these books from several previous essays and talks in Yiddish and Hebrew. In 1959 he had commemorated the Kotzker rebbe's hundredth Yahrzeit with a talk in Yiddish to the Rabbinical Assembly on "a Dissenter in Hasidism." At that time, the *New York Times* reported that just the fact that Heschel used Yiddish created a small tempest. Soon afterward, Heschel's essay in Hebrew about the Kotzker rebbe and the Baal Shem Tov appeared in *Hadoar*. There he contrasted the benevolence of Medzibozh with the brutal demands of Kotzk. The Kotzker's teachings had created a revolution in the Hasidic world, stirring unrest in the Jewish soul.[15]

Several years later, in 1968, Heschel placed a short piece in Hebrew in the Israeli quarterly *Sedemot*, published by the Union of Kibbutzim. Another essay in Hebrew appeared in Pinchas Peli's weekly journal *Panim el Panim* early the next year. Heschel also sent a two-part essay to *Die goldene Keyt,* the Tel Aviv Yiddish periodical edited by Abraham Sutzkever; it was published in 1969 and 1970. Heschel's recognition as an academic authority on the rebbe was confirmed by his invited contribution to the English-language *Encyclopaedia Judaica.* In this foundational reference work, he highlighted the cultural antithesis between the worlds of the Baal Shem and the Kotzker rebbe: "While Medzibozh emphasized love, joy, and compassion for this world, Kotzk demanded constant tension and an unmitigated militancy in combating this egocentricity." The Kotzker's banner was *emet* (truth). Anticipating a broad readership, Heschel compared the Kotzker rebbe with Søren Kierkegaard (1813–1855), the Christian father of existentialism, another tormented master.[16]

The books contained Heschel's most explicit self-analysis, illuminating tendencies he had expressed more discreetly over the years. For the first time, he wrote of his ancestry and explained how two forces, representing opposite traditions, had battled in his personality since the age of nine, when his father died and he was introduced to the relentless demands of Kotzk. His autobiographical preface to the English volume summarized the extremes: "I was taught about inexhaustible mines of meaning by the Baal Shem; from the Kotzker I learned to detect immense mountains of absurdity standing in the way."[17]

The focus on the Kotzker rebbe allowed Heschel to display an unexpected negativity, as in his grim diagnosis of religion, which was even more pessimistic than it had been in the 1950s: "Gone for our time is the sweetness of faith. . . . We are frightened by a world that God may be ready to abandon. What a nightmare to live in a cosmic lie, in an absurdity that makes pretensions to beauty." Although Heschel had always been passionate in his stands, in this book he raged against mediocrity as never before. One perceptive reviewer speculated that Heschel was atoning for his role as a "court prophet," admired as a holy man and accepting praise from a community he despised. Or perhaps Heschel was frustrated by his inability to effect real change.[18]

Kierkegaard and the Kotzker were extremists, religious radicals, "outsiders" who had "little compassionate consideration for the human condition and its natural limitations." Both men were alienated from normal society, subject to depression, and "haunted by mysterious states of anguish, the price they had to pay for their penetrating insights." Heschel rationalized these afflictions as payment for their "passion for truth." Heschel also shared with

Kierkegaard and the Kotzker rebbe "a predilection for sarcasm, irony, satire, and polemic. No one in the history of Jewish piety was more biting [than the Kotzker] in exposing the subterfuges of man. His language was abrasive." Heschel, too, was reproached for his demeaning sarcasm, such as calling modern rabbis "page boys" (who announced page numbers) and condemning the suburban synagogue as "a graveyard where prayer is buried."[19]

The Kotzker's battle with metaphysical absurdity unveiled more heroic efforts: "So many of us are haunted by the ugly futility of human effort, the triumph of brute force, of evil, and man's helpless misery. Is not any form of hopefulness false, unreal, self-deceiving?" In his chapter on the Kotzker and Job, Heschel advanced a post-Holocaust, post-Hiroshima faith, a reason to live and love the world: "meaning beyond absurdity in living as a response to an expectation." That hope, according to Heschel, was "the promise of messianic redemption."[20]

In an incandescent paragraph Heschel anticipated his own self-sacrifice to the causes that were his passion as he asserted that we must believe in God in spite of God: "The agony of our problem foments like a volcano, and it is foolish to seek finite answers to infinite agony. . . . The pain is strong as death, cruel as the grave. But perhaps it will be in the grave, the dwelling place of Truth, that our own death will somewhat hasten its resurrection."[21]

The Teacher and His Students

The political climate in which Heschel developed these daunting reflections was becoming increasingly contentious. On 10 March 1970, five American soldiers were court-martialed for war crimes committed at the village of My Lai in Vietnam. On 30 April the United States invaded Cambodia. Barely a week later, several student protesters were killed or wounded by National Guard at Kent State University. In response to the Cambodian invasion and the Kent State massacre, CALCAV cosponsored a mobilization in Washington on 9 May. Still recuperating from his heart attack and hepatitis, Heschel was not able to attend.

That spring, Heschel was elected to the American Academy of Arts and Sciences, along with the theology professor H. Richard Niebuhr, brother of Reinhold, the CBS news commentator Eric Sevareid, the writers Norman Mailer and Günter Grass, Duke Ellington, and Charlie Chaplin, among a total of 107 new members. Chancellor Finkelstein wrote to compliment Heschel for that "distinction made important by your inclusion in the group."[22]

Heschel was also asked to contribute to a Festschrift honoring John Coleman Bennett. Heschel's essay, "God, Torah, and Israel," was the only Jewish reflection in the volume, which was balanced toward liberal Christian theology, Protestant and Catholic. Heschel abstracted his carefully documented article from the manuscript of the uncompleted third volume of his Hebrew study of the Talmud. For the interfaith readership, he drew a parallel between the trinity of God, Christ, and the Holy Spirit and the Jewish hierarchy of God, Torah, and the Jewish people, giving priority to the divine.[23]

Meanwhile, at JTS, Heschel was receiving long-overdue support. Despite the dismissal of his approach to scholarship by the institution's authorities, Heschel brought distinction to the Seminary. Heschel was finally allowed to offer a course on Hasidism as part of the Rabbinical School curriculum. Finkelstein had at long last given his unacknowledged rival this measure of trust. The gesture may also have been an acknowledgment that Heschel's teaching was no longer perceived in a negative light. In the past, he had given informal seminars on Hasidism, deeply influencing some individuals while putting off most students by his lax pedagogy. In one such seminar, Heschel gave talks on major books of Hasidism and asked students for oral reports, but they were never required to submit their research, an omission that some found frustrating. As Arthur Green complained, "When I wanted a rebbe he was a professor, and when I wanted a professor he was a rebbe."[24]

Such was not the case during the 1970–71 academic year. The JTS students now embraced him as a celebrity, but more important, they honored him as a great Jew, a model of what they wanted to become as rabbis. Many who had avoided his classes on Maimonides and Judah Halevi registered for his course on Hasidism. When it opened, Heschel read from his manuscript on the Kotzker rebbe. In the past, this had been a bad sign. Now students were thrilled. Heschel also presented the ethical and religious treatises *Menorat ha-Maor* (Candlestick of light, fourteenth century), *Orchot Tzaddikim* (Ways of the righteous, fifteenth century), and Bahya Ibn Paquda's classical work, *Hovot ha-Levavaot* (Duties of the heart, eleventh century) as literary efforts to transform souls.

Sympathetic students appreciated Heschel as a religious philosopher capable of communicating life-transforming insights. He was pleased, even flattered, that he had suddenly become popular at the Seminary. A second generation of Heschel followers emerged. Most of these were not disciples in the conventional sense but thinkers inspired by his teaching and example. From the early to mid-1960s they included David Novak, Sol Tanenzapf, Ray

Heschel teaching at the Jewish Theological Seminary, ca. 1972. Courtesy of the Ratner Center for the Study of Conservative Judaism, Jewish Theological Seminary of America.

Scheindlin, Arthur Green, and Reuven Kimelman. Later Harlan Wechsler, William Berman, Hillel Levine, Larry Meyers (Aryeh Meir), and Byron Sherwin joined the group. Other followers included individuals who were inspired by private conversations in his office but were not students at the Seminary: Michael Lerner, Arthur Waskow, Arnold Eisen, the Catholic scholar Eva Fleischner, and myself. In Heschel's final years, the students closest to him were Pinchas Peli, Harold Kasimow, and Jacob Teshima.

One of Heschel's JTS pedagogical successes was a seminar for which he chose the students. Even the seating arrangement reflected his sensitivity to class dynamics. Heschel sat at his desk next to an L-shaped table, with two students at his left and two others directly in front of him. One year Novak and Tanenzapf, who were interested in classical philosophy, sat on one side, with Green and Kimelman, more interested in religious experience, on the other. Subtly and skillfully Heschel played one group against the other to enliven the debate.[25]

Heschel was more responsive to questions than he had been in the past. When pressed to explain something, he would back up his philosophical arguments with his enormous knowledge of classical Jewish texts. Many students felt that Heschel could have produced many more followers had he taught as effectively earlier in his career. Even so, he did not impress everyone. He had scheduled a seminar for special Talmud students, Yochanan Muffs, Ben Zion Gold, and David Weiss. After one session they found excuses not to return, while retaining their admiration of the man.[26]

Heschel remained at his best with active seekers. In the fall of 1970 a Japanese Christian, Jacob Yuroh Teshima, entered JTS after completing advanced Judaic studies at the Hebrew University in Jerusalem. Teshima became Heschel's closest student in the two years before his death. His attraction to Judaism had been inspired by his father, Ikuroh A. Teshima, the charismatic founder of the Original Gospel Movement, or Makuya (Non-Church or Tabernacle), a Japanese Christian sect whose followers revered the Hebrew Bible and the state of Israel. Their symbol was the menorah, signifying worship, rather than the cross, which signified suffering. Makuya leaders studied for up to three years in Israel to perfect their Hebrew and to imbibe the spirit of the holy sites.[27]

Jacob Teshima first went to Israel intending to study with Martin Buber, who had influenced his father. When he found that Buber had retired, he took the advice of Gershom Scholem to follow a strict academic program. In 1967 Teshima returned to Japan with a degree in philosophy and the Bible; for the next three years he helped his father lead the Makuya movement. Teshima had heard Heschel speak in Israel in 1965, and he entered the JTS graduate program to study the Bible with H. L. Ginsberg and philosophy with Heschel.

Teshima was disappointed by Heschel's class on rabbinic theology since Heschel simply read from *Heavenly Torah* and asked students to summarize its contents. He did not correct or return their papers. But Heschel's class on the Kotzker rebbe made up for the other class's shortcomings. Here students read original Hasidic texts and wrote a research paper on one of them. All discussions were in Hebrew. Heschel stressed the conflict between *ahavah* (love), represented by his ancestor the Apter rebbe, and criticism, represented by the Kotzker.

Heschel was impressed by the Japanese student's paper in fluent Hebrew, and he took a liking to this devout and original personality, who combined a sense of humor, thoughtful independence, and reverence for his teacher. The Heschels became close to Jacob and his wife, Tamiko (Tammy), a concert pianist like Sylvia, and their baby daughter. Teshima often accompanied Heschel home from his office late at night. After earning a DHL (Doctor of Hebrew Letters) with a thesis on Zen Buddhism and Hasidism, Teshima returned to Japan with his family. He stopped working for the Makuya movement and

Heschel with Tamiko Teshima and her daughter Elize, 14 November 1970.
Courtesy of Jacob Yuroh Teshima.

Heschel and Jacob Teshima, November 1971. Courtesy of Jacob Yuroh Teshima.

*Heschel and Susannah, 1971. Courtesy
of Jacob Yuroh Teshima.*

earned a living in business, with a mission to "convey the message of Judaism
to secular Japanese society." Teshima translated Heschel's works into Japanese along with his own teachings.[28]

The New Year began with loss. On Thursday, 31 December 1970, Heschel's older brother, Rabbi Jacob Heshel, died of a heart attack in London at age
sixty-seven. He was buried a few hours after death, following Orthodox custom
and because of the coming Sabbath. Heschel remained in New York for the
memorial week of shiva, holding services every day at his apartment through
Friday morning, 8 January 1971. Heschel and Yankele (as Heschel called his
brother in Yiddish) had been close and affectionate, though Jacob Heshel was
not an intellectual. He was beloved as a sweet, generous, and devout Jew. He
immigrated in 1929 from Nazi-occupied Vienna to London with his wife and
daughter Thena, learned English quickly, and became the rabbi of an Orthodox congregation and headmaster of a religious school. Governed by a forthright view of right and wrong, he saw the best in people. He did not dress in
Hasidic garb, but he introduced ancestral stories into his sermons and published a scholarly article, "The History of Hasidism in Austria."[29]

Heschel's brother, Rabbi Jacob Heshel,
Edgeware, London, 10 September 1967, at
the wedding of his daughter Thena. Courtesy
of Thena Heshel Kendall.

The following month Heschel was honored by B'nai B'rith, which presented him with its annual Jewish Heritage Award. Students, friends, and colleagues gathered at the Waldorf-Astoria Hotel to recognize his accomplishments. At the award luncheon John C. Bennett, now president emeritus of Union Theological Seminary, explained Heschel's importance to Christians, stressing his combination of piety and activism. He read several passages from Heschel's works that were used by Christians in their devotions as he recalled Heschel's success as the Fosdick visiting professor.[30]

Lou H. Silberman, professor of Jewish literature and thought at Vanderbilt University Divinity School, and a former student of Heschel's at Hebrew Union College, movingly evoked the vulnerable immigrant of past years: "Sad-eyed and, despite what goodwill there may have been, sadly alone, not at home among our noisy crew." He recalled Heschel's admitting that a person can possess only one language and his was Yiddish. People had trouble understanding Heschel because they expected a clear, logical professor's discourse, whereas Heschel was a rebbe who *zogt Toyreh* (spoke words of Torah).[31]

Later the guests went to study sessions on Heschel's writings. The interpreters included three former JTS students who were now colleagues, Fritz Rothschild, Seymour Siegel, and Avraham Holtz, and two younger academics: Heschel's former JTS student Byron Sherwin, now assistant professor of religious philosophy at Spertus College of Judaica in Chicago, and me, at that time instructor of French at Barnard College. We all went on to publish significant studies. Elie Wiesel was also present with his wife, Marion.[32]

A Public Audience with the Pope

Despite his still fragile health, Heschel returned to Italy in March for a lecture tour arranged by the Italian Cultural Association, accompanied by his wife, Sylvia. He also scheduled an audience with Pope Paul VI to confirm his high standing with the Vatican. Heschel gave addresses in several cities using material from *Who Is Man?* His lectures in English were simultaneously translated into Italian by Elena Mortara, who accompanied him to Turin, Milan, and Rome. His audiences were enthusiastic, and he relished the stimulating European environment.[33]

Speaking in Rome at the Eliseo Theater, Heschel's slow, impassioned manner struck the imagination of a writer for *Shalom,* the Jewish community magazine. The listener imagined that Heschel looked "as though he had hurled himself into a mythological challenge with Titans. . . . So fragile, so vulnerable behind his beard, eyes shining, intent on making us aware, making us expand that inner light." At a dinner party hosted by the Ruffinis, a revered family of antifascists, Heschel spoke about his childhood in Poland and his writing on the Kotzker rebbe. He recounted a witticism of a boyhood teacher who scolded him for preferring adult conversation to that of his peers: "If you act like an old man now, when you grow up you will become a child." The group included Christina Campo, who wrote an introduction to Heschel's first translated book, the historian Lidia Storoni, and Guido Ceronetti, a writer and Bible translator, and his wife.[34]

Elena Mortara especially enjoyed the Heschels "at home," released from social protocol. At the end of the lecture tour, tired of eating out every night, they invited her to their hotel room for cold food from a kosher delicatessen. Amid the paper plates and plastic forks, they "spent a cheerful evening, chattering and laughing like a group of students, a moment of real relaxation." Heschel's

Italian translator discovered the simple person, "a warm man, who in his quiet way seemed able to imprint each moment of his life with meaning."[35]

On 17 March (a Wednesday), the Heschels were received ceremoniously by Pope Paul VI. As if to prepare for subsequent interviews, Heschel afterward wrote a memorandum to himself that emphasized his central role in the ritualized meeting. The theme was set by the pontiff's warm greeting: "When he saw me he smiled joyously, with a radiant face, shook my hand cordially with both his hands—he did so several times during the audience. He opened the conversation by telling me that he was reading my books, that my books are very spiritual and very beautiful, and that Catholics should read my books." Heschel gave him a signed copy of the recently published Italian translation of *Who Is Man?*[36]

After Heschel thanked the pope "for what he had done for the Jewish people through the Ecumenical Council," he underscored the importance of Jerusalem to Jews everywhere: "All of Jewish history is a pilgrimage to Jerusalem, and the union of the Jewish people and the city of Jerusalem we regard as a sign of divine grace and providence in this age of darkness. The Pope then said: 'I will remember your words,' and added: 'I hope that you and I will meet together in Jerusalem.'"

The pope commemorated the occasion with photographs. Heschel continued in his memorandum: "Mrs. Heschel started to move away, the Pope took her hand and then my hand, placed them on the arms of his chair, and a picture was taken." Thus, Heschel successfully completed the "summit meeting" he had mishandled in secret six years earlier.

This photograph and another one showing only Heschel and the pope were distributed to Jewish and Catholic publications around the country. Both communities used it to advance interfaith relationships that had been carefully built up since the promulgation of *Nostra Aetate* in 1965. The image of the Heschels standing on either side of the pope was interpreted in *The Pilot*, the official paper of the Boston Diocese, as symbolizing the pontiff's high regard for the Jewish people in general and for Rabbi and Mrs. Heschel in particular. Heschel and the pope were featured on the cover of *United Synagogue Review* (fall 1971, the High Holy Day issue), which went to all Conservative congregations. The report quoted the pope as saying that he would meet Heschel again in "the Holy City."[37]

When Heschel returned to the United States, the JTS Media Relations Office began to promote him as a celebrity. In May he did a radio interview with the novelist and television writer Harold Flender. (Transcripts were available from JTS for fifty cents.) Heschel recapped his recent trip to Italy and touched

The Heschels with Pope Paul VI, Rome, 1971. Courtesy of the Ratner Center for the Study of Conservative Judaism, Jewish Theological Seminary of America.

on his relationships with Christians, the Middle East situation, and his friendships with Martin Luther King, Jr., and the controversial Daniel Berrigan. Heschel praised the Jesuit militant as "a genuine poet, a person of great charisma, who lacks what most of us have, namely the readiness to be indifferent, the readiness to compromise with evil." He went on to justify his own tendency to challenge authority: "Most Americans have by now forgotten what was so vital to me as youngster, namely America as the great hope in a dark world and a reactionary world."[38]

Then, answering a question about Soviet Jewry, Heschel gave in to his increasing tendency to elevate his role in historic events: "I believe I was the very first man who . . . initiated the movement for the Jews in Soviet Russia. At the beginning there were very few individuals who responded to my appeal, and it took several years finally to awaken the organized Jewish community." Ego was not the only reason for Heschel's somewhat exaggerated boast. Taking credit was an indirect way of expressing anger at the apathy of American Jews with regard to Vietnam, Israel, civil rights, and other calls to personal responsibility.[39]

That same month Heschel published an extensive essay in *Hadoar*, another excerpt from the incomplete manuscript of volume 3 of *Heavenly Torah*. The title, "Have You Acted Faithfully?" came from a Talmudic passage on the questions a person is asked upon entering heaven. Heschel expressed dismay at the shortcomings of contemporary faith: "The Divine Presence is gone and love has stopped, heresy is gone and in its place is levity, apathy; . . . The malady of the generation is not denial of God but a denial of the possibility of faith." Renewal of faith could only come from recognizing and overcoming pessimism: "There is no noble life without spiritual exertion. A person who has not felt the sting of doubts, has an unripe faith. . . . We say to God, You are our father despite Auschwitz."[40]

Honoring His Elders

One of Heschel's most important friendships came to an end when Reinhold Niebuhr died on 2 June 1971, at age seventy-eight. After moving from New York into a retirement home in Stockbridge, Massachusetts, Niebuhr and his wife, Ursula, had begun planning his funeral. They decided to invite Heschel to give the only eulogy. Heschel's participation would reaffirm Reinhold's closeness to prophetic Judaism, his love for the Hebrew Bible and the Jewish people.

On Sunday, 4 June, Heschel and Seymour Siegel went to the memorial service at the First Congregational Church in Stockbridge. Niebuhr's body was not present; it had been donated to Harvard Medical School. The two hundred mourners included the historian Arthur Schlesinger, Jr., the labor leader and civil rights activist Joseph Rau, the historian William L. Shirer, and the literary and cultural critics Lionel and Diana Trilling.

Heschel spoke from the heart: "This is a critical moment in the lives of many of us, in the history of religion in America: to say farewell to the physical existence of the master and to pray: Abide, continue to dwell in our midst, spirit of Reinhold Niebuhr." Niebuhr "combined heaven and earth," said Heschel, referring to the theologian's synthesis of spirituality and activism: "For all his profundity, prophetic radicalism, insight into the ultimate aspects of human destiny, Reinhold Niebuhr maintained a concern for the immediate problems of justice in society and politics, of the here and now." After remembering Niebuhr as "a staunch friend of the Jewish people and the State of Israel, of the poor and the down-trodden everywhere," Heschel quoted a passage from the Book of Job that was commonly recited at Christian and Jewish funerals: "The Lord has given / The Lord has taken, Praised be the name of the Lord." Heschel concluded by celebrating Niebuhr's life as "a song in the form of deeds, a song that will go on for ever."[41]

The following week, Heschel paid tribute to another giant of American religious life, Mordecai Menahem Kaplan, a theological rival but also a respected friend, still very much alive. It had become customary to honor each decade of the Reconstructionist patriarch's life, and this gala dinner celebrated Kaplan's ninetieth year. For the first time Kaplan invited Heschel to speak. Heschel wondered how to deal with his ambivalent feelings: he loved Kaplan the man but repudiated his ideas. Heschel's spontaneous performance that evening revealed his tension. It was an illustration of Freud's theory that wit liberated forbidden thoughts.[42]

The Jewish elite were present, most of whom agreed with Kaplan's religious naturalism. Worried about what to say, Heschel sought advice from Wolfe Kelman, and they had a few drinks. Heschel did not prepare his speech; he rarely did. By the time the master of ceremonies, Philip Klutznik, former president of the B'nai B'rith, had called on Heschel to give remarks before the dinner, he was already a bit tipsy. With a string of witticisms intended to relax the audience, and himself, Heschel teased Kaplan, playing on his key ideas.

Humorously, Heschel chided Reconstructionism for abandoning its feminist principles (the movement was the first to establish the bat mitzvah and ordain female rabbis). "Kaplan is the founder of 'Women's Lib' in Jewish life," quipped Heschel, "but there is a major inconsistency: there are so few 'ladies' seated at the head table!" He went on in this vein. There was uncontrolled laughter at certain points, shared by audience and speaker, which betrayed the tensions. Heschel's next joke, long and convoluted, concerned the pursuit for a title for his speech. noting that it could not be called an "after dinner speech" since he was speaking before the meal. Heschel sought precedents, for example of the Passover seder: "First we chant the aggadah, then we eat the *knaylakh*" (matzoh balls). The second precedent was biblical. When the angels visited Abraham and Sarah, she prepared a wonderful dinner ("though it wasn't kosher"). The angels gave a before-dinner speech and announced that the 90-year-old Sarah would have a child (pause . . . remember, it was Kaplan's ninetieth birthday). Everyone laughed. Heschel lost control. With repeated efforts, he regained his composure. Then he said, "This speech for Kaplan must be pregnant with meaning." (More laughter.)

It was obvious that Heschel had been drinking, and that he was improvising, brilliantly. But the audience wasn't sure whether Heschel would, or could, complete his speech. He recovered, playing on the titles of Kaplan's famous books: "Professor Kaplan without Supernaturalism." But that title was no good because it would mean no miracles, and Mordecai Kaplan is marvelous! How about "Professor Kaplan as a Civilization"? After all, he is one of the most civilized beings on the faculty of JTS. "Religion as Ethical Personality"? But to do a mitzvah requires effort; it has to hurt a little. In this case, the mitzvah of "love thy neighbor as thyself" is easy because Mordecai Kaplan is so easy to love.

Heschel's joking praise was sincerely meant. Kaplan took his religion personally and seriously, noted Heschel, and he compared his friend with Jewish mystics who remain awake for *tikkun hatzot* (all-night study sessions). "Kaplan stays up past midnight worrying about the Jewish people." Such was Kaplan's "magnificent obsession," one that Heschel shared. Heschel ended his speech gracefully, expressing his affection with another humorous title, appropriate for Kaplan's 120th birthday, the traditional Jewish wish: "The Greater Kaplan in the Making." Kaplan and his son-in-law Ira Eisenstein were delighted with the performance.

By this time Heschel himself was receiving a number of honors. In addition to an honorary degree from Upsala College, a small, private liberal arts institution in East Orange, New Jersey, affiliated with the Lutheran Church, Heschel was given the Democratic Legacy Award of the Anti-Defamation League. In early November, the day after he appeared on an ABC national television interview with Frank Reynolds, Heschel became the first rabbi to receive the prestigious ADL commendation. (Previous recipients included former chief justice Earl Warren and Presidents Truman, Eisenhower, Kennedy, and Johnson.)[43]

The award ceremony took place at Grossinger's, the famed Catskills resort hotel. Guest speakers were Eugene Carson Blake, general secretary of the World Council of Churches (which had more than 400 million members), and Edward H. Flannery, assistant director of the Institute of Judeo-Christian Studies at Seton Hall University and executive secretary of the Secretariat for Catholic-Jewish Relations of the Bishops' Committee for Ecumenical and Interreligious Affairs. Blake described Heschel as "an 'authentic saint' who was helping to bring about 'the miracle of mutual understanding and greater cooperation' which is bridging religious differences." Father Flannery, the author of an influential book on anti-Semitism, *The Anguish of the Jews* (1965), praised Heschel's ability to expound the Jewish view of Israel and the Hebrew Bible.[44]

Heschel's prestige at the Vatican was proclaimed by a message from Pope Paul VI, received as a telegram from John Cardinal Wright, formerly of Chicago, now in Rome as prefect of the Sacred Congregation for the Clergy. The past forgotten, the pope praised the "sometimes lonely witness of the great and wise rabbi scholar."

Heschel responded to this acclaim of his spiritual radicalism with criticism of "do-gooders": Jews who were beginning to withdraw from the civil rights movement. The anti-Semitism of some black militants could not excuse it, explained Heschel. As a child in Poland he knew "what it means to live in a country where you are despised. Blacks have the same feelings here." Referring to the Knapp Commission's inquiry into police brutality and corruption, he warned his audience: "'If a few filthy guttersnipes put a fire to a synagogue, we all feel alarmed, and rightly so. But when we are told that police serve as patrons of deadly crimes, the community remains unconcerned.'" As Jews we must "keep our tongues and souls clean." Both Christian and Jewish listeners were moved by the half-hour talk. The *ADL Bulletin* underscored the appreciation of his audience for Heschel's "soft, accented voice sprinkled with Hebrew and Yiddish expressions."[45]

The traumatic year was coming to an end. Rabbi and Mrs. Heschel were given a surprise party at their Riverside Drive apartment on Saturday evening, 11 December 1971, after Shabbat, to honor their twenty-fifth wedding anniversary. The embossed invitation cited the Song of Songs (4:1–8, 5:10–16, 6:3):

> Behold, thou art fair, my love; behold thou art fair;
> Thine eyes are as doves behind thy veil;
> Thy hair is as a flock of goats. . . .
> His head is as the most fine gold, His locks are curled,
> And black as a raven.

Heschel's hair had by now become white, though retaining its luxurious abundance.

I add the following lines (8:6), which recall how close Heschel came to death two years earlier:

> Set me for a seal upon thy heart,
> As a seal upon thine arm;
> For love is strong as death.[46]

19
Summation of a Life (1972)

It would have been abnormal if a life possessed of such unbearable
tensions had remained normal. And it required extraordinary strength
not to subside into total mental derangement.
Is melancholy always a symptom of madness, or can it be a sign of deep
anxiety about the madness that has overtaken so-called normal society?
—Heschel, *A Passion for Truth* (1973)

HESCHEL TURNED SIXTY-FIVE ON 11 JANUARY 1972, BUT HE APPEARED FAR
older than his years. His face was deeply furrowed and his walk had lost vigor;
he shuffled, slightly dragging his feet. Yet he remained forceful as a speaker,
conscious that his long white hair and beard enhanced his image and through
it his ability to communicate. Despite his recent brush with death, he accepted too many invitations to travel and to speak, in addition to maintaining
his teaching load at JTS. He also contended with his illness as he struggled to
complete his two books on the Kotzker rebbe.

Heschel's resilience was weakened by the news of the massive human suffering inflicted by U.S. bombings in Southeast Asia, reported in the *New York
Times* in gruesome detail. Jacob Teshima would massage his teacher's shoulders and back to ease the tension brought on by the daily horrors: "His mus-
cles were like wood," Teshima remembered. People close to Heschel noticed
that he drank more than usual, sometimes traveling with a bottle of whiskey.
He felt constant stress and appeared to be lonely and sad. In an almost un-
canny way, during his final year he month by month—and sometimes week by
week—gave closure to major areas of his calling, demonstrating the inclusiveness of his concerns and putting the last touches on his spiritual legacy.[1]

Reconciliations of the Spirit

Heschel summarized his devotion to racial equality on a national television
program honoring Martin Luther King, Jr. On 9 January, he was the Jewish dis-
cussant along with two African American clergymen, the Protestant pastor Jesse
L. Jackson, a close associate of King's in the Southern Christian Leadership
Conference, and a Catholic priest, George R. Clements. The moderator was
ABC correspondent Frank Reynolds, who had recently interviewed Heschel.
Heschel and Jackson were especially telegenic, the venerable rabbi with his
white hair and beard and black skullcap, the youthful Jackson with a full Afro.[2]

In a somber tone, Heschel praised King's nonviolence, keen intelligence,
powerful presence, and grasp of complex sociological factors: "This combination of an inspired man and a sophisticated man is indeed unique." Heschel
also asserted that the nation's spiritual health depended, to a large extent, on
the quality of prayer he had experienced in African American religious services: "If there is an American Christianity, a living faith and a knowledge of
the art of praying, it is still preserved in the black churches."[3]

Elsewhere, Heschel focused his efforts on the antiwar movement's new goal
of national reconciliation, while continuing to protest the U.S. bombings of

Vietnam, Cambodia, and Laos. He contributed to an interfaith conference on peace that took place 14–16 January in Kansas City, arranged by the National Council of Churches, CALCAV, and other religious organizations. It was Henry Siegman who had proposed Heschel to the Reverend Robert S. Bilheimer, executive director of the Council's Department of International Affairs, as a speaker who could "plumb the depths of the action which we need to take." Heschel's affirmative answer and his preliminary statement were worthy of the Kotzker rebbe: "The cruelties committed by our armed forces in Southeast Asia were made possible by an unprecedented campaign of deceiving the American people. . . . The hour may have come to realize that falsehood, deception, is at the root of evil." The *New York Times* reported that the conference was "the most comprehensive religious gathering ever assembled in the United States over the peace issue, largely because of increased support among Catholics." Heschel offered a personal account of how he became involved in the peace movement.[4]

The following week Heschel flew to Jerusalem for the 28th World Zionist Congress. Addressing this international gathering, he reviewed his hopes for the Jewish state and the Diaspora. It was a troubled time for Zionists, who considered dissent highly suspect. The mood of the conference was more contentious than usual: the invitation to give the keynote address had been withdrawn from Nahum Goldmann, president of the World Jewish Congress, because he supported Jews who chose to remain in the Soviet Union. Contesting the tenet that all Jews must eventually settle in Israel, Goldmann claimed that he had passed "beyond Zionism."[5]

Some potentially disruptive leaders were demanding to speak. On the left was Kovachi Shemesh, of the Israeli "Black Panthers," who, on behalf of the poor, wished to denounce police brutality. (The previous evening police had harshly suppressed a small demonstration. Mounted officers dispersed the crowd, while others wielded clubs and high-pressure hoses.) Shemesh was eventually allowed to testify on Israel's social problems before a special committee. On the right, the belligerent American rabbi, Meir Kahane, insisted that he be allowed to represent the viewpoint of his Jewish Defense League.[6]

Nearly a thousand delegates and observers met at the Jerusalem Concert Hall for the opening session on 19 January. There were standing ovations for former premier David Ben-Gurion, President Zalman Shazar, and Premier Golda Meir. Shazar gave the opening address. The question of immigration was high on the agenda, with excitement at the prospect of a mass aliyah of Jews from the Soviet Union.

In the discussions, Heschel presented his flexible but deliberate religious viewpoint, deploring the gulf between Orthodox Jews, whose lives and politics were governed by halakhah, and Jews with modern, humanist approaches to life. Repeating the advice he had given both Israeli and Diaspora Jews for years, Heschel regretted the fact that each tendency was one-sided: Reform disregarded Torah and Israel for "ethical monotheism" while the ultra-Orthodox stressed "the supremacy of the Torah, equating Torah with *Shulhan Arukh* [Code of Jewish Law], in disregard of God and Israel, frequently leading to religious behaviorism." Heschel proposed a synthesis.[7]

Criticizing the hostility of secular Zionists to religion, he pointed out that the original conception of Zionism included spirit as well as politics, quoting in German: "'*Zionism is the return to Judaism even before returning to the land of the Jews*,' said Herzl in his opening address at the first Congress. Indeed, Judaism without *halakhah* is like a tree cut off at its roots." At the same time, Heschel firmly opposed civil authority for the Orthodox establishment. Above all, he insisted, Israel must uphold ethics over rigid legalism: "I am grateful to God that in the official establishments and hotels *kashrut* is observed. But what hurts is the question why it is only required for butcher-stores to be under religious supervision. Why not insist that banks, factories and those who deal in real estate should require a *hekhsher* [kosher certification] and be operated according to religious law?" His examples struck a raw nerve for Israelis, recently alerted to scandals in their banking and construction industries: "When a drop of blood is found in an egg we abhor eating the egg. But often there is more than one drop of blood in a dollar or a lira [Israeli pound] and we fail to remind the people constantly of the teachings of our tradition." The Jewish state must be a light unto the nations: "For the sake of God, for the sake of Israel and the world, the people Israel and the State of Israel must emerge as religious witnesses, to keep the consciousness of the God of Abraham and the reverence for the Bible alive in the world."[8]

Less than two weeks later, on 3 March, Heschel's Israeli friend Yehiel Hofer, his closest childhood companion from Warsaw, died in Tel Aviv at age sixty-six. Heschel wrote to Hofer's widow in Yiddish: "I am crushed and broken. . . . But please do not forget your wonderful love and invaluable spiritual devotion, which kept this beautiful man of the spirit alive for so many years." Gone was another witness to Heschel's youth.[9]

That same month, on 26–27 March, Heschel joined other dissenters in Washington to call for a general amnesty for all draft resisters. Their goal was to resolve America's internal conflicts and enable social reconciliation. As the organizers explained, denying young men the right to refuse service in a specific war was "a major source of the moral crisis of tens of thousands who saw themselves with no choice but exile or prison." Heschel's carefully documented paper, "The Theological, Biblical, and Ethical Considerations of Amnesty," was never published, but it circulated widely in antiwar and civil liberties communities. His immediate goal was to alleviate the nation's affliction: "The youth of America have gone through the shock of a moral earthquake. Young men differed widely as to what loyalty to our country demands." He urged the Justice Department to help heal the nation by promoting forgiveness.[10]

Heschel justified amnesty as a devout Jew, citing the Talmud: "The law of the secular government must be strictly obeyed in civil affairs (*Babba Kamma*, 113A). . . . However, if the law of the state is in conflict with the religious and moral laws, one must obey the Master of all of us and disobey the state." His final authority was Rashi, "the classical Jewish source," who forbade a man to murder another, even if he were ordered to do so by the town governor: "How could you say that your life is dearer to God than his?" Civil disobedience, in fact, could be halakhically justified. Heschel demanded that the government liberate the more than one hundred thousand young Americans exiled or imprisoned for obeying their moral judgment: "They are guilty of seeing earlier what all honest men should now see (when it is rather late) that the war in Vietnam was a stupid, immoral, absurd adventure for which it is not worthwhile shedding the blood of a single soldier."[11]

On 4 June, another of Heschel's conflicts was resolved—his strained relationship with the Hebrew Union College. In 1945 his abrupt departure from Cincinnati had created some hard feelings. Since that time he had made no secret of his disdain for some basic concepts of Reform, denouncing its "customs and ceremonies" as folklore, not religion. But by the 1970s the Reform seminary had recognized Heschel's value for all Jews. In March, in one of his first acts as the new president of HUC, Rabbi Alfred Gottschalk (a German student whose life had been saved by President Morgenstern) invited Heschel to receive an honorary doctorate of humane letters at ordination exercises in New York. Heschel was delighted and accepted immediately: "Becoming an honorary alumnus will only deepen my relationship to the College."[12]

At the graduation ceremony in Temple Emmanuel on Fifth Avenue, Heschel addressed the newly ordained rabbis and challenged their consciences on the crisis in America's cities. Alluding to the Jewish Defense League, which had recently committed their movement to violent reprisals, he warned Jews not to withdraw from society. If they did, "the mood of despair in the Jewish community will only be deepened and the charlatans with their demagogic slogans will be hailed as the spokesmen of our people." At the luncheon that followed, Heschel spoke again to encourage Jewish activism, rejecting fears that the nation's failure in Vietnam, the racial crisis, and economic problems would spur a new wave of anti-Semitism. He deplored predictions of another Holocaust as symptoms of "an unprecedented crisis of self-confidence, borderline hysteria and massive depression." At the same time, Heschel dealt cautiously with the contentious issue of affirmative action, which had led many Jewish liberals to abandon the civil rights movement. Heschel urged Jews to continue to fight for blacks and other minority groups, but "not by gimmickry and quotas."[13]

During the summer in Los Angeles, his last, Heschel devoted himself to his two books on the Kotzker rebbe. In July he sent a nearly completed manuscript of the English volume, with the provisional title *A Passion for Sincerity*, to Roger Straus, who turned it over to Robert Giroux. Giroux had worked on some of Heschel's previous books and was not overly impressed: "It is certainly a worthy book, and very moving in many parts, but I found it diffuse and repetitive. It would gain from judicious editing and cutting, and I have every feeling that the author might consider every word sacrosanct."[14]

Straus conveyed this evaluation to Heschel in a diplomatic letter, adding details about royalties, distribution, and the reissuing of *Man Is Not Alone* and *God in Search of Man* under Farrar, Straus's Octagon imprint. Overall, Heschel had a lot to be pleased about, as well as significant revisions to undertake, when he returned the signed contract for *A Passion for Sincerity* on 9 August.[15]

As for the Yiddish manuscript on the Kotzker rebbe, following Heschel's tendency to proliferate ideas, it had expanded into two volumes. Heschel dated the preface 1 Elul 5732 (11 August 1972). This book in Yiddish brought closure to the most intimate, and the least known, dimension of his life, his first thirty-three years in Europe. In the dedication, he memorialized six men who supported him at crucial stages of life: Bezalel Levy, his tutor in Warsaw, who inculcated the severe integrity of Kotzk; Yitzhak Levin, a family friend and a disciple of the Kotzker who helped support Heschel's incipient secular studies financially; Leo Hirsch a writer in Berlin who promoted Heschel's poetry; David Koigen, who led a philosophy seminar that inspired Heschel to interpret Hasidism for moderns; the publisher Erich Reiss, who commissioned Heschel's biography of Maimonides and subsidized the publication of his doctoral dissertation on the prophets, without which Heschel would not have qualified for the life-saving academic position in the United States; and, finally, the sole American, the JTS professor Levi (Louis) Ginzberg, who hired Heschel and promoted his first American books.[16]

Children of Abraham

Heschel's intense writing program in Los Angeles was interrupted by an extraordinary invitation. For the first time in his life, he was asked to participate in an interfaith conference that included Muslims. This unpublicized four-day meeting on "a Spiritual Charter for Jerusalem" would take place in Rome from 29 August through 1 September. Heschel was frail and overworked. His friends, the physician Victor Goodhill and his wife Ruth, whose home he often visited, urged him not to attend. But driven by his passionate hope for peace, he could not refuse. Until then, Heschel had had little contact with Arabs, and he publicly supported the Israeli occupation of Arab territories conquered in 1967, though privately he shared doubts with his daughter and a few others. This was a chance to speak directly with Arabs. So Heschel made his final trip to Rome.[17]

At the conference Heschel reconnected with the ideals of Henry Corbin, a scholar of Islamic mysticism whom he had first met in Berlin in 1936. Corbin recognized in Heschel a kindred spirit: so impressed was Corbin with the Jewish scholar's unifying vision that in 1939 he translated large sections of Heschel's doctoral thesis on prophetic inspiration. Their interrupted dialogue about Judaism and Islam could now be completed.[18]

The Jerusalem project was initiated by George Appleton, an Anglican archbishop and metropolitan in Jerusalem, who for several years had traveled on peace missions to Arab countries and Israel, and by Paul Johnson, director of the American Friends Service Committee (AFSC) in the Middle East. Appleton consulted with Pope Paul VI, who approved the meeting, although the Curia did not permit official Vatican sponsorship. Organizers then conferred with Jerusalem's mayor, Teddy Kollek; Israeli Foreign Office officials; and Christian and Muslim figures in Jerusalem, Cairo, and Beirut. The AFSC was the official sponsor of the conference, with tacit Vatican support. [19]

The meetings took place at the Center for Mediterranean Studies on the piazza Cardelli. The twenty-five participants represented eight nationalities and included nine Christians, four Muslims, and six Jews; there were several observers, some from the Vatican. No reporters were present, no formal report was produced, and brief summaries released to the press did not name the participants. Prominent among the Jewish speakers were Rabbi Arthur Hertzberg, chairman of the American Jewish Congress, and R. J. Zwi Werblowsky, professor of comparative religions at the Hebrew University and president of the Interfaith Committee of Israel. Two of the Muslims were also academics, Serif Mardin (a Sunni), professor of political science at the Bogazici University in Istanbul and visiting professor at Princeton University, and Seyyed Hossein Nasr (a Shia or Sufi), vice chancellor and dean of faculties at Arymehr University in Tehran. (There were no Arab Muslims.)[20]

In such a contentious time, it was necessary to emphasize the possibility of a spiritual charter. To disarm potential disputes, the convener, Archbishop Appleton, developed a contemplative focus. "Each session began with a few moments of meditation, a reading from the Bible or the Koran, and existential, often unspoken reminders of the chairman that there was some transcendental value to the search for all present." Each session ended with a period of silence. Organizers reformulated political issues with such questions as "Is religion something of and by itself, or only the handmaiden of nationalism? Do we love Jerusalem, or do we love only the possession of Jerusalem?" Mayor Teddy Kollek made a particularly deep impression when he described the pluralistic makeup of the city.[21]

Heschel's role was to intervene informally in the deliberations. Pleased that the conference surpassed "religious politics," he was charming and at ease, especially in individual conversations. Above all, he hoped that sharing "spiritual anxiety" about Jerusalem would open hearts: "It is important for me to remember now that while I have prayed from the heart for the Muslims all my life . . . I have never been face-to-face with them to talk about God! This is *very* important. We must go further."[22]

Heschel led the opening devotions at the fourth and final session, on Friday, 1 September. He took the opportunity to dramatize the Jews' attachment to Jerusalem. Stating that the Haftarah portion from Isaiah would be read that Sabbath by Jews throughout the world, he recited the English text, which begins, "I will greatly rejoice in the Lord" (61:10), softly underscoring the final verses: "For Zion's sake, I will not hold my peace, and for Jerusalem's sake, I will not rest, until her triumph go forth as brightness and her salvation as a torch that burneth!" (62). He concluded with the passage on the Suffering Servant: "So He was their Savior. In all their affliction, He was afflicted, and the angel of His presence saved Him; in His love and His pity, He redeemed them" (63:8–9). Simply by reciting the sacred text, Heschel evoked his people's millennial exile from Jerusalem and their hope for its redemption.[23]

The prayers ended, Heschel sat down without another word. The room was silent. In this atmosphere the closing session began. Zwi Werblowsky and Serif Mardin each gave a talk, and John Coombs, an Australian Anglican priest and writer, discussed the spiritual charter. Archbishop Appleton closed the conference with a magnanimous summary: "Whatever may be the political settlement finally agreed, the pluralistic nature of Jerusalem will continue. The challenge is to have a love for the city and also a possibility of embracing all who love her."[24]

As Heschel slowly shuffled out, most of the others had already left, but the two Muslim professors remained. Serif Mardin pressed Heschel's hand and walked away without saying a word. Seyyed Hossein Nasr, now alone with Heschel, took his hand and said, "This is an unforgettable moment for me. I have read everything you have written I could find. God give you strength."[25]

Heschel and Nasr had been seated next to each other for most of the sessions and had developed a special understanding. Heschel was familiar with Nasr's books on Sufism and Islamic mysticism; Nasr knew Heschel's writings from when he and Corbin had taught them at Tehran University. These two scholars of Islam appreciated that Heschel's approach to religion was "not totally Westernized and Germanized like so many other Jewish philosophers who came out of Middle Europe." Nasr believed that Heschel's phenomenology of prophetic consciousness was analogous to the Arabic *kashfal-mahjub* (casting aside the veil of the veiled).[26]

During the conference, Heschel and Nasr had discussed their common mission to teach religion as a reality. In the future, they agreed, Jews and Muslims should develop their dialogue separately from Christians. Judaism and Islam had a spiritual continuity in common, while Christianity, imbued with Greek thought and Western secularism, had lost much of its Semitic character over the centuries. Jews and Muslims might begin with the patriarch Abraham, who in the Qur'an is called *chalil allah*, God's friend.

Returning to New York, Heschel shared his enthusiasm for the conference with his students. He asked Judith Herschlag at the ADL to airmail a copy of *Israel: An Echo of Eternity* to Nasr in Tehran. Heschel then wrote to Archbishop Appleton saying that he hoped to have the book translated into Arabic. Heschel soon found translators in Israel and immediately sent Appleton a $250 check to help him pay them. Heschel was a step closer to his lifelong dream of ultimate reconciliation: "The God of Israel is also the God of Syria, the God of Egypt. The enmity between the nations will turn into friendship."[27]

But Heschel had little time to savor these aspirations. Hopes for peace between Israel and its neighbors were crushed on 5 September when Arab terrorists (the term "Palestinian" was not yet current) infiltrated the Olympic Village in Munich, killing two Israeli athletes and taking nine others hostage. After twenty-four tense hours, German police and soldiers were able to kill the gunmen, but they had already murdered their captives, in what became known as the Munich Massacre. Rosh Hashanah began at sundown on 8 September, and Jews throughout the world mourned the slain athletes. The *New York Times* headlined the inevitable counterattack: "Scores of Israeli Planes Strike at 10 Guerrilla Bases in a Reprisal for Munich." The malignant cycle of violence was continuing.[28]

Jewish Infighting

In August, before he left for Rome, Heschel became involved in a humiliating squabble with the Jewish Theological Seminary over office space. After enduring more than twenty years in his uncomfortably crowded office, Room 603 in the Teachers Institute building, he proposed to David Kogen, the JTS administrative vice chancellor, that the Seminary allow him to move next door, to the larger Room 605, which was used by researchers in Talmud. Kogen told Heschel that he had no authority to grant his request and asked him to contact Finkelstein, who had retired as chancellor of the Seminary that June but still controlled that room.[29]

Heschel, frustrated and discomfited, and finding the situation demeaning, delayed. It was two months before he wrote to Finkelstein, pointing out the obvious fact that, "spending nearly all of my waking hours in my study at the Seminary," he needed more space to organize his "books and the vast collection of research materials and reflection, the fruit of so many years." The room was "crowded to suffocation" and he had even lost several pages of a manuscript that had been sent to a publisher. Could Finkelstein arrange a trade between Heschel and Rabbi Liss, who occupied Room 605?[30]

Finkelstein answered immediately, and in detail. He explained his obligation to retain the room as the Maxwell Abbell Research Room, named after a donor "whose heart was in Talmudic studies." Abbell had donated to the Seminary a building in Chicago worth about 20 million dollars. "Obviously,

I would have no right to take away a room set aside in his memory for a purpose which he cherished. Indeed, when I retired, I made it a condition that this room remain as it was intended to, unless replaced with another new building then planned."[31]

To placate Heschel, the Seminary constructed two bookcases outside his office, and the director of the Columbia University library was asked to allow Heschel "the use of a cubicle in your Library for his scholarly work," as if the dark stacks in Butler could compensate for the cramped quarters at JTS. This indignity typified numerous affronts Heschel had endured at JTS for years under the authority of Louis Finkelstein and Saul Lieberman. Once again, Heschel's creative life was troubled by associates devoted to academic Talmud research.[32]

Heschel became further alienated from JTS, this time quite openly, because of his support for presidential candidate George McGovern. Heschel believed that McGovern, a man of moral integrity, would be more beneficial to Americans—and to the Jews, as the saying goes—than the crafty Nixon and Kissinger. His advocacy of the liberal senator put him at odds with his inner circle, Seymour Siegel, Fritz Rothschild, and Wolfe Kelman.

On 4 August, the *Times* published an article whose headline told the whole story: "3 Jewish Leaders Back Nixon; Cite Policy on Israel as Reason." The three were Dr. William A. Wexler, chairman of the World Conference of Jewish Organizations; Rabbi Herschel Schacter, former chairman of the American Jewish Conference on Soviet Jewry and the Religious Zionists of America; and Seymour Siegel, a former Democrat who had now become committed to conservative politics. Siegel championed Nixon in a letter to the editor of the *New York Times* that was an answer to Rabbi David Greenberg, who felt that Jewish institutions should not be associated with specific political views. Referring tacitly to Heschel, Siegel defended his own support for the Republican Party: "It is also strange that Rabbi Greenberg did not object when others, including a world-famous theologian, urged the Jewish community to vote for Senator McGovern. If I can use a theological phrase, it depends on whose ox is being gored."[33]

Many other Jews faulted Heschel's political involvement, some in print. Months earlier, an unsympathetic Jewish journalist from the *Village Voice* had portrayed Heschel as careless at a McGovern speech on Israel at a Reform temple on the Upper West Side. The candidate had introduced Heschel as "the greatest living Jewish theologian," and the reporter noted that one of Heschel's admirers had flattered him by recalling McGovern's compliment. He then pointed out that when Heschel left the hall he didn't notice that his black yarmulke had fallen to the floor; the insinuation was that Heschel was not sincere.[34]

On 9 October several articles in the *New York Times* focused on the division among Jews. Page 1 reported, "G.O.P. Intensifies Drive to Attract Jews to Nixon," while the headline banner of the op-ed section announced the day's topic in bold type, "The Question of the Jewish Vote." Conspicuous was a provocative photograph of a young, bearded Jewish Defense League activist with fist raised and a placard reading, "Never Never, Never Never, Never Again!" The same page reprinted two opposing essays that were originally published in *Sh'ma*, the Jewish opinion journal. Eugene Borowitz, editor of *Sh'ma* and a leading theologian of Reform Judaism, supported McGovern and

Heschel and Senator George McGovern at Congregation Shaarei Tefillah in Manhattan. Photograph copyright © 1972 Diana Mara Henry / dianamarahenry.com.

criticized the Israel lobby. Borowitz deplored the "shameful self-interest" of Jews seeking to protect their economic privileges. Seymour Siegel praised Nixon: "McGovern's election would bring to power those whose morality would be very different than the majority of Americans."

Heschel was dismayed by both essays. He dispatched an indignant letter to the *Times,* which appeared on 27 October. The views expressed by his "former students"—Borowitz at HUC and Siegel at JTS—he stated, "depressed me deeply by the absence of any reference to the war in Vietnam, by the highly exaggerated claim of 'pressure the Israelis have put on US Jewry,' and above all, by the lack of any reference to the fundamental commitments that characterize Jewishness." Religious thinking must inform politics. Would Isaiah and Amos, he asked rhetorically, "accept the corruption in high places, the indifferent way in which the sick, the poor, and the old are treated?" The Hebrew prophets, Heschel claimed, would support gun-control legislation and oppose the war in Vietnam. "God's law" was an authority higher than nationalism, and McGovern was the candidate most likely to confront the violence of American society, on television, in the movies, on the streets. Heschel mailed out dozens of copies of his statement.

A rebuttal of Heschel's letter to the editor by Isaac Lewin, professor of history at Yeshiva University, appeared on 5 November, right before the election. Lewin praised Nixon for making "heroic efforts . . . to reach an agreement on Vietnam and to stop the violence." He deplored Heschel's contention that "Isaiah and Amos might be campaigning against the re-election of President Nixon and would be 'standing amidst those who protest against the violence of the war in Vietnam, the decay of our cities, the hypocrisy and falsehood that surround our present Administration.'" The professor concluded with a severe reprimand: "To accuse him [Nixon] of hypocrisy and falsehood is unfair and certainly not in the spirit of the Jewish sages who said (Talmud, tractate Berakoth 31a): 'One who suspects his neighbor of a fault which he has not committed must beg his pardon, nay more, he must bless him.'"

The conservatives had the last word. On 7 November 1972, President Richard Nixon won a landslide victory over George McGovern, who carried only Massachusetts and the District of Columbia. At Nixon's inauguration, on 20 January 1973, Rabbi Seymour Siegel pronounced a blessing in Hebrew and in English. Siegel had chosen the blessing that the Talmud prescribes for the appearance of a king and his court. He altered the prayer slightly but was still criticized for his choice. Heschel was not alive to witness it.[35]

Rabbi to the World

The opprobrium of many Jews was somewhat soothed for Heschel by the admiration of Christians, among whom he had achieved iconic stature. The day before the election, 6 November, Heschel received an honorary Doctorate of Humane Letters from the College of Saint Scholastica, a coeducational Benedictine institution in Wisconsin. The degree was awarded at an impressive ceremony at the University of Wisconsin, Superior, at which six colleges and universities were represented by their presidents, chancellors, and other officers. Father Francis X. Shea, the president of Saint Scholastica, read the citation to Heschel as "Rabbi to the World"—"because Christian belief in the incarnate God remains a development of Jewish humanism, because you stand as the latest and strongest voice of Jewish teaching in our contemporary world." Heschel responded, "To be honored is the way to learn how to honor others. And man is the instrument most important in uniting mankind." This was one of Heschel's last public appearances.[36]

The JTS Media Relations Office continued to promote Heschel. On 10 December, the Seminary and the National Broadcasting Company recorded an hour-long interview with Carl Stern, "Conversation with Doctor Abraham Joshua Heschel," as part of the *Eternal Light* television series. (It was aired in February the following year.) No one could predict that Heschel would die just two weeks later. Yet in this interview his body language betrayed considerable tension. With bags under his eyes, he sat stiffly on the edge of his chair, shuffling his file cards, as he often did when delivering a lecture or a speech. At one point his black yarmulke fell off his head; he didn't retrieve it until later, so absorbed he was in summarizing his life and thought for posterity.[37]

Heschel's final days of life were filled with drama. His last public act was a symbolic gesture of solidarity with Daniel and Philip Berrigan, an association that Heschel's critics deplored. Heschel's long-standing, though not uncritical, friendship with Daniel Berrigan had endured even after their ways had diverged. A founding member of Clergy Concerned About Vietnam, Daniel, along with his brother Philip, had soon moved beyond lobbying and mobilizations. The two launched a campaign of symbolic "crimes," such as splattering blood on Selective Service files, damaging missiles or airplanes at military bases, and burning draft cards with napalm. After the Berrigans and their allies became defendants in highly politicized trials, Daniel went "underground" to defy government authority. He was finally captured in August 1970 at the Block Island home of William Stringfellow, who had been a respondent to Heschel at the 1963 "Conference on Religion and Race."[38]

Heschel and other mainstream clergy admired the Berrigans' spirit of protest, without condoning their tactics and ideology. After they began to serve sentences in the Danbury Correctional Institution for destroying draft records, a group that included Heschel; Balfour Brickner; Lawrence M. Jones, acting president of Union Theological Seminary; and George W. Webber, president of New York Theological Seminary, appealed to authorities to allow the imprisoned clerics to distribute written or taped sermons to the outside—although Heschel strongly disagreed with Daniel Berrigan that serving time in prison was an effective way to bear witness. Better to work on the outside. In this respect, Heschel was a moderate who respected the rule of law and practical action. He did invite Berrigan to his class at JTS, where they and students debated these issues.[39]

On Wednesday morning, 20 December, Philip Berrigan was due to be released from the Danbury prison after completing a thirty-nine-month sentence. Heschel wanted to bear witness at the rally of his supporters. By this time Heschel's personal isolation was such that when he asked Wolfe Kelman to substitute for him in class he did not explain why. Because of their disagreement over Vietnam, Heschel had felt he had to hide the truth from his closest confidant. Thinking that his friend had a medical appointment Kelman quickly agreed. (Heschel's students, also uninformed about this act of moral protest, walked out of class and wrote a letter to the chancellor, Gerson Cohen, complaining of their teacher's neglect.)[40]

Well before dawn on Wednesday, which was cold and snowy, Daniel Berrigan and Tom Lewis, an artist and a Catholic activist, picked Heschel up at his apartment. Heschel asked permission to say his morning prayers in the car and was assured that the others would not be embarrassed. His worship moved the Catholics, who listened respectfully.[41]

At Danbury, Philip Berrigan emerged from the prison, giving a clenched-fist salute to the inmates at the windows. Then he and Daniel waved to the more than three hundred followers who had come to greet him, among them Heschel's daughter, Susannah, who came from Trinity College in Hartford. Pete Seeger sang protest songs and, with other notables, Heschel and the Berrigans walked about a mile to the Amber Room restaurant, where they held a religious service and a news conference in the ballroom. As Heschel left, he invited the brothers to tea at his apartment for Shabbat, 23 December.[42]

Heschel returned to JTS late that morning. His class was over, and as Kelman left the room, he saw Heschel standing in the corridor, shivering, out of breath. Heschel admitted that he had gone to Danbury and stood out in the cold waiting for Philip Berrigan's release. Kelman was hurt and angry; he practically carried Heschel, exhausted, back to his office.[43]

In his last week Heschel finished correcting the galley proofs of his most intimate book, the Yiddish biography of the Kotzker rebbe, *Kotzk: A Struggle for Integrity* (Kotsk: in gerangl far emesdikeyt). In addition, he was frantically completing the manuscript of the English-language version, *A Passion for Sincerity*, whose title he had discussed with several people, hesitating between *Sincerity* and *Truth*. The day before he died, Heschel brought Roger Straus the 580-page manuscript, which still required considerable editing.[44]

On Friday Jacob Teshima met Heschel in the hallway. Heschel was ecstatic; he had just mailed the corrected proofs of his Yiddish book to the publisher in Tel Aviv and delivered his manuscript in English to Farrar, Straus. That afternoon, Heschel told Fritz Rothschild about his plans to leave that Sunday for a two-week winter vacation with Sylvia and Susannah in Los Angeles.

Heschel and Daniel Berrigan on their way to greet Philip Berrigan,
who was being released from the Danbury Correctional Institute,
20 December 1972. Photograph © Tom Lewis. This is the
last known photograph of Heschel.

*Philip Berrigan on his release from prison, with
Daniel Berrigan, 20 December 1972. Courtesy of
the Swarthmore Peace Collection, Swarthmore,
Pennsylvania.*

Heschel at his desk, 1972. Photograph by Jacob Yuroh Teshima.

On the way to California, Heschel would stop in Chicago to perform the marriage of his former student Byron Sherwin. He told Teshima that he expected to visit Japan after February.[45]

The Heschels had invited several guests for Shabbat dinner. The list included a not unusual mixture: the family dentist Stanley Batkin and his wife, who were active in their Conservative synagogue in New Rochelle; the actor Joseph Wiseman and his wife, the dancer and choreographer Pearl Lang, who were good friends from the Yiddish-speaking and artistic worlds; and daughter Susannah with a friend from Trinity College.

After dinner Heschel, in a pensive mood, took his book of Yiddish poetry from a shelf and asked Joseph Wiseman to read "God follows me everywhere . . ." (Got geht mir nokh umetum . . .), which includes these mystical lines: "I go with my reveries as with a secret. . . . And sometimes I glimpse high above me, the faceless face of God." Eventually the guests left. We cannot fathom the turmoil in Heschel's spirit, as he went to bed. He did not wake up. He left this world peacefully, a sanctified departure on the Sabbath, between darkness and dawn. Like Moses, Heschel died with the kiss of God.[46]

20
A Pluralistic Legacy

*The Kotzker is still waiting for his disciples, for individuals who will
make explicit in concrete language what he hinted at by subtle
suggestion. They will be willing to stake their existence on the worth of
spreading his ideas from person to person through the generations,
guarding them from trivialization or desecration.*
—Heschel, *A Passion for Truth* (1973)

HESCHEL NOW BELONGED TO THE AGES. THE DIVERSE INDIVIDUALS AND COM-
munities he inspired, each according to their needs or understanding, began
immediately to honor him and promote his ideals. As a final irony, Heschel's
death was accompanied by Nixon's "Christmas bombings" of North Vietnam.
That very morning, 23 December 1972, page 1 of the *New York Times* announced: "U.S. to Continue Bombing; Says Next Move Is Hanoi's."

It was on Shabbat morning that Sylvia and Susannah discovered Heschel's
lifeless body. They rushed downstairs to tell the doorman and also went to Saul
Lieberman, who lived in the building. Then they began to call Christian
friends, who would not be in synagogue. Richard John Neuhaus was among
the first. Sylvia Heschel also telephoned the Berrigan brothers and asked
them to come at once and remain until others arrived.[1]

Neil Gillman and Seymour Siegel were at the JTS chapel when they were
asked to fetch Kelman, who was attending a bar mitzvah at the Spanish Por-
tuguese synagogue on Central Park West. After services they met Kelman on
the sidewalk and told him of Heschel's death. Despite the Sabbath prohibition
on traveling in a car, the three jumped into a cab and raced to the Heschel
apartment, where Sylvia and Susannah were still distraught. Pastor Neuhaus
was kneeling in prayer beside Heschel's bed. The Berrigan brothers arrived
soon thereafter; they too prayed at the bedside.

Kelman took over. He, Sylvia, and Susannah made telephone calls to family, close friends, and students, also informing the *New York Times*. As soon as
evening fell (early, in mid-winter), they called Heschel's Hasidic relatives in
Brooklyn (who would not answer the telephone on Shabbat). Soon afterward
Rabbi Moses Heschel, the young Kopitzhinitzer rebbe and a son of Heschel's
first cousin, arrived with other men to prepare the body for burial. Kelman
went out of his way to accommodate the Hasidim, who arranged everything
according to the strictest laws and customs. The body was removed from the
apartment carefully, to be returned to his ancestors.

It was later reported that two books lay on Heschel's night table, David
Halberstam's exposé of Nixon's war cabinet, *The Best and the Brightest,* and
the *Keter Shem Tov,* a Hasidic classic. These two books symbolized the dynamic coexistence of Heschel's two spheres of action, piety and political responsibility. The morning after Heschel's death, however, Sylvia Heschel
admitted to a friend that she had deliberately positioned the books there, re-
placing the *Newsweek* of 25 December 1972, which Heschel had been reading. (The cover story was on Paul Moore, Jr., who had just been consecrated
the Episcopal bishop of New York. Heschel knew Moore as a 1960s civil

rights and antiwar activist.) Sylvia felt that the books would be more appropriate. The mythologizing of Heschel had begun.[2]

The Funeral

Jews are usually buried within twenty-four hours of their death, but Heschel had made no specific arrangements for his funeral. Lieberman remembered that Heschel had once expressed the hope to be buried in Israel, but there were no documents verifying this. Kelman soon learned that Heschel had told his cousin Jacob Perlow that he wished to be buried near his uncle Yehudah Aryeh Leib Perlow, the Novominsker rebbe of Williamsburg.[3]

Kelman wanted the funeral to be conducted at the Jewish Theological Seminary, but there were difficulties. The next logical place would be the Conservative Park Avenue Synagogue, whose rabbi, Judah Nadich, was a close family friend. But the Hasidim would not enter a Conservative chapel. It was finally decided to hold the funeral on neutral territory, at Park West Memorial Chapel on 79th Street. The service began at 1:45 on Sunday, 24 December. Mayor John Lindsay, in an exceptional decision, ordered the street closed to traffic.

The overflow crowd testified to Heschel's many worlds. According to the *New York Times* there were five hundred people, including Mayor Lindsay; Christopher Mooney, president of the Jesuit Woodstock College; Samuel Belkin, president of Yeshiva University; Louis Finkelstein, chancellor emeritus of the Jewish Theological Seminary; Alfred Gottschalk, president of the Hebrew Union College; J. Brooke Mosley, president of Union Theological Seminary; and numerous colleagues, friends, and students.[4]

Many people had to remain outside the packed chapel. The coffin was placed in a small side room where black-suited Hasidim were chanting *tehillim* (psalms) over the body, according to Jewish custom and law. Fritz Rothschild, Yochanan Muffs, and Samuel Dresner, who flew in from Chicago, met in the room to pay their last respects, while Jacob Teshima checked to make sure that the white linen had been wrapped correctly to enshroud his beloved mentor. Sylvia and Susannah were distressed that their close friend, and Heschel's ally in the antiwar movement, William Sloane Coffin had not been invited to give the eulogy. He was an inspiring speaker, and he had loved Heschel. But Kelman felt that it was inappropriate for a Christian clergyman to participate in the ceremony. In addition, Reb Moses Heschel also insisted that Coffin not be included, and most of Heschel's colleagues at JTS disapproved of the minister's politics.[5]

It was a thoroughly traditional service. Susannah read from the Book of Chronicles in a trembling voice: "And thou Solomon, My son, know thou the God of thy father, and serve Him with a whole heart and a willing mind." This was the passage her father had cited in his dedication to her of *Who Is Man?* Elie Wiesel recited a Yiddish poem that Heschel had published in 1933, "God follows me everywhere . . . ," coincidentally the same poem Heschel had asked Joseph Wiseman to present at his last Shabbat gathering.[6]

Kelman gave the eulogy. As Heschel's closest friend and the executive vice president of the Rabbinical Assembly, he spoke of Heschel as both an individual and a model Jew. Quoting selections from Heschel's own 1945 *hesped* (eulogy) "for the slaughtered Jews of Eastern Europe," Heschel's reflections on aging from his speech at the 1961 White House conference, and other talks, Kelman praised Heschel's participation in the Selma–Montgomery march, his "reaffirming the integrity of Jerusalem and the holiness of the land of Israel," and his witness for peace in Vietnam.

Heschel's personality was both benevolent and judgmental, Kelman explained: "Above all, he loved and lived passionately. He hated sham and hypocrisy. . . . He had an unsurpassed gift for friendship and we who were blessed and touched by it are bereft." Heschel's love for, even veneration of, all human beings was the most palpable motive of his impassioned social action: "Repeatedly, he would remind me, as he emphasized in his writing, that the one unforgivable sin is *halbanat panim,* to cause the face of another human being to blanch by humiliating him. To shame another person is like murder, for it drains blood from the face and heart of the shamed and the downtrodden. . . . He wept for the humiliated and the massacred in Treblinka, Alabama, Haiphong, everywhere." Kelman concluded with the three final paragraphs of *Man Is Not Alone*: "For this act of giving away is reciprocity on man's part for God's gift of life. For the pious man it is a privilege to die."[7]

After the eulogy Samuel Dresner, Heschel's closest disciple, read from Psalm 15 (which Heschel had planned to read before the Selma–Montgomery march):

> Lord, who shall sojourn in Thy tabernacle?
> Who shall dwell upon Thy holy mountain?
> He that walketh uprightly, and worketh righteousness,
> And speaketh truth in his heart;
> That hath no slander upon his tongue,
> Nor doeth evil to his fellow.

Fritz Rothschild, Heschel's foremost interpreter, recited Psalm 42, a song of mystical longing, in both Hebrew and English:

> As the hart panteth after the water brooks,
> So panteth my soul after Thee, O God.
> My soul thirsteth for God, for the living God:
> "When shall I come and appear before God?"

To close the service, one of the Kopitzhinitzer Hasidim chanted in Hebrew the *El moley rahamim,* the plaintive petition of Jewish funeral services: "Lord of mercy, bring him under the cover of Thy wings, and let his soul be bound up in the bond of eternal life. Be Thou his possession, and may his repose be peace. Amen."[8]

When the service was over, according to custom, the coffin was carried for two blocks down the middle of 79th Street to the waiting hearse. The cortège to the Beth David Cemetery in Elmont, Long Island, was slowed by heavy traffic, and perhaps also because of the police escort. The trip took a full hour, and many people were lost along the way. The gravediggers were on strike, and it was feared that the burial place would not be ready.

The scene at the cemetery was pitiful and grotesque, reminiscent of Saul Anski's macabre play "The Dybbuk" or Japanese kabuki theater. It was raining and cold; mounds of wet dirt were scattered around; the ground was muddy and slippery. The hole was so big that some of the Hasidim worried that "their rebbe's grave" (the grave of Heschel's uncle) had been disturbed. As the black-suited pallbearers—among whom was a tall, thin Hasid who resembled Heschel, with white hair and goatee—lowered the coffin into the ground, someone slipped, the tapes twisted, and the coffin fell to the bottom of the pit, opening up, and exposing the white shrouds (*takhrikhin*) and tallit in which Heschel was wrapped. Heschel's ultimate helplessness was appalling.

In the ensuing consternation, Jacob Teshima realized that as a Gentile he could close the coffin (strictly Orthodox Jews considered it a defilement to touch an open coffin). He leapt into the open grave and closed the lid. Although one of the young Hasidim yelled in Yiddish, "Get the 'orel' [Gentile] out of the grave," Reb Moses told him that the Japanese Christian was worthy to restore the dignity of his teacher. The sorrow was unspeakable. The coffin was secured, and the widow and daughter, and other family members, friends and colleagues, in turn shoveled dirt into the grave, until it was completely filled. Seymour Siegel led the graveside service, and a Kopitzhinitzer Hasid slowly said the Kaddish one more time. Many cars returned to the city, while for those remaining there was a Minha (afternoon) prayer service at the cemetery administrative building.[9]

It was now time to sit shiva. A Jewish family in mourning remains at home for a week, receiving visits from friends and family. At the Heschel apartment on Riverside Drive there were three prayer services a day. As a woman, Susannah was not allowed to join the minyan: she and her mother had to stay in another room while the men prayed for the comfort of her father's soul. This ritual, with its painful exclusion, confirmed her commitment to feminism, which her father had supported.[10]

But the spirit of inclusiveness did have a place. At the end of shiva, Sylvia and Susannah took Teshima to another room to speak with Reb Moses Heschel. Teshima was afraid that he might have done something to offend the Orthodox Jews. Instead, the rebbe praised his spiritual sensitivity: "I have observed you for the entire week of *shiva*, and no one else has shown as much *kavanah*. I name you Reb Yaacov, and you are one of us, part of our family." This strictly Orthodox leader was one with his uncle's open spirit.[11]

Heschel for Posterity

An obituary in the *New York Times* appeared on the day of the funeral, along with a long article by Robert D. McFadden and excerpts from Heschel's writings. The *Jerusalem Post* of 29 December carried a life summary by Pinchas Peli, accompanied by Heschel's preface to his books on the Kotzker rebbe, which were about to appear in Israel and New York. Heschel was celebrated in the *Wall Street Journal*, *Time*, and *Newsweek*. Martin Marty announced in the *Christian Century*, "A Giant Has Fallen."[12]

In New York, a traditional memorial gathering took place on 21 January 1973, the thirtieth day (*shloshim*), in the presence of Heschel's widow and daughter at the Park Avenue Synagogue. Rabbi Judah Nadich led the proceedings, which brought together Jewish and Christian speakers: JTS chancellor Gerson Cohen; Fritz Rothschild; W. D. Davies, now professor at Duke University, who recalled Heschel's year at Union Seminary; and Coretta Scott King, who spoke of Heschel's partnership with her husband. The Israeli consul read a message from President Zalman Shazar, who praised Heschel's forthcoming books on the Kotzker rebbe.

In Rome, the pope confirmed Heschel's spiritual stature for people of all faiths. A Vatican communiqué printed in the *New York Times* on 2 February explained that "in an address to pilgrims attending the weekly general audience

in the Vatican, Pope Paul VI quoted a Jewish theologian, the late Rabbi Abraham J. Heschel of New York. The pontiff, who rarely quoted non-Christian
writers, used the words, 'before we have moved to seek for God, God has come
in search of us' from Rabbi Heschel's book *God in Search of Man*." Whatever
Heschel's weaknesses during Vatican II, his final legacy was one of positive
influence.[13]

Longer essays honoring Heschel soon appeared. The first was in the Jesuit
weekly *America*, whose editor, Donald R. Campion, S.J., stressed that this was
the first time a Christian magazine had devoted an entire issue "to contemporary Jewish religious thought and life." A dramatic drawing of Heschel (taken
from a Lotte Jacobi photograph) graced the red and black cover; inside were
essays by Louis Finkelstein, Fritz Rothschild, and Seymour Siegel from JTS,
and the Protestants John Bennett, W. D. Davies, and Jacob Neusner, of Brown
University, who contributed the powerful article "Faith in the Crucible of the
Mind." Father John C. Haughey, S.J., associate editor of *America*, wrote on
Heschel and prayer.[14]

A commemorative issue of *Conservative Judaism* included Heschel's essay
on death and the first English translation of one of his German articles on the
metaphysics of Ibn Gabirol. I contributed an interpretive essay, along with Edmond Cherbonnier, Avraham Holtz, and James Sanders; in addition the essays
by Finkelstein and Rothschild from *America* were reprinted. There was also a
tribute in Yiddish by Yudel Mark, Hebrew and English poems by Pinchas Peli,
and reminiscences by Moshe Starkman, Jacob Teshima, and Judith Herschlag
Muffs (who was now known as Yocheved; she had married one of Heschel's former students, Yochanan Muffs). The written expressions of grief and admiration
bore witness to the transformed lives of Heschel's disciples of the future.[15]

In February, the hour-long interview recorded on 10 December was broadcast nationally on NBC television. JTS made mimeographed transcripts available, and, eventually, videotapes. The conversation, with U.S. Supreme Court
correspondent Carl Stern, summarized Heschel's life and legacy. After surveying Heschel's Hasidic childhood, his openness to surprise, the paradox of God
in search of man, and the centrality of the Bible, Stern asked Heschel whether
he was a prophet. Heschel demurred: "I won't accept this praise. . . . It is a
claim almost arrogant enough to say that I'm a descendant of the prophets,
what is called *B'nai Nevi'im*. So let us hope and pray that I am worthy of being
a descendant of the prophets."[16]

Heschel and Stern spoke about civil rights, the dehumanization of politics,
the demands God makes on human beings, and religious pluralism as the will

of God. Heschel explained that he believed himself to be accountable to God: he "could not always control my mean leanings" without belief in God. When asked about life after death, Heschel answered curtly: "We believe in an afterlife. But we have no information about it. . . . I think that's God's business— what to do with me after life."[17]

When Stern brought up Heschel's role in the Second Vatican Council, Heschel completed his personal version of his summit meeting with Pope Paul VI by proudly recalling his "very strong rebuke" about choosing death in Auschwitz over conversion to Christianity. Then, contradicting Zachariah Schuster's secret eyewitness accounts and his own previous leaks, Heschel proclaimed: "And I succeeded in persuading even the Pope, the head of the Church, you realize; he personally crossed out a paragraph in which there was a reference to conversion or mission to the Jews. The Pope himself. And the declaration published by the Ecumenical Council—if you study it carefully,

Left to right: *Wolfe Kelman, Jacob Teshima, and Levi Kelman at Heschel's grave.* *Photograph by Morton Leifman, courtesy of Jacob Yuroh Teshima.*

you will notice the impact of my effort." Consciously or not, Heschel was idealizing his role in this historical event and placing it at the center.[18]

As the hour came to an end, Heschel addressed a message to the youth of America that he had prepared in advance. Telling young people, "There is a meaning beyond absurdity," Heschel identified the current trend of "drug addiction" as evidence of a widely felt search for exaltation. "Above all," he urged, "remember that the meaning of life is to build a life as if it were a work of art."[19]

It is customary to let a year pass before a headstone is placed on the grave of a Jew, but Heschel's grieving widow and daughter took longer. When Jacob Teshima visited the unadorned tomb of his mentor, he constructed a temporary memorial out of clay, which stated simply: "Abraham Joshua Heschel (1907–1972)." He drove to the cemetery with Morton Leifman, Wolfe Kelman, and Kelman's son Levi, and the four men said Kaddish over the makeshift tomb.[20]

Heschel's gravestone, to the right of the grave of his cousin Aaron Perlow; the grave of his uncle Rabbi Yehuda Aryeh Leib Perlow is behind them. Courtesy of Yitzhak Meir Twersky.

Some time later, with the help of Heschel's Hasidic family, a traditional stone was erected that listed his illustrious ancestry (yikhus) in Hebrew—adding, at Susannah Heschel's request, her grandmother's name:[21]

Here is buried
Abraham Joshua Heschel
the son of sainted Master
Our Rabbi Moshe Mordecai and Reizel Heschel
the grandson of the holy Rabbi
Baal Ohev Yisrael
and the holy Rabbi of Ruzhin
and the holy Rabbi of Berditchev
and of great sanctity
the Maggid of Mezritch
Who left this life on
18 Tevet 5733
May his soul be bound up
in the bond of everlasting life

Heschel joined his Hasidic ancestors, embodying in death as in life their spiritual aspirations for the modern world.

Notes

Part One. Cincinnati, The War Years

1. See Michael Meyer, "The Refugee Scholars Project of the Hebrew Union College," in Korn 1976, 359–75, and Michael Meyer, "A Centennial History," in Karff 1976, 123–28. See also Irving A. Mandel, "Lights in Exile," *Hebrew Union College Monthly* (February 1942): 12, 17; Julius Lewy, "Hitler's Contribution to the Teaching Staff of the Hebrew Union College," *Hebrew Union College Bulletin* (February 1945): 1–2, 15.

2. See Felix A. Levy, letter to Cyrus Adler, president of JTS, 17 September 1937, about Elbogen's wish to emigrate; William Rosenau, letter to Adler, 7 October 1937, enclosing a letter from Elbogen's son; letter from Rosenau to Adler, 25 October 1937; Louis Finkelstein, letter to Ismar Elbogen, 14 April 1938: "As for the Seminary itself, the fact is that with our limited faculty and diminishing financial resources we simply cannot do as much as we would like with regard to the situation"; Finkelstein, letter to Elbogen, 18 April 1938: "It would not be in the interest of the rabbinate in America or Judaism in America, or Judaism in the world

that these standards should be altered. I am sure you recognize this," JTS General Files, Faculty Records, 3B, 1–9.

3. Julian Morgenstern, letter to the Honorable A. M. Warren, 2 July 1939, 1–2, American Jewish Archives, Cincinnati. The original list submitted by Morgenstern included ten names: Eugen Täubler, Franz Landsberger, "Dr. Walter Gottschalk, former Instructor in Semitics at the University of Heidelberg, more recently head of the Near-East Department of the Berlin Staatsbibliotek," Isaiah Sonne, "Dr. Albert Lewkowitz, for 24 years Professor of Jewish Philosophy and Theology at the Jewish Theological Seminary in Breslau," Alexander Guttmann, Max Weiner, Arthur Spanier, and Franz Rosenthal. Heschel was ninth on the list. Lewkowitz chose to go to Palestine; Spanier, who did not receive a visa, was deported to Bergen-Belsen and murdered. See Susannah Heschel 1996, xviii–xix.

Chapter 1. First Year in America

1. *New York Times,* 22 March 1940; interview with Arnold Jacob Wolf, who witnessed Heschel's conversation, in Yiddish, with the father of Eugene Borowitz about the incident on the dock. Rabbi Borowitz does not remember this conversation and doubts that it occurred, but I consider the anecdote plausible.

2. Heschel, letter to Morgenstern, 21 March 1940, American Jewish Archives, Cincinnati. See Kaplan and Dresner 1998, 302–3. Burrows's review is in *Journal of Biblical Literature* 56 (1937): 398–400. Millar Burrows, ordained at Union Theological Seminary, later led the team of scholars who published the Dead Sea Scrolls.

3. In a letter to Buber of 11 June 1938, Heschel used a favorite analogy from mathematics to characterize his job at HUC as a temporary stabilizing force: Martin Buber Archive, Jerusalem, MsVar. 290:15. All of Heschel's letters to Buber are in this archive. See Kaplan and Dresner 1998, 270. Finkelstein, letter to Heschel, 16 March 1938, JTS General Files. See Kaplan and Dresner 1998, 269.

4. Finkelstein 1973, 203–4; Heschel, letter to Morgenstern, 27 March 1940; Heschel, letter to Mordecai Kaplan, 29 March 1940; Morgenstern, letter to Heschel, 1 April 1940; Heschel, letter to Morgenstern, 8 April 1940, American Jewish Archives, Cincinnati.

5. Interview with Eugene Borowitz.

6. Interviews with Eugene Borowitz, Albert Plotkin.

7. Heschel, letter to Buber, 16 April 1940, MsVar 290:38.

8. Ibid.; Heschel, letter to Eduard Strauss, 21 April 1940, Leo Baeck Institute Archives, New York. Even before Heschel was expelled from Germany on 28 October 1938, he kept in touch with Eduard Strauss by mail. Heschel's letters to Strauss are preserved at the Leo Baeck Institute Archives.

9. Meyer, "Centennial History," in Karff 1976, 126–27.

10. Julius Lewy, "Hitler's Contribution," *Hebrew Union College Bulletin* (February 1945): 15.

11. Albert Plotkin took the streetcar with Heschel to the black neighborhood. Heschel also took Samuel Dresner to Harris's church. Interviews with Samuel Dresner, Arnold Jacob Wolf, Albert Plotkin; Larry D. Harris, letter to author.

12. In 1930 Heschel's philosophy professor at the Hochschule, Julius Guttmann, moved to Cincinnati to teach at HUC but, finding it incompatible, quickly returned to Berlin. See Meyer, "Centennial History," in Karff 1976, 110.

13. Plaut 1980, 3.

14. Sefton D. Temkin, "A Century of Reform Judaism in America," *American Jewish Year Book* (1973): 3–75 (quotation on p. 60).

15. Interviews with Stanley Dreyfus, Eugene Borowitz.

16. Interview with Jacob Rader Marcus; see also Elinor Grumet, "A Moment Interview with Jacob Rader Marcus," *Moment* (March–April 1981), A75–A85; Silberman 1971.

17. Interview with Albert Plotkin.

18. The HUC catalog of 1940–41 praised the library's important collection as its greatest resource after the faculty. Dresner 1985, "Heschel as a Hasidic Scholar."

19. Krome 2002; Meyer, "Centennial History," in Karff 1976, 73, 118–19.

20. See Deutsch 1995–96, vol. 2, pp. 84–88, 90–91, 104; Ezra Spicehandler, "A Survey of Scholarly Contributions," and "Hebrew and Hebrew Literature," in Karff 1976, 462; and Michael Meyer, "Refugee Scholars," in Korn 1976. Wilensky kept up his relationship with Rabbi Schneerson, to whom he willed his personal book collection.

21. Note of Samuel Dresner, Heschel Archive.

22. Declaration of intention to become a U.S. citizen, Certification no. 9–24996, 15 May 1940. Heschel acquired the official Petition for Naturalization, no. 17894, on 28 May 1945 at the District Court of the United States, Cincinnati, Ohio. Witnesses were Amy Blank, 201 Lafayette Circle, Cincinnati, and Bertha Feinberg, 3562 Lee Place, Cincinnati, who certified that they had known Heschel since 5 April 1940; signed 17 April 1945. United States District Court, Southern District of Ohio. Duplicates from U.S. Department of Justice, Immigration and Naturalization Service, Washington, D.C. See Chapter 2 for more on Blank and Feinberg and their friendships with Heschel.

23. Preliminary announcement of "Conference on Science, Philosophy, and Religion in Their Relation to the Democratic Way of Life," held on 9, 10, 11 September 1940 at the Jewish Theological Seminary, press release, JTS General Files. See Fred W. Buettler, "For the World at Large: Intergroup Activities at the Jewish Theological Seminary," in Wertheimer 1997, vol. 2, pp. 667–736. Einstein alluded to a famous Kantian dictum: "Thoughts without content are empty, intuitions without concepts are blind" (Kant, *Critique of Pure Reason*, trans. Norman Kemp Smith [New York: Modern Library, 1958], A51, B75). In *Man Is Not Alone*, Heschel countered

with his version: "*Faith without reason is mute; reason without faith is deaf*" (Heschel 1951, 173).

24. Stenographic transcript of "Proceedings: Conference on Science, Philosophy and Religion in Their Relation to the Democratic Way of Life," microfilm, JTS General Files, 9–11 September 1940, boxes 2, 3.

25. Einstein's article appeared in the 13 September 1940 issue of *Aufbau*, which was published by the German-Jewish Club. Heschel's essay appeared the following week, 20 September 1940. Einstein's essay is reprinted in *Science, Philosophy and Religion: A Symposium* (1941; New York: Kraus Reprint, 1971), 209–14.

26. Albert Einstein, "God's Religion or Religion of the Good?" *Aufbau*, 13 September 1940, cited in Heschel 1940, "Antwort an Einstein." I thank Susannah Buschmeyer for translating Einstein's article for me.

27. Heschel 1940, "Antwort an Einstein," trans. Susannah Buschmeyer. Further quotations in the text are from this source. Heschel's ironic epigraph—"The Goddess of truth dwells in the temple of nature"—targeted a materialistic pantheism derived from Ernst Haekel, the nineteenth-century German zoologist-philosopher whose 1899 *Riddles of the World,* was the "gospel" of materialistic Darwinism. Heschel rejected Haekel's vague monism or animism in which spirit and nature appear to be identical.

28. Heschel, letter to Eduard Strauss, 17 November 1940, Leo Baeck Institute Archives; Eugene Mihaly, letter to Samuel Dresner, 6 March 1979: "I do have a faint recollection that some 15 or 20 years ago I was asked to look at [Diesendruck's] manuscript with a view towards editing it. At that time, however, I found it in such a disorganized and incomplete state that I did not feel that I could devote the several years which would have been required to get the manuscript ready for publication," Heschel Archive.

29. Heschel had earlier explored this same territory in his 1934 tribute to David Koigen, his deceased mentor from Berlin. Kaplan and Dresner 1998, chap. 13, "Spiritual and Intellectual Biographies: Koigen and Maimonides," 194–97.

30. Heschel 1941–42, "Zevi Diesendruck." Further quotations in the text are from this source. See also Meyer, "A Centennial History," in Karff 1976, 110, 111, 131; Lou H. Silberman, "Theology and Philosophy: Some Tentative Remarks," in Karff 1976, 408–15, 417; Ezra Spicehandler, "Hebrew and Hebrew Literature," in Karff 1976, 461, 468.

Chapter 2. Hebrew Union College

1. The other refugee professors, though not on the faculty, were designated "special instructors," a higher position than "fellow." HUC catalog, 1940–41, Registrar's roster, and letter from Rosalind Chaiken, HUC registrar, American Jewish Archives, Cincinnati.

2. HUC catalog, 1941–42, 1–3; Julius Lewy, "Hitler's Contribution to the Teaching Staff of H.U.C.," part 2, *Hebrew Union College Bulletin* (April 1945): 8–10.

3. See Gerhart Saenger, "The Psychology of the Refugee," *Contemporary Jewish Record* 3 (1940): 264–73 (orig. "Strangers Within Our Gates," *American Scholar* [spring 1940]); the Hellenist Eugen Täubler was particularly judgmental, according to Marcus: "The HUC faculty treated Täubler kindly, and he despised them," interview with Jacob Rader Marcus. Ordained at HUC in 1920, after completing a doctorate at the University of Berlin, Marcus eventually created the entire discipline of American Jewish history. See Martin A. Cohen, "History," in Karff 1976, 436–40.

4. See Kaplan and Dresner 1998, chap. 3, "The Blessings of Humiliation," 37–55.

5. Interview with Albert Plotkin; Lou Silberman, "Theology and Philosophy," in Karff 1976, 415–17. "Morgy," as the president was called on campus, was the quintessential Reform rabbi of his generation. Born in St. Francisville, Illinois, into a poor family of German Jewish origin, he was "confirmed" at age thirteen and entered HUC the same year. After completing eight years of study and an undergraduate degree at the University of Cincinnati, he was ordained at HUC in 1902. Morgenstern went on to earn a doctorate at the University of Heidelberg, with a thesis on Babylonian religion. After serving a congregation in Indiana, he returned to HUC to teach Bible, specializing in the prophetic Book of Amos (hence the quip, "Amos 'n' Morgy," after the popular radio program *Amos 'n' Andy*). He became HUC president in 1921 (defeating David Philipson, who actively sought the post) and from then on devoted his life to the college. He was involved in all decisions large or small and was responsible for forming the institution as Heschel knew it. See Michael Meyer, "American Rabbis for American Israel," in Karff 1976, 85–136, the best short history of Morgenstern's presidency.

6. Interview with Jacob Rader Marcus.

7. Interview with Albert Plotkin.

8. Ibid. Plotkin sometimes accompanied Heschel to the symphony. Heschel also developed a friendship with James G. Heller, the rabbi of the more moderate Reform congregation, B'nai Jeshurun, another music lover, who wrote program notes for the orchestra.

9. Interview with Jacob Rader Marcus. Marcus admitted that he and Heschel "were not close," a huge understatement. See also conversations with Sylvia Heschel; Susannah Heschel 1996, xx.

10. *Day Book of Service at the Altar as Lived by Samuel S. Cohon* (Los Angeles: Harelich and Ruth, 1978), 20–21. On Cohon see Meyer, "American Rabbis," in Karff 1976, 95; Michael Meyer, "Samuel S. Cohon: Reformer of Reform Judaism," *Judaism* 15 (1966): 319–28. Cohon wrote *What We Jews Believe* (1931) and was theology editor of the *Universal Jewish Encyclopedia* (1939).

11. *Day Book of Service*, 20–21. Cohon felt unappreciated by his colleagues and students at HUC, despite his prominence in the Reform rabbinical association. In addition,

he may have sensed that his extensive theological writings lacked coherence and clarity. According to the sympathetic but discriminating Lou Silberman, "[Cohon's] understanding of the Holy One in philosophical terms as transcendent, in ethical terms as the numinous, never came together in a compelling and commanding unity. The word awaited seemed always behind his lips, never on them," Lou Silberman, "Samuel S. Cohon: Holiness as Feeling," in Karff 1976, 407.

12. Interview with Miriam Blank Sachs; see also Sheldon Blank, "Bible," in Karff 1976, esp. 296–300.

13. Interviews with Stanley Dreyfus, Arnold Jacob Wolf, Maurice Davis; Dresner memorandum, 31 August 1999, Heschel Archive; Michael Meyer, letter to Samuel Dresner, 1 September 1999. See Meyer, "American Rabbis," in Karff 1976, 93–94.

14. Brav 1965, 137.

15. Abraham Cronbach, "The Social Training of the Rabbi," *Hebrew Union College Bulletin* 3, 3 (March 1944): 1–2, 8; for a profile of Cronbach, see pp. 7–8.

16. Dresner memorandum, 31 August 1999, Heschel Archive.

17. Frances Fox Sandmel, "Reminiscence of HUC Faculty-Student Gatherings," *CCAR Journal* (Autumn 1976): 91; interview with Maurice Davis.

18. Interview with Shulamit Eden.

19. Works Projects Administration Writers' Program, eds., *The Ohio Guide* (New York: Oxford University Press, 1940), 214; interview with Pesach Krauss.

20. See Dresner 1970, 32–36, and Krauss 1988, 143–44; interview with Albert Plotkin.

21. Dresner memorandum, June 1989, Heschel Archive.

22. Silver did not appreciate the Conservative movement either. In 1935 the Agudat Harabonim issued a herem against a legal innovation by the Conservative movement regarding the vexed issue of *agunah*, women who were unable to obtain a religious divorce from their husbands and so were unable to remarry. See Rakeffet-Rothkoff 1981, 114–15; Sarna 2004, 240–42.

23. Rakeffet-Rothkoff 1981, 163.

24. See Zuroff 2000; Rakeffet-Rothkoff 1981, 156–69, 192 ff.

25. Interviews with Shulamit Eden, Ada Brodsky (David's widow). Brodsky soon enlisted in the American army. After the war, in 1946, he immigrated to Palestine, supported by the G.I. Bill, to study at the Hebrew University.

26. Archival documents pertaining to Heschel's Midrasha are rich: Simcha Kling, letter to Samuel Dresner, 23 June 1988; interviews with Hanna Grad Goodman, Hanna Rosen, Nehama (Levin) Weiner, Pesach Krauss, Heschel Archive.

27. Interview with Hanna Rosen.

28. Krauss 1988.

29. Interview with Arnold Jacob Wolf.

30. Hannah Grad Goodman, letters to Samuel Dresner, 28 February 1983, 15 January 1984. She left Cincinnati in 1944 to join her husband, who had been transferred to Washington, D.C.

31. See Lipstadt 1986; Heschel, letter to Eduard Strauss, 30 March 1941, Leo Baeck Archives.

32. Heschel 1939, "Das Gebet als Äusserung und Einfühlung"; Heschel 1941, "'Al Mahut ha-Tefillah"; Heschel 1941, "Das Gebet"; both articles appeared the following spring: Heschel 1942, "An Analysis of Piety"; Heschel 1942, Review of Salo Wittmayer Baron's *Essays on Maimonides.*

33. Heschel 1941, "A Concise Dictionary of Hebrew Philosophical Terms," intro.

34. Heschel, letter to Eduard Strauss, 21 January 1942, Leo Baeck Institute Archives.

35. The copyright page of *Man Is Not Alone* carried this note: "My thanks are due to Doctor Fritz Kaufmann of the University of Buffalo for his kindness in reading the manuscript."

36. See Kaplan and Dresner 1998, 258–59.

37. *Hebrew Union College Bulletin* (March 1942), 16.

38. Krome 2002; Heschel, letter to Buber, 1 March 1942, MsVar. 290:39.

39. Heschel, letters to Buber, 2 June 1942, 1 March 1943, MsVar. 290:40–41. See Sarna 1989.

40. Heschel, letter to Buber, 2 June 1942, MsVar. 290:40.

41. Dresner 1985, xxvii–xxix; Heschel 1942, "An Analysis of Piety," 302–3.

42. Heschel 1942, "An Analysis of Piety," 298; see Edward Kaplan 1996, chap. 3, "Learning to Think Religiously," 33–43.

43. Heschel 1942, "An Analysis of Piety," 307.

44. Heschel, letter to Strauss, 24 October 1941, Leo Baeck Institute Archives.

45. The full title of John Dewey's book was *The Quest for Certainty: A Study of the Relation Between Knowledge and Action.* That same year Louis Finkelstein edited a volume on Saadia for the Jewish Theological Seminary, featuring articles by the faculty, including Alexander Marx, Abraham S. Halkin, Ben Zion Bokser, and Robert Gordis. See the sympathetic and meticulous review of Heschel's and Finkelstein's volumes by Nahum Glatzer of Boston Hebrew Teachers College in *The Review of Religion* 9, 1 (November 1944): 56–62. See also Jonathan Sarna, "Two Traditions of Seminary Scholarship," in Wertheimer 1997, 2:53–80. Heschel 1944, *The Quest for Certainty in Saadia's Philosophy,* 45. Heschel continued, using one of his favorite images: "This view was not a tactical stratagem. What Saadia did might be described, if we were allowed to speak figuratively, as the setting up of a system of co-ordinates, with faith as an abscissa and reason as an ordinate, which should determine the validity of any thought, religious or secular." See also Heschel, letter to Buber 11 June 1938, and Heschel 1951, *Man Is Not Alone.*

46. Heschel 1944, *The Quest for Certainty in Saadia's Philosophy,* 55, 25.

1. HUC catalog, 1942–43.
2. Interview with Jacob Rader Marcus.
3. Interview with Celia Atlas.
4. *Encyclopaedia Judaica*, s.v. "Atlas," 829; interview with Stanley Dreyfus. In Berlin, Atlas began a lifelong friendship with Rabbi Yechiel Weinberg, rector of the Orthodox Rabbinical Seminary and considered one of the most outstanding Talmudic *poseks* (legal decision makers) of his era. See Marc B. Shapiro, "Scholars and Friends: Rabbi Yechiel Jacob Weinberg and Professor Samuel Atlas," *Torah U-Madda Journal* 7 (1997): 105–21.
5. Rubenstein 1974, 89–90.
6. HUC, faculty minutes, 2 February 1942, American Jewish Archives, Cincinnati.
7. *Hebrew Union College Bulletin* (November 1942), "Campus Chatter," 9–11; HUC, faculty minutes, 2 February 1942, American Jewish Archives, Cincinnati.
8. Material from several interviews with Arnold Jacob Wolf.
9. Interview with Samuel Dresner; numerous conversations with Dresner and his wife, Ruth, as well as Dresner memoranda in Heschel Archive. Rabbi Elliot Gertel has collected Dresner's sermons; he also wrote an excellent obituary of Dresner. See my introduction to Dresner's posthumous *Heschel, Hasidism, and Halakha* (2002), ix–xiii.
10. Gertel, "Remembering Rabbi Samuel H. Dresner," *National Jewish Post and Opinion* (24 May 2000), 12.
11. Interviews with Albert Plotkin, Sidney Brooks, Arnold Jacob Wolf, Richard D. Hirsch, Eugene Borowitz.
12. Interview with Marvin Fox.
13. Interview with Arnold Jacob Wolf.
14. Interview with Albert Plotkin. Heschel shared another Berlin experience with his daughter: one evening he was attending the opera when Adolf Hitler entered. Everyone rose to their feet, except Heschel, refusing to look at the man who defiled God's image (Susannah Heschel 1996 xiv).
15. Interview with Albert Plotkin.
16. Interview with Eugene Borowitz. Borowitz became Reform Judaism's preeminent theologian. He still dresses carefully, with the awareness of *hiddur Torah*, honoring the Torah, that he learned from Heschel.
17. Interview with Maurice Davis.
18. Interview with Albert Plotkin.
19. Faierstein 1999, 272–74. The interview with Gershon Jacobson was originally published in Yiddish in the *Day-Morning Journal*, 13 September 1963.
20. Penkower 1985, 97–98. See also Medoff 1996.
21. Penkower 1985, 98; Faierstein 1999, 272.

22. Faierstein 1999, 272.

23. Hayim Greenberg, "Under the Axis" and "The Plan of Destruction," *Jewish Frontier* (19 November 1942), 3, 4–9.

24. Greenberg 1964, 5. See also obituary of Hayim Greenberg, *New York Times*, 15 March 1953, 93.

25. Greenberg 1964, 8, 5.

26. From the cover of *The Reconstructionist* (3 November 1944), in which part 1 of Heschel's article "Faith" appeared; interview with Ira Eisenstein. See Scult 2002.

27. Heschel, letter to Mordecai Kaplan, 3 February 1943, Heschel Archive.

28. Heschel 1943, "The Meaning of This War," 2. Unless otherwise indicated, future quotations in the text are from this version. See Edward Kaplan 1996, 188n10.

29. Interview with Arnold Jacob Wolf.

30. Heschel 1944, "The Meaning of This War," 20.

31. *Jewish Currents* (April 1991): 4.

32. Susannah Heschel 1996, xix; Erwin L. Herman, letter to Samuel Dresner, 12 December 1978, Heschel Archive.

33. Interview with Albert Plotkin.

34. Heschel 1943, "The Holy Dimension," 117.

35. Ibid., 120–21.

36. HUC, faculty minutes, 11 April 1943; HUC, faculty minutes, 23 April 1943, American Jewish Archives, Cincinnati.

37. HUC, minutes of the Board of Governors, 12 May 1943, American Jewish Archives, Cincinnati.

38. HUC, faculty minutes, 20 May 1943. Other relevant events are recorded, including that a "petition dated October 28th [1943], signed by 35 members of the Student Body, requesting that a course in Yiddish be introduced into the curriculum, was considered by the Faculty." The petition was referred to the Committee on Curriculum, which was asked to report back as soon as possible to the faculty: American Jewish Archives, Cincinnati.

39. After praising the other European scholars, Morgenstern wrote: "Abraham Heschel adds a great philosophical background to the reputation of the Hebrew Union College. . . . Pedagogically he makes use of several of his manifold accomplishments by offering his students a rare insight into the fields of Bible, Commentaries, Modern Hebrew and Philosophy," *Hebrew Union College Bulletin* (November 1943), 4–5.

40. HUC, report prepared by Murray Seasongood, Hiram B. Weiss, and James G. Heller, discussed at the faculty meeting of 11 April 1943, 1–2, American Jewish Archives, Cincinnati.

41. Ibid. Morgenstern responded to the humbling alumni survey skillfully. At the April 1943 meeting of the Board of Governors he presented an ambitious policy statement, which he set before the faculty on 12 May. In it he developed a concise

overview of the college from 1930 to 1943 and asserted that HUC "occupies an outstanding and leading position" among Jewish institutions, including the Hebrew University in Jerusalem (Report of the President to the Board of Governors, 30 April 1943, faculty minutes, American Jewish Archives, Cincinnati).

Chapter 4. Architecture of a New Theology

Note to epigraph: This cry of anguished faith resounds throughout Heschel's works: see Heschel 1970, "On Prayer," 7; Edward Kaplan 1996, 150–51.

1. Penkower 1985, 100–107, no. 10, on the failed rescue resolution; Greenberg 1964.
2. Rakeffet-Rothkoff 1981, chap. 8, "The Va'ad Hatzala in Despair and Reconstruction," 217 ff. The following year, Silver admonished President Roosevelt about the Auschwitz concentration camp, 223. See Zuroff 2000, for a more complex view.
3. See "Rabbis Present Plea to Wallace," *New York Times*, 7 October 1943, 7; Sarna 2004, 263–64; and Arthur Hertzberg, introduction to a special project of the David S. Wyman Institute for Holocaust Studies, 21 January 2005; Rafael Medoff, "The Day the Rabbis Marched," the David S. Wyman Institute for Holocaust Studies, both at wymaninstitute.org/special/rabbimarch/pg08p.
4. "Rabbis Present a Plea to Wallace," 14.
5. HUC catalog, 1944–45; see Kaplan and Dresner 1998, 291–92; Rothschild 1973.
6. See Kaplan and Dresner 1998, 262; Finkelstein, letters to Heschel, 23 March 1942 and 7 June 1943, JTS General Files.
7. *Hebrew Union College Bulletin* (January 1944), 8. In the same issue it was announced that "Drs. Abraham Heschel and James G. Heller eulogized Saul Tchernikovsky at a recent memorial meeting held at the Cincinnati Rockdale Temple Annex. In tribute to his memory, Dr. Heschel spoke eloquently in Hebrew." Heschel, letter to Morgenstern, [August 1944]; Morgenstern, letter to Heschel, 18 August 1944, American Jewish Archives, Cincinnati. In March, Heschel gave two lectures in Chicago, "Prayer and the Inner Life of Man" and a talk relating to his Hebrew work, "The Prophetic Experience in the Middle Ages," *Hebrew Union College Bulletin* (March 1944), Faculty Notes, 13, American Jewish Archives, Cincinnati. Heschel's two foundational monographs, published in Hebrew in 1945 and 1950, did not appear in English translation until 1996, in *Prophetic Inspiration After the Prophets.*
8. *Hebrew Union College Bulletin* (January 1944), 8. In 1967 Abraham Weiss settled in Israel.
9. Contributors to the Schorr volume included Samuel Atlas, Julius Lewy, and Julian Morgenstern of HUC; Louis Finkelstein, Saul Lieberman, and Louis Ginzberg of JTS; Abraham Weiss of Yeshiva University; Salo W. Baron of Columbia University; and Chanokh Albeck, Judah Bergmann, Umberto Cassuto, and Harry Torczyner (Tur-Sinai) of the Hebrew University in Jerusalem: *Kovež Madda'i le-Zekher Moshe Schorr*

(Studies in Memory of Moses Schorr, 1874–1941), ed. Louis Ginzberg and Abraham Weiss (New York: Professor Moses Schorr Memorial Committee, 1944). The text published by Heschel was not appreciated by specialists until Moshe Idel, the innovative interpreter of Kabbalah and Jewish mysticism, cited it in his 1976 doctoral dissertation for the Hebrew University. See Moshe Idel, "Ramon Lull and Ecstatic Kabbalah: A Preliminary Observation," *Journal of the Warburg and Courtauld Institutes* 51 (1988): 171n11.

10. Finkelstein, letter to Heschel, 7 August 1944; Heschel, letter to Finkelstein, 11 August 1944, JTS General Files; Heschel 1944, Review of Gershom Scholem's *Major Trends in Jewish Mysticism*.

11. See Edward Kaplan 1996, chap. 9, "Metaphor and Miracle: Modern Judaism and the Holy Spirit," 133–46.

12. Heschel 1944, "Faith," pt. 1, pp. 10, 13.

13. Ibid., pt. 2, pp. 13, 14.

14. Ibid., 16.

15. Heschel, letter to Morgenstern, August 1944 ("I managed to find a large and very beautiful room [on Riverside] Drive. I work at home most of the time and have finished my study on "Prophecy after the cessation of prophecy"); Morgenstern, letter to Heschel, 18 August 1944, American Jewish Archives. Susannah Heschel 1996, xvii–xix. Spanier was arrested in Holland in 1942 and sent to Bergen-Belsen, where he was murdered.

16. Heschel, letter to Finkelstein, 30 January 1945, JTS General Files; *Newsletter of the YIVO* (February 1945): 5. For the best analysis of this episode with precise bibliographical references, see Shandler 1993, 268–84. See also Neusner 1981, 82–96. The final session began with a scholarly paper by Harry Orlinsky of the Jewish Institute of Religion, followed by activist representatives of the Workman's Circle, the Pioneer Women's Organization, the Sholem Aleichem Folk Institute, the Central Yiddish Culture Organization, and the International Ladies' Garment Workers' Union; see *New York Times*, 8 January 1945, 17. About 1,400 persons were an attendance. *Newsletter of the YIVO* (December 1944 and February 1945).

17. See Kaplan and Dresner 1998, 261; Shandler 1993, 269n41, 271.

18. Heschel 1946, "The Eastern European Era in Jewish History," 89 ("Frequently, in Ashkenazic literature, the form is shattered by the overflow of feeling, by passion of thought, and explosive ecstasy"), 94.

19. Ibid., 105.

20. Ibid., 106.

21. *Newsletter of the YIVO* (February 1945), 5.

22. "When [Heschel] finished speaking, the audience of several thousands was moved to tears, and a spontaneous Kaddish was uttered by many who were committed secularists and nonbelievers," Deborah Dash Moore 1990, preface; cf. Shandler 1993, 275n60; Rabbi Philip R. Alstat, review of *The Earth Is the Lord's*,

Jewish Examiner (24 March 1950). (A brief article in the *New York Times* of 8 January 1945 headlined Joseph Lestchinsky's account of the 6 million European Jews who had been exterminated, which was also presented at that final session.) It is likely that memories of Heschel's first speech were confused with impressions surrounding the address he gave two years later, at the twenty-first annual YIVO meeting—this time, in fact, at the opening session and to a larger audience. Nearly 3,000 persons heard Heschel consider "The Meaning of Jewish Existence" at the Hunter College Assembly Hall on 18 January 1947. See *News of the YIVO* (February 1947): 1–2 for a summary of the session (note the change in the name of the newsletter).

23. Shandler 1993.

24. Heschel, letter to Ravitch, 24 January 1945, Melekh Ravitch Archive. Thanks to Yossel Birstein for his translation of these letters and his help in research and background, as well as for sharing his wide knowledge of Ravitch and Yiddish literature with me.

25. Ravitch, letter to Heschel, 14 February 1945, Ravitch Archive.

26. Heschel, letter to Ravitch, 18 February 1945, Ravitch Archive. For further correspondence see Heschel's letters to Ravitch of 2 February and 6 March 1945.

27. Heschel 1945, "Prayer," 158.

28. Ibid., 156.

29. Ibid., 164.

30. Ibid., 167. In one of his 1933 poems, "Lonely," he confessed to this same isolation: "I would like to scream to myself through all the gates—'Where are you?' / but I can't speak intimately enough with myself for that" (literally, say *Du*, "thou," to myself), Heschel 2004, *The Ineffable Name of God: Man*, 127.

31. Heschel 1945, "Prayer," 168.

32. Hartstein, letter to Heschel, 15 February 1945, Hartstein Administrative Files, Collection 4.

33. "Clarification of Sol[oveitchik] situation. Should be consulted?" Handwritten memorandum by Hartstein, undated; Hartstein, letter to Heschel, 10 April 1945, Hartstein Administrative Files, Collection 4. It is possible that Belkin actually opposed Heschel: interview with Bernard Perlow, 17 February 1981. No other evidence is available.

34. It is unlikely that Heschel and Soloveitchik knew each other in Berlin. Soloveitchik submitted his doctoral dissertation on the neo-Kantian philosopher Hermann Cohen in July 1930; the following year he left for the United States. Heschel defended his dissertation on the prophets in February 1933. According to available evidence, Heschel and Soloveitchik did not meet until 1962, during the American Jewish Committee's preparations for the Second Vatican Council in Rome. Interview with Haym Soloveitchik, the rabbi's son. See also Kimelman 2004.

35. Interview with Sylvia Ettenberg, 5 January 1988.

36. Interview with Pesach Krauss, June 1999.

37. See Shuly Rubin Schwartz, "The Schechter Faculty: The Seminary and 'Wissenschaft des Judentums' in America," in Wertheimer 1997, vol. 1, pp. 293–326.

38. *Louis Ginzberg Jubilee Volume* (New York: The American Academy for Jewish Research, 1945); Louis Finkelstein, "Louis Ginzberg," in *American Jewish Year Book* (1955): 573–79; Herbert Parzen, "Louis Ginzberg, the Proponent of Halakhah," *Architects of Conservative Judaism* (New York: Jonathan David, 1964), 128–54; Eli Ginzberg, "Address in Honor of L.G.," *Proceedings of the Rabbinical Assembly* 28 (1964): 109–19; interview with Eli Ginzberg; Ginzberg 1966.

39. Conversation with Sylvia Heschel; Roundtable: David Novak, 58.

40. See Michael Greenbaum, "Finkelstein and His Critics," *Conservative Judaism* 47, 4 (Summer 1995): 3–78; Baila R. Shargel, "The Texture of Life During the Finkelstein Era," in Wertheimer 1997, vol. 1, pp. 537–38.

41. Interview with Louis Finkelstein; Finkelstein, letter to Heschel, 24 May 1945 (copy not in files), information from Heschel, letter to Finkelstein, 29 May 1945, JTS General Files. The JTS catalog of 1947–48 lists Heschel as associate professor of Jewish ethics and mysticism in the Rabbinical School and in the Teachers Institute.

42. Heschel's letter of resignation to Morgenstern, dated 3 May 1945, is reproduced in "Minutes of the Board of Governors," 9 May 1945, 6–7, American Jewish Archives, Cincinnati. The same letter, undated, was published in Gottschalk 1973.

43. Morgenstern, letter to Heschel, dated 19 May 1945, I believe erroneously, since he stated that the meeting took place "yesterday." Morgenstern probably dictated the letter the same afternoon, after the morning meeting of 9 May. The HUC president concluded his business with Heschel with his customary tact. On 14 May 1945, he answered Heschel's earlier request to find a substitute teacher for his course (dated 18 March), addressing him for the first time as "My dear Dr. Heschel," informing him that Samuel Atlas would "not only take over the Philosophy course in the summer term, but likewise give special instruction in Talmud 5 to the two students," American Jewish Archives, Cincinnati.

44. Interviews with Albert Plotkin, Celia Atlas; see Rubenstein 1974, 73–74, 89; interview with Richard L. Rubenstein.

45. Rubenstein 1974. Kaufman later married Aviva Gootman, one of Heschel's enthusiastic Midrasha students.

46. Heschel, letter to Hartstein, 3 June 1945; Hartstein, letter to Heschel, 8 June 1945, Hartstein Administrative Files, Collection 4.

47. Certificate of Arrival no. 9–24996c. Amy Blank and Bertha Feinberg signed as witnesses on 17 April 1945. Petition for Naturalization, Certificate number 6475263. Documents from District Court of the United States, Cincinnati, Ohio, Southern District of Ohio.

Part Two. Rescuing the American Soul

1. Heschel 1973, *A Passion for Truth*, xiv.
2. For the most complete history of the Jewish Theological Seminary see Wertheimer 1997.
3. The photograph is reproduced in Wertheimer 1997, vol. 1, p. 354.

Chapter 5. First Years in New York

Epigraph. Heschel 1948, "After Majdanek" in Faierstein 1999, 268. I have slightly modified the translation.

1. Heschel, letter to Finkelstein, 29 June 1945, JTS General Files. Heschel enclosed an offprint of his Yiddish article on East European Jewry from *YIVO Bleter*. Other speakers at the symposium included Mordecai Kaplan, Israel Goldstein, Abraham Menes, Samuel Cohon, Menachem Ribalow, Jacob Agus, Robert Gordis, Hayim Greenberg, Paul Weiss, Salo W. Baron, Meir Grossman, and Max Weinreich: Finkelstein, letter to Heschel, 22 June 1945, JTS General Files.
2. Heschel, letter to Simon Greenberg, 23 August 1945, JTS General Files; Heschel, letter to Morgenstern, 29 August 1945, American Jewish Archives, Cincinnati. The JPS translation of the verse continues: "O God of Israel, who brings victory" (Isaiah 45:15).
3. See Michael B. Greenbaum, "The Finkelstein Era," Wertheimer 1997, vol. 1, pp. 162–232; Jonathan Sarna, "Two Traditions of Seminary Scholarship," Wertheimer 1997, vol. 2, pp. 53–80.
4. Finkelstein, letter to Heschel, 27 September 1940, JTS General Files. Ginzberg considered Mordecai Kaplan's interpretation of Judaism heretical (interview with Louis Finkelstein). See David Kaufman, "Jewish Education as a Civilization," Wertheimer 1997, vol. 1, pp. 602–9.
5. Rela Mintz Geffen, "The Shaping of a Cultural and Religious Elite," Wertheimer 1997, vol. 1, pp. 632–53; Kaufman, "Jewish Education as a Civilization," 566–629.
6. Abraham Halkin married a daughter of Rabbi Meir Berlin (Bar-Ilan), who was also the father of Saul Lieberman's wife, Judith. See David Kaufman, "Jewish Education as a Civilization: A History of the Teachers Institute," Wertheimer 1997, vol. 1, pp. 596–97.
7. See Alan Mintz, "Divided Fate of Hebrew and Hebrew Culture at the Seminary," Wertheimer 1997, vol. 2, pp. 99–104 (translation by Mintz, pp. 100–101). See Naomi W. Cohen, "'Diaspora plus Palestine, Religion plus Nationalism,'" Wertheimer 1997, vol. 2, pp. 114–76; Eli Lederhendler, "The Ongoing Dialogue," Wertheimer 1997, vol. 2, pp. 178–270.
8. Heschel 1962–63, "Hillel Bavli: In Memoriam," 71.

9. Guest lists dated 20 February 1946; Heschel's addendum dated 28 February, JTS General Files. The JTS archives preserved only the invitations, guest lists, and the title of Heschel's address, but not the text itself.

10. Statement by the faculty of the Jewish Theological Seminary of America, marked in pencil: "Confidential, Draft subject to revision, not for pub. or dist.," JTS General Files, IC-47-6: 1945–46 Faculty Folder. Further quotations in the text are from this source. Cf. the beginning of Heschel's 1944 essay "The Meaning of This War": "Emblazoned over the gates of the world in which we live is the escutcheon of the demons. The mark of Cain in the face of man has come to overshadow the likeness of God. There have never been so much guilt and distress, agony and terror. At no time has the earth been so soaked with blood," reprinted in Heschel 1996, *Moral Grandeur and Spiritual Audacity,* 209.

11. Cf. Heschel, "The Meaning of This War": "Let us forever remember that the sense for the sacred is as vital to us as the light of the sun. There can be no nature without spirit, no world without the Torah, no brotherhood without a father, no humanity without God," reprinted in Heschel 1996, *Moral Grandeur and Spiritual Audacity,* 211.

12. Cf. ibid., 212: "Either we make it an altar for God or it is invaded by demons. There can be no neutrality. Either we are ministers of the sacred or slaves of evil. Let the blasphemy of our time not become an eternal scandal."

13. See Kaplan and Dresner 1998, 73–96.

14. Ibid., 214.

15. Heschel, letter to Max Arzt, 10 September 1952, JTS General Files: "I have in the past few years helped him [Hofer] out of my personal means but the help needed now far exceeds anything I can do for him. Let me add that he is one of the finest human beings I have met in my life and had throughout his life given help to other people. The sum of $1000 will be needed to tide him over the present emergency and perhaps even to save his life." See Prof. F. Schneurson [*sic*], M.D., "Aliments [sic] of Contemporary Political Psychology," Publication No. 1, "Al Domi," Tel Aviv, undated [before 1948], 6. In terms similar to Hayim Greenberg's editorial "Bankrupt," Schneersohn wrote about a cancer, a "malady" of humankind: a moral paralysis that set in following World War I and "the frightful and 'surprising' annihilation of nearly one million Armenians in Turkey," Martin Buber Archive, MsVar. 350:699. For Heschel's relationship with Schneersohn, see Kaplan and Dresner 1998, 2–55.

16. See Kaplan and Dresner 1998, 58, 314n32, and genealogical charts, xi–xiii. For Rabbi Nahum Mordecai, see pp. 34, 58, 314. Heschel was buried adjacent to Rabbi Yehuda Aryeh Leib Perlow.

17. Interview with Abraham Perlow.

18. Interviews with Bernard Perlow and Rabbi Jacob Perlow, Heschel Archive.

19. For Rabbi Israel Friedman (1797–1850) and for the interrelationships of the Heschel and Friedman clans, see Kaplan and Dresner 1998. See also Mintz 1992,

13–20. For Abraham Joshua Heschel (1888–1967), the rebbe of Kopitzhinitz, see Kaplan and Dresner 1998, 22, 32, 33, 240, 263–64, 302, 320n34, 352n1.

20. Interview with Gary Apfel.

21. Interview with Baruch Feder.

22. Translated by Yossel Birstein from Ravitch 1945, 1947, vol. 2, pp. 21–23. Further quotations from the conversation are from this source. See Kaplan and Dresner 1998, 64–67; in an interview, Khone Shmeruk said that Heschel "walked like a rebbe."

23. Ravitch refers to a letter Heschel wrote him about his first volume of his memoirs; Ravitch, letter to Heschel, 18 February 1946, interview questions; Heschel, letter to Ravitch, 31 January 1947. Heschel was offended by Ravitch's letter. Ravitch Archive, Jerusalem.

24. Susannah Heschel 1996, xx; conversations with Sylvia Heschel.

25. Heschel 2004, *The Ineffable Name of God: Man,* "In the Most Distant Closeness," 109.

26. Information on the Straus family from interviews with Barbara Straus Kessler Reed and a privately published family book by Irene G. Shur, *From Kulno to Cleveland* (West Chester, Pa.: Sylvan, 1994?).

27. Finkelstein, letter to Frank D. Fackenthal, 8 November 1946, JTS General Files.

28. The Heschels were married by Rabbi Eliezer Adler at 556 N. Flores Street, Los Angeles, 10 December 1946. The marriage certificate read: "Abraham Heschel, age last birthday: 39; birthplace: Poland; occupation: teacher. . . . Sylvia Straus, age last birthday: 29; occupation: pianist." Certificate No. 39849, County of Los Angeles, Registrar-Recorder, County Clerk. Thanks to Rabbi Harvey Fields for this document. The 1920 U.S. Census lists Sylvia Straus's birthdate as 1913 and her first name as Cecilia, Ancestry.com. See *Boston Globe,* obituary of Sylvia Strauss Heschel (27 March 2007).

29. The talk was given on Saturday evening, 18 January 1947. See *News of the YIVO* (February 1947), 1–2, for a summary of the session. See the previous issue, no. 18 (December 1946), 6–7, for the announced program. All the speakers related the Holocaust to ways in which Jews coped with past crises. Max Weinreich opened the evening by reflecting on the present and urging people to support the work of YIVO. The Yiddish writer Abraham Menes, co-editor of *Zukunft* and columnist for the Yiddish newspaper *Daily Forward,* presented a historical paper, "Jewish Reconstruction After the Massacres in the Ukraine in 1648."

30. *Yidisher Kemfer,* 12 September 1947, 25–28; four years later, the piece was translated in the inaugural issue of *Zionist Quarterly* 1, 1 (Summer 1951): 78–84, repr. in Heschel 1996, *Moral Grandeur and Spiritual Audacity,* 3–11 (quotations on pp. 3, 4).

31. Heschel 1948, "After Majdanek," trans. in Faierstein 1999, 264–71. I have modified the translation slightly.

32. Ibid., 267. Three years later, Heschel inserted this phrase from the 1947 Yiddish essay—"When we were blinded by the light of our European civilization, we could not appreciate the value of the tiny flame of our eternal light"—into *The Earth Is the Lord's:* "In the spiritual confusion of the last hundred years, many of us have overlooked the incomparable beauty of our poor, old homes. . . . Dazzled by the big city lights we lost our inner vision" (Heschel 1950, 105).

33. See Roundtable.

34. This group included Dresner (the leader), Seymour Siegel, Hershel Matt, Fritz Rothschild, and, somewhat later, Marshall Meyer, Seymour Fox, Moshe Greenberg, Arthur Cohen, Ivan Caine, Jules Harlow, Neil Gillman, Eugene Weiner, and Jack Riemer.

35. Information on Kelman from interviews with Wolfe Kelman, David Szoni, and Morton Leifman. See also Roundtable.

36. Interview with Seymour Siegel.

37. Ibid. A month later, on 15 May 1948, Israel declared its independence.

38. Interviews with Marc Tanenbaum; see Tanenbaum 2002.

39. Rothschild, letter to Buber, 18 October 1943; Buber, letter to Rothschild, 21 November 1943, in Buber 1991, 500–504.

40. Interview with Fritz Rothschild. Each member of the Institute for Theology became prominent in his academic field: Although Arthur Cohen died early he wrote incisive articles and books and was the founder of Noonday Press; Moshe Greenberg taught the Bible at the Hebrew University in Jerusalem; David Winston, an expert on Greek and Philo, taught at Columbia University and then the Graduate Theological Union; Arthur Hyman became a specialist in medieval Jewish philosophy; and Rothschild became Heschel's foremost interpreter.

41. See Rothschild 1959, Introduction to *Between God and Man*. Rothschild did not complete his dissertation on Heschel, but instead transferred to JTS, where he earned a doctorate in Hebrew letters with a dissertation on the idea of God as king in the Book of Genesis.

42. Interview with David Novak. Heschel called Martin Buber "the most erudite" man he ever met.

43. Roundtable: David Novak, 69–70, who originally heard it from Wolfe Kelman. See Baker 1978.

Chapter 6. Books of Spiritual Rescue

1. Finkelstein 1949. Publication of the volumes was delayed; Joan Leff, assistant to Dr. Finkelstein, letter to Heschel, 18 June 1947, JTS General Files.

2. Heschel 1949, "The Mystical Element," repr. in Heschel 1996, *Moral Grandeur and Spiritual Audacity,* 166. Heschel's magisterial study of the Talmud, 1962, 1965, 1990, *Torah min Hashamayim* (trans. in Heschel 2005, *Heavenly Torah as*

Refracted Through the Generations), provides abundant documentation for the classic sources of Heschel's own theology.

3. Heschel 1949, "The Mystical Element," repr. in Heschel 1996, *Moral Grandeur and Spiritual Audacity.*

4. Heschel's booklet was published by the Baronial Press. I quote from "Pikuach Neshama" (To save a soul), in Heschel 1996, *Moral Grandeur and Spiritual Audacity*, 54–67; the text was originally translated by Aryeh Cohen, emended by Samuel Dresner and edited by Susannah Heschel. My thanks to Aharon Appelfeld for a penetrating conversation on this text.

5. Ibid., 55, 58–60.

6. Ibid., 67: "The millions of Jews who were destroyed bear witness to the fact that as long as people do not accept the commandment 'Remember the Sabbath to keep it holy,' the commandment 'Thou shalt not kill' will likewise fail to be operative in life" (66).

7. Heschel 1954, *Man's Quest for God*, 44n30 (citing *Seah Sarfe Kodesh*, vol. 2). For an explanation of the prayers see Donin 1980, 202–10.

8. Gershon Jacobson, "Interview with Prof. Heschel About Russian Jewry," in Yiddish *Day-Morning Journal* (13 September 1963), 1; translated in Faierstein 1999, 272–74.

9. *Commentary* evolved from the American Jewish Committee's wartime news digest *Contemporary Jewish Record*, which excerpted detailed information from the world press. See esp. Nathan Abrams, "A Significant Journal of *Jewish* Opinion? The Jewishness of *Commentary* Magazine," *American Jewish Archives Journal* 60, 1 (2003): 35–62; Cohen 1972, 263–64.

10. Heschel 1948, "The Two Great Traditions," 416.

11. Ibid., 418–19; 417–18. In conversation with me, Samuel Dresner remembered Heschel showing him the manuscript of *The Earth Is the Lord's* and asking him to comment on the meter.

12. Heschel 1948, "The Two Great Traditions,"419, 422.

13. Ibid., 420–21; Ismar Elbogen, *Der jüdische Gottesdienst in seiner geschlichtlichen Entwicklung* (Leipzig: Fock, 1913), translated as *Jewish Liturgy: A Comprehensive Survey* (Philadelphia: Jewish Publication Society; New York: Jewish Theological Seminary, 1993).

14. Theodore Wiener, "The Two Traditions," and Ernst Simon, "Sephardim and Ashkenazim," *Commentary* (July 1948), 86, 384; Jacob Sloan, "No More Than Human: Four Reflections on Judaism," *Commentary* (June 1949), 576. Whether deliberate or not, the publication of Sloan's whimsical essay a year after Fiedler's "Hasidism and the Modern Jew" demonstrates an antireligious editorial decision. Jacob Taubes introduced chapters from Maimonides' *Mishneh Torah*, translated by Jacob Sloan, with this comment: "To understand revelation as far as the limits of

reason allow, means: to understand prophecy out of the nature of man," *Commentary* (May 1949), 482. Any "supernaturalism" was anathema.

15. Leslie Fiedler, "Hasidism and the Modern Jew," *Commentary* (February 1949), 196–98, a review of recent books by Martin Buber, including *Tales of the Hasidim: The Later Masters* and *Hasidism.*

16. Herberg 1947; Herberg 1949, 455. See David Dalin, "Will Herberg," Katz 1993, 113–30.

17. Henry Schuman, letter to Finkelstein, 22 December 1949; Finkelstein, letter to Schuman, 29 December 1949, JTS General Files. Finkelstein first suggested to Schuman that he publish an English translation of Heschel's German book on Maimonides. But Heschel needed too much time to revise it, and the opportunity fell through, Heschel, letter to Finkelstein, 4 January 1950, JTS General Files; interview with Marc Tanenbaum; Heschel, letter to Finkelstein, 4 January 1950, JTS General Files.

18. Interview with Marc Tanenbaum.

19. Heschel 1950, *The Earth Is the Lord's*, 10. The reference to Heschel's original speech at YIVO was eliminated from the reissue by Jewish Lights, and the subtitle was changed to the "The Inner Life of the Jew in Eastern Europe" (instead of "East Europe").

20. Heschel 1950, *The Earth Is the Lord's*, 14.

21. Ibid., 54.

22. Ibid., 75.

23. Ibid., 98, 103–4, 108.

24. Sol Liptzin, review of *The Earth Is the Lord's, Jewish Social Studies* 12 (1950): 415–16; Alfred Werner, review of *The Earth Is the Lord's, New York Times*, 4 June 1950; see also the following appreciative responses: Bernard Cohen, *Sociology and Social Research* 35 (1950): 140–41; Antoni Gronowicz, *Saturday Review of Literature* 5 (August 1950): 25; *U.S. Quarterly Book Review* 6 (Spring 1950): 293; Melville Jacobs, *Annals of the American Academy* (July 1950): 197.

25. Irving Kristol, "Elegy for a Lost World," *Commentary* (May 1950), 490–91.

26. Immanuel Lewy, "A Romantic Version of Hasidic Life in East Europe, *The Reconstructionist* (16 June 1950): 27–28. Herbert Parzen, in *Bulletin of the Rabbinical Assembly of America* (June 1960), 6, offered a more balanced, though equally simplistic, reading.

27. Marvin Lowenthal, "The Jewish Community: What It Means to the West," *New York Herald Tribune*, 2 July 1950, 5. Lowenthal refers to Morris Raphael Cohen, *Reflections of a Wondering Jew* (Boston: Beacon, 1950).

28. Heschel, letter to the editor, and Lowenthal, rejoinder, *New York Herald Tribune*, 13 August 1950.

29. Maurice Samuel, "The Monument to European Jewry," *Congress Weekly* (27 March 1950), 7–9 (quotations on pp. 7, 9). Kristol dismissed Samuel as another

idealizer: "We have already been instructed in the life of the 'onion-peddlers' in Maurice Samuel's books on Sholem Aleichem and Peretz. Now we are given an insight into the people of the midnight lament," "Elegy for a Lost World," 491.

30. Maurice Samuel: "It may be called—for the sophisticate—the inversion of the *moshel* [*mashsal,* parable] and the *nimshul,* the illustration and the substance, the example and the rule" ("Monument to European Jewry," 9). Heschel 1950, *The Earth Is the Lord's,* 15.

31. Friedman 1987; see also Friedman, letter to Heschel, 2 August 1950, JTS General Files.

32. Friedman 1987, 7–8.

33. Heschel, letter to Finkelstein, 11 October 1950: "Dr. Friedman is endowed with rare gifts of mind and spirit and, if properly guided, he may make an important contribution to religious thinking," JTS General Files.

34. Although see the severe critique by Jacob Neusner, *Why There Never was a "Talmud of Caesarea": Saul Lieberman's Mistakes* (Atlanta: Scholars, 1994).

35. Schochet and Spiro 2005, 16; Solomon Spiro, "The Moral Vision of Saul Lieberman: A Historiographic Approach to Normative Jewish Ethics," *Conservative Judaism* 46, 4 (Summer 1994): 64–84; Michael Greenbaum, "The Finkelstein Era," Wertheimer 1997, vol. 1, pp. 161–232. For a bibliography of Lieberman's writings see David Golinkin, "The Influence of Seminary Professors on Halakhah in the Conservative Movement, 1902–1968," Wertheimer 1997, vol. 2, pp. 450–52, 472–74nn35–37.

36. Interview with Wolfe Kelman. See Jonathan Sarna, "Two Traditions of Seminary Scholarship," Wertheimer 1997, vol. 2, pp. 53–80. Lieberman once introduced Gershom Scholem to a JTS audience with the words, "Nonsense (*narishkeit*) is nonsense, but the history of nonsense can be great scholarship," interview with David Novak.

37. See Judith Berlin Lieberman's autobiographical essay in Finkelstein 1953, 159–76; Heschel, letter to Finkelstein, 11 August 1948, JTS General Files; Heschel, letter to Solomon Grayzel, 3 August 1948; Maurice Jacobs, letter to Heschel, 5 August 1948, JPS Archives; conversations with Sylvia Heschel. See Schochet and Spiro 2005, 223–28, on the man's harsh personality.

38. Maurice Jacobs, letter to Heschel, 19 July 1948; Heschel, letter to Grayzel, 28 July 1948, JPS Archives.

39. See Sarna 1989 and esp. Sarna 2004.

40. Jacobs, letter to Grayzel, 5 August 1948, JPS Archives; Heschel, letter to Finkelstein, 26 July 1948; Grayzel, letter to Finkelstein, 5 August 1948; Finkelstein, letter to Heschel, 9 August 1948, JTS General Files; Grayzel, letter to Finkelstein, 5 August 1948; Grayzel, letter to Jacobs, 8 August 1948; Finkelstein, letter to Grayzel, 3 August 1948, JPS Archives.

41. Morgenstern, letter to Grayzel, 7 October 1948; Milton Steinberg, letter to Grayzel, 11 October 1948; Freehof, letter to Jacobs, 26 August 1948, JPS Archives.

42. Louis L. Kaplan, letter to Grayzel, 27 October 1948, JPS Archives.

43. Louis Ginzberg's statement was excerpted from a memorandum on "New Manuscripts" submitted to the JPS Publications Committee on 7 November 1948. Maurice Jacobs, letter to Heschel, 14 February 1949; Heschel, letter to Jacobs, 15 February 1949; Jacobs, letter to Heschel, 1 April 1949. On 24 January 1950, Heschel finally received the contract with an advance royalty check; Jacobs, letter to Heschel, 24 January 1950. All in JPS Archives.

44. Grayzel, letter to Heschel, 15 November 1948, JPS Archives.

45. Heschel, letter to Grayzel, 10 May 1949; Grayzel, letter to Heschel, 10 June 1949; Heschel, letter to Grayzel, 12 July 1949 ("Please, do not consider the manuscript in its present form as absolutely final. Your comments and criticisms will be most welcome. On my part, I am planning to go over the manuscript several times and there will be some changes and corrections. There is also a problem in which order to publish the various chapters."), JPS Archives.

46. Grayzel, letter to Heschel, 18 July 1949; several letters between Heschel and Grayzel, August and October 1949. In Grayzel, letter to Heschel, 13 October 1949, he acknowledged receiving the chapter "The Problem of Living." Heschel sent Grayzel part of the chapter tentatively called "The Attributes of God." A few days later, he sent the chapter on faith, then the first part of the chapter on God, entitled "The Sense of the Ineffable." By mid-October, Heschel had finished "The Problem of Living." All in JPS Archives.

47. Grayzel, letter to Heschel, 29 July 1949, JPS Archives.

48. Grayzel, letter to Heschel, 16 November 1949; Heschel, letter to Grayzel, 28 November 1949; Grayzel, letter to Heschel, 5 December 1949, JPS Archives. Heschel asked to meet with Grayzel to discuss "the final arrangements for the publication of my book": Heschel, letter to Grayzel, 30 May 1950, JPS Archives.

49. Roger Straus, letter to Grayzel, 30 June 1950, JPS Archives.

50. Heschel, letter to Grayzel, 2 July 1950; Grayzel, letter to Heschel, 4 July 1950; Grayzel, memorandum to the Executive Committee of the JPS, 7 July 1950; Heschel, letter to Grayzel, 11 July 1950, apologizing for the misunderstanding; Grayzel memorandum to the Executive Committee, 7 July 1950, JPS Archives.

51. Heschel, letter and enclosure to Grayzel, 11 July 1950; Grayzel, letter to Heschel, 14 July 1950; Grayzel, letter to Bernard Frankel, 25 July 1950; Roger Straus, letters to Grayzel and Lesser Zussman, executive secretary of the JPS, 26 July 1950, JPS Archives. Heschel's table of contents as of 11 July 1950 was

Part I
The Ultimate Question
    The Sense of the Ineffable
    One God
    The Divine Concern

Faith

The Holy Dimension

The Problem of Living

Human Needs

The Vision of Ends

What Is Jewish Religion?

The Way

A Pattern for Living

The Great Yearning

Part II

God in the Bible

The Dignity of Deeds

The Duties of the Heart

The Ladder of Learning

The Mystery of Integrity

Prayer

The Jewish Day

The Jewish Year

The Ethical Minimum

An Analysis of Piety

The People of Israel

52. Roger Straus, letter to Grayzel and Zussman, 26 July 1950, JPS Archives; contracts, Farrar, Straus and Giroux Archives; Zussman, letter to Straus, 17 August 1950; Straus, letter to Zussman, 18 August 1950; Heschel, letter to Grayzel, 22 August 1950 ("the ms. book is about ready to go to press"); Straus, letter to Heschel, 3 October 1950, giving publication date of 20 February; Straus, letter to Grayzel, 6 October 1950, all in JPS Archives.

53. Grayzel, letter to Straus, 27 July 1950, JPS Archives. Heschel, Grayzel, and Straus were still "fooling around with titles," *A Philosophy of Religion* for volume 1 and *A Philosophy of Judaism* for volume 2, with the subtitle *Man Is Not Alone* for both volumes.

54. The first official publication date was 20 February 1951: minutes of the meeting of the Board of Trustees, JPS of America, 9 October 1950; Heschel, letter to Grayzel, 15 November 1950, JPS Archives.

55. Heschel, letter to Grayzel, 15 November 1950, JPS Archives. The final decision on the title was made at the Farrar, Straus sales conference: "They want us to call the book MAN IS NOT ALONE with the subtitle of A Philosophy of Religion. And the next book to be called MAN IS NOT ALONE, A Philosophy of Judaism" (the second volume was eventually titled *God in Search of Man: A Philosophy of Judaism*): Straus, letter

to Grayzel, 16 November 1950; Shirley Kuller (from Farrar, Straus), letter to Grayzel, 19 December 1950; Grayzel, letter to Kuller, 20 December 1950; Straus, letter to Grayzel, 4 January 1951, JPS Archives. The extended publication date was 19 March 1951: Grayzel, letter to Straus, 5 February 1951; Kuller, letter to Grayzel, 5 February 1951, JPS Archives.

Chapter 7. Theological Revolution

1. Interviews with Pearl Twersky, several conversations with Sylvia Heschel, Morton Leifman, and others.
2. Heschel, letter to Finkelstein, 18 January 1951. Heschel was hurt by Finkelstein's response, 24 January 1951: "Unfortunately, it looks as though the evening of February 15th will—like most of my evenings—have to be spent on Seminary business," JTS General Files.
3. Conversation with Morton Leifman; *New York Times*, 16 February 1951, 20, signed "H.C.S."; *New York Herald Tribune*, 16 February 1951, signed "J.B.H."; "E.S.B.," *Musical Courier*, 1 March 1951, 23. *Musical America* (March 1951), 18, 20, also had a moderately supportive review.
4. Heschel, letter to Grayzel, 4 March 1951, JPS Archives; Finkelstein, letter to Heschel, 9 October 1950; see Heschel, letter to Finkelstein, 11 October 1950, JTS General Files.
5. Heschel 1951, *Man Is Not Alone*, 67–79. See Edward Kaplan, "Mysticism and Despair" (1977), revised and reprinted in Edward Kaplan 1996.
6. Only years later did scholars define the phenomenological function of Heschel's hybrid style: see Rothschild 1968; Edward Kaplan 1973; Edward Kaplan 1985; Edward Kaplan 2001.
7. Reinhold Niebuhr, "Masterly Analysis of Faith," *New York Herald Tribune Book Review*, 1 April 1951, 12. Later that year Niebuhr praised Will Herberg's first major book, *Judaism and Modern Man*, in similar terms: Herberg's book "may well become a milestone in the religious thought of America," *New York Herald Tribune*, 16 December 1951. See David Dalin, "Will Herberg," Katz 1993, 118, 128n8.
8. Niebuhr, "Masterly Analysis of Faith," 12; See Goldy 1990 for the most detailed account of this post-1945 development of Jewish theology.
9. Jacob Agus, review of *Man Is Not Alone*, *Congress Weekly* (16 April 1951), 12–13.
10. The Association for Jewish Studies was founded in 1969.
11. Interview Marvin Fox, who provided the correspondence; Irving Kristol, letter to Marvin Fox, 10 April 1951, Heschel Archive.
12. Kristol, letter to Fox, 10 April 1951, Heschel Archive.
13. Kristol, letter to Fox, 28 June 1951, Heschel Archive; Marvin Fox, "A Modern

Mystic," *Commentary*, August 1951, 193–95. Quotations in the text are from this source.

14. Eugene Kohn, review of *Man Is Not Alone*, *The Reconstructionist* (15 June 1951): 27–30. Further quotations in the text are from this source. With fellow Reconstructionist leaders Mordecai Kaplan and Ira Eisenstein, Kohn edited a controversial Passover Haggadah (1941) and the Reconstructionist Prayer Book (1948); with Kaplan and J. Paul Williams, he produced *Faith of America*, a book of readings for celebrating American holidays, published by Henry Schuman in 1951.

15. See a similarly ambivalent review by Ira Eisenstein in the *Hadassah Newsletter*, July–August 1951.

16. Alexander J. Burnstein, *Bulletin of the Rabbinical Assembly of America* (June 1951): 4. He concluded with a double-edged compliment: "I wish the author would concern himself, in the book yet to follow, less with nebulous prolegomena and more with the direct exposition of the central teachings of Judaism. This he does particularly well (16).

17. See Goldy 1990, 50–51; Robert Gordis, "The Genesis of *Judaism:* A Chapter in Jewish Cultural History," *Judaism* 30, 4 (fall 1981): 390–95. Included in the inaugural issue were Milton Konvitz, professor of industrial and labor relations at Cornell University; Will Herberg; the sociologist C. Bezalel Sherman; Jacob B. Agus; and Nahum N. Glatzer.

18. See Fackenheim 1948; Fackenheim 1950. After the June 1967 war Fackenheim became prominent as a post-Holocaust theologian. See "Jewish Faith and the Holocaust" (1968), Fackenheim 1970. See also Goldy 1990, chap. 7, "The Question of Jewish Theology in Heschel, Fackenheim, and Soloveitchik," 66–86.

19. Emil Ludwig Fackenheim, review of *Man Is Not Alone*, *Judaism* 1, 1 (January 1952): 85–89. Further quotations in the text are from this source.

20. See Edward Kaplan "Reverence and Responsibility," Tirosh-Samuelson 2002.

21. Heschel 1951, *Man Is Not Alone*, 151. Fackenheim hoped that Heschel, in his announced companion volume, would provide "a fusion" of mysticism and historical consciousness. Another reviewer, Philip Louis Seman of the University of Judaism in Los Angeles and a national leader in Jewish social work, who liked the book, was immune to the dualistic thinking that caused readers to view Heschel as hostile to science, reason, and ethics: *Social Science* (June 1952), 166–68.

22. Before immigrating to Palestine in 1920, Bergman, a librarian at the University of Prague, became friends with Buber at the Bar Kochba Jewish student organization in Prague, where Buber later delivered his famous *Drei Reden über des Judentum*. Bergman also met Franz Kafka in Prague. S. Hugo Bergman, "Der Mensch ist nicht allein," *Mitteilungsblatt der Hebräschen Universität* (18 May 1951), trans. Stephanie Wollny; further quotations in the text are from this source. This review was republished in *Människan är icke allena: Judisk Tidskrift* (June–July 1951): 160–63.

See Baruch Shohetman, ed., *The Writings of Shmuel Hugo Bergman: A Bibliography, 1903–1967* (Jerusalem: Magnes Press, 1968), no. 1016. Cf. Shmuel (Samuel) Hugo Bergman, *Dialogical Philosophy from Kierkegaard to Buber*, trans. Arnold A. Gerstein (Albany: State University of New York Press, 1991).

23. In June 1951 a brief, eulogistic article by Ludwig Lewisohn on the book appeared in *Circle in Jewish Bookland*. See also the brief review by Rabbi Felix Levy in the *Chicago Sunday Tribune*, 28 July 1951, 4.

24. Interview with Jack Riemer.

25. Heschel, letter to Grayzel, 26 June 1951, JPS Archives.

26. Grayzel, letter to Heschel, 28 June 1951; Heschel, letter to Grayzel, 5 July 1951; Roger Straus, letter to Grayzel, 5 July 1951; Grayzel, letter to Roger Straus, 9 July 1951, JPS Archives.

27. Roger Straus, letter to Grayzel, 10 July 1951, JPS Archives.

28. Roger Straus, letter to Grayzel, 24 September 1951; Grayzel, letter to Straus, 27 September 1951; John Meyer of Farrar, Straus and Young, letter to Grayzel, 2 October 1951, JPS Archives; Everett R. Clinchy, president of the National Conference of Christians and Jews, to John Meyer, 3 October 1951, Farrar, Straus and Giroux Archives; Grayzel, letter to Heschel, 8 October 1951, JPS Archives. Heschel returned Grayzel's good wishes for Rosh Hashanah on 4 October and explained that *The Sabbath* would probably be ready on 26 or 29 October: JPS Archives.

29. Heschel, "Between Civilization and Eternity: An Ancient Debate and an Allegorical Interpretation," *Commentary*, October 1951, 375–78 (quotation on p. 378). The essay was split into two chapters that also incorporated material from *The Sabbath*. In the book, Heschel deleted the word *tragic* in "the [tragic] problem of civilization" (Heschel 1951, *The Sabbath*, 48).

30. Heschel, "Architecture of Time," *Judaism* 1, 1 (January 1952): 44–51. I quote from the reprint in Heschel 1990, *To Grow in Wisdom*, 71–81. The footnote to this passage reads: "This is one of the aspects which distinguishes the religious from the aesthetic experience" (73–74). See Heschel 1951, *The Sabbath*, 6.

31. Heschel 1990, 73; see Heschel 1951, *The Sabbath*, 6.

32. In October 1956, Les Editions de Minuit, the famous Parisian Resistance publisher, agreed to publish a volume entitled *Les Bâtisseurs du temps* (The builders of time), made up of chapters from *The Sabbath* and *The Earth Is the Lord's*. The book became Heschel's classic work in France and formed his European reputation: Farrar, Straus and Giroux Archives.

33. Will Herberg's lead article, "Prophetic Faith in an Age of Crisis," implicitly supported Heschel's mission to import Jewish holiness into American culture. Herberg's subtitle defined their common perspective: "God-Centered Religion Meets the Challenge of Our Time," *Judaism* 1, 3 (July 1952): 198. Heschel, "Space, Time, and Reality: The Centrality of Time in the Biblical World-View,"

Judaism 1, 3 (July 1952): 262–69, reprinted in Heschel 1990, *To Grow in Wisdom*, 83–95.

34. *Judaism* 1, 3 (July 1952): 277–78.

35. Twenty years later, Weiss-Rosmarin still labeled Heschel "a poetico-mystical expositor of Jewish teachings and way of life in ecstatic language," anything but a philosopher or theologian. See "Jewish Theology," *Jewish Spectator* (January 1961): 25, and debate between Weiss-Rosmarin and Jakob Petuchowski, pp. 23–25.

36. Nahum N. Glatzer, review of *The Sabbath*, *Judaism* 1, 3 (July 1952): 283–86 (quotation on p. 284).

37. Ibid., 285. Glatzer ended his review with an interpretation of Schor's wood engravings. For Glatzer, Schor's combination of folkloric and abstract conceptions fitly symbolized Heschel's attempt to insert a sense of eternal holiness into contemporary thinking.

38. Ira Eisenstein, "Of Time and the Sabbath," *The Reconstructionist* (22 February 1952): 23–24.

39. Jacob B. Agus, review of *The Sabbath*, *Bulletin of the Rabbinical Assembly of America* (April 1952): 6–7. Milton Konvitz, in review of *The Sabbath*, *Jewish Social Studies* 14, 3 (July 1952): 254, found the book more successful in conveying a balanced view of space and time and celebrating the Sabbath. See also Charles O'Conor Sloane, review of *The Sabbath*, *Catholic Biblical Quarterly* 15 (1953): 270: "His book is on the side of the angels."

40. Will Herberg, "Space, Time, and the Sabbath," *Commentary* (June 1952), 610–12.

41. Interview with Yaakov Rosenberg.

42. Hillel Halkin, "Making Heschel a Tzaddik for All Seasons," *Forward*, 7 August 1998, 11–12.

43. Interviews with Nahum Sarna, Fritz Rothschild; Roundtable.

44. "A Trumpet for All Israel," *Time*, 15 October 1951, 52–59. See Baila Shargel, "Texture of Seminary Life," Wertheimer 1997, vol. 1, pp. 537–55 .

45. Interview with Wolfe Kelman.

46. Interview with Morton Leifman, 2005. See Schochet and Spiro 2005, 223–28, on Lieberman's dark side. See Grade 1976. Heschel once characterized Mussar as the Jewish *krechts*, a groan or a sigh.

47. Heschel 1973, *A Passion for Truth*, "Why I Had to Write This Book," xv. See Kaplan and Dresner 1998, 39–43.

48. Gerry J. Rosenberg, quoted in "Reminiscences by Heschel's Former Students," *Conservative Judaism* 50, 2–3 (winter–spring 1998): 175; interview with Avraham Holtz, 19 April 1988.

49. Interview with Neil Gillman.

50. Dresner 2002, 112.

51. Neal Rose (12 December 1997), "AJH: Twenty-fifth Yahrzeit Tribute" 1998, 174.

52. Information from several interviews with Marshall Meyer. Letters quoted are from his personal papers. See also Richard A. Freund, "'Somos Testigos—We Are Witnesses': The Jewish Theology of Liberation of Rabbi Marshall T. Meyer," *Conservative Judaism* 47, 1 (fall 1994): 27–38. On Rosenstock-Huessy's relationship to Rosenzweig, see Rosenstock-Huessy 1969.

53. The Jewish Theological Seminary sponsored three public lectures by Buber to be given in the Unterberg Auditorium: "The Appeal to Religion" (15 November 1951), "Judaism and Civilization" (19 November), and "The Dialogue Between Heaven and Earth" (27 November), JTS General Files.

54. We do not possess any records of Heschel and Buber's conversations, although Roger Straus, Heschel's publisher, remained grateful that Heschel introduced him to Buber. The old German Jew reminded the urbane Straus of his grandfather, who was also a small, bearded, distinguished man: interview with Roger W. Straus, Jr.; interview with Marshall Meyer; J. William Petty, "Dr. Buber Talks of Jung and Religion; Holds Informal Discussion Period," *The Dartmouth*, 14 November 1952, 1.

55. For the speech, "Hope for This Hour," see Friedman 1983, *The Later Years*, 303–6; quotation from Buber, "Hope for This Hour" (1952), Buber 1957, 222. The following year Buber collected his American lectures into a powerful book, *Eclipse of God: Studies in the Relation Between Religion and Philosophy* (1952). There he explained how Hegel, Kierkegaard, Nietzsche, Heidegger, and Sartre prepared the notion of an eclipse of God and the fashionable "death of God theology," both of which Buber opposed.

56. "A. J. Heschel Addresses GI [Great Issues course] This Evening, *The Dartmouth*, 28 April 1952; J. Dickerson May, "Seniors' Spiritual Values Emphasized by Speaker," *The Dartmouth*, 29 April 1952.

57. Sylvia Heschel received internal injuries during the birth, and after two operations it was determined that she could no longer bear children: conversation with Sylvia Heschel. Heschel, letter to Louis Finkelstein, 15 May 1952, JTS General Files; Heschel, letter to Marshall Meyer, 15 May 1952, Marshall Meyer, personal papers; Susannah Heschel, email to the author, 3 January 2001.

Chapter 8. Critique of American Judaism

1. Heschel debated the issue of symbolism in David Koigen's 1930 philosophy seminar in Berlin. See Kaplan and Dresner 1998, chap. 7, "A Jewish Philosophical Mentor," 121–39, and chap. 15, "Alliance with Martin Buber," 218–28; F. Ernest Johnson, letter to Heschel, 17 June 1952; Heschel, letter to Johnson, 20 June 1952, JTS General Files; Heschel, letter to Marshall Meyer, 15 August 1952; Marshall Meyer, personal papers.

2. On 18 November 1952 Heschel presented his paper at the Jewish Theological Seminary. Heschel was pleased that he could lecture from notes written on file

cards or sheets of paper. A stenographer recorded and typed his oral delivery, which he then revised for the published version of the conference. See Johnson, letter to Heschel, 25 September 1952; Heschel, letter to Johnson, 3 October 1952, JTS General Files. It is reprinted in Heschel 1954, *Man's Quest for God*, "Symbolism," 117–44; repr. in Heschel 1990, *Moral Grandeur and Spiritual Audacity*, 80–99. Quotations in the text are from Heschel 1954, "Symbolism and Jewish Faith."

3. Heschel 1954, "Symbolism and Jewish Faith," 54, 56, 58–59.

4. Ibid., 62–63.

5. Ibid., 70, 72.

6. Ibid., 55–56.

7. Ibid., 53, 59–60.

8. Mordecai Kaplan, "The Future of Religious Symbolism: A Jewish View," Johnson 1955, 203–17 (quotation on p. 204).

9. Interviews with Wolfe Kelman, Fritz Rothschild, and Samuel Dresner. See Knight 1947, which refers to Heschel only once, on p. 138. See E. W. Heaton, review of H. Wheeler Robinson's *Two Hebrew Prophets* and Harold Knight's *The Hebrew Prophetic Consciousness*, *Theology* 51, 338 (August 1948): 308–9. In 1943 Knight had published "The Problem of Divine Possibility and Prophetic Theology," *Theology* 46, 272 (February 1943): 25–32, in which he briefly alluded to "A recent writer (Heschel, *Das profetische Bewusstsein*)," 26.

10. William L. Savage, letter to Solomon Grayzel, 2 February 1953, JPS Archives.

11. Heschel, letter to Grayzel, 12 February 1953; Julius Bewer, letter to Grayzel, 14 February 1953; H. L. Ginsberg, letter to Grayzel, 17 February 1953; Sheldon H. Blank, letter to Grayzel, 26 March 1953, JPS Archives. Grayzel wrote to Scribner's that the translation needed to be read by "several of our own readers." JPS Archives.

12. Minutes, Meeting of the JPS Publications Committee, 11 October 1953; William Savage, letter to Grayzel, 1 December 1953, JPS Archives. A letter from Straus was sent to Grayzel and Lesser Zussman, in charge of JPS production, thanking them for "your reconsideration of Heschel's problems"; Roger Straus, letter to Grayzel and Lesser Zussman, 15 December 1953, JPS Archives.

13. Heschel 1953, "The Divine Pathos," 64.

14. Heschel 1953, "The Moment at Sinai," repr. in Heschel 1990, *Moral Grandeur and Spiritual Audacity*, 13. The Zionist Organization of America was an advocate for Hebrew culture in the United States, sponsoring summer camps and the Young Judea youth movement, as well as Zionist education in Israel.

15. Heschel 1954, "A Preface to the Understanding of Revelation," 28, 33.

16. Arthur Cohen, letter to Heschel, 5 March 1953, Heschel Archive. Cohen also felt that Heschel went too far with his comparison of Christianity and Judaism as

antitheses. The expression for God as "the most moved mover" came originally from Fritz Rothschild from whom Heschel obtained permission to use it in his own name. It was obviously circulating among Heschel's students in several forms. Interview with Fritz Rothschild. After Cohen left the Seminary, he founded Meridian Books, which distributed paperbacks of the Jewish Publication Society. He also edited and wrote several books of his own, including *Martin Buber* (1959) and an analysis of contemporary Jewish thought, *The Natural and Supernatural Jew* (1962), in which he formulated an insightful interpretation of Heschel's rhetoric.

17. The opening session was Saturday evening, 14 February 1953. Heschel spoke the next day. See Heschel 1953, "The Spirit of Jewish Education." A significantly revised version was published as "Jewish Education" in Heschel 1966, *The Insecurity of Freedom*, 223–41.

18. Heschel 1953, "The Spirit of Jewish Education," 11–12, 15, 16–17.

19. Ibid., 18–19, 62.

20. Ibid., 62.

21. Ibid., 13–14.

22. While Heschel was trying to reinvigorate the American Jewish community, he was losing many friends from his Yiddish-speaking immigrant world. On 14 March 1953, Hayim Greenberg, editor of *Yidisher Kemfer* and *Jewish Frontier*, died at age sixty-three. On 31 March, Abraham Reisen, known as "the dean of Yiddish poets," died at age seventy-seven. Reisen was born in Koidanov, Russia, the home of Heschel's maternal relatives. In addition to these personal losses, Heschel was dismayed by the execution on 19 June of Julius and Ethel Rosenberg for espionage. The officiating rabbi at their funeral two days later was Abraham Cronbach, Heschel's friend from Hebrew Union College.

23. "Communists must be exposed for what they are; but it is a rejection of true religion to deny that repentance is possible," *Proceedings* 1953, 148.

24. Heschel 1953, "The Spirit of Jewish Prayer," *Proceedings* 1953, 151. Heschel incorporated a revised version of the speech into chapter 3 of *Man's Quest for God*, "Spontaneity is the Goal," 49–89. All quotations in the text are from the original *Proceedings* version, which contains a number of Hebrew words, phrases, and quotations.

25. A simplistic reading of Soloveitchik's foundational essay, "Halakhic Man," might suggest that it was only necessary to follow the rules; one did not have to strive for attachment to God: Soloveitchik 1983.

26. In the printed version, Heschel referred in a footnote (*Proceedings* 153, 156n3) to Josiah Royce's *The Problem of Christianity* (1913), rather than Kaplan's *Judaism as a Civilization* (1934) when citing a Kaplanian axiom: God is a symbol of social action, "the spirit of the beloved community."

27. "A discussion of this view, which is so popular today, is found in I. [Joseph] Segond, *La prière, étude de psychologie religieuse*, Paris, 1911, p. 52": *Proceedings* 1953, 158n7a.

28. Heschel is referring to Joseph Zeitlin, *Disciples of the Wise: The Religious and Social Opinions of American Rabbis* (New York: Teachers Institute, Columbia University, 1945), 76. See also *Proceedings* 1953, 163: "Decisive is not the mystic experience of our being close to Him; decisive is not our feeling but our certainty of His being close to us."

29. *Proceedings* 1953, 164, citing Heschel's footnote to *Man Is Not Alone*, chap. 23.

30. Eugene Kohn, "Prayer and the Modern Jew," *Proceedings* 1953, 184–85. According to a note, "This address now constitutes the last chapter of Rabbi Eugene Kohn's 'Religion and Humanity.'"

31. Ibid., 187–88.

32. Lehrman's remarks in *Proceedings* 1953, 192–93. Further quotations from the audience discussion will be from this source, pp. 194–217. Referring to a recent Billy Graham revival meeting in Miami that attracted more than thirty thousand young people who wanted to pray, not just to hear the preacher, Lehrman agreed with Heschel that American Jews were ready for "a renaissance of the spirit of prayer."

33. Eisenstein had a more fluid definition of prayer: "Prayer does not emerge from a conception of God but from a belief in God, from some vague sense that there is a reality beyond ourselves, and though we may not insist that this reality is the God of Abraham, Isaac and Jacob. Nevertheless the prayer can be a sincere and genuine expression," *Proceedings* 1953, 207–8.

34. Heschel, letter to Marshall Meyer, undated [June 1953], Marshall Meyer, personal papers; Irving Spiegel, *New York Times*, 24 June 1953, 26.

35. Rothschild 1953, 455.

36. Interview with Ira Eisenstein.

37. Samuel S. Cohon, "The Existentialist Trend in Theology," *CCAR* 1953, 348–85 (quotations on pp. 352–53, 373, 385, 363). Especially useful was Rosenzweig's "new thinking," as found in *The Star of Redemption* (which still was not available in English), and the example of the man's final years, in which he continued to teach and write despite his debilitating terminal illness.

38. David Polish, "Current Trends in Jewish Theology," *CCAR* 1953, 420–30 (quotations on pp. 413, 418, 422–23, 423–24, 423). Polish quoted a passage from Heschel 1944, *The Quest for Certainty in Saadia's Philosophy*. Cf. Heschel 1951, *Man Is Not Alone*, 173: "An essential disagreement between reason and revelation would presuppose the existence of two divine beings, each of whom would represent a different source of knowledge. Faith, therefore, can never compel the reason to accept that which is absurd."

39. Heschel 1953, "Toward an Understanding of Halacha," 387. This was revised, with significant deletions, in Heschel 1954, *Man's Quest for God*, "Continuity Is the Way," 93–114 (repr. in Heschel 1996, *Moral Grandeur and Spiritual Audacity*, 127–45).

40. Heschel 1953, "Toward an Understanding of Halacha," 389.

41. Ibid., 388–91. See Kaplan and Dresner 1998, chaps. 6–9.

42. Ibid., 393–96, 399. Heschel's religious standards were practical: "The highest peak of spiritual living is not necessarily reached in rare moments of ecstasy; the highest peak lies wherever we are and may be ascended in a common deed" (404).

43. Ibid., 390.

44. Ibid., 405–6n7 (quoted from Morton M. Berman, *The Survey of Current Reform Practice by Laymen*, delivered at the forty-second General Assembly of the Union of American Hebrew Congregations, 22 April 1953), 406n8 (long quotation in Hebrew). See the exchange of letters between Berman and Heschel in *Jewish Frontier* (June 1954).

45. Heschel 1953, "Toward an Understanding of Halacha," 407–9.

46. That August, Heschel returned to Estes Park, to speak about belief in God at a B'nai B'rith Institute for rabbis of all tendencies. See Heschel, letter to Marshall Meyer, 24 August 1953, Marshall Meyer, personal papers. This debate was picked up by Trude Weiss-Rosmarin, who satirized Heschel's "failure of reason" in *Jewish Spectator* (November 1954): 5–6. A public challenge to Heschel's criticism of Reform Judaism appeared in the April 1954 *Jewish Frontier*, in which a version of Heschel's talk to the CCAR had previously appeared. See Rabbi Morton Berman's letter of 22 April 1954 in *Jewish Frontier* (June 1954) and Heschel's reply of 21 May 1954 in the same issue.

47. I have found no accounts of this talk, which took place some time in 1954 at HUC in Cincinnati, other than the text and an audio tape recording. "Heschel Address to Students of Hebrew Union College," edited and with an introduction by Samuel H. Dresner, remains unpublished; the parable is quoted, with slight modifications, from this typescript. Audio tapes available from the American Jewish Archives, Cincinnati. See Samuel E. Karff, letter to Samuel Dresner, 23 June 1982, Heschel Archive.

Chapter 9. A Jewish Summa Theologica

1. For overviews of the debates within American Judaism see Goldy 1990; Eisen 1982; Staub 2002. Important contributions to the debate include Herberg 1947; Herberg 1949; Fackenheim 1948; Fackenheim 1950; Emanuel Rackman, "Orthodox Judaism Moves with the Times: The Creativity of Tradition," *Commentary* (June 1952): 545–50; Jakob J. Petuchowski, "The Question of Jewish Theology," *Judaism* 7 (winter 1958): 49–55.

2. Charles Raddock, "Judaism and the 'Lost' Intellectuals," *Jewish Forum* (July 1952), 95–98; ibid., 98. Raddock also castigated Franz Rosenzweig, Max Brod, Franz Kafka, Simone Weil, Franz Werfel, Henri Bergson, Scholem Asch, and other modern Jews who, in his view, had abandoned or betrayed true Judaism. Years later Raddock became editor of the magazine.

3. Responses by Zeitlin (130), Gutkind (128–29), Howe (130), Kaufmann (133), Fackenheim (132), "Judaism and the 'Lost' Intellectuals (A Symposium)," *Jewish Forum* (September 1952).

4. Al-Yahud 1952–53, pt. 1, pp. 137, 139.

5. Ibid., p. 141; Al-Yahud 1952–53, pt. 2, pp. 48–49. Al-Yahud's identity has remained a mystery, but he was formed in Orthodox Judaism, involved in contemporary debates, and probably an immigrant. (The only other article by Dayyan Al-Yahud I found was "Professor [Chaim] Tschernowitz and His Magnum Opus," *Jewish Forum* [May 1952], 71–72, suggesting, perhaps, that he was a Hebraist who knew Heschel well.) Heschel ignored his corrections, never fixing these mistakes in subsequent editions of his books.

6 On Heschel's own scholarly collection in Europe see Bernard Mandelbaum, memorandum to Louis Finkelstein, 27 March 1947: "Doctor [Salo] Baron has advised Doctor Heschel to communicate with the United States Embassy in Warsaw to retrieve his books"; Finkelstein, letter to the Honorable Stanton Griffiths, United States Ambassador, Warsaw, 8 April 1947: "I understand that Professor Heschel has sent you detailed information about his library. The importance of many of the volumes and manuscripts in his library cannot be overemphasized": JTS General Files. On the YIVO archive, see Zalman Alpert, "A Chasidic Archive That Never Came to Be," *Chasidic Historical Review* 1, 2 (February 1996): 8, 9. Heschel described the process in Heschel 1952, "Umbakante dokumentn tsu der geshikhte fun khasidus."

7. The rabbis' letter is reproduced in Alpert, "Chasidic Archive." See Dresner 1985, "Introduction." Heschel also published a request for materials in *Hadoar*, 8 September 1950.

8. Heschel rejected the hypothesis of Scholem and Joseph Weiss that Hasidism originated in the Sabbatean heresy of the false messiah. See Faierstein 1987; Faierstein 1990. "Once after Scholem gave a lecture on the origins of Hasidism at the Seminary, Heschel took two scholars to his office to show them that he had the manuscripts [Scholem used in his lecture] already," interview with Moses Shulvass.

9. Heschel 1949, "Reb Pinkhes Koritser." See Katz 1980 and corrections in Klein 1980 and Heschel 1987, *I Asked for Wonder*. Heschel 1950–51.

10. Heschel 1952, "Umbakante dokumentn tsu der geshikhte fun khasidus." An unpublished translation by Zanvel Klein is in the Heschel Archive. In 1952 Heschel also published a major study in Hebrew, "Rabbi Pineas of Koretz and the Maggid of Mezeritch" (Heschel 1952).

11. Heschel originally put Louis Ginzberg on his list, but he passed away: Heschel,

letter to James F. Mathias of the Guggenheim Foundation, 3 December 1953, Guggenheim Archives.

12. Schneider letter, Guggenheim Archives.

13. Roger Straus, letter to Thomas Yoseloff (of the Jewish Book Guild), 1 December 1953, Farrar, Straus and Giroux Archives. Roger Straus, letter to Henry Allen Moe, 7 January 1954, Guggenheim Archives.

14. Henry Allen Moe, letter to Heschel, 19 April 1954; Heschel, letter to Moe, 21 April 1954; Letter of Appointment, 1 November 1954, Guggenheim Archives; "Guggenheim Fund Grants $1,000,000," *New York Times*, 3 May 1954, 32; Finkelstein, letter to Heschel, 3 May 1954, JTS General Files.

15. Interview with Arthur Green. A student at Union Seminary, Charles Brewster, remembers Heschel watching the flames with "his eyes filled with tears and he couldn't speak," Brewster, letter to Carline Glick, 7 June 1989, Heschel Archive. On the archive see *News of the YIVO* (Summer 2000), 12. This collection concerns religious Jewish life in the Borough Park section of Brooklyn, New York.

16. Heschel, letters to Grayzel, 21 April 1954, late September 1954, JPS Archives.

17. See Marmur 2005.

18. Straus requested a speedy process without additional readers, "believing naturally that any work by Dr. Heschel on such a subject would be first rate": Roger Straus, letter to Grayzel, 25 May 1954; Shalom Spiegel, letter to Grayzel, 25 May 1954; Grayzel, letter to Spiegel, 26 May 1954; Heschel, letter to Grayzel, 11 June 1954; Heschel, letter to Grayzel, 18 June 1954, accepting Grayzel's invitation; Minutes of the JPS Publications Committee, 31 October 1954, JPS Archives.

19. Heschel, letter to Max Arzt, 12 July 1954, JTS General Files. See also Heschel, letter to Jessica Feingold, 25 July 1954, asking for copyright permission to include his article on symbolism for the Finkelstein volume: JTS General Files. The two articles were Heschel 1939, "Das Gebet als Äusserung und Einfühlung," and Heschel 1945, "Prayer." See Kaplan and Dresner 1998, 300–301. On the book's publication see Lesser Zussman, letter to Heschel, 15 November 1954, JPS Archives. Finkelstein, letter to Heschel, 21 October 1954, JTS General Files.

20. Heschel distinguished between *descriptive* and *indicative* words; see Heschel 1955, *God in Search of Man*, 181–83; Kaplan 1973; Kaplan 1996, chap. 4. Heschel 1954, *Man's Quest for God*, 26, 27, 25.

21. Heschel 1954, *Man's Quest for God*, 39–40.

22. Ibid., 150. Thanks to Martin Kavka for this important detail.

23. New York Regional Round Table on "The Responsibility of Higher Education for Judeo-Christian Values in American Culture," 26–27 November 1954, at Earl Hall, Columbia University. See Herman E. Wornom, General Secretary of the Religious Education Association, letter to Heschel, 31 December 1954, with application for membership enclosed, Religious Education Association Archive, Yale Divinity School Library, New Haven. See Schmidt 1983, 156nn26,27.

24. Nash K. Burger, "Very thoughtful and deeply spiritual messages," *Kirkus* (1 October 1954). Burger also placed a short notice in the *New York Times* of 21 November 1954. See also *Saturday Review* (5 March 1955). Herberg, review of *Man's Quest for God, Theology Today* (October 1955), 404–6. Herberg included some advance information, not all correct, about the publication of the second volume of the "Philosophy" (the "Philosophy of Judaism"), as yet unnamed, and *Die Prophetie* ("soon to appear in English translation").

25. Friedman 1955, 18–20.

26. Edward A. Synan, S.J., "Abraham Heschel and Prayer," *The Bridge: A Yearbook of Judeo-Christian Studies,* ed. John M. Oesterreicher (New York: Pantheon, 1955), 256–65. *The Bridge* was put out by the Institute of Judeo-Christian Studies, inspired by the words of Pope Pius XII, "Spiritually we are Semites."

27. Ira Eisenstein, "Book Notes," *The Reconstructionist* (30 December 1955), 24–26.

28. See Marmur 2005.

29. Lesser Zussman, letter to Heschel, 8 November 1954, JPS Archives.

30. Roger Straus, letter to Grayzel, 22 March 1955, JPS Archives. The title was still under discussion. See Zussman, letter to Straus, 23 March 1955; Straus, letter to Zussman, 24 March 1955, JPS Archives; Memorandum from Roger Straus of 28 March 1955 to P.M., cc to HV and J. Peck: "It has now been definitely agreed that the title of the book will be PHILOSOPHY OF JUDAISM, with the subtitle "God in Search of Man." The subtitle should be played up and the main title played down. This has been approved by Grayzel and Heschel": Farrar, Straus and Giroux Archives. Finally, Straus suggested a definitive title: *God in Search of Man: A Philosophy of Judaism.*

31. Heschel 1955, "The Last Years of Maimonides"; repr. Heschel 1966, *The Insecurity of Freedom.* The biography was first translated into French in 1936. A Spanish version appeared in 1969, and the entire book was not translated into English until 1982.

32. Memorandum from J. Peck to Mrs. Pat Van Doren, 2 August 1955; Pat Van Doren, letter of 4 August 1955 to Zussman; Lesser Zussman, letter to Pat Van Doren, Farrar, Straus and Giroux Archives; H. D. Vursell, production manager of Farrar, Straus and Cudahy, letter to Lesser Zussman, 19 September 1955; Grayzel, letter to Heschel, 4 October 1955; Van Doren, letter to Zussman, 28 November 1955, JPS Archives. In October 1955, Heschel wrote optimistically to Grayzel that he expected to complete the translation by March or April 1956. Would it be possible for JPS to distribute the book in the fall of 1956? Heschel letter to Grayzel, 16 October 1955, JPS Archives. But the following June he revised his schedule: "Let me inform you that I have been working hard on my book on the prophets. It is not going to be a translation at all but a completely rewritten work. I hope that the book will be ready for publication in January or February 1957. As you recall, the book has been accepted by the Jewish Publication Society, and I think you could sched-

ule its publication for the fall of 1957": Heschel, letter to Grayzel, 26 June 1956, JPS Archives.

33. S. Feld, Farrar, Straus Subsidiary Rights, letter to Elliot E. Cohen, editor of *Commentary*, 6 October 1955; Martin Greenberg, managing editor of *Commentary*, letter to S. Feld, 13 October 1955; Zussman, letter to Roger Straus, 1 November 1955, Farrar, Straus and Giroux Archive.

34. *Library Journal* (1 December 1955); Kirkus Review Service (1 January 1956), 38. See also *Book Review Digest* (1 January 1956), 345.

35. Heschel 1955, *God in Search of Man*, 138, 143n5. See Edward Kaplan 1996, chap. 9, "Metaphor and Miracle: Modern Judaism and the Holy Spirit." Heschel 1945, "Did Maimonides Strive for Prophetic Inspiration?"; Heschel 1950, "'Al ruah ha-kodesh bimey ha-beynayim" trans. in Heschel 1996, *Prophetic Inspiration After the Prophets*.

36. Heschel 1955, *God in Search of Man*, 258–59; cf. "The cardinal sin in thinking about ultimate issues is *literal mindedness*" (178–79). Around 1960–62 Heschel completed two volumes in Hebrew dealing with the multiple interpretations of divine revelation among the rabbis of the Talmud. See Heschel 1962, 1965, 1990, *Torah min ha-shamayim;* trans. in Heschel 2005, *Heavenly Torah As Refracted Through the Generations*. Heschel 1955, *God in Search of Man*, 244.

37. Heschel 1955, *God in Search of Man*, 317–19n3.

38. Ibid., 341.

39. Ibid., 369.

40. Ibid., 425.

41. Ibid., 421, 425–26.

42. Lynn Caine, director of publicity, letter to Philip Slomovitz of the *Jewish News* (Detroit), 2 January 1956, Farrar, Straus and Giroux Archives. Roger Straus sent letters with advance copies of the book to H. Richard Niebuhr of Yale University and Paul Tillich of Harvard Divinity School on 6 January 1956: Farrar, Straus and Giroux Archives. A. Powell Davies, "Revelation and the Needs of Man," *New York Times*, 12 February 1956, 5.

43. Unsigned article (probably by the religion editor, John Elsen), *Time* (19 March 1956), 64; Reinhold Niebuhr, "The Mysteries of Faith," *Saturday Review* (31 April 1956), 18. See Reinhold Niebuhr, letter to Roger Straus, 9 February 1956, Farrar, Straus and Giroux Archives. Straus sent the quotation from Niebuhr's essay to Heschel, letter of 10 February 1955; see William D. Patterson, letter to Roger Straus, 30 March 1956, Farrar, Straus and Giroux Archives.

44. Will Herberg, "Converging Trails," *Christian Century* (18 April 1956), 486. Heschel sent a copy of this review to Roger Straus; see Straus, letter to Heschel, 5 April 1956, Farrar, Straus and Giroux Archives. Jack Riemer, review of *God in Search of Man, The Torch* (1956), 23–24; Marshall T. Meyer, "A Matter of Life and Death," *Jerusalem Post*, 15 June 1956, 8. On the other side, a skeptical review by

Paul Vishny appeared in *Congress Weekly* which included a number of common misunderstandings of Heschel's ideas, such as his "refusal to accord reason a substantial role in the act of believing": Paul Vishny, "The Priority of Faith," *Congress Weekly* (14 May 1956), 14–15.

45. James Muilenburg, review of *God in Search of Man, Religious Education* (July–August 1956), 315. Muilenburg ended by recognizing differences: "In Christianity the sense of sin is more pronounced and 'tragic,' the need for redemption more imperative, the hope for an outcome or resolution, the eschatological hope more insistent and strong. . . . the centrality of the Christ dominates the faith and gives to it a different atmosphere and quality" (316).

46. Maurice Friedman, review of *God in Search of Man, Religious Education* (July–August 1956), 317.

47. Herbert Schneider, review of *God in Search of Man, Review of Religion* 21, 1–2 (November 1956): 31–38. See also Friedman 1955.

48. There was still no academic Orthodox journal in the United States, but Orthodox Jews had begun to form a centralized rabbinic association. See Charles S. Liebman, "A Sociological Analysis of Contemporary Orthodoxy," *Judaism* 13, 3 (summer 1964): 285–304.

49. Joseph H. Lookstein, "The Neo-Hasidism of Abraham J. Heschel," *Judaism* 5, 3 (summer 1956): 248. See Heschel 1955, *God in Search of Man*, 251–52. Rabbi Lookstein founded the Ramaz school, an Orthodox Jewish Day School, and was its principal for thirty years. Heschel sent his daughter, Susannah, there.

50. Emanuel Rackman, "Can We Moderns Keep the Sabbath?" *Commentary* (September 1954), 211–20; Rackman, "Dr. Heschel's Answer," *Jewish Horizon* (October 1956), 16.

51. Rackman, "Dr. Heschel's Answer," 17–18. See also Zalman M. Schachter, "Hasidism and Neo-Hasidism," *Judaism* 9, 3 (summer 1960): 216–21, and the later debate: Marvin Fox, "Heschel, Intuition and the Halakhah," *Tradition* 3, 1 (fall 1960): 5–15; Zalman Schachter, "Two Facets of Judaism," *Tradition* 3, 2 (spring 1961): 191–202.

52. Material about Horwitz from Horwitz, letter to Samuel Dresner, 2 March 1989, Heschel Archive; interview with Rivka Horwitz.

53. Scholem 1941, 337; interview with Fritz Rothschild.

54. *God in Search of Man*, however, was not published in Hebrew translation until 2002: *Elohim mevakesh et ha-adam: filosofyah shel ha-Yahadut.* Trans. Meir-Levi 'Azan. Jerusalem: Magnes Press, Hebrew University.

Part Three. Spiritual Radical

1. Sanders 1973.

Chapter 10. Building Bridges

1. Heschel 1956, "Teaching Religion to American Jews," 4, also in Heschel 1996, *Moral Grandeur and Spiritual Audacity*, 149. This essay was drawn from interviews and books, probably by the magazine's editors. Chapter 38 of *God in Search of Man*, "The Problem of Integrity," 387–95, is also relevant to Heschel's public statements on Jewish education.

2. Heschel 1956, "The Biblical View of Reality," repr. in Heschel 1996, *Moral Grandeur and Spiritual Audacity*, 354, 361, 365.

3. Heschel lectured on 5, 6, 7 February 1957. The interview was with Nan Rosenthal, *Sophian*, 21 February 1957, Smith College Archives, Northampton, Massachusetts.

4. Heschel 1956, "A Hebrew Evaluation of Reinhold Niebuhr." Other contributors included Rabbi Alexander J. Burnstein of New York City; Emil Brunner, International Christian University, Tokyo; Paul Tillich, Harvard University; Paul Ramsey, Princeton University; Gustave Weigel, S.J., Woodstock College; John C. Bennett, Union Theological Seminary; Arthur Schlesinger, Jr., Harvard University; and Daniel D. Williams, the University of Chicago. For Heschel's sources see Heschel 1955, *God in Search of Man*, chap. 36, "The Problem of Evil," and chap. 37, "The Problem of the Neutral," and references to Reinhold Niebuhr, *Nature and Destiny of Man* (380n5), and *An Interpretation of Christian Ethics* (381n19). Rabbi Alexander J. Burnstein, "Niebuhr, Scripture, and Normative Judaism," Charles Kegley and Robert Bretall, eds., *Reinhold Niebuhr: His Religious, Social, and Political Thought* (New York: Macmillan, 1956), 412–28, countered Niebuhr's pessimism with Jewish sources that were more "optimistic" than those cited by Heschel.

5. Heschel 1956, "A Hebrew Evaluation of Reinhold Niebuhr," 399, 405, 406–7, quoting *An Interpretation of Christian Ethics:* "the possibilities of evil grow with the possibilities of good."

6. Interview with Wolfe Kelman, 5 January 1988.

7. Niebuhr's address to the joint JTS and Union Theological Seminary faculty meeting, "The Relations of Christians and Jews in Western Civilization," was incorporated into his *Pious and Secular America* (New York: Scribner's, 1958). See Seymour Siegel, "Reinhold Niebuhr: In Memoriam," *American Jewish Year Book* (1972): 605–10.

8. Ursula Niebuhr, "Notes on a Friendship: Abraham Joshua Heschel and Reinhold Niebuhr," Merkle 1985, *Abraham Joshua Heschel*, 35–43.

9. Heschel 1957, "Sacred Images of Man," repr. in *Religious Education*, 97. Heschel's fellow speakers at the assembly were Gustave Weigel, S.J., professor of Ecclesiology at Woodstock College, representing the Catholic view, and Roger L.

Shinn, professor of Christian Ethics at the Vanderbilt University Divinity School, representing the Protestant view.

10. Ibid., 100.

11. Ibid., 102, the final lines. See also Heschel 1962, *The Prophets*, 185–86; Heschel 1966, *The Insecurity of Freedom*, "Sacred Image of Man," 165–66; and below, chap. 16, p. 315.

12. Heschel 1965, *Who Is Man?* notes: "Many important aspects of the problem of man have not been discussed in this volume, while others have been dealt with too briefly. But the volume will serve as a prolegomena to a more comprehensive study in which I have been engaged for some time." Heschel 1960, "The Concept of Man in Jewish Thought."

13. Heschel 1958, "The Religious Message," 252.

14. Ibid. When the speech was revised for his 1966 collection *The Insecurity of Freedom*, Heschel added, "Religion is not for religion's sake but for God's sake. Who is 'gracious and merciful . . . good to all, and His compassion is over all that he has made'" (Psalm 145:8 ff.), 9.

15. Heschel 1958, "The Religious Message," 264. Packard had addressed the 1957 convention of the Religious Education Association at which Heschel spoke on "Sacred Images of Man." See Vance Packard, "Images and Morals in the Mass Manipulation of Human Behavior," *Religious Education* (March–April 1958), 127–33.

16. Heschel 1958, "The Religious Message," 270.

17. Reported in Finkelstein, letter to Heschel, 9 June 1958, JTS General Files.

18. Finkelstein, letter to Heschel, 5 January 1959, JTS General Files.

19. Heschel, "Some Basic Issues of Jewish Education," plenary talk given to the "Fifth Annual Pedagogic Conference, Institute of Jewish Studies," 9 February 1958 (Cleveland Bureau of Jewish Education, mimeographed booklet), 3–12. Further quotations in the text will be from this source.

20. Heschel, "The Relevance of Prophecy," seminar given to the "Fifth Annual Pedagogic Conference, Institute of Jewish Studies," 9 February 1958 (Cleveland Bureau of Jewish Education, mimeographed booklet), 13–19. Further quotations in the text will be from this source.

21. Heschel first published this passage in the final paragraph of Heschel 1950, "'Al ruah ha-kodesh bimey ha-beynayim" (in Hebrew, Prophetic inspiration in the Middle Ages), trans. in Heschel 1996, *Prophetic Inspiration After the Prophets*, 67. See Heschel 1955, *God in Search of Man*, 138; Edward Kaplan 1996, chap. 9. See also below, chap. 11, text at n. 32, for a similar passage.

22. "Even before Israel becomes a people, the land is preordained for it. What we have witnessed in our days is a reminder of the power of God's mysterious promise to Abraham and a testimony to the fact that the people kept its promise: 'If I forget thee, O Jerusalem, let my right hand wither' (Psalms 137:5)": Heschel 1955,

God in Search of Man, 425. It was also true that Gershom Scholem prevented Heschel from receiving a visiting appointment to any Israeli university.

23. Heschel 1951, "To Be a Jew," 81, repr. in Heschel 1996, *Moral Grandeur and Spiritual Audacity*, 7. The Yiddish original of Heschel's article appeared in 1947 in the newspaper *Yidisher Kemfer*.

24. Conversation with Sylvia Heschel. The state of Israel was proclaimed on 14 May 1948.

25. Interview with Wolfe Kelman.

26. On Tova Perlow see Kaplan and Dresner 1998, 50–52, 60, 69, 72. Heschel, letter to Wolfe Kelman, 4 August 1957; Kelman, letter to Heschel, 7 August 1957, Kelman personal files, which were uncataloged at JTS when I consulted them. All JTS General Files.

27. Eva Grunebaum, "Jewish Mystic, Modern Scholar," *Jerusalem Post*, 15 August 1957.

28. Heschel 1961, "The Individual Jew and His Obligations," 10. The original Hebrew speech, Heschel 1957, "The Nation and the Individual," was reprinted in various forms, including an English translation. See the References. This translation has been coordinated with the edited version in Heschel 1966, *The Insecurity of Freedom*, 187–211. Heschel 1961, "The Individual Jew and His Obligations," 26, Heschel 1966, *The Insecurity of Freedom*, 210.

29. Heschel 1961, "The Individual Jew and His Obligations," 12, Heschel 1966, *The Insecurity of Freedom*, 189.

30. Heschel 1961, "The Individual Jew and His Obligations," 12–13, Heschel 1966, *The Insecurity of Freedom*, 191 (passage revised); Heschel 1961, "The Individual Jew and His Obligations," 16, Heschel 1966, *The Insecurity of Freedom*, 198.

31. Heschel 1961, "The Individual Jew and His Obligations," 17–18, Heschel 1966, *The Insecurity of Freedom*, 199–200; Heschel 1961, "The Individual Jew and His Obligations," 26, Heschel 1966, *The Insecurity of Freedom*, 210.

32. *Jerusalem Post*, 16 August 1957.

33. Heschel 1958, "Yisrael: Am, Eretz, Medinah," 119.

34. Ibid., 118–19. Heschel spoke on 29 April.

35. Ibid. This was Heschel's second public condemnation of racism in America.

36. Ibid., 126, 136.

37. The Israeli government made the responses available in mimeographed form. The participants included the world's most respected Jewish thinkers. The American rabbis were Aaron Kotler of Lakewood, New Jersey, Menachem Mendel Schneerson, Hayyim Heller, Joseph Soloveitchik, Louis Finkelstein, and Solomon Freehof, a Reform rabbi from Pittsburgh. Heschel was placed among the American scholars with Mordecai Kaplan, Saul Lieberman, Alexander Altmann from Brandeis University, and Harry A. Wolfson. Among the Israeli rabbis were Yitzhak Isaac Herzog and Shlomo Goren; European rabbis included Jacob Kaplan of France, the Beth Din [Rabbinic Court] of London, Sabato Toaff of Rome, Yechiel Y. Weinberg of

Switzerland. Scholars from Israel included Samuel Hugo Bergman, Ernst Simon, and Ephraim E. Urbach.

38. Ben-Gurion's letter and virtually all the replies were in Hebrew. I quote from Hoenig and Litvin 1965. Heschel's answer was dated 18 December 1958 (7 Tevet 5719) and is reprinted as "Answer to Ben Gurion," Hoenig and Litvin 1965, 229–31 (quotation on p. 229). See Heschel 1959, "Answer to Ben Gurion," for reprints in both English and Hebrew.

39. Heschel, "Answer to Ben Gurion," Hoenig and Litvin 1965, 229.

40. Ibid., 230: "All that remain to us [are] the Torah, and one's heart's desire to find a road to a life which would have an aspect of eternal life."

41. Ibid., 231.

42. Joseph Soloveitchik and Hayyim Heller, Hoenig and Litvak 1965, 117 (all responses were untitled and written in the form of a letter to the prime minister).

43. Louis Finkelstein, Hoenig and Litvak 1965, 121; Mordecai Kaplan, Hoenig and Litvak 1965, 235.

44. Heschel 1960, "Should the United Synagogue of America Join the World Zionist Organization?" 77 (I corrected several typographical errors). The meeting took place 15–19 November 1959 at the Concord Hotel, Kiamesha Lake, New York. See *New York Times*, 18 November 1959; *The Torch* titled its article "The Great Debate." Heschel's experiences in Europe, before and during Hitler's rise to power, had given him an unmovable suspicion of political thinking. In 1939 he complained to Martin Buber that people in Poland were limited by "an exclusively political orientation." See Kaplan and Dresner 1998, 282–83.

45. *New York Times*, 18 November 1959. The paper featured a photograph of a younger, beardless Heschel and identified him as the instigator of the split.

46. Heschel announced in a publicity memorandum dated January 1959 that two books were "scheduled to appear in the near future": *The Idea of Mosaic Revelation in Jewish History* and *The Prophets of Israel*, Marc H. Tanenbaum, personal papers, American Jewish Archives. See Rothschild 1959, Introduction to *Between God and Man:* "The Battle of the Book, a documented history of the manner in which Jewish rabbis and thinkers wrestled with the problems of Mosaic revelation" (9). Articles on Heschel included Maurice Friedman, "Abraham Joshua Heschel: Toward a Philosophy of Judaism," *Conservative Judaism* 10, 2 (Winter 1956): 1–10 (see also Friedman 1955); Herbert Schneider, "On Reading *God in Search of Man:* A Review Article," *Review of Religion* 21, 1–2 (November 1956): 31–38; J. Lookstein, "The Neo-Hasidism of Abraham J. Heschel," *Judaism* 5, 3 (summer 1956): 248–55. Jakob Petuchowski, "Faith as a Leap of Action," *Commentary* (May 1958), 390–97; Edmond La B. Cherbonnier, "Abraham Joshua Heschel and the Philosophy of the Bible: Mystic or Rationalist?" *Commentary* (January 1959), 23–29. Heschel cited Cherbonnier's *Hardness of Heart: A Contemporary Interpretation of the Doctrine of Sin* (London: Gollanz, 1956) in *The Prophets*.

47. Petuchowski, "Faith as a Leap of Action," 390; Cherbonnier, "Heschel and the Philosophy of the Bible," 23.

48. Rothschild 1959, "God and Modern Man." Heschel was at this time a contributing editor of the journal, along with Salo W. Baron, Hugo Bergman, Martin Buber, Emil Fackenheim, Marvin Fox, Nahum Glatzer, Emanuel Rackman, Ernst Simon, Harry Wolfson, and others. Felix A. Levy, a leading Reform rabbi in Chicago (and Wolfe Kelman's father-in-law), was the editor. Rothschild was identified as a rabbi in Philadelphia.

   In the bibliography of the first edition Rothschild omitted Heschel's first book, a collection of Yiddish poems, *Der Shem Hameforash: Mentsh* (1933), and he cited Harold Knight's book, which had plagiarized Heschel, as "an exposition in English of the ideas presented in *Die Prophetie.*" In his biographical summary, Rothschild did not mention Heschel's diploma from the Realgymnasium of Vilna, something he learned about only after Heschel's death. Rothschild's bibliography was last revised in 1975.

49. Rothschild 1959, Introduction to *Between God and Man*, 22, 24.

50. Ibid., 30; interview with Fritz Rothschild.

51. Arthur A. Cohen, review of *Between God and Man, Christian Century* (24 June 1959), 751. In 1961 Reinhold Niebuhr contributed a laudatory notice on the Rothschild anthology to *Conservative Judaism* 25, 3 (spring): 45.

Chapter 11. A Prophetic Witness

1. After 1961 Tanenbaum headed interreligious affairs at the American Jewish Committee, a position from which he helped Heschel extend his international presence. See Tanenbaum 2002.

2. Memorandum dated 6 April 1960 from Morris Fine and Samuel Fishzohn, director of AJC's youth division; conference program; Heschel's untitled address is quoted from a mimeographed copy dated 27 March 1960, AJC/NY Archives.

3. *New York Times*, 28 March 1960, 1, 23.

4. *Washington Post*, 29 March 1960, A1. Heschel also suggested that the government supplement compulsory military service in peacetime with "compulsory adult education for leisure time for the sake of spiritual security." Later in the week about 1,400 youth delegates, supported by Kenneth Clark of the New York Youth Commission and Buell Gallager, president of the City College of New York, urged delegates to uphold the Supreme Court decision to desegregate the public schools and to support peaceful sit-down demonstrations in favor of black students: *New York Times*, 31 March 1960, 27; 1 April 1960, 25; 2 April 1960, 25.

5. Memoranda and other preparatory materials for the 1960 "White House Conference" from AJC/NY Archives; Heschel 1960, "Call of the Hour."

6. Heschel, letter to Finkelstein, 1 May 1959, JTS General Files. Susannah attended the public school and a synagogue Hebrew School: Susannah Heschel, postcard to Jessica Feingold, undated, JTS General Files.

7. Interviews with Louis Milgrom, David Cooperman; Heschel, letter to Wolfe Kelman, 8(?) April 1960, JTS General Files. A month after his arrival, the student newspaper published an interview with Heschel: Bev Kees, "Rabbi Heschel Says, Words Are Vessels of the Spirit," *Minnesota Daily*, 4 May 1960.

8. Interview with David Cooperman.

9. Ibid.

10. The meeting took place on 23 April 1960. Heschel, "The Moral Challenge to America," mimeographed transcript, 312, from Marc H. Tanenbaum, personal papers, American Jewish Archives. Published in Heschel 1959, "Who Is Man," *Proceedings of the 53rd Annual Meeting of the American Jewish Committee*. The speech began with a dire warning: "Man may be dying but there will be no one to write his history. This is the problem that shatters all complacency, 'Is man obsolete?'" (transcript, 292). The answer, he argued, was for intellectual leaders to formulate a positive definition of the human. Heschel's speech borrows many elements and passages from Heschel 1958, "The Religious Message."

11. Heschel 1960, "Depth Theology." The term *depth theology* appears both hyphenated and open in Heschel's works. Except in quotation, I use *depth theology* throughout. Heschel first introduced the term in *God in Search of Man*, chap. 1, subsection "Depth-Theology," 7–8. J. Cunneen, editorial, *CrossCurrents* (fall 1960), 313.

12. Heschel 1960, "Depth Theology," 318–20.

13. *New York Times*, 11 January 1961, 1, 18, 19; *New York Times*, 13 January 1961, 16; *New York World Telegram and Sun*, 31 December 1960; internal report of the Synagogue Council of America (January–February 1961), 3–4, Heschel Archive; Tanenbaum, letter to Warren Roudebusch, 5 April 1961, AJC/NY.

14. Heschel 1961 "To Grow in Wisdom," repr. Heschel 1990, *To Grow in Wisdom*, 179–91 (quotations on pp. 179, 180). The speech was considerably revised for Heschel 1966, *The Insecurity of Freedom*, 70–84.

15. Heschel 1990, *To Grow in Wisdom*, 181. Heschel set the emphasized phrase at the end of the essay when he revised it for *The Insecurity of Freedom* (Heschel 1966, 84):

"It takes three things to attain a sense of significant being:
> God
> A Soul
> And a Moment.
And the three are always here.
Just to be is a blessing. Just to live is holy."

16. Representative John E. Fogarty of Rhode Island placed the speech in the 21 March 1961 *Congressional Record;* it also appeared in the 14 June 1961 issue.

17. While he was still committed to the University of Minnesota, Heschel had accepted the invitation to take up a visiting professorship from Robert Michaelsen, director of the School of Religion at the University of Iowa. Heschel asked whether he could postpone his visit: Michaelsen, letter to Heschel, 14 May 1959; Heschel, letters to Michaelsen, 22 May 1959, 25 November 1959. Having met Heschel at the University of Minnesota, Michaelsen wrote to Louis Finkelstein on 18 May 1960 to get his agreement to the appointment. The official letter of appointment was dated 22 June 1960, and Heschel's acceptance of it dated 24 June 1960: University of Iowa Archives. Kay Armstrong, "Indifference to Evil Biggest Evil, Rabbi Heschel Says," *Daily Iowan*, 9 February 1961, front page. See above, chap. 10, p. 182, on Heschel's speech at the November 1957 convention of the Religious Education Association in Chicago, in which he quoted the same passage. See also below, chap. 16, p. 315.

18. Sherman 1970, an excellent introductory volume in the series on contemporary theologians directed by Martin Marty. See also Sherman 1963. Heschel, letter to Michaelsen, 4 June 1961, responding to Michaelsen, letter to Heschel, 1 June 1961, University of Iowa Archives.

19. Obituary of Ilya Schor, *New York Times*, 8 June 1961, 35; Heschel's obituary of Bavli in *Hadoar*, 8 December 1961, translated for *Conservative Judaism* 17, 1–2 (fall–winter); see Kaplan and Dresner 1998, 195–97.

20. Heschel 1961, "Ilya Schor." See Ilya Schor's essay in the same issue, "A Working Definition of Jewish Art" (translated from the Yiddish by Harry Z. Sky), *Conservative Judaism* 16, 1 (fall 1961): 28–33.

21. Heschel 1962–63, "Hillel Bavli: In Memoriam."

22. Remarks by Greenberg, Schafler, Kelman, *Proceedings* 1962.

23. Heschel, "The Values of Jewish Education," *Proceedings* 1962, 83–85; comments by Simcha Kling and David Lieber, *Proceedings* 1962, 101–9. Heschel spoke on Tuesday evening, 22 May 1962. Seymour Fox was decisively influenced by Heschel and introduced his approach into the curriculum at the Teachers Institute.

24. Heschel, "The Values of Jewish Education," 86. As an example, Heschel quoted and applied a Midrash: "Revelation gives us an answer to the fundamental, vital question: is the ultimate Being good or evil? Judaism is a way of thinking. And we must be committed, and we are committed, in spite of Auschwitz" (88).

25. Ibid., 93, 98.

26. Heschel, "'Arakim ba-hinukh hayehudi" (The values of Jewish education), *Proceedings of the International Biennial Convention* (May 1962), 72, 75 (address given to the International Biennial Convention, World Council of Synagogues, Jerusalem, 29–31 May 1962). This international meeting included Simon Greenberg; Georges Lévitte, from Paris, who translated *The Earth Is the Lord's* and *The Sabbath* into French; Heschel's former student and disciple Marshall Meyer, recently settled in Buenos Aires; Ernst Akiva Simon from Israel; Yitzhak Ben-Zvi,

president of Israel; and Moshe Sharett, chairman of the World Zionist Organization. Files of World Council of Synagogues.

27. Bernard Siegel, Alfred Hirschberg, responses, *Proceedings of the International Biennial Convention* (May 1962), 81–82.

28. Heschel, "Idols in the Temples," *Religious Education* (March–April 1962), 127–37. Repr. in Heschel 1966, *The Insecurity of Freedom*, 52–69. The meeting took place 18–20 November 1962.

29. Heschel 2005, *Heavenly Torah As Refracted Through the Generations*, 255. The title page in English of the first edition reads, *The Theology of Ancient Judaism*. The first volume (295 pages) appeared in 1962, and volume 2 (440 pages) in 1965.

30. Interviews with Fritz Rothschild.

31. Heschel published excerpts from the introduction in Meisel's newspaper as "Two Methods in Jewish Religious Thought" (Hebrew), *Hadoar*, 8 February 1963, 244–46, and 15 February 1963, 262–63. Note from Samuel Dresner, Heschel Archive; Sylvia Heschel 1990; Susannah Heschel 2005.

32. From the Hebrew volume, Heschel 1962, 1965, 1990, *Torah min ha-shamayim be-aspaklaryah shel ha-dorot*, vol. 1, pp. xliii, 180, as cited by Leonard Levin, "Heschel's Homage to the Rabbis: *Torah Min Hashamayim* as Historical Theology," *Conservative Judaism* 50, 2–3 (winter–spring 1998): 56–66 (quotation on p. 61). Heschel summarized these contrasts in chaps. 1–2, "Introduction" and "Two Approaches to Torah Exegesis," Heschel 2005, *Heavenly Torah as Refracted Through the Generations*, 1–64. See chap. 10, p. 187, on Heschel's seminar to the Cleveland teachers, in which he noted, "How marvelous that we have both interpretations. They supplement each other," seminar given to the "Fifth Annual Pedagogic Conference, Institute of Jewish Studies," 9 February 1958 (Cleveland Bureau of Jewish Education, mimeographed booklet), 19.

33. Heschel 2005, *Heavenly Torah as Refracted Through the Generations*, 34, 35. Cf. Louis Finkelstein's biography, *Akiba: Scholar, Saint and Martyr* (Philadelphia: Jewish Publication Society of America, 1936).

34. See Levin, "Heschel's Homage to the Rabbis"; Rebecca Schorsch, "The Hermeneutics of Heschel in *Torah min Hashamayim*," *Judaism* 43, 3 (summer 1991): 301–8; Kaplan and Dresner 1998, 43–45, on the Novominsker rebbe of Warsaw.

35. The discussion in this paragraph was inspired by Eisen 2003. Tucker translated the last phrase as "May their Souls be bound up in the bond of life." See Kaplan and Dresner 1998, 306, and Eisen 2003, 217. For similar reflections see Heschel 1969, *Israel*, 112; Heschel 1973, *A Passion for Truth*, "The Kotzker and Job," 261–303.

36. Interview with Fritz Rothschild, 10 May 1989, who had the story from Wolfe Kelman. Neither note has been located.

37. Louis Jacobs, review of *Torah min ha-shamayim be-aspaklaryah shel ha-dorot*, *Conservative Judaism* 18, 2 (Winter 1964): 59–61; David Shlomo Shapiro, "Hashkafah hadashah al shitoteihem shel Rabbi Ishmael ve-Rabbi Akiva" (A new view on the systems of Rabbis Akiva and Ishmael), *Hadoar*, 27 September 1963, 769; Neusner 1966.

38. Ya'akov Levinger, "He'arot le-Torah min hashamayim" (Notes on *Torah min hashamayim*), *De'ot*, Winter 1966, 45–48; Rivka Horwitz, "'Iyyun hadash be-makhshevet ha-t'annaim [ma'amar bikoret]," (A new study in Tannaitic thought: a critical article), *Molad*, 1965: 239–42. See Gordon Tucker, preface to Heschel 2005, *Heavenly Torah as Refracted Through the Generations*, xxvn5.

   Heschel suffered at the hands of the Israeli academic establishment. Ephraim Urbach's introduction to his groundbreaking synthesis of rabbinic thought, *The Sages*, criticized Heschel unfairly for ignoring "philological examination and form-criticism of the sources." The note cited Heschel's book as providing "numerous examples of the neglect of these principles." Urbach denigrated Heschel's demonstration that the Talmud itself was a locus of original theology: "In truth the author attempts to adumbrate in it a theology of his own, in the same way as his book *God in Search of Man*": Ephraim Urbach, *Hazal: Pirkei Emunot Vedeot* (Jerusalem: Magnes, 1971), 14n26; English trans.: Israel Abrahams, *The Sages: Their Concepts and Beliefs* (Cambridge: Harvard University Press, 1987), 695n20. For a critical appraisal of Urbach's classic book and its reputation see Jacob Neusner, "Urbach's *Hazal* Revisited on the Occasion of a Reprint, After Fifteen Years," *Religious Studies and Theology* 8 (January–May 1988): 66–74.

   On a more banal note, his monumental work allowed Heschel to squeeze out a concession from his home institution. He sent Finkelstein the first volume and requested improvements to his onerous teaching schedule. Heschel was relieved of five out of six hours at the Teachers Institute so that he could develop a weekly seminar in the Rabbinical School on sources of Jewish thought: Heschel, letter to Finkelstein, 24 June 1962; David C. Kogen, letter to Heschel, 28 August 1962, JTS General Files.

39. Heschel, letter to Grayzel, 26 June 1956; Grayzel, letter to Heschel, 17 July 1956, JPS Archives. See Sarna 1989.

40. The excerpts were: Heschel 1962, "Prophetic Inspiration," "The Religion of Sympathy," and "Le judaïsme concerne-t-il l'homme américain?"; and Heschel 1963, "Prophétie et poésie" and "The Israelite Prophet in His Relation to God and the People." Heschel, letter to Grayzel, 28 June 1962, JPS Archives. On the need for an outside editor see interview with Fritz Rothschild; Hugh Van Dusen, letter to the author. I found nothing in the Harper and Row archives.

41. Heschel 1962, *The Prophets*, xii. Around this time, Heschel's address to a group of Quakers at Frankfurt-am-Main in February 1938, "Search for a Meaning" (Versuch einer Deutung), was published for the first time: see Heschel 1962, "Versuch einer Deutung"; Edward Kaplan 1996, app. 2: "Heschel in Germany," 163–66.

42. Heschel 1962, *The Prophets*, xii.

43. Cf. Heschel 1951, *Man Is Not Alone*, chap. 16, "The Hiding God."

44. Heschel 1962, *The Prophets*, 14–16 (subsection entitled, "Few Are Guilty, All Are Responsible"), in the chapter "What Manner of Man Is the Prophet?"

45. Ibid., 18. This chapter continued Heschel's old debate with Martin Buber about the prophet as more than an ethical symbol; for Heschel, Hosea scorned offered a "glimpse into the inner life of God" (50–60): see Edward Kaplan 1996, "Sacred versus Symbolic Religion: Social Science or God's Will?" 75–89. See Kaplan and Dresner 1998, 218–28, on Heschel and Buber.

46. Heschel 1962, *The Prophets*, 90.

47. Ibid., 126.

48. Ibid., 143, 151 ("Suffering as chastisement is man's responsibility; suffering as redemption is God's responsibility"). In chapter 10, "Chastisement," Heschel defined a biblical equivalent of a post-Holocaust theology of God's absence: God's punishment of the defiant people was a chastening of the ego, paradoxical, but effective: "Out of despair, out of total inability to believe, prayer bursts forth" (191–92).

49. Ibid., 488.

50. Muilenburg announced the book's forthcoming publication in *Christian Century* (30 January 1963), 147; Gerald B. Cooke, review of *The Prophets*, *Christian Century* (13 March 1963), 337–38; Bruce Vawter, C.M., review of *The Prophets*, *America* (2 March 1963), 309–10.

51. Brevard S. Childs, review of *The Prophets*, *Journal of Biblical Literature* 82 (September 1963): 328–29. Childs disagreed with some of Heschel's definitions, such as "sympathy with God" for *daat elohim*, on scholarly grounds and he regretted the inconsistent quality of references to scholarly sources. On the other hand, James Muilenburg, in *Conservative Judaism* 17, 3–4 (spring–summer 1963): 114–15, praised Heschel's interpretation of *daat elohim* (114). Samuel Terrien, "The Divine Pathos," *Interpretation* 17 (1963): 482–88, 485. Two other sympathetic reviewers pointed to problems Heschel had not yet solved. In *Religious Education* (March–April 1964), 189–90, Norman Gottwald admonished Heschel for "the almost total misunderstanding of ecstasy and mysticism which are categorically excluded from prophecy . . . He falls back on the old stereotypes about mysticism." After a masterful summary of the book, with astute criticism of detail, Maurice Friedman's comprehensive review in *Judaism* 13 (1964): 115–21, criticized Heschel's incomplete response to Martin Buber's philosophy of dialogue (121).

52. David Daiches, "Doom and Love," *Commentary* (June 1963), 537–40. Daiches apparently ignored Heschel's citation of Psalm 44 and the chapter on "Chastisement," which raised the question of undeserved suffering.

53. Ibid., 539–40; Eliezer Berkovits, "Dr. A. J. Heschel's Theology of Pathos," *Tradition* 6, 2 (spring–summer 1964): 70. Berkovits goes on to refute the validity of

this idea, which he has misattributed to Heschel. See E. Munk, letter to the editor, *Tradition* 7, 2 (summer 1965): 143–44. Heschel's discussion of metaphorical language in *God in Search of Man* and *The Prophets* should have eliminated these erroneous charges of literalism. See Edward Kaplan 1973; Kaplan 1996, 176n19.

54. David Shlomo Shapiro, "Haneviim" (The Prophets), *Hadoar*, 4 September 1964, 665–67; see also Shapiro, "A New View on the System of Rabbis Akiva and Ishmael," *Hadoar*, 27 September 1963, 769–72. See Nathan Rotenstreich, "On Prophetic Consciousness," *Journal of Religion* 54, 3 (July 1974): 185–98, the first serious study of *Die Prophetie* and the English revision.

Chapter 12. We Shall Overcome

1. Heschel 1964, "The White Man on Trial," repr. in Heschel 1966, *The Insecurity of Freedom*, 107. King was named man of the year for 1963 by *Time* magazine.
2. Heschel 1958, "Yisrael: Am, Eretz, Medinah," 118; this line was not included in edited version, "Israel and the Diaspora," that Heschel published in *The Insecurity of Freedom* (1966).
3. Minutes of Program Committee Meeting, 7 August 1962, 1–3, AJC/NY, folder "Conf. on Religion and Race." See also official letters of invitation from Mathew Ahmann to Heschel, 5 October 1962, and to M. L. King, 4 October 1962; unpublished memorandum by Rabbi Balfour Brickner, director, Interfaith Activities, and associate director, Commission on Social Action, Union of American Hebrew Congregations (Reform), 15 pp., AJC/NY, folder "Conf. on Religion and Race"; Tanenbaum 2002.
4. Program, "National Conference on Religion and Race," Chicago, 14–17 January 1963.
5. I quote from Heschel's reading manuscript (identified as "1963 MS"), marked with his pauses, underlined words, cut and pasted pages, and corrections, AJC/NY. See also Heschel 1963, "The Religious Basis of Equal Opportunity."
6. Heschel 1963 MS, 5a, Heschel 1963, "The Religious Basis of Equal Opportunity," 58–59 (Heschel used this example the previous year at the Rabbinical Assembly: see above, chap. 11, text at n. 25); Heschel 1963 MS, 17, Heschel 1963, "The Religious Basis of Equal Opportunity," 68; Heschel 1963 MS, 18, Heschel 1963, "The Religious Basis of Equal Opportunity," 70.
7. William Stringfellow, remarks, memorandum of Balfour Brickner, AJC/NY.
8. Albert Vorspan, remarks, memorandum of Balfour Brickner, AJC/NY.
9. See Susannah Heschel 2000.
10. Mimeographed copy of King's speech, "A Challenge to the Churches and Synagogues," from files of Taylor Branch, personal communication; I quote from the published version in Ahmann 1963, 155–69 (quotations on pp. 155, 157–58).

Thanks to Taylor Branch for a portion omitted from *Pillar of Fire* (1998) dealing with this conference; see also Branch 1988.

11. *Time* (23 January 1963), 66.

12. This telegram was not made public until Heschel's daughter, Susannah, reprinted it at the beginning of her introduction to her 1996 anthology, *Moral Grandeur and Spiritual Audacity*. Email from Jules Harlow, who also attended, to the author; guest lists, White House diary entry, photographs, and transcript available at the JFK Library.

13. *New York Times*, 22 February 1964, 24.

14. Heschel, "The White Man on Trial," repr. in Heschel 1966, *The Insecurity of Freedom*, 101–2. "The White Man on Trial" is also printed in "Proceedings of the Metropolitan Conference on Religion and Race," typescript AJC/NY; reprinted in *Jewish World* (March 1964).

15. Heschel, "The White Man on Trial," 105–6.

16. Heschel, John C. Bennett, Mgsr. Gregory L. Mooney, "Crisis in Education," letter to the editor dated 29 January 1965, *New York Times*, 2 February 1965, 32; conversation with David Rogers, February 2005.

17. *New York Times*, 10 March 1965, 23. See also Garrow 1986, 396–400.

18. Information on the demonstration from FBI files, memorandum, NYO 100-153735, 9 March 1965, Subject: Freedom March Sponsored by Student Non-Violent Coordinating Committee to FBI: Racial Matters; memorandum (100-442529) to FBI director J. Edgar Hoover. See also *New York Times*, 10 March 1965, 23.

19. The advertisement was dated 10 March 1965; FBI files, memorandum from SAC, WFO (100-231150), to SAC, Chicago, dated 18 May 1965.

20. See John Lewis 1998, 342.

21. Interviews with Wolfe Kelman, Everett Gendler, and Andrew Young; "thoughts on Heschel," Maurice Davis, Heschel Archive.

22. John Lewis 1998, 341–47; Roy Reed, "Freedom March Begins at Selma: Troops on Guard," *New York Times*, 22 March 1965, 1. I was present at the march. Susannah Heschel, 1996, xxiii–xxiv: "He wrote in an unpublished memoir that he had intended to read Psalm 15, 'O Lord, who shall sojourn in thy tent [tabernacle]?,' but changed his mind after he arrived in Selma." Psalm 27 continues with an image that recalls Heschel's Yiddish poetry: "Hear, O Lord, when I call with my voice, / And become gracious unto me, and answer me. / In Thy behalf my heart has said: 'Seek ye My face'; / Thy face, Lord, will I seek. / Hide not Thy face from me" (Ps. 27:8–9).

23. Interview with Marc Tanenbaum. See Garrow 1986, 410–13. Susannah Heschel, "Following in My Father's Footsteps: Selma 40 Years Later," *Vox of Dartmouth, Vox Home*, 4 April 2005, dartmouth.edu/~vox/0405/0404.

24. Incidents at the airport from interview with Maurice Davis.

25. John Lewis 1998, 345–47; an unpublished memoir cited by Susannah Heschel 1996, xxiii. See also S. Heschel, "Following in My Father's Footsteps."

26. Wolfe Kelman, "Report of the Executive Vice-President," *Proceedings* 1961, 124–25.

27. Memorandum (undated), "Factual Report: Activities of the Synagogue Council of America Regarding the Soviet-Jewish Question," mimeographed copy, 2 pp., Heschel Archive.

28. Interview with Wolfe Kelman, 22 April 1988; accounts of the conference and speech from the following sources: news release of 6 October 1963, lecture by Heschel 6 October 1963 at Temple B'nai Shalom, Rockville Centre, "The Spiritual Legacy of Russian Jewry," press release from "Seven Arts Feature Syndicate" with a selection from speech, without the Talmudic and biblical references, dated 4 October 1963, JTS Public Affairs Files; Heschel 1963, "A Momentous Emergency—The Russian Jewry." These articles were reprinted and distributed by the Synagogue Council of America as a broadside. A French version appeared in *L'Arche* (August–September 1964), 23–29. Heschel also appeared around that time in a videotape produced by the Cleveland Council on Soviet Anti-Semitism, "Before Our Eyes."

29. Heschel 1963, "A Momentous Emergency": his biblical references were Leviticus 21:1–9 and Deuteronomy 21:1–9.

30. Heschel, "A Call to Conscience," 1964, repr. in Heschel 1966, *The Insecurity of Freedom*, 274–84 (quotation on p. 278).

31. Ibid., 281, 283, repeating the ending of his previous speech: "I do not want future generations to spit on our graves, saying: 'Here lies a community which, living in comfort and prosperity, kept silent while millions of their brothers were exposed to spiritual extermination.'" Also quoted in *New York Times*, 17 May 1966, 10.

32. *Jewish Times* (Baltimore), 17 June 1966. Heschel was scheduled to speak on "The Prerequisites of Faith" at 8:30 on Monday, 16 May, after an afternoon session at which Elie Wiesel spoke on "World Jewry and Russian Jewry: A Paradox." See *Proceedings* 1966. Finkelstein spoke on the disastrous fire at JTS that destroyed or damaged fifty thousand books.

33. Elie Wiesel, "World Jewry and Russian Jewry: A Paradox," *Proceedings* 1966, 44; Irving Spiegel, "Inaction Charged to Western Jews on Soviet Issue," *New York Times*, 17 May 1966, 10. See also *Jewish Telegraph Agency News Bulletin*, 17 May 1966, 27 May 1966. Wiesel visited the Soviet Union during the High Holy Days, September–October 1965. See Elie Wiesel 1966.

34. See, e.g., *Long Island Jewish Press*, June 1966.

35. *Jewish Week*, editorial, 23 June 1966; Jerry Zenick Lyndhurst, letter to the editor of *Jewish News* (Cleveland), 8 July 1966.

36. Clipping from *New York Times*, 8 December 1966, 30, in FBI files, SAC, Newark

(100-42359), Subject: CP, USA, Counterintelligence Program, IS-C; memo dated 16 December 1966 to Director FBI (100-3-104-31), from SAC, Newark (100-42359); FBI memorandum on Washington D.C., demonstration of 3 June 1971 for Soviet Jews, sponsored by the Synagogue Council of America.

37. Documents on the Raymond Fred West Memorial Lectures from Department of Special Collections, Stanford University Libraries.

38. *Stanford Daily,* 6 May 1963, 8 May 1963, 9 May 1963.

39. Branch 1998, 119–20; Armin Rosencranz, letter to Allard Lowenstein, 13 May 1963, Allard Lowenstein Papers, Library of the University of North Carolina at Chapel Hill, b8f289.

40. Heschel 1965, *Who Is Man?* vii.

41. Ibid., 27.

42. Ibid., 33.

43. Ibid., 69, 97.

44. Ibid., 111, 119.

45. Review of *Who Is Man? Booklist* (15 February 1966), 545. See also *Library Journal* (1 October 1965), 4088. Marvin Fox, "Heschel's Theology of Man," *Tradition* 8, 3 (fall 1966): 79–84. See also John Weborg 1979, "Abraham Joshua Heschel: A Study on Anthropodicy," *Anglican Theological Review* 61, 4 (October): 483–97.

46. Edmund Epstein, letter to Heschel, 21 January 1964; Roger Straus, letter to Heschel, 19 February 1964; Straus, letter to Grayzel and Zussman, 21 February 1964; Straus, internal memorandum, 10 November 1964: "We have decided to postpone THE INSECURITY OF FREEDOM: Essays in Applied Religion until late August 1965," Farrar, Straus and Giroux Archives.

47. Edmund Epstein, letter to Heschel, 21 January 1964; see Roger Straus, letter to his uncle Harry Guggenheim, asking for financial support for Heschel, 4 December 1963; Straus, letter to Heschel, 9 February 1964; Straus, letter to Solomon Grayzel and Lesser Zussman, 21 February 1964, memorandum from Robert Giroux to Roger Straus, 28 February 1964. By November 1964 the table of contents was established: memorandum from Roger Straus to everyone, 10 November 1964. Straus, letter to Grayzel, 26 April 1965, and numerous letters dated September–October 1965. All Farrar, Straus and Giroux Archives.

48. For reviews, see George Adelman in *Library Journal* (1 April 1966), 1901; *Choice* (November 1966), 790; Will Herberg, "Man of Faith," *New York Times Book Review,* 24 April 1966, 34–35; Jacob B. Agus, "Abraham Joshua Heschel, *The Insecurity of Freedom,*" *Jewish Social Studies* 29, 2 (April 1967): 120–22. Roger Shinn of Union Theological Seminary praised Heschel as a prophet in *Conservative Judaism* 21, 1 (fall 1966): 83–84.

49. "The Last Years of Maimonides" was first published in June 1955 in the *National Jewish Monthly.* Heschel 1966, *The Insecurity of Freedom,* "The Last Years of Maimonides," 290.

50. Roger Straus, letter to Elie Wiesel, 25 March 1966; Straus, letter to John Cogley of the *New York Times,* 28 March 1966, Farrar, Straus and Giroux Archives.

Part 4. Apostle to the Gentiles

1. Pius XII's actions may have been motivated in part by an attempt to atone for his inaction during World War II, when he raised no objections to the deportation of Italian Jews to the death camps. See Susan Zuccotti, *Under His Very Windows: The Vatican and the Holocaust in Italy* (New Haven: Yale University Press, 2000).

Chapter 13. Confronting the Church

1. Gerald Nachman, "Vatican Liberal," *New York Post,* November 1964. See symposium in Bea's honor: *Simposio Card. Agostino Bea (16–19 dicembre 1981),* with articles in French, English, German, and Italian (Rome: Pontificia Università Lateranense, 1983).
2. My narrative is drawn primarily from unpublished documents preserved in the American Jewish Committee archives, in particular, a draft "White Paper": "The Vatican Decree on Jews and Judaism and the American Jewish Committee: A Historical Record" (marked "strictly confidential"), 28 August 1964, 95 pp. I coordinated this institutional narrative with the raw data of numerous memoranda and letters. For the official AJC narrative see the two-part article by Judith Hershcopf (Hershcopf 1965 and Hershcopf 1966). See also Oesterreicher 1967; Schmerker n.d.; Tanenbaum 1986. Information about the AJC's consultants is in "The Vatican Decree on Jews and Judaism," 18, AJC/NY.
3. Zachariah Shuster obituary, *New York Times,* 16 February 1986, 44; Shuster, letter to John Slawson, 28 October 1960, AJC/NY.
4. Tanenbaum, letters to Joseph B. Soloveitchik, Abraham Heschel, 11 May 1961; letter to Louis Finkelstein, 12 May 1961; memorandum from Dr. A. Lichtenstein, undated; Tanenbaum, memorandum to Slawson, 15 May 1961, with copies to Shuster and others; Tanenbaum, memorandum to Slawson, D. Danzig, S. Segal, Shuster, J. Hershcopf, AJC/NY.
5. Shuster, memorandum to Slawson, 7 July 1961; various letters and memoranda, AJC/NY.
6. See John Slawson, report on "Journey to Paris, Frankfurt and Bonn," 9–15 July 1961, 5 pp.; Heschel, letters to Cardinal Bea, 14 December 1961, 18 December 1961, in German; Slawson memorandum to Tanenbaum, 1 December 1961; Heschel, meeting in Slawson's office, 30 November 1961, reporting on his trip, AJC/NY.
7. Details on the meeting from Shuster's memorandum to the AJC Foreign Affairs Department, 1 December 1961, 2–3, AJC/Paris.

8. Heschel soon received a letter from Cardinal Bea, dated 9 January 1962; see also article by Gershon Jacobson, *Day-Morning Journal*, 20 December 1960, translated from the Yiddish, AJC/NY. Shuster, letter to Heschel, 2 December 1961, AJC/Paris.

9. Heschel reported on the meeting to Shuster: see Slawson, memorandum to Tanenbaum, 1 December 1961, AJC/NY.

10. Shuster, letter to Tanenbaum, 1 December 1961; Shuster, report to Tanenbaum and Slawson, 1 December 1961; also Shuster, memorandum to AJC Foreign Affairs Department, 1 December 1961; Shuster, letter to Heschel, 2 December 1961; Shuster memorandum to Slawson, 14 December 1961; Shuster, letter to Heschel, 2 December 1961, AJC/Paris.

11. Interview with Malachi Martin; Martin, letter to the author; see also Shuster file, not yet catalogued when I consulted it, AJC/NY.

12. Tanenbaum memorandum, "Zachariah Shuster's request for AJC Policy re Ecumenical Council, Pro Deo, etc.," to Slawson, Danzig, et al., 29 December 1961; Shuster, letters to Tanenbaum and Heschel, 27 February 1962; Heschel, letter to Shuster, 2 March 1962, dictated by telephone; Tanenbaum, memorandum to Slawson et al., 8 March 1962; Judith Hershcopf, memorandum to Tanenbaum, 9 March 1962; draft outline, 2 March 1962; Tanenbaum, letter to Shuster, 13 April 1962, on Finkelstein and Soloveitchik (he met with Soloveitchik about the memorandum), AJC/NY.

13. Tanenbaum, draft memorandum, 6 August 1962, 23–25, AJC/NY.

14. Quotations from Heschel's typed memorandum, "On Improving Catholic-Jewish Relations: A Memorandum to His Eminence Agostino Cardinal Bea, President, the Secretariat for Christian Unity," 5 pp., 22 May 1962, Marc H. Tanenbaum, personal papers, American Jewish Archives, and AJC/NY.

15. Hershcopf, memorandum to Tanenbaum, 6 June 1962, AJC/NY. Goldmann made his announcement on 12 June: see Hershcopf 1965, 111–12.

16. Shuster, memorandum, 21 September 1962; draft of chronology, AJC/NYC.

17. Cardinal Cushing spoke at a press conference: *Jewish Telegraphic Agency*, 11 October 1962, draft, AJC/NY; Hershcopf 1965, 112.

18. Gershon Jacobson, "The Ecumenical Council and the Jews," *Day-Morning Journal*, 17, 20 December 1962, translated for the AJC by Eliezer Greenberg, AJC/NY.

19. Interview with Gershon Jacobson. When Küng learned that Jacobson had reported this conversation in the Yiddish press, he denied ever talking to him.

20. The original list included brief descriptions of the participants: "Rabbi Joseph B. Soloveitchik, Prof. of Talmud, Yeshiva University, one of the foremost living Talmudic authorities and Aristotelian scholars. Rabbi Solomon B. Freehof of Pittsburgh, Pres. of the World Union for Progressive Judaism, leading Reform authority on Responsa literature. Rabbi Samuel Belkin, New York, Pres. of Yeshiva Univ., noted authority on Philo. Rabbi Nelson Glueck, Cincinnati, Pres. Hebrew Union

College, Jewish Inst. of Religion (Reform), nationally known Biblical Archeologist. Rabbi Louis Finkelstein, New York, Pres. Jewish Theological Seminary of America, theologian and authority on the Pharisees. Rabbi Leo Jung of New York, Rabbi of the Jewish Center, scholar, author of numerous works. Dr. Salo Baron of New York, Prof. of Jewish History and Institutions, Columbia Univ., author of the major studies of the social, economic and political history of the Jews. Prof. Harry Wolfson of Harvard Univ., Boston, noted authority on the Church Fathers and Philo. Skuliner Rebbe, distinguished Hasidic leader. Dr. Julius Mark of New York, pres. Synagogue Council of America." Tanenbaum memorandum to David Danzig, 5 March 1963, AJC/NY. Tanenbaum, memorandum to Slawson et al., 11 March 1963; see draft letter from Heschel to Dr. Julius Mark, inviting him to attend the meeting; Heschel, letter to Emmanuel Rackman, 26 March 1963, AJC/NY.

21. Tanenbaum, memorandum to Slawson et al., 18 April 1963, 3 pp, and draft of chronology, AJC/NY.

22. Tanenbaum, memorandum to Slawson et al., 18 April 1963, AJC/NY.

23. Information from the outline of Heschel's introductions and discussion, 10 pp.; "Conversation of Cardinal Bea with Jewish Scholars and Theologians, Summary of the Main Ideas," 12 pp., AJC Summary. See also Segal, summary of the German conversation, AJC memorandum, 7 March 1963, 3 pp., all AJC/NY.

24. Simon Segal, memorandum to Tanenbaum, 5 April 1963, on Meeting with Cardinal Bea; AJC Summary, AJC/NY.

25. Segal, memorandum to Tanenbaum, 5 April 1963, AJC/NY.

26. Carbon copy of Cardinal Bea's statement, 1–2, AJC/NY. See George Dugan, "Papal Advisor Terms Vatican Supporter of Religious Liberty," *New York Times*, 2 April 1963, 26.

27. Copy of Cardinal Bea's statement, 2, AJC/NY.

28. "A Jewish Response," *Catholic News* (4 April 1963), 4. Address given on 1 April 1963 to Cardinal Bea. See *Jewish Chronicle* (London), 5 April 1963; article by Milton Bracker, *New York Times*, collected in AJC/NY. Heschel's speech was reprinted as "The Ecumenical Movement" in Heschel 1966, *The Insecurity of Freedom*, 179–83 (quotations on pp. 179, 180, 182).

29. AJC memorandum, 4 April 1963, AJC/NY.

30. *Washington Post*, 1 July 1963, A1, A10.

31. The American delegation, headed by Supreme court chief justice Earl Warren, included Finkelstein, Senate majority leader Mike Mansfield (D-Montana), and Charles W. Engelhard, a businessman from Newark, New Jersey: *New York Herald Tribune*, 28 June 1963; Felix Morlion, letter to David Danzig, 28 June 1963, AJC/NY.

32. The AJC director, John Slawson, wrote Heschel a letter of apology: Slawson, letter to Heschel, 1 July 1963; see also Tanenbaum, letter to Rabbi Samuel Silver, 8 August 1963, AJC/NY. Apparently news of the mix-up got around.

33. Shuster, letter to Heschel, 12 September 1963, AJC/Paris. On 9 October 1963, Shuster sent a top-secret copy of the new declaration to Simon Segal at the AJC in New York, warning him not to copy it and to show it only to the inner circle: AJC/Paris.

34. Heschel, letter to Shuster, 16 September 1963, AJC/NY. The draft was entitled "On the Catholic Attitude Toward Non-Christians, and Especially Toward Jews." It included positive statements such as: "The church owes its origins to Judaism. . . . Roman Catholics should never forget that Jesus was a Jew. . . . The guilt for the death of Jesus falls more properly on all humanity than on the Jews. . . . The church disapproves of the anti-Semitism of the past and of the present." Milton Bracker, "Vatican Council Paper Decries Blaming of Jews in Jesus's Death," *New York Times*, 17 October 1963, 1. See Hershcopf 1965, 114–23.

35. Memorandum from Sonneband to Members of Key Leadership Groups, 17 October 1963, 3 pp., AJC/NYC.

36. Tanenbaum, memorandum to Slawson, Danzig, et al., 22 October 1963, from telephone call of Heschel to Tanenbaum, AJC/NY.

37. Immediately after the meeting, on 22 November 1963, Heschel wrote a formal but forthright letter to Bea from the Hotel Mediterraneo; see also Shuster, memorandum to New York office, 9 December 1963, both in AJC/Paris.

38. See Hershcopf 1965, 116–22.

39. Shuster, letter to Tanenbaum, 12 December 1963. See also Tanenbaum, memorandum to Shuster, 4 December 1963: "I have been in regular touch with Dr. Heschel and Dr. Finkelstein, both of whom are very much depressed by what has happened." AJC/Paris.

40. Hershcopf 1965, 118–22; Shuster, letter to Tanenbaum, 27 December 1963; Tanenbaum memorandum to Shuster, 23 December 1963, AJC/Paris. See Heschel 1996, *Moral Grandeur and Spiritual Audacity,* "No Religion Is an Island," 246, on his final conversation with Weigel. See Patrick W. Collins, *Gustave Weigel, S.J.: A Pioneer of Reform* (Collegeville, Minn.: Liturgical Press, 1992); Weigel obituary, *New York Times,* 4 January 1964, 1, 23.

41. Shuster, letter to Heschel, 12 March 1964: "I am now asking him [Malachi Martin] for definite and final instructions with regard to his position on advance payments from the publishers, and I shall communicate with you as soon as I hear from him," AJC/Paris. Hans Küng found the book "teeming with facts and worth considering," adding wryly in parentheses, "it is able to put itself in Papa Montini's position": Küng, *My Struggle for Freedom* (Grand Rapids, Mich.: Eerdmans, 2003), 383. *The Pilgrim* was reviewed with three other books on the Vatican by John Cogley, "Religion: Ecumenism Assessed," *New York Times Book Review,* 13 June 1965, E11. A highly unfavorable review in *Commonweal* (24 July 1964), 517–18 identified Serafian as "Malachy [sic] Martin, a priest once associated with the Biblical Institute in Rome." Interview with Roger Straus.

42. This and the following quotation from *Jewish Chronicle* (London), 7 February 1964. See also *National Jewish Post and Opinion* (5 June 1964), article on Soloveitchik. See Tanenbaum, letter to Soloveitchik, 18 June 1964; *Rabbinical Council Record* (June 1964), 8; chronological draft. Tanenbaum, memorandum to Slawson, 15 June 1964; see also Tanenbaum, letter to Soloveitchik, 18 June 1964; Tanenbaum, memorandum to Slawson, 19 June 1964: "I have just talked with Jack Weiler who told me that he discussed the Soloveitchik matter with Rabbi Belkin. There will be no statement by Rabbi Soloveitchik at the Rabbinical Council of America Convention which begins on June 22, Weiler said with certainty. Soloveitchik sent a message through one of his disciples to me this morning that he would like to meet with me." All collected in AJC/NY. *New York Times*, 23 June 1964, 29; AJC answer, *New York Times*, 28 June 1964, 37.

43. Internal AJC chronology, 11 May 1964, and list of participants, Catholic, Protestant, and Jewish, 2 pp., AJC/NY.

44. Confidential account of the audience, dated 4 June 1964, from Dr. Slawson's office, 7 pp., AJC/NY.

45. Tanenbaum, memorandum to Slawson, 25 June 1964, items 4 and 5; AJC Chronology; declaration dictated by Cardinal Bea for communication to the AJC leaders received by Pope Paul VI on May 30, 1964, dated 5 June 1964; Tanenbaum, memorandum to Slawson et al., 9 June 1964, AJC/NY.

46. Robert C. Doty, "Text on the Jews Reported Muted," *New York Times*, 12 June 1964, 1, 7.

47. Tanenbaum, memorandum to Slawson, 25 June 1964: "the following information was shared in strictest confidence with Rabbi Heschel. He in turn has passed this on to us in that same spirit," AJC/NY.

48. See especially Shuster, memorandum to New York office, 11 June 1964, 4 pp.; Shuster, letter to Heschel, 16 June 1964. Heschel and the AJC also tried to enlist the help of the venerable Protestant theologian Karl Barth in Basel; he was supportive but finally decided not to act. Shuster, letter to Heschel, 18 June 1964; Shuster, letter to Karl Barth, 18 June 1964, following a telephone conversation; Shuster, memorandum to New York office, 19 June 1964; Shuster, letter to Heschel, 23 June 1964; Heschel, letter to Shuster, 25 June 1964; Karl Barth, letter in German to Shuster, 26 June 1964; minutes of a telephone call from Heschel to Slawson, 7 July 1964; Shuster, letter to Slawson, 10 July 1964, Heschel, report on a telephone call to Tanenbaum on 6 August 1964, all in AJC/Paris.

49. Heschel, letter to Shuster, 7 July 1964, AJC/Paris; interviews with Flavian Burns, Patrick Hart. See Merton 1997, 126–27, 142–43; Edward Kaplan 2004, "'Under My Catholic Skin,'" plus letters of Heschel and Merton, and Brenda Fitch Fairaday, "Thomas Merton's Prophetic Voice: Merton, Heschel, and Vatican II," Bruteau 2004, 217–31, 269–81.

50. Merton 1997, entry for 14 July 1964, 126–27.

51. Ibid.; interview with Flavian Burns.

52. Merton, letter to Cardinal Bea, 14 July 1964; Merton, letter to Heschel, 27 July 1964, quoted in Fairaday, "Merton's Prophetic Voice," 221–22.

Chapter 14. Vulnerable Prophet

1. *New York Herald Tribune*, 3 September 1964; Irving Spiegel, "Jewish Group Concerned," *New York Times*, 4 September 1964, 2. Spiegel cites Heschel's acerbic response to the draft, noted below.

2. Spiegel, "Jewish Group Concerned," 2.

3. Memorandum, 3 September 1964, 2, AJC/NY; *Time* (11 September 1964), 58; Heschel, mimeographed statement to the Second Vatican Council, 3 September 1964, AJC/NY, published in Bruteau 2004, 223–24.

4. Heschel, statement to the Vatican Council, Bruteau 2004, 223–24. Professor R. L. Zwi Werblowsky of the Hebrew University reported a conversation with Cardinal Willebrands about Judaism as *preparatio evangelica*, to which Heschel retorted: "If this is going to be in the Vatican document, I prefer going to Auschwitz": Werblowsky, letter to the author, 20 August 1994.

5. Heschel, statement to the Vatican Council, Bruteau 2004, 223–24.

6. Merton, letter to Heschel, 9 September 1964, Bruteau 2004, 225; Merton, journal entry, Bruteau 2004, 226, and Merton 1997, 142–43.

7. "Statement Adopted by the Rabbinical Council of America at the Mid-Winter Conference," 3–5 February 1964: "Any suggestion that the historical and meta-historical worth of a faith community be viewed against the backdrop of another faith, and the mere hint that a revision of basic historic attitudes is anticipated, are incongruous with the fundamentals of religious liberty and freedom of conscience and can only breed discord and suspicion," 28–29, AJC/NYC; J. B. Soloveitchik, "Confrontation," *Tradition* 6, 2 (spring–summer 1964): 5–29.

8. Tanenbaum, memorandum to Shuster, 10 September 1964, AJC/NY.

9. Finkelstein 1973, 20–21. Cardinal Cushing first received a cablegram from Monsignor Mario Nasalli Rocca, maestro di camera di sua Santita, giving "Rabbi Heschel" a private audience with the pope at 11:00 A.M. on Saturday, 12 September, at Castel Gandolfo, the pope's residence: chronology and documents, Slawson, letter to Monsignor Edward C. Murray, 11 September 1964; chronology, AJC/NY. Sidney R. Rabb, a Boston businessman, active AJC member, and friend of Cardinal Cushing and other Catholic officials, was also consulted.

10. Shuster, "Comments Concerning Dr. Heschel's Interview with *Ma'ariv*," confidential memorandum to John Slawson, undated [4 January 1965], comments numbered 1–9, 3 pp., AJC/Paris.

11. My considerably abridged presentation of this audience is based on the following archival documents, which I designate Shuster Report 1 and Shuster Report 2.

Shuster Report 1: "Audience with the Pope of Dr. Heschel and Mr. Shuster on September 14, 1964," 4 pp., unsigned, included in Slawson, letter to Sidney Rabb, 18 September 1964; a draft of that same report, typed in italics, by Heschel and Shuster; log of a telephone call from Shuster to Slawson, 14 September 1964; log of a telephone call from Heschel to Slawson? 14 September 1964; Shuster, letter to Slawson, 15 September 1964; "Addendum to White Paper Pamphlet," 22 September 1964, all in folders Documents, Chronological, AJC/NY.

Shuster Report 2: "Notes on Audience with Paul VI, September 14, 1964, 5 pp., single spaced; Shuster, memorandum to Tanenbaum, 10 September 1964; Shuster, letters to Slawson and Heschel, 15 September 1964, both with official report; Morlion, letter to Slawson, 18 September 1964, AJC/Paris. I found Shuster's highly confidential, candid account in the files of the AJC Paris office conserved at YIVO.

12. The following, official version of the meeting is from Shuster Report 1, "Audience with the Pope," AJC/NY.

13. "Memorandum respectfully submitted and with firm hope to His Holiness Pope Paul VI concerning the proposed declaration on the Jews," 3 pp., AJC/Paris.

14. The following version of the meeting is from Shuster Report 2, "Notes on Audience with Pope Paul VI," AJC/Paris.

15. The Talmudic principle is *mipnei darchai shalom*, "due to the ways of peace." Thanks to Herbert Dreyer for this insight and reference.

16. Paul C. Marcinkus was Pope Paul's translator when he met with President Lyndon Johnson and other dignitaries. Originally from a Lithuanian immigrant family in Cicero, Illinois, Marcinkus was known for his bluntness and skill in organization; he became Pope Paul's advance man in his various travels and was promoted to bishop in 1969. Eventually appointed head of the Vatican Bank, he resigned in 1982 under shadow of scandal. See *New York Times*, 4 January 1969, 19; 8 July 1982, A4; obituary, *Boston Globe*, 22 February 2006.

17. Interview with Malachi Martin; Shuster Report 2, "Notes on Audience with Pope Paul VI," 5.

18. Deut. 28:66. See Heschel 1969, "Teaching Jewish Theology," 5. Ursula Niebuhr remembered that in September 1964, the day before he met the pope, Heschel wrote to the Niebuhrs from Rome. Soon after his return, Heschel left a bottle of brandy wrapped in foil with their doorman. Ursula Niebuhr, "Notes on a Friendship," Merkle 1985.

19. Reported by the Jewish Telegraphic Agency on 15 September 1964, quoting Rabbi Soloveitchik, AJC/NY.

20. Morlion, letter to Slawson, 18 September 1964, AJC/Paris.

21. *Day-Morning Journal*, 2 October 1964, 1, 9.

22. *Jewish Chronicle* (London), 9 October 1964.

23. Shuster, memorandum to Slawson, 9 October 1964, AJC/Paris.

24. "The Audience That Was," *Jewish World*, (October 1964), 23–24, 68. The article stated that Heschel returned home on Tuesday, 15 September (a misprint had September 14).

25. "The Audience That Was," 23.

26. Ibid., 24.

27. Ibid., 68. The vacillation of Pope Paul was mentioned, as well as his criticism of "*the way the matter has been aired in public.*"

28. Hershcopf 1965, 99. The larger declaration on non-Christian religions passed by 1,651 to 99, with 242 in favor with reservations: Hershcopf 1966, 46–47, 126–27. For details see Xavier Rynne [Fr. Francis Xavier Murphy, CSSR], *Vatican Council II* (Maryknoll, N.Y.: Orbis, 1999), 303–5, 415–25. Shuster, letters to Willebrands and Stransky, 24 November 1964; Shuster, telegram to Cardinal Bea, 24 November 1964, AJC/Paris.

29. Shuster, letter to Tanenbaum, 7 December 1964, AJC/Paris.

30. Tanenbaum, letter to Shuster, 9 December 1964, AJC/Paris.

31. "Unyielding Israeli Warrior," *New York Times,* 31 July 1980, A8. Years later, Cohen became an extreme right-wing member of the Knesset, the Israeli Parliament. She was the only member not to applaud Egyptian president Anwar Sadat's historic speech in November 1977. Interview with Geula Cohen. See Geula Cohen, *Woman of Violence: Memoirs of a Young Terrorist, 1943–48* (New York: Holt, Rinehart and Winston, 1966). See *New York Times*, 7 June 1946, 14, on her prison sentence.

32. Shuster, "Comments Concerning Dr. Heschel's Interview with *Ma'ariv*," memorandum to Slawson, 2, AJC/Paris.

33. AJC translation of *Ma'ariv* interview, dated 4 January 1965, 3, AJC/Paris. I also consulted the following documents: "Report on Vatican Reactions to Heschel Interview with *Ma'ariv*," 3 pp., dated 4 January 1965, sent by Shuster only to John Slawson; Shuster, "Dr. Heschel's Interview in *Ma'ariv*," memorandum, "strictly confidential" to Marc Tanenbaum, 4 January 1965; original clipping of the published interview; Shuster, letter to John Slawson, "personal and confidential," 5 January 1965; Shuster, "Comments concerning Dr. Heschel's Interview with *Ma'ariv*," memorandum to Slawson. None of the AJC documents mention Geula Cohen by name, referring to her only as journalist or she. All documents from AJC/Paris.

34. AJC translation of *Ma'ariv* interview, 2, AJC/Paris.

35. Ibid., 3.

36. Ibid., 4. Heschel was willing to play the traditional role of *shtadlan*, peacefully mediating between the Jews and the enemy: "There was an old custom in the communities of the Jewish diaspora that the rabbis used to go to speak to priests on the eve of a disastrous event. I have therefore not had a shadow of a doubt, either from the point of view of Halakhah or Agaddah, in undertaking to do something in order to dam up one source of hatred of Jews."

37. Ibid.

38. Ibid., 5.

39. Ibid.

40. Ibid., 6.

41. Shuster telephoned and wrote to Slawson, who was away, and to Tanenbaum, urging him to convey his comments to Heschel: Shuster, "Comments Concerning Dr. Heschel's Interview with *Ma'ariv*," memorandum to Slawson; Shuster, letter to John Slawson, personal and confidential, 5 January 1965; Shuster, "Dr. Heschel's Interview in *Ma'ariv*," memorandum to Tanenbaum. See also AJC translation of *Ma'ariv* article, dated 4 January 1965. All AJC/Paris.

42. "Report on Vatican Reactions." See also Shuster, "Dr. Heschel's Interview in *Ma'ariv*," memorandum to Tanenbaum: "Cardinal Bea was . . . painfully concerned with the ultimate fate of the Jewish document." Both AJC/Paris.

43. "Report on Vatican Reactions," 1, 2. Shuster went on, "Give this man [Heschel] no encouragement. No contact. This could be worse than the Wardi incident. The interview-article will be translated and commented. He has no sense of propriety or proportion. He is a child playing with dynamite. Another mistake like this and it will signal the end of all hopes. Haven't we enough prejudice in high places to contend with already?"(3). See also Shuster, letter to Tanenbaum, 4 January 1965, AJC/Paris.

44. Shuster, "Comments Concerning Dr. Heschel's Interview with *Ma'ariv*," memorandum to Slawson, AJC/Paris.

45. Ibid.

46. Morris Abram, letter to Cardinal Bea, 19 March 1965, AJC/Paris.

47. Among the abundant literature on self-deception, see Herbert Fingarette, *Self Deception* (London: Routledge and Kegan Paul; New York: Humanities Press, 1969); Alfred R. Mele, "Self-Deception," *Philosophical Quarterly* 33, 133 (October 1983): 365–77; Robert Lockie, "Depth Psychology and Self-Deception," *Philosophical Psychology* 16, 1 (2003): 127–48; Alfred Mele, *Self-Deception Unmasked* (Princeton: Princeton University Press, 2001).

48. Heschel, unsigned memorandum, AJC/NY, quoted in *New York Herald Tribune*, 1 October 1965, which also reported: "American bishops insist at a news conference that the new text is an improved statement. Nevertheless, heated debate is expected, both at Council sessions and behind the scenes."

49. Robert C. Doty, "Council's Final Approval Voted for Text on Jews," *New York Times*, 16 October 1965, 1.

50. For the entire text, "Declaration on the Relation of the Church to Non-Christian Religions," see Hershcopf 1966, 75–77. See James M. Somerville's comparison of the versions of *Nostra Aetate* in English and in Latin in "The Successive Versions of *Nostra Aetate:* Translation, Outline Analysis, Chronology, Commentary," Bruteau 2004, 341–71.

51. Pope Paul VI himself publicly received Rabbi and Mrs. Heschel at the Vatican in 1971; he later became the first pope officially to cite a Jewish thinker when he quoted from Heschel's work. See *United Synagogue Review* (fall 1971), 2; *The Pilot* (29 May 1971), 3; below, Chapter 20, pp. 381–82.

52. Joseph Roddy, "How the Jews Changed Catholic Teaching," *Look* (25 January 1966), 18–23. For reactions to the article, see Tanenbaum, memorandum to Area Directors, 7 January 1966, 44 pp., AJC/NY; Shuster, memorandum to New York office, 10 January 1966; Tanenbaum, memorandum to Shuster, 26 January 1966; Robert McAfee Brown, letter to Tanenbaum, 22 January 1966; John M. Oesterreicher to editors of *Look* (14 January 1966); Shuster, letter to Tanenbaum, 31 January 1966: "It is really fortunate that this miserable description of a great event has caused much less damage than we feared." All in AJC/Paris. See also Joseph L. Lichten, "The Statement on the Jews," *Catholic World* 202 (1966): 357–63, in AJC/Paris.

53. Cushing's friend, the Boston businessman and active AJC member Sidney R. Rabb, admonished the AJC not to flatter Cardinal Cushing, a truly "humble man who doesn't realize how great he really is." Cushing was a "standard bearer" for all righteous Christians, Rabb explained, "because of his willingness to stand for what he believes is Godly and right." Sidney R. Rabb, letter to Marc Tanenbaum, 8 October 1964, AJC/NY.

Chapter 15. Interfaith Triumphs

1. Interview with John C. Bennett; Heschel 1963, "Idols in the Temples."
2. Reinhold Niebuhr, "The Crisis in American Protestantism," *Christian Century* (4 December 1963), 1486; Heschel 1963, "Protestant Renewal," 1501–2.
3. Handy 1987, 260–69; Bennett, letter to Heschel, 5 November 1964; Heschel, answer to Bennett, 11 November 1964; see news release, Union Theological Seminary, 10 March 1965, Burke Library.
4. Union Theological Seminary catalog with announcement of courses, 1965–66.
5. Jessica Feingold, letter to Heschel, 9 December 1964, JTS General Files.
6. Roger Shinn, dean of instruction, memorandum to John C. Bennett, 27 January 1965; Bennett, response to Shinn, 11 February 1965; Minutes of the Meeting of the Board of Directors, 9 March 1965, Burke Library.
7. News release, 3 pp., 10 March 1965; Bennett, letter to Heschel, 22 March 1965; Heschel, answer to Bennett, 24 March 1965; Memorandum, Provisional Schedule for Dr. Abraham Heschel, dated 30 July 1965, Burke Library. Heschel's topics included: Mystery and Meaning; Depth Theology, Prerequisites of Faith; About Our Reasons for Believing in the Realness of God; The Prophets of Israel; The Theology of Pathos; The Meaning of Biblical Revelation; Who is Man?; The Patient as a Person; Religion in a Free Society; Sanctification of Time; Prayer; Religion and

Race; Religious Education; Major Trends in Ancient Jewish Theology; Faith and
Interfaith.

8. Susannah Heschel email to the author, 3 January 2001. On bat mitzvah ceremonies in the United States, see Sarna 2000, 287–88. Thanks to Jonathan Sarna
for describing the ceremony he attended with his parents.

9. The Torah portion that week was Emor (Leviticus 21–24) and Haftarah was Ezekiel
44:15–31. David Kogen, letter to Heschel, 29 April 1965; Finkelstein, letter to
Heschel, 5 May 1965, JTS General Files.

10. Conversation with Sylvia Heschel; Jessica Feingold, memorandum, 8 November
1965; Feingold, letter to John Bennett, 11 November 1965; note re telephone conversation with Mrs. Abraham Heschel, 11 November 1965, JTS General Files.

11. Heschel 1966, "No Religion Is an Island," repr. in Heschel 1996, *Moral Grandeur
and Spiritual Audacity,* 235–50 (quotation on p. 235).

12. Ibid., 236.

13. Ibid., 239–40.

14. Ibid., 243, 246–47n1: Reinhold Niebuhr, *Pious and Secular America* (1958), 108;
Paul Tillich, *Christianity and the Encounter of the World Religions* (1963), 95.

15. Heschel 1996, *Moral Grandeur and Spiritual Authority,* "No Religion Is an Island," 244, 247, 250.

16. Interview with Yochanan Muffs, 12 May 1988. Also interview with Jules Harlow.

17. The manuscript he first submitted was not completely revised; several pages appeared to be thrown together. Charles E. Brewster, letter to Samuel Dresner, 7 June
1989, Heschel Archive. Heschel repeated the substance of this speech for the
R.A. convention in Toronto, 15 May 1966. See Heschel 1967, "From Mission to
Dialogue?" Heschel also gave a brief lecture on the Bible at an interfaith program
sponsored by Union on 10 January 1966, "The Bible—Antiquated and Contemporary," with an opening statement by John Bennett, Burke Library, transcript and
audiotape.

18. Undated memorandum, "Dr. Heschel's dietary scruples," Burke Library.

19. Union Theological Seminary catalog, 1965–66, 87.

20. Ibid., 93.

21. Charles E. Brewster, letter to Samuel Dresner, 7 June 1989, Heschel Archive.

22. Lincoln S. Dring, Jr., letter to Samuel Dresner, 5 December 1988, Heschel
Archive.

23. William Lad Sessions, professor of philosophy, Washington and Lee University,
letter to Samuel Dresner, 3 January 1990, Heschel Archive.

24. Ibid.

25. Ibid.

26. Samuel Rutherford Todd, letter to Samuel Dresner, 29 November 1988, Heschel
Archive.

27. Interview with Sarah Terrien.

28. Handy 1987, 230; interview with W. D. Davies. See Davies, "My Odyssey in New Testament Interpretation," *Bible Review* (June 1989): 10–18, and Davies, *Setting of the Sermon on the Mount* (Cambridge: Cambridge University Press, 1966). This major book contextualizes the sermon in the Mishnah, as part of the Pharisaic tradition.

29. Davies, "My Odyssey," 16.

30. Interview with W. D. Davies, 18 June 1991. See Davies' commemorative essay on Heschel, "Conscience, Scholar, Witness," *America* (10 March 1973), 213–15.

31. Interviews with James A. Sanders.

32. See Sanders 1973.

33. Interview with W. D. Davies.

34. Woodward's admiring unsigned essay, "What God Thinks of Man," was accompanied by a photograph captioned "Heschel: A Radical Judaism," *Newsweek* (31 January 1966), 57.

35. *Jubilee* (January 1966), cover and Heschel essay (37–39).

36. Heschel 1966, "Choose Life!" 38, 39.

37. Program of special academic convocation, Saint Michael's College, 7–8 March 1966; John D. Donoghue, director of public relations, Saint Michael's, letter to John C. Bennett, 10 March 1966, and press release, Burke Library. See also John Donoghue, letter to Finkelstein, 10 March 1966; Finkelstein, letter to Donoghue, 14 March 1966, JTS General Files. *New York Times*, 24 March 1966, 20; clippings (some unidentified), program, and other materials, University of Notre Dame Archives. See especially John P. Thurin, "Vatican II Epilogue," *Insight: Notre Dame* (summer 1966), 8–19.

38. Conference program, University of Notre Dame Archives, PNDP 1302–1966a.

39. Theodore Hesburgh, letters to Heschel, 25 August 1967, 8 September 1967; Heschel, letter to Hesburgh, 5 September 1967, University of Notre Dame Archives. The event took place at the Americana Hotel in New York on 9 October 1967.

40. Heschel 1967, "Abraham Joshua Heschel," 70, 73. Also included in the book were interviews with Robert McAfee Brown, John Bennett, Karl Rahner, Jaroslav Pelikan, and others.

41. Ibid., 75.

42. Ibid., 81, 82.

43. The conference was sponsored by the Canadian Catholic Bishops and organized by the Pontifical Institute of Saint Michael's College. See L. K. Shook, CSB, ed., *Renewal of Religious Thought: Proceedings of the Congress on the Theology of the Church Centenary of Canada, 1867–1967* (Montreal: Palm, 1968), 379–80, for the complete listing of participants. Jeanette Jardine of the Pontifical Institute, email to the author, 29 January 2004; L. K. Shook, letter to Heschel, 19 May 1966, Farrar, Straus and Giroux Archives.

44. Programme and in-house collection of post-presentation discussion, 19–20, 21,

Archives of the Canadian Conference of Catholic Bishops; Monsignor Peter Scho-
nenbach, P.H., letter to the author, 9 February 2004; discussion report, 19. See
Edward A. Synan, S.J., "Abraham Heschel and Prayer," *The Bridge: A Yearbook of
Judeo-Christian Studies*, ed. John M. Oesterreicher (New York: Pantheon, 1955):
256–65.

45. Heschel 1968, "The Jewish Notion of God," 105.
46. Ibid., 110: The Jewish people is "God's stake in human history, regardless of merit
and often against our will." Ibid., 115.
47. Ibid., 123–24.
48. Discussion report, 19–21, Archives of the Canadian Conference of Catholic Bishops, Pontifical Institute of Medieval Studies, Toronto. For Heschel's Descartes
revision, see above, chap. 12, pp. 231–32.
49. Ibid.

Part 5. Final Years

1. Heschel 1962, *The Prophets*, 4–5.

Chapter 16. Vietnam and Israel

1. Heschel 1973, "The Reasons for My Involvement in the Peace Movement," repr. in
Heschel 1996, *Moral Grandeur and Spiritual Audacity*, 224.
2. Ibid., 225, 226; Heschel, quoted in "Battle of Conscience," *Newsweek* (November
15, 1965), 78, quoted in Hall 1990, 15. Cf. Heschel 1955, *God in Search of Man:*
"There is a passion and drive for cruel deeds which only the awe and fear of God
can soothe; there is a suffocating selfishness in man which only holiness can venti-
late," 169.
3. John Sibley, "Clergymen Defend Right to Protest Vietnam Policy," *New York Times*,
26 October 1965, 10; Hall 1990, 14–15; interview with Richard John Neuhaus;
Hall 1990, 14n40.
4. *New York Times*, 28 November 1965. See also FBI files, FBI/NYO 100-154786
4076, DHL:plr., quotation from p. 100. This packet of more than two hundred
pages contains clippings of antiwar activities from both the leftist and the mainstream press, in addition to reports from informants. See the *National Guardian*,
4 December 1965, p. 9, col. 3, and 18 December 1965, p. 9, col. 2, "Round-up of
Anti-War Activities." The FBI cited a follow-up article in the *Guardian*, and a
New York Times advertisement of 12 December 1965, "protesting the reassign-
ment of Father Daniel Berrigan, a Jesuit priest, poet, and opponent of the Vietnam
war, to South America." Two other Jesuits, Francis Keating and Daniel Kilfoyle,
were ordered to remove their names as sponsors of the antiwar organization: Hall
1990, 15.

5. My account of Clergy and Laymen Concerned About Vietnam (CALCAV) follows Hall 1990; we often use the same primary sources, such as newspaper articles, FBI reports, archival documents. For a detailed chronology see Hall 2000. On the origins of CCAV see Hall 1990, 22; statement dated 18 April 1966, Swarthmore Peace Collection; Coffin 1977; Coffin understood the complexities of government espionage firsthand. In 1943 he had joined military intelligence, under whose auspices he learned Russian; he was appalled by the brutality meted out to Russian prisoners who had been forcibly repatriated after the war. At the outbreak of the Korean War he joined the CIA but left the service to pursue a religious vocation; Coffin 1977, 115–17.

6. Telegram, CALCAV records, 11 January 1966, 24 January 1966; Fernandez, "Proposal. Clergy and Laymen Concerned about Vietnam—a National Emergency Com—Its History and Future," 21 September 1966, CALCAV records, series 2, box 2, Swarthmore Peace Collection.

7. Hall 1990, 20–21; Heschel, letters to Hans J. Morgenthau, 8 April 1966, and 25 April 1966; Heschel, letter to J. Robert Oppenheimer, 8 April 1966; Morgenthau, letter to Heschel, 17 April 1966, Swarthmore Peace Collection.

8. Hall 1990, 19–20; obituary of Robert McAfee Brown, *Boston Globe*, 7 September 2001.

9. Interview with Richard John Neuhaus.

10. John Dear, ed., *Apostle of Peace: Essays in Honor of Daniel Berrigan* (Maryknoll, N.Y.: Orbis, 1996), introduction, 1–17; interview with Reuven Kimelman; Roundtable.

11. See Hall 1990.

12. Ibid., 18; Coffin 1977, 209–29, 115–17; interview with William Sloane Coffin. Inspired by the Hillel chaplain, Rabbi Richard Israel, Coffin pressured Yale's president Whitney Griswold to create policies and living conditions favorable to the admission and matriculation of observant Jews: Coffin 1977, 137–38.

13. This first meeting and the Sabbath dinner in Coffin 1977, 217–23, confirmed by interview with William Sloane Coffin.

14. See Hall 1990, chap. 2, "Taking the Middle Ground (March 1966–September 1967), 26–52.

15. Hall 1990, 29–30; *New York Times*, 4 July 1966, 2; *Long Island Press*, 5 July 1966; *Christian Science Monitor*, 9 July 1966.

16. Heschel, letters to Kivie Kaplan, Rabbi Richard Hirsch, 24 September 1966; Heschel, mimeographed letter, 9 September 1966, personal papers of the author. Al Vorspan and Balfour Brickner were also informed of Heschel's words. Heschel 1966, "The Moral Outrage of Vietnam," 24. Further quotations in the text will be from this source.

17. FBI files, FBI report to Director FBI (105-138315) from SAC, New York (105-

153827-16), dated 17 June 1966. Town Hall meeting in FBI/NYO 100-154786, p. 199, and FBI/NYO memorandum, 17 June 1966, 105-153827-16.

18. FBI files, FBI memorandum, FBI/NY 100-154786, pp. 202–3, which noted an article in the "East Coast Communist newspaper" paper "The Worker," "Women, Clergy to March Against the War" 18 October 1966, 3. See *New York Times*, 20 October 1966.

19. Interview with Seymour Melman; CALCAV 1968. See Edward B. Fiske, "Clerics Accuse U.S. of War Crimes," *New York Times*, 4 February 1968, 1; interview with Richard Fernandez.

20. Interview with Richard Fernandez.

21. Mimeographed report written by Edward Kaplan in February 1967, when I was a graduate student at Columbia University, personal papers of the author. Cf. Coffin 1977, 224–29.

22. "Service of Witness in Time of War," New York Avenue Presbyterian Church, program, personal papers of the author.

23. Heschel's speech quoted from a pamphlet printed and distributed by CALCAV entitled "Vietnam: The Clergymen's Dilemma," published in Heschel 1966, "The Moral Outrage of Vietnam," in *Vietnam: Crisis of Conscience*, 51–52. Heschel took the story from *The Golem*, a play by the Yiddish writer Halper Levik.

24. *New York Times*, 2 February 1967. The *Times* also reported that earlier the same day seven CALCAV representatives met with Walt W. Rostow, the president's adviser on national security affairs. See also memoranda in LBJ Library.

25. See Hall 1990, 37–38; Coffin 1977, 226–29.

26. Coffin 1977, 229.

27. I wrote to Robert McNamara on 21 August 1992 describing the incident and asking for his reactions to it; McNamara responded with a handwritten note on 25 August: he did not remember the incident but he would not have thought Heschel to be "stupid and impractical": personal papers of the author. See McNamara 1995.

28. Coffin 1977, 229; interview with William Sloane Coffin.

29. Hall 1990, 40–45.

30. Ibid., 41–45; for King's entry into the antiwar movement see Garrow 1986, 449–557.

31. Martin Luther King, Jr., "Beyond Vietnam," *Dr. Martin Luther King, Jr., Dr. John Bennett, Dr. Henry Steele Commager, Rabbi Abraham Heschel Speak on the War in Vietnam* ([New York:] Clergy and Laymen Concerned About Vietnam, [1967]), 10, 11.

32. Henry Steele Commager and John Bennett, untitled speeches in *King, Bennett, Commager, Heschel Speak on the War in Vietnam*, 17–19, 19–20.

33. Heschel, untitled speech in *King, Bennett, Commager, Heschel Speak on the War in Vietnam*, 20.

34. Heschel 1966, "The Moral Outrage of Vietnam," repr. in *Vietnam: Crisis of Conscience*, 52, 56–57. The important paragraph on "engaged Buddhism" was omitted from this reprint. *Vietnam: Crisis of Conscience* also contained a bibliography, official statements from the Synagogue Council of America and the Central Committee of the World Council of Churches, excerpts from the encyclical *Christi Matri* of Pope Paul VI, a statement by the American Roman Catholic bishops, and an appeal from the General Assembly of the National Council of Churches. See Hall 1990, 47.

35. See Staub 2002, chap. 4, "Vietnam and the Politics of Theology," 112–52. In 1966 *Tradition* featured an article by Michael Wyschogrod, philosophy professor at the City College of New York, who candidly advocated for "Jewish self-interest," "The Jewish Interest in Vietnam," *Tradition* 8, 4 (winter 1966): 5–18. The reply of Charles S. Liebman, professor of political science at Yeshiva University—written just before but published soon after the June 1967 war—registered his "profound disagreement with the logic and conclusions of [Wyschogrod's] article." Liebman, "Judaism and Vietnam: A Reply to Dr. Wyschogrod," *Tradition* 9, 1–2 (spring–summer 1967): 155–60; reply of Michael Wyschogrod, "Jewish Interest in Vietnam," *Tradition* 9, 3 (Fall 1967): 154–56.

36. Interviews with Balfour Brickner and Wolfe Kelman (who was present at the meeting with the Israeli delegate); Elie Wiesel, "When We Deal with Nuclear Issues, the Jewish Community Turns Off," *Shalom* (fall–winter 1986–87): 1–3 (quotation on p. 2).

37. See Oren 2002.

38. Interview with Penina Peli.

39. The talk was later published as Heschel 1967, "*Ginzey ha-yesha*" (The hidden sources of redemption), *Hadoar*, 11 August 1967, 643–45. Translation by Karen Chernick. Further quotations in the text are from this source.

40. See above, chap. 10, p. 182, in which Heschel quotes Isaiah 19:23–25 on the reconciliation of Egypt, Assyria, and Israel: "All three will be equally God's chosen people," Heschel 1957, "Sacred Images of Man," repr. in *Religious Education*, 102. See also chap. 11, p. 203. Heschel quotes this passage with references to a myriad of biblical sources in Heschel 1962, *The Prophets*, 185–86.

41. Heschel, "An Echo of Eternity," *Hadassah* (September 1967), 4–6.

42. Note from the editors, *Christian Century* (26 July 1967), 955.

43. Willard G. Oxtoby, "Christians and the Mideast Crisis," *Christian Century* (26 July 1967), 961–65.

44. David Polish, "Why American Jews Are Disillusioned," *Christian Century* (26 July 1967), 965–67.

45. Sanders, "Urbis and Orbis: Jerusalem Today," *Christian Century* (26 July 1967), 967–70. Sanders took his title from *Urbis et Orbis*, "to the city and to the world," the pope's annual Easter homily to world Christians. This article was followed by

another article strongly supporting the Jewish perspective, "Again, Silence in the Churches. I. The Case for Israel," by Roy and Alice Eckhardt, 970–73.

46. Interview with James Sanders.

47. Description of meeting in his apartment, Sanders email to the author, 1 February 2004. See also Sanders, "Intertextuality and Dialogue," *Biblical Theology Bulletin* 29, 1 (1999): 37; interview with James Sanders.

48. A week or so before the High Holy Days (Rosh Hashanah 5728 began on 5 October 1967), two of Heschel's closest allies in the antiwar movement defined the essential disagreement between Christians and Jews. See Balfour Brickner, "No Ease in Zion for Us," and John Bennett, "A Response to Rabbi Brickner," *Christianity and Crisis* (18 September 1967), 200, 204–5.

Chapter 17. Dismay and Exaltation

Epigraph. Heschel 1966, "The Moral Outrage of Vietnam," rpt. in *Vietnam: Crisis of Conscience.*

1. FBI files, FBI memorandum, 123656-57; FBI document 123661; teletype, FBI/NYO, 19 January 1968, 123660, to Mr. Deloach for the Director. CC: R. Sullivan; Douglas Robinson, "Dr. King Calls for Antiwar Rally in Capital, Feb. 5–6," *New York Times,* 13 January 1968; CALCAV flyer in FBI Files, 123658. All in King Library, Special Collections. Among the signers of the flyer were John Bennett, Daniel Berrigan, Robert McAfee Brown, William Sloane Coffin, Heschel, Maurice Eisendrath, Harvey Cox, and Martin Luther King, Jr.

2. CALCAV 1968. Each chapter is headed by selections from international treatises. Edward Fiske, "Clerics Accuse U.S. of War Crimes," *New York Times,* 4 February 1968, 1.

3. Edward Kaplan, mimeographed report, February 1968, personal papers of the author. The following account of the mobilization is based on this report, FBI files, newspaper articles, original documents of CALCAV, and secondary sources.

4. Richard Hirsch, memorandum to Eisendrath, Heschel, Brickner, 30 January 1968, Swarthmore College Peace Collection; Kaplan, mimeographed report, February 1968, personal papers of the author.

5. Heschel's address is reprinted in the brochure "In Whose Name?" that was distributed by CALCAV, personal papers of the author. Heschel gave a photocopy of his speech to the author.

6. Also on 6 February, about 1,000 people attended a session on "The Religious Community and the Draft," while 350–400 attended the session presided over by Richard Neuhaus, "The Religious Community and Politics, 1968," at the Lincoln Memorial Temple. Kaplan, mimeographed report, February 1968; clippings from *Evening Star* (6 February 1968), *Times Herald* (7 February 1968), *Washington Post*

(7 February 1968), and *Catholic Virginian* (16 February 1968), some with excellent photographs, collected in FBI reports, 123570–72, Swarthmore Peace Collection; see also typewritten memorandum by LeRoy Moore, Jr., Hartford Seminary Foundation, Swarthmore Peace Collection.

7. FBI report, 123570, Swarthmore Peace Collection; the newspaper articles have a different wording, which I think is incorrect: "In this period of absolute silence, let us pray." In Mark 15:34 Christ's words are given in Aramaic. Heschel's interfaith gesture was criticized after the *New York Times* mistakenly transcribed the words from Psalm 22 in the Aramaic of Jesus; see *New York Times*, 7 February 1968, and the correction in *New York Times*, 16 February 1968, 18.

8. "A Turning Point, Peace or War?" and "How Much Do You Value Free Speech?" *New York Times*, 11 February 1968, E5, E7. Heschel was honorary chair of the Civil Liberties Legal Defense Fund. "Clergyman's War Protest," letter to the editor from David C. Kogan, Wolfe Kelman, Seymour Siegel, Arthur Hertzberg, *New York Times*, 11 February 1968, E13.

9. Rabbi Alexander M. Schindler, vice president of the UAHC, memorandum to members of the UAHC Board of Directors, 4 April 1968; attached were Freehof, letter to Eisendrath, 23 February 1968, Hirsch, memorandum to Eisendrath, 20 February 1968, notes of a telephone conversation with Heschel, personal papers of the author. Interview with Balfour Brickner. Hirsch, memorandum to Eisendrath, 20 February 1968. Ezekiel ben Judah Landau (1713–1793), born in Opatow, Poland, was one of the greatest Jewish figures of his time. He was rabbi of Prague and the whole of Bohemia and the author of numerous responsa.

10. Hirsch, memorandum to Eisendrath, 20 February 1968, personal papers of the author.

11. See *Proceedings* 1968.

12. Heschel 1968, "Conversation with Martin Luther King," 1. King, quoted ibid., 2. Four years earlier, Heschel had been instrumental in persuading the Jewish Theological Seminary to confer an honorary Doctor of Laws on King. See *Seminary Progress* (spring 1968), an in-house publication, for photographs.

13. King, quoted in Heschel 1968, "Conversation with Martin Luther King," 12.

14. Ibid., 15.

15. Edmond Cherbonnier, "Heschel as a Religious Thinker," *Conservative Judaism* 23, 1 (fall 1968), 25–39.

16. Fritz A. Rothschild, "The Religious Thought of Abraham Heschel," *Conservative Judaism* 23, 1 (fall 1968), 12–24.

17. Seymour Siegel, "Abraham Joshua Heschel's Contributions to Jewish Scholarship," *Proceedings* 1968, 78, 84.

18. Heschel 1968, "The Theological Dimensions of Medinat Yisrael," 91. The speech was edited and reprinted with subtitles as Heschel 1969, "Christian-Jewish Dialogue and the Meaning of the State of Israel." Another version was

presented at Saint Louis University, conference on "Theology and the City of Man," 15–17 October 1968.

19. Heschel 1968, "Theological Dimensions," 93, 96; see Heschel 1951, *Man Is Not Alone:* "The major folly of this view seems to lie in its shifting the responsibility for man's plight from man to God," 151; Heschel 1968, "Theological Dimensions," 96.

20. Heschel 1968, "Theological Dimensions," 97, 101–2.

21. *Proceedings* 1968, 104–9, 106–7, 107–8. Heschel also reminded the rabbis of German Catholics who did not want to oppose Hitler in order to protect the church.

22. Heschel quoted from the Revised Standard Version, with some changes: compact disk of the funeral at the King Papers Project at Stanford University. Heschel's apparent choice of the Suffering Servant text irked the eminent Yiddish poet and writer Yaakov (Jacob) Glatstein, who criticized him in the Yiddish *Day-Morning Journal* for reading from the New Testament. When he was informed that the Gospels had adopted the passage from Isaiah, he apologized. Interview with Seymour Siegel. Description of King's funeral can be found in the *New York Times* (9–10 April 1968), which includes transcripts of the eulogies; King 1969, 328 ff. and appendix; Oates 1982, 493–96; and John Lewis 1998, 390–94. For a disenchanted view see David L. Lewis 1970.

23. Heschel's two-hour talk, with discussion, was transcribed and edited by Pesach Schindler: Heschel 1969, "Teaching Jewish Theology in the Solomon Schechter Day School." Some capitalizations were changed for consistency. Schindler translated Yiddish or Hebrew expressions in brackets.

24. Ibid., 19, 24–26.

25. Kenneth Woodward in *Newsweek* (30 December 1968), 38.

26. In 1969 Zolla published an Italian translation (by Elena Mortara) of chapter 4 of *God in Search of Man*, "La meraviglia" (Wonder) in *Conoscenza religiosa* 1 (1969): 4–18, with a "Note on Heschel." In 1971 Zolla published a translated excerpt from the manuscript of *A Passion for Truth: Conoscenza religiosa* 4 (1971): 337–53, "Il chassidismo e Kierkegaard."

27. Interview with Elémire Zolla; Zolla, letter to Samuel Dresner, 20 March 1979, Heschel Archive. See also Zolla article in *Corriere della sera*, 14 April 1986.

28. Interview with Elémire Zolla.

29. In the wake of the abduction of Edgardo Mortara international leaders including Napoleon III tried unsuccessfully to intervene with Pope Pius IX for the child's return to his family. Only after Rome and Vatican City fell to the French army in 1870, ending the pope's secular power, was Mortara freed. By then he had become a priest, entered the Augustinian order, and begun a career as "apostolic missionary." He died in 1940. Elena Mortara di Veroli published an article about Heschel's talk, "Heschel, risposta all'ebreo di oggi"(Heschel: An answer to today's Jew), in *Shalom* (January 1969), the monthly magazine of the Rome Jewish community.

30. Interview with Gianfranco Tedeschi.

31. *Proceedings of the First International Congress on Genesis of Sudden Death and Re-animation*, ed. Vincenzo Lapiccirella (Florence: Marchi and Bertolli, 1970). The conference was held 10–14 January 1969. Heschel also participated in the round-table discussion at the end of the conference, organized by Italian television (RAI-TV). See *Proceedings of the First International Congress*, 627–61.

32. Heschel 1969, "Reflections on Death," 534, 542. See Heschel 1951, *Man Is Not Alone*, 296.

33. As usual the FBI and related agencies kept themselves informed, mainly through public documents and direct observation. FBI documents 121362–63 and others when noted; the cover sheet for the collection (124351) stated that the following of-ficials would receive copies: the president; secretary of state; director, CIA; direc-tor, defense intelligence agency; department of the army; department of the air force; Secret Service (PID) by plaintext teletype; attorney general (by messenger). Unclassified. An eleven-page teletype document summarizes the entire event, 121250–276; and a typewritten copy, 124269–273. All in King Library, Special Collections.

34. The 1969 Position Paper of Clergy and Laymen Concerned About Vietnam, "The Reconciliation We Seek: Consequences and Lessons of the Vietnam War," from FBI files, 121277–80, King Library, Special Collections.

35. *New York Times*, 5 February 1969, 10; FBI file, 124339, King Library, Special Col-lections; Ben A. Franklin, "Opponents of Vietnam War Meet with Kissinger," *New York Times*, 6 February 1969, 17; Coffin 1977, 294–98; interview with Coffin.

36. Interviews with Richard Fernandez, Richard John Neuhaus, Heschel Archive. Henry Kissinger was a literate Jew who was reared in an observant family. His father was a Hebrew teacher.

37. FBI report, 121261, p. 6; FBI report, 124275, King Library, Special Collections.

38. On 21 February CALCAV sent an open letter to President Nixon, on the eve of his departure for Europe, urging him to negotiate an end to the war. Signers included Heschel, John Bennett, Coretta Scott King, James Shannon, and Philip Sharper: clipping dated 22 February 1969, from "Daily World," FBI Files, 21 February, King Library, Special Collections. On the rally see FBI Files, 100–445003; FBI/NYO 100–156717, 11 June 1969, 7 pp.; Appendix on American Veterans for Peace in "Guide to Subversive Organizations and Publications," revised and pub-lished 1 December 1961 by the Committee on Un-American Activities, U.S. House of Representatives. The FBI report was widely distributed: the U.S. attor-ney, Southern District of New York, 108th Military Intelligence Group, Naval In-vestigative Service Office (NISO), Office of Special Investigations (OSI), and Secret Service, New York City.

39. The ADL program director, Oscar Cohen, and Solomon Bernards, director of

interreligious cooperation, had been in touch with Heschel since 1964 on matters of Jewish-Christian dialogue: see Bernards, letters to Heschel, 2 December 1964, 10 June 1966, 10 December 1966; Cohen, letter to Heschel, 27 December 1966; Bernards, letters to Heschel, 12 January 1967, 24 January 1967, ADL files.

40. Judith Herschlag Muffs, "A Reminiscence of Abraham Joshua Heschel," *Conservative Judaism* 28, 1 (fall 1973), 53–54; interview with Yocheved Muffs. Roger Straus, letter to Heschel, 30 January 1968; Straus, letter to Lesser Zussman, Jewish Publication Society, 21 March 1968, Farrar, Straus and Giroux Archives. The occasion for the symposium was the university's sesquicentennial.

41. Heschel 1969, "Jewish-Christian Dialogue and the Meaning of the State of Israel," 409.

42. Ibid, 418. See Heschel 1955, *God in Search of Man:* "Even before Israel becomes a people, the land is preordained for it. What we have witnessed in our own day is a reminder of the power of God's mysterious promise to Abraham and a testimony to the fact that the people kept its promise; 'If I forget thee, o Jerusalem, let my right hand wither' (Psalms 137:5)," 425. Heschel 1969, "Jewish-Christian Dialogue and the Meaning of the State of Israel," 414, 425.

43. Judith Herschlag, letter to Heschel, 18 June 1968, ADL files; Stan Wexler, Publications Department of ADL, letter to John Peck, Farrar, Straus, 29 October 1968, Farrar, Straus and Giroux Archives.

44. Invitation to the launch of *Israel: An Echo of Eternity,* Anti-Defamation League of B'nai B'rith, Thursday, 20 February at 4:00 o'clock, Lexington Avenue, New York; Julie Coryn, director of publicity of Farrar, Straus, letter to Marc Tanenbaum, 5 February 1969, with a longer list of names. Information added in Coryn, letter to Marshall Meyer, 5 February 1969; Roger Straus, letter to David Salten, 30 January 1969. Permission was granted to *Catholic Digest* to publish an excerpt of pp. 161–67: Roger Straus, memorandum to JFC, 27 January 1969. All in Farrar, Straus and Giroux Archives.

45. Jim F. Anderson, "Israel and the Holy War," *National Catholic Reporter* (19 February 1969), 13.

46. David Lieber, letter to Robert G. Hoyt, 4 March 1969, ADL files.

47. *Time* (14 March 1969). See also A. Roy Eckardt, review of Heschel's *Israel, Conservative Judaism* 23, 4 (summer 1968): 70–73; Zvi Zinger, "Humanize the Sacred, Sanctify the Secular," *Jerusalem Post,* 8 August 1969, 14. A Hebrew translation of Heschel's book was published soon after the author's death: see review by Pinchas Lapide in *Jerusalem Post,* 11 January 1974.

48. See below, chap. 19, pp. 366–67.

49. Heschel 1969, *Israel,* 14. See also: "Jerusalem is not divine, her life depends on our presence. Alone she is desolate and silent, with Israel she is a witness, a proclamation. Alone she is a widow, with Israel she is a bride" (ibid.).

Chapter 18. Stronger Than Death

1. The conference took place on 25–28 August 1969. Some 2,500 people attended the opening session at the Milwaukee Arena, which ended with a multimedia extravaganza, a liturgical dance, and a mass set to rock music. See L. I. Steli, "The Road Show of Hope," *Tempo*, (15 October 1969), 3; *Catholic Herald Citizen* (29 March 1969), and articles by Ethel Gintoft, "Speaker [Robert McAfee Brown] Defines Meaning of Liturgy as 'Work People Do,'" *Catholic Herald Citizen* (30 August 1969), and "Rabbi Reminds Conference of Need for Prayer Along with Activity," *Catholic Herald Citizen* (6 September 1969). Robert McAfee Brown, "Backdrop for Hope," *Tempo* (15 October 1969), 7.

2. Steli, "Road Show of Hope," 3; Gintoft, "Rabbi Reminds Conference of Need for Prayer." Heschel's speech was excerpted in *Tempo* (15 October 1969), 8, 11. The most complete version, "On Prayer," appeared in *Conservative Judaism* 25, 1 (fall 1970), 1–12, from which I quote.

3. Heschel 1970, "On Prayer," 2–3, 4.

4. Ibid., 5, 7; Gintoft, "Rabbi Reminds Conference of Need for Prayer."

5. On 28 August 1969, Heschel was completing his stay in Milwaukee at the Liturgical Conference; Fritz Rothschild, letter to his sister, 31 December 1972, Heschel Archive. Interview with Wolfe Kelman, 23 August 1987; conversations with Sylvia Heschel.

6. Fernandez, memorandum to CALCAV Steering Committee, 5 September 1969, Swarthmore College Peace Collection; Kogan, memorandum to JTS faculty, 3 September 1969; photocopy of Heschel's note given to author by Wolfe Kelman.

7. Interview with Joshua Shmidman. Thanks to Laurence Kaplan for this story and this contact.

8. David Kogan, *Daily Bulletin*, 15 September 1969, JTS General Files. Interview with Jacob Perlow, February 1979.

9. After Heschel's death in 1972, Sylvia Heschel's brother Reuben Straus, a pathologist, spoke with Heschel's cardiologist, who expressed surprise that Heschel had survived as long as he did: conversation with Sylvia Heschel, 2004.

10. Announcement and program of Moratorium by Roberta Kiel, 13 October 1969, JTS General Files.

11. Heschel, letter to the author, Sylvia Heschel, letter to the author, both dated 26 January 1970, personal papers of the author. Sylvia Heschel wrote: "Every morning I walk for 25 minutes to Rabbi Kronish's temple where I have the privilege of practicing on their well-worn grand piano—and that makes Florida possible for me. Without it, everything seems so meaningless and empty." Finkelstein, letter to Heschel, at Mount Sinai Hospital, Miami Beach, 3 March 1970, JTS General Files.

12. Conversation with Sylvia Heschel.

13. Heschel 1973, *Kotsk,* manuscript of the translation by Jonathan Boyarin, 3, unpublished.

14. Heschel's article in the *Encyclopaedia Judaica* glossed over the most controversial event of the Kotzker's life, the so-called Friday Night Incident, an act of blasphemy that led to the rebbe's withdrawal from his community for the last twenty years of his life. See Faierstein 1991.

15. Heschel's talk was "The Kotzker Rebbe: A Dissenter in Chassidism," 20 May 1959, at a session in honor of Boaz Cohen, JTS professor of rabbinics: *Proceedings* 1959, 23; Kalman A. Siegel, "Jewish Scholars Sift Man's Role," *New York Times,* 21 May 1959, 18; Heschel 1959, "Rabbi Mendel mi-Kotzk."

16. Heschel's articles: 1968, "Rabbi Mendel mi-Kotzk"; 1969, "Kotzk"; 1969–70, "Der Kotsker rebbe." See Heschel, letters to Abraham Sutzkever, YIVO Archives. During this time, Heschel corresponded with Father Damasus Winzen of the Benedictine Priory in Weston, Vermont, where his friend Leo Rudloff was abbot. Later, Heschel dedicated an essay in English on the Kotzker and Kierkegaard to Father Damasus: Heschel 1972, "Søren Kierkegaard and the Rabbi of Kotzk." Heschel, "Kotzk, Menahem Mendel of," *Encyclopaedia Judaica* 10: 1222–24; the piece was published in 1971, but submitted years earlier. See Green 1979.

17. Heschel completed both versions of the book before he died, and they appeared posthumously. The Yiddish book (two volumes, total 694 pages) bore the same relation to the English volume (323 pages) as the two Hebrew tomes of *Heavenly Torah* (Torah min Ha-shamayim) bore to *Man Is Not Alone* and *God in Search of Man:* in both cases Heschel wrote in the language of his original sources in order to authenticate the theology and ethics he developed in English for a broader readership. For Heschel's childhood see Kaplan and Dresner 1998, 39–41; a similar autobiographical statement is the passage on Berlin in *Man's Quest for God,* originally presented in 1953 to Reform rabbis. (I limit the following comments to *A Passion for Truth,* which Heschel wrote for speakers of English, Jewish and Christian.) Heschel 1973, *A Passion for Truth,* xiv.

18. Heschel 1973, *A Passion for Truth,* 320; Zvi Yaron, review of *Kotsk, Jerusalem Post,* 30 August 1974, 15. The final section of *A Passion for Truth,* "The Kotzker Today," gives ample evidence of Heschel's pessimism.

19. Heschel 1973, *A Passion for Truth,* 167, 204, 206, 210.

20. Ibid., 287–88, 290, 298.

21. Ibid., 301.

22. Press release, American Academy of Arts and Sciences, 13 May 1970, JTS Publicity Files; Finkelstein, letter to Heschel, 18 May 1970, JTS General Files.

23. Heschel 1970, "God, Torah, and Israel." Heschel revised the translation by his student Byron Sherwin.

24. Interview with Harlan Wechsler; Harlan Wechsler, letter to Samuel Dresner, 2 May 1983; interview with Arthur Green.

25. Roundtable: David Novak, Sol Tanenzapf, 3.

26. Interview with Fritz Rothschild. Heschel probably read from his book.

27. Interviews with Jacob Teshima, starting 17 April 1988; Israel Shenker, "Japanese Christian Is Awarded a Doctorate by Jewish Seminary," *New York Times,* 31 May 1977, 25. See the special issue of *Light of Life on the Original Gospel Movement* (Tokyo, November 1968). Also Ikuro Teshima, *Introduction to the Original Gospel Movement* (Japan, 1970); Carlo Caldarola, "The Makuya Christian Movement," *Japanese Religions* 7, 4 (December 1972): 18–34. Teshima studied in Israel from 1963 to 1967.

28. Jacob named his son, who was born in New York, Wolfe Heschel Teshima. Interview with Jacob Teshima, 1988. Ikuro Teshima, letter to Roger Straus, 14 July 1971; Peter Hinzmann, letter to Jacob Teshima, 23 July 1971; Yoji Iwashita, letters to Lila Karp, Subsidiary Rights, 20 July 1972, 31 July 1972: "We held our annual summer conference this year at the foot of the Japan Alps in the last part of July, which was attended by a little more than 4,000 people, and [Heschel's] books were sold out during the conference." All in Farrar, Straus and Giroux Archives.

29. David Kogan, memorandum to the JTS faculty, 4 January 1971; JTS General Files; memoir by Felice Morgenstern, niece of Jacob Heshel. This and other documents from Thena Heshel Kendall, Jacob's daughter. Jacob Heshel, "The History of Hasidism in Austria," in Josef Fraenkel, ed., *The Jews of Austria* (London: Vallentine Mitchell, 1967), 347–60.

30. The event took place on 20 February 1971. John C. Bennett, "A Prophet for Our Day," *Jewish Heritage* (fall 1971): 43–46.

31. Lou H. Silberman, "Rebbe for Our Day," *Jewish Heritage* (fall 1971): 39–43 (quotation on p. 39).

32. My paper, "Form and Content in Abraham J. Heschel's Poetic Style," was published in the *CCAR Journal* (Kaplan 1971).

33. Heschel's apparent lack of preparation worried the organizers, since he provided translators with only a long typescript that contained almost the entire text of *Who Is Man?* Elena Mortara, letter to Samuel Dresner, 13 December 1987, Heschel Archive.

34. Marcello Molinari, "Spazio interiore" (Interior space), *Shalom* (March 1971), quoted in Mortara 1973; Mortara, translation of Mortara 1973, Heschel Archive.

35. Ibid.

36. *United Synagogue Review* 24, 3 (fall 1971). See interview with Seymour Siegel, Heschel Archive. The account is taken from Heschel, memorandum, 3 pp., Heschel Archive, cited in part in Susannah Heschel 1996, xxvi–xxvii.

37. *The Pilot,* 29 May 1971, 3, Religious News Service photo. As a reminder of Heschel's moral authority, this same *United Synagogue Review* included his essay on

Captain William Calley, who had been condemned by a military tribunal for his responsibility for the My Lai massacre: Heschel 1971, "Required: A Moral Ombudsman."

38. Flender's weekly program was sponsored by JTS. See Heschel 1971, *The Eternal Light* (quotations from pt. 1, pp. 3, 5–6).

39. Ibid., 7.

40. Heschel 1971, "Nasa'ta ve-natata be-'emunah?" (Have you acted faithfully?), trans. Aryeh Cohen, unpublished, Heschel Archive, 8, 12. Heschel's footnote quoted the story of a refugee from the Spanish expulsion who admonished God after his entire family perished: "You are doing much to force me to leave my religion. Know therefore, that despite those who reside in heaven I am a Jew, and a Jew I will remain."

41. "Friends Officiate at Service for Niebuhr," *Berkshire Eagle*, 5 June 1971; Heschel 1971, "Reinhold Niebuhr: A Last Farewell"; Seymour Siegel, article, announcement, *New York Times*, 3 June 1971, 42; Fox 1985, 292–93.

42. Accounts of the evening from interviews with Ira Eisenstein, Wolfe Kelman; quotations from the audiotape of Heschel's speech, Heschel Archive.

43. JTS Publicity File; Frank Reynolds interview, "A Conversation with Rabbi Abraham J. Heschel," 21 November 1971, ABC. *ADL Bulletin* (December 1971), personal papers of the author. Letters and ADL press release, 4 November 1971, ADL files.

44. *ADL Bulletin*, December 1971, 3.

45. ADL press release, ADL files.

46. Invitation, Heschel Archive.

Chapter 19. Summation of a Life

1. Interview with Jacob Teshima, 20 September 2001, personal papers of the author; interviews with Thena Heshel Kendall, Seymour Siegel, Wolfe Kelman, Jane Kronholz. Heschel Archive.

2. "The Heritage of Martin Luther King, Jr.," ABC, 9 January 1972.

3. Ibid.

4. Robert Bilheimer, letter to Heschel, 8 November 1971; Heschel, statement dictated to Siegman's secretary (see Siegman, letter to Heschel, 29 October 1971); Bilheimer, letter to Heschel, 8 November 1971, Heschel Archive. Edward B. Fiske, "Religious Assembly Terms Vietnam Policy Immoral," *New York Times*, 17 January 1972, 35; Heschel 1973, "The Reason for My Involvement in the Peace Movement."

5. Press releases of the Jewish Telegraph Agency (JTA) daily news bulletin, 18–26 January 1972, Hebrew College Library, Newton, Mass.; Berel Lang, "Zionism or Zionisms?" *Midstream* (May 1972), 28–32.

6. See Janet L. Dolgin, *Jewish Identity and the JDL* (Princeton: Princeton University Press, 1977).

7. Heschel 1972, "A Time for Renewal," 46–47: I quote from the *Midstream* essay with some changes according to a translation of the Hebrew provided by Samuel Dresner. Cf. Heschel 1951, "To Be a Jew: What Is It?"; JTA, 21 January 1972; see also "World Zionist Congress Highlights," JTA, 26 January 1972, 4, Hebrew College Library, Jerusalem.

8. Heschel 1972, "A Time for Renewal," 50–51.

9. Heschel, letter quoted in book edited by Hofer's widow, Yehiel Hofer, *Lider fun shpisal un lider fun der nacht* (Tel Aviv: ha-Menorah, 1976), 101.

10. Ronald Taylor, "Group of Clergy Supports Amnesty for Everyone but War Criminals," *Washington Post*, 28 March 1972, A8; Eleanor Blau, "Amnesty for Dissenters on War Is Backed by Religious Leaders," *New York Times*, 28 March 1972, 16; see Hall 1990, 161–65. The document was drafted by a committee headed by William Sloane Coffin, Jr. Heschel 1972, "The Theological, Biblical, and Ethical Considerations of Amnesty," copy given to the author by Henry Schwarzschild of the American Civil Liberties Union, personal papers of the author.

11. Heschel cited Maimonides, *Laws Concerning Kings* (III, 8, 9), as a basic authority. The Rashi citation is "*Pesahim* 25A, see *Sanhedrin* 74A."

12. Gottschalk, letter to Heschel, 20 March 1972; Heschel, letter to Gottschalk, 24 March 1972, American Jewish Archives, Cincinnati. Also receiving honorary degrees were the Yiddish writer Chaim Grade and the Hebrew poet Gabriel Preil: Eleanor Blau, "1st Woman Rabbi in US Ordained," *New York Times*, 4 June 1972, 76.

13. News release by Gunther Lawrence, Abraham Heschel Nearprint, Biography File, American Jewish Archives, Cincinnati.

14. Heschel and his family remained in Los Angeles until after the High Holy Days: Abraham and Sylvia Heschel, New Year's card to the author, postmarked 21 September 1972. Robert Giroux, memorandum to Roger Straus, 19 July 1972, Farrar, Straus and Giroux Archive.

15. Roger Straus, letter to Heschel, 20 July 1972, Farrar, Straus and Giroux Archive.

16. On the five Europeans see Kaplan and Dresner 1998, 71, 306–7.

17. Original documents at the AFSC Archive. Interviews with Sayyed Hossein Nasr, Serif Mardin, letters from E. A. Bayne, Teddy Kollek, George Appleton. Susannah Heschel 1997: "Only later, in the few years before his sudden death in December, 1972, did my father begin to speak out on behalf of the Palestinians and with great criticism of certain Israeli government actions," xxviii. Interview with Seymour Melman.

18. See Kaplan and Dresner 1998, 234–36, 257–58, 300.

19. Interview with Sayyed Hossein Nasr.

20. Nasr immigrated to the United States after the Iranian revolution. He published

many distinguished books, among them *Islam and the Plight of Modern Man* (Malaysia: Longman, 1975). Interview with Sayyed Hossein Nasr.

21. E. A. Bayne, "Staff Memorandum" stamped confidential, 8 September 1972, 6 pp. (quotation on p. 5); Johnson memorandum, summary of seminar, dated 5 September 1972, 3, both in AFSC Archive. See Archbishop Appleton's assessment, "The Spiritual Nature of Jerusalem," undated, 3 pp., marked confidential, AFSC Archive. Werblowsky, letter to the author, 12 December 1991.

22. E. A. Bayne, "Abraham Joshua Heschel," *Mediterranean Report, Bulletin of the Center for Mediterranean Studies of the American Universities Field Staff in Rome, Italy* (Spring–Summer 1973), 8.

23. Victor Goodhill, letter to Samuel Dresner, 15 March 1982; corrected by letter from Appleton to Dresner, 25 November 1982, and E. A. Bayne, letters to Dresner, 29 December 1982, 3 February 1983, Heschel Archive.

24. Apppleton, summary of meeting, 3, 1972, AFSC Archive.

25. Goodhill, letter to Dresner, 15 March 1982; Dresner, unpublished note, 27 April 1982, Heschel Archive.

26. Interview with Sayyed Hossein Nasr.

27. Interview with Jacob Teshima, 20 September 2001; Heschel, letter to Judith Herschlag Muffs, 13 September 1972; Appleton, letter to Heschel, 19 October 1972; Judith Herschlag Muffs, memorandum to Abraham H. Foxman, 22 January 1973; Appleton, letter to Heschel, 19 October 1972: the archbishop suggested some revisions, "a paragraph put here and there in a slightly different way so as not to hurt the sensitivity of Arabs." Heschel 1969, *Israel*, 218. See above, chap. 10, p. 182, and chap. 11, p. 203.

28. Terrence Smith, "Mrs. Meir Speaks," *New York Times*, 6 September 1972, 1; Irving Spiegel, "Rosh ha-shanah Starts at Sundown with Prayers for Israelis Slain in Munich," *New York Times*, 8 September 1972, 13. Juan de Onis, "Lebanon Raided by Israeli Patrol," *New York Times*, 8 September 1972, 1. Terrence Smith, "Scores of Israeli Planes Strike 10 Guerrilla Bases in a Reprisal for Munich," *New York Times*, 9 September 1972, 1.

29. David Kogen, memorandum to Gerson Cohen, 25 August 1972, JTS General Files.

30. Heschel, letter to Finkelstein, dated 5 October 1972 (but sent 5 November, according to Finkelstein's answer), JTS General Files.

31. Finkelstein, letter to Heschel, 6 November 1972, JTS General Files.

32. Menahem Schmelzer, letter to Warren J. Haas, director Columbia University Library Office, 22 November 1972, JTS General Files.

33. Frank Lynn, "3 Jewish Leaders Back Nixon; Cite Policy on Israel as Reason," *New York Times*, 4 August 1972, 35; Seymour Siegel, letter to the editor dated 14 August 1972, *New York Times*, 25 August 1972, 32. Siegel was answering Greenberg's letter of 11 August.

34. Ron Rosenbaum, "A Tale of Two Rabbis," *Village Voice*, 29 June 1972, 10–11, 76.

35. Israel Shenker, "Rabbi to Give Nixon a Kingly Blessing," *New York Times*, 19 January 1973, 16.

36. Press releases from JTS Publicity Files; the Superior *Evening Telegram*, 7 November 1972, 16. Audiotape of Heschel's speech, Heschel Archive.

37. Heschel 1972, "Conversation with Doctor Abraham Joshua Heschel."

38. Fritz Rothschild, letter to his sister, 31 December 1972; Samuel Dresner, memorandum, undated, both in Heschel Archive. Daniel Berrigan's negative reputation among many Jews began after Heschel's death, when soon after the "Yom Kippur War" of October 1973, Berrigan, then teaching at the University of Manitoba in Winnipeg, spoke critically of Israel to a meeting of the Association of Arab-American University graduates. See Polner and O'Grady 1997, 303–24 and bibliography. See also *The Great Berrigan Debate* (New York: Committee on New Alternatives in the Middle East, 1974). Daniel Berrigan, "Israel, as Presently Constituted," *Poetry, Drama, Prose* (New York: Orbis, 1988), 159–65. Interviews with Daniel Berrigan. Heschel took credit for getting Daniel Berrigan involved in CAL-CAV: Heschel 1971, *The Eternal Light*, pt. 1, p. 3. See Philip Nobile, "The Priest Who Stayed Out in the Cold," *New York Times*, 28 June 1970, 177. The most famous trials of the Berrigans and their associates were those of the Baltimore Four (October 1967), the Catonsville Nine (May 1968), the Milwaukee Fourteen (September 1968), and the Chicago Eighteen (May 1969).

39. Peter Kihiss, "Religious Leaders Back Berrigans on Sermons," *New York Times*, 11 November 1970, 16. See Berrigan 1987, 179; Daniel Berrigan, "My Friend" [on Heschel], Kasimow and Sherwin 1991, 68–75; Edward Bristow, ed., *No Religion Is an Island: The "Nostra Aetate" Dialogues* (New York: Fordham University Press, 1998), the section entitled "Abraham Joshua Heschel: Prophet of Social Activism," 153–179, includes essays by Dan Berrigan, John Healey, Eugene Borowitz, Susannah Heschel. See Roundtable: Reuven Kimelman for Berrigan at JTS.

40. Interview with Wolfe Kelman, 5 January 1988; Lawrence Fellows, "Berrigan Freed After 39 Months: Says in Danbury He Will Continue Antiwar Fight," *New York Times*, 21 December 1972, 40; undated memorandum from Samuel Dresner, "The Last Week of Heschel's Life was Filled with Trauma," Heschel Archive.

41. Interviews with Daniel Berrigan.

42. Communication from Susannah Heschel.

43. Interview with Wolfe Kelman.

44. Roger Straus wrote to Edmond Fuller, the author of an important essay on Heschel in the *Wall Street Journal*, that Heschel had turned in the manuscript "the morning of the day he died." (Heschel died after midnight on Saturday morning, 23 December.) Straus, letter to Fuller, 2 February 1973. On the editing, see the manuscript editor's reports: Wayland Schmitt, letter to Robert Giroux, 25 January 1973, with a list of concerns and corrections; Giroux, letter to Mrs. Abraham Joshua Heschel, 5 February 1973; my letters to Giroux, 19 April 1973, 23 April 1973 (I was one of

the people who corrected the proofs); Giroux, letter to me, 4 May 1973, naming the title *A Passion for Truth*. All in Farrar, Straus and Giroux Archives. The book was officially published in October 1973.

45. Interviews with Jacob Teshima; Fritz Rothschild, letter to his sister, 31 December 1972, Heschel Archive; Teshima 1973, 52–53.

46. Stanley Batkin, letter to Samuel Dresner, 14 December 1978; interviews with Stanley Batkin, Joseph Wiseman, and Pearl Lang; Rothschild, letter to his sister, 31 December 1972, Heschel Archive. Heschel 2004, *The Ineffable Name of God*, poem dedicated "to my teacher David Koigen, May his soul be in paradise," 57.

Chapter 20. A Pluralistic Legacy

1. The account of Heschel's death and funeral preparations is from interviews with Neil Gillman; Rothschild, letter to his sister, December 1972, Heschel Archive.

2. See Samuel Dresner, letter to Pinchas Peli, 15 January 1973: "He died with two books at his side, one lying by his side was David Halberstam's bestseller on Viet Nam, and the other in his hand was the Keter Shem Tov. Who else combined these two worlds as he?" The friend to whom Sylvia Heschel confided the story chose to remain anonymous.

3. Heschel, last will and testament, dated 21 May 1965, with Proskauer Rose Goetz & Mendelsohn, Counselors at Law, contains no mention of his burial. On his wish to be buried next to his uncle, see chapter 18, p. 341.

4. I attended the funeral and rode in the limousine with Wolfe Kelman and others to the cemetery.

5. Interview with Jacob Teshima, 20 September 2001: Teshima kept this secret until he confided it to me. Coffin had handwritten an eloquent eulogy on sheets of yellow paper, which he left with Sylvia Heschel; it began: "I called him Father Abraham because he was as a father to me. He was warm, wise and he gently instructed me with his humor. It was always a joy to be with him. I loved him because he was the most biblical man I knew. He knew that reverence for God meant a certain irreverence for all institutions, including and particularly the State. Yet his judgments were always tempered with prophetic mercy." William Sloane Coffin, Jr., eulogy, 2 pp., Heschel Archive.

6. *New York Times*, 25 December 1972, 20.

7. The eulogy was published later: Wolfe Kelman, "Abraham Joshua Heschel: In Memoriam," *Congress Bi-Weekly* (12 January 1973), 2–3.

8. English translation of the Hebrew in booklet provided by Park West Memorial Chapel.

9. Interview with Jacob Teshima, 20 September 2001; interview with Zusya Heschel, the son of the late Kopitzhinitzer rebbe, Abraham Joshua Heschel, and brother of Moses; Rothschild, letter to his sister, December 1972, Heschel Archive.

10. See Susannah Heschel 1983; Susannah Heschel, "Judaism," Arvind Sharma and Katherine Young, eds., *Her Voice, Her Faith* (Cambridge, Mass.: Westview, 2003), 145–67.

11. Teshima, conversation with the author, 2005.

12. Robert D. McFadden, "Rabbi Abraham Joshua Heschel Dead," *New York Times*, 24 December 1972, 40; the funeral was described the following day: "Homage Paid to Rabbi by 500 at Traditional Service," *New York Times*, 25 December 1972, 20; Pinchas Peli, "Ancient Prophet with a Message for Today," and "Heschel's Last Words," *Jerusalem Post*, 29 December 1972; "A Militant Mystic," *Time* (8 January 1973), 43; Kenneth L. Woodward, "A Foretaste of Eternity," *Newsweek* (8 January 1973), 50; Robert Fuller, "Rabbi Heschel's Heritage of Wonder and Awe," *Wall Street Journal*, 2 February 1973, 8; Martin Marty, "A Giant Has Fallen," *Christian Century* (17 January 1973), 87.

13. James F. Clarity, "Notes on People," *New York Times*, 2 February 1973, 37.

14. *America* (10 March 1973).

15. *Conservative Judaism* 28, 1 (fall 1973).

16. Heschel 1972, "Conversation with Doctor Abraham Joshua Heschel," repr. in Heschel 1996, *Moral Grandeur and Spiritual Audacity*, "Carl Stern's Interview with Dr. Heschel," 395–412 (quotation on p. 400).

17. Ibid., 411.

18. Ibid., 405.

19. Ibid., 412.

20. Interview with Morton Leifman, 14 July 2005; email from Jacob Teshima, 18 July 2005.

21. Pearl Twersky, conversation with the author, 27 March 2007.

References

For the most complete listing of Heschel's publications before 1940 see Edward K. Kaplan and Samuel H. Dresner, "Abraham Joshua Heschel: Prophetic Witness" (New Haven: Yale University Press, 1998), and the bibliography of Heschel's works and criticism in Abraham Joshua Heschel, "Between God and Man," ed. Fritz A. Rothschild (1959; rev. ed. New York: Macmillan, 1975).

Archives

American Friends Service Committee [AFSC] Archives, Philadelphia.

American Jewish Archives, Hebrew Union College, Cincinnati, Ohio.

American Jewish Committee Archives, New York [AJC/NY], Paris [AJC/Paris]. Some New York and Paris files are preserved at YIVO.

Anti-Defamation League [ADL] files, B'nai B'rith, New York.

Leo Baeck Institute Archives, New York.

Martin Buber Archive, Jewish National and University Library, Givat Ram, Jerusalem.

Burke Library, Union Theological Seminary, New York.

Henry Corbin, Personal Papers, Bibliothèque nationale, Paris.

Farrar, Straus and Giroux Archives, New York Public Library, New York.

Federal Bureau of Investigation [FBI] files: I received thirty-eight pages of copied material from the files of the New York office [NYO]; forty pages were withheld. A search of the central records system failed to reveal a main file for Abraham Joshua Heschel, but there were thirty-one documents (82 pp.) with relevant material [file description: AJH cross references]. I also consulted FBI files at the Margaret I. King Library, Special Collections, University of Kentucky, Lexington, and at the Swarthmore Peace Collection, Swarthmore, Pa.

Archives of the John Simon Guggenheim Memorial Foundation [Guggenheim Archives], New York.

Jacob I. Hartstein Administrative Files, Yeshiva University Archives, New York.

Abraham Joshua Heschel Archive, Jewish Theological Seminary of America, New York.

Jewish Publication Society [JPS] Archives, Balch Institute for Ethnic Studies, Philadelphia Jewish Archives Center.

Jewish Theological Seminary of America [JTS], General Files, Public Affairs Files, and Publicity Files, the Library of the Jewish Theological Seminary of America and the Ratner Center for the Study of Conservative Judaism, New York.

Lyndon Baines Johnson [LBJ] Library and Museum, Austin, Tex.

Thena Heshel Kendall, London, family papers.

John F. Kennedy [JFK] Presidential Library and Museum, Boston.

Margaret I. King Library, Special Collections, University of Kentucky, Lexington.

Melekh Ravitch Archive, Jewish National and University Library, Givat Ram, Jerusalem.

Swarthmore College Peace Collection, Swarthmore, Pa.

Marc H. Tanenbaum, personal papers, American Jewish Archives, Cincinnati, Ohio.

United States National Archives, Washington, D.C.

University of Iowa Archives, Iowa City.

University of Minnesota Archives, Minneapolis.

University of Notre Dame Archives, South Bend, Ind.

YIVO Archives, New York.

Zionist Archives and Library, New York.

Interviews and Correspondence

Unless otherwise indicated, interviews after 1989 were done by the author or under his direction. Transcripts and tapes are deposited at the Heschel Archive.

Abrams, Jerry, interview, n.d.

Apfel, Gary, interview, 22 June 1999.

Apfel, Willy, interview, 23 June 1999.

Appleton, George, letter to Samuel Dresner, 25 November 1982.

Atlas, Celia, interviews, 5, 7 January 1990.

Batkin, Stanley, and Selma Batkin, interview, 6 November 1991.

Bayne, E. A., letters to Samuel Dresner, 29 December 1982, 3 February, 5 September 1983.

Bennett, John C., interview, 18 January 1988.

Berkowitz, William, interview, 13 July 1990.

Berrigan, Daniel, interviews, 12 January 1988, 8 January 1991, January 1999.

Berrigan, Philip, interview, 23 May 1991.

Borowitz, Eugene, interviews, n.d.

Brewster, Charles E., letter to Samuel Dresner, 7 June 1989.

Brickner, Balfour, interview, 4 May 1988.

Brodie, Joseph, interview, 28 December 1987.

Brodsky, Ada, Jerusalem, interview, 1999.

Brooks, Sidney, interview, 15 August 1990.

Burns, Father Flavian, interview, 24 April 1998.

Chaiken, Rosalind, letter to author, 9 August 1990.

Cherbonnier, Edmond La B., interview, 11 April 1984.

Coffin, William Sloane, Jr., interview, 9 December 1987.

Cohen, Gerson D., interviews, 15, 17 January, 1 November 1990.

Cohen, Geula, Israel, interview, March 1998.

Cooperman, David, interview, before 1989.

Cywiak, Leib, interview, 14 November 1987.

Davies, W. D., interviews, 12, 18 June 1991.

Davis, Maurice, interview, 27 April 1988.

Davis, Moshe, interview, May 1988.

Derczansky, Alexandre, Paris, interview, 14 June 1992.

Dresner, Ruth, several conversations with the author, n.d.

Dresner, Samuel H., several conversations with the author, n.d. See also Roundtable.

Dreyfus, Stanley, interview, 10 August 1990.

Dring, Lincoln S., Jr., letter to Samuel Dresner, 5 December 1988.

Eden, Shulamit (Gootman), interview, 11 November 1987.

Eisenstein, Ira, interview, 18 January 1988.

Elberg, Yehuda, Montreal, interview, 22 June 1997.

Ettenberg, Sylvia, interviews, 5 January 1988, 16 March 1999.

Fackenheim, Emil, Jerusalem, interview, 11 May 1992.

Feder, Avraham, Jerusalem, interview, May–June 1999.

Feder, Baruch, interview, 16 March 1999.

Feingold, Jessica, interview, 3 March 1991.

Fernandez, Richard, interview, 2 June 1988.

Finkelstein, Louis, interview, 6 October 1987.

Fox, Marvin, interview, before 1989.

Fox, Seymour, interviews, 2 June 1988, 4 December 1998.

Fleischner, Eva, interview, 11 May 1983.

Friedman, Israel, interviews, 19 April 1988, 12 January 1990.

Gelbtuch, Joseph, interview, 21 July 1986.

Gendler, Everett, interview, 16 April 1990.

Gershfield, Edward, interview, 21 December 1987.

Gillman, Neil, interview, 20 April 1988. See also Roundtable.

Ginzberg, Eli, interview, 21 August 1996.

Giroux, Robert, interview, 8 March 1989.

Goodhill, Victor, letter to Samuel Dresner, 15 March 1982.

Goodhill, Victor, and Ruth Goodhill, interview, 28 April 1988.

Goodman, Hanna Grad, letters to Samuel Dresner, 28 February 1983, 15 January 1984.

Goodman, Naomi, interview, 15 August 1990.

Green, Arthur, interviews and conversations, n.d. See also Roundtable.

Greenberg, Simon, interviews, 28 December 1987, 7 January 1990.

Handy, Robert, interview, 25 August 1987.

Harlow, Jules, interviews, including 15 December 1987, 19 December 1989.

Harris, Larry D., letter to the author, 2 September 1990.

Hart, Patrick, interviews, n.d.

Heifetz, Ronald, interview, 19 November 1992.

Heschel, Abraham Joshua, conversations with Samuel H. Dresner, 1942–72, and the author, 1966–72.

Heschel, Abraham Joshua (b. 1974, son of R. Moses Mordecai), interview, 27 October 1998.

Heschel, Israel (son of the Kopitzhinitzer rebbe, Brooklyn, N.Y.), interview, 20 June 1990.

Heschel, Sylvia Straus, several conversations with the author, 1990–2005.

Heschel, Susannah, several conversations, emails to the author.

Hirsch, Richard D., interview, n.d.

Holtz, Avraham, interviews, 3 February, 19 April 1988.

Hoon, Paul, letter, 1 August 1987.

Horwitz, Rivka, interview, 8 October 1991.

Jacobson, Gershon, New York, interview, 21 April 1988.

Johnson, William, interview, 18 May 1989.

Kasimow, Harold, interview, 27 May 1988.

Kelman, Levi, Jerusalem, interview, 10 May 1992.

Kelman, Wolfe, New York, interviews, 5 May, 23 August 1987; 5 January, 22 April 1988; 21 October, 14 December 1989; 7, 10 January, 25 May 1990; letter to the author, 4 May 1982.

Kendall, Thena Heshel, London, several interviews, including 1 March, 28 June 1992; 27 June, 1994; letters to the author.

Kimelman, Reuven, interviews with the author, n.d. See also Roundtable.

Kogen, David C., interview, 9 December 1987.

Krauss, Pesach, Jerusalem, interview, 3 May 1988, June 1999.

Krents, Milton, interview, 20 May 1987.

Kronholtz, Jane, interview, 24 December 1989.

Leifman, Morton, interview, 17 July 2001, conversations with the author, n.d.

Lerner, Michael, interview, 2 January 1998.

Levine, Hillel, interview, 10 December 1987, follow-up letter, 28 October 1988.

Lieber, David L., interview, 28 May 1988.

Lukinsky, Joseph, interview, 30 December 1987.

Mandelbaum, Bernard, interview, 8 January 1990.

Marcus, Jacob Rader, interview, 9 November 1987.

Mardin, Serif, interview, 20 June 1991.

Margolis, Daniel, interview, March 2000.

Margolis, Patricia, interview, 6 February 2000.

Martin, Malachi, letter, 15 August 1990; interview 16 January 1991.

Melman, Seymour, interview, after 1989.

Meyer, Marshall, New York, interviews, 13 January 1988; 3, 10 January, 15 March 1991, 10 March 1992.

Milgrom, Louis, interview, 24 December 1987.

Miller, Israel, interview, 21 June 1999.

Mortara di Veroli, Elena, Rome, interviews with the author, after 1989.

Muffs, Yochanan, interviews, 12 May 1988, 8 January 1991, 13 November 1992.

Muffs, Yocheved (Judith Herschlag), interviews, 14 April, 12 May 1988, 6 September 1990.

Nadich, Judah, interview, January 1988.

Nasr, Sayyed Hossein, interviews, 27 June 1990, 15 November 1993.

Neuhaus, Richard John, interview, 9 September 1987.

Neusner, Jacob, interview, ca. 1990.

Novak, David, interview, 8 March 1988. See also Roundtable.

Paul, Shalom, interview, 18 February 1988.

Peli, Penina, interview, 13 March 1990.

Peli, Pinchas, interview, 12 February 1988.

Perlow, Abraham (son of Aaron Perlow, grandson of the Novominsker rebbe of Warsaw), interview, 15 April 1992.

Perlow, Bernard (son of Nahum Mordecai Perlow). Chicago, interviews, 17 February 1981, September 1983.

Perlow, Rabbi Jacob (son of Nahum Mordecai, Novominsker rebbe of Williamsburg, and grandson of the Novominsker rebbe of Warsaw). Borough Park, Brooklyn, N.Y., interviews, February 1979, 15 November 1987.

Plaut, Gunther, Montreal, letter to the author, 1988; telephone interview, after 1989.

Plotkin, Albert, interview, 6 December 1990.

Porter, Jack Nusan, interview, 12 March 1999.

Rabinowicz, Harry M., London, interview, ca. 1989.

Ran, Leyzer, interviews, 11 December 1987, 24 May 1989.

Reed, Barbara Straus Kessler, interviews, 5 June, 7 September 1998.

Riemer, Jack, interview, 10 February 1988.

Rogers, David, conversations, February 2005, April 2006.

Rosen, Hanna, interview, 22 May 1998.

Rosenak, Michael, interview, 7 June 1988.

Rosenberg, Yaakov, interview, 28 May 1987.

Roskies, David, interview, 17 December 1987.

Rothschild, Fritz A., New York, interviews, 10 May, 5, 20 October 1989; 7 January 1990; 3 February 1998; September 1992; letter to his sister, 31 December 1972. See also Roundtable.

Rottenberg, Ephraim, Los Angeles, interviews, 21 July 1986, 12 June 1990.

Roundtable: discussion organized by Jack Wertheimer and Samuel Dresner, August 1987. Participants: Samuel H. Dresner, Neil Gillman, Arthur Green, Reuven Kimelman, David Novak, Fritz A. Rothschild, Sol Tanenzapf. Transcript, 125 pp., Heschel Archive.

Rozenberg, Yakov, Jerusalem, interview, May-June 1992.

Rubenstein, Richard L., interview, 5 January 2001.

Ruskay, John, interview, ca. 1988.

Sachs, Miriam Blank, interview, 13 March 2000.

Sanders, James A., 30 April 1987, 18 August 1999.

Sarna, Nahum, interview, ca. 1987.

Schachter-Shalomi, Zalman, interview, 6 November 1997.

Schafler, Samuel, interview, 21 January 1991.

Scheindlin, Raymond, interview, 14 April 1988.

Schor, Resia, interview, 15 December 1989.

Schulman, Elias, letter, 15 March 1979.

Schulweis, Harold, interview, 28 May 1988.

Schulvass, Moses, interviews, December 1987, September 1988.

Scult, Mel, interview, 12 April 1988.

Seidman, Hillel, interviews, 8, 25 May 1990.

Sessions, William Lad, letter to Samuel Dresner, 3 January 1990.

Sherwin, Byron, interviews, July; 8, 9 November 1987; August; 9 November 1988; 27 December 1990.

Shinn, Roger, interview, 17 August 1987.

Shmeruk, Khone, interview, 29 March 1990.

Shmidman, Joshua, interview, 12 September 2002.

Siegel, Seymour, interview, July 1987.

Siegman, Henry, interview, 30 August 1990.

Silverman, David, interview, ca. 1987.

Stransky, Thomas, interview, 25 July 1988.

Straus, Jack and Barbara Straus, interview, 28 April 1988.

Straus, Roger W., Jr., interview, 8 March, May 1989.

Szoni, David, interview, ca. 1987.

Tanenbaum, Marc H., interviews, 13 December 1989, 10 January, 12 June 1990.

Tanghe, Warren, interview, 1991.

Tedeschi, Gianfranco, Rome, interview, ca. 1987.

Terrien, Sarah, interview, 2004.

Teshima, Jacob Yuroh, Japan, conversations, emails to the author, beginning 17 April 1988.

Ticktin, Max D., interview, 14 June 1988.

Todd, Samuel Rutherford, letter to Samuel Dresner, 29 November 1988.

Tucker, Gordon, interview, 7 June 1991.

Twersky, Isadore, interview, ca. 1987.

Twersky, Pearl, New York, interviews, 4 January, 6 December 1990, and conversations.

Twersky, Yitzhak Meir, several conversations with the author, 1989–95.

Van Dusen, Hugh, letter to the author, 28 February 1992.

Waskow, Arthur, interview, 27 September 1997.

Waxman, Mordecai, interview, 10 December 1987.

Wechsler, Harlan, interview, 27 January 1988.

Weiner, Gershon, Jerusalem, interview, May–June 1999.

Weiner, Nechama, Jerusalem, interview, May–June 1999.

Werblowsky, R. J. Zvi, letters to the author, 12 December 1991, 20 August 1994.

Wiesel, Elie, New York, interview, April 1988.

Wiseman, Joseph, and Pearl Lang, interview, 6 June 1991.

Wolf, Arnold Jacob, interviews, June, July, August 1990.

Wurtzberger, Walter S., interview, 25 February 1999.

Wyler, Marjorie, interview, 29 December 1987.

Young, Andrew, interview, 7 October 1988.

Zolla, Elémire, interview, 14 April 1986.

Selected Works of Abraham Joshua Heschel

1933. *Der Shem Hameforash: Mentsh* (in Yiddish, God's ineffable name: man). Warsaw: Farlag Indzl. Trans. Zalman Schachter-Shalomi. Winnipeg, Canada: distributed privately, 1973. Authorized trans.: Heschel 2004, *The Ineffable Name of God: Man*.

1934. "David Koigen." *Jüdische Rundschau* (27 February): 5.

1935. *Maimonides: Eine Biographie.* Berlin: Erich Reiss Verlag. English trans.: *Maimonides: A Biography.* Trans. Joachim Neugroschel. New York: Farrar, Straus and Giroux, 1982.

1936. *Die Prophetie.* Kraków: Polish Academy of Sciences and Letters. Mémoires de la Commission Orientaliste, 22.

1937. "Der Begriff des Seins in der Philosophie Gabirols." *Festschrift Jakob Freimann zum 70 Geburtstag,* 68–77. Berlin. English trans.: "The Concept of Being in Gabirol's Philosophy." Trans. David Wolf Silverman. *Conservative Judaism* 28, 1 (fall 1973): 89–95.

1937. *Don Jizhak Abravanel.* Berlin: Erich Reiss Verlag. Abridged English trans.: "Don Isaac Abravanel." Trans. William Wolf. *Intermountain Jewish News* (19 December 1986): 5, 8–12.

1938. "Der Begriff der Einheit in der Philosophie Gabirol" (The concept of unity in Gabirol's philosophy). *Monatsschrift für die Geschichte und Wissenschaft des Judentums* 82: 89–111.

1938. "David Koigens Sinndeutung der jüdischen Geschichte" (David Koigen's interpretation of Jewish history). *Jüdische Rundschau,* 7 October, 4–5.

1939. "Das Gebet als Äusserung und Einfühlung" (Prayer as expression and empathy). *Monatsschrift für die Geschichte und Wissenschaft des Judentums* 83: 562–67. Confiscated by the Nazis and not published until September 1941.

1939. "Das Wesen der Dinge nach der Lehre Gabirols" (The status of the thing in Gabirol's teaching). *Hebrew Union College Annual* 14: 359–85.

1940. "Antwort an Einstein." *Aufbau,* 20 September, 3. English trans.: "Answer to Einstein." Trans. Susannah Buschmeyer. *Conservative Judaism* 35, 4 (summer 2003): 39–41.

1941. "A Concise Dictionary of Hebrew Philosophical Terms." Mimeograph. (October). Cincinnati: Hebrew Union College.

1941. "Das Gebet" (Prayer). *Bulletin of Congregation Habonim at Central Synagogue* (September), 2–3.

1941. "'Al Mahut ha-tefillah" (in Hebrew, On the essence of prayer). *Bitzaron Hebrew Monthly* (February), 346–53. Prepared for the Mayer Balaban Festschrift (Warsaw, 1939), but confiscated by the Nazis before publication. See also Heschel 1960, "On the Essence of Prayer."

1941–42. "Zevi Diesendruck" (obituary). *American Jewish Year Book* 43: 391–98. Philadelphia: Jewish Publication Society of America.

1942. "An Analysis of Piety." *Review of Religion* 6, 3 (March): 293–307. Excerpts: "Piety." *Hamigdal* (September–October, 1946), 12–13; Hebrew trans.: "Yir'at shamayim." *Sefer Hashnah lihudey Amerikah,* 61–72. New York: Histadruth Ivrith, 1942. Repr. in Heschel 1996, *Moral Grandeur and Spiritual Audacity,* 305–17.

1942. Review of Salo Wittmayer Baron, ed., *Essays on Maimonides: An Octocentennial Volume. Review of Religion* 6, 3 (March): 315.

1942. Review of *Rashi Anniversary Volume. Review of Religion* 7, 1 (November): 105.

1942. Review of Chaim W. Reines, *Personality and Community in Judaism. Historia Judaica* 4: 115–16.

1943. "The Holy Dimension," *Journal of Religion* 23, 2 (April): 117–24. Repr. in Heschel 1996, *Moral Grandeur and Spiritual Audacity*, 318–27.

1943. "The Meaning of This War." *Hebrew Union College Bulletin* (March), 1–2, 18. Revision in *Liberal Judaism;* see Heschel 1944, "The Meaning of This War," and Heschel 1962, "Versuch einer Deutung."

1943. "The Quest for Certainty in Saadia's Philosophy." Part 1. *Jewish Quarterly Review* 33, 2–3: 263–313.

1944. "A Cabbalistic Commentary to the Prayerbook" (in Hebrew, text of Abulafia). In *Koveż Madda'i le-Zekher Moshe Schorr* (Studies in memory of Moses Schorr, 1874–1941), 113–26. Ed. Louis Ginzberg and Abraham Weiss. New York: Professor Moses Schorr Memorial Committee.

1944. "Faith." Part 1: *The Reconstructionist* 10, 13 (3 November): 10–14; Part 2: *The Reconstructionist* 10, 14 (17 November): 12–16. Repr. in Heschel 1996, *Moral Grandeur and Spiritual Audacity*, 328–39.

1944. "The Meaning of This War," *Liberal Judaism* (February), 18–21. Repr. in Heschel 1954, *Man's Quest for God*, "The Meaning of This Hour,"147–51, and Heschel 1996, *Moral Grandeur and Spiritual Audacity*, 209–12.

1944. *The Quest for Certainty in Saadia's Philosophy.* Pamphlet. New York: Philip Feldheim, 67 pp.

1944. "The Quest for Certainty in Saadia's Philosophy: Reason and Revelation." *Jewish Quarterly Review* 34, 4: 391–408.

1944. Review of Gershom Scholem, *Major Trends in Jewish Mysticism. Journal of Religion* 24: 140–41.

1945. "Did Maimonides Strive for Prophetic Inspiration?" (in Hebrew). In *Louis Ginzberg Jubilee Volume*, 159–88. New York: American Academy for Jewish Research. English trans.: Heschel 1996, *Prophetic Inspiration After the Prophets*, 69–139.

1945. "The Eastern European Era in Jewish History" (in Yiddish). *YIVO Bleter* 25, 2 (March–April): 163–83. Hebrew trans.: "Ha-Yehudi shel Mizrah Eropa." Trans. Yehudah Yaari. *Luah ha-Aretz 1947–1948*, 98–124. Tel Aviv: Haim, 1947.

1945. "Prayer." *Review of Religion* 9, 2 (January): 153–68. Repr. in Heschel 1996, *Moral Grandeur and Spiritual Audacity*, 340–53.

1946. "The Eastern European Era in Jewish History." Probably trans. from the Yiddish by Shlomo Noble. *YIVO Annual of Jewish Social Science* 1: 86–106. New York: Yiddish Scientific Institute–YIVO. Repr. in part as introductory essay to Roman Vishniac, *Polish Jews: A Pictorial History*, 7–17. New York: Schocken, 1947. Abridged: *Jewish Spectator* (May 1947), 16–20.

1946. *Der mizrakh-eyropeisher yid.* New York: Schocken, 45 pp.

1947. "To Be a Jew: What Is It?" (in Yiddish). *Yidisher Kemfer*, 12 September, 25–28. English trans.: *Zionist Quarterly* 1, 1 (summer 1951).

1948. "After Majdanek: On the Poetry of Aaron Zeitlin" (in Yiddish). *Yidisher Kemfer*, 1 October, 28–30. English trans.: Faierstein 1999, 264–71.

1948. "The Two Great Traditions." *Commentary* (May), 416–22.

1949. "The Mystical Element in Judaism." In Finkelstein 1949, vol. 1, pp. 602–23. Repr. in Heschel 1996, *Moral Grandeur and Spiritual Audacity*, 164–84.

1949. *Pikuach Neshama* (in Hebrew, To save a soul). New York: Baronial Press. English trans.: Heschel 1996, *Moral Grandeur and Spiritual Audacity*, 54–67. Trans. Aryeh Cohen and Samuel Dresner. Ed. Susannah Heschel.

1949. "Reb Pinkhes Koritser" (in Yiddish). *Yivo Bleter* 33: 9–48. Hebrew trans.: "Letoldot R. Pinhas mi-Koretz," *'Alei 'Ayin: The Salman Schocken Jubilee Volume*, 213–44. Jerusalem, 1951–52. English trans.: Heschel 1985, *The Circle of the Baal Shem Tov*, 1–43.

1950. *The Earth Is the Lord's: The Inner Life of the Jew in East Europe*. New York: Henry Schuman.

1950. "'Al ruah ha-kodesh bimey ha-beynayim" (in Hebrew, Prophetic inspiration in the Middle Ages). In *Alexander Marx Jubilee Volume*, 175–208. New York: Jewish Theological Seminary of America. English trans.: Heschel 1996, *Prophetic Inspiration After the Prophets*, 1–67.

1950–1951. "Rabbi Gershon of Kuty" (in Hebrew). *Hebrew Union College Annual* 23, 2: 17–71. English trans.: Heschel 1985, *The Circle of the Baal Shem Tov*, 44–112.

1951. *Man Is Not Alone: A Philosophy of Religion*. New York: Farrar, Straus and Young; Philadelphia: Jewish Publication Society of America.

1951. *The Sabbath: Its Meaning for Modern Man*. New York: Farrar, Straus and Young.

1951. "To Be a Jew: What Is It?" *Zionist Quarterly* 1, 1 (summer): 78–84. Repr. in Heschel 1996, *Moral Grandeur and Spiritual Audacity*, 3–11.

1952. "Architecture of Time." *Judaism* 1, 1 (January): 44–51.

1952. "Rabbi Pineas of Koretz and the Maggid of Meseritch" (in Hebrew). In *Hadoar: Thirtieth Anniversary Jubilee Volume*, 279–85. New York: Histadruth Ivrith of America.

1952. "Space, Time, and Reality: The Centrality of Time in the Biblical World View." *Judaism* 1, 3 (July): 262–69.

1952. "Umbakante dokumentn tsu der geshikhte fun khasidus" (in Yiddish, Unknown documents in the history of Hasidism). *Yivo Bleter* 36: 113–35.

1953. "The Divine Pathos: The Basic Category of Prophetic Theology." Trans. William Wolf. *Judaism* 2, 1 (January): 61–67. Excerpt from Heschel 1936, *Die Prophetie*, pt. 3, chap. 1.

1953. "The Moment at Sinai." *American Zionist* (5 February), 18–20. Repr. in Heschel 1996, *Moral Grandeur and Spiritual Audacity*, 12–17.

1953. "The Spirit of Jewish Education." *Jewish Education* (fall), 9–20. Hebrew trans.:

In *Hadoar*, 23 December 1955, 151–53, and 30 December 1955, 166–68. Trans. M. M. [Moshe Maisels]. Repr. in Heschel 1966, *The Insecurity of Freedom*, "Jewish Education," 223–41.

1953. "The Spirit of Jewish Prayer." *Proceedings* 1953, 151–77. Hebrew trans.: In *Megillot* (March 1954), 3–24. Trans. "Alef Lamed" (A. L.). Repr. in Heschel 1996, *Moral Grandeur and Spiritual Audacity,* 100–126.

1953. "Toward an Understanding of Halacha." *Yearbook of the Central Conference of American Rabbis* 63: 386–409. Repr. in part in *Jewish Frontier* (April 1954), 22–28. Repr. in Heschel 1996, *Moral Grandeur and Spiritual Audacity,* 127–45.

1954. *Man's Quest for God: Studies in Prayer and Symbolism.* New York: Scribner's.

1954. "A Preface to the Understanding of Revelation." In *Essays Presented to Leo Baeck on the Occasion of His Eightieth Birthday,* 28–35. London: East and West Library. Repr. in Heschel 1996, *Moral Grandeur and Spiritual Audacity,* 185–90.

1954. "Symbolism and Jewish Faith." In Johnson 1955, 53–79. Also in Heschel 1954, *Man's Quest for God,* chap. 5, "Symbolism," 117–44. Repr. in Heschel 1996, *Moral Grandeur and Spiritual Audacity,* "Symbolism and Jewish Faith," 80–100.

1955. *God in Search of Man: A Philosophy of Judaism.* New York: Farrar, Straus and Cudahy; Philadelphia: Jewish Publication Society of America.

1955. "In tog fun has" (in Yiddish, Day of hate). In *Nusah Vilne.* Commemorative brochure on the twenty-fifth anniversary of Yung Vilne. (March), 45–46. Orig. pub. in Warsaw, May 1933.

1955. "The Last Years of Maimonides." *National Jewish Monthly* (June), 7, 27–28. Trans. of Heschel 1935, *Maimonides: Eine Biographie,* chap. 25.

1956. "The Biblical View of Reality." In Harold A. Basilius, ed., *Contemporary Problems in Religion,* 57–76. Detroit: Wayne State University Press. Repr. in Heschel 1996, *Moral Grandeur and Spiritual Audacity,* 354–65.

1956. "A Hebrew Evaluation of Reinhold Niebuhr." In Charles Kegley and Robert Bretall, eds., *Reinhold Niebuhr: His Religious, Social, and Political Thought,* 391–410. The Library of Living Theology 2. New York: Macmillan. Repr. in Heschel 1966, *The Insecurity of Freedom,* "Confusion of God and Evil," 127–49.

1956. "Teaching Religion to American Jews." *Adult Jewish Education* (fall), 3–6. Repr. in Heschel 1996, *Moral Grandeur and Spiritual Audacity,* 148–53.

1957. "The Hebrew Prophet in Relation to God and Man" (in Hebrew). In Zevi Adar, ed., *The Old Testament Conception of God, Man and the World,* 215–24. Tel Aviv: Massadah.

1957. "The Nation and the Individual" (in Hebrew). *Molad* 15, 107–8 (July–August): 237–44. Abridged: "The Problem of the Individual." *Hadoar,* 4 April 1958, 396–99. Expanded, as "The Problem of the Individual," *Proceedings of the Ideological Conference in Jerusalem (Sefer ha-kinnus ha-iyyuni ha-'olami), Hazut,* Jerusalem: *Ha-sifriyah ha-tziyonit* 4 (1958): 312–19. English trans.: Heschel 1961, "The Individual Jew and His Obligations."

1957. "Rabbi Yitzhak of Drohobitsh" (in Hebrew). *Hadoar Jubilee Volume* 37, 28 (31 May): 86–94. English trans.: Heschel 1985, *The Circle of the Baal Shem Tov*, 152–81.

1957. "Sacred Images of Man." *Christian Century* (11 December), 1473–75. Repr. in *Religious Education* (March–April 1958), 97–102. Repr. in Heschel 1966, *The Insecurity of Freedom*, 150–67.

1957. "The Task of the Hazzan." *Conservative Judaism* 12, 2 (winter 1958): 1–8. Repr. in Heschel 1966, *The Insecurity of Freedom*, 242–53.

1958. "The Religious Message." In John Cogley ed., *Religion in America: Original Essays on Religion in a Free Society*, 244–71. New York: Meridian. Repr. in Heschel 1966, *The Insecurity of Freedom*, "Religion in a Free Society," 3–23.

1958. "Yisrael: Am, Eretz, Medinah: Ideological Evaluation of Israel and the Diaspora." *Proceedings* 1958, 118–36. Repr. in Heschel 1966, *The Insecurity of Freedom*, "Israel and the Diaspora," 212–22.

1959. "Answer to Ben Gurion" (in Hebrew). *Hadoar*, 9 October, 741. Repr. in Solomon S. Bernards, ed., *Who Is a Jew: A Reader*, "We Cannot Force People to Believe," 38–39. New York; Anti-Defamation League of B'nai B'rith. Repr. in Heschel 1996, *Moral Grandeur and Spiritual Audacity*, 44–46.

1959. *Between God and Man*. Ed. Fritz A. Rothschild. New York: Free Press. Rev. bib., 1975.

1959. "Prayer and Theological Discipline." *Union Seminary Quarterly Review* (May): 3–8.

1959. "Rabbi Mendel mi-Kotzk" (in Hebrew). *Hadoar*, 5 June, 519–21.

1959. "Who Is Man?" *Jewish Chronicle* (London), 9 October, 23–25. Repr. in *Proceedings of the 53rd Annual Meeting of the American Jewish Committee*, "The Moral Challenge to America," 62–77. New York: American Jewish Committee, 1960.

1960. "Call of the Hour." *Law and Order: The Independent Magazine for the Police Profession* (May), 14–15, 18–22, 25. Repr. in Heschel 1966, *The Insecurity of Freedom*, "Children and Youth," 39–51.

1960. "The Concept of Man in Jewish Thought." In S. Radhakrishnan and P. T. Raju, eds., *The Concept of Man*, 108–57. London: Allen and Unwin.

1960. "Depth Theology." *CrossCurrents* (fall), 317–25. Repr. in Heschel 1966, *The Insecurity of Freedom*, 115–26.

1960. "On the Essence of Prayer" (in Hebrew, 'Al Mahut ha-tefillah). In Joseph Heinemann, ed., *Ha-Tefillah*, 3–15. Jerusalem: Amanah. Repr. in Jakob Petuchowski and Ezra Spicehandler, eds., *Essays in Judaism* (Perakim ba-yahadut), 37–44. Cincinnati: Hebrew Union College Press; Jerusalem: M. Newman. See Heschel 1941, "'Al Mahut ha-tefillah."

1960. "Should the United Synagogue of America Join the World Zionist Organization? No." *Proceedings of the 1959 Biennial Convention of the United Synagogue of America*, 76–85. New York: United Synagogue of America. Repr. as "The Great

Debate." *The Torch* (winter). Repr. in Milton Berger, Joel Geffen, and M. David Hoffman, eds., *Roads to Jewish Survival*, "Should the United Synagogue of America Join the World Zionist Organization? No, Says Rabbi Abraham Joshua Heschel," 330–42. New York: Bloch, 1967.

1961. "Hillel Bavli" (in Hebrew). *Hadoar*, 8 December, 81. English trans.: Heschel 1962–63, "Hillel Bavli: In Memoriam."

1961. "Ilya Schor." *Conservative Judaism* 16, 1 (fall): 20–21.

1961. "The Individual Jew and His Obligations." Trans. Simcha Kling and Samuel H. Dresner. *Conservative Judaism* 15, 3 (spring): 10–26. Repr. in Heschel 1966, *The Insecurity of Freedom*, 187–211. See Heschel 1957, "The Nation and the Individual."

1961. "To Grow in Wisdom." In *New York American Examiner* (February). Repr. *Congressional Record: Proceedings and Debates of the 87th Congress*, First Session, 21 March, Appendix A, 1973–75, and 14 June, Appendix A, 4364–67. Extracts in the Jewish Theological Seminary of America's *The Beacon* (June 1961), 5, 19–20. Distributed as a pamphlet by Synagogue Council of America (New York, 1961) and the Utah Religious Committee (Salt Lake City, 1963). Repr. with significant revisions in Heschel 1966, *The Insecurity of Freedom*, 70–84.

1962. "Le Judaïsme concerne-t-il l'homme américain?" *L'Arche* (Paris) (August–September), 64–67.

1962. "Prophetic Inspiration." *Judaism* 11, 1 (winter): 3–13. Excerpts from Heschel 1962, *The Prophets*, chap. 25.

1962. *The Prophets*. New York: Harper and Row; Philadelphia: Jewish Publication Society of America.

1962. "The Religion of Sympathy." In Menahem Kasher, Norman Lamm, and Leonard Rosenfeld, eds., *The Leo Jung Jubilee Volume: Essays in His Honor on the Occasion of his Seventieth Birthday*, 105–13. New York: N.p. Excerpt from Heschel 1962, *The Prophets*, chap. 18.

1962. "The Values of Jewish Education." In *Proceedings* 1962, 83–100. Hebrew trans.: "'Arakhim ba-hinukh hayehudi," *Gesher* 8, 1–2 (30–32): 54–60. For another version see Heschel 1963, "Idols in the Temples."

1962. "Versuch einer Deutung" (in German, Search for a meaning). In *Begegnung mit dem Judentum: Ein Gedenkbuch* (Encounter with Jewry: A Memorial Book, Voices of [the Society of] Friends in Germany). Ed. Margarethe Lachmund, vol. 2, pp. 11–13. Bad Pyrmont. First publication of an address delivered to a group of Quakers at Frankfurt-am-Main in February 1938.

1962, 1965, 1990. *Torah min ha-shamayim be-aspaklaryah shel ha-dorot* (in Hebrew; English title in the volume: Theology of Ancient Judaism). 3 vols. Vol. 1: London: Soncino, 1962. Vol. 2: London: Soncino, 1965. Vol. 3: Jerusalem: Jewish Theological Studies, 1990. English trans.: Heschel 2005, *Heavenly Torah As Refracted Through the Generations*.

1962–63. "Hillel Bavli: In Memoriam." *Conservative Judaism* 17, 1–2 (fall–winter): 70–71.

1963. "Idols in the Temples." *Religious Education* (March–April): 127–37. Repr. in Heschel 1966, *The Insecurity of Freedom*, 52–69.

1963. "The Israelite Prophet in His Relation to God and the People" (in Yiddish). *Davke (Precisamente)* 50 (Buenos Aires) (July–December), 203–16. Excerpts from Heschel 1962, *The Prophets*.

1963. "A Jewish Response." *Catholic News* (4 April), 4. Address given on 1 April 1963 to Cardinal Bea. Repr. in Heschel 1966, *The Insecurity of Freedom*, "The Ecumenical Movement," 179–83.

1963. "A Momentous Emergency—The Russian Jewry." *Day-Morning Journal*, 12, 13 September, 12 October. Repr. as broadside by the Synagogue Council of America. Repr. in Heschel 1966, *The Insecurity of Freedom*, 262–73.

1963. "Prophétie et poésie." *Evidences* (Paris) (January–February), 45–50. French trans. of excerpts from Heschel 1962, *The Prophets*, chap. 22.

1963. "Protestant Renewal: A Jewish View." *Christian Century* (4 December), 1501–4. Repr. in Heschel 1966, *The Insecurity of Freedom*, 168–78.

1963. "The Religious Basis of Equality of Opportunity: The Segregation of God." In Ahmann 1963, 55–71. Abridged: *United Synagogue Review* (spring 1963). Repr. in Heschel 1966, *The Insecurity of Freedom*, "Religion and Race," 85–100.

1963. "Two Methods in Jewish Religious Thought" (in Hebrew). *Hadoar*, 8 February, 244–46, and 15 February 1963, 262–63. Excerpts from the introduction of Heschel 1962, 1965, 1990 *Torah min ha-shamayim be-aspaklaryah shel ha-dorot*, vol. 1.

1964. " '*Iyunim ba-midrash*" (in Hebrew, Studies in midrashic literature). In *The Abraham Weiss Jubilee Volume*, 349–60 (Hebrew section). Ed. Samuel Belkin. New York: N.p.

1964. "The Meaning of the Spirit." In *The Clarement Church Lectures* (2 February). Claremont, Calif.: Claremont Community Church of Seventh-day Adventists, 21 pp.

1964. "Modern Man" and "The Eastern European Jew" (in Hebrew). Trans. from English by Ovadiah Margaliot in *Sheviley ha-emunah ba-dor ha-aharon*, 11–15, 328–46. Tel Aviv: Mahbarot Lesifrut.

1964. "The Moral Dilemma of the Space Age." In Lilian Levy, ed., *Space: Its Impact on Man and Society*, 176–79. New York: Norton. Repr. in Heschel 1996, *Moral Grandeur and Spiritual Audacity*, 216–18.

1964. "The Patient as a Person." Manuscripts of Addresses Presented to the American Medical Association's 113th Convention, San Francisco, California, 21 June, 23–41. Chicago: Department of Medicine and Religion, American Medical Association. Repr. *Conservative Judaism* 19, 1 (fall 1964): 1–10. Abridged: "The Sisyphus Complex." *Ramparts* (October 1964), 45–49. Repr. in Heschel 1966, *The Insecurity of Freedom*, "The Patient as a Person," 24–38.

1964. "The Plight of Russian Jews." *United Synagogue Review* (winter), 14–15, 26–27. Repr. in Heschel 1996, *Moral Grandeur and Spiritual Audacity*, 213–15.

1964. "A Visit with Rabbi Heschel." Interview with Arthur Herzog. *Think* (January–February), 16–19. Abridged: *Jewish Digest* (December 1968), 15–19.

1964. "The White Man on Trial." *Proceedings of the Metropolitan New York Conference on Religion and Race*, 100–110. New York: New York City Youth Board. Repr. in Heschel 1966, *The Insecurity of Freedom*, 101–11.

1965. "Existence and Celebration." Pamphlet. New York: Council of Jewish Federations and Welfare Funds, 24 pp. Repr. in Heschel 1996, *Moral Grandeur and Spiritual Audacity*, 18–31.

1965. "Rabbi Nahman of Kossov, Companion of the Baal Shem" (in Hebrew). In Saul Lieberman et al., eds., *The Harry A. Wolfson Jubilee Volume*, 113–41. New York: American Academy for Jewish Research. English trans.: Heschel 1985, *The Circle of the Baal Shem Tov*, 113–51.

1965. "Who Is Man?" *Stanford Today* (July), 12–16. Excerpts from Heschel 1965, *Who Is Man?*

1965. *Who Is Man?* Stanford: Stanford University Press. Revision of the Fred West Lectures delivered at Stanford University, 1963.

1965. "Yom Kippur." In *Mas'at Rav*, a professional supplement to *Conservative Judaism* (August): 13–14. Repr. in Heschel 1996, *Moral Grandeur and Spiritual Audacity*, 146–47.

1966. "Choose Life!" *Jubilee* (January): 37–39. Repr. as "Why Not Choose Life?" *Dominion* (October 1966), 9–16. Repr. in Heschel 1996, *Moral Grandeur and Spiritual Audacity*, "Choose Life!" 251–56.

1966. *The Insecurity of Freedom: Essays on Human Existence.* New York: Farrar, Straus and Giroux.

1966. "The Moral Outrage of Vietnam." *Fellowship* (September), 24–26. Repr. in Robert McAfee Brown, Abraham J. Heschel, Michael Novak, *Vietnam: Crisis of Conscience*, 48–61. New York: Association Press, Behrman House, Herder and Herder, 1967.

1966. "Moses Maimonides." *Jubilee* (January), 36–41. Excerpt from Heschel 1966, *The Insecurity of Freedom*, chap. 20.

1966. "No Religion Is an Island." *Union Seminary Quarterly Review* 21, 2, pt. 1 (January): 117–34. Inaugural lecture as Harry Emerson Fosdick Visiting Professor at Union Theology Seminary, New York, November 1965. Repr. in *The Graduate Journal: The University of Texas* 7 (1966), supplement: 65–82. Repr. in Kasimow and Sherwin 1991, 3–22. Repr. in Heschel 1996, *Moral Grandeur and Spiritual Audacity*, 235–50. For another version see Heschel 1967, "From Mission to Dialogue."

1967. "Abraham Joshua Heschel." Interview with Patrick Granfield, OSB. In Patrick Granfield, ed., *Theologians at Work*. New York: Macmillan, 69–85. Repr. in Heschel

1996, *Moral Grandeur and Spiritual Audacity,* "Interview at Notre Dame," 381–93.

[1967]. *Dr. Martin Luther King, Jr., Dr. John Bennett, Dr. Henry Steele Commager, Rabbi Abraham Heschel Speak on the War in Vietnam* ([New York:] Clergy and Laymen Concerned About Vietnam). Pamphlet of addresses given at Riverside Church on the Vietnam War, 4 April.

1967. "From Mission to Dialogue." *Conservative Judaism* 21, 3 (spring): 1–11.

1967. *"Ginzey ha-yesha"* (in Hebrew, The hidden sources of redemption). *Hadoar,* 11 August, 643–45.

1967. "Man—Who Is He?" In Clarence Walton, ed., *Today's Changing Society: A Challenge to Individual Identity,* 50–56. New York: Institute of Life Insurance.

1967. "Our Heritage from Eastern Europe." In Milton Berger, Joel Geffen, and M. David Hoffman, eds., *Roads to Jewish Survival,* 390–95. New York: Bloch. Excerpt from Heschel 1950 *The Earth Is the Lord's,* chap. 15, "The Untold Story."

1967. "What Ecumenism Is." *Jewish Heritage* (spring), 1–4. Repr. in Lily Edelman, ed., *Face to Face: A Primer in Dialogue.* Washington, D.C.: B'nai B'rith Adult Jewish Education. Repr. in Heschel 1996, *Moral Grandeur and Spiritual Audacity,* 286–89.

1967. "What We Might Do Together." *Religious Education* (March–April), 133–40. Repr. in Heschel 1996, *Moral Grandeur and Spiritual Audacity,* 290–300.

1968. "Conversation with Martin Luther King." *Conservative Judaism* 22, 3 (spring): 1–19.

1968. Foreword to Ronald I. Rubin, ed., *The Unredeemed: Antisemitism in the Soviet Union,* 13–16. Chicago: Quadrangle.

1968. "The Jewish Notion of God and Christian Renewal." In L. K. Shook, CSB, ed., *Renewal of Religious Thought: Proceedings of the Congress on the Theology of the Church Centenary of Canada, 1867–1967,* 105–29. Montreal: Palm. Repr. in Heschel 1996, *Moral Grandeur and Spiritual Audacity,* "The God of Israel and Christian Renewal," 268–85.

1968. "Rabbi Mendel mi-Kotzk" (in Hebrew). *Shedemot* (Tel Aviv) 29 (spring): 87–94.

1968. "The Theological Dimensions of Medinat Yisrael." *Proceedings* 1968, 91–103; discussion, 104–109.

1968. "The Theology of Pathos." In Edward Quinn and Paul Dolan, eds., *The Sense of the Sixties,* 297–310. New York: Free Press. Excerpt from Heschel 1962, *The Prophets.*

1969. "Christian-Jewish Dialogue and the Meaning of the State of Israel." *CrossCurrents* (fall), 409–25. Repr. in John W. Padberg, ed., *Theology and the City of Man: A Sesquicentennial Conference,* 409–25. West Nyack, N.Y.: CrossCurrents, 1970.

1969. Foreword to James Parkes, *Prelude to Dialogue: Jewish-Christian Relationships,* vii. London: Vallentine Mitchell.

1969. *Israel: An Echo of Eternity.* New York: Farrar, Straus and Giroux.

1969. "Kotzk" (in Hebrew). *Panim el Panim* (Jerusalem) (7 February), 10–11, 18.

1969. "Reflections on Death." In *Proceedings of the First International Congress on Genesis of Sudden Death and Reanimation. Clinical and Moral Problems Connected* (Genesi della morte improvisa e rianimazione), Florence, Italy, 10–14 January, 533–42. Ed. Vincenzo Lapiccirella. Florence: Marchi and Bertolli, 1970. Abridged: *Conservative Judaism* 28, 1 (fall 1973): 3–9; Repr. in Jack Riemer, ed., *Jewish Reflections on Death*, "Death as Homecoming," 58–73. New York: Schocken, 1974. Repr. in Heschel 1996, *Moral Grandeur and Spiritual Audacity,* "Death as Homecoming," 366–78.

1969. "The Restoration of Israel." *Catholic Digest* (May): 21–23. Excerpt from Heschel 1969, *Israel: An Echo of Eternity.*

1969. "Teaching Jewish Theology in the Solomon Schechter Day School." Transcribed and ed. Pesach Schindler. *Synagogue School* (fall), 1-33. Repr. in Heschel 1996, *Moral Grandeur and Spiritual Audacity,* "Jewish Theology," 154–63, without the discussion.

1969–1970. "Der Kotsker rebbe" (in Yiddish). *Die goldene Keyt: Periodical for Literature and Social Problems* (Tel Aviv) 65 (1969): 138–56, and 71 (1970): 60–70.

1970. "A brokhe dem nosi" (in Yiddish, Greetings to President Zalman Shazar on his eightieth birthday). *Die goldene Keyt: Periodical for Literature and Social Problems* (Tel Aviv) 68: 26.

1970. Foreword to Moshe Decter, ed., *A Hero for Our Time: The Trial and Fate of Boris Kochubiyevsky,* 3. New York: Academic Committee on Soviet Jewry, Conference on the Status of Soviet Jews.

1970. "God, Torah, and Israel." Trans. from Hebrew manuscript of Heschel 1962, 1965, 1990, *Torah min ha-shamayim be-aspaklaryah shel ha-dorot,* vol. 3, by Byron L. Sherwin. In Edward Long and Robert Handy, eds., *Theology and Church in Times of Change: Essays in Honor of John Coleman Bennett,* 71–90. Philadelphia: Westminster. Repr. in Heschel 1996, *Moral Grandeur and Spiritual Audacity,* 191–208.

1970. "On Prayer." *Conservative Judaism* 25, 1 (fall): 1–12. Excerpts: National Council of Churches, New York, publication *Tempo* (15 October 1969), 8, 11. Repr. in Jakob Petuchowski, ed., *Understanding Jewish Prayer,* 69–83. New York: KTAV, 1972. Repr. in Heschel 1996, *Moral Grandeur and Spiritual Audacity,* 257–67.

1970. "The Sabbath: Its Meaning for Modern Man" (in Hebrew). *Petahim* (Jerusalem) 15 (November): 307. Excerpts from Heschel 1951, *The Sabbath.*

1970. "What Scripture Really Says About Jewish Restoration in Israel." *Jewish Digest* 15, 5 (February): 19–21. Extract from Heschel 1969, *Israel: An Echo of Eternity.*

1971. "Il chassidismo e Kierkegaard" (in Italian). *Conoscenza religiosa* (Florence) 4: 337–53. Trans. of excerpt of manuscript of Heschel 1973, *A Passion for Truth.*

1971. "A Conversation with Rabbi Abraham J. Heschel." Interview with Frank Reynolds. ABC, broadcast 21 November.

1971. "In Search of Exaltation." *Jewish Heritage* (fall), 29, 30, 35. Repr. in Heschel 1996, *Moral Grandeur and Spiritual Audacity,* 227–29.

1971. "Kotzk, Menahem Mendel of." *Encyclopaedia Judaica,* vol. 10, coll. 1222–24. Jerusalem: Keter.

1971. "Man's Search for Faith." *United Synagogue Review* (spring), 14, 15, 24.

1971. "Nasa'ta ve-natata be-'emunah?" (in Hebrew, Have you acted faithfully?). *Hadoar,* 28 May, 496–97. Trans. Aryeh Cohen. Personal papers of the author. Excerpt of manuscript of Heschel 1962, 1965, 1990, *Torah min ha-shamayim be-aspaklaryah shel ha-dorot,* vol. 3, but not published in that volume.

1971. *The Eternal Light:* "Two Conversations with Abraham Joshua Heschel." Radio interview with Harold Flender. Part 1 broadcast 9 May; part 2 broadcast 16 May. Transcript in Heschel Archive. Excerpted in *Women's American ORT Reporter* (January–February 1971), 7, 8, 11.

1971. "A Prayer for Peace." *Jewish Heritage* (spring–summer), 7–11. Excerpt of Heschel 1966, "The Moral Outrage of Vietnam." Repr. in Heschel 1996, *Moral Grandeur and Spiritual Audacity,* 230–34.

1971. "Reinhold Niebuhr: A Last Farewell." *Conservative Judaism* 24, 4 (summer): 62–63. Repr. in Heschel 1996, *Moral Grandeur and Spiritual Audacity,* "Reinhold Niebuhr," 301–2.

1971. "Required: A Moral Ombudsman." *United Synagogue Review* (fall), 4, 5, 28, 30. Repr. in Heschel 1996, *Moral Grandeur and Spiritual Audacity,* 219–23.

1972. "Celebration and Exaltation." *Jewish Heritage* (summer), 5–10.

1972. "A Conversation with Doctor Abraham Joshua Heschel." Interview with Carl Stern. *The Eternal Light,* NBC, broadcast 4 February 1973. Repr. in Heschel 1996, *Moral Grandeur and Spiritual Audacity,* 395–412.

1972. "Hasidism as a New Approach to Torah." *Jewish Heritage* (fall–winter), 4–21. Repr. in Heschel 1996, *Moral Grandeur and Spiritual Audacity,* 33–39.

1972. "The Heritage of Martin Luther King, Jr." Interview with Frank Reynolds, Jesse Jackson, and George Clements. ABC, broadcast 9 January.

1972. " 'Perakim le-'inyan 'torah mi-sinay" (in Hebrew, Did Moses incorporate into the Pentateuch pre-Sinaitic laws?"). In Menahem Zohori, Arie Tartakover, and Haim Ormian, eds., *Hagut Ivrit Ba-Amerika* (Studies on Jewish themes by contemporary American scholars). 3 vols. Vol. 1, pp. 308–17. Tel Aviv: Yavneh-Brit Ivrit Olamit. Excerpts of manuscript of Heschel 1962, 1965, 1990, *Torah min ha-shamayim be-aspaklaryah shel ha-dorot,* vol. 3.

1972. "Søren Kierkegaard and the Rabbi of Kotzk." Mount Savior Monastery, Pine City, New York, publication, *Monastic Studies* 8 (spring): 147–51. Excerpts from manuscript of Heschel 1973, *A Passion for Truth.*

1972. "The Theological, Biblical, and Ethical Considerations of Amnesty." Unpublished manuscript, 6 pp., Heschel Archive.

1972. "A Time for Renewal" (in Hebrew). Address given to the 28th World Zionist Congress, Jerusalem, 18–28 January, on 19 January. English trans.: *Midstream* 18, 5 (May): 46–51. Repr. in Heschel 1996, *Moral Grandeur and Spiritual Audacity*, 47–53.

1973. "Heschel's Last Words." *Jerusalem Post Weekly*, 1 January, 14. Excerpt from Heschel 1973, *A Passion for Truth*, intro.

1973. *Kotsk: In gerangl far emesdikayt* (in Yiddish, The struggle for integrity). 2 vols. Tel Aviv: Hamenora.

1973. *A Passion for Truth.* New York: Farrar, Straus and Giroux.

1973. "The Reason for My Involvement in the Peace Movement." *Journal of Social Philosophy* 4 (January): 7–8. Repr. in Heschel 1996, *Moral Grandeur and Spiritual Audacity*, 224–26.

1974. Preface to Layzer Ran, ed., *Jerusalem of Lithuania* (in Yiddish, English, and Russian). New York: Vilner albom komitet.

1975. *The Wisdom of Heschel.* Ed. Ruth Marcus Goodhill. New York: Farrar, Straus and Giroux.

1985. *The Circle of the Baal Shem Tov: Studies in Hasidism.* Ed. Samuel H. Dresner. Chicago: University of Chicago Press.

1987. *I Asked for Wonder: A Spiritual Anthology.* Ed. Samuel H. Dresner. New York: Crossroad.

1990. *To Grow in Wisdom: An Anthology of Abraham Joshua Heschel.* Ed. Jacob Neusner and Noam Neusner. Lanham, Md.: Madison.

1996. *Moral Grandeur and Spiritual Audacity: Essays by Abraham Joshua Heschel.* Ed. Susannah Heschel. New York: Farrar, Straus and Giroux.

1996. *Prophetic Inspiration After the Prophets: Maimonides and Other Medieval Authorities.* Trans. David Wolf Silverman and David Shapiro. Ed. Morris Faierstein. Preface Moshe Idel. Hoboken, N.J.: KTAV. Trans. of Hebrew articles in Heschel 1945, "Did Maimonides Strive for Prophetic Inspiration?" and Heschel 1950, "'Al ruah ha-kodesh bimey ha-beynayim."

2004. *The Ineffable Name of God: Man. Poems.* Trans. Morton Leifman. New York: Continuum. Trans. of Heschel 1933, *Der Shem Hameforash: Mentsh.*

2005. *Heavenly Torah As Refracted Through the Generations.* Ed. and trans. Gordon Tucker, with Leonard Levin. New York: Continuum. Trans. of Heschel 1962, 1965, 1990, *Torah min ha-shamayim be-aspaklaryah shel ha-dorot.*

Secondary Sources

Agus, Jacob B. 1941. *Modern Philosophies of Judaism: A Study of Recent Jewish Philosophies of Religion.* New York: Behrman Jewish Book House.

Ahmann, Mathew, ed. 1963. *Race: Challenge to Religion.* Chicago: Henry Regnery.

"AJH: Twenty-fifth Yahrzeit Tribute." 1998. "Abraham Joshua Heschel: A Twenty-fifth Yahrzeit Tribute." *Conservative Judaism* 50, 2–3 (winter–spring). Special issue.

"AJH: Yahrzeit Tribute." 1973. "Abraham Joshua Heschel: A Yahrzeit Tribute." *Conservative Judaism* 28, 1 (fall). Special issue.

Al-Yahud, Dayyan [pseudonym]. 1952–53. "Professor Heschel, the Creative Thinker: A Critical Study of His Works." *Jewish Forum.* Part 1: (September 1952), 137–41. Part 2: (November 1952), 189–90. Part 3: (January 1953), 16–18. Part 4: (March 1953), 48–49.

America. 1973. Special issue on Heschel. (10 March).

Baker, Leonard. 1978. *Days of Sorrow and Pain: Leo Baeck and the Berlin Jews.* New York: Oxford University Press.

Baron, Salo W., and Alexander Marx. 1943. Obituary of Ismar Elbogen. *American Jewish Year Book,* xxiv–xxv.

Bergman, Shmuel [Samuel] Hugo. 1991. *Dialogical Philosophy from Kierkegaard to Buber.* Trans. Arnold A. Gerstein. Albany: State University of New York Press. Hebrew original, 1974.

Berrigan, Daniel. 1987. *To Dwell in Peace. An Autobiography.* New York: Harper and Row.

Branch, Taylor. 1988. *Parting the Waters: America in the King Years, 1954–1963.* New York: Simon and Schuster.

———. 1998. *Pillar of Fire: America in the King Years, 1963–65.* New York: Simon and Schuster.

Brav, Stanley R., ed. 1965. *Telling Tales out of School: Seminary Memories of the Hebrew Union College–Jewish Institute of Religion.* Cincinnati: HUC–JIR Alumni Association.

Bruteau, Beatrice, ed. 2004. *Merton and Judaism: Recognition, Repentance, and Renewal; Holiness in Words.* Louisville, Ky.: Fons Vitae.

Buber, Martin. 1947. *Tales of the Hasidim.* Vol. 1.: *Early Masters.* New York: Schocken.

———. 1948. *Tales of the Hasidim.* Vol. 2.: *Later Masters.* New York: Schocken.

———. 1952. *Eclipse of God: Studies in the Relation Between Religion and Philosophy.* New York: Harper and Row.

———. 1954. *The Prophetic Faith.* New York: Macmillan.

———. 1957. *Pointing the Way: Collected Essays.* Trans. and ed. Maurice Friedman. London: Routledge and Kegan Paul.

———. 1991. *The Letters of Martin Buber: A Life of Dialogue.* Ed. Nahum Glatzer and Paul Mendes-Flohr. New York: Schocken.

CALCAV. 1968. *In the Name of America: The Conduct of the War in Vietnam by the Armed Forces of the United States as Shown by Published Reports, Compared with the Laws of War Binding on the United States Government and on Its Citizens.* Director of research, Seymour Melman. Research associates, Melvyn Baron and Dodge Ely. [New York:] Clergy and Laymen Concerned About Vietnam.

CCAR. 1953. *Central Conference of American Rabbis Yearbook.* Volume 63: Sixty-fourth Annual Convention. New York: Central Conference of American Rabbis.

Chester, Michael A. 2005. *Divine Pathos and Human Being: The Theology of Abraham Joshua Heschel.* London: Vallentine Mitchell.

Coffin, William Sloane, Jr. 1977. *Once to Every Man.* New York: Atheneum.

Cohen, Arthur A. 1962. *The Natural and the Supernatural Jew: A Historical and Theological Introduction.* New York: Pantheon.

Cohen, Naomi W. 1972. *Not Free to Desist: A History of the American Jewish Committee, 1906–1966.* Philadelphia: Jewish Publication Society of America.

——— 1997. "'Diaspora plus Palestine, Religion plus Nationalism': The Seminary and Zionism, 1902–1948." In Wertheimer 1997, vol. 2, pp. 114–76.

Deutsch, Shaul Shimon. 1995–96. *Larger Than Life: The Life and Times of the Lubavitcher Rebbe, Rabbi Menachem Mendel Schneerson.* 2 vols. New York: Chassidic Historical Productions.

Donin, Hayim Halevy. 1980. *To Pray as a Jew: A Guide to the Prayer Book and the Synagogue Service.* New York: Basic.

Dresner, Samuel H. 1957. *Prayer, Humility, and Compassion.* Philadelphia: Jewish Publication Society.

———. 1960. *The Zaddik.* New York: Abelard-Schuman.

———. 1970. *The Sabbath.* New York: Burning Bush.

———. 1974. *Levi Yitzhak of Berditchev: Portrait of a Hasidic Master.* New York: Hartmore House.

———. 1981. "Hasidism and Its Opponents." In Raphael Jospe and Stanley Wagner, eds., *Great Schisms in Jewish History,* 119–75. New York: KTAV.

———, ed. 1983. *I Asked for Wonder: A Spiritual Anthology.* New York: Crossroad.

———. 1985. "Heschel the Man." In Merkle 1985, *Abraham Joshua Heschel,* 3–34.

———. 1985. "Introduction: Heschel as a Hasidic Scholar." In Heschel 1985, *The Circle of the Baal Shem Tov,* vii–xlv.

———. 2002. *Heschel, Hasidism, and Halakha.* New York: Fordham University Press.

Eisen, Arnold M. 1982. "Theology, Sociology, Ideology: Jewish Thought in America, 1925–1955." *Modern Judaism* 2: 91–103.

———. 1997. *Taking Hold of Torah: Jewish Commitment and Community in America.* Bloomington: Indiana University Press.

Eisen, Robert. 2003. "Abraham Joshua Heschel's Rabbinic Theology as a Response to the Holocaust." *Modern Judaism* 23, 3 (October): 211–25.

Elbogen, Ismar. 1944. *A Century of Jewish Life.* Philadelphia: Jewish Publication Society of America.

Fackenheim, Emil L. 1948. "Can We Believe in Judaism Religiously? An Ethical Faith Is Not Enough." *Commentary* (November), 521–27.

———. 1950. "The Modern Jew's Path to God: Inviting the Great Encounter." *Commentary* (May), 450–57.

————. 1968. "Jewish Faith and the Holocaust." *Commentary* (August), 30–36.

————. 1970. *God's Presence in History: Jewish Affirmations and Philosophical Reflections.* Northvale, N.J.,: Jason Aronson.

Faierstein, Morris. 1987. "Gershom Scholem and Hasidism." *Journal of Jewish Studies* (Oxford) 37, 2 (autumn): 221–33.

————. 1990. Review of Abraham Joshua Heschel, *The Circle of the Baal Shem Tov. Judaism* 39, 2 (spring): 250–51.

————. 1991. "Hasidism: The Last Decade in Research." *Modern Judaism* 11: 111–24.

————. 1999. "Abraham Joshua Heschel and the Holocaust." *Modern Judaism* 19: 255–75. Appendix 1: trans. of Heschel, "After Majdanek: On Aaron Zeitlin's Poetry," 264–71. Appendix 2, "Interview with Professor Heschel about Russian Jewry," by Gershon Jacobson, 272–75.

Finkelstein, Louis, ed. 1949. *The Jews: Their History, Culture, and Religion.* 2 vols. New York: Harper and Brothers; Philadelphia: Jewish Publication Society of America.

————, ed. 1953. *Thirteen Americans: Their Spiritual Autobiographies.* New York: Harper and Brothers; New York: Institute for Religious and Social Studies.

————. 1973. "Three Meetings with Abraham Heschel." *Conservative Judaism* 28, 1 (fall): 19–22.

Fox, Richard Wightman. 1985. *Reinhold Niebuhr: A Biography.* New York: Pantheon.

Friedman, Maurice. 1955. "The Thought of Abraham Heschel." *Congress Weekly* (14 November), 18–20.

————. 1960. *Martin Buber: The Life of Dialogue.* New York: Harper.

————. 1983. *Martin Buber: His Life and Work; The Later Years, 1945–1965.* Detroit: Wayne State University Press.

————. 1983. *Martin Buber: His Life and Work; The Middle Years, 1923–1945.* New York: Dutton.

————. 1987. *Abraham Joshua Heschel and Elie Wiesel: You Are My Witnesses.* New York: Farrar, Straus and Giroux.

Garrow, David J. 1986. *Bearing the Cross: Martin Luther King, Jr., and the Southern Christian Leadership Conference.* New York: Random House.

Geffen, Rela Mintz. 1997, "The Shaping of a Cultural and Religious Elite: Alumni of the Teachers Institute, Seminary College and Graduate Schools, 1930–1995." In Wertheimer 1997, vol. 1, pp. 632–53.

Ginzberg, Eli. 1966. *Keeper of the Law: Louis Ginzberg, a Personal Memoir.* Philadelphia: Jewish Publication Society of America.

Goldberg, Hillel. 1989. *Between Berlin and Slobodka: Jewish Transition Figures from Eastern Europe.* Hoboken, N.J.: KTAV.

Goldstein, Warren. 2004. *William Sloane Coffin, Jr.: A Holy Impatience.* New Haven: Yale University Press.

Goldy, Robert G. 1990. *The Emergence of Jewish Theology in America.* Bloomington: Indiana University Press.

Gottschalk, Alfred. 1973. "Abraham Joshua Heschel, a Man of Dialogues." *Conservative Judaism* 28, 1 (fall): 23–26.

Grade, Chaim. 1976. *The Yeshiva.* Trans. Curt Leviant. Indianapolis: Bobbs-Merrill.

Green, Arthur. 1979. *Tormented Master: A Life of Rabbi Nahman of Bratslav.* New York: Schocken.

Greenbaum, Michael B. 1997. "The Finkelstein Era." In Wertheimer 1997, vol. 1, pp. 162–232.

Greenberg, Hayim. 1964. "Bankrupt." *Midstream* (March), 5–10. Yiddish original, 1943.

Hall, Mitchell K. 1990. *Because of Their Faith: CALCAV and Religious Opposition to the Vietnam War.* New York: Columbia University Press.

———. 2000. *The Vietnam War.* New York: Longman.

Handy, Robert T. 1987. *A History of Union Theological Seminary in New York.* New York: Columbia University Press.

Herberg, Will. 1947. "From Marxism to Judaism," *Commentary* (January), 25–32.

———. 1949. "Has Judaism Still Power to Speak? A Religion for an Age of Crisis," *Commentary* (May), 447–57.

Hershcopf, Judith. 1965. "The Church and the Jews: The Struggle at Vatican Council II." *American Jewish Year Book* 66: 99–136.

———. 1966. "The Church and the Jews: The Struggle at Vatican Council II." *American Jewish Year Book* 67: 45–77.

Heschel, Susannah, ed. 1983. *On Being a Jewish Feminist: A Reader.* New York: Schocken.

———. 1996. Introduction to Heschel 1996, *Moral Grandeur and Spiritual Audacity,* vii–xxx.

———. 1997. Introduction Heschel 1969, *Israel: An Echo of Eternity,* xvii–xxix.

———. 2000. "Theological Affinities in the Writings of Abraham Joshua Heschel and Martin Luther King, Jr." In Yvonne Chireau and Nathaniel Deutsch, eds. *Black Zion: African American Religious Encounters with Judaism.* New York: Oxford University Press.

———. 2005. Foreword to Heschel 2005, *Heavenly Torah As Refracted Through the Generations,* xvii–xx.

Heschel, Susannah, Samuel H. Dresner, and Pinchas Peli. 1985. *Prayer and Politics: The Twin Poles of Abraham Joshua Heschel.* Ed. Joshua Stampfer. Portland, Oreg.: Institute for Judaic Studies.

Heschel, Sylvia Straus. 1982. Foreword to Heschel 1982, *Maimonides: A Biography,* ix–x.

———. 1990. Foreword to Heschel 1962, 1965, 1990, *Torah min ha-shamayim be-aspaklaryah shel ha-dorot,* vol. 3, p. 170.

Heshel, Jacob. 1967. "The History of Hasidism in Austria." In Josef Fraenkel, ed., *The Jews of Austria: Essays on Their Life, History and Destruction,* 347–60. London: Vallentine Mitchell.

Hoenig, Sidney B., and Baruch Litvin, eds. 1965. *Jewish Identity: Modern Responsa* and Opinions on the Registration of Children of Mixed Marriages. David Ben-Gurion's Query to Leaders of World Jewry. New York: Feldheim.

Holtz, Avraham. 1970–71. "Hillel Zeitlin: Publicist and Martyr." Jewish Book Annual 28: 141–46.

Hundert, Gershon, ed. 1991. Essential Papers on Hasidism: Origins to the Present. New York: New York University Press.

Idel, Moshe. 1988. Kabbalah: New Perspectives. New Haven: Yale University Press.

Johnson, F. Ernest, ed. 1955. Religious Symbolism. New York: Institute for Religious and Social Studies, Harper and Brothers.

Kaplan, Edward K. 1971. "Form and Content in Abraham J. Heschel's Poetic Style." CCAR Journal 18, 2 (April): 28–39.

———. 1973. "Language and Reality in Abraham J. Heschel's Philosophy of Religion." Journal of the American Academy of Religion 41, 1 (March): 94–113.

———. 1985. "Abraham Heschel's Poetics of Religious Thinking." In Merkle 1985, Abraham Joshua Heschel, 103–19.

———. 1994. "Sacred Versus Symbolic Religion: Abraham Joshua Heschel and Martin Buber." Modern Judaism 14: 213–31.

———. 1996. Holiness in Words. Albany: State University of New York Press.

———. 1998. "Readiness Before God: Abraham Heschel in Europe." Conservative Judaism 40, 2–3 (winter–spring): 22–35.

———. 2001. "Heschel as Philosopher: Phenomenology and the Rhetoric of Revelation." Modern Judaism 21, 1 (February): 1–14.

———. 2003. "Heschel's First American Controversies: Einstein, War, and the Living God." Conservative Judaism 55, 4 (summer): 26–41.

———. 2004. "'A Humanly Impoverished Thirst for Light': Thomas Merton's Receptivity to the Feminine, to Judaism, and to Religious Pluralism." Merton Annual Studies in Culture, Spirituality, and Social Concerns 17: 137–52.

———. 2004. Introduction to Heschel 2004, The Ineffable Name of God: Man, 7–18.

———. 2004. "Revelation and Commitment: Abraham Joshua Heschel's Situational Philosophy." In P. Amodio, G. Giannani, G. Lissa, eds., Filosofia e critica della filosofia nel pensiero ebraico, 199–222. Naples: Giannini Editore.

———. 2004. "'Under My Catholic Skin': Thomas Merton's Opening to Judaism and to the World." In Bruteau 2004, 109–25.

Kaplan, Edward K., and Samuel H. Dresner. 1998. Abraham Joshua Heschel, Prophetic Witness. New Haven: Yale University Press.

Kaplan, Mordecai M. 1934. Judaism as a Civilization. Toward a Reconstruction of American-Jewish Life. New York: Macmillan.

Karff, Samuel, ed. 1976. Hebrew Union College–Jewish Institute of Religion at 100 Years. Cincinnati: Hebrew Union College Press.

Kasimow, Harold, and Byron Sherwin, eds. 1991. *No Religion Is an Island: Abraham Joshua Heschel and Interreligious Dialogue*. New York: Orbis.

Katz, Steven T. 1980. "Abraham Joshua Heschel and Hasidism." *Journal of Jewish Studies* 31 (spring): 82–104.

———. 1993. *Interpreters of Judaism in the Late Twentieth Century*. Washington, D.C.: B'nai B'rith Books.

Kaufman, David. 1997. "Jewish Education as a Civilization: A History of the Teachers Institute." In Wertheimer 1997, vol. 1, pp. 566–629.

Kavka, Martin. 2006. "The Meaning of That Hour: Prophecy, Phenomenology and the Public Sphere in the Early Writings of Abraham Joshua Heschel." In Clayton Crockett, ed., *Religion and Violence in the Secular World: Toward a New Political Theology*, 108–36. Charlottesville: University of Virginia Press.

Kimelman, Reuven. 2004. "Rabbis Joseph B. Soloveitchik and Abraham Joshua Heschel on Jewish-Christian Relations." *Modern Judaism* 24 (2004): 251–71.

King, Coretta Scott. 1969. *My Life with Martin Luther King, Jr.* New York: Holt, Rinehart and Winston.

Klein, Zanvel. 1980. "Heschel as a Hasidic Scholar." *Journal of Jewish Studies* 31 (spring): 212–14.

Knight, Harold. 1947. *The Hebrew Prophetic Consciousness*. London: Lutterworth.

Korn, Bertram W., ed. 1976. *A Bicentennial Festschrift for Jacob Rader Marcus*. Waltham, Mass.: Jewish Historical Society; New York: KTAV.

Krauss, Pesach. 1988. *Why Me? Coping with Grief, Loss, and Change*. Toronto: Bantam.

Krome, Frederic. 2002. "Correspondence Between Martin Buber, Hans Kohn, Abraham Joshua Heschel, and Adolph Oko." *Jewish Culture and History* 5, 1 (summer): 121–34.

Lederhendler, Eli. 1997. "The Ongoing Dialogue: The Seminary and the Challenge of Israel." In Wertheimer 1997, vol. 2, 177–270.

Lewis, David L. 1970. *King: A Biography*. New York: Praeger.

Lewis, John. 1998. *Walking with the Wind: A Memoir of the Movement*. New York: Simon and Schuster.

Lipstadt, Deborah E. 1986. *Beyond Belief: The American Press and the Coming of the Holocaust, 1933–1945*. New York: Free Press.

Liptzin, Sol. 1985. *A History of Yiddish Literature*. New York: Jonathan David.

Magid, Shaul. 1998. "Abraham Joshua Heschel and Thomas Merton: Heretics of Modernity." *Conservative Judaism* 1, 2–3 (winter–spring): 445–61.

———. 2005. "A Monk, a Rabbi, and 'The Meaning of This Hour': War and Non-Violence in Abraham Joshua Heschel and Thomas Merton." *CrossCurrents* (summer), 184–213.

Marmur, Michael. 2005. "Heschel's Rhetoric of Citation: The Use of Sources in *God in Search of Man*." Ph.D. diss. The Hebrew University, Jerusalem.

McNamara, Robert S. 1995. *In Retrospect: The Tragedy and Lessons of Vietnam.* New York: Random House.

Medoff, Rafael. 1996. "New Perspectives on How America, and American Jewry, Responded to the Holocaust." *American Jewish History* 84, 3: 253–66.

Mendes-Flohr, Paul. 1991. *Divided Passions: Jewish Intellectuals and the Experience of Modernity.* Detroit: Wayne State University Press.

Merkle, John C., ed. 1985. *Abraham Joshua Heschel: Exploring His Life and Thought.* New York: Macmillan.

———. 1985. *The Genesis of Faith: The Depth Theology of Abraham Joshua Heschel.* New York: Macmillan.

Merton, Thomas. 1997. *The Journals of Thomas Merton.* Vol. 5: *Dancing in the Water of Life: Seeking Peace in the Hermitage.* Ed. Walter E. Daggy. San Francisco: HarperSanFrancisco.

Meyer, Michael A. 1976. "The Refugee Scholars Project of the Hebrew Union College." In Korn 1976, 359–75.

———. 1988. *Response to Modernity: A History of the Reform Movement in Judaism.* New York: Oxford University Press.

Mintz, Alan. 1989. *Banished from Their Father's Table.* Bloomington: Indiana University Press.

Mintz, Jerome. 1992. *Hasidic People: A Place in the New World.* Cambridge: Harvard University Press.

Moore, Deborah Dash, ed. 1990. *East European Jews in Two Worlds.* Evanston, Ill.: Northwestern University Press.

Moore, Donald, J. 1989. *The Human and the Holy: The Spirituality of Abraham Joshua Heschel.* New York: Fordham University Press.

Mortara di Veroli, Elena. 1969. "Heschel, risposta all'ebreo di oggi"(in Italian, Heschel: An answer to today's Jew). *Shalom* (January).

———. 1973. "Ricordi di Heschel" (In Italian, Memories of Heschel), *Rassegna mensile di Israel* (Rome) (February), 3–11.

Neusner, Jacob. 1966. Review of Abraham Joshua Heschel, *Torah Min Ha-shamayim. Conservative Judaism* 20, 3 (spring): 66–73.

———. 1981. *Stranger at Home: "The Holocaust," Zionism, and American Judaism.* Chicago: University of Chicago Press.

———. 1990. "Abraham Joshua Heschel: The Man," and "The Intellectual Achievement of Abraham Joshua Heschel," in Heschel 1990, *To Grow in Wisdom,* 3–22.

Niebuhr, Reinhold. 1932. *Moral Man and Immoral Society.* New York: Scribner's

Oates, Stephen B. 1982. *Let the Trumpet Sound: The Life of Martin Luther King, Jr.* New York: Harper and Row.

Oesterreicher, John M., ed. 1955. *The Bridge: A Yearbook of Judeo-Christian Studies.* Vol. 1. New York: Pantheon.

————. 1967. "Declaration on the Relationship of the Church to Non-Christian Religions: Introduction and Commentary," 1–136. In Herbert Vorgrimler, ed., *Commentary on the Documents of Vatican II*. New York: Herder and Herder.

Oren, Michael. 2002. *Six Days of War: June 1967 and the Making of the Modern Middle East*. London: Oxford University Press.

Penkower, Monty. 1985. "American Jewry and the Holocaust: From Biltmore to the American Jewish Conference." *Jewish Social Studies* 47, 2: 95–114.

Plaut, W. Gunther. 1980. "Reform Judaism: Past, Present, and Future." *Journal of Reform Judaism* 27, 3 (summer): 1–11.

————. 1981. *Unfinished Business: An Autobiography*. Toronto: Lester and Orpen Dennys.

Polner, Murray, and Jim O'Grady. 1997. *Disarmed and Dangerous: The Radical Lives and Times of Daniel and Phillip Berrigan*. New York: Basic.

Proceedings. 1953. *Proceedings of the Rabbinical Assembly of America* 17. New York: Rabbinical Assembly of America.

Proceedings. 1958. *Proceedings of the Rabbinical Assembly of America* 22. New York: Rabbinical Assembly of America.

Proceedings. 1959. *Proceedings of the Rabbinical Assembly of America* 23. New York: Rabbinical Assembly of America.

Proceedings. 1961. *Proceedings of the Rabbinical Assembly of America* 25. New York: Rabbinical Assembly of America.

Proceedings. 1962. *Proceedings of the Rabbinical Assembly of America* 26. New York: Rabbinical Assembly of America.

Proceedings. 1966. *Proceedings of the 66th Annual Convention of the Rabbinical Assembly* 30. New York: Rabbinical Assembly of America.

Proceedings. 1968. *Proceedings of the Rabbinical Assembly*, 68th annual convention, 32. New York: Rabbinical Assembly of America.

Rakeffet-Rothkoff, Aaron. 1981. *The Silver Era in American Jewish Orthodoxy: Rabbi Eliezer Silver and His Generation*. Jerusalem: Feldheim.

————. 1999. *The Rav: The World of Rabbi Joseph B. Soloveitchik*. Hoboken, N.J.: KTAV.

Ravitch, Melekh. 1945, 1947. *Mayn leksikon* (in Yiddish). 2 vols. (Vol. 1, 1945; vol. 2, 1947). Montreal: Aroysgegeben fun A Komitet.

Rosenstock-Huessy, Eugen, ed. 1969. *Judaism Despite Christianity: The "Letters on Christianity and Judaism" Between Eugen Rosenstock-Huessy and Franz Rosenzweig*. New York: Schocken.

Rosenzweig, Franz. 1965. *On Jewish Learning*. New York: Schocken.

————. 2005. *The Star of Redemption*. Trans. Barbara E. Galli. Madison: University of Wisconsin Press.

Rotenstreich, Nathan. 1974. "On Prophetic Consciousness." *Journal of Religion* 54: 185–98.

Rothschild, Fritz A. 1953. "Conservative Judaism Faces the Need for Change." *Commentary* (November), 447–55.

———. 1959. "God and Modern Man: The Approach of Abraham J. Heschel." *Judaism* 8, 2 (spring): 112–20

———. 1959. Introduction to Heschel 1959, *Between God and Man*, 7–32.

———. 1967. "Abraham Joshua Heschel." In Thomas E. Bird, ed., *Modern Theologians*, 169–82. Notre Dame, Ind.: Notre Dame University Press.

———. 1968. "The Religious Thought of Abraham Joshua Heschel." *Conservative Judaism* 23, 1 (fall): 12–24.

———. 1973. "Abraham Joshua Heschel (1907–1972)." *American Jewish Year Book* 74: 533–44.

———. 1973. "Architect and Herald of a New Theology." *Conservative Judaism* 28, 1 (fall): 55–60.

———, ed. 1990. *Jewish Perspectives on Christianity: Leo Baeck, Martin Buber, Franz Rosenzweig, Will Herberg, and Abraham J. Heschel.* New York: Crossroad.

Rubenstein, Richard L. 1966. *After Auschwitz: Radical Theology and Contemporary Judaism.* Indianapolis: Bobbs-Merrill.

———. 1974. *Power Struggle. An Autobiographical Confession.* New York: Scribner's.

Sanders, James. 1973. "An Apostle to the Gentiles." *Conservative Judaism* 28, 1 (fall): 61–63.

Sarna, Jonathan. 1989. *JPS, the Americanization of Jewish Culture, 1888–1988: A Centennial History of the Jewish Publication Society.* Philadelphia: Jewish Publication Society of America.

———. 2000. With Jonathan J. Golden. "The Twentieth Century Through American Jewish Eyes: A History of the *American Jewish Year Book*, 1899–1999." *American Jewish Year Book 2000*, 100: 3–102. New York: American Jewish Committee.

———. 2004. *American Judaism: A History.* New Haven: Yale University Press.

Schachter-Shalomi, Zalman. 1991. *Spiritual Intimacy: A Study of Counseling in Hasidism.* Northvale, N.J.: Jason Aronson.

Schmerker, Miriam R. N.d. "Abraham Joshua Heschel's Encounter as Theologian-Activist During the Second Vatican Council." Ph.D. diss. Jewish Theological Seminary.

Schmidt, Stephan A. 1983. *A History of the Religious Education Association.* Birmingham, Ala.: Religious Education Press.

Schochet, Elijah Judah, and Solomon Spiro. 2005. *Saul Lieberman: The Man and His Work.* New York: Jewish Theological Seminary.

Scholem, Gershom. 1941. *Major Trends in Jewish Mysticism.* 3d rev. ed. New York: Schocken, 1961.

Scult, Mel. 1993. *Judaism Faces the Twentieth Century: A Biography of Mordecai M. Kaplan.* Detroit: Wayne State University Press.

————. 2002. "Kaplan's Heschel: A View from the Kaplan Diary." *Conservative Judaism* 54, 4 (summer): 3–14.

Shandler, Jeffrey. 1993. "Heschel and Yiddish: A Struggle with Signification." *Journal of Jewish Thought and Philosophy* 2: 245–99.

Sherman, Franklin. 1963. "Abraham J. Heschel: Spokesman for Jewish Faith." *Lutheran World* (October), 400–408.

————. 1970. *The Promise of Heschel.* Philadelphia: Lippincott.

Silberman, Lou H. 1971. "Rebbe for Our Day." *Jewish Heritage* (fall): 39–43.

Soloveitchik, Joseph Baer. 1983. *Halakhic Man.* Trans. Lawrence Kaplan. Philadelphia: Jewish Publication Society of America.

Staub, Michael E. 2002. *Torn at the Roots: The Crisis of Jewish Liberalism in Postwar America.* New York: Columbia University Press.

Stern, Harold. 1983. "A. J. Heschel, Irenic Polemicist." *Proceedings of the Rabbinical Assembly,* 169–77. New York: Rabbinical Assembly of America.

Strauss, Herbert A., ed. 1987. *Jewish Immigrants of the Nazi Period.* Vol. 6. New York: Saur.

Tanenbaum, Marc H. 1986. "A Jewish Viewpoint on *Nostra Aetate.*" In Eugene J. Fisher, James Rudin, and Marc Tanenbaum, eds., *Twenty Years of Jewish-Catholic Relations,* 39–60. New York: Paulist.

————. 2002. *A Prophet for Our Times: An Anthology of the Writings of Rabbi Marc H. Tanenbaum.* Ed. Judith Hershcopf Banki and Eugene J. Fisher. New York: Fordham University Press.

Teshima, Jacob Yuroh. 1973. "In Memory of My Teacher." *Light of Life* (Japan): 49–55.

Tikkun. 1998. Special issue on Heschel. (January–February).

Tirosh-Samuelson, Hava, ed. 2002. *Judaism and Ecology: Created World and Revealed Word.* Cambridge: Harvard University Press.

Wertheimer, Jack, ed. 1997. *Tradition Renewed: A History of the Jewish Theological Seminary of America.* 2 vols. New York: Jewish Theological Seminary.

Wiesel, Elie. 1966. *The Jews of Silence: A Personal Report on Soviet Jewry.* Trans. Neil Kozodoy. New York: Holt, Rinehart and Winston.

Zipperstein, Steven J. 1993. *Elusive Prophet: Ahad Ha'am and the Origins of Zionism.* Berkeley: University of California Press.

Zuroff, Efraim. 2000. *The Response of Orthodox Jewry in the United States to the Holocaust.* Hoboken, N.J.: KTAV.

Permissions and Credits

497

The following are reprinted by permission of the Rabbinical Assembly of America: excerpts from Abraham Joshua Heschel, "The Spirit of Jewish Prayer," *Proceedings of the Rabbinical Assembly of America* 17 (1953): 151–215; excerpts from Abraham Joshua Heschel, "Yisrael: Am, Eretz, Medinah. Ideological Evaluation of Israel and the Diaspora," *Proceedings of the Rabbinical Assembly of America* 22 (1958): 118–36; excerpts from Abraham Joshua Heschel, "The Values of Jewish Education," *Proceedings of the Rabbinical Assembly of America* 26 (1962): 83–100; excerpts from Abraham Joshua Heschel, "From Mission to Dialogue," *Conservative Judaism* 21, 3 (Spring 1967): 1–11; excerpts from Abraham Joshua Heschel, "On Prayer," *Conservative Judaism* (Fall 1970): 1–12.

The following is reprinted by permission of the Central Conference of American Rabbis: excerpts from Abraham Joshua Heschel, "Toward an Understanding of Halacha, *Yearbook of the Central Conference of American Rabbis*, vol. 63 (1953): 386–409.

Photographic Credits

Title page: Abraham Joshua Heschel in New York in 1972. Photograph by Joel Orent.

Page 1: Abraham Joshua Heschel at Hebrew Union College in Cincinnati, 1943. Photograph by Bill Liebschutz.

Page 67: Gates of the Jewish Theological Seminary, New York. Courtesy of the Ratner Center for the Study of Conservative Judaism, Jewish Theological Seminary of America.

Page 175: Heschel with Martin Luther King, Jr. (left), and Ralph Bunche, former U.S. ambassador to the United Nations, at the Selma to Montgomery march, 1965. Courtesy of the Ratner Center for the Study of Conservative Judaism, Jewish Theological Seminary of America.

Page 235: Heschel and Pope Paul VI. Cover, *United Synagogue Review*, fall 1971. Reproduced with permission.

Page 295: Heschel in 1972. Photograph by Joel Orent.

Acknowledgments

It has been almost two decades since Rabbi Samuel Dresner invited me to write the biography of his teacher Abraham Joshua Heschel, whom he considered the zaddik of his generation. The project of which he dreamed has been completed with this second and final volume. Rabbi Dresner passed away in 2000, so my writing could not benefit from his knowledge and boundless enthusiasm for the project. I am deeply grateful for his confidence and encouragement over the years, and for that of his widow, Ruth Rapp Dresner, who has remained a wise companion to my efforts.

Sylvia Straus Heschel, Heschel's widow, who passed away on 26 March 2007, extended her hospitality to me over forty years of friendship. May her memory be for a blessing. Although this is not an authorized biography, Mrs. Heschel and her daughter, Susannah, herself a Judaic scholar and activist, provided valuable information and support, as did Heschel's nieces and cousins, Thena Heshel Kendall, Pearl Twersky, Yitz Twersky, and other members of the Heschel and Perlow clans.

Interviewing Heschel's friends, acquaintances, relatives, students, and colleagues was the most moving aspect of my research. My gratitude extends to Fritz Rothschild, who made the systematic study of Heschel possible, for hours of piquant conversation and crucial insights. Heschel's closest friend, Wolfe Kelman, generously and selflessly shared his memories with me; he was especially gracious during the last weeks of his fatal cancer, when he apologized that he could not be more helpful. Marc H. Tanenbaum and Marshall Meyer each in his own way exemplified the multicultural Jewish personality they admired in Heschel, and their life and work fully reflect Heschel's deepest ideals.

The public availability of several archives made it possible for me to write this biography, and I thank the following for their invaluable assistance. Helen Ritter and Miriam B. Kranis guided me through the superbly organized archives of the American Jewish Committee; Franklin C. Muse of the Philadelphia Jewish Archives Center made available the records of the Jewish Publication Society; Roger Straus, Jr., opened the archives of Farrar, Straus and Giroux for me before they went to the New York Public Library; Kevin Profitt helped me at the American Jewish Archives in Cincinnati; Jack Wertheimer authorized my research in the General Files of the Jewish Theological Seminary, before they were completely cataloged; and Julie Miller and Ellen Kastel of the Ratner Center for the Study of Conservative Judaism provided photographs and precious advice. Taylor Branch, the epic biographer of Martin Luther King, Jr., also shared information with me. Georgette Bennett, the widow of Marc Tanenbaum, gave me access to her husband's personal files before they were sent to the American Jewish Archives in Cincinnati. Jessica De Cou helped obtain materials from the University of Iowa Archives, as did Katherine Levin from the University of Minnesota, and Seth Kasten and Andrew Kadel from Burke Library at Union Theological Seminary. Leonid Kelbert did superb interviewing in Jerusalem. Morton Leifman shared vivid stories with me.

Material and institutional support were provided by my academic home, Brandeis University, whose president, Jehuda Reinharz, a historian of Zionism and biographer of Chaim Weizmann, supported this project from the beginning. The university has been remarkably receptive to my role as a scholar of French literature committed also to religious studies, and aided this long project with generous faculty research funds. James Rosenblum and Nancy Zibman of the Judaica section of the Goldfarb Library gave practical help. I am particularly grateful to the Lucius T. Littauer Foundation, and especially Pamela Ween Bromberg, for their long-standing support.

Among the research assistants who helped me for this volume, I want first to thank Baila Round Shargel, who did excellent interviewing for Rabbi Dresner, transcribing and analyzing interviews in an exemplary fashion; for me she read portions of the manuscript and offered corrections and suggestions for improvement. Adina Anflick, Elyssa Auster, Karen Chernick, Veronica Kavin, and Andrew Sugerman helped with essential technical matters. And Hadassah Margolis gave a sharp critical reading of an early draft of the manuscript, a turning point in my writing process.

Several people examined the entire manuscript, or several chapters, at various stages of revision, offering corrections, criticism, suggestions for improvement, and well-needed encouragement: Roberta Apfel, Ruth Rapp Dresner, Herbert Dreyer, Michael Fishbane, Erich Goldhagen, Bob Jampol, Lucien Miller, David Novak, Jonathan Sarna, Adam B. Seligman, Bennett Simon, Carol Wool, and Steven Zipperstein. My wife, Janna Kaplan, read the manuscript at its worst and trusted me to improve. I dedicate this book to her with love. My children, Jeremy Kaplan and his wife, Rebecca Ballantine (and their son, Eli), Aaron Emmanuel Kaplan, and Simona Chava Kaplan, did not read the manuscript but they shared the sacrifice that an author makes for the benefit of his work.

To Jonathan Brent at Yale University Press, gratitude for his support for this biography over many years, and for his patience. My admiration to Susan Laity for her insightful editing of the manuscript, bringing it gracefully into print during the centenary year of Heschel's birth. Painfully aware of its omissions and shortcomings, I take full responsibility for the final book.

Index

Page numbers of illustrations appear in italic.

286, 308, 345, 350, 383; and Union
Theological Seminary, 279

Bergman, Shmuel (Samuel) Hugo, 125,
410n22

Berkovits, Eliezer, 213, 432–33n53

Berlin, 41, 78, 182, 185, 243, 394n14;
Heschel's acquaintances from, 14,
44, 61, 75, 118, 160, 330, 363–64,
398n34; Hochschule at, 2, 5, 8,
10–11, 31, 39, 54, 95, 124, 173;
University of, ix–xi, 21, 36, 37, 61,
154, 210, 239, 284, 289, 299,
391n3

Berman, Morton M., 155, 417n46

Berrigan, Daniel, *374;* and CCAV (later
CALCAV), 300–301, 305, 307; as
genuine poet, 353; and Heschel,
302, 371–73, *373,* 377; and radical
protest, 302, 371–72, 449n4,
464nn38, 39

Berrigan, Philip, 301, 371–73, *374*

Bialik, Hayim Nahman (1873–1934),
25, 74

Bible, Hebrew: Christian reverence for,
287–88, 347, 354; desanctification
of, 279; as ethical model, 17, 23–24,
59, 182, 207, 230, 302, 326; as
God's anthropology, 120, 125, 182;
holiness of, 59, 98, 168, 180, 207,
217, 239, 241, 278–79, 282, 288,
337, 361; interpretation of, 155,
168, 187, 292, 356; as paradigm for
Israel, 337; as still being written,
59, 314, 327; teaching of, 9, 28, 40,
49–50, 93, 196, 237

Biography: Glatzer's of Rosenzweig,
153; Heschel's obituary of
Diesendruck, 18; Heschel's of
Abravanel, 100; Heschel's of the
Kotzker rebbe (*see* Heschel,
Abraham Joshua: works; Kotzker

rebbe, Menahem Mendl); Heschel's
of Maimonides, 31, 166, 364

Blake, Eugene Carson, 335, 356

Blank, Amy K., 23, 65, 389n22, 399n47

Blank, Sheldon H., 10, 23, 142

Blasphemy: charge of deicide as, 247;
Israel as recompense for Holocaust,
327–28; by the Kotzker rebbe,
459n14; racism as, 216

Bohnen, Eli H., 324–25, *325*

Borowitz, Eugene, 39, 42, 369, 388,
394n16

Bracker, Milton, 252, 255

Brand plucked from the fire, image of,
190, 282

Brickner, Balfour, 302, 320, 372

Brodsky, David, 26–27, 392n25

Brown, Robert McAfee, 290, 301,
307–9, 313–14, 339

Buber, Martin (1878–1965): American
lecture tour of, 134–36; criticism of,
290–91; dialogue concept of, 60,
118, 126, 142–43, 149; Friedman
on, 107–8, 165; and Hasidism, 102,
172; Heschel and, x, 6–7, 32, 53,
79, 103, 138, 161–62, 188, 388n3,
403n42, 413n54; Oko and, 14;
philosophy of religion of, 152–53,
158; and Rosenstock-Huessy,
133–34; and Rosenzweig, 22, 118,
121, 133, 142, 152, 153, 159, 170;
and search for publishers, 14,
31–32, 103

—works: *Between Man and Man,* 195;
The Eclipse of God, 153; *I and Thou,*
xii, 118, 126; *The Prophetic Faith,*
32; *Tales of the Hasidim,* 405n15

Bunche, Ralph, *175,* 177, 223–25

Callousness, 143, 169, 186, 199,
211–12, 309, 335, 340

Catholics. *See* Christianity and Christians; Vatican Council, Second

Celebration, as faith, 99, 202–3, 231–32, 285, 336

Central Conference of American Rabbis (CCAR, Reform rabbinical association), 43, 138, 146, 152, 156, 164, 221

Certainty: personal God as Heschel's primary, 16; quest for, 33–34, 393*n*45; religious, 120, 224, 326–29, 416*n*38

Cherbonnier, Edmond La B., 195, 326, 382

Childs, Brevard S., 212, 432*n*51

Chosen people, 169, 182, 292, 304

Christian Century, 170, 182, 196, 212, 278, 316, 381

Christianity and Christians: affirmations of Christians with regard to Jews, 249, 252, 256–57, 260, 277, 283, 289; African American, 10, 24, 176, 219, 359; anti-Judaism, 236–37, 240–44, 259, 274, 279; Catholic peace activists, 300–301, 309, 321, 372; Christians and Israel, 314–18, 335–36; Christian scholars, 142, 171, 212–13, 287; Heschel admired by, 120, 165, 180, 195, 204, 371; Heschel's addresses to, 255–56, 278–79, 292–93, 335–36, 339–40; Heschel's rebuke to Catholics, 260, 270, 290; mission to the Jews, 181, 253, 259–60, 262, 283, 288, 304, 383; and the Soviet Union, 225–26. *See also* Bea, Augustin Cardinal; Union Theological Seminary; Vatican Council, Second

Cicognani, Amleto Giovanni Cardinal, 256, 273

Cincinnati, Ohio: Avondale area, 3, 24–27; Bureau of Jewish Education, 27–29; Clifton area, 3, 38; Conservative synagogue in, 25; Heschel's departure from, 37, 64, 362; Heschel's *Midrasha* in, 27–28, 62; musical life, 22; Orthodox synagogue in, 44; Reform synagogue in, 23; as segregated American city, 3, 10; University of Cincinnati, 10, 37. *See also* Hebrew Union College

Civil Rights movement, 176–77, 183, 199, 220, 425*n*35; and affirmative action, 324, 363; "National Conference on Religion and Race" (1963), 215. *See also* King, Martin Luther, Jr.; Racism

Clergy and Laymen Concerned About Vietnam (CALCAV), 300–313, 319–24, 332–34, 344, 360, 370. *See also* Vietnam War

Clergy Concerned About Vietnam (CCAV). *See* Clergy and Laymen Concerned About Vietnam

Coffin, William Sloane, Jr., 301, 302–4, *306,* 308, 309–11, 333, 378, 450*nn*5,12

Cohen, Arthur A., 95, 149, 196, 403*n*40

Cohen, Gerson D., 372, 381

Cohen, Geula, 269–74, *270,* 444*nn*31, 33

Cohen, Hermann, 101, 128, 152, 159, 398*n*34

Cohon, Samuel Solomon, 10, 22–23, 28, 37, 39, 152–53, 391–92*n*11, 400*n*1

Cold War, 68, 136, 138, 172, 176, 216, 250, 265, 299, 300

Columbia University, xii, 15, 30, 72, 74, 83, 85, 134, 152, 162, 165, 179, 196, 229, 240, 307, 368, 403*n*40

Commentary (magazine), 100–105, 121–26, 129, 152, 172, 194–95, 213, 404*n*9

Commitment: ethical and political, xiii, 217, 299, 332; Heschel's religious, 154; personal, 23, 133, 152, 230; radical, 217, 283, 370; spiritual, 38, 122, 151, 190

Communism: and anti-Semitism, 29, 308; as enemy, 299, 300, 313, 323, 415*n*23; FBI and, 229, 334; McCarthy hearings, 138, 158, 176, 221–22; Rosenberg execution, 415*n*22

Community: Heschel's true, 302, 324, 343; Jewish immigrant, 44, 52, 77–80; New York, 75–76; Yiddish-speaking, 16, 78, 91, 425*n*22

Compassion: American Jews' lack of, 44, 320; of the Baal Shem Tov, xi, 342–43; for God, 83, 213; God's, 124, 169, 183, 282, 320–21; Heschel's, 92, 141, 192–93, 296–97; as moral guide, 51, 226, 312

Complacency, 75, 216–17, 219, 278, 428*n*10

Concepts: ideas of God, 82, 279, 326; mental abstractions, 55, 118, 120, 143, 151, 195, 389*n*23. *See also* Depth theology

"Conference on Science, Philosophy, and Religion" (1940), 16, 429*n*22

Conscience: of American Jews, 227–29, 320, 363; arousing, 185–86, 283, 289, 312, 321; and moral responsibility, 46, 183, 226, 260; prisoners of, 334

Conservative Judaism. *See* Judaism

Conservative Judaism (journal), 88, 194, 198, 209, 382

Consumer culture, critique of, 183–84, 191–92, 228, 289, 332–33, 370

Contradictions, xi, 36, 146, 169, 208

Conversion of the Jews: as Christian mission, 260, 268, 271, 290; Heschel's debate with Coffin on, 304–5; Heschel's statement regarding, 260, 271

Cooperman, David, 200–201

Copernican revolution, Heschel's. *See* Recentering of subjectivity

Corbin, Henry, 31, 53, 330, 364, 366

Covenant, 46, 47, 98, 125, 181, 188, 249, 260, 292, 304, 306, 309, 327

Creed versus faith, xi–xii, 34, 55–56, 202. *See also* Faith

Cronbach, Abraham, 10, 23–24, 42, 215, 222, 224

Culture wars, Jewish, xiv, 105–6, 122, 139, 158

Cushing, Richard Cardinal, 245, 246, 261–62, 268, 276, 303

Customs and ceremonies, 12, 73, 155–56, 185, 205–6, 329, 362

Daiches, David, 213

Dartmouth College, xiii, 133–36, 209

Davies, W. D. (William David), 286–87, 288, 381–82

Davis, Maurice, 24, 222–25

Davis, Moshe, 62, 74

Day-Morning Journal (*Der Tog-Morgen Zhurnal,* Yiddish newspaper), 227, 240, 246, 267, 455*n*22

Dayyan al-Yahud (pseudonym), 159, 166, 172, 418*n*5

Death: "First International Conference on Sudden Death and Reanimation" (1969), 331–32; Heschel's loss of brother Jacob Heshel, 349; Heschel's loss of Eduard Strauss,

Esthetics: beauty, 101, 148, 205; Heschel and, 37, 154; religion versus, 59, 121–22, 139, 155, 411n30

Ethics: commitment to, 88, 152, 332; military, 278, 307; piety and, 17, 33, 85, 120, 121, 145, 202, 213, 289, 302; prayer and, 60, 80, 164, 308–9; Reform idea of "ethical monotheism," 12, 24, 361; and the secularizing of religion, 102; teaching, 10, 154. *See also* Sacred humanism

Evil: anti-Semitism, 263, 282; evil drive, 70, 169; falsehood as root of, 360; human responsibility, 46, 77, 120, 232; mixture of good and, 169, 180, 323; racism, 214, 216; reality of, 17, 48, 124, 148, 180, 192; sensitivity to, 186, 203, 296, 344; war as, 46, 299. *See also* Mitzvah; Redemption

Exile (Hebrew, galut): Diaspora as, 292–93, 327, 366; dissent and, 363; Heschel's idea of God (Shekhinah) in, 83, 98, 149, 339; spiritual vulgarity as, 191–92; war as unredeemed, 192

Existentialism: Buber and Rosenzweig, 102; Cohon and Polish, 152–53; depth theology, 282–83; Fackenheim, 124; Herberg, 153; Heschel against, 231–32; Heschel as Jewish existentialist, 172; Kierkegaard, 341, 343; Sartre, 153

Exodus from Egypt, 171, 219, 223

Expediency, 183–84, 194

Extermination camps, 43–44, 100, 236, 325–27. *See also* Nuclear warfare

Extremism, 23, 101, 138, 159, 211, 221, 275, 311, 328

Fackenheim, Emil Ludwig, 124–25, 159, 291–93

Faith: of black churches, 359; and creed, 34, 151, 168, 292; crisis of, 150, 154, 170, 282, 327; cultivating, 185, 193–94; and despair, 30, 282, 343–44, 354; and doubt, 329, 354; and ethics, 143; Heschel's writings on, 28, 46, 53, 55–56, 102, 111; after the Holocaust, 212; insufficiency of, 150, 190, 283, 317; and Israel, 327–28; Jewish culture wars, 139–40; in the living God, 17, 122, 148, 231, 287, 328; moments of, 337, 383; need for, 71, 121, 164, 185, 240; reason and, 33–34, 125, 150, 153, 155–56, 389–90n23; and science, 16, 138. *See also* Creed versus faith; Depth theology; Saadia Gaon

Falsehood (lying), xi, 48, 145, 156, 258, 340, 360, 370

Federal Bureau of Investigation (FBI), 221–22, 229, 300, 307, 320, 334

Feinberg, Bertha, 25, 65

Feinberg, Louis, 25–27, 41, 65, 75

Fellowship of Reconciliation, 306–9, 313, 381

Feminism, 355, 381

Fernandez, Richard, 304, *305*, 307–8, 311, 331, 333, 340

Fiedler, Leslie, 101–2

Finkelstein, Louis (1895–1991), *91, 109;* affronts to Heschel by, 117, 129–30, 134, 280–82, 367–68; and American Jewish Committee, 240, 243, 246, 248, 251; background of, 72–73; courtship of Heschel, 6–7, 16, 53, 54–55, 63–64; envy of Heschel, 130, 181, 184; and European refugees, 2, 94, 387n2; and

Guilt: as general condition during World
War II, 35, 46, 76; and universal
responsibility, 211, 299, 305
Guttmann, Alexander, 8, *9*, 10, 37
Guttmann, Julius, 54, 172–73, 389*n*12

Hadoar (Hebrew-language newspaper),
75, 204–13, 342, 354
Halakhah (Jewish law): and aggadah,
169, 172, 207; critique of Buber
over, 291; as essence of Judaism, xi,
61, 62, 146, 193, 361; in Heschel's
writings, 79, 192–93; versus
Kavanah, 60, 99; as necessary duty,
154–56, 191; overemphasis on, 190,
192, 361; problem for moderns, 146,
159, 361; and traditional practice,
10–11. *See also* Aggadah
Halberstam, Chaim, 160, 377
Halevi, Judah (1085–1140), 28, 74,
283, 345
Halkin, Abraham, 33, 75, 129, 400*n*6
Halkin, Simon, 75
Häring, Bernard, 290
Harris, Larry D., 10, 215, 329
Hartstein, Jacob I. 61, 65, 75
Hasidism: Baal Shem Tov and, xi, 14,
24, 100, 104, 131, 160–62; Buber
and, 102, 153, 290–91; Heschel's
Hasidic relatives, 5, 26, 78–82;
Heschel's seminars on, 87, 101,
129, 345–47; joy as teaching of,
107; Kotzker rebbe and, xi, 60, 131,
153, 339, 342, 347; neo-, xiii, 86,
101–2, 153, 172–73, 180, 363–64;
New York community of Hasidim,
ix, xi, 39; opponents of, 29, 36, 101,
129; Scholem and, 173
Hayes, Thomas Lee, *334*, 336
Hebrew, modern culture, 13, 18, 25,
27–28, 33, 57, 73–75, 187, 243

Hebrew Union College: American
faculty of, 8, 10–11; crisis at, 49–50;
curriculum at, 9–10, 20, 48, 49;
Heschel as classroom teacher, 20,
39–42, 62; Heschel's adjustment
to, 12–14; Heschel's alienation at,
10–11; Heschel's disciples at,
37–40; refugee professors (College
in Exile) at, 7–8, 9, 388*n*3, 391*n*3;
as students at, 8–10
Heidegger, Martin (1889–1976), 153,
231–32
Heller, Hayyim, 193, 425*n*37
Herberg, Will, 102, 129, 152–53, 170,
183, 207, 411–12*n*53
Herschlag, Judith (Yocheved Muffs),
335, 382
Hertzberg, Arthur E., 323, 365, 396
Hesburgh, Theodore Martin, 290, 336
Heschel, Abraham Joshua (1888–
1967, Kopitzhinitzer rebbe of New
York, first cousin and brother-in-law),
5, 26, *79*, 80–81, 91, 136, 160,
256, 261
Heschel, Abraham Joshua
(1907–1972), *1, 9, 15, 76, 79, 81,
84, 89, 90, 91, 94 119, 135, 140,
175, 189, 233, 235, 247, 281, 295,
305, 306, 317, 322, 328, 334, 346,
348, 349, 353, 369, 373, 374;*
academic promotions of, 36, 48, 53,
63–64, 184; acquisition of English
by, x, 7, 13, 14, 18, 20, 30; activism
of, xiii, 145, 177, 201, 208, 232–33,
324, 350; ambition of, xi, 21, 31,
114, 125, 162; ancestry (yikhus) of,
78–80, 343, 385; appearance,
physical, 28, 36, 82, 176–77, 188,
201, 359; charisma of, xiii, 198,
285, 303; as child prodigy, xi, 13,
39, 131, 208; contradictions in

Heschel, Abraham Joshua (continued)
nature of, xi, 21, 68, 169, 208, 328,
331, 343; creative method of, 34,
102, 112, 129, 196, 207–8, 230;
death and burial of, xi, 297, 339,
340–42, 357, 359, 373–84, 458n9;
disciples of, xiii, 39, 88, 173,
345–47, 379, 382; doctoral
dissertation of, 41, 210, 364,
398n34; expelled from Germany, x,
388n8; extremism of, 60, 101, 138,
159, 211, 275, 328, 343;
Guggenheim Fellowship awarded to,
161–62; heart disease of, 7, 47,
340–41, 349; honors awarded to,
130, 180–81, 279, 289–90, 324–27,
345, 350, 356, 357, 362–63, 371,
377, 382; humor of, 42–43, 65, 84,
131–32, 156, 186, 200–201, 224,
342, 355–56, 465n5; as iconic
figure, x, xiii, 58, 87, 223, 371, 378;
inferiority complex of, 21, 131;
interpretation of works of, 121,
194–96; lecture topics of, 136,
179–80, 199, 280, 284–85, 446n7;
loneliness of, 18, 60, 148, 171, 202,
211, 299, 357, 359, 398n30; love of
music of, 21–22, 55–56, 83, 110,
117, 202, 218, 304, 342, 391n8;
marriage of, 84–85, 402n28;
mastery of Talmud of, 36, 78,
207–11; as moderating influence,
221, 224, 307, 328, 372; narcissism
of, 21, 62, 131, 223, 258, 271–74,
275, 296–97, 352–53, 383–84;
naturalization of, 14–15, 23, 65,
389n22, 399n47; outbursts of, 311,
333; poetry of, 59, 78, 83, 136, 289,
363, 375, 379, 427n48; polemic
style of, 17, 57, 100, 106, 138–40,
144, 150, 155, 207, 275, 344;

reticence of, 29, 43, 90; sarcasm of,
17, 40, 145, 149, 155, 184–85,
227–28, 343–44; self-deception of,
xi, 258, 275; shyness of, xi, 13, 21,
29, 38, 43, 90, 198; as student in
Berlin, ix, 21, 55, 61, 154–55; as
student in Vilna, 13, 16, 78, 81,
188, 299; study of, at Israeli
universities, 210, 431n38; as
teacher, xi, 20, 39–42, 48, 62,
86–89, 132–34, 144, 204, 284–86;
at Union Theological Seminary, 237,
281–91; at University of Iowa, 203,
240; at University of Minnesota,
199, 201; vulnerability of, xi, 86,
106, 212, 237, 274–75, 350, 351
—works: "After Majdanek: On the
Poetry of Aaron Zeitlin" (1948), 70,
86, 102; "An Analysis of Piety"
(1942), 19, 30, 31, 32–33, 40, 45,
53, 102, 110, 111, 112, 146, 332,
407–8n51; "Answer to Ben Gurion"
(1959), 192–93; "Answer to
Einstein" (1940), 4, 16–17; "The
Biblical View of Reality" (1956),
179, 278; "A Cabbalistic
Commentary to the Prayerbook"
(1944), 54; "On Children and
Youth" (1960), 199, 427n5; "Choose
Life!" (1966), 289; "The Concept of
Man in Jewish Thought" (1960),
182; "A Concise Dictionary of
Hebrew Philosophical Terms"
(1941), 30; "Conversation with
Martin Luther King" (1968),
325–26; "David Koigen" (1934), 18,
390n29; "Depth Theology" (1960),
201–2, 428n11; "Did Maimonides
Strive for Prophetic Inspiration?"
(1945), 53–54; "The Divine Pathos"
(1953), 124; *The Earth Is the*

Lord's (1950), 58–59, 68, 93, 97, 102–6, 127, 403n32; "The Eastern European Era in Jewish History" (1945, 1946), 56–59, 397n18; "The Essence of Prayer" (1939), 30; "Faith" (1944), 46, 53, 55–56, 59, 102, 110; "From Mission to Dialogue" (1967), 284, 447n17; "God follows me everywhere . . ." (1929, 1933), 375, 379; *God in Search of Man* (1955), 125, 136, 142–43, 157–58, 166–72, 180, 187, 331, 335, 363, 382, 420n30, 449n2, 457n42; "God, Torah, and Israel" (1970), 345; "The Great Debate" (1960), 194; "Have You Acted Faithfully?" (1971), 354, 461n40; *Heavenly Torah As Refracted Through the Generations* (1962, 1965, 1990, trans. 2005), 174, 177, 207, 208–11, 213, 284, 431n38; "A Hebrew Evaluation of Reinhold Niebuhr" (1956), 180, 278; "Hidden sources of Redemption" (1967), 315; "Hillel Bavli: In Memoriam" (1962), 75; "The Holy Dimension" (1943), 47, 53, 56, 164; "I and Thou" (1929, 1933), xii, 118, 126; Ibn Gabirol studies (1937–39), 31, 100, 382; "Idols in the Temples" (1963), 207, 278; "Ilya Schor" (1961), 103, 126, 204, 336; "The Individual Jew and His Obligations" (1957, 1961), 189–91, 425n28; *The Ineffable Name of God: Man* (1933; trans. 2004), 16, 78, 83, 289, 398, 427n28, 465n46; *The Insecurity of Freedom* (1966), 177, 183, 232–34; *Israel: An Echo of Eternity* (1969), 182, 315, 336–37, 366–67, 463n77; "The Jewish Notion of God and

Christian Renewal" (1968), 292–93; "A Jewish Response [to Cardinal Bea]" (1963), 250; "Kotzk" (1969), 343; *Kotzk: Struggle for Integrity* (1973), 373, 459n17; "Kotzk, Menahem Mendel of" (1971), 459n16; "Der Kotzker rebbe" (1969–1970), 339, 363, 373, 381; "The Last Years of Maimonides" (1955, 1966), 166, 232–33; *Maimonides: A Biography* (1935; trans. 1982), 31, 364; *Man Is Not Alone* (1951), 31, 34, 51, 110, 114–15, 117–25, 148, 163, 278, 332, 379; *Man's Quest for God* (1954), 99, 158, 164–66, 182; "The Meaning of This War" (1943, 1944), 35, 46–47, 76, 120, 401nn10,11; "The Moment at Sinai" (1953), 143; "The Moral Outrage of Vietnam" (1966), 298, 306–7, 309, 313, 319; "The Mystical Element in Judaism," (1949), 71, 98, 102; "No Religion Is an Island" (1965), 236, 277, 281–84; *A Passion for Truth* (1973), xi, 68, 258, 296, 338, 342–44, 358, 363–64, 373, 376; "The Patient as a Person" (1964), 232; "Pikuach Neshama" (To Save a Soul, 1949), 94, 98–99; "Prayer" (1945), 59; "On Prayer" (1970), 339; "Prayer and Theological Discipline" (1959), 278; "Prayer as Expression and Empathy" (1939, 1941), 59–60; Preface to Layzer Ran, ed., *Jerusalem of Lithuania* (1974), 78; "A Preface to the Understanding of Revelation" (1954), 137, 143–44; *Prophetic Inspiration After the Prophets* (1996), 187, 396, 421n35; "Prophetic Inspiration in the Middle

Heschel, Gittel (d. 1942, sister), 5, 47, 209

Heschel, Hannah Susannah (b. 1952, daughter), xiii, *135*, 136, 188, *189*, 199, 222, 230, 280, *281*, 304, 340, 342, *349*, 373, 375, 377–79, 381, 385, 422*n*49, 434*n*22

Heschel, Israel (1911–94, first cousin and nephew), *79*, 81

Heschel, Moses Mordecai (Moyshe, son of the Kopitzhinitzer rebbe of New York, 1927–1975), 81, 377–78, 380–81

Heschel, Moshe Mordecai (1873–1917, the Pelzovizna rebbe, father), 131, 217, 385

Heschel, Rivka Reizel Perlow (1874–1942, mother), 5, 47, 136, 209, 385

Heschel, Sarah Bracha (1891–1964, sister, wife of the Kopitzhinitzer rebbe of New York), 5, 256

Heschel, Sylvia Straus (1913–2007, wife): beauty of, 83, birth of daughter of, 136, 413*n*57; family of, 83; and Heschel's death, 377–78; and Heschel's illness, 340–42, 458*n*11; marriage of, 83–85, *84*, 402*n*28; meets Heschel, 22; performance career of, 116–17, *116*; travels of, 188–89, 199, 351

Heshel, Jacob (1903–1970, brother), 188, 261, 349, *350*

Heshel, Thena (b. 1934). *See* Kendall, Thena Heshel

Hiroshima. *See* Auschwitz; Nuclear warfare

Hirsch, Richard G., 323–24, 394*n*1

History: and Christianity, 252; God's involvement in, 137, 168, 180, 194, 211, 236, 244, 282; of Hasidism, 14, 160–62, 349; and Jewish experience, 291, 293; of Judaism, 10, 57–58, 106, 208; meaning of, 17, 68, 103, 124, 128, 352; mountain of (Sinai) image, 46, 215, 220, 250; prophecy and, 211, 213, 227, 242

Hofer, Yehiel, 78, 361

Holiness: as beyond ethics, 169, 449*n*2; Bible, words of, 168–69; evoking awareness of, 40, 96, 107, 160; as God's gift, 140; insensitivity to, 200–201; and Jewish mission, 190, 194, 249, 411*n*33; of Land of Israel, 172, 379; and piety, xi, 33–36, 76–77, 183; versus social custom, 12, 58, 101; time and, 128–29

Holocaust: American responses to, 43, 46, 100, 143, 279, 325; apathy about, 143, 212, 401*n*15; as divine punishment, 99; faith after, 59, 99, 143, 327–29, 327, 343–44, 354; Greenberg's responses to, 44; Heschel's responses to, 45–48, 57–59, 68, 85–86, 231; Heschel's review of Zeitlin, 86; and Israel, 313–14, 324, 327–28; meaning of, 211, 231–32, 432*n*48; memory of, 190, 260, 291; and nuclear warfare, 71; Pope John XXIII, 236; Soviet Jewry and, 225, 228

Holtz, Avraham, 132, 351, 382

Horkheimer, Max, 241–42

Horwitz, Gertrude Rivka, 172, 173, 210

Humanism, sacred. *See* Sacred humanism

Humility and contrition, xi, xii, 180, 190, 244, 250, 257, 283, 309, 312

Ibn Gabirol, Solomon (ca. 1021–1058), 21, 100, 382

Idolatry, 176, 197, 205, 236

Ineffable: as beyond words and thoughts, 60, 86, 104, 123, 156, 164, 285; human embarrassment in the face of, 232; presence of God, 55, 115, 121, 124–25; reverence as, 118

Insight and intuition: in Ashkenazic culture, 100; as goal of teaching, 87, 120, 196, 200; Heschel's brief notations of, 77, 112; and immediate cognition, 55–56, 179; and prayer, 60, 155; and prophetic revelation, 186; religious knowledge through, 34, 55, 118–20, 151, 162; and religious thinking, 42, 209, 231. *See also* Depth theology; Radical amazement

Interfaith initiatives: American Jewish Committee, 199, 215; "Conference on Religion and Race," 215–16; Finkelstein, 138, 140–41; Heschel as interfaith theologian, 218, 288–93, 345; Heschel's confrontational stance at, 138; joint JTS and UTS faculty meeting, 180–81; limitations of, 288, 316; Muslims and, 364–67; pluralism, 201–2, 278, 281–82; in public life, 182–84, 202, 219–20; REA panel on, 165; Soloveitchik opposed to, 260–61, 266; three-faith meetings, 63, 126, 138, 181, 215–16, 219–20, 250, 255; and worship, 308–9, 321–22, 333–34. *See also* Religious Education Association; Union Theological Seminary; Vatican Council, Second

Inwardness, x, xii, 144, 168–69, 180, 282, 286, 339

Isaac, Jules, 236, 240

Islam, 31, 182, 250, 260, 283, 330–31; Muslims, xiv, 284, 364–67

Ismael ben Elisha, Rabbi (90–135), 24, 208–9, 284, 307

Israel: aliyah, 315; as ancient homeland, 45; citizenship of, 192–93; commitment to, 187, 314, 328, 337; criticism of, 316–17, 369–70; and Diaspora, 187–92; Heschel's book on, 318, 327, 336; Heschel's defense of, 314, 317–18, 335–36; and Holocaust, 328; Judaism and, 190–91; King's support for, 326; Land of, 327; Orthodox hegemony in, 174, 327; peace for, 203, 325, 337, 364; restoration of, 292, 315, 328, 336; Shazar, 187–88, 360, 381; as spiritual ideal, 101, 159–60, 315, 327–28, 337, 360–61; Vatican's recognition of, 247; and Vietnam War, 313, 321. *See also* Diaspora; Jerusalem; Six-Day War; Zionism

Jackson, Jesse L., 321, 359

Jacobi, Lotte, 259, 321

Jacobs, Louis, 209

Jacobson, Gershon, 43–44, 227, 245–46, 259, 267–68

Jerusalem: Christian views of, 288, 292, 315–17, 336; conference on, 364–67; Hebrew University, 54, 78, 125; restoration of, 292–93, 352

Jerusalem Post (newspaper), 171, 180, 189, 191, 381

Jesus, 59, 181, 236, 249, 275–76, 279, 286, 292, 304, 322, 336, 440n34, 454n7

Jewish Chronicle (London newspaper), 254, 267, 441n42

Jewish Defense League (JDL), 360, 363, 369

Jewish Publication Society of America (JPS), 31–32, 110–14, 126, 142, 163, 166–71, 210. *See also* Grayzel, Solomon

Jewish Theological Seminary of America (JTS): Admissions Committee of, 88, 131–32; Bavli at, 74–75; under Finkelstein, 71–73, 110; Ginzberg at, 71; Heschel as teacher at, 74, 86–89, 132–33; Heschel's appointment at, 68; Heschel's inaugural lecture at, 75–77; Heschel's teaching schedule at, 74; history of, 68; Kaplan at, 73; power shift at, 108–10; Rabbinical School at, 74, 109, 173, 345; Teachers Institute at, 45, 73–74, 431*n*38. *See also* Finkelstein, Louis; Lieberman, Saul

Jewry: Ashkenazic, 57, 100–107, 307*n*18; German, 3, 12, 16, 25, 27, 30, 95, 100–101, 118, 158, 165, 172, 256, 391*n*5; German Jewish American, 16, 25, 78, 95; Hasidic, ix, xi, 26, 39, 78–82; Polish, 15, 27, 43, 53–54, 82, 100, 103, 107, 128; secular, xi, 16, 21, 57–59, 82–83, 98, 102, 104, 109; Sephardic, 27, 57–58, 100–101, 106; Soviet, x, 43, 176, 220, 225–29, 232, 242, 246, 353, 360–61

Jewry, American: culture wars among, 100, 104–8, 122; customs of, 42; example for Israel, 192; Heschel's critique of, 100–102, 146; moral failures of, 43–44, 47, 52, 226–27, 228–29; Orthodox, 158–60; rationalism of, 123, 128, 138; reconstruction of, 73; religious

education of, 2, 98, 144, 179, 184, 205; spiritual emergency of, 69, 104

Job, Book of, 287, 354

John XXIII, Pope (Angelo Giuseppe Roncalli, 1881–1963), 215–16, 236–40, 245, 247, 250–51, 276

Johnson, Lyndon Baines, 220–25, 296, 299–301, 311–12, 356, 364

Journal of Religion, 47, 52, 182

Joy: of concentration, 13; of friendship, 30; Hasidism and, 107, 131, 343; and healing, 212; in Jewishness, 104, 152, 191; in music, 21

Jubilee (periodical), 54, 284

Judaism: American, 137–66, 147–49; Columbus Platform, 12, 22; Conservative, 2, 25, 57, 68, 72–73, 89, 152; Orthodox, xi, 10–11, 25–26, 34, 38, 41, 52–53, 61–62, 158–62; Pittsburgh Platform, 11–12; Reconstructionist, 45, 62, 73, 122–23, 128, 139, 147–49; Reform (or Liberal), 2, 3, 10–11, 21–23, 42, 43, 46–47, 152–56

Judaism: A Quarterly Journal, 123–24, 127–28

Jüdisches Lehrhaus (Frankfurt), x, 3, 7, 28, 75, 93, 138

Jung, Leo, 210, 439*n*20

Kabbalah, 38, 58, 63, 86, 104, 139, 196, 201, 207, 330

Kant, Immanuel, 36, 120, 139, 152, 154, 289–90*n*23

Kaplan, Mordecai Menahem (1881–1983), 147, 151–53, 191–94, 283, 327, 355–56

Kaufmann, Fritz, 30, 159

Kavanah (inner intention): and halakhah, 60, 155, 168; Heschel's difficulty achieving, 150–51; and

Militarism, x, 212, 256, 270, 278, 298, 305, 313

Miracle, 73, 173, 284, 356

Mishnah, 9, 25, 37, 54, 64, 95, 128, 156, 209

Mitnagid (opponent of Hasidism), 29, 36, 62, 109, 172

Mitzvah (plural, *mitzvot:* deed, commandment): divine will and, 139–40, 154, 168, 185; as historically relative, 11; and Jewish obligation, 82, 180, 321, 331, 356. *See also* Customs and ceremonies; Halakhah

Montreal, 59, 82, 291–92

Moore, Paul, Jr., 308, 377–78

Morgenstern, Julian: as administrator, 49; background of, 391n5; Bible class of, 10, 49; and HUC crisis, 49–50; and rescue of refugee scholars, 2–3, 21, 56, 362, 395n39; supports Heschel, 5–6, 42, 56, 71, 111, 161. *See also* Hebrew Union College

Morlion, Felix, 241, 243, 246, 250–51, 266

Mortara, Elena di Veroli, 331, 351–52

Mortara case, 455n29

"Most (great) moved mover," 144, 196, 414–15n16

Mourning, 25, 85–86, 256, 354, 381

Muffs, Yochanan, 347, 378, 382

Muffs, Yocheved. *See* Herschlag, Judith

Muilenburg, James, 171, 181, 212

Music, 11, 12, 27, 29, 55–56, 73, 101, 117, 202

Mussar movement, 29, 108, 131, 412n46

Mystery: awe and, 153, 202; and end of time, 272; humility at, xi–xii, 190; meaning beyond, 212, 285, 332; reductionism and, 211

Mysticism: Buber's, 153; ethics and, xii, 63–64, 98, 102; Heschel's, x, 44, 54, 56, 70; Islamic, 330, 364, 366, 432n51; Jewish, 54–55, 61, 72, 327; objections to, 105–6, 110, 123, 124, 128; prophecy and, 98, 432n51; reason and, 195, 410n21; Scholem and, 55, 123, 173; Zohar, 71, 139. *See also* Revelation, divine

Nadich, Judah, 378, 381

Nahman of Bratslav (1772–1810), 300, 312

Nasr, Seyyed Hossein, 365–67

Nasser, Gamal Abdel, 245, 268, 313–14

"National Conference on Religion and Race" (1963), 176, 215–19, 325, 372

National Council of Churches, 226, 278, 301, 304, 312, 360

Naturalism, 17, 100, 151, 355

Nature, 17, 33, 70, 77, 149, 200, 390n27, 401n11

Nazism: atheism of, 190; Catholic Church compared with, 272–73; dehumanization of, 17, 144–45, 182; extermination policy of, 43–44, 99, 244; Heidegger as Nazi, 231; Jewish resistance to, 27, 47, 95, 105, 304; Kristallnacht, 220; and memories of Germany, 183, 256, 313–14

Neo-Kantianism, 36, 120, 134, 154, 398n34. *See also* Rationalism

Neuhaus, Richard John: at antiwar protest, *334*, 336; background, 302; co-founds CCAV (later CALCAV), 300–302, 304, 305, 309; at Heschel's death, 377; visit to Kissinger, 333; visit to McNamara, 310–11

Neusner, Jacob, 209, 382

Newsweek (periodical), x, 289, 296, 330, 377, 381

Niebuhr, H. Richard, 302, 344, 421*n*42

Niebuhr, Reinhold: cultivation of by Finkelstein, 130; friendship with Heschel of, 181, 286; Heschel at funeral of, 354–55; Heschel's interpretation of, 180, 232, 423*n*4; influence on Herberg, 102; influence on King, 217; as model for Judaism, 152; neo-Orthodoxy of, 102, 180; opposition to racism of, 216, 278; opposition to Vietnam War of, 301, 312, 314; rejection of Christian conversion of Jews by, 181, 283; support for Heschel by, x, 120–21, 161, 170, 181, 183

Nixon, Richard Milhous, 138, 332–34, 368–70, 377

Nostra Aetate (In our times, 1965), 237, 276, 352. *See also* Vatican Council, Second

Novak, David, 345–46

Novak, Michael, 309, 313

Novominsk (Minsk Mazowieck, Poland), 78, 225

Nuclear warfare: as antithetical to God, 250; Dresner opposes, 88; fear of, 68, 176, 186, 250; Heschel's "kosher atomic bomb" example, 132; Hiroshima and Nagasaki associated with Holocaust, 71, 138; public apathy over, 289; Test Ban Treaty, 227

Observance: crisis of among American Jews, 69, 139, 146; Heschel's promotion of, 98, 104, 107, 152, 154–56; Heschel's traditional,

22–25, 39; at HUC, 10–12, 42–43; and inner life, 61, 120, 139, 168; ladder of, 192; and Reform policy, 22; as response to God's will, 12, 139; and Sabbath, 99, 104, 110, 127, 241, 331; sociological approach to, 140; Soloveitchik on, 61

Oesterreicher, John Maria, 165, 239

Oko, Adolph S., 14, 32

Ontology, 153, 195–96, 202

Orthodox Judaism. *See* Judaism: Orthodox

Oxtoby, Willard Gurdon, 316

Packard, Vance, 183

Palestine: Buber in, 14; European refugees in, 52, 56, 78, 388; Heschel's critique of, 101; Heschel's support for, 24–25, 26, 74–75, 335–36; as Jewish homeland, 12, 25, 52, 57, 74–76, 121. *See also* Israel; Zionism

Paradox, 98, 180, 382, 432*n*48

Pauk, Wilhelm, 134, 165

Paul VI, Pope (Giovanni Battista Montini, 1897–1978), 251–56, *265*, 268–70, 276, 282, 303, *353*, 357, 364, 381–82; Heschel's public audience with, 351–52; Heschel's secret audience with, 261–76, 288, 292, 383–84, 442*n*7, 442–43*n*11

Peace: between Arabs and Jews, 315, 326, 336–37, 364–67; halakhah and, 264, 444*n*36; Isaiah's vision of, 182, 192, 203, 309, 315, 334; and opposition to Vietnam War, 301, 309, 311–12, 319, 360, 379; prophetic vision of, 192, 309, 334; worship for, 308–9, 321–24

Peli, Pinchas, 14, 335, 342, 346, 381–82

Peoplehood, 73, 193, 301, 365, 370

Perlow, Aaron (1902–1963, Heschel's first cousin), 79, *80*, 384

Perlow, Alter Israel Shimon (1874–1933, Novominsker rebbe of Warsaw), 32, 78, 161, 208–9, 341

Perlow, Jacob (d. 1981, son of the Novominsker rebbe of Williamsburg), 341, 378

Perlow, Nahum Mordecai (1896–1976, Novominsker rebbe of Borough Park), 78, 80, 127

Perlow, Tova (Gittel) (1908–1956, Heschel's first cousin), 188

Perlow, Yehuda Aryeh Leib (1877–1960, Novominsker rebbe of Williamsburg), 26, 78, 80, 160, 378

Petuchowski, Jakob Josef, 155, 195, 412*n*35

Phenomenology: analysis of consciousness, 31–33; mystical illumination, 122; piety and, 32, 47, 170; of prophetic consciousness, 32, 55, 210, 366

Philipson, David, 11–12, 21, 22, 32, 48

Philosophy: criticism of Heschel's, 122, 124–25; existential, 152, 153, 231–32; of the human, 181–82, 229–33; of Judaism, 31, 75, 142, 162–63, 166, 285; neo-Kantian, 36, 154; rationalism, 34, 36, 55, 100, 120, 146, 155; situational, 168, 195; at University of Berlin, ix, 14, 61, 154, 172–73, 363

Piety (*hasidut*): analysis of, 32–33, 112; as cultural ideal, 58, 93, 104, 122; and ethics, 76; German Jewish, 95; Kaplan on Heschel's essay, 45; opponents of, 82, 109–10; personal, 25; and spiritual awareness, 19, 75. *See also*

Heschel, Abraham Joshua, works: "An Analysis of Piety"

Pius XII, Pope (Eugenio Pacelli, 1876–1958), 236, 239, 251, 325, 437*n*1

Pluralism: Heschel's affirmation of, 180, 183, 250; prewar Jewish diversity, 82; in Talmud, 207–8, 327; and will of God, 238, 283

Poetry: Goethe poem, 154; and Heschel's writing style, 32, 55, 59, 75; inspirational, 117, 121, 168; philosophy and, 111, 210; prayer and, 164; vocation of, 86–87; Yiddish, 136, 363

Poets: Akiva (Akiba ben Joseph), 208; Bavli, 75; D. Berrigan, 300; Blank, 23; S. Halkin, 86; Merton, 256; Ravitch, 59; Zeitlin, 75

Poland: anti-Semitism in, 217, 243, 291, 351, 357; failure of American Jewry toward Polish Jews, 43–44, 52; German invasion of, 26; Hasidism in, 14, 26, 103, 161; Heschel's birthplace, 2, 15; and Holocaust memories, 86, 328; liberation of by Soviets, 56; march on Washington for, 52–53; murder of Jews in, 43–44, 46–47, 71; Orthodox Jewry in, 16–25; rescue of Polish Jews, 26; secularization of Jews in, 179; Zionists in, 187. *See also* Jewry: Polish; Warsaw, Poland

Polarities, 127, 168–69, 180, 208, 285–86

Poverty, 217, 220, 300, 311–12, 326, 354, 360, 370

Prayer: debate on, at Rabbinical Assembly conference (1953), 146–52, 416*n*33; ethics and, 106–7; Feinberg and, 25–26; as greatest joy,

21; *havdalah,* 39; Heschel on African Americans', 359; Heschel's critique of American Jews', 146–56, 163–66, 205–6, 344; Heschel's writings on, 30, 53, 54, 59–61, 95–96; power of, 96; prayer book, 45, 54, 146, 148–49, 155; and protest, 225, 305; Ravitch against, 82; as song, 99; as subversive, 339–40; as way to overcome despair, 44. *See also* Kavanah

Prinz, Joachim, 228

Pro Deo University (Rome), 240–41, 250, 255

Prophets, Hebrew: Amos, 213, 370; Buber's book on, 32; and continuous revelation, 55, 187; God of, 143; Heschel's German and English studies of, 6, 41, 98, 141–42, 184, 194–95, 197, 210–13, 216, 218, 222, 241, 256, 263, 265, 278, 299, 398n34, 420–21n32, 427n48; Heschel's physical resemblance to, 177, 201, 303; Heschel's public role as prophet, 222–23, 229, 242, 292, 301, 343; Heschel's teaching of, 184–87, 199, 203; Hosea, 211–12, 432n45; Isaiah, 42, 71, 180, 182, 200, 228, 315, 365, 370; Islamic prophecy, 366; Jeremiah, 41, 211–12; King as prophet, 325–26; Malachi, 250, 263; need to emulate, 211; 354; Second Isaiah, 210–12, 329; Zecharia, 190–91

Psalms: *15,* 379, 434n22; *22,* 322, 454n7; *27,* 223, 434n22; *42,* 380, 434n52; *44,* 211; *137,* 424n22, 457n42; *145,* 424n14

Quakers, 42–44, 46, 57, 308, 364–65

Rabb, Sidney R., 276, 442n9, 446n53

Rabbi Akiva. *See* Akiva, Rabbi

Rabbi Ishmael. *See* Ismael ben Elisha

Rabbinical Assembly of America (Conservative): defense of Heschel by, 229; Heschel honored by, 326–27; Heschel's Yiddish address to, 342; Kelman and, 89–90, 198, 225–26, 379; King honored by, 324–25; meeting of, *1953,* 146–52; meeting of, *1958,* 191–92, 215; meeting of, *1962,* 205–6; meeting of, *1966,* 228; meeting of, *1968,* 324–29, 335; on Soviet Jewry, 225–26

Rabbinical Council of America (modern Orthodox), 240, 248, 254–55, 260–61, 441n42, 442n7

Racism: American, x, 10, 215–16, 219–21, 363; as evil, 214; throughout Jewish history, 227; Nazi, 17. *See also* Civil Rights movement

Rackman, Emanuel, 171–72, 248

Raddock, Charles, 158–59

Radhakrishnan, Sarvepalli, 182

Radical amazement, xii, 42, 47, 118, 179, 191, 231

Randall, John Herman, 95, 196

Rashi (Rabbi Shlomo Itzhaki, 1040–1105), 20, 36, 38, 41, 53, 87, 104, 159, 168, 362

Rationalism: as cultural norm, 57, 118; of Descartes, 231–32; as dogma, 55, 152; and empiricism, 34; Heschel's critique of Einstein's, 17; Heschel's disparagement of, 123; limits of, 155, 166; of Rabbi Ishmael, 208; versus religious thinking, 34, 55, 122–25, 139, 142–43. *See also* Neo-Kantianism

Rattner, Abraham, 336

Ravitch, Melekh, 59, 82

Recentering of subjectivity, 32–33, 56, 60, 102

Reconstructionism. *See* Judaism: Reconstructionist

Reconstructionist (journal), 45–46, 55, 105, 123, 128, 165

Redemption, 124, 192, 232, 244, 277, 293, 315, 344, 366, 432*n*48, 422*n*45

Reform Judaism. *See* Judaism: Reform

Reiss, Erich, 75, 364

Religion: and the arts, 21; and depth theology, 168, 179–80, 187, 202, 282–83, 326; and ethics, 102; and experience, 125; idolatry, 236; and the ineffable, 123; pragmatic, 124; and science, 16–17, 63; secularization of, 17, 27, 105, 190; social science as, 62, 73, 138; teaching of, 2, 98, 144–45, 179, 184–87, 205; trivialization of, 46. *See also* Depth theology; Faith

Religious Education Association, 165, 171, 179, 181–82, 205, 211, 207, 327

Renewal: Christian, 215, 232, 276, 278–79, 292–93; Heschel as model of, 123; Jewish, xiii, 138, 314–15, 327

Repentance, 261, 266, 293, 305, 310, 321

Responsibility: ethical, 136, 120, 211, 230, 289; for God's presence, 153, 164; and public life, 179, 299, 305; for redemption, 232, 242; the Sabbath and, 126–27; for victims of Holocaust, 226, 270–71, 274. *See also* Prophets, Hebrew

Revelation, divine: Buber's idea of, 330–31; as continuous, 55, 104; Heschel's analysis of, 34, 137, 143–44, 153, 168–69; interpretation of, 187, 208; versus intuition, 186–87; Islamic, 330–31; and the mitzvot, 12; reality of, xi, 171, 185; and reception of by readers, 118, 125, 168; rejection of, 11, 140, 213, 404*n*14

Reverence: for the Bible, 282, 361; for God, 98, 185; for Heschel, 93, 347; for human beings, 24, 182–84, 199, 250, 274, 289; for Israel, 191; for Judaism, 288; for parents, 202. *See also* Radical amazement

Review of Religion (journal), 30–31, 59, 163, 171

Reynolds, Frank, 356, 359

Riemer, Jack, 144, 170, 173

Roosevelt, Franklin Delano, 43, 52, 61, 72, 198

Rosenstock-Huessy, Eugen, 133–34

Rosenthal, Franz, 8, 9, 20

Rosenzweig, Franz, 22, 101, 118, 128, 159, 173

Rosh Hashanah, 71, 158, 261, 275, 340, 367

Rothschild, Fritz, *94;* advises Heschel, 95, 163, 207, 317, 373; background of, 93; *Between God and Man,* 195–96; at Heschel's funeral, 378, 380, 381; immigration of, 93–94; as interpreter of Heschel, 53, 95, 152, 171, 326, 351, 382; at JTS, 94–95; "Most Moved Mover," 196; political conservatism of, 313, 368

Rubenstein, Richard Lowell, 7, 39, 64, 206

Rubinstein, Arthur, 83, 303

Rudloff, Leo Alfred, 239, 459*n*16

Ruzhin, Israel Friedman, rebbe of, 5, 79, 173, 385

Saadia Gaon (Saadia ben Joseph, 882–942): in *Man Is Not Alone*, 55, 102, 153; on reason and faith, 33–34, 393n45; on reason and revelation, 153, 416n3

Sabbath: additional soul received on, 145, 161; at the Feinbergs, 23; halakhic adjustments to Sylvia Heschel's observance of, 110; *havdalah*, 39; Heschel's death on, 375; Heschel's *Midrasha* in Cincinnati, 27–28; Heschel's observance of, 57, 80, 99, 110, 172, 222, 241, 251, 255, 261, 267, 275, 331, 349; Heschel's *The Sabbath*, 79, 125–28, 129; at HUC, 11–12; idea of time not space, 337; Jewish consciousness of, 99; in Jewish history, 128, 304; and return to Jewish life, 104, 169, 192; secularization of, 192; Seventh-day Adventists, 43; as way to peace, 404n6

Sacred humanism: Christian, 371; and the divine image, 24, 154, 181–83, 282–83, 371; and existential philosophy, 229–34; as foundation for common ground for Jews and Christians, 182, 206; Hitler's violation of, 394n14; and human holiness, 140, 181–82; versus secular humanism, 24, 118, 138; and spirituality and ethics, 98, 326; Stanford lectures on, 229–34; and reverence for humanity, 182, 206, 216, 218, 274; in Zohar, 98

Salanter, Israel (1810–1885), 29

Samuel, Maurice, 106–7

Sanders, James Alvin, 286–87, 316, 382

Schachter-Shalomi, Zalman, xiii, 422n51

Schechter, Solomon (1847–1915), 62, 68, 73, 113, 329

Schmidt, Stefan, 241, 245–46

Schneersohn, Fishl, 78, 187, 401n15

Schneerson, Menachem Mendel, 14

Schneider, Herbert Wallace, 162, 171

Schocken, Shelomoh Salman, 167

Schocken, Theodore, 75

Scholem, Gershom (Gerhard): Heschel hurt by, 173; Heschel's competition with, 160–61, 418n8; Heschel's review of *Major Trends in Jewish Mysticism*, 55; Horwitz and, 173; Lieberman on, 406n36; Teshima and, 347; work of, 54, 123, 139, 143, 159, 161

Schor, Ilya, 103, 126, 204, 336

Schorr, Moses, 54

Schuman, Henry, 93, 103

Secularization, Jewish: American, 17, 27, 105–6, 138, 143, 179; Fackenheim against, 124; Herberg against, 102. *See also* Judaism: Reconstructionist

Self-deception, xi, 49, 258, 275

Shannon, James Patrick, 321, 322, 339, 456

Shapiro, David Shlomo, 209, 213

Sharper, Philip, 301, 336

Shazar, Zalman (Schneor Zalman Rubashov, 1889–1974), 187–88, 360, 381

Shekhinah, 98, 145, 149, 160, 339

Sherman, Franklin, 204

Sherwin, Byron L., 346, 351, 375

Shmidman, Joshua, 340–41

Shoah. *See* Holocaust

126, 162–67, 170, 232, 254, 335, 363, 373

Straus, Samuel (father of Sylvia Heschel), 402*n*28

Straus, Sylvia. *See* Heschel, Sylvia Straus

Strauss, Eduard, 7, 15, 20, 75

Stringfellow, William, 217, 371–72

Student Non-Violent Coordinating Committee (SNCC), 220–22, 334

Suffering: caused by Christians, 260, 263, 272; chastisement and, 432*n*48; cross as symbol of, 347; God's, 211–12; and human callousness, 199; of innocent human beings, 82–83, 359; of Israel's enemies, 92; of the Jewish people, 68, 99, 193, 236, 249; Jews as God's Suffering Servant, 212, 329, 365–66, 455*n*22; in Vietnam, 321

Symbolism: and esthetic religion, 12, 136, 138, 155; Heschel's debate with Buber on, 138, 432*n*45; idols, 143; as a replacement of God, 166; in the Torah, 324. *See also* Customs and ceremonies; Sacred humanism

Synagogue Council of America (umbrella organization of all denominations), 43, 198, 203, 206, 216, 225–26, 248

Synan, Edward A., 165, 171, 292

Talmud: Brisk method, 25, 61; burnings of, 274; citations of passages from, 167, 216, 264, 354, 362, 370; Finkelstein as scholar of, 16, 109; Heschel's expertise in, 36, 57, 78, 110, 196, 207–8; as interpretive discipline, 331; Kelman's knowledge of, 88;

Lieberman as scholar of, 68, 72, 108, 209; pilpul, 104; pluralism in, 207–9, 283, 327, 421*n*36; Rashi's commentaries, 41, 104; reverence for, 304; and Shekhinah, 98; Siegel as instructor of, 92. *See also* Heschel, Abraham Joshua, works: *Heavenly Torah As Refracted Through the Generations;* Lieberman, Saul

Tanenbaum, Marc, *247, 271;* background of, 92; bond with Heschel, 92–93; and "Conference on Religion and Race," 215; involvement in Second Vatican Council negotiations, 240, 242, 266–71; joins AJC, 237; and Kelman, 93, 215; mediates with Soloveitchik, 254; meets Cardinal Bea, 246–47; at Notre Dame University, 290; and promotion of Heschel, 198, 202, 232; and Schuman, 103; and Shuster, 240, 242, 253, 262, 269; and summary of Declaration on the Jews, 243–44; and Synagogue Council, 198, 206

Täubler, Eugen, 8

Täubler-Stern, Selma, 8, 143

Tedeschi, Giancarlo, 331

Terrien, Samuel, 212–13, 287

Terrorism, 52, 92, 270, 314, 367

Teshima, Jacob Yuroh, 346–49, *348,* 359, 373, 375, 378–81, 383, *383,* 384

Theology: American Jewish, x, 148; biblical, 278, 326; Cohon on, 22, 152–53; death of God, 206, 288, 292, 327–28, 413*n*55; of divine pathos, 98, 142, 208; and ethics, 33; of God as subject, 211; of God in exile, 83; Herberg's crisis theology, 102; Heschel's construction of, 31, 53;

Theology (continued)
  Heschel's critique of Christian,
    278–79; and JPS list, 113; Kohn's
    view of, 149; Lieberman's rejection
    of, 110; *Man Is Not Alone* as
    theological revolution, 115–25;
    neo-Kantian, 36; Niebuhr's, 180;
    Polish's survey of, 153–54; process,
    73, 143–44, 147–49, 151, 153;
    reduced to esthetics, 139; as
    response to Holocaust, 231. *See also*
    Depth theology; God
Thich Nhat Hanh, 307
Tillich, Paul, 134, 136, 183, 195, 283,
    326
Time (periodical), 93, 103, 170, 179,
    218, 260, 278, 337
Time versus space, 104, 126–28,
    159, 169, 199, 202–3, 272,
    288
Tisserant, Eugene Cardinal, 245, 255,
    269
Toaff, Elio, 240
Tone, 101, 147, 211, 273, 333, 339,
    359
Torah: blessing over, 145; in cemetery,
    321, 323–24; as divine revelation,
    206; dressing to honor, 42; God,
    Torah, Israel, 190, 193, 345, 361;
    Heschel as personification of, 287;
    hold sefer Torah, 103, 204; as holy
    teaching, 350–51; interpretation of,
    208, 284; Jews' forced acceptance
    of, 46; scrolls of not intrinsically
    holy, 139–40; Torah-true Jews, 155,
    172, 361
*Tradition: A Journal of Orthodox
    Thought*, 213, 232
Transcendence, 73, 107, 112, 118,
    139–40, 148–51, 199, 212, 214,
    231, 236, 289

Translation: Buber on Hasidism, 102;
    creed as, 55–56; of Heschel's
    works, 31, 46, 58–59, 141–42, 162,
    166, 167, 174, 208, 210, 337, 349,
    352, 364; as way to bridge cultures,
    102–3, 205, 249, 314; of word
    ceremonies, 155
Translators: Bavli, 74, 204; Buber,
    32, 159, 291; Corbin, 364;
    Diesendruck, 18; Friedman, 108;
    Knight, 141; Liebman, 31; Mortara,
    331, 351; Saadia, 34; Samuel, 106;
    Teshima, 349; Zolla, 330

Union of American Hebrew
    Congregations (UAHC, Reform
    Jewish lay organization), 46, 217,
    302, 323
Union Theological Seminary: Heschel
    as visiting professor at, 237, 278–91;
    Heschel's faculty friends at, 286–88;
    and Heschel's funeral, 378; and
    Heschel's JTS inauguration, 75;
    joint meeting with JTS faculty,
    181; *Newsweek* article on Heschel,
    289. *See also* Bennett, John
    Coleman
United Synagogue of America
    (Conservative lay organization),
    125, 194, 281, 352, 426n44
Unity of the Jewish people, 206, 260,
    315, 328
University of Iowa, Heschel as
    visiting professor at, 203–4,
    240
University of Minnesota, Heschel as
    visiting professor at, 199–201,
    429n17
University of Notre Dame, 37–38,
    289–93
Urbach, Ephraim, 287

Vatican Council, Second (Vatican II, 1962–65): American Jewish Committee and, 177, 198, 236–39, 239–74; Declaration on the Jews of, x, 239–46, 252–61, 266–69; first and second sessions of, 245–57; third session of, 268–75; fourth session of, 275–76. *See also* Deicide, charge of against Jews; John XXIII, Pope; Paul VI, Pope; Shuster, Zachariah

Vienna, 5, 29, 59, 80, 88, 349

Vietnam War: American war crimes, 307–8, 320, 344; callousness of, 212; escalation of, 296, 377; Jewish support for, 299, 368–70; patriotic duty to oppose, 299; prayer as dissent to, 340; religious opposition to, 298–313, 319–24, 332–34. *See also* Clergy and Laymen Concerned About Vietnam

Vilna, (Vilnius), Lithuania, xi, 13, 16, 62, 74, 78, 108, 188, 299

Vilna Gaon, Elijah ben Solomon Zalman (1720–1797), 62

Visa, immigrant, x, 2–6, 8, 36, 79, 93, 161, 243, 315, 360, 388n3

Vorspan, Albert, 217

Warsaw, Poland: ghetto in, 5, 29, 43, 56; Heschel's childhood in, ix, xi, 13, 16, 21, 39, 187, 207, 291, 299; Heschel's companions from, 77–78, 79, 82, 160, 188, 361, 363; Heschel's identity as a wounded Jew from, 275, 282, 342; Heschel's library in, 160; Heschel's return to (1938–39), x, 16, 30, 36, 42, 54; liberation of by Red Army, 59; Novominsker rebbe of, 32, 78, 161, 208–9, 341; uprising and

liquidation of ghetto in, 47, 105; Yiddish of, 82, 341

Waskow, Arthur, xiii, 346,

Weigel, Gustave, 183, 254

Weinreich, Max, 57, 75

Weiss, Abraham, 54, 75

Weiss-Rosmarin, Trude, 127–28, 159, 412n35, 417n46

Werblowsky, Raphael Juda Zwi, 365–66

"White House Conference on Aging" (1961), 202

"White House Conference on Children and Youth" (1960), 176, 198

Wiesel, Elie, 228, 313, 314, 351, 379

Wilensky, Michael, 9, 14

Willebrands, Johannes Cardinal, 241–42, 246, 253–69

Wise, Isaac Mayer (1819–90), 3, 155

Wiseman, Joseph, 375, 379

Wissenschaft des Judentums (scientific historical Jewish scholarship): academic neutrality of, 54; Heschel's criticism of, 101; Heschel's practice of, 33, 160–61; historical method of, xi, 2; as JTS ideal, 68. *See also* Berlin

Wolf, Arnold Jacob, 38–39

Wolfson, Harry Austryn, 33, 54, 63, 240

Wonder, 40, 47, 118, 185, 202, 231. *See also* Radical amazement

Woodward, Kenneth L., 289

Words: blasphemous, 288; degradation of, 183; Heschel's sensitivity to, 13, 38, 46, 164; and holiness, 168, 351; individual, 151; as ineffable, 55, 60, 225; poetry, 164, 204; of the prophets, 185–86, 210–11

World war, fear of a third, 306

World War I, 152

World War II: Cronbach's pacifism during, 23; failures of American Jews during, 43–44, 52; first mention of in HUC catalog, 20; Greenberg's reports on imminent genocide, 44; liquidation of Warsaw Ghetto, 46–47; march on Washington, 52–53; "The Meaning of This Hour," 164; rescue efforts during, 26; spiritual meaning of, 35, 46, 76, 152–53. *See also* Holocaust; Militarism; Peace

Worship: and action, xiii, 225; Christian, 290; duty of, 154; interfaith, 33–34, 308–9, 321, 333; Isaiah on reconciliation of Egypt, Assyria, and Israel, 182, 203, 315; psychological approach to, 148; theological approach to, 150; as way to expand presence of God, 148, 164. *See also* Observance; Prayer

Wright, John J. Cardinal, 290, 357

Yeshiva University, 54, 75, 171–72, 240–41, 248, 370; Belkin at, 61, *81*, 376; Hartstein at, 61, 65, 75; Heschel's attempt to get position at, 61, 65; JTS students from, 72, 92; Soloveitchik at, 61

Yiddish: *Day-Morning Journal* (newspaper), 227, 246, 267; *Di goldene Keyt* (Tel Aviv periodical), 343; Heschel's accent, 40, 224; as Heschel's essential identity, 342, 350, 373; as Heschel's mother tongue, 13, 42, 82, 329, 341, 350;

Heschel's writings in, 13, 59, 160, 342, 363; as natural language of East European culture, 100–101, 102–3; poems in, 83, 136, 375, 379; speakers of, 43, 56–57, 75, 77, 78, 91, 92, 105, 106–7, 227, 240, 243, 375, 379, 382; Yiddish words, 104, 320; *Yidisher Kemfer* (newspaper), 44, 57, 85; *Yivo Bleter* (journal), 58–59, 161, 400n1

YIVO (Yidisher Visenshaftliker Institut, Jewish Scientific Institute), 16, 75, 78, 160–62, 341; Heschel's speeches at, 57–59, 85, 98, 103

Young, Andrew Jackson, Jr., 222–23, 311, 321, 326, 339

Youth: groups, 27, 29, 62, 93; Heschel as, 86, 139, 299, 361; Heschel on, 362, 384; of the 1960s, 363

Zaddik, 39, 88, 173

Zeitlin, Aaron, 70, 77–78, 86, 102, 185

Zionism: Heschel's commitment to, 187, 314–15, 328, 365; Heschel's speeches to Zionist congresses, 188–91, 360–61; Jewish opposition to, 26, 75, 187; Labor, 28, 315; religious, 110, 368; right-wing, 270; secular, 361; Zionist publications, 188, 315. *See also* Diaspora; Israel

Zohar, 13, 71, 98, 139, 323

Zolla, Elémire, 330–32

Zolli, Eugenio (orig. Israel Zoller, 1881–1956), 263–66